Stage 2

Business and Company Law

Examination Text

British Library Cataloguing-in-Publication Data

A catalogue record for this book is available from the British Library.

Published by AT Foulks Lynch Ltd
Number 4
The Griffin Centre
Staines Road
Feltham
Middlesex
TW14 0HS

ISBN 0 7483 3407 6

© AT Foulks Lynch Ltd, 1996

Acknowledgements

We are grateful to the Chartered Institute of Management Accountants, the Chartered Association of Certified Accountants and the Institute of Chartered Accountants in England and Wales for permission to reproduce past examination questions. The answers have been prepared by AT Foulks Lynch Ltd.

CONTENTS

Page

Preface (iv)

Syllabus and syllabus guidance notes (v)

Hotline to the examiner (xii)

May 1997 examinations - syllabus changes (xiv)

Contract

Chapter 1	Contract: The nature of a contract	1
Chapter 2	Contract: Offer and acceptance	5
Chapter 3	Contract: Consideration	22
Chapter 4	Contract: Intention, capacity, form, illegality	36
Chapter 5	Contract: Mistake and misrepresentation	54
Chapter 6	Contract: Terms	83
Chapter 7	Contract: Discharge	118
Chapter 8	Contract: Remedies for breach	134

Agency

Chapter 9	Agency	152

Negligence

Chapter 10	Tort: General principles	178
Chapter 11	Tort: Negligence	194
Chapter 12	Tort: Other torts	223

Employment

Chapter 13	The contract of employment	231
Chapter 14	Statutory regulation	250
Chapter 15	Termination of employment	270
Chapter 16	Health and Safety	293

Company formation

Chapter 17	Incorporation	300
Chapter 18	Publicity	332
Chapter 19	Memorandum of Association	349
Chapter 20	Articles of Association	373

Corporate finance

Chapter 21	Raising of share capital	402
Chapter 22	Maintenance of share capital	421
Chapter 23	Loan capital	443

Corporate management

Chapter 24	The board	467
Chapter 25	Directors' duties	493
Chapter 26	Company secretary & auditors	517

Shareholders

Chapter 27	Company meetings	530
Chapter 28	Rights	546

Table of cases 575

Index 580

PREFACE

The 1996 edition of this textbook has been specifically written for paper 8, Business and Company Law for the CIMA examinations.

CIMA base the examinations set in November 1996 and May 1997 on legislation at 1 June 1996, and this Textbook has been fully updated where necessary for such legislation.

We have also analysed the syllabus guidance notes and the various clarifications issued by CIMA to ensure that all the appropriate items contained therein have been incorporated into the text. CIMA have also kindly provided us with an advance copy of the new syllabus guidance notes to be published in August 1996 and the syllabus changes to be effective from May 1997, and we have incorporated these notes into the text where appropriate.

The text has been written to cover the syllabus in great detail giving appropriate weighting to the various topics. Our texts are, however, very different from a reference book or a more traditional style text book. The texts are focused very closely on the examinations and are written in a way that will help you assimilate the information easily and give you plenty of practice at the various techniques involved.

Particular attention has been paid to producing an interactive text that will maintain your interest with a series of carefully designed features.

- **Activities**. The text involves you in the learning process with a series of activities designed to arrest your attention and make you concentrate and respond.

- **Definitions**. The text clearly defines key words or concepts and where relevant we do of course use CIMA's official terminology. The purpose of including these definitions is **not** that you should learn them - rote learning is not required and is positively harmful. The definitions are included to focus your attention on the point being covered.

- **Conclusions**. Where helpful, the text includes conclusions that summarise important points as you read through the chapter rather than leaving the conclusion to the chapter end. The purpose of this is to summarise concisely the key material that has just been covered so that you can constantly monitor your understanding of the material as you read it.

- **Self test questions**. At the end of each chapter there is a series of self test questions. The purpose of these is to help you revise some of the key elements of the chapter. The answer to each is a paragraph reference, encouraging you to go back and re-read and revise that point.

- **End of chapter questions**. At the end of each chapter we include examination style questions. These will give you a very good idea of the sort of thing the examiner will ask and will test your understanding of what has been covered.

All in all a textbook which will teach you, involve you, interest you and help you revise and, most importantly of all, a textbook that is focused on the examinations.

THE SYLLABUS

ABILITIES REQUIRED IN THE EXAMINATION

Each examination paper contains a number of topics. Each topic has been given a number to indicate the level of ability required of the candidate.

The numbers range from 1 to 4 and represent the following ability levels:

Ability level

Appreciation

To understand a knowledge area at an early stage of learning, or outside the core of management accounting, at a level which enables the accountant to communicate and work with other members of the management team.

1

Knowledge

To have detailed knowledge of such matters as laws, standards, facts and techniques so as to advise at a level appropriate to a management accounting specialist.

2

Skill

To apply theoretical knowledge, concepts and techniques to the solution of problems where it is clear what technique has to be used and the information needed is clearly indicated.

3

Application

To apply knowledge and skills where candidates have to determine from a number of techniques which is the most appropriate and select the information required from a fairly wide range of data, some of which might not be relevant; to exercise professional judgement and to communicate and work with members of the management team and other recipients of financial reports.

4

EXAMINATION PROCEDURE

The examination will be set in accordance with the provisions of relevant UK legislation passed and case law established *up to and including 1 June* preceding the examination. This is especially relevant to the following five papers:

- Business Environment and Information Technology (Stage 1)
- Financial Accounting & Business and Company Law (Stage 2)
- Financial Reporting & Business Taxation (Stage 3)

This means that the Business Taxation paper will be set in accordance with the Finance Act 1996 for both the November 1996 and May 1997 examinations and with the Finance Act 1997 for the November 1997 examination.

The examination will also be set in accordance with relevant Statements of Standard Accounting Practice and Financial Reporting Standards issued up to and including 1 June preceding the examination. These are especially relevant to the following papers:

- Financial Accounting
- Financial Reporting

This criterion also applies to material contained in Exposure Drafts which are especially relevant to the Financial Reporting paper.

Where examinations are not based on UK legislation and practice, overseas candidates may take appropriate opportunities to cite examples of local practice in their answers. Such examples should be supported with references which will validate the answers.

Stage 2, Paper 8: BUSINESS AND COMPANY LAW

Syllabus overview

This syllabus enables students to acquire a sound understanding of those aspects of law which affect businesses. It assumes a basic understanding of key legal concepts and the operation of the legal system included in Business Environment at Stage 1. The more technical accounting aspects of company law will be followed up in Financial Reporting in Stage 3.

Aim

To test the candidate's ability to:

- explain the principles of business and company law (including insolvency law as appropriate) which underpin competence in management accounting

- apply legal principles to business problems

- advise managers and directors on the main legal issues which arise in the course of a management accountant's work.

Content	*Ability required*	*Chapter where covered in this text*
8a CONTRACT (study weighting 30%)		
Agreement, intention to create legal relations, certainty, consideration, form; contractual terms, including those implied by statute (eg, for the sale of goods)	3	1, 2, 3, 4, 6
Standard form contracts and exemption clauses	3	1, 6
Mistake, misrepresentation and contracts in restraint of trade	3	5, 6
Discharge of contract; remedies for breach	3	7, 8
8b AGENCY (study weighting 10%)		
Legal relationships between the parties to agency agreements with special reference to the authority of persons to act on behalf of others, particularly in companies and partnerships	3	9
8c NEGLIGENCE (study weighting 10%)		
The basic concepts of negligence in order to assess and guard against liability in negligence with special reference to professional advice, product liability, industrial accidents and dangerous premises	3	10, 11
Strict liability; breach of statutory duty; defences; vicarious liability; remedies	3	10, 11, 12

Content		Ability required	Chapter where covered in this text
8d	**EMPLOYMENT (study weighting 10%)**		
	The contract of employment: engagement, terms (including wages), dismissal; health and safety requirements and the consequences of breach	3	13, 14, 15, 16
8e	**COMPANY FORMATION (study weighting 10%)**		
	Types of company formed under the Companies Acts	2	17
	Corporate personality, 'lifting the veil' of incorporation	2	17
	Company registration, publicity, accounts and filing; Memorandum and Articles of Association	2	17, 18, 19, 20
	Corporate capacity to contract	2	19
8f	**CORPORATE FINANCE (study weighting 10%)**		
	Share Capital: types of shares, raising share capital, maintenance of capital, increase and reduction of share capital, purchase by a company of its own shares, financial assistance in the purchase of shares	3	21, 22
	Loan Capital: raising loan capital, secured and unsecured loans, fixed and floating charges, registration of charges, priority of charges	3	23
	Distribution of profit	3	22
8g	**CORPORATE MANAGEMENT (study weighting 10%)**		
	Directors: appointment, retirement, removal and disqualification; powers and duties; the liability of directors to shareholders, creditors and employees; fraudulent and wrongful trading	3	24, 25
	The company secretary: powers and duties	3	26
	Auditors: powers and duties; issues in corporate governance	2	24, 25, 26
8h	**SHAREHOLDERS (study weighting 10%)**		
	Company meetings: conduct, resolutions, the relationship between the board and the general meeting	3	27
	Shareholder's rights: class rights and their variation, transfer, transmission and mortgage of shares, the protection of minority shareholders	3	28

SYLLABUS GUIDANCE NOTES

STAGE 2

Paper 8

Business and Company Law (LAW)

Introduction

It is clearly important that chartered management accountants should have a knowledge of the legal framework within which they work. The main aim of the syllabus, therefore, is to enable candidates to obtain a good understanding of the key business and company law rules which underpin competence in management accounting.

Law is a technical subject. It follows that candidates will be expected to demonstrate good technical knowledge of the relevant rules and principles. It will not be sufficient for candidates to attempt to answer as intelligent laymen without supporting answers with detailed knowledge of the law.

The examination paper

The examination paper will consist of three sections.

Section A will contain one compulsory question composed of ten multiple-choice sub-questions. They will range across the whole syllabus and are designed to test candidates' knowledge of important business and company law rules.

Section B will consist of four questions on business law, taking the form of problems and essays.

Section C will contain three questions on company law, again taking the form of problems and essays.

Candidates will be required to answer four questions from Sections B and C, including at least one question from each section.

As a general principle, it may be assumed that the subject matter of the paper will follow the study weightings listed in the syllabus. Thus, for example, as the law of contract is afforded a 30% study weighting, approximately 30% of the questions on the examination paper as a whole will relate to the law of contract.

Questions may require candidates to play the role of finance director, company secretary etc and to present their answers in the form of a report, internal memorandum or letter.

Content

8 (a) Contract (study weighting 30%)

Questions will commonly take the form of problems which require candidates to advise one of the parties of the legal position.

In the examination, candidates may be required to:

- demonstrate a knowledge of, and an ability to apply, the following:

    (i)   the essential elements of a valid simple contract

    (ii)   when a statement becomes a term of the contract

    (iii)   the status of those terms, including those implied by statute

    (iv)   how a contract may be brought to an end by performance, frustration, agreement and breach

    (v)   situations in which a party may avoid a contract as a result of a misrepresentation, mistake, duress or undue influence

    (vi)   the remedies available to innocent parties in the event of a breach of contract

- demonstrate an awareness of those transactions that require a special form of contract, eg contracts for the sale of land which must be in writing, and of the rules relating to privity of contract.

The following items are **not** examinable:

- assignment

- negotiation.

8 (b) Agency (study weighting 10%)

Candidates must know the legal rules governing:

- the relation between the principal and the agent

- the relation between the principal and the agent on the one hand, and a third party on the other.

8 (c) Negligence (study weighting 10%)

In the examination, candidates may be required to:

- demonstrate a knowledge of the basic concepts of the tort of negligence, such as duty of care, breach, and damage or injury

- display a knowledge of how the tort of negligence affects the liability of professionals to those who rely on their expertise.

8 (d) Employment (study weighting 10%)

In the examination, candidates may be required to:

- distinguish between employees and independent contractors, and understand the importance of the distinction

- demonstrate a knowledge of what normal and implied terms are to be found in contracts of employment, including the right not to be discriminated against on the grounds of sex or race

- demonstrate a knowledge and understanding of the rules relating to wrongful and unfair dismissal, with particular emphasis on the latter because of its greater practical importance

- demonstrate a knowledge of how employers and employees are affected by health and safety legislation, including the consequences of a failure to comply.

8 (e) Company formation (study weighting 10%)

In the examination, candidates may be required to:

- demonstrate a knowledge of the situations in which the courts may be prepared to 'lift the veil' of incorporation, and those in which legislation requires the veil to be lifted

- demonstrate a knowledge of the nature and significance of the documents which must be submitted to the Registrar

- demonstrate an awareness of alternative methods of company formation, such as the purchase of 'off the shelf' companies

- distinguish between public and private companies.

8 (f) Corporate finance (study weighting 10%)

In the examination, candidates may be required to:

- demonstrate a knowledge of the rules relating to the issue of shares including:

    (i)   issue at a discount and premium
    (ii)   issue for a non-cash consideration
    (iii)   when such consideration must be valued
    (iv)   to whom the shares must be offered
    (v)   the powers of directors to issue shares

- demonstrate an understanding of the rules relating to the maintenance of capital principle, including increases and reductions of capital and how the principle is affected by a company's ability to purchase, redeem and provide financial assistance for the purchase of its own shares

- in the context of loan capital and the validity of floating charges, demonstrate a knowledge of Section 245 of the Insolvency Act 1986.

The following item is **not** examinable:

- listing particulars and prospectuses.

8 (g) Corporate management (study weighting 10%)

It should be noted that there is some overlap between the topic of directors item and section **(b)** **Agency**, in that the board of directors is the agent of a company, so that many of the rules covered in section **(b)** will also be of relevance here.

In the examination, candidates may be required to:

- know how directors may incur personal liability in respect of their dealings, including those which take place prior to the liquidation of the company, eg in respect of fraudulent and wrongful trading, and in respect of 'transactions at an undervalue' and 'preferences'.

8 (h) Shareholders (study weighting 10%)

In the context of the protection of minority shareholders, the modern tendency is for minority actions to be based on s.459, rather than the exceptions to *Foss v Harbottle*. An answer to a question on minority protection would be regarded as complete, therefore, even if it was restricted to s.459. The exceptions to *Foss v Harbottle* may, of course, provide examples of situations where a minority shareholder would today utilise s.459.

In the examination, candidates may be required to:

- understand how the law seeks to protect minority shareholders in their dealings with the majority, with particular reference to statutory protection.

HOTLINE TO THE EXAMINER

AT Foulks Lynch, in common with other training organisations, maintains regular contact with the CIMA examiners to seek clarification of the syllabus. CIMA publishes all such questions and the examiners' answers, and we are grateful to CIMA for permission to reproduce the key questions and answers below.

1   **Is contractual capacity examinable (8a)?**

Contractual capacity is examinable: it is included under 'essential elements of a valid simple contract'.

2   **Could the Examiner confirm that illegal contracts are not examinable (8a)?**

Contracts void for illegality is examinable: this topic is included under 'essential elements of a valid simple contract'. Void contracts other than for mistake or restraint of trade are not examinable.

3   **Could the Examiner confirm that assignment is not examinable?**

Assignment is not examinable.

4   **Is negotiability examinable?**

Negotiability is not examinable.

5   **Is limitation of action examinable?**

Yes: the Examiner would include this when considering 'remedies available'.

6   **Are remedies of debenture holders examinable?**

Yes: under 'the distinction between fixed and floating charges' (8f).

7   **Could the Examiner confirm that the Sale of Goods Act (SGA) 1979 is only examinable under the head of implied contract terms (8a)?**

The required depth of knowledge of SGA 1979 is those terms implied by Sections 12 to 15, and the extent to which they may be excluded. This may, of course, lead to other related Sections of this Act, for example Section 35.

8   **Will questions require knowledge of the Supply of Goods and Services Act 1982, the Supply of Goods (Implied Terms) Act 1973 and the Consumer Credit Act 1974?**

Knowledge will be required of the first Act mentioned here, but not of the other two.

9   **Could the Examiner confirm that redundancy is not examinable (8d)?**

Candidates will be expected to have an outline knowledge of redundancy.

10 **The syllabus states as one of its aims 'to explain the principles of business and company law including insolvency law as appropriate'. To what extent will insolvency law be tested? In particular, will the following topics be examined: liquidations; just and equitable winding up; receivership; administration?**

The expression 'insolvency law as appropriate' is used to cover those situations where it is impossible meaningfully to teach/understand a particular topic without reference to insolvency law. Examples include:

(i)   the basic fact of limited liability under 'corporate personality' in 8e;

(ii)   'priority of charges' in relation to debentures in 8f;

(iii) '. . . how directors may incur personal liability in respect of their dealings, including those that take place prior to the liquidation of the company . . .' ie, in respect of preferences, transactions at an undervalue etc (see 8g). In addition, 'just and equitable winding up' is examinable as a possible remedy of minority shareholders, ie, '. . . how the law seeks to protect minority shareholders in their dealings with the majority, with particular reference to statutory protection' (see 8h).

11 **To what extent are listing particulars and prospectuses examinable?**

These are not examinable.

12 **Are candidates required to have a knowledge of the Financial Services Act 1986 and of the Stock Exchange 'Listing Requirements'?**

No, these are not examinable.

13 **Issues in corporate governance - is this mainly concentrated on the Cadbury Committee (8g)?**

By stating that candidates '. . . should have some knowledge of topical issues of company law relating to corporate governance', the Examiner means, for example, the division of power between the board and the general meeting; the Cadbury Report; the ability of the shareholders to control the board etc.

14 **Would the Examiner please give specific guidance on the registration of charges provisions of the Companies Acts 1985/89, particularly in view of the probability that the 1989 provisions will never be brought into operation in their current form.**

This is a continuing problem. Although the 1989 Act contained a number of changes, they have not yet been implemented. Furthermore, according to Companies House, the changes are unlikely to ever be implemented! The problem is exacerbated by the fact that although the majority of textbooks contain the new rules, lecturers may choose to teach the rules which are still in force. Therefore, when examining registration of charges, the Examiner takes the view that both the existing and CA 1989 rules are acceptable. Candidates may therefore use either set of rules.

15 **More guidance is required about the depth of knowledge required for all aspect of the Company Law part of the syllabus, eg on the rules on the maintenance of share capital, loan capital and in particular, how much knowledge is required on receivership, loans to directors and meetings.**

Suggested answers have now been published for both the pilot and the May 1995 papers, in addition to the syllabus guidance notes. The Examiner assumes, therefore, that a greater understanding of the depth of knowledge is being acquired.

MAY 1997 EXAMINATIONS - SYLLABUS CHANGES

CIMA have announced some minor alterations to certain syllabuses to take effect from May 1997 onwards.

There are no alterations to the syllabus for this paper.

1 CONTRACT: THE NATURE OF A CONTRACT

INTRODUCTION & LEARNING OBJECTIVES

Syllabus area 8a. The nature of a contract. (Ability required 3).

Contracts are a central feature of modern life. Not only do they affect entire nations (treaties are effectively contracts) they also feature in ordinary daily life: the purchase of a drink in a public house; the boarding of a bus; the ordering of goods; the booking of a course of study - all constitute contracts. The law of contract is therefore of fundamental importance to the activities of virtually all kinds of business. A contract is in effect a mini legal system, in that **its** provisions govern the rights and obligations of the parties. This and the next seven chapters deal with the detail of this mini legal system.

When you have studied this chapter you should be able to do the following:

- Explain why all contracts are agreements but that not all agreements are contracts.

- Identify the five elements essential to the formation of a contract.

- Understand what a lawyer means when he uses such words and phrases as 'specialty contract', 'void' and 'voidable'.

---

1 WHAT IS A CONTRACT?

> **Definition** A contract is an agreement between two or more parties which is enforceable by the law.

Although all contracts are agreements not all agreements are contracts. This is because some agreements we might make are not enforceable at law. For example if two friends agree to go out to dinner together this is not a contract: neither could sue the other in court should one of them back out.

2 OUTLINE OF CONTRACT LAW

The law of contract is concerned with three basic questions.

(a) Is there a contract? The answer to this question lies in the rules relating to **formation** of a contract. In order for a legally binding contract to exist the following elements must be satisfied.

- **Agreement ie, offer and acceptance**

    There must be an offer by one party which the other accepts without qualification. For example, if John offers to sell his car for £500 to Bill by word of mouth and Bill verbally accepts, then a contract exists, provided the other essential elements are satisfied.

- **An intention to create legal relations**

  The agreement must be intended to be subject to an action in a court of law if a dispute arises between the parties, as opposed to a mere domestic or social arrangement such as agreeing to dine at a restaurant with a friend.

- **Consideration**

  This means that each party to the contract must suffer a loss or detriment, in return for the benefit received. For example, in a contract of sale the buyer acquires the goods and pays the price, whilst the seller receives the price in return for the goods handed over. The law enforces bargains made by the parties, not gratuitous promises.

- **Capacity**

  Each party must have the legal power to bind himself contractually to the agreement concluded. For example, the Crown, corporations, persons under the age of eighteen (minors) and persons of unsound mind or under the influence of drink have limitations on their power to contract.

- **Form**

  Some contracts are required to be made in a particular form such as writing. For most contracts, however, there is no special requirement and an oral agreement is just as much binding in law as a written agreement.

(b)   Is the agreement one which the law should recognise and enforce? Some contracts will be wholly or partly **invalid** at law because of a **vitiating factor** such as mistake and misrepresentation.

(c)   When do the **obligations** of the parties come to an end and what are the **remedies for breach** of contract? The most common method of termination of a contract is when each party performs his contractual obligations and this necessarily requires knowledge of exactly what each party undertook to do ie, the terms of the contract. Remedies for breach of contract include monetary compensation (called damages), an action for the price, and the court orders of specific performance and injunction.

3   BASIC PRINCIPLES AND DEFINITIONS

The following chapters will deal with all the above aspects in detail. It is useful, however, at the outset to mention two general principles and 3 sets of definitions which run through all aspects of the law of contract, and all other branches of law based primarily on contract eg, sale of goods, consumer credit agreements, employment, partnership, and agency.

3.1   General principles

(a)   **Freedom of contract**

The essence of contract is bargain; the parties are free to make their own bargain and the terms of the contract must be decided on by the parties to the contract. There are some restrictions on this principle:

- **Standard form contracts** - a person faced with a standard form cannot usually bargain; he must take it or leave it eg, conditions of rail travel.

- **Implied terms** - where the parties have failed to express all the terms of their contract, the court may imply terms into the agreement based on the presumed but unexpressed intention of the parties. Sometimes, such terms are implied by statute eg, implied conditions as to fitness and quality in sale of goods and implied conditions as to periods of notice in contracts of employment.

- Prohibitions on clauses excluding liability in certain transactions eg, the Unfair Contract Terms Act 1977.

Despite these restrictions, the principle of freedom of contract is still important, especially in commercial transactions where parties who negotiate are on an equal footing.

(b)   **Sanctity of contract**

The agreement of the parties cannot be interfered with either by the parties themselves, by the court or by third parties. Once the parties have made their agreement each must abide by it, unless released by the other, even though circumstances change so as to affect their expectations. The parties may make a good or a bad bargain - the courts will not interfere and renegotiate the terms for them. The fact that a party is not in any way at fault does not excuse him from his obligation to perform the contract. Thus in a contract for the sale of goods a shop is under a contractual obligation to sell goods which are of merchantable quality. If the goods are defective the customer has an action against the shop for breach of contract. It is no excuse for the shop to plead that the defect was the fault of the person who manufactured the goods.

There are some restrictions on the application of this principle of sanctity of contract:

- Restrictive interpretation placed on exemption clauses in contracts.
- Lawful excuses for non-performance of a contractual obligation eg, frustration.

3.2   Definitions

- **Specialty/simple**

A contract made by deed is called a specialty contract. In order to make a contract in the form of a deed it must be in writing, must state on its face that it is a deed, must be signed by each party, each party's signature must be witnessed and the witness must also sign, and it must be delivered. It is normal, although not necessary, to employ a solicitor to draw up a contract in the form of a deed.

Any contract which is not a specialty contract is a simple contract.

You will see that these two types of contract are treated differently:

-     in order for a specialty contract to exist consideration is not necessary

-     the time limit (called the limitation period) for suing for breach of contract is 6 years for simple contracts and 12 years for specialty contracts.

- **Bilateral/unilateral**

A contract whereby both parties make promises and are bound is a **bilateral contract** (the usual type of contract eg, a contract for sale of something, where the seller promises to transfer legal title to the buyer and the buyer promises to pay).

A contract whereby one person makes promises and is bound and the other person is free to perform or not as he chooses is a **unilateral contract.** This is a reward type situation, where one person promises to pay another if the other does something as in **Carlill v Carbolic Smoke Ball Company [1893]** where the Carbolic Smoke Ball Company in an advertisement promised to pay £100 to anyone who bought their smokeball, used it and still got influenza. Mrs Carlill bought and used the smokeball and caught influenza. She successfully claimed the £100. The promisor is bound if the promisee does the act which the promisor promised to reward.

You will see that the rules on offer and acceptance are sometimes different for bilateral and unilateral contracts.

- **Void/voidable**

A contract may be **vitiated** (flawed) by a number of factors eg, mistake, misrepresentation, duress, undue influence, illegality, in which case the contract is either **void** or **voidable.**

Void: a void contract has no legal effect on either party - it is as if there is no contract. Any property which is transferred under a void contract must be handed back to the transferor, as he remains the owner of it; if the transferee keeps the goods he could be sued by the real owner for wrongful detention of goods ie, conversion.

Voidable: a voidable contract exists unless and until it is brought to an end at the option of one of the parties, usually at the option of the innocent party. The act by which the innocent party avoids a voidable contract is called rescission.

4   Activity

In 1993 Clare orally agreed to sell her car to Fred for £6,000. Fred does not pay even though he has taken possession of the car. In what year does Clare's action for the price become statute-barred?

5   Activity solution

1999: since this is a simple contract Clare has 6 years in which to sue Fred for breach of contract.

6   SELF TEST QUESTIONS

6.1   List the 5 essential elements necessary for the formation of a contract (2)

6.2   State 2 vitiating factors (2)

6.3   How is a deed made? (3.2)

6.4   Distinguish between a void contract and a voidable contract (3.2)

2 CONTRACT: OFFER AND ACCEPTANCE

INTRODUCTION & LEARNING OBJECTIVES

Syllabus area 8a. Agreement. (Ability required 3).

This chapter covers the first essential element in the formation of a contract: that of agreement. The two components of agreement are that an **offer** has been made by one party (called the offeror) which the other party (called the offeree) has **accepted.** To put it another way: in order for a legally binding contract to exist there must be both offer and acceptance.

When you have studied this chapter you should be able to do the following:

- Define an offer and be able to distinguish it from an invitation to treat.
- Understand the effect of a counter-offer.
- Understand and apply the rules on revocation of an offer.
- Outline the rules on tenders and auctions.
- Define and describe acceptance.
- Understand the rules on communication of acceptance and in particular the postal rule.

1   THE OFFER

> **Definition**   An offer is a definite and unequivocal statement of willingness to be bound by contract.

1.1   Form of the offer

(a)   The offeror can make the offer expressly. This is where a person makes the offer orally or in writing.

(b)   The offeror can make the offer impliedly (ie, by conduct). This is where a person's behaviour implies the offer. An example of this would be a person filling his tank with petrol, at a petrol station. It is implicit in his behaviour that he is offering to buy the petrol.

In order to be valid the offer must have certain elements. Without these elements the offer does not legally exist and so cannot be accepted.

The requirements of a valid offer are set out below.

1.2   Definite and unequivocal

The offer must be a definite and unequivocal statement of willingness to be bound in contract. It cannot be vague or uncertain in its interpretation. So, an offer to sell someone a particular car for £5,000 will be an offer. But a statement that a person will sell: "... one of my cars for about £5,000" will not be an offer.

1.3   Clear intention to be bound

There must be a clear intention of present willingness to be bound by the offer. The offeror must not merely be negotiating. All the offeree has to do is to accept the terms as laid down by the offeror and the contract will be complete.

Gibson v Manchester City Council [1979]

Facts: the Council sent a letter to Gibson stating 'The corporation may be prepared to sell the house to you at the purchase price of £2,725 . . .'

Held: this was not an offer to sell the house, capable of acceptance by Gibson. (The letter is what is commonly called an 'invitation to treat' - a starting point in negotiations.)

1.4   Persons to whom an offer may be made

The offer can be made to a particular person, to a class of persons or even to the whole world.

An example of an offer made to the whole world arose in the leading case of **Carlill v Carbolic Smoke Ball Co [1893]**

Facts: the manufacturers of a medicinal 'smoke ball' advertised in a newspaper that anyone who bought and used the ball properly and nevertheless contracted influenza would be paid a £100 reward. Mrs Carlill used the ball as directed and did catch 'flu. The manufacturers claimed that they did not have to pay her the £100 as an offer could not be made to the whole world.

Held: that an offer could be made to the whole world, that the wording of the advert amounted to such an offer, and that Mrs Carlill had accepted it by properly using the smoke ball.

Another example of an offer to the world at large is a more typical advert for reward, say when someone has lost their cat and they offer a financial incentive for the finder to return it.

1.5   Communication of the offer

The offer must actually reach the person to whom it was made. In other words the offeree must know of it. An offer will not be valid unless the offeror has clearly communicated it to the offeree and that person is aware of it.

R v Clarke [1927]

Facts: the Government of Western Australia offered a free pardon to the accomplices of certain murderers if they gave evidence that would lead to their arrest and conviction. Clarke provided the information but admitted that he was not aware of the reward at the time he gave the information to the authorities.

Held: he could not claim the reward because he was not aware of the offer at the time he gave the information.

The rule is also relevant to cross-offers. Suppose for example: A writes to B offering to sell certain property at a stated price. B writes to A offering to buy the same property at the same price. The letters cross in the post. The majority of the judges in **Tinn v Hoffman [1873]** were of the opinion that there would be no contract in this situation.

1.6   Termination of an offer

The offer must be 'open' (ie still in force) when the offeree accepts it. It is important to note that when an offer has been terminated it can no longer be accepted.

(a)   **Revocation of offer**

One of the most important ways in which an offer can be terminated is by revocation by the offeror.

An offer can be revoked at any time before it has been accepted by the offeree. The revocation may be by express words or it may be implied from the offeror's conduct - **Dickinson v Dodds [1876]**

- The critical thing to note for examination questions is that the revocation will not take effect until the revocation has been received and clearly understood by the offeree. Until then, it remains open, and can be accepted.

   Byrne v Leon Van Tienhoven [1880]

   Facts: an offer was posted by the defendant in Cardiff on 1 October. It was received by the plaintiff in New York on 11 October. He at once cabled an acceptance (effectively accepting on this date). In the meantime the defendant had changed his mind and had sent a letter of revocation from Cardiff on 8 October. This letter of revocation reached New York on 15 October. The question before the court was whether the offer had been accepted or revoked.

   Held: the revocation was not complete until it had been communicated to the offeree. This was on the 15 October. In the meantime, however, the offer had been accepted. As a result, the revocation was ineffective and the contract did exist. The defendant was therefore liable under the contract.

- The revocation can be communicated by the offeror or by a reliable third party:

   Dickinson v Dodds [1876]

   Facts: the defendant, on 10 June, gave the plaintiff a written offer to sell a house for £800, "to be left over until 12 June at 9.00am". On 11 June the defendant sold the house to a third party for £800, and that evening another person told the plaintiff of the sale. Before 9.00am the next day the plaintiff accepted the offer.

   Held: as the plaintiff knew that the defendant was no longer in the position to sell the property to him the defendant had validly withdrawn his offer. If a reasonable person would have been aware of this withdrawal the offer is withdrawn.

- With unilateral contracts ie, where an offer is to be accepted by conduct, the offer cannot be revoked once the offeree has begun to try and perform whatever act is necessary to constitute acceptance.

   Errington v Errington [1953]

   Facts: a man offered to transfer his house to his son and daughter-in-law if they cleared the mortgage debt by paying all instalments when due. The couple began paying the instalments but when the man died his personal representatives attempted to withdraw the offer.

Held: the couple were entitled to continue paying the instalments and claim the house when the mortgage debt had been paid off. The father's offer could not be revoked once the couple commenced the act of acceptance: it would however cease to bind him if they left it incomplete and unperformed.

- The rule that an offer can be revoked at any time before acceptance applies even though the offeror has stated that he will keep the offer open for a stated time.

Routledge v Grant [1828]

Facts: Grant offered to buy Routledge's horse and gave him six weeks to decide whether or not to accept. Before the six weeks had elapsed, Grant withdrew his offer.

Held: in the absence of Routledge already having accepted, Grant was entitled to revoke his offer.

To safeguard his position in such a situation the offeree might choose to pay the offeror to keep the offer open. This, an option, is a separate binding contract. Thus, if during the period of the option, the offer is revoked the offeror commits a breach of contract for which damages are recoverable by the offeree.

(b)   **Rejection of an offer**

An offer can be terminated by a rejection. This is the action of the offeree turning down the offer. This is either outright, by the offeree stating that he will not accept it, or by a counter-offer.

(Definition)   A counter-offer is an offer made in response to an offer.

An example of a counter-offer is where the offeree offers a lower price or in any other way barters with the offeror. This is imposing conditions on the acceptance and, as we will see, an acceptance must be unconditional. This counter-offer, in the same way as an outright rejection, terminates the original offer.

Hyde v Wrench [1840]

Facts: Wrench offered to sell Hyde a farm for £1,000. Hyde made a counter-offer, by offering £950. Wrench rejected this. Later Hyde came back and said that he now accepted the original offer of £1,000. Wrench rejected it.

Held: Hyde could no longer accept the original offer. It had been terminated by the counter-offer and was no longer capable of acceptance. His 'acceptance' was merely a fresh offer which Wrench was free to turn down.

Note that a mere request for further details does not constitute a counter-offer.

Stevenson v McLean [1880]

Facts: M offered, in writing, to sell a quantity of iron to S at a given price. S replied querying delivery times, but before receiving a reply sent a further letter accepting the offer. This acceptance crossed in the post with a letter of revocation from M to S. M refused to supply the iron to S, arguing that S's query was a counter-offer.

Held: M could not treat the query as a counter-offer. S had not intended to prejudice M's position, just to establish the parameters of the deal. Therefore M's offer was still open when S wrote accepting it.

(c)   **Lapse of an offer**

An offer can also be terminated by **lapse**.

- If the offer is stated only to be open for a specific time period it will end after the expiration of this time. If there is no specific period of time mentioned by the offeror the offer will lapse after a reasonable length of time. If there is a dispute about the time period the court will decide what is reasonable. It is a question of fact to be decided in each case.

- If the offer was made subject to a condition it will lapse on failure of that condition. An example of this would be an offer to supply an establishment with alcohol as long as it had a licence to sell alcohol. If the establishment for any reason lost its licence, the offer would lapse and would no longer be capable of acceptance.

- If the offeror dies the offer can no longer be accepted once the offeree knows of the death.

- If the offeree dies the offer cannot be accepted by his personal representatives (who step into the shoes of the deceased and administer the estate after death). If the deceased had a will they are called 'executors' and if the deceased has died intestate (ie, with no will) they are known as 'administrators'.

1.7   Activity

Gail offers to sell Clare her dog for £10. Clare is not sure and wants to check with her husband first. She gives Gail £1 on Gail's promise to keep the offer open for 2 days. Before the 2 days have elapsed Gail sells the dog and tells Clare.

Advise Clare.

1.8   Activity solution

Clare cannot accept Gail's offer to sell to the dog because the offer has been terminated by an effective revocation. However, Clare can sue Gail for damages for breach of the collateral contract to keep the offer open.

1.9   Activity

P offers to sell his car to Q.

(a)   Q accepts P's offer and then dies
(b)   Q dies and his executors purport to accept P's offer.

In each situation, is there a binding contract?

1.10   Activity solution

(a)   Q made a binding contract before he died. Therefore Q is contractually bound to buy the car from P. (Since Q is dead it is his personal representatives who will have to carry out his pre-death obligations and actually buy the car).

(b)   Q's death causes P's offer to lapse. There is therefore no offer which Q's executors can accept and accordingly no binding contract.

1.11

[Conclusion]   In order to be valid the offer must be:

- clear, definite and unequivocal;
- one that the offeror intends to be bound by;
- made to a person, a group of persons or to the whole world;
- communicated to the offeree;
- open when it is accepted.

Until all of these conditions are present the offer will not be valid and so cannot be accepted.

2   SITUATIONS WHERE THERE IS NO OFFER

2.1   Introduction

When considering an examination question it is vital to decide whether or not the facts amount to an offer. Not all statements amount to an offer and only an offer can be accepted, so leading to a contract. It is vital to distinguish the offer from the other possibilities in the exam question.

2.2   Invitation to treat

[Definition]   An invitation to treat is not an offer in itself but is an invitation to others to make an offer.

An invitation to treat is often the starting point of the negotiations - **Gibson v Manchester City Council [1979]**.

- **Shop displays**

Pharmaceutical Society of Great Britain v Boots Cash Chemists [1953]

Facts: statute requires that the sale of certain pharmaceuticals must be carried out under the supervision of a qualified pharmacist. Boots operated a store where the drugs were sold on a self-service basis and the customers paid at a cash desk for the goods they had selected. A pharmacist was present at the cash desk but not at the shelves where the goods were displayed with a price tag. The Pharmaceutical Society claimed that the statute was being contravened.

Held: the display of goods in a shop was not an offer but an invitation to treat. It was the customer who made the offer and Boots could either accept or reject this offer at the cash desk (in the presence of a qualified pharmacist). The act constituting the acceptance is the ringing up of the price on the till by the cashier and at that moment a binding contract of sale is made.

Fisher v Bell [1960]

Facts: the Restriction of Offensive Weapons Act 1959 creates a criminal offence of 'offering for sale' certain offensive weapons. A shopkeeper was prosecuted under this statute for displaying a flick knife in his shop window.

Held: a window display was not an offer of sale but only an invitation to treat. So the display did not infringe the law.

- **Advertisements**

Sometimes an advertisement is an offer, sometimes it is an invitation to treat.

The general position is that it will be an invitation to treat because further negotiations are intended or expected.

Partridge v Crittenden [1968]

Facts: the appellant inserted an advertisement in a periodical 'Bramblefinch cocks and hens, 25s each'. It was **held** this was an invitation to treat not an offer.

It will be an offer if no further negotiations are intended or expected. This is the position with rewards - **Carlill v Carbolic Smoke Ball [1893]**

- **Catalogues and prospectuses**

These are invitations to treat, not offers.

2.3   A mere statement of intention

An offer must be distinguished from a mere statement of intention.

Harris v Nickerson [1873]

Facts: an auction sale of furniture was advertised in a newspaper. A London broker saw the advert and travelled up to attend the sale in order to bid for various lots. Unknown to him the items had been withdrawn from the sale before he arrived. He claimed that his actions of turning up at the auction sale amounted to an acceptance of the offer contained in the advertisement. As a result he claimed that the auctioneers had breached the contract in not selling the items of furniture. He then sued for damages to cover his loss.

Held: the advertisement did not amount to an offer:

- It was not clear, definite or unequivocal from the advertisement that the auctioneers wanted to sell the items of furniture to the broker;

- The auctioneers had no intention to be bound to this broker.

Accordingly, the critical pre-requisites for an offer were not all present and this advertisement was a mere statement of intention.

2.4   A statement of price

An offer must be distinguished from a mere supplying of information.

The statement of a price in answer to an enquiry is not necessarily an offer to sell at that price.

Harvey v Facey [1893]

Facts: a telegram was sent by Harvey to Facey asking: **"Will you sell us Bumper Hall Pen? Telegram lowest cash price".** Bumper Hall Pen was a piece of land owned by Facey. A telegram was sent in reply stating: **"Lowest cash price for Bumper Hall Pen £900".** Harvey responded by sending a further telegram stating: **"We agree to buy Bumper Hall Pen for £900 asked by you"**. There were no further communications and Harvey then claimed that Facey was bound by an enforceable contract to sell the land for £900.

Held: that a concluded contract had not been negotiated. The first telegram was a request for information and the second telegram was merely an answer to the question posed in the first telegram. The final telegram embodied an offer to buy the land for £900, but the offer was not accepted by the landowner to bring a contract of sale into existence.

2.5   Activity

John sees a car displayed on a garage forecourt with a sticker on the windscreen 'For Sale. £999'. He walks in and says to the manager that he is buying the car for £999. The manager refuses to sell it to him. Has John a contractual right to the car?

2.6   Activity solution

No. The display of the car is not an offer. His statement he will buy is therefore not an acceptance, it is an offer which the manager has chosen to reject. There is no binding contract.

Note: under criminal law it is an offence for a business to display goods for a price at which it is unwilling to sell. It is likely then that the garage here could be prosecuted and fined. This does not, however, have any bearing on the law of contract which is civil law.

3   ACCEPTANCE

3.1   Definition

Definition   Acceptance is the unconditional assent to all the terms of the offer.

We have already seen that if an offeree attempts to change the terms of the offer or qualify it in any way it will terminate the offer and be classed as a counter-offer. This is as in the case of **Hyde v Wrench** above. It is only when the offeree has accepted the offer unconditionally that the parties can be said to be in agreement. This complete agreement about the terms and conditions of the contract is fundamental in English contract law.

Remember that not all enquiries about the terms of the contract will amount to a counter-offer by the offeree. The offeree may only be enquiring about delivery times or other less essential terms of the contract. Only that which amounts to a complete rejection of the terms suggested by the offeror will terminate the offer, rendering it incapable of acceptance. However, an enquiry about the price will almost certainly be a counter-offer. It depends upon the facts of the question and what the parties consider are the conditions (or fundamental terms) of the contract.

The acceptance must also not be 'subject to contract'. This phrase is frequently used in the buying and selling of land. The phrase 'subject to contract' denotes that the parties have reached a degree of agreement but there will be no binding commitment until they enter into a formal contract, usually in writing. (In English law this will be at the 'exchange of contracts' stage.)

3.2   Form of acceptance

- Any form of acceptance is valid whether it be oral, written or merely inferred from the conduct of the parties. An example of the last occurred in **Carlill v Carbolic Smoke Ball [1893]** where Mrs Carlill was held to accept the company's offer by using the smoke ball in the prescribed manner. Another example is

Brogden v Metropolitan Railway [1877]

Facts: the company submitted a draft agreement to Brogden for the supply coal. Brogden sent back the document to the company having added new terms. The company did not expressly agree these new terms but coal was supplied on these amended terms.

Held: mere mental assent by the company was not a valid acceptance but the parties had, by their conduct, agreed to act on the basis of the amended draft contract and so it had become binding. A contract existed either from the moment the company placed its first order for coal with Brogden after he returned the amended document, or, at the very latest, when the first order was completed by delivery of the coal.

- An offeror may stipulate a mode or method of acceptance.

If he makes his stipulation mandatory (eg, by stating that acceptance **must** be in writing) then no other form of acceptance would be valid.

If he makes his stipulation as a request any other equally advantageous form of acceptance is valid.

Yates Building v R J Pulleyn & Sons [1975]

Facts: the offeror asked for the offer to be accepted by registered or recorded delivery letter. The offeree accepted by an ordinary letter, which arrived promptly.

Held: the offeror had suffered no disadvantage in the way that the offer had been accepted. As the offeror had not specified that the acceptance could only be made by recorded or registered letter the acceptance was in as quick and as reliable a form and so was valid.

- An offeror may not stipulate that silence shall amount to acceptance.

Felthouse v Bindley [1863]

Facts: F wrote to his nephew offering to buy the nephew's horse for £30 15s and adding "If I hear no more about him, I consider the horse mine at that price". The nephew never replied.

It was **held** that there was no contract: an offeror cannot impose contractual liability on an offeree merely by proclaiming that silence shall be deemed acceptance.

The modern day format of the **Felthouse v Bindley** principle is 'inertia selling' as where a tradesman sends unsolicited goods to a customer accompanied by a letter stating that if the goods are not returned within ten days it will be assumed they are bought. The common law decision in **Felthouse v Bindley** is that the customer cannot have a contract imposed on him in this way. The Unsolicited Goods and Services Act 1971 takes matters further by providing that if unsolicited goods are sent with the intention that the recipient shall either purchase or hire them from the sender then the recipient may keep the goods as an unconditional gift provided 6 months have elapsed and the sender has not taken steps to retrieve the goods. The Act also makes it a criminal offence to demand payment for unsolicited goods.

3.3   Communication of acceptance

- Acceptance is not effective until and unless it is communicated to the offeror. Mere mental assent (silence) is not acceptance - **Brogden v Metropolitan Railway [1877]**.

- The communication must be carried out by the offeree or by his authorised agent.

    Powell v Lee [1908]

    Facts: at a meeting the managers of a school decided to accept Lee's offer to be headmaster. Acting on his own initiative one of the managers informed Lee of the decision.

    It was **held** that there was no contract because there had been no communication of the acceptance by the managers as a body nor communication by a person authorised by them.

- There are two exceptions to the rule that acceptance must be communicated.

3.4   Dispensation by the offeror

The offeror may expressly or impliedly dispense with the need for communication. He may dispense altogether with communication or merely dispense with communication to himself.

- **Express dispensation**

    For example, an offeror may, if he so wishes, ask for a message of acceptance to be left on his telephone answering machine. It would seem that a contract exists from the moment such a message is left and even though the offeror never plays back his messages.

    It is probable also in the **Felthouse v Bindley** situation that, having been given the option of silence constituting acceptance, the offeree could choose to accept by non-reply.

- **Implied dispensation**

    The terms of the offer may imply that communication of acceptance is unnecessary. This will be the case in unilateral contracts such as **Carlill v Carbolic Smoke Ball [1893]**.

3.5   The postal rule

 The postal rule states that the acceptance will be complete and effective when the letter is posted or placed into the hands of the relevant postal authorities - **Adams v Lindsell [1818]**

The postal rule will only apply when acceptance by post is either the chosen, obvious or reasonable method of acceptance. It will be the chosen method of acceptance where the offeree has stipulated that posting the acceptance is the only acceptable method. It will be the obvious method of acceptance in a standard business situation or where the parties are communicating at a distance and the offeror requires a record of the reply. Also where the offer was by letter. It will be the reasonable method of acceptance if an ordinary person, looking at all the circumstances would assume that to reply by post was the proper way.

Household Fire Insurance v Grant [1879]

Facts: Grant applied for shares in a company. The company posted a letter of allotment (ie accepting his offer) to Grant. He never received it. Later, the company went into liquidation and Grant was sued for the balance owing on the shares.

Held: the acceptance was complete as soon as the letter of acceptance was posted. As a result Grant was liable under the contract to pay the existing balance.

Holwell Securities v Hughes [1974]

Facts: Holwell Securities had been granted an option by Hughes to purchase some property. This option was to be exercised by 'notice in writing'. Holwell Securities sent Hughes a letter giving notice of their intention to exercise the option. This letter was lost in the post.

Held: the words **'notice** in writing' mean that the notice must actually be received and that posting it was not enough in this instance.

The letter must be properly stamped addressed and posted. Handing a letter to a postman who is authorised to deliver is not equivalent in law to posting a letter.

Re London and Northern Bank ex parte Jones [1900]

Facts: in this case a letter of acceptance (to buy shares in a bank) was handed to a postman. Before the letter reached the offeror, he revoked the offer and a question arose as to whether the acceptance letter had been 'posted' for the purpose of the postal rule.

Held: handing letters to a post office worker is not the same as 'posting' them and so the postal rule does not apply in this situation. Acceptance is communicated when the offeror receives the letter.

The postal rule extends to telegrams but not to telex. Being effectively a telegraphic medium telex is treated in the same way as other instantaneous communications. As a result the normal rule of acceptance applies.

Entores v Miles Far East Corporation [1955]

Facts: the offeror, in London, sent an offer by telex to the offeree, in Amsterdam. The offeree then sent an acceptance, also by telex.

Held: the postal rule did not apply. Therefore, under the general rule, the acceptance was complete when the telex was printed out on the offeror's machine in London, and not when it was typed in to the offeree's machine in Amsterdam.

3.6   Activity

Alan accepted a business offer by posting a letter in a post box in the country. He knew, by reading the local paper, that the postal service in his area had been suspended due to the ill health of two of the postal workers. The letter never arrived at the premises of the offeror.

Was the offer accepted by Alan's actions?

3.7   Activity solution

No. The postal rule will not apply in this situation as it is not a reasonable method of acceptance. As Alan knows of the suspension in the postal service he cannot reasonably state that he considered this an acceptable way to reply.

As a result the usual rules on acceptance apply and as Alan's letter never reached its destination it was never accepted. No contract.

4   CONCLUSION

In order to be a proper acceptance it must be:

- Clear, absolute and unqualified;

- Communicated to the offeror either orally, in writing or by conduct; (unless acceptance by conduct is appropriate or the postal rule applies);

- Communicated in the precise way stipulated by the offeror, unless an equally quick, efficient or reliable method is chosen.

5   FURTHER MATTERS

5.1   Tenders

Definition   A tender is an offer to supply specified goods or services at a stated cost or rate.

Tenders are often used in commercial situations. An example would be where a local authority or government body invited various suppliers to bid for a contract, say to supply heating oil for the region's schools. Competing businesses would then, as offerors, send in a bids or tenders to do the work and these would be the offers.

- If the tender is an offer to work on a 'one-off' job, such as building a by-pass, it is an offer that can be accepted immediately by the relevant local authority. The contract would then be complete when the local authority accepts the tender in the usual way.

- A tender can be in the form of a standing offer.

Definition   A standing offer tender is a response to an invitation to supply a series of things, such as school meals or refuse collection services, if and when required. The tender is open to a series of acceptances whenever an order is placed.

Each acceptance completes a distinct contract. The standing offer can be revoked at any time unless there is a binding obligation to keep it open for a certain period of time. This obligation to keep the offer open has to be supported by consideration or be embodied in an agreement under seal, which needs no consideration.

Great Northern Railways v Witham [1873]

Facts: Witham successfully tendered for the contract to supply iron goods to GNR for the period of one year. The wording of the tender was to supply such quantities as GNR may . . "order from time to time". GNR placed several orders but after a time Witham refused to service the orders.

Held: Witham's tender was a standing offer which GNR accepted every time it placed an order. A a result Witham was bound to supply orders that had already been placed, but he was free to revoke the standing offer in the usual way. Witham was not liable to supply any iron after the revocation had been clearly received by the offeree.

5.2   Auctions

The rules on offer and acceptance at auctions require explanation as they have featured in examination questions in the past.

The auctioneer who holds the auction sale makes an invitation to treat (although it may be treated as a mere statement of intention as in the case of **Harris v Nickerson**).

At the auction sale each bid is an offer which the auctioneer is free to accept or reject. It is important to note here that the person who passes the item to the auctioneer for sale may indicate a 'reserve price'. This is the lowest price that he will accept from one of the bidders. The auctioneer is effectively selling the item as an agent for the owner. Reaching the stated reserve price at the sale will be a 'condition precedent' to the contract of agency coming into existence. Until the sale price has been reached in the bidding the contract between the owner and the auctioneers will not be effective.

At the auction sale each bidder is free to revoke his bid, as long as he does so in the usual way; clearly and before the bid has been accepted. A bid will lapse when a higher bid is made.

The auctioneer will accept the bid when his hammer hits the gavel. At this time the contract is complete. No new terms can be imposed after this time and the auctioneer is contractually bound to sell the item to the highest bidder, whose bid he has accepted.

Payne v Cave [1789]

Facts: in this case the defendant was bidding for goods at an auction sale. He made the highest bid but withdrew it before the hammer fell.

Held: the Court held that there was no contract in this situation. This is because the bid (the offer) had been revoked before the acceptance came (by the drop of the hammer). The usual rules of offer and acceptance (and so revocation) apply. The bidder had clearly withdrawn his offer by way of revocation before the acceptance was complete.

5.3   Battle of forms

A further problem related to offer and acceptance is what has now become known as the **battle of forms,** where the contracting parties both purport to act on their own written standard terms. In a sale of goods the seller may offer to sell the goods on his (seller's) terms and the buyer may accept on his (buyer's) terms. If a strict analysis were placed on this situation then the seller's terms would constitute an offer and the buyer's terms a counter-offer - so there would be no contract. In **Butler v Ex-Cell-O Corp [1979]** the above situation occurred. However, at the foot of the buyer's order was a tear-off acknowledgement or order slip, and this was completed by the seller and returned to the buyer. The court held that this constituted an acceptance of the buyer's counter-offer; thus, there was a contract on the buyer's standard terms. It was fortuitous that there was an acknowledgement slip. If there had not been one, perhaps delivery and/or acceptance of the goods would have constituted acceptance.

6   Activity

Will a contract exist in the following situations?

(1)   Jules offers Sam a room in his hotel for £50.00 but insists that Sam accepts by midday the next day in writing. Sam drives round to Jules hotel the next day but because of heavy traffic does not arrive until 2.00pm to pass over his letter of acceptance.

(2)   Susie offers Alan her pony for £500. She says that she will assume Alan accepts if she hears nothing from him by Saturday. Alan, who does not wish to accept, does not reply.

(3)   Mark posts an acceptance to a postal business offer only a few hours before a postal strike begins. Mark knew of the possible strike.

(4)   Tim sends for some shoes from a mail order company but the company has run out of shoes in his size. They return his money.

6.1   Activity solution

(1)   No. The offer is terminated by lapse - passage of stipulated time.

(2)   No. The offeror cannot stipulate that silence shall constitute acceptance - **Felthouse v Bindley**.

(3)   the postal rule does not apply since it would not be reasonable to use the post as a means of communication. There will however be a contract - when and if the letter is received.

(4)   No. The mail order catalogue (or advertisement if this is what Tim responded to) is an invitation to treat. Tim's sending away is an offer. The company's sending back of his money is a rejection of his offer.

7   CHAPTER SUMMARY

In order for a legally binding contract to exist there must be both offer and acceptance. Together they amount to an agreement.

In order to be valid an offer must be:

- clear, definite and unequivocal;
- one that the offeree intends to be bound by;
- made to a person, a group of persons or to the world;
- communicated to the offeree;
- open when it is accepted.

An offer should be distinguished from an invitation to treat, an mere statement of intention and a statement of price. No offer occurs in these situations and so they are not capable of acceptance.

In order to be valid an acceptance must:

- be an unconditional assent to all the terms of the offer (and not amount to a counter-offer);

- be made either verbally, in writing or by conduct;

- be made in the way that the offeror has expressly stipulated or in a way that is equally quick, efficient and reliable;

- be clearly communicated to the offeror by the offeree. However the **postal rule** will render the acceptance complete once the letter of acceptance has been posted. The rule will **only** apply where acceptance by letter is within the contemplation of the parties as a means of communication.

8   SELF TEST QUESTIONS

8.1   Define an offer. (1)

8.2   At what point in time will a revocation terminate an offer? (1.6)

8.3   What effect will a counter-offer have on an offer? (1.6)

8.4   What is an invitation to treat? (2.2)

8.5   Define an acceptance. (3.1)

8.6   In what different ways can an acceptance be validly made? (3.2)

8.7   Whose responsibility is it to ensure that an acceptance is properly communicated? (3.3)

8.8   State the two exceptions to the rule that acceptance must be communicated (3.4 and 3.5)

8.9   When will the postal rule apply? What is the rule? (3.5)

9   EXAMINATION TYPE QUESTION

9.1   Mark and Daniel

Mark wants to stay in Daniel's hotel for three nights. Daniel explains that he only has one room left for that particular period and that he will let Mark have the room under two conditions. Firstly, that Mark pays him £75.00 per night and secondly, that Mark accepts this offer in writing by first class post to be received by the next day.

Advise the parties on the following:

(a)   Is Daniel's offer valid? What are the pre-requisites for a valid offer?

(5 marks)

(b)   What would happen if Mark arrived the next day with a written acceptance which he delivers to Daniel but Daniel informs him that he sent a fax purporting to revoke the offer the previous day? Mark never received the fax.

(5 marks)

(c)   What if Mark sends his acceptance on the same day that the offer is made but the letter gets lost in the post? Would your answer be the same if a postal strike had started on the day the offer was made?

(5 marks)

(d)   What if there is no postal strike but Mark sends the letter of acceptance by second class post which does not arrive until the day after the one specified by Daniel?

(5 marks)

(Total: 20 marks)

10   ANSWER TO EXAMINATION TYPE QUESTION

10.1   Mark and Daniel

(a)   In order for Daniel's offer to provide a room in his hotel for £75.00 per night to be valid it must satisfy the legal conditions for such an offer:

- it must be a definite and unequivocal statement of willingness to be bound in contract to Mark. There can be little question on the facts that the offer to provide a room in a hotel for a fee is certain.

- there must be a clear intention to be bound. Daniel must not be merely negotiating with Mark. Again there is little doubt that if Mark agrees to pay £75.00 per night there will be a contract.

- the offer is made to a person. It is clearly made to Mark; there is no legal problem with this.

- the offer must reach the person to whom it is made. It is the responsibility of the offeror to ensure that the offer reaches Mark. Daniel appears to have explained the terms to Mark and they have been properly communicated.

- the offer must be open when it is accepted by the offeree. There is no question, at this stage, that the offer is open. For the purposes of this part of the question the offer is open.

As a result of all of the above elements being present Daniel's offer to Mark is a valid one and it is capable of acceptance.

(b)   Mark is the offeree in this question. It is his legal responsibility to ensure that the acceptance is properly communicated to the offeror, Daniel. In this situation Daniel has specified a particular mode of acceptance, namely by first class post.

The facts here raise two issues:

- was the offer revoked by Daniel's actions, or was it still capable of acceptance by Mark?

- as Mark did not accept in the way stipulated is his acceptance (ie, by personal delivery) a reasonable acceptance?

Dealing with the first issue. In order for Daniel's purported revocation to be effective it must reach the offeree before the acceptance is complete. Daniel has to ensure that Mark receives and understands the fact that the offer is terminated.

In the case of **Byrne v Van Tienhoven** the Court held that the acceptance of the offer (by post) was effective before the revocation was complete. The offeror could not claim that there was not a contract. In the present case Mark did not receive the fax and so the revocation was not adequately communicated to him. He was still in a position to accept the offer.

Dealing with the second issue. If a method of acceptance has been specified by the offeror the acceptance must be effected in this specific way or in a way that is equally quick, efficient and reliable. It must also be reasonable to have accepted in another way.

It could be the case that Daniel requested that the offer be accepted by first class post because this is the way his bookings are always dealt with. Or it could be that he wants to receive the acceptance first thing in the morning. Either way this would mean that hand delivering the acceptance the next day is arguably not a efficient as the specified method and that the acceptance will not be adequate.

Note: it is not critical to reach a conclusion in a law answer of this type. As long as the law relevant to the facts is discussed and the possibilities considered the marks will be awarded for the answer.

(c)   The rule for the acceptance of an offer is that it is the responsibility of the offeree to ensure that the acceptance is received. The acceptance will only be effective from the time the offeree properly communicates the acceptance to the offeror.

However, an exception to that rule is the postal rule. If acceptance by post is the chosen, obvious or reasonable method of acceptance the rule will apply. In this situation it is not only a reasonable method of acceptance but it is also chosen as the method of acceptance by the offeror. Where the rule applies the offer is deemed to be accepted, as long as the reply is properly addressed and posted, as soon as the letter is posted or placed into the hands of the relevant postal authorities. This is as per the case of **Household Fire Insurance v Grant**.

On the first part of the facts Mark's acceptance will be complete as soon as his letter is posted irregardless of the fact that the letter did not arrive.

However, on the second part of the facts; if Mark was at all aware of the postal strike it would not be reasonable for him to use this method of acceptance (even if stipulated by Daniel) and the postal rule would not apply. In this situation the offer would be accepted only when the acceptance is communicated to the offeror and if this is delayed by the strike there may be no contract here.

(d)   In this final scenario it has to be decided whether or not the postal rule applies. Daniel specified that the acceptance should be in writing to be received by him the next day.

As discussed above the postal rule will only operate when it is the chosen, obvious or reasonable way to accept the contract. To accept by second class post is not reasonable on these facts as, with the best will in the world, it is unlikely that the letter will arrive, as required, by the next day.

If the postal rule does not apply the usual rule of acceptance prevails. This is that the acceptance will be complete as soon as it is clearly communicated to the offeror. The letter of acceptance does not arrive until the day after the day specified by Daniel on these facts so the acceptance falls foul of the conditions laid down. There is no acceptance and so there is no contract for Mark to rely upon.

Note: not all of the answers have to be the same length. The important consideration is to answer the question that is asked. If that can be adequately done in less time do not be afraid to finish the answer at that point and go on. This is especially the case in a question such as this one where the points have been dealt with fully in previous parts of the answer.

3 CONTRACT: CONSIDERATION

INTRODUCTION & LEARNING OBJECTIVES

Syllabus area 8a. Consideration. (Ability required 3).

This chapter introduces and explains the second pre-requisite for a contract - consideration. An agreement requires 5 things before it amounts to a binding contract:

- Offer and acceptance
- Consideration
- Intention to create legal relations
- Capacity
- Form

Consideration is a highly examinable topic and should be carefully learnt.

When you have studied this chapter you should be able to do the following:

- understand what consideration is

- understand the terms 'valuable' consideration 'sufficient' consideration and 'past' consideration

- apply these concepts to the 'part payment problem'

---

1 NATURE OF CONSIDERATION

1.1 The basic rule

Every simple contract must be supported by consideration.

1.2 Specialty contracts

Contracts made by deed do not require consideration

1.3 Activity

Jane wishes to make a deed. List for her the necessary legal steps.

1.4 Activity solution

- all the terms must be written

- the document must state it is a deed

- Jane (and any other party) must sign it

- a witness to each signature must sign

- the deed must be delivered (eg, if each party signs a copy they must hand over the copies to each other)

1.5   Definition of consideration

The case of **Currie v Misa [1875]** laid down the accepted definition of consideration. It can be defined as: 'some right, interest, profit or benefit accruing to one party, or some forbearance, detriment, loss or responsibility given, suffered or undertaken by the other'.

This can be difficult to understand and to quote but in an examination question there are some key words that can be used to show the examiner that you do understand the concept. It is essentially where one person (being a party to the contract) does something, omits to do something or promises to do or omit something in **exchange** for another person (the other party) doing, omitting or promising something.

It must be an exchange; one person does something, etc **because** the other person does something. A simple everyday example is where a person purchases a drink from a vending machine. One party inserts the money into the machine and in **exchange** for this receives the canned drink. Both parties are receiving a benefit (the person inserting the money, takes the canned drink, and the vending machine company takes the money), and simultaneously they are each being detrimented. The purchaser is losing the purchase price and the drinks company the can that has been vended.

A more modern definition, and one which reflects more the importance of respective promises, rather than the concept of benefit/detriment is: 'consideration is an act or forbearance (or the promise of it) on the part of one party to a contract as the price of the promise made to him by the other party to the contract': **Dunlop v Selfridge [1915]**.

1.6   Executed and executory consideration

'Executed' consideration is given where a promise is made in return for the performance of an act. For example, where an offer of reward is made, one party promises to pay if and when another performs the specified act.

Carlill v Carbolic Smokeball Co Ltd [1893]

Facts: the company promised to pay £100 to any person complying with various conditions. Mrs Carlill made no reciprocal promise, she merely complied with the terms of the offer.

Held: here the consideration, provided by Mrs Carlill, was the doing of the act ie, **executed** consideration.

'Executory' consideration is given where there is an exchange of promises to do something in the future. Executory means 'yet to be done'. There is a contract even though at the time it is concluded or agreed neither of the parties has actually done the thing that they have promised to do.

An example is where you get into a taxi and ask to be taken to a particular destination. You have given your promise to pay the fare when you arrive at your destination and the taxi driver has promised to take you there.

2   THE RULES

There are two rules

(a)   Consideration must be valuable and sufficient but need not be adequate
(b)   Consideration must move from the promisee

Each is now analysed.

2.1   Consideration need not be adequate but must be valuable

In law, the parties to a contract are free to conclude their bargain on whatever terms they think are appropriate.   The courts will not question the adequacy of the consideration agreed upon by balancing the respective promises or acts of the parties to ascertain whether the agreement is fair in an objective or commercial sense, but they must be satisfied that there is something of real value provided by the parties. As long as the parties are of equal bargaining power and there is no duress they will not investigate the motives behind the transaction or check the consideration given.

Valuable consideration means money or money's worth, that is to say something upon which a monetary value can be placed such as rendering a service.

The consideration provided must be valuable in the sense that it must have some value, however slight. In **Thomas v Thomas [1842]** a promise to convey a house to a widow on her promise to pay £1 per year rent and keep the house in repair was binding; the promise to pay £1 per year and keep the house in repair were valuable consideration.

Chappell & Co v Nestle Co Ltd [1960]

Facts: Nestle offered records for sale to the public for 1s 6d and three chocolate wrappers each.

Held: the chocolate wrappers were part of the consideration even though they were of minimal value and, in fact, thrown away by Nestle as soon as received.

However, where the consideration for a transaction is highly inadequate it may raise a suspicion of fraud, duress or undue influence on the part of the person gaining the advantage.

Valuable consideration must be distinguished from consideration in the moral sense. For example, a promise from feelings of natural love and affection for the promisee is not legally enforceable, as where a father promises to buy a house for his daughter who is homeless after her husband's death.

White v Bluett [1853]

Facts: The alleged consideration was a son's promise to his father that he would cease complaining to him.

Held: such a promise could not be measured in value and was too insubstantial to amount to real consideration.

2.2   Consideration must be sufficient

The consideration provided must be 'sufficient' in the sense that it must be something the law recognises as consideration.

(a)   **Performance of existing duty imposed by law**

Where a person has to do something by law the discharge of that duty will not amount to consideration and cannot support a contract.

Collins v Godefroy [1831]

Facts: a witness, subpoenaed (legally required) to attend court, was promised payment if he would attend court and give evidence. He attended court and sued for the payment promised.

Held: he had not provided consideration, as he was legally obliged to attend under the subpoena. He had done no more than he was legally obliged to do already so had not provided sufficient consideration for a contract to exist.

However, if an act is performed over and above that required by law or public duty, that act is sufficient consideration for any promise to confer a benefit in return.

Glasbrook Brothers Ltd v Glamorgan County Council [1925]

Facts: Glasbrook Brothers Ltd, promised to pay the police authority if it stationed police officers on company premises to protect that property from apprehended damage during a miners' strike. The company had rejected a recommendation by the superintendent in charge that a mobile force movable to any trouble spot constituted an adequate safeguard.

Held: the police authority was entitled to payment of the promised remuneration. The police have a public duty to provide only that degree of protection that is reasonably necessary in the circumstances of the individual case. A permanent force of policemen on company property was an additional protection which provided the consideration necessary to enforce the promise to pay.

(b) **Performance of an existing contractual duty**

If a person is obliged to perform an act under an existing contract and the other party then promises to pay him an additional sum of money to ensure that he finishes the work on time there will be no new contract in respect of the extra sum of money.

This is because the person doing the work has provided no new consideration (no 'sufficiency' of consideration). He has done no more than he is already obliged to do under the pre-existing contract. Without this consideration there can be no contract and so he cannot make a claim that this new contract has been breached.

Stilk v Myrick [1809]

Facts: a ship's captain, unable to replace two deserting seamen from the crew, promised those remaining that if they completed the voyage the wages of the deserters would be divided amongst them, in addition to their contractually agreed wage.

Held: the extra payment need not be paid since the remaining seaman, by completing the voyage, did no more than they were originally contractually obliged to do.

This case may be compared with:

Hartley v Ponsonby [1857]

Facts: a high number of desertions from a merchant ship rendered the vessel unseaworthy since it was now undermanned. Extra pay was offered to the crew if they remained loyal.

Held: the promise of extra money was recoverable by the seamen who remained loyal since they were now working in a dangerous situation not contemplated by their original contractual undertaking, (ie they were doing more than required by their original contract).

Performance of an existing contractual obligation is sufficient consideration to support a promise from a third party.

Shadwell v Shadwell [1860]

Facts: C promised his nephew, A, an allowance if he would marry his fiancée, B (in those days an agreement to marry was legally binding).

Held: the promise was binding, even though A was already obliged to marry B. A had provided consideration for the uncle's promise as he was initially under a duty to the fiancée not to the uncle.

The following recent case is rather difficult to reconcile with **Stilk v Myrick**.

Williams v Roffey Brothers [1990]

Facts: Williams agreed to do some carpentry in a block of flats for Roffey at a fixed price of £20,000. There was an agreed date by which the work was to be completed. The work ran late and Roffey agreed to pay an extra £10,000 to ensure that the work was completed on time. If the work was not completed on time Roffey would have suffered a penalty in his own contract with the owner of the flats.

Held: the Court of Appeal decided that even though Williams was in effect doing nothing over and above the original agreement to complete the work by a completed time there was a new contract here for the £10,000. The court decided that both Williams and Roffey benefited from the new contract. Two reasons were given:

- the consideration given by Williams was enabling Roffey to avoid the penalty sum (and not merely finishing the work on time). As such he had provided 'something new'.

- Roffey's promise to pay the extra £10,000 had not been extracted by fraud or pressure. (It was Roffey who had approached Williams and had volunteered the extra money). It would be inequitable to go back on his promise.

(c)   **Past consideration**

The act or promise of one party and the act or promise of the other must constitute one single transaction. One party must do something because the other party is doing something. If one party makes a promise in return for an act or promise which has already been performed unilaterally, the two promises are not a response to one another and do not support a contract. Past consideration is insufficient.

Re McArdle [1951]

Facts: a man and his wife spent £488 on improvements to a bungalow in which they resided with the husband's mother. When the mother died the house would become the joint property of the husband, and his brothers and sisters. The man attempted to enforce a promise, to repay the cost of the improvements, made by the brothers and sisters after completion of the work.

Held: since all the work had been carried out before the promise was made, this past consideration could not support the later promise to reimburse the cost so as to bring a binding obligation into existence. Past consideration is no consideration.

Past consideration must be distinguished from the situation where a service is requested, then carried out, then a promise of payment is made. The court may be persuaded to treat the request as carrying an implied promise to pay: the later actual promise then being treated as merely the fixing of the amount. The court will be persuaded to follow this analysis where it is proved that the parties throughout contemplated that some payment should be made.

Re Casey's Patents [1892]

Facts: Casey spent two years promoting a patent jointly owned by two persons who encouraged him so to act. Later, Casey was given a written assurance that he would receive a one-third share of the patent in payment for his work.

Held: this assurance was legally binding; an implication existed when Casey agreed to work for the owners that he would ultimately be paid for his services.

However, there are exceptions to the rule that consideration must not be past:

- Bills of exchange can be supported by antecedent (past) consideration: S27 Bills of Exchange Act 1882. A bill of exchange is a written order by one person to another to pay a sum of money to the former or to another person (eg, a cheque is a bill of exchange drawn on a banker and payable on demand).

- Past consideration is sufficient to support a written acknowledgement of a debt in order to re-start time running for the purposes of the Limitation Act 1980 (this topic is covered later in the chapter 'Contract: Remedies for breach').

(d)   **Illegal consideration**

The doing of, or promise of doing, an illegal act is insufficient to amount to consideration.

2.3   Consideration must move from the promisee

A person wishing to enforce a contract must show that he personally provided consideration. It is not enough that someone else provided consideration to the party being sued. For example, Alan services Brian's car in return for Brian's promise to pay the agreed charge of £20 to Colin. If Alan completes the service Colin cannot sue for payment of the £20 since, as promisee, he did not personally supply consideration to Brian. Only Alan can sue Brian.

This principle is often confused with the rule called 'privity of contract' - (covered later in detail in the chapter 'Contract: Remedies for breach') that only a party to a contract can enforce it, but, although interconnected, the two rules operate independently of each other.

For example, Jim has recently married Margaret and their respective fathers each promise to pay Jim £5,000. Each father suffers a detriment, and also receives a benefit in the form of an equivalent payment by the other father to make suitable provision for their children, whom they wish to see settled for life. If only Jim's father pays, then he may sue Margaret's father for failing to implement his promise. Jim cannot sue however, since he did not provide any consideration in return for his father-in-law's promise. Further, Jim might not be a party to the contract between his father and his father-in-law. Even if Jim had been expressly joined as a party to a written contract he could not have enforced his father-in-law's promise, since he did not provide any consideration in return. On the other hand, if the agreement is concluded by deed and if Jim is joined as a party to the deed, then he may personally enforce his father-in-law's promise. Not only is he a party to the contract, but also his failure to supply consideration is immaterial in a specialty contract.

Tweddle v Atkinson [1861]

Facts: the plaintiff's father and father-in-law agreed with each other to pay the plaintiff £100 and £200 respectively in consideration of his then intended marriage and after the marriage had taken place they confirmed their agreement in writing. The £200 was not paid and the plaintiff sued his father-in-law's executor to recover this sum.

Held: his action must fail as no stranger to the consideration can take advantage of a contract, although made for his benefit. A promisee cannot bring a successful action unless the consideration for the promise moved from him.

3   THE PART-PAYMENT PROBLEM

3.1   The rule in Pinnel's case

The rule in **Pinnel's case [1602]** states that payment of a lesser sum in satisfaction of a greater sum, cannot be any satisfaction for the whole sum. This rule has been affirmed by the House of Lords in

Foakes v Beer [1884]

Facts: Mrs Beer obtained a judgement against Dr Foakes for a sum of £2,090 with interest. She agreed to payment of the debt in instalments and also promised that further proceedings on the judgement would not be taken. After receiving the £2,090, Mrs Beer sued for £360 interest on the judgement debt which Dr Foakes refused to pay.

Held: the interest was recoverable. Payment of the debt and costs, a smaller sum, was not consideration for the promise to accept this amount in satisfaction of a debt, interest and costs, a greater sum. The debtor had not provided any consideration for the promise not to claim interest.

A creditor who agrees to accept £50 from a debtor in payment and satisfaction of a debt for £100, does not receive any benefit for his promise not to claim the balance; consequently the creditor's promise is unenforceable at common law. The creditor cannot be restrained from breaking his promise and taking legal action to recover the balance of the debt still unpaid.

This is really an example of the rule that a promise to do something one is already bound to do by contract is insufficient consideration to enforce a promise. But note:

(a)   **The rule only applies to liquidated claims** ie, claims for fixed amounts eg, the price of goods, and not for unliquidated amounts eg, damages for defective goods.

(b)   **The rule only applies to undisputed claims;** where the claim is disputed in good faith, the value is again uncertain. Unless this were so, all legal actions compromised to avoid litigation could be reopened at a later stage.

It seems unfair that a party can apparently dupe another party into accepting a smaller sum in full and final settlement of his claim and then go back and sue for the full amount. So the law has found ways around the problem.

3.2   Exceptions

(a)   **Variation of terms at the creditor's request (accord and satisfaction)**

Where the payment of a lesser sum in discharge of a greater debt is accompanied by the introduction of some new element at the creditor's request, the new element is sufficient consideration to support the creditor's promise not to claim the balance of the debt still unpaid. This is often called accord and satisfaction. The accord is the agreement to accept less and the satisfaction is the new consideration.

The new element introduced at the creditor's request, which is the consideration he receives for not claiming the balance, may take a number of forms, for example:

* payment of the debt on a date earlier than that originally agreed;

* payment at a different place to that stipulated in the agreement; or

* payment of a smaller sum accompanied by the transfer of another item (eg, £10 plus a book in satisfaction of a £15 debt).

D&C Builders v Rees [1966]

Facts: the defendant owed £482 to the plaintiff (a building company) for work carried out. The defendant, knowing the plaintiff was in desperate need of money to stave off bankruptcy, offered £300 by cheque in settlement of the debt saying that if the plaintiff refused it would get nothing. The plaintiff accepted the £300 reluctantly in settlement.

Held: the plaintiff could successfully sue for the balance. Several reasons contributed to the court's decision, amongst them were:

* in view of the pressure put on the plaintiff and the plaintiff's reluctance there was no **true** accord

* payment by cheque and cash are, in these circumstances, no different. Therefore the payment by cheque did not amount to consideration: it conferred no benefit over and above payment in cash.

If the promise to accept less than is owed, or nothing at all, is made by deed it will be binding. Remember that an agreement made by deed does not require consideration. So if the agreement to accept a lesser sum is made by deed no satisfaction is required to make that accord binding.

(b)   **Part-payment by a third party**

A creditor, who has agreed to accept a smaller sum from a third party in full satisfaction of a debtor's obligation to pay a larger sum, is prevented from claiming the balance of the debt from the debtor himself, since this would be a fraud on the third party.

Hirachand Punamchand v Temple [1911]

Facts: the defendant had given the plaintiff a promissory note (this is evidence of a promise to pay the bearer a certain sum of money in the future). The plaintiff accepted a smaller sum from the defendant's father in full and final settlement of the debt.

Held: the plaintiff could not sue the defendant for the balance. The position was as if the promissory note had been cancelled as the original debt had been discharged by payment by another person of the smaller sum.

(c)   **Composition with creditors**

A debtor who is unable to pay his debts in full may make an arrangement with his creditors in consequence of which they all agree to accept part-payment of outstanding debts in full satisfaction of their claims.

If an individual creditor went back on his promise by attempting to sue for the balance of his debt, this would constitute a fraud on the other creditors who were observing the composition.

The consideration between the creditors themselves, supporting their individual promises not to sue, is the promise of each creditor not to claim the full debt so that no creditor benefits at the expense of the others.

The debtor's consideration is the procuring of a promise from each individual creditor to accept less than the full amount so that creditors generally will share whatever property is available.

3.3   Equitable doctrine of promissory estoppel

Another way around the part-payment problem is to apply the principle of equity or fairness. As has already been seen, the rule that a gratuitous promise is unenforceable (unless it is given by deed) can produce hardship.

There is no question that if a certain sum is owed under a contract, the party owed the money can invoke the common law to sue for the debt. This is the case even if it appears unfair to go back on his word as in **Foakes v Beer**.

However we have seen that equity can act to interpret or modify the common law where it appears harsh or inflexible.

The equitable concept of estoppel, referred to as **promissory** estoppel, may operate to prevent a person going back on his promise to accept a lesser amount. The promise which the plaintiff is prevented by equity from resiling from is a promise relating to his future conduct.

Central London Property Trust Ltd v High Trees House Ltd [1947]

Facts: in 1937, the plaintiff company ('the lessor') let a block of flats in London to the defendant company ('the lessee') on a ninety-nine year term, at a ground rent of £2,500 per year. During the war, because of the blitz, few flats could be let to tenants by High Trees House Ltd, and the lessor agreed to reduce the rent by one-half. By 1945, all the flats had been let and the lessor claimed full rent for the last two quarters of 1945.

Held: the lessor's claim should be allowed since the wartime conditions giving rise to the promise to reduce the rent had now ended and the agreement was no longer operative.

Although the plaintiffs were not claiming the full rent during the war the court commented on whether they could have claimed it. (This was *obiter dicta*). The lessee had not provided any consideration for the lessor's promise to reduce the rent, but if payment of full rent had been demanded for the years during which the flats were unoccupied, then the doctrine of equitable estoppel would have barred any such claim. The promise not to claim the full rent was 'intended to be acted upon, and in fact acted upon, is binding so far as its terms properly apply. It is binding as covering the period down to 1945, and from that time full rent is payable.' In this way Lord Justice Denning let promissory estoppel in through the back door of *obiter dicta*.

It must be clear that one party has made an unequivocal representation whether by words or conduct, which he intends the other party to rely upon.

The exact scope of promissory estoppel is not clear and there are difficulties with it as it does conflict with the rule in **Pinnel's** case. Partially as a result of this confusion, certain limitations have been put on the principle.

(a)   **It is 'a shield not a sword'** (ie, it is a defence, it does not create new rights)

The **High Trees** doctrine may be used by a defendant as a defence to an action claiming the debt which the plaintiff promised to waive, but promissory estoppel cannot be used by a person in the position of a plaintiff to demand rights not supported by consideration.

Combe v Combe [1951]

Facts: a husband entered into an agreement promising to pay his wife £100, free of income tax, after their divorce. The wife did not apply to the court for a maintenance order, but when the husband failed to implement his promise she sued to enforce the agreement relying on his promise and the doctrine of promissory estoppel.

Held: the agreement was unenforceable by the wife for lack of consideration on her part, since the equitable doctrine did not create a new cause of action where none existed before.

(b)   **It may have only a suspensory effect**

The obligations imposed by the original contract, later modified by mutual agreement, may be reverted to after the promisor has given sufficient notice to the promisee of his intention to do so, or where the situation giving rise to the modification comes to an end. The future relationship between the parties is then governed by their original contractual undertaking.

The effect of the principle on periodic payments such as rent or hire-purchase instalments is clear, ie,, arrears which have been waived are irrecoverable but future payments may be demanded in full. This was the actual decision in the **High Trees** case.

(c)   A party relying on promissory estoppel must also have acted fairly and in accordance with equitable principles

D & C Builders v Rees [1966]

Facts: the plaintiff company pressed for payment of £482 in respect of building work undertaken at the defendant's request. The builders were on the verge of bankruptcy. £300 was offered and accepted in full and final settlement of the outstanding debt. The plaintiff company was forced to issue a receipt acknowledging payment in completion of the account. The balance of the debt was now claimed.

Held: the remainder of the debt still unpaid was recoverable. The plaintiff company's consent to variation of the original contractual obligation had been secured under pressure. The equitable principle of promissory estoppel is not available to a debtor who holds his creditor to ransom by intimidating him into acceptance of an unfavourable settlement.

Equity relies upon fairness and we have already seen the principle that 'he who comes to equity must come with clean hands'.

3.4   Activity

Bev offers to sell Raman her car for £12,000.   Raman accepts and promises to pay in two instalments; the first instalment due in 3 months and the balance after a further 3 months. Raman pays the first instalment but then loses his job and he realises that he will be unable to pay the balance.

He approaches Bev and asks her if she will accept a further £4,000 in full and final settlement of all of her claims. She agrees and he pays her a cheque.

The next day Bev issues proceedings in the County Court for the outstanding £2,000. Her action is based on the original contract. Raman's serves a defence upon her which is based upon the fact that the money is not, in fact, owed at all. He claims that there is a new contract in which she has agreed to accept £10,000 in full and final settlement of all claims. Raman says that this is contractually binding.

Write a brief summary of the competing contractual claims in this situation concentrating upon the matters surrounding the mutual consideration.

3.5   Activity solution

Bev claims that there is no consideration for the new contract:

- Raman did not offer her anything other than that which he was contractually obliged to do (ie, pay money under the existing contract (£12,000 was owed)

- as a result there was insufficient consideration to support the new contract and it did not exist.

- the case of **Stilk v Myrick** applies: Raman has not exceeded his existing contractual duty and so is still bound by the original contract.

Raman is claiming that there is a new contract. He can support this claim as follows:

- by paying the smaller sum early he has provided new consideration (under the rules of 'accord and satisfaction'.) Being paid earlier is valuable and so it will be regarded as sufficient consideration

- in the alternative the doctrine of promissory estoppel may apply. The creditor has waived part of the original consideration in exchange for no new consideration. She has promised not to go back on her word and if Raman can fairly show that he has in some way been detrimented by her action she will be estopped by the court from going back on her promise.

4   SELF TEST QUESTIONS

4.1   Give a definition of consideration. (1.5)

4.2   What is the difference between executory and executed consideration? (1.6)

4.3   In the case of **Nestle v Chappell** why was it held that three chocolate wrappers could be regarded as consideration? (2.1)

4.4   What were the two key reasons as to why it was decided that Roffey should be paid the extra £10,000 by Williams even though it appears on the facts of the case that he in fact provides nothing new? (2.2)

4.5   What is the rule in **Pinnel's** case? (3.1)

4.6   What was the name of the case in which Lord Justice Denning introduced the concept of promissory estoppel? (3.3)

4.7   What does the phrase 'promissory estoppel is a shield not a sword' mean? (3.3)

5   EXAMINATION TYPE QUESTIONS

5.1   Paul

Explain whether Paul is required by the law of contract to fulfil his promises in the following situations:

(a)   He promises to sell an expensive car to Arthur for £10.

(4 marks)

(b)   He returns home to find that his house windows have been cleaned by Bernard and he promises to pay Bernard £1 for his work.

(4 marks)

(c)   He agrees to pay Charles £100 for painting his house within three weeks and he later promises a further £20 if Charles finished the job on time.

(4 marks)

(d)   He promises to deliver goods to David in return for a payment to him of £50 by Eric.

(4 marks)

(e)   He promises to release Frank from a debt of £500 if Frank pays him £400.

(4 marks)

(Total: 20 marks)

5.2   Payment of a lesser sum

Is payment for a lesser sum ever satisfaction of a larger amount?

(10 marks)

6   ANSWERS TO EXAMINATION TYPE QUESTIONS

6.1   Paul

Every simple contract must be supported by consideration. A simple contract is one not in the form of a deed. In each situation Paul will be legally bound by each promise only if consideration was given for it. Consideration may be defined as an act or forbearance, promised or actual.

(a)   Consideration must be valuable but need not be adequate. The word 'valuable' means that the consideration must be of some economic or monetary value, such as a motor car and money. 'Need not be adequate' means that the consideration given by each party does not have to match in value - **Chappell v Nestle**. Thus £10 in return for an expensive car is consideration even though inadequate. Accordingly Paul is bound by his promise to Arthur.

(b)   Consideration must be sufficient. This means that what is offered as consideration must be capable in law to amount to consideration. In law past consideration is insufficient - **Re McArdle**. Consideration is past where it is wholly executed before the other party makes his promise. Thus Bernard's cleaning of the windows, having been done before Paul made his promise of payment, is past. Accordingly Paul is not bound by his promise to Bernard.

Tutorial note: of course, the answer here may well have been different had the facts indicated that Paul had previously requested Bernard to clean the windows - see **Re Casey's Patents**. This point is not required for the answer to this question - remember: do not invent facts, keep to what the examiner has given.

(c)   Performance of an existing duty is insufficient to amount to consideration. As in **Stilk v Myrick**, Charles is already contractually obliged to paint the house by a given date and the mere doing of this by Charles is insufficient unless some extra benefit is thereby conferred on Paul - **Williams v Roffey**. The given facts do not suggest any extra benefit. Accordingly Paul is not bound on his promise of £20.

(d)   Consideration must move from the promisee. This means that a party who wishes to enforce a promise must himself provide consideration - **Tweddle v Atkinson**. Thus David cannot enforce Paul's promise because David provided no consideration for it.

The doctrine of privity of contract states that only the parties to a contract can sue on it. Thus in order for Eric to enforce Paul's promise Eric must show that it was to him that Paul made the promise.

(e)   Since performance of an existing contractual duty is insufficient it follows that performance of less than a contractual duty is also insufficient. This is the basis of the rule in **Pinnel's** case (also called the rule in **Foakes v Beer**) which states that payment of a lesser sum does not discharge a debt of a greater amount. Although there are exceptions to the rule, the given facts do not here suggest any might be of relevance. Accordingly Paul is not bound by his promise of release.

6.2   Payment of a lesser sum

The rule in **Pinnel's Case** is that payment of a lesser sum is not satisfaction of a greater sum. The rule stems from the basic rule in contract that a promise is only binding if supported by consideration. A person who promises to accept a lesser sum in satisfaction of a greater sum will not be bound by his promise unless consideration is given for the promise.

The rule relates to undisputed liquidated claims ie, claims for amounts which are fixed eg, the price of goods which is not disputed. Thus, it will not apply to a situation where someone has purchased goods which he considers to be defective and therefore is paying a reduced amount to take into account the breach by the supplier of the goods and the supplier accepts the reduced amount.

There are, however, other situations where a promise to accept a lesser sum may be binding. These exceptions are as follows:

(a)   a promise to accept a lesser amount together with some item of property as consideration for the promise is given in the form of the property;

(b)   a promise to accept a lesser sum at a date earlier than the date the larger sum was due as consideration is given by making payment earlier.

(*Note:* that in both these cases the alterations must be at the creditor's request or at the very least his completely unfettered acceptance.)

(c)   a promise under seal to accept a lesser sum as no consideration is required;

(d)   a promise to a third party that if he pays a lesser sum the creditor will not seek the remainder from the debtor. Here the creditor is bound by his promise to the third party;

(e)   a composition with creditors whereby the debtor and all his creditors agree how much each creditor will get in full satisfaction of the debt owed to him. Here the creditors are bound by their promises to each other;

(f)   where **promissory estoppel** can be invoked by the debtor. The limits on this doctrine are uncertain but it will arise where the creditor has made a promise to the debtor who had relied on the promise. The creditor is then 'estopped' or prevented from denying his promise. It is generally thought to relate only to promises to accept smaller instalment payments and not to lump sum debts.

4 CONTRACT: INTENTION, CAPACITY, FORM, ILLEGALITY

INTRODUCTION & LEARNING OBJECTIVES

Syllabus area 8a. Intention to create legal relations. (Ability required 3).

Form. (Ability required 3)

This chapter introduces and explains the three final pre-requisites for a contract - intention to create legal relations, capacity and form. As we have seen an agreement requires five things before it amounts to a binding contract:

- Offer and acceptance
- Consideration
- Intention to create legal relations
- Capacity
- Form

Even if the above essential elements are present the agreement will nevertheless be void if it is illegal.

Examination questions are often asked on the topic area of Intention particularly in a problem type question also involving consideration or offer and acceptance. It is essential to look out for where relatives or good friends are entering into an agreement to do something: this is usually a hint that the examiner is expecting a reference to the relevant intention to make that agreement legally binding. Questions on Capacity and Form are much less common. In problem questions the word 'children' or 'minor' should alert you to the topic of Capacity and the words 'oral' and 'house' or 'land' should alert you to the topic of Form.

When you have studied this chapter you should be able to do the following:

- Describe intention to create legal relations

- Recognise what the presumptions are and when they apply

- Recognise how the law provides protection for infants who are contracting or attempting to contract

- State the general rule that a contract may be in any form and realise that statute provides exceptions

- Recognise in outline situations where a contract might be illegal.

1 INTENTION TO CREATE LEGAL RELATIONS

1.1 Introduction

Some agreements are not intended to be legally enforceable, their nature being such that a reasonable man viewing the words and conduct of the parties objectively would not conclude that they intended to create legal relations. For example, a reasonable man would not expect an enforceable legal obligation to spring from a mere social engagement, such as an invitation to lunch, despite the presence of all the other essential elements necessary to create a binding agreement.

1.2 Domestic and social arrangements

In domestic and social arrangements there is a presumption that there was no intention that the agreement be legally binding. Arrangements in a domestic or social context include agreements made between members of a family and between friends. A presumption means that the plaintiff in the action need not prove certain matters on a balance of probabilities; the court presumes that they exist.

Balfour v Balfour [1919]

Facts: the defendant, who was about to go abroad, promised to pay his wife £30 per month in consideration of her agreeing to support herself without calling on him for any further maintenance. The wife contended that the defendant was bound by his promise.

Held: there was no legally binding contract between the parties. As it was a domestic agreement it was presumed the parties did not intend to be legally bound.

However this presumption may be rebutted. Thus the court may reach a contrary conclusion after examining words used and surrounding circumstances.

Simpkins v Pays [1955]

Facts: Pays and her granddaughter, together with Simpkins, a paying lodger, submitted an entry each week in a fashion competition appearing in the Sunday Empire News. All three devised a separate solution to the competition, but they were submitted on one coupon only, in Pays' name. The entry fees and postage were shared equally. The granddaughter made a correct forecast and Pays received a price of £750. Simpkins claimed a one-third share of the prize money.

Held: although this was an arrangement in a domestic context the presumption was rebutted: it was **a legally enforceable joint enterprise** and the parties clearly intended to share any prize money. 'There was mutuality in the arrangements between the parties and an intention to create legal relations' It was decided that on the facts this went beyond a mere friendly agreement and became a joint enterprise.

The presumption will be rebutted where the evidence shows that the parties made formal and/or detailed financial arrangements.

Parker v Clark [1960]

Facts: Mrs Clark wrote to her niece Mrs Parker suggesting that she and her husband might consider selling their own home in Sussex and living with Mrs Clark and her husband in their large house in Torquay. The letter set out detailed financial arrangements for sharing household expenses. Mrs Clarke promised that the house in Torquay and its contents would be devised by will to Mrs Parker. This offer was accepted in writing by Mrs Parker and the agreement implemented. Following continued unpleasantness between the two couples the Parkers left.

Held: there was an intention to create legal relations since by selling their home the Parkers had 'burned their boats' and relied on the enforceability of the agreement. Further, when Mr Clark altered his will to implement the promise made to the Parkers, he clearly regarded their arrangements as legally binding. £1,200 damages were awarded to the Parkers jointly, representing the value of rent-free accommodation in Torquay (assessed at £300 per annum multiplied by four years, being the life expectancy of the Clarks). Mrs Parker was awarded £3,400 assessed as the value of her expected inheritance.

The usual presumption that agreements between spouses living happily together are not legally enforceable does not apply when they are about to separate, or have already separated.

Merritt v Merritt [1970]

Facts: a husband, separated from his wife, wrote and signed a document stating that, in consideration of the wife paying off the outstanding mortgage debt of £180 on their matrimonial home, he would transfer the house standing in their joint name into her sole ownership. The wife implemented her promise, but the husband refused to transfer title in the house to her, alleging that his promise was a domestic arrangement not giving rise to legal relations.

Held: the husband's promise was enforceable, the agreement having been made when the parties were not living together amicably. A legal relationship is contemplated where a husband deserts his wife and an agreement is concluded on ownership of the matrimonial home occupied by the wife and children.

1.3   Commercial agreements

In the case of ordinary commercial dealings (for example buying goods in a shop) there is a strong presumption that the parties intended it to be legally binding. This presumption can be rebutted if a contrary intention is *clearly* expressed in the agreement itself.

Jones v Vernon's Pools Ltd [1938]

Facts: Jones contended that he had forwarded a winning entry to the defendant company of football pools promoters, but they denied having received it. In order to deal with this type of eventuality, a clause was printed on the pools coupon which Jones had signed, stating that 'any agreement........entered into....shall not.....give rise to any legal relationship....but....is binding in honour only'.

Held: a contact did not exist between the parties, since the wording of the agreement clearly negated any such intention. Jones could not, therefore, sue the pools company for breach of contract.

Edwards v Skyways [1964]

Facts: an employer agreed to make an '*ex-gratia*' payment to a redundant employee. *(Ex- gratia means non-contractual and at the will of one of the parties.)*

Held: the use of the term *ex-gratia* was only a denial of a previous liability and did not rebut the presumption that the parties intended that the agreement was legally binding.

It is common in business for 'letters of comfort' to be given: in general they are not intended to be legally binding.

Kleinwort Benson Ltd v Malaysia Mining Corp [1989]

Facts: the plaintiff bank had agreed to make a loan facility of up to £10m available to the defendant's wholly owned subsidiary, M, which was trading in tin on the London Metal Exchange. The defendants had refused to give a formal guarantee but had written a letter to the plaintiff stating: 'It is our policy to ensure that the business of M is at all times in a position to meet its liabilities to you under the loan facility agreement'. When the world tin market collapsed, M went into liquidation and the bank sought to recover the amount of the outstanding debt from the defendants.

Held: the wording of the letter of comfort showed that it constituted a statement of the defendant's present policy: it was not intended to amount to a contractually binding promise for the future. Therefore the letter imposed no legal obligation on the defendant to meet M's debts, merely a moral obligation with which the law is not concerned.

Carlill v Carbolic Smoke Ball Co [1893]

Facts: an advertisement stated that the Carbolic Smoke Ball Company were depositing £1,000 at a bank to show 'their sincerity' in the matter.

Held: this was sufficient to show an intention to create legal relations.

1.4 Collective bargaining agreements

Definition A collective agreement is defined as an agreement or arrangement made by, or on behalf of , one or more trade unions and one or more employers' associations, concerning working conditions of the employees.

Collective agreements are conclusively presumed not to have been intended by the parties to be legally enforceable unless there is a written term stating that the agreement is intended to be wholly or partially enforceable by legal action, then it is conclusively presumed to be so to the extent indicated: Trade Union and Labour Relations (Consolidation) Act 1992.

In practice, trade unions and employers resist agreeing to the legal enforceability of a collective agreement to which they are party, especially if it embodies a clause restricting the right of the workers to strike or take other forms of industrial action. Such agreements are binding in honour only and the terms agreed upon may be violated without giving rise to any right of legal redress for the innocent party.

1.5

Conclusion Where an examination question asks about intention to create legal relations deal with social or domestic arrangements and commercial arrangements separately. State the presumption for each. Then look for evidence (in a problem question) or give examples (in a bookwork question) which might rebut the relevant presumption.

For example: where an agreement is made in a social context (which is the most likely in examination questions) the presumption is that there is no intention to create legal relations. This presumption may be rebutted

- where there is evidence of a joint enterprise between the parties; eg, **Simpkins v Pays**

- where the parties are separated or divorced (if it is a marital situation): eg, **Merritt v Merritt**

- where the arrangements have been formalised or otherwise committed to writing: eg, **Parker v Clark**

1.6   Activity

Is there an intention to create legal relations in the following circumstances?

(a)   Exe Ltd enter into an agreement with USDAW in which the union agrees not to strike.

(b)   Sally agrees that her cousin can come and stay with her whilst she is in the UK on a holiday from her home in Australia. A week before her cousin arrives in the UK Sally asks her boyfriend to move in with her and the room is no longer available.

(c)   Phillippe goes into a cycle repair shop to get a small puncture mended. The repair work only takes 3 or 4 minutes but the shop charge him £5. Phillippe does not want to pay because he claims that the person who did his repair was on his lunch break.

(d)   Christine promises to pay her estranged husband £50 per day to child mind their 18 month old son. The son is living with Christine.

(e)   Edward commissions his uncle, who is a professional artist, to paint a portrait of his mother. He gives him some fairly precise instructions but does not want to pay the fee of £150 that his uncle later asks him for.

1.7   Activity solution

(a)   No: this is a collective agreement. The conclusive presumption is there is no intention to be legally bound.

(b)   No: they are family and this appears to be a promise from one family member to another. There is no evidence to rebut the presumption that they do not intend to be legally bound.

(c)   Yes: this is a commercial situation and the presumption is that an intention exists. There are no persuasive rebutting factors here.

(d)   Yes: this is a domestic situation but the couple are estranged and so the presumption of no intention is rebutted by the situation.

(e)   Yes: although the parties are relatives this agreement appears to have been made in a business or commercial context *(Note:* the indicative words 'commissions' and 'professional'). The presumption is that the parties intend to be legally bound.

2   CAPACITY TO CONTRACT

In order for a contract to be valid the parties must have the legal capacity (or ability) to contract. Those who are deemed incapable by the law to contract include:

(a)   Minors

(b)   Companies (in certain situations)

(c)   The mentally disordered

(d)   Drunkards

The next section will deal with the necessary detail.

3   MINORS

3.1   Introduction

Definition   A person who is under 18 years old (sometimes called an 'infant')

A minor must be protected by the law from the financial consequences of entering into commercially unsound contracts and to discourage adults from taking unfair advantage of the minor's inexperience in business affairs. Consequently, not all contracts negotiated by a minor are binding on him.

3.2   Contracts for necessary goods and services

Strictly speaking, a minor is incapable of concluding a legally enforceable contract, but if his needs are satisfied by contracting for and receiving the benefit of **necessary** goods and services on credit, then the law imposes a **quasi-contractual** duty to pay. The minor must pay a **reasonable price** which may be less than the agreed contract price if the minor has been overcharged by a trader taking advantage of his inexperience.

Definition   S3 Sale of Goods Act 1979 defines necessary goods as:

(a)   goods suitable to the condition in life of the minor; and also

(b)   to his actual requirements both at the time of sale and at the time of delivery.

Nash v Inman [1908]

Facts: Inman, a Cambridge undergraduate not yet of full age (ie, under 18), purchased eleven fancy waistcoats from Nash, a Saville Row tailor. When Inman failed to pay for these garments, the supplier sued for the agreed purchase price.

Held: on the evidence presented to the Court, the minor was already adequately supplied with clothes suitable to his station in life. Although eleven fancy waistcoats might be considered as necessary items of clothing in the circumstances, since he came from a wealthy family and was expected to have an ample supply of fashionable clothes, they were surplus to the minor's actual needs both at the time of sale and also at the time of delivery.

The concept of necessary goods and services is not confined solely to the bare essentials of life, such as food and clothing. It also includes rent, medical and legal expenses, payment for educational courses and funeral expenses for a deceased spouse.

The burden for proving that the goods are necessaries lies with the seller. He must show that the goods are capable of being necessaries and that they are necessary for the minor in question.

If a minor is married he may validly contract to purchase necessaries for his wife and children as well, their needs being judged by the station in life and needs of the husband.

A minor is not liable on an executory contract for necessary goods. This means he is not liable on a contract where the goods to be acquired have not yet been delivered. The trader may keep the goods, but he cannot claim the contract price. However, such contracts for services are enforceable.

Roberts v Gray [1913]

Facts: Roberts, a famous billiard player, agreed to take Gray, a minor on a world billiards tour, paying his expenses, with the object of teaching Gray the profession of billiards. Roberts made preparation for the tour but Gray repudiated the contract before the tour began.

Held: Roberts could recover damages: the contract would have benefited Gray and was therefore enforceable against him.

An adult is liable on an executory contract to supply necessaries, if sued by the minor for failure to perform the agreement in the manner stipulated.

Even if the contract is one for necessaries the Court may still refuse to enforce it against the infant if it contains an onerous term which places him at an unfair disadvantage.

3.3   Contracts of employment

Any contract of employment or apprenticeship negotiated while under age is usually binding on the minor in exactly the same manner as an adult, since he must be allowed to earn a livelihood, provided that as a whole the agreement can be regarded as beneficial to the minor.

Doyle v White City Stadium [1935]

Facts: D, a minor who was a professional boxer, held a licence from the British Boxing Board, under the terms of which his money was to be withheld should he be disqualified. Following a subsequent disqualification, his money was stopped and D sued to recover it.

Held: D could not recover as the contract, enabling him to earn his living as a boxer, was for his benefit and thus a binding contract.

However, this does not extend to simple trading contracts even if profitable to the minor and therefore beneficial. (In **Cowern v Nield** a contract to deliver hay was not enforceable against a minor who was a hay and straw dealer).

It is not necessary for the employer wishing to enforce the contract to establish that every single term in the contract is beneficial provided that when viewed as a whole it is substantially beneficial.

Clements v London and North Western Rail Co [1894]

Facts: the plaintiff, an infant, entered the service of the defendant railway company as a porter and agreed to join the company's insurance scheme which involved his giving up his right of action for personal injury under the **Employer's Liability Act 1880**. The scheme applied to more types of accident but compensation under the Act was more generous. The plaintiff was injured and sought to say the contract was void so that the Act would apply instead.

Held: although parts of the contract were not to the advantage of the plaintiff the contract as a whole, on the facts, was. It was binding.

A non-beneficial contract of employment is voidable at the minor's option. He may continue to regard the contract as binding and enforceable by himself and the employer, or alternatively, it may be rescinded during minority or within a reasonable time after attaining majority, which is usually interpreted as within a six month period.

De Francesco v Barnum [1889]

Facts: the minor had entered a dancing apprenticeship contract under which he had agreed not to take any professional engagement without his employer's consent nor to marry without such consent. The employer was not bound to find engagements of work for the minor, who might receive no remuneration for periods of time.

Held: the contract was unenforceable as it was not beneficial to the minor, since it placed him entirely at his employer's disposal. Benefits are assessed in the material sense only.

3.4 Purchase or exchange of non-necessary goods

Generally, a minor is not liable to pay for non-necessary goods or services. However the following exceptions apply:

(a)   Where a trader supplies goods or services to a minor in return for a cash consideration, whether they are necessaries or luxuries, no problem arises. The contract having been fully executed by the parties, the assistance of the court is not required by the adult to enforce it against the minor. If the goods or services are defective in any way the minor may sue the adult for breach of contract in the usual way.

(b)   A trader is bound to supply non-necessaries to a minor in accordance with their contractual agreement, if the minor is willing to pay the agreed price, although the supplier may be reluctant to do so if the market price has risen since contracting. The minor may claim damages for breach of contract if the trader fails to implement his promise.

(c)   Title to goods can pass under such contracts so that a minor, who buys non-necessaries **on credit**, can keep the goods **and** refuse to pay for them.

4   MINORS AND VOIDABLE CONTRACTS

4.1 Introduction

Definition   A voidable contract is one which is valid unless the minor chooses to avoid (or repudiate) it. This can be done whilst he is still a minor or within a reasonable time of 'achieving his majority'. This means that he has to choose whether or not to end the contract before or soon after his 18th birthday. These contracts are those which are of a continuing nature.

The minor may enter into a contract for the acquisition of a proprietary interest involving rights and duties of a continuing nature, such as purchasing stocks and shares, or entering a partnership.

On repudiation within the time allowed, the minor is freed from all further liability under the voidable agreement.

The minor cannot recover money he paid before repudiation of the voidable contract to meet his obligations under it, unless there has been a total failure of consideration.

Corpe v Overton [1833]

Facts: Corpe, a minor, contracted to enter a partnership in the following January with a tailor for the sum of £1,000. Corpe repudiated the contract on attaining majority and before the partnership actually came into existence, when he discovered that Overton had misrepresented the extent of his business. Corpe sued to recover £100 already paid over as security.

Held: he was entitled to do so since the partnership agreement had not yet taken effect and at the time when the contract was repudiated the consideration for payment of the money had failed completely.

When a minor becomes a partner in a firm he cannot be held liable for partnership debts incurred during his minority, whether they are the result of the minor's actions or those of a fellow partner, since trading debts are always void as against a minor. However, the minor's share of profits and capital may be debited with his share of trading debts. Debts contracted during the partner's minority cannot be enforced against the minor's personal estate at the instance of creditors.

If a minor purchases shares in a public company the total purchase price is often payable on acquisition. The shares are then fully paid for and the minor, like any other shareholder, cannot be required to make any further financial contribution to the company's assets, even if it goes into liquidation with substantial debts that cannot be fully paid.

If the shares are not fully paid for, the shareholders, including minors, must pay the balance of the purchase price when requested by the company, referred to as a **call** on shares. A minor can avoid future liability for calls by repudiating the shares, but cannot recover calls already paid.

Steinberg v Scala (Leeds) Ltd [1923]

Facts: a minor purchased part-paid shares in a company. She subsequently repudiated the contract, thereby avoiding liability to meet any future call on the shares. She sought to reclaim her original part-payment

Held: whilst the contract was in force (ie whilst she was a member) she had enjoyed the benefits of membership (eg rights to vote in general meetings and to receive dividends). Thus she had received consideration under the contract, and could not recover her money.

4.2   Minors and void contracts

Definition   A void contract is one which never existed. Legal title can never pass under such a contract in respect of minors. The law has been simplified and is contained within the Minors Contracts Act 1987.

The law is as follows:

(a)   Contracts for loans and non necessaries are enforceable by the minor but unenforceable against him.

(b)   Ratification (or adopting) of such a contract by the minor after majority is allowed.

(c)   A creditor of a minor will be able to enforce a fresh agreement or ratification after majority of a previously unenforceable loan, debt or contract

A minor is not liable if a cheque or bill of exchange, given in payment of necessary or non-necessary goods or services supplied to him, is not duly paid, where, for example, the minor has insufficient money in his account to meet the required payment: S22 Bills of Exchange Act 1882

Any trading contract to which a minor is a party is void, even if its terms are beneficial to him, on the ground that a minor who trades may lose the capital he has invested in the business enterprise. As a result, where a minor sets up in business on his own account he is not liable for:

(a)   failing to supply goods already paid for by the purchaser; and

(b)   the purchase price of goods supplied to him on credit in the course of his trade, even though he has resold them to a third party. Goods not yet resold are recoverable by the supplier only if the minor acted fraudulently in securing them, as by misrepresenting his age.

Conclusion | Voidable contracts include things such as the purchase of shares or rights in a partnership. A minor can end such a contract either whilst still a minor or within a reasonable time after his 18th birthday.

Void contracts include contracts for loans and non-necessaries and any trading contract to which the minor is a party. Such contracts are unenforceable against the minor but enforceable by him and the contract can be adopted by the minor after he becomes 18.

4.3   Remedy of restitution

S3 Minors Contracts Act 1987 provides that where an adult enters into a contract with a minor which is unenforceable against the minor or which the minor repudiates, the court may, if it is just and equitable to do so, require the minor to transfer to the adult any property the minor acquired under the contract.

The minor may be ordered to restore not only the actual property he received under the contract but 'any property representing it' but the meaning of this provision is not clear. It may be that the minor could be ordered to transfer to the adult the proceeds of sale of any property he had obtained under the contract. So if the minor obtained goods, sold them and retained the money, the adult could claim that money if he could show that the money represented the property acquired by the minor under the contract.

4.4   Indirect enforcement of a void contract

Persons dealing with an infant may attempt to enforce their contract indirectly by suing him in tort for deceit or negligence, rather than on the contract itself. A minor cannot be sued for damages in tort where the cause of action is so closely connected with the contract that it constitutes an indirect method for enforcing an otherwise void contract.

A minor may be successfully sued for damages in tort, however, where the cause of action is separate and distinguishable from the situation supporting a contractual claim. Compare the following cases:

Jennings v Rundall [1799]

Facts: an infant hired a horse for riding. He rode it so hard that he injured it.

Held: what he had done was an act contemplated by the contract, ie, riding, although excessive. He would not be held liable in contract and he could not therefore be made indirectly liable on the contract in tort.

Burnard v Haggis [1863]

Facts: the defendant, who was under age, went to the stables of the plaintiff and hired a horse to ride on the road. The plaintiff stipulated that the horse was not to be ridden by anyone but the defendant and was not to be used for jumping. The defendant let his friend ride the horse and the friend forced the animal to attempt a fence but the jump was unsuccessful. The horse fell and was injured.

Held: the plaintiff was entitled to damages in tort as such conduct was not contemplated by the contract and had in fact been specifically forbidden.

4.5   Activity

Written below are two extracts from contracts with Charlene who is 16 years old. Please state whether they are valid or invalid:

(a)   .....'at the age of 18 Charlene will enter the family business taking over her late father's share of the equity. This amounts to a 33% profit share. As a result of this Charlene will become the managing partner and will take up all duties and responsibilities concomitant with that role. She will assume responsibility for all debts of the partnership which were previously related to this share of the business (id est: the share of 33% belonging to....her father)

(b)   .....'the driver of the hired vehicle (being a Ford Surpriso 1600 cc) will be the only driver of the vehicle for the entire period of hire (see clause 13) and if s/he either directly or indirectly permits anyone else to drive the vehicle s/he will be liable to reimburse the hirer for any resulting damage in the law of tort as well as breach of contract....'

4.6   Activity solution

(a)   Invalid - when a minor becomes a partner in a firm she cannot be held liable for partnership debts incurred during her minority. (However, her share of the profits may be debited with the share of the trading debts).

(b)   Valid - this is almost certainly a void contract (vehicle hire at the age of 17 will not be regarded as a 'necessary'). As in the case of **Burnard v Harris**, however, if the driving of the hired vehicle by another person is not contemplated by the (void) contract the hirer will be entitled to damages in tort.

5   CORPORATIONS

A corporation is a recognised legal person having a distinct legal personality. As such it has the capacity to make contracts in its own name.

A corporation is required to have a formal statement of its activities (in a document called a Memorandum of Association). If a corporation makes a contract which is unconnected with those stated activities the contract is said to be *ultra vires* (ie, beyond the powers) the corporation and at common law an *ultra vires* contract is void. Thus the corporation cannot sue the other party on the contract nor can the other party sue the corporation. Exceptionally the common law effect of the *ultra vires* rule does not apply to contracts made by corporations created by registration under the Companies Act 1985 (such a corporation is commonly referred to as a company). Thus if a company makes an *ultra vires* contract that contract is not void for lack of capacity.

No corporation has contractual capacity before it is formed. A corporation becomes a legal person on the date it is incorporated. Before that date it does not exist as a legal person so cannot make contracts - **Kelner v Baxter [1866].** Any person who acts on behalf of a company not yet formed will generally be personally liable on the contract by virtue of the Companies Act.

6   PERSONS MENTALLY DISORDERED

If a party is suffering from such a degree of mental disorder that he is incapable of understanding the nature of the contract then it is voidable by him provided his disability was known or ought to have been known to the other party. The burden is on him to show he was mentally disordered **and** that the other party knew this.

It is worth noting:

(a)   He is always bound by contracts made during a lucid interval.

(b)   A mentally disordered person must always pay a reasonable price for necessaries supplied to him: S3 Sale of Goods Act 1979.

(a) and (b) are both irrespective of the state of knowledge of the other party.

Persons who are 'patients' within the meaning of the Mental Health Act have no contractual capacity.

7   INVALID CONTRACTS AND DRUNKARDS

(a)   If one party is so drunk that he does not know what he is doing the contract is voidable by him provided the other party knew of his condition.

(b)   A similar duty to pay a reasonable price for necessaries is imposed on him as on the mentally disordered by S2 Sale of Goods Act 1979.

(c)   The drunk may ratify the contract on becoming sober.

8   FORM OF A CONTRACT

8.1   Common law rule

The general rule is that a contract may be in any form whatsoever. Thus a contract is valid whether it is made orally, in writing or even by conduct.

In practice the parties will choose to put important contracts in writing so that there can be no argument as to their terms.

8.2   Statutory exceptions

(a)   **Contracts which must be by deed**

Examples include:

- a conveyance of land
- an assignment of a lease (where the lease is for three years or more)
- the transfer of a ship or a share therein

(b)   **Contracts which must be in writing**

Examples include:

- bills of exchange (eg, a cheque) and promissory notes (eg, a bank note)
- contracts of marine insurance
- regulated consumer credit agreements (eg, a hire purchase agreement)
- transfers of shares in registered companies
- legal assignments of debts
- contracts for the sale or other dispositions of land

(c)   **Contracts which must be evidenced in writing** (although the contract itself may be oral)

   The sole example here is the contract of guarantee.

Transfers of shares and legal assignments of debts are dealt with later. The special positions regarding land and guarantees are set out immediately below.

8.3   Land

The stages in the sale of land are:

(a)   **The precontractual stage**

   When the owner of land advertises its sale, he is making an invitation to treat. He is not making an offer to sell at the price stated.

   On a sale of land preliminary communications and statements of intention are usually expressly stated to be **subject to contract**. This means that neither party wishes to be bound by any statement made until a formal and binding contract has been drawn up. The parties are given an opportunity to reflect on the proposed transaction before being finally committed to it.

(b)   **Exchange of contracts**

   Eventually each party signs a copy of the contract of sale and the parties then exchange contracts. The buyer has a copy of the contract with the seller's signature and vice versa. At this stage the purchaser usually pays a deposit, which is normally 10% of the purchase price. The contract is that the seller will transfer title and the buyer will pay the balance of the purchase money on the completion date (usually about one month later).

   It is this stage which is the contract for the sale of land and which, by the Law of Property (Miscellaneous Provisions) Act 1989, must be made in writing and must incorporate all the terms expressly agreed either in one document or where contracts are exchanged, in each document. The document(s) must be signed by or on behalf of each party to the contract. If this required form is not used the contract is void.

(c)   **Completion**

   Completion of the transaction takes place when the purchaser hands over the balance of the agreed price and the seller hands over a conveyance or transfer deed to the purchaser together with the title deeds to the property or the land certificate.

   This stage, being a conveyance of the land, must be in the form of a deed - Law of Property Act 1925. If this required form is not used the conveyance is void ie, ownership does not vest in the transferee.

8.4   Activity

Jane orally agrees to sell her house to John with completion to be in a month's time.

Jane is now refusing to sign a deed conveying ownership to John. Can John compel her to do?

8.5   Activity solution

No. The contract, being an oral contract for the sale of land, is void - Law Reform (Miscellaneous Provisions) Act 1989.

8.6   Contracts of guarantee

One party, the guarantor, promises to be answerable to the other party for the debt, default or miscarriage of another person.

For example, if Ian wishes to borrow money the bank may be unwilling to lend to him because they doubt his ability to repay, unless he can find a financially sound guarantor, say Carl, whom the bank can trust. In effect Carl, the guarantor, says to the bank, 'let Ian borrow £1,000, then if he fails to settle his indebtedness with you I will settle on his behalf.' In this type of situation three contracts exist:

(a)   as between the principal debtor (Ian) and the principal creditor (the bank) there is a contract giving rise to the debt;

(b)   as between the guarantor (Carl) and the principal creditor (the bank) there is a contract of guarantee under which Carl makes himself secondarily liable to settle the principal debtor's loan if it is not repaid by the principal debtor; and

(c)   as between the guarantor and the principal debtor there is always an implied contract, and often an express agreement, whereby the principal debtor promises to repay the guarantor any money that he has to hand over to the principal creditor.

It is (b) above which is the contract of guarantee.

The main effect of a guarantee is that the principal debtor is able to raise a loan that would otherwise be denied him, while the principal creditor transfers any risk of loss onto the shoulders of the guarantor, a person not expected to default if called upon to meet payment of the debt.

The **Statute of Frauds 1677** requires a contract of guarantee to be evidenced in writing. It provides that no action shall be brought unless the agreement or some memorandum or note thereof is in writing and signed by the party to be charged (ie, the guarantor) or some other person lawfully authorised by him.

Thus, the contract itself need not be committed to writing at the time when the parties conclude their agreement, but a note or memorandum in writing, signed by the party charged or by his duly authorised agent, setting out the main terms of the contract, must exist when one party seeks the court's assistance to enforce his rights by legal action, with the following details:

(a)   The parties to the contract must be named or sufficiently described in order to be identifiable.

(b)   The subject matter of the contract must be described in such a way that it can be identified.

(c)   All material terms of the contract must be set out.

The memorandum need not be in any special form and may be contained in more than one document. But documents not signed by the defendant may be introduced as evidence only if documents which are signed refer to them expressly or by implication.

Note that a contract of guarantee which is not evidenced in writing is not void, merely **unenforceable** (ie, no court action may be brought). Thus if the guarantor refuses to pay under an oral guarantee which is not evidenced by writing, the creditor cannot sue him to make him do so. The guarantor may, however, choose to pay and can then sue to recover the money from the creditor.

9   ILLEGALITY

9.1   Introduction

[Definition]   **Illegal** here is not confined to what is criminally illegal. Some agreements are declared illegal by statute or by the common law. They are a nullity, ie, absolutely void of legal effect, and therefore no action can be based on them.

9.2   Contracts illegal at common law

A contract is illegal at common law, as being harmful to the interests of society, if it offends against the concepts of public policy set out below:

(a)   An agreement knowingly made to further a sexually immoral purpose: **Pearce v Brooks [1866]** (a contract to hire a horse-drawn carriage to a prostitute where it was known she would use it to attract clients)

(b)   Where the direct or indirect object is to commit a crime or a tort, such as attempts to defraud the Inland Revenue or local authority of taxes or rates: **Miller v Karlinsky [1945]**.

(c)   A contract which tends to promote corruption in public affairs: **Parkinson v College of Ambulance [1925]**(money donated to charity in return for a promised knighthood).

(d)   Contemplated actions in a friendly foreign country which violate its law thereby disrupting international goodwill: **Foster v Driscoll [1929]** (smuggling alcohol into the USA during the prohibition era).

(e)   Contracts with enemy aliens: **Daimler Co Ltd v Continental Tyre & Rubber Co (GB) Ltd [1916]** (purchase of tyres during the First World War from a German-owned company).

(f)   Interference with the administration of justice: **John v Mendoza** (bribery of a creditor to desist from bankruptcy proceedings against his debtor).

9.3   Contracts illegal under statute

A statute or a statutory instrument may expressly or impliedly declare a certain type of contract or other transaction to be illegal.

The particular statute will often state the precise effects of illegality: if it does not it will generally be void and of no legal effect and therefore cannot be sued on. An example, from company law, is S151 Companies Act 1985 which states that it is illegal for a company to give financial assistance for the acquisition of its own shares. If the assistance is given, for example, by way of a 'loan contract' the company cannot sue on the contract to recover its money. As we shall see though, there are other legal principles which can be relied on in order to enable the company to recover.

10   SELF TEST QUESTIONS

10.1   What is the presumption in respect of intention to contract in a situation between husband and wife? (1.2)

10.2   What facts in the case **Simpkins v Pays** distinguished it from other cases which have held that agreements between friends are not generally legally enforceable? (1.2)

10.3   How are 'necessary goods' defined under S3 Sale of Goods Act 1979? (3.2)

10.4   Is a contract of employment or apprenticeship which has been negotiated whilst a person is under 18 binding on the minor in the same way as it would be on an adult? (3.3)

10.5   What are the rules laid down by the Minors Contracts Act 1987 in respect of void contracts? (4.2)

10.6   What is the general common law rule regarding form of a contract? (8.1)

10.7   Name the Act of Parliament which requires a contract for the sale of land to be in writing (8.3)

10.8   What does the Law of Property Act 1925 require to be in the form of a deed? (8.3)

10.9   What does the Statute of Frauds 1677 require? (8.6)

10.10   What, in general, is the effect of an illegal contract? (9.1)

11   EXAMINATION TYPE QUESTIONS

11.1   A - sale of car

(a)   Explain whether the intention to create legal relations is an essential element in a binding contract.

(10 marks)

(b)   A advertised his car for sale for £5,000 in a local newspaper. B saw the advertisement and telephoned A offering him £4,500 for the car. A eventually offered to sell B the car for £4,800 and B said he would need to drive the car before he could agree such a price. They agreed a time to meet at A's house at the weekend for a test-drive. On Friday A sold the car to X for £4,500.

Discuss.

(10 marks)

(Total: 20 marks)

11.2   Infant's contractual capacity

In outline, what is the contractual capacity of an infant?

(10 marks)

12   ANSWERS TO EXAMINATION TYPE QUESTIONS

12.1   A - sale of car

(a)   A contract is a legally binding agreement. Consequently, it is essential that the parties intend the agreement to be legally binding. However, where contracts are made in the commercial sphere it is presumed that the parties intend to create a legal relationship and therefore this need not be positively proved by the plaintiff. It is possible though, to rebut the presumption that an agreement in the commercial sphere is legally binding. For example, if a party agrees to make an *ex gratia* payment or enters a gentleman's agreement such arrangements are binding in honour only.

In the case of agreements between husband and wife and other domestic and social agreements the position is different. If a husband and wife make an agreement at a time when they are happily married, there is a presumption against an intention to create a legal relationship. Thus, in **Balfour v Balfour**, where a husband agreed, at a time when they were happily married, to pay his wife £30 a month whilst he was abroad on military service, and later failed to pay this £30, the agreement was not enforceable in a court of law. However, if agreements are made between spouses at a time when the marriage is on 'rocky grounds' such as when they are about to separate **(Merritt v Merritt)** it is presumed they do intend the agreement to be legally binding.

Turning to other social and domestic agreements such as those between friends or persons who live under the same roof, once again there is a presumption that they are not intended to create legal relations. This presumption may, however, be rebutted by evidence to the contrary. For example, in **Simkins v Pays** a grandmother, her granddaughter and a lodger regularly entered a Sunday newspaper competition. They took it in turns to enter the competition in one of their names but agreed whose ever name had been entered, the prize, if won, would be shared between the three of them. On a week in which the competition was entered into in the grandmother's name, a prize was won, but the grandmother refused to pay one third of the winnings to the lodger. On account of the evidence of the formalities that the three women had kept to in rigorously taking it in turns to enter the competition in each one's name and having the responsibility for posting it, the court was satisfied there was an intention to be bound.

(b)   The question is whether there is a binding contract between A and B for the sale of the car and whether A made an offer to B which he was at liberty to revoke. Offer and acceptance are necessary for a binding contract. An offer is a proposition made by one party to another with the intention of being bound. It needs to be distinguished from an 'invitation to treat' which is merely a preliminary proposition which cannot be accepted. The advertisement in the newspaper is merely an 'invitation to treat'. B has made an offer to buy at £4,500. This offer appears to have been rejected. Once an offer is rejected it no longer stands. In its place A has made an offer to sell the car to B for £4,800. This, it seems, is a standing offer as A has agreed that B should be able to test-drive the car at the weekend. However, the agreement to hold the offer open is not supported by a consideration on the part of B, and as such it is revocable at any time up until acceptance. It is therefore necessary to decide whether B has accepted the offer so as to create a binding contract. Acceptance must be a final and unqualified assent on the terms of the offer. B has not made an unqualified acceptance of the offer to sell at £4,800 because his acceptance is subject to a satisfactory test drive at the weekend. Consequently there is no contract and as the standing offer was not supported by consideration on the part of B, A is at liberty to sell the car to X for £4,500.

12.2   Infant's contractual capacity

A minor is a person under eighteen years of age. The law protects minors (or infants – the terms are used interchangeably in contract) against the possibility of adults taking unfair advantage. Thus some contracts which are binding on an adult are not binding on a minor.

The law protects minors by providing that a minor has no capacity to enter certain contracts and therefore is not bound by such agreements purely because he is a minor. Thus, if he had been an adult the contract would be binding on him.

However, the law does not allow minors to escape liability on all contracts. There are several different types of contracts which are treated differently when a minor is a party. The law is not consistent, nor is there a comprehensive set of rules. The basic types of contracts only are therefore discussed.

The type of contract which is most 'binding' on an infant is a contract for necessaries sold and delivered to him: S3 Sale of Goods Act 1979. The minor will be compelled to pay a reasonable price for such goods which may be below the contract price. The Act also defines necessaries as goods and services suitable to the minor's condition in life and to his actual requirements. The burden of proving this is on the seller. Thus, in **Nash v Inman**, a minor purchased some waistcoats and the seller sued him. The seller was able to prove that the waistcoats were suitable to the infant's condition but not to his actual requirements as he already had a number of them.

Another type of contract which is 'binding' on a minor is a contract of employment, provided the contract as a whole is beneficial to the minor. Thus, contracts of apprenticeship and employment which provide the minor with the opportunity to train or learn a skill will be binding even though some of the terms are not particularly to his advantage. Thus, in **Doyle v White City Stadium** a minor under contract as a boxer was held to his contract as it did provide an opportunity for him to learn the trade even though one of the terms was not advantageous to him.

Some contracts of a continuing nature, such as a contract giving a minor a share in a partnership or shares in a company, are valid and enforceable against him unless he repudiates them. He must repudiate them while still a minor or within a short time of reaching majority. If he does repudiate the contract he will escape future but not past liabilities. Thus, if he buys shares in a company which are not fully paid he will be liable for any calls made before he repudiated but not those made after. He cannot recover any money paid under the contract unless there has been a total failure of consideration: **Steinberg v Scala**, where the court held that merely holding the shares is consideration.

Some contracts are void against the minor. The Minors Contracts Act 1987 has recently altered the law on this and it is not absolutely clear where it now stands. However, examples of void contracts are loans to infants and supplies of non-necessaries.

5 MISTAKE AND MISREPRESENTATION

INTRODUCTION & LEARNING OBJECTIVES

Syllabus area 8a. Mistake, misrepresentation. (Ability required 3).

This chapter looks at the factors that 'vitiate' or invalidate a contract once it has been formed. The most examinable topics are misrepresentation and mistake.

Examination questions in this area do not require the candidate to discuss the features of how a contract is formed, but to recognise that one of the parties is claiming that the contract (or part of it) should not exist and what remedies are being sought as a result.

When you have studied this chapter you should be able to do the following:

- know what a misrepresentation is, be able to define it and understand the difference between the three different types of misrepresentation

- know the remedies for a misrepresentation: including the equitable remedy of rescission and when it is lost, and when damages that can be claimed either as well as or instead of rescission

- understand the meaning of mistake: in particular why it is so hard to prove and what the effect of claiming that a contract has been formed due to a mistake is

- know the three different types of mistake

- be able to distinguish between the effect of a contract being void (for mistake) and voidable (for misrepresentation)

- understand the twin concepts of duress and undue influence and know that, like misrepresentation, they render the contract voidable

---

1 MISREPRESENTATION

1.1. Definition of misrepresentation

A misrepresentation may be defined as a false statement of material fact made by one of the contracting parties before or at the time of entering into the contract which was intended to and did induce the other party to make the contract.

The definition of misrepresentation can be broken down. It must be

(a)   a **statement**
(b)   of **fact**
(c)   which is **false**
(d)   made by one **contracting party**
(e)   and it **induced** the contract

1.2   Statement

The representation may be express or implied by conduct. The general rule is that **silence does not constitute** a misrepresentation. There are exceptions to this general rule:

(a)   Where silence distorts a positive representation: a half truth may be false because of what it leaves unsaid.

Nottingham Patent Brick v Butler [1886]

Facts: the potential purchaser of a house asked if there were any restrictive covenants in relation to the property. (A restrictive covenant in this context is an agreement attaching to the title of the property which, for example, would not allow for any further building works on the land). The solicitor replied that he was 'not aware' of any such covenants. This was a true statement because the solicitor had not actually looked for any covenants when he had searched the title, ie checked the title deeds, etc. He should have done this type of search; if he had done so he would have discovered certain restrictions.

Held: this statement amounted to a misrepresentation because it was a misleading statement in the context it was given.

(b)   Where a party makes a representation during the course of negotiations which is true, but which becomes false before the making of the contract is concluded, he is under a duty to disclose this fact to the other party. If he does not the original statement has become a misrepresentation.

With v O'Flanagan [1936]

Facts: O'Flanagan correctly told With that his medical practice produced an income of £2,000 a year, but when With bought it some four months later it was practically worthless, owing to neglect while O'Flanagan was ill during that period.

Held: failure to correct his earlier statement amounted to a misrepresentation.

(c)   In contracts of utmost good faith (*uberrimae fidei*) where one party only is in possession of vital information it must be communicated to the other party so that he can assess the advisability of entering into a contractual relationship.

There is a duty to disclose all relevant facts. Taking insurance contracts as an example of a contract of utmost good faith. A person takes out policies of insurance to guard against such things as the financial problems that arise on the destruction of, or damage to, his house, or on his premature death before the normally anticipated life span has elapsed. The person taking out the policy possesses full knowledge of the material facts. Upon these facts, such as defects in the house or the history of his health, the risk is calculated by the insurance company.

The person taking out the insurance (the insured) must make full disclosure to the insurer of every material circumstance known to him which would influence the judgement of a prudent insurer in determining whether to accept the risk. Failure to do so renders the policy voidable at the instance of the insurer and it is immaterial that no loss has been suffered as a result of non-disclosure.

(Definition)   A voidable contract is one which can be rescinded by one of the parties.

(d)   In some fiduciary relationships the nature of the relationship imposes a duty to make full disclosure: eg, partners, promoters of a company and the company, principal and agent, and in arrangements between members of a family. Equity imposes the duty of disclosure in order to prevent abuse of confidence.

> **Definition**   A fiduciary relationship is a relationship of trust and confidence.

(e)   In contracts for the sale of land - in these contracts the seller is under a duty to disclose all matters affecting **title** to the land: he is not obliged to tell anything else (eg, existence of physical defects) because the purchaser should find those out for himself under the *caveat emptor* rule.

> **Definition**   *Caveat emptor* ('let the buyer beware') is the general legal principle obliging buyers of land, goods, etc to satisfy themselves as to the value of their bargains.

(f)   Note also that conduct may amount to misrepresentation eg, if a shop offers a discount to accountancy students and a person who is not a student of Training Co X goes into the shop wearing a Training Co X sweatshirt and obtains the discount, he is liable for misrepresentation.

1.3   Statement of fact - not law, opinion or intention

(a)   **Law**

A statement of law is not a statement of fact and thus a false statement of law will not amount to a misrepresentation.

(b)   **Opinion**

Bisset v Wilkinson [1927]

Facts: Bisset agreed to buy a farm from Wilkinson, allegedly relying on a representation that the farm would support about 2,000 sheep if properly worked. In fact, to the knowledge of both parties, the farm had never been used for this particular purpose. Bisset claimed rescission on ascertaining that the farm would not support anywhere near the suggested number of sheep.

Held: rescission could not be granted since there had not been any misrepresentation in law. Although the seller's erroneous assertion induced the contract, it was not a statement of fact but a mere opinion.

> **Definition**   the effect of rescission is to restore the parties to their original positions.

If the basic facts concerning the subject matter of the contract are not equally well known to both parties then a statement of opinion by the party in possession of relevant facts often involves a statement of material fact, for he impliedly asserts that he is aware of facts that support his opinion.

Smith v Land and House Property Corporation [1884]

Facts: a vendor of property described the existing tenant as 'very desirable', when he knew that the rent was in arrears and the tenant's bankruptcy might occur in the near future.

Held: this was a statement of fact in the circumstances, and being untrue amounted to a misrepresentation.

(c)   **Intention**

Like a statement of opinion, a statement of a person's intention is not a statement of fact. A genuinely stated intention therefore cannot amount to a misrepresentation if it is not adhered to.

However, a false statement of an intention which is not genuinely held is considered to be a misrepresentation of fact. For example, if A induces B to lend money to his company by stating that he intends to use it to expand the business when in fact he intends to use it to pay off the debts of the company, there is a misrepresentation of fact as he is stating an intention which he does not, in reality, hold.

Edgington v Fitzmaurice [1885]

Facts: the directors of a company invited loans from the public stating that the money would be used to improve the company's business. The directors' real intention was to pay off the company's existing debts.

Held: the statement of intention was also a statement of fact. The directors had made a misstatement of their present intention as to their future conduct.

(d)   **Advertising Puff**

A tradesman's praise of his wares is usually regarded as a mere puff and not a representation, eg 'this product washes clothes whiter than white'.

Dimmock v Hallet [1866]

Facts: an auctioneer described some land as 'fertile and improvable' when it was in part useless and abandoned.

Held: this was not a misrepresentation but merely a 'flourishing description'. (Note however that recent legislation requires estate agents to describe property accurately.)

1.4   False

A statement is false not only if it is untrue but also where it is true but misleading in the context. See for example **Nottingham Patent Brick v Butler [1886]**.

1.5   Made by one contracting party

The statement must be made by the contracting party or his agent. **Nottingham Patent Brick v Butler [1886]** is an example of the latter. A statement made by a contracting party which reaches the other party indirectly is actionable provided the misrepresentor intended it to reach the misrepresentee.

Philmore v Hood [1838]

Facts: Hood, wishing to sell his pub, told the prospective buyer, X, that takings were more than they in fact were. X could not afford to buy the pub but he passed the information re takings to Philmore with Hood's knowledge, and Philmore did buy.

Held: the representation was intended by Hood to induce Philmore to enter the contract.

1.6   Inducement

The misrepresentation must have **induced** the other party to enter the contract. Thus, the innocent party cannot avoid the contract if:

(a)   It was made after the contract had been entered into

(b)   He did not know of the misrepresentation.

Horsfall v Thomas [1862]

Facts: Horsfall made a gun for Thomas which had a defect which Horsfall concealed. However, Thomas did not examine the gun before paying for it.

Held: as Thomas was unaware of the misrepresentation (the concealment of the defect) it had not induced him to enter into the contract.

(c)   He knew the statement was false.

(d)   He did not rely on the statement eg, he ignored it or made his own independent investigation.

Attwood v Small [1838]

Facts: Small, who was interested in purchasing a mine and iron works from Attwood, made inquiries concerning its earning capacity. Attwood's reply was an exaggeration of the true position, but Small appointed his own agents to make a survey, and they confirmed the view already expressed by the seller. On discovering the inaccuracy six months after completing the sale, Small attempted to rescind the contract.

Held: the buyer was not entitled to rescind the sale since he had not relied upon the seller's misrepresentation, but on his own independent investigation.

However, the fact that the party misled had the means, of which he did not avail himself, of discovering the falseness of the representation, is immaterial, because he was entitled to rely on the representation.

Redgrave v Hurd [1881]

Facts: a solicitor advertised for a partner. The advertisement described his practice as moderate with extensive connections in a populous town. Another solicitor answered the advertisement and at an interview the advertiser stated that the business was worth about £300 pa. No accounts had been kept but the prospective partner inspected various papers which showed that the business produced a gross income of £200 pa and an agreement was concluded. In fact the practice was worthless.

Held: the new partner was entitled to rescission as he had been induced to enter into a contract by representation which turned out to be untrue. It was not an answer to his claim to say that if he had exercised due diligence he would have discovered the real situation.

The misrepresentation need not be the sole inducement.

Edgington v Fitzmaurice [1885]

Facts: a man was induced to take debentures in a company partly because of a misstatement in the prospectus and partly because of his own mistaken belief that he would have a charge on the company's assets.

Held: the fact that the misrepresentation was not the sole inducement did not disentitle him to rescission for misrepresentation.

A misrepresentation will be actionable by the party relying on it to his detriment, only if it has been made by the representor with that intention in mind. It is not sufficient if the representor intended to mislead someone else.

Peek v Gurney [1873]

Facts: Peek bought shares in a company on the stock market, relying upon false statements in the prospectus issued by Gurney and his fellow directors. Peek sued the directors on discovering the misrepresentation.

Held: Peek was remediless since the false statements were intended by the directors to mislead investors purchasing shares direct from the company at the time when they were first allotted. Once the public had subscribed for the shares the false statements had spent their force. Subsequent purchasers of shares from original shareholders could not rely on the falsity as the basis of an action against the directors responsible for it. (Note that the Financial Services Act 1986 now gives a remedy in damages to persons in Peek's position. However, the common law principle in this case still applies in other situations).

However, realise that the representation may be to the public generally, for example, in an advertisement.

| Conclusion | A misrepresentation is a statement made by one of the contracting parties which turns out to be false (it need not be deliberately false). |

It should be:

- a material statement of fact

    - not opinion
    - not law
    - not intention

- made at the outset of the contract (during negotiations, etc) what was intended to induce the innocent party (the misrepresentee) to enter into the contract

- and did induce the decision to contract

1.7   Activity

Which of the following would amount to a misrepresentation under the definition expounded above?

(a)   Michael is applying for motor vehicle insurance. He states that he has no penalty points on his driving licence: a true statement. However, before the policy is issued he gets stopped by the police and the Magistrates Court convict him of Careless Driving. He has 5 penalty points endorsed on his licence but he does not inform the insurance company.

(b)   Lesley bought a Hover mower on the basis that she saw an advertisement for the mower which said that it was equally effective on wet or dry grass. She now discovers that although not completely useless the mower is, in fact, much more effective when mowing her lawn when it is dry.

(c)   Jim bought a car from Ron. Ron told Jim that the mileage on the odometer was absolutely genuine, even though it was unusually low for a car of that age. The truth is that Ron had interfered with the car's instrumentation and he knew that he was telling a lie. Unbeknown to Ron, Jim had known the previous owner and knew that, in fact, the mileage must be higher than Ron was admitting to.

1.8   Activity solution

(a)   Yes - this is a contract that relies upon the latin maxim *uberrimae fidei*. When the facts changed the driver should have told the insurance company as the risk had changed.

(b)   No - this is almost certainly mere advertising puff. It was more of a description than a representation.

(c)   No - the statement must induce the misrepresentee to enter into the contract. Here Jim knew of the lie that Ron had told and so could not be said to have entered into the contract due to this attempted inducement.

2   TYPES OF MISREPRESENTATION AND REMEDIES

2.1   Fraudulent misrepresentation

A misrepresentation is fraudulent if the person making the statement did not honestly believe it to be true, either because he knew it to be false or because he made it recklessly, not caring whether or not it was true.

Derry v Peek [1889]

Facts: the Plymouth, Devonport and District Tramways Co was authorised to make certain tramways by special Act of Parliament which provided that the carriages might be moved by animal power and, with the consent of the Board of Trade, by steam or any mechanical power for fixed periods and subject to the regulations of the Board. The company issued a prospectus stating that it had the right to use steam or mechanical power, instead of horses. The plaintiff bought shares on the faith of this advertisement but the Board of Trade afterwards refused their consent to the use of steam power and the company was wound up. At the time of issuing the prospectus the company honestly believed the consent would be granted as a matter of course.

Held: the statement contained in the prospectus was not a fraudulent misrepresentation since the company entertained an honest belief that it was true.

Remedies for fraudulent misrepresentation are:

(a)   rescission of the contract (although he may elect not to rescind but rather to affirm the contract). Rescission is an equitable remedy. It puts the parties back into their exact precontractual positions.

(b)   a claim for damages based on the common law tort of deceit as in the above case of **Derry v Peek.**

2.2   Negligent misrepresentation

This is a misrepresentation made when the party making the misrepresentation (known as the misrepresentor) has a duty to take care when making the statement but breaches this duty by failing to take reasonable care. This should be considered in an examination question when the misrepresentor is in a position of trust (such as a professional person or someone who is regarded as an expert) and makes a statement without properly and fully checking the facts (eg an art dealer saying...."this painting is by Constable", If the painting is in fact a forgery but the dealer did not know this it could be regarded as a negligent misrepresentation).

Remedies for negligent misrepresentation are:

(a)   rescission of the contract (although he may elect not to rescind but rather to affirm the contract).   Note that S2(2) Misrepresentation Act 1967 authorises the court to award damages instead of rescission if it would be equitable to do so (ie, if it would be too severe a penalty to impose rescission on a person guilty of a relatively minor negligent misrepresentation); and/or

(b)   a claim for damages under S2(1) Misrepresentation Act 1967.

Under the Misrepresentation Act 1967, where a party has been induced to enter into a contract after a misrepresentation has been made to him, and as a result has suffered loss, then if the person making the statement would be liable for damages had the misrepresentation been made fraudulently, that person should still be liable unless he proves that he had **reasonable grounds to believe and did believe up to the time of the contract** that the facts represented were true: S2(1) MA 1967.   The misled party is more likely to bring an action for negligent rather than fraudulent misrepresentation as the former is much easier to prove, the onus being on the representor to disprove negligence.

(c)   a claim for damages at common law in the tort of negligence.   The tort of negligence is covered in detail in later chapters.   In brief the plaintiff has the duty of proving

   •   that the defendant owed him a duty of care.   This means that there must be a special relationship between the parties.   For an example see **Esso Petroleum v Mardon [1976]** (below)

   •   that the defendant has breached his duty of care by failing to exercise reasonable care.   Notice here the burden of proof is on the plaintiff: compare this with S2(1) Misrepresentation Act 1967

   •   that as a result the defendant has suffered loss which is not too remote.

Esso Petroleum v Mardon [1976]

Facts: during pre-contractual negotiations for the 3 year lease of a petrol filling station L (an expert with over 40 years experience acting on behalf of Esso) forecast the throughput of the station by the third year as 200,000 gallons.   Mr Mardon suggested that 100,000 gallons might be more realistic but his doubts were quelled by L's expertise and experience and Mardon took the lease.   In the event the throughput in the third year was only 86,000 gallons and Mr Mardon lost all his capital. Esso sued Mr Mardon for arrears of rent and Mr Mardon counterclaimed for damages in the tort of negligence.

(1)   It was **held** the action in tort for negligent mis-statement succeeded.   A duty of care existed because there was a special relationship between the parties based on proximity and reasonable foreseeability.   Breach of duty and resultant loss were also proved.

(2)   The Court of Appeal also stated that the plaintiff's statement was a misrepresentation in the law of contract, because although it was strictly a statement of opinion it implied an underlying knowledge of fact known to the expert but not to Mr Mardon and would therefore be treated as if it were a statement of fact.   Thus if Mr Mardon had sued in contractual misrepresentation he would have been awarded damages under the Misrepresentation Act 1967.   *Note:* Mr Mardon did not sue under the MA 1967 because Esso made the statement in 1963 and the MA only applies to statements made after 1967.

2.3   Innocent misrepresentation

In this case the representor had reasonable grounds for his statement but it was nonetheless untrue.

The sole remedy for innocent misrepresentation is rescission of the contract (although the injured party may elect not to rescind but rather to affirm the contract). Note that due to S2(2) MA 1967 the court may award damages in lieu of rescission (as for negligent misrepresentation).

> **Definition**   Affirmation is any act by a party entitled to rescind which has the effect of showing his continuing intention to be bound, eg voting with shares bought under a voidable contract.

The court has no power under S2(2)MA 1967 to award damages in lieu of rescission where the right to rescission has been lost. If there is no longer a right to rescind there can be no award of damages in lieu. Thus if rescission is not available eg, because the parties cannot be restored to their original position or because the contract has been affirmed, there is no remedy available for an innocent misrepresentation.

3   RESCISSION

3.1   What is rescission?

Rescission is an equitable remedy which restores the parties to their exact pre-contractual position.

Rescission can mean a formal order of the court or the act of a party cancelling or 'avoiding' the contract.

Car & Universal Finance v Caldwell [1964]

Facts: a man was induced by fraud to sell his car to a crook called Norris, who paid by cheque. His cheque was dishonoured and he disappeared. The seller notified the police and the Automobile Association immediately and asked them to try to find the car.

Held: he had successfully rescinded the contract as he had done all that he could in the circumstances.

Note: where a party pays by cheque this is a representation that the cheque will be paid.

3.2   The bars to rescission

Rescission is an equitable remedy. In practice the right to rescind is of less importance than it might appear because it is lost in the following circumstances:

(a)   **Affirmation**

This is where a party, knowing of the misrepresentation, shows an intention nevertheless to continue with the contract. For example

Long v Lloyd [1958]

Facts: the plaintiff bought a lorry from the defendant as a result of the defendant's representation that it was in excellent condition. On the plaintiff's first journey the dynamo broke and he noticed several other serious defects. On the next journey the lorry broke down and the plaintiff, realising that it was in very bad condition, sought to rescind the contract.

It was **held** by the Court of Appeal that he could not now rescind: the second journey constituted affirmation.

Affirmation may also be inferred where a plaintiff, who has discovered the misrepresentation, does nothing to exercise his rights to rescind.

(b)   **Lapse of time**

All equitable remedies must be sought within a reasonable time. 'Delay defeats the Equities'. What is a reasonable time will vary according to the circumstances.

Leaf v International Galleries [1950]

Facts: 5 years had elapsed before the purchaser discovered that the painting he had bought was not, as he had been led to believe, by Constable.

Held: he was barred from rescission by lapse of time.

Note: the misrepresentor had made an innocent misrepresentation and since damages are not available where the misrepresentation is innocent Leaf was left with no remedy in the law of misrepresentation.

It is likely that lapse of time is not a bar to fraudulent misrepresentation.

(c)   **Restitution is impossible**

The parties can no longer be restored to their original position eg, the goods have been consumed or deteriorated.

(d)   **Intervention of innocent third party rights**

A third party has acquired rights which would be prejudiced by rescission eg, if he has bought the contract goods from the party who made the misrepresentation.

Lewis v Averay [1972]

Facts: Lewis offered his car for sale. A rogue agreed to buy it and induced L to accept payment by cheque by claiming to be Richard Green, a well-known television actor. The rogue sold the car to Averay who took it in good faith. The rogue's cheque 'bounced' and Lewis sought to recover the car from Averay.

Held: the first contract was voidable for fraudulent misrepresentation but Averay had purchased the car before Lewis took steps to rescind the contract. Averay kept the car.

Conclusion   The remedies for misrepresentation can be summarised as follows;

- fraudulent misrepresentation: the misrepresentee can rescind the contract and/or claim damages under the tort of deceit

- negligent misrepresentation: the misrepresentee can rescind the contract and/or claim damages under S2(1) Misrepresentation Act 1967 or under the tort of negligence

- innocent misrepresentation: the misrepresentee can rescind the contract.

- if (whatever the type of misrepresentation) the contract is still executory ie, yet to be carried out, the misrepresentee may refuse to perform it

- sometimes a representation will also be a term of the contract in which case the innocent party will not only have remedies for misrepresentation but also remedies for breach of contract. This matter is covered in the later chapter 'Contract Terms'.

3.3   Activity

Susan goes into an Indian Restaurant. She says that she will only purchase a curry if the staff can assure her that all of the ingredients are fresh that day. She is assured that they are.

She orders her meal on the basis of this statement and when she is half way through eating it she starts to feel ill and discovers that some of the food has gone off. She says that she intends to rescind the contract. Can she?

3.4   Activity solution

Rescission is only available where the parties can be returned to their exact pre-contractual position. As she has eaten part of her meal this is no longer possible.

She can claim damages if the misrepresentation was either fraudulent or negligent. However, if the misrepresentation was completely innocent and the restaurant genuinely and reasonably believed that the food was fresh, as rescission is no longer possible she can get no remedy in misrepresentation. (Later you will see that Susan will have a remedy for breach of an implied term of the contract).

4   MISTAKE

4.1   Effect of mistake

Since a contract is made by acceptance of an offer the parties are, in principle, bound by the terms which have been agreed between them. As a general rule neither can escape liability by saying afterwards that what was agreed is not what was intended ie, that he was mistaken.

Tamplin v James [1880]

Facts: the defendant had bid successfully at an auction sale for a public house believing that the property offered for sale included an adjoining field, which had always been used by the publican.

Held: the court decided that the sale particulars clearly excluded the field. The defendant was bound by the contract.

However, there are some exceptional situations where a mistake operates to vitiate the contract. The significance of mistake in contract is twofold.

First there is the obvious question of whether a party is bound by a contract to which he did not, when the true position is discovered, intend to commit himself.

[Definition]   An operative mistake is one which the common law recognises as being so fundamental as to destroy any intention on the part of the person mistaken to be bound by the contract.

If mistake is an **operative mistake** at common law then the contract is **void**, the mistake nullifying the consent.

Definition   A void contract is one which has no legal effect. It cannot be enforced. Assets mistakenly transferred can be recovered.

However, even if the mistake is not operative at common law, **equity may sometimes grant relief** eg, rescission (allow the innocent party to avoid). This relief is always discretionary and may be granted on terms laid down by the court.

Secondly the other party may, before the true position is discovered, have resold the goods to an innocent third party. What then is the position of the third party?

If the contract was **void for mistake** the other party had **no title** to the goods and therefore could give none on resale. This is the principle known as *nemo dat quod non habet* - one cannot transfer that which one does not have. This means that the third party does not own the goods and would have to return them to the true owner. (There are some exceptions to this rule but they are not within your syllabus).

If, on the other hand, the contract was **not void for mistake** but is **merely voidable** (eg for misrepresentation) then the party misled **may be entitled to avoid** or rescind the contract, but until he does so it is a valid but voidable contract under which **title to goods passes** and can be passed on under a resale to an innocent purchaser. If the misled party avoids the contract after the resale it is too late ie, he cannot recover the goods from the third party who purchased them although he may still claim damages from the dishonest party. It is a question of which innocent person is to suffer the loss caused by the dishonesty of the party who made the misrepresentation.

4.2   Summary

In the exam be able to contrast:

(a)   **operative mistake** at common law which renders a contract **void**;

(b)   the **equitable relief of rescission** under which the contract is **voidable;** and

(c)   misrepresentation which renders a contract **voidable**

4.3   Types of mistake

There are several different types of mistake. These are:

(a)   Common mistake - where both parties have made the same mistake. Each knows the other's intention but both are mistaken about the same thing. Not all common mistakes are operative.

(b)   Mutual mistake - where the parties believe that they have agreed but in fact there is a misunderstanding. Mutual mistakes are operative.

(c)   Unilateral mistake - where there is again misunderstanding but one party is aware of it and may indeed have dishonestly induced it by misrepresentation. Unilateral mistake is frequently concerned with the identity of the parties. Not all unilateral mistakes are operative.

5   COMMON MISTAKE

5.1   Introduction

[Definition] An agreement may be reached on the basis of a mistake which is common to both parties, and thus they are both labouring under exactly the same misapprehension. Since the terms of both the offer and the acceptance correspond with one another, an agreement does exist. It must then be determined whether the underlying mistake affects the validity of the contract concluded (ie, is it an operative mistake?)

[Definition] An operative mistake is one which at common law renders the contract void.

5.2   Common mistake as to the existence of the subject matter

Both parties may believe that the subject matter of the contract is in existence at the time when the agreement is concluded, whereas in fact the property has been destroyed or does not exist. In this case, there is an operative mistake because the mistake is fundamental and the contract is void. The buyer is not required to pay for the goods, and any payment already made may be recovered.

Couturier v Hastie [1852]

Facts: some corn on board a ship travelling between two countries was sold while in transit. Unknown to either buyer or seller, the cargo had become overheated, and therefore dangerous, in the course of voyage. Consequently the captain had sold it at a port of call. The buyer repudiated the sale on learning the true facts, but the court had to decide whether an obligation to pay for the goods still existed.

Held: there was a basic assumption by both parties at the time of contracting that the goods being sold were still in existence, whereas in fact this was not true. The parties had made a contract which was void and destitute of effect since they were negotiating about goods which no longer existed.

Galloway v Galloway [1914]

Facts: the parties, believing themselves to be married, made a separation deed making provision for the wife on separation from the husband. In fact they were not married because the husband's first wife was still alive and not divorced from the husband.

Held: there was no contract. The mistake was fundamental. The separation deed was void and the second 'wife' could not claim under it.

Cooper v Phibbs [1867]

Facts: a party agreed to take on a lease a property that he already owned (though neither party knew this).

Held: the contract was void since there was a complete absence of any contractual subject matter.

5.3   Common mistake as to the quality

A common mistake by the parties, concerning the quality of the subject matter of the contract does not render the agreement void at common law, since the parties have agreed in the same terms on the same subject matter.

Bell v Lever Bros [1932]

Facts: Lever Brothers appointed Bell to be managing director of a subsidiary company for a period of five years. Owing to an amalgamation he became redundant before the end of that time and Lever Bros paid him £30,000 compensation. Subsequently, they discovered that he had innocently committed breaches of duty which would have entitled them to dismiss him without compensation. He was not aware of this when he accepted the compensation. The company sued for the return of the money.

Held: contracts are void only for mistakes which are sufficiently fundamental. This one was not because the parties had achieved what they set out to do (ie, the severance of their relationship): Lever Bros had merely paid too much. Therefore Lever Bros' action failed.

Leaf v International Galleries [1950]

Facts: Leaf brought a picture of Salisbury Cathedral from the Galleries for £85. At the time of the purchase the Galleries innocently but erroneously asserted that it had been painted by Constable. When he realised that it was a forgery, Leaf attempted to claim the contract was void for mistake.

Held: there was a mistake about the quality of the subject matter, because both parties believed the picture to be a Constable. There was no fundamental mistake about the subject matter of sale merely its quality. Therefore the contract was not void.

5.4   Relief in equity

Where a common mistake is not operative, relief in equity may be available provided that the party seeking relief is not personally at fault in failing to detect his error. Usually the court imposes terms that are fair to both parties, rather than casting the loss wholly on the shoulders of one party.

Solle v Butcher [1950]

Facts: a flat was leased for £250 per annum, since the parties mistakenly believed that it was not covered by the Rent Restrictions Acts. In fact, it was subject to a controlled rent of £140 per annum and Solle claimed excess rent payments made over the two previous years. Butcher counterclaimed for rescission of the lease since, before granting it, he could have served a statutory notice and charged a rent of £250 per annum because of extensive repair work to the premises. However, once the lease had been granted at £140 per annum, the rent could not subsequently be increased.

Held: there had been a mistake of fact as to the quality of the flat and the contract was not void at common law. The lease was voidable in equity however. Butcher was entitled to relief, based on just and equitable terms which regulated the position that had arisen between the two parties. It was inequitable simply to rescind the lease since Solle would be dispossessed. He was given the choice of either surrendering the lease entirely or remaining in possession at the full rent of £250 per annum, as if the landlord had served the statutory notice at the proper time. The rent overpaid was irrecoverable.

`Conclusion`   Common mistake is where both parties make the same mistake.

In order to operate to render the contract void the mistake must go to the very root of the agreement and be fundamental to its existence. It will not be sufficient if it is merely a mistake as to the quality of the subject matter.

5.5   Activity

Which of the below examples are instances of common mistake?

(a)   Roger sells his boat to Chay when they both believe that it is of ocean going class. It is not.

(b)   Bella contracts to sing in a music hall in Manchester for two evenings. At the time the contract was signed neither of the parties were aware that the hall had been destroyed by fire the previous weekend.

5.6   Activity solution

(a)   Yes - but as it is as to quality the mistake is not operative

(b)   Yes - this is as to existence of subject-matter: the contract is void

6   MUTUAL MISTAKE

Definition   **Mutual mistake** is where the parties are at cross purposes although neither party is aware of this. For example, one party offers a horse for sale and the other believes he is offering a house. In such cases the court resolves the confusion by looking **objectively** at the parties' conduct to determine whether the actions of the parties support one interpretation rather than the other.

The court is not concerned with intention but with conduct, so if someone conducts himself so that a reasonable man would infer the existence of a contract in a given sense, the court notwithstanding the mistake will hold the contract binding, and the party who correctly understood the contract is then able to enforce it eg, **Tamplin v James** (explained above).

The attitude of the court is that where there has been no misrepresentation and no ambiguity in the terms of the contract the defendant cannot be allowed to evade the performance of the contract by the simple statement that he has made a mistake.

However, if the contract is so ambiguous that it could mean what either party asserts, there is no agreement between them and therefore the contract is void.

Raffles v Wichelaus [1864]

Facts: the defendants agreed to buy **125 bales of Surat cotton...to arrive ex Peerless from Bombay.....** The ship mentioned in the agreement was intended by the defendants to be the 'Peerless' which sailed from Bombay in October, whereas the plaintiff offered 125 bales of Surat cotton from another ship called the 'Peerless' which sailed from Bombay in December.

Held: there was no binding contract between the parties, as there was ambiguity on one objective test.

If the contract is unambiguous but A, who was not mistaken, must have known that B was mistaken as to the terms of the contract, A cannot hold B to an agreement which A knew did not exist. This is a case of unilateral mistake.

It is not easy to prove that one party is knowingly taking advantage of the other's mistake.

Smith v Hughes [1871]

Facts: A sold oats to B. B had seen a sample and believed that the oats were old oats. In fact they were new.

Held: only if the seller knew that the buyer wrongly thought that the seller had warranted oats to be old would mistake operate to avoid contract.

Scriven v Hindley [1913]

Facts: a bidder at an auction of ropes made a bid for tow, which was obviously excessive (for tow), under the impression that the lot offered was hemp. The auction particulars were confusing and ambiguous.

Held: there was no contract here. The auctioneer must have realised the bidder had mistaken the terms of the contract ie, what was offered for sale.

> Conclusion Mutual mistake is where the parties are at cross-purposes. Literally one party thinks that the contract is to do one thing and the other party thinks it is to do another.
>
> A contract requires consensus (agreement) in order to be binding on the parties. If there is no agreement because the parties are at cross-purposes there can be no contract. Since the parties' mutual mistake is fundamental it is operative.

7   UNILATERAL MISTAKE

7.1   Introduction

> Definition A unilateral mistake occurs when one party is mistaken as to the terms of the contract whilst the other knows of his mistake. In such cases the mistake negates the consent and the contract is void. In this context a man is deemed to know what would be obvious to a reasonable man in the circumstances.

Webster v Cecil [1861]

Facts: a vendor of land, who had refused an offer of £2,000, wrote a letter offering to sell at £1,250 which was a mistake for £2,250. The purchaser was quick to accept before the mistake was corrected.

Held: the court said that he plainly knew that a mistake had been made and there was no contract.

7.2   Mistaken identity

Most cases of unilateral mistake have been cases of mistaken identity. In this type of case, A, a rogue, persuades B, the seller, to sell goods on credit to A by falsely pretending to be C, a creditworthy person. A then resells to D, an innocent third party, and disappears. Is the contract between B and A void for mistake or merely voidable for misrepresentation? The difference will determine which of two innocent parties will suffer the loss caused by the rogue A. Any mistake is unilateral since A himself deliberately induced it.

If the contract is void for mistake, there would be no contract. A would never own the goods and could not pass title to D. D would therefore be obliged to return the goods to B (D suffers the loss).

However, if the contract is not void for mistake but merely voidable for misrepresentation, A would obtain good title to the goods, and if D bought the goods before B rescinded the contract, D would have title to the goods and could keep them, (B suffers the loss).

To establish that the contract is void for mistake over identity of the other party, the seller must show that:

(a)   he intended to sell to some person other than the actual buyer;

(b)   the buyer was aware of the mistake ie, it was unilateral;

(c)   the identity of the buyer was a matter fundamental to the contract: and

(d)   he (the seller) took reasonable steps to check the identity of the person with whom he was dealing.

The decided cases are not easy to reconcile.

If the contract was made **by correspondence** so that the parties did not meet, the seller can apparently satisfy the tests above, including (d), by showing that the offer to purchase apparently came from a person known to him.

Cundy v Lindsay [1878]

Facts: a rogue called Blenkarn ordered goods and signed his letter in such a way that the signature appeared to be **Blenkiron & Co,** and he wrote from an address in the same street (but not the same number in the street) as the premises of Blenkiron & Co, a respectable firm known to the seller.

Held: this was a fundamental mistake of **identity** of buyer. The contract was void.

King's Norton Metal Co v Edridge, Merrett & Co [1897]

Facts: in this case the seller did not know the purported buyer; the name given was entirely fictitious. The letterhead used gave an ambitious picture of a non-existent factory.

Held: the seller intended to contract with the actual buyer although mistaken as to his **attributes**. Hence, the contract was not void but voidable for misrepresentation.

Where the parties have met **face to face** before the contract is finally made it is almost impossible for the seller to establish that he did not intend to sell to the party whom he had met.

Phillips v Brooks [1919]

Facts: the buyer (a rogue) described himself to a jeweller as **Sir George Bullough of St James's Square.** Before accepting his cheque and allowing him to take away jewellery, the jeweller checked from a directory that Sir George Bullough (a well-known society figure) did live at the address given.

Held: the mistake made the contract voidable for misrepresentation and not void for mistake. The jeweller intended to deal with the person in the shop; his identity was only relevant in deciding whether to take a cheque from him.

The results of these 'face-to-face' cases are usually justified and distinguished from the correspondence cases on the basis that the plaintiff intended to make a deal with the person present in the shop, his identity being of only secondary importance This is sometimes expressed by saying that the plaintiff's mistake is one of creditworthiness rather than identity. So it is not a mistake about subject-matter but about quality.

Lewis v Averay [1972]

Facts: Lewis offered his car for sale. A rogue agreed to buy it and induced L to accept payment by cheque by claiming to be Richard Green, a well-known television actor. The rogue sold the car to Averay who took it in good faith. The rogue's cheque 'bounced' and Lewis sought to recover the car from Averay.

Held: the first contract had been voidable for fraud but Averay had purchased the car before Lewis took steps to rescind the contract. Averay kept the car. The contract was not void for mistaken identity, as this feature of the rogue was only relevant to the method of payment, not to the contract itself.

7.3   Mistake as to the nature or effect of a signed document

As a general rule, a person is bound by his signature to a document whether he reads or understands it or not. Exceptionally his mistake is operative to render the document void if he can plead '*non est factum*'.

> **Definition**   *Non est factum* (it is not my deed) is a plea available to a person who wishes to avoid a contract on the basis of its being completely different in nature from that which he intended.

Saunders v Anglia Building Society [1970]

This case is also often referred to by its Court of Appeal title of **Gallie v Lee**. It is a decision of the House of Lords which established clear principles from the confused case law.
Facts: Mrs Gallie, a widow, had agreed to transfer her house as a gift to her nephew on condition that she was to remain in occupation for the rest of her life. The nephew asked Lee, a solicitor's clerk, to prepare the transfer. However, he prepared a transfer of sale to himself and persuaded Mrs Gallie, at a time when her spectacles were broken, to sign the document which she had not read. He then mortgaged the house to a building society. It was argued, on the basis of earlier decisions, that Mrs Gallie (and after her death Saunders, her executor) could treat the transfer as void.

Held: a successful plea of non est factum requires 3 conditions:

(a)   He is mistaken as to 'the object of the exercise' for which the document is required ie, what he signed was a fundamentally different document from that which he thought he signed, and

(b)   His signature was obtained by a trick, and

(c)   The mistake was not caused by carelessness.

Mrs Gallie's claim failed under the first condition. Mrs Gallie knew that she was transferring the ownership of her house and that the nephew might, subject to her rights of occupation, use it as security to raise money. The House was divided on the question of whether or not Mrs Gallie had been careless.

Note: the assignment was however voidable because of the fraud inducing Mrs Gallie's signature, but it was too late to set aside the contract when the third party rights in the property for value were acquired by the building society without notice of Mrs Gallie's claim.

A plea of *non est factum* (this is not my deed) renders the contract void for unilateral mistake on the grounds that the signatory's mind did not accompany his act.

Lewis v Clay [1897]

Facts: Clay was tricked into signing promissory notes in favour of Lewis, having been given reasonable grounds to believe that he was merely witnessing the trickster's will.

Held: Clay could plead *non est factum* to avoid liability on the notes. On the facts he had acted reasonably and had not given his signature to support this type of contract.

8   RECTIFICATION OF WRITTEN AGREEMENT

8.1   Explanation

Where parties have reached an oral agreement and have subsequently embodied it in a written document but the document contains a mistake in recording the terms, the court may grant an order of rectification to cause the document to reflect accurately the agreement reached. This is a form of equitable relief for mistake.

Strong evidence is required to show that the document does not accurately reflect the intentions of the parties.

Joscelyne v Nissen [1970]

Facts: Joscelyne, who shared a house with Nissen, his daughter, proposed to her that she should take over his car hire business. In the ensuing conversations, it was made clear that, if the proposal were accepted, she should pay all the household expenses in respect of the part of the house occupied by her father. The terms were included in a written contract which placed no liability on the daughter to pay the household expenses. The daughter refused to pay the expenses.

Held: rectification of the document was ordered by the court on the grounds that there was an original oral bargain which set out the common intention of the parties

8.2   Activity

Sandra goes into a shop which is selling porcelain. She sees a piece which is described by a label as 'An original 17th Century piece by the Angelina Factory in Venice.' This makes the piece very highly sought after. She asks the manager of the shop about the piece. He introduces himself as Ricardo Angelina, the great great great great grandson of the original designer and assures her on this basis that the piece is absolutely genuine.

It turns out to be a fake but before she takes the piece back she has it independently valued and tries to sell it to the person who values it.

Briefly summarise the legal actions that Sandra may consider taking.

8.3   Activity solution

Sandra will first consider the law of mistake:

- if operative this renders the contract void (so irregardless of the fact that she may have delayed or may have acted inconsistently with her intention to rescind the contract she can still get the purchase price back)

- it would have to be a unilateral mistake as the owner was clearly lying. It would be very hard to prove as the mistake must be fundamental and go to the very root of the very existence of the subject-matter and not merely be a mistake about quality. (See the case of **Leaf v International Galleries**).

- here it is a matter of quality, not subject-matter and she would almost certainly fail in this action

Sandra will then consider fraudulent misrepresentation:

- the misrepresentor was lying (a complete absence of honest belief)

- the remedy here is to seek rescission of the contract: however, it could be argued that to attempt to sell the piece was to act in a way inconsistent with her intention to rescind ie, affirmation

- damages in the tort of deceit seems the only alternative

   (There has also been a breach of S13 Sale of Goods Act 1979 - see the later chapter 'Contract: Terms')

9   CONSENT - DURESS AND UNDUE INFLUENCE

A contract may have been concluded to all outward appearances. However, there may be a vitiating element which prevents the agreement from correctly reflecting the intentions of the parties. As explained before, to vitiate a contract is to destroy its validity.

A contract concluded under duress or undue influence is **voidable** at the option of the coerced or influenced party, since that person does not freely consent to the agreement made.

10   DURESS

Definition   The old common law doctrine of duress was narrow in scope, being limited to contracts entered into as a result of the use of **violence, fear of unlawful imprisonment, or threatened violence** to the contracting party or his immediate family. Modern cases extend the concept to include **economic duress**. The doctrine applies to contracts and to gifts.

Cumming v Ince [1847]

Facts: an old lady was threatened by a relative that she would be put in a mental home if she did not transfer property to the relative.

Held: the transfer would be set aside as having been made under duress.

The common law once rejected the view that threats to property could amount to duress, yet the notion of economic duress (ie, threat to property, finance) has now been firmly accepted. Its precise scope, however, remains unclear as yet.

Universe Tankships of Monrovia v ITWF [1982]

Facts: the plaintiffs, who were owners of a ship, entered into an agreement with the defendant trade union, whereby they agreed to pay certain sums of money to the union's welfare fund, in return for the union's agreement to end blacking of the ship. Twelve days after the release of the ship the plaintiff reclaimed the money on the grounds that it had been extorted under economic duress

Held: the money paid to the union could be reclaimed.. Although the conduct of the union was not in itself unlawful, its effect upon the plaintiff was such that it amounted to illegitimate pressure (economic duress).

While the courts now clearly recognise the concept of economic duress, it remains to be seen what action will amount to illegitimate pressure or commercial pressure that vitiates free will. Although it will certainly include some threats to break a contract, it will not include all.

There is a very thin line between economic duress and legitimate commercial pressure.

Atlas Express v Kafco [1989]

Facts: the plaintiffs were carriers who contracted with the defendants to deliver baskets to one of the defendant's important customers, Woolworths, for an agreed price. In due course the plaintiff's depot manager refused to collect the goods unless the defendants signed an agreement to pay more for the carriage.

The defendants signed under protest.

Held: the plaintiffs could not enforce the higher rate since the defendant's consent had been obtained by economic duress. Factors which, taken together, led the court to decide that there had been illegitimate pressure amounting to duress rather than 'hard bargaining' (which is legitimate) were:

- the plaintiff knew that fulfilment of the basket contract with Woolworths was vital to the survival of the defendant's business

- on the day the plaintiff's lorry driver arrived with the new contract he had been instructed not to take the baskets unless the new contract was signed

- and on that day the plaintiff's depot manager deliberately made himself unavailable for contact by the defendant

- the plaintiff knew that the defendant would be unable to find an alternative carrier at such short notice at such a busy time of the year.

Note: the court also gave another reason for its decision, viz that plaintiffs had not given consideration for the new agreement as they were already obliged to deliver the goods under the original contract. This case could therefore be cited in a question on 'sufficiency of consideration'.

11   UNDUE INFLUENCE

11.1   Introduction

A person who has been induced to enter into a transaction by the undue influence of another (the wrongdoer) is entitled in equity to set that transaction aside as against the wrongdoer: the transaction is **voidable.**

Equity regarded the common law doctrine of duress as very narrow and therefore developed the wide concept of undue influence to cover cases where one party enters into a transaction under influence which prevents him from freely deciding for himself upon the advisability of the transaction. Like duress the concept applies to contracts and gifts.

(Definition)   The courts have avoided defining undue influence since the existence of a rigid definition might limit the scope of the doctrine. Undue influence is based on the concept that one party has a stronger mind (or will) than the other such that the other is unable to exercise free and independent judgement: the essence, then, is mental coercion.

The law on undue influence was reviewed and restated in 1993 by the House of Lords in **Barclays Bank v O'Brien** and **CIBC Mortgages v Pitt**.

Contracts which may be rescinded for undue influence fall into two categories: first, those where no fiduciary relationship exists between the parties; second, those where a fiduciary relationship exists. In the first case, undue influence must be proved as a fact, in the second it is presumed to exist. The two categories are not mutually exclusive and it is quite possible in litigation for the complainant to allege, and successfully, both that undue influence should be presumed and that it existed in fact.

11.2   Class 1: actual undue influence

In cases where no fiduciary relationship exists between the parties it is necessary for the claimant to prove affirmatively that the wrongdoer exerted undue influence on the complainant to enter into the transaction.

CIBC Mortgages plc v Pitt [1993]

Facts: Mr Pitt wished to speculate on the stock exchange and to borrow money for this purpose secured by mortgage on a house jointly owned by he and his wife. Mrs Pitt was not happy about this suggestion and made her feelings known to her husband. As a result he embarked on a course of conduct putting pressure on Mrs Pitt. Eventually she agreed to a joint loan secured by mortgage on the house.

Held: Mrs Pitt signed the necessary paperwork under the actual undue influence of Mr Pitt.

11.3   Class 2: presumed undue influence

In these cases the complainant only has to show that there was a relationship of trust and confidence between the complainant and the wrongdoer of such a nature that equity will presume that the wrongdoer abused that relationship in procuring the complainant to enter into the transaction. Here there is no need to produce evidence that actual undue influence was exerted: once the confidential relationship has been proved the burden then shifts to the wrongdoer to prove that the complainant entered into the transaction freely, for example by showing that the complainant had independent advice.

Such a confidential relationship can be established in two ways, viz:

Class 2A. Certain relationships as a matter of law raise the presumption that undue influence has been exerted. Case law shows that these relationships include:

(a)   Solicitor and client

(b)   Trustee and beneficiary

(c)   Medical advisor and client

(d)   Religious advisor and disciple

(e)   Parent and child

Class 2B. Where the complainant proves the existence of a relationship under which the complainant **generally** reposed trust and confidence in the wrongdoer, there then arises a presumption of undue influence in relation to the **particular** transaction.

Lloyds Bank v Bundy [1974]

Facts: Bundy, an elderly farmer with little business experience, had banked with the local branch of Lloyds for many decades and assumed that he would be advised only to his advantage. His son's business (which also banked at the same bank) got into difficulty and Bundy guaranteed the overdraft. The guarantee was secured by a mortgage on his farmhouse, which was his home and only asset. When the son's business failed the bank sought to enforce the mortgage.

Held: this was a Class 2B relationship because, on the particular facts, the farmer generally reposed trust and confidence in the bank. Therefore undue influence would be presumed in relation to the guarantee and mortgage and, since it was to Bundy's manifest disadvantage, it would be set aside.

Note: this case was decided on its particular facts - not every customer reposes complete trust in his bank manager and assumes the bank always acts in his (the customer's) interests.

Note: there was no allegation of actual undue influence by the bank ie, there was no suggestion that the bank put any pressure on Bundy to sign.

11.4   Effect of undue influence

The remedy for undue influence is the equitable one of rescission ie, the complainant may have the transaction set aside.

Where undue influence is presumed the complainant cannot set aside the transaction unless it is manifestly disadvantageous to him: whether or not the transaction is manifestly disadvantageous is not material to the setting aside of a transaction induced by actual undue influence.

Being an equitable remedy the right to rescind for undue influence will be lost if:

(a)   A reasonable time has elapsed since removal of the influence inducing the agreement.

Allcard v Skinner [1887]

Facts: Allcard, on entering a convent, agreed whilst in the grip of her own religious fervour, to transfer money to the convent. She left the convent ten years later but waited a further six years to reclaim the money.

Held: her right to have the gift set aside was lost.

(b)   Restitution is impossible.

(c)   The contract has been expressly or impliedly affirmed by the party influenced.

(d)   Rights in the property transferred to the dominant party had been acquired by a third party for value, without notice of the exercise of undue influence.

11.5   Undue influence and third parties

The effect of undue influence is that the complainant can set aside any transaction between himself and the dominant party. The matter which is now considered is where the complainant (W), acting under the undue influence of a dominant party (H), is thereby induced to enter into a transaction with a third party (B): the question often before the courts is can W set aside the transaction with B? The most common example of this scenario nowadays is where a wife (or cohabitee) mortgages her share of the matrimonial home to a bank to secure her husband's business liabilities. Should the business then fail she will wish to prevent the bank enforcing the mortgage (ie, repossessing the matrimonial home). In many situations she will be under the undue influence of her husband, whether actual or presumed (Class 2B) and this would entitle her to set any transaction she has with the husband aside but in the above example the transaction the wife wishes to set aside is the mortgage contract with the bank. As a general rule she cannot claim to set aside the transaction with the bank on the ground of her husband's undue influence. To this rule there are two exceptions:

- where the dominant party is the agent of the third party

- where the third party has notice, actual or constructive, of the dominant party's undue influence. A third party should be put on enquiry (ie, has constructive notice) where (a) the transaction on its face its not to the financial advantage of the complainant, and (b) the complainant and the dominant party are cohabitees such that there is a substantial risk that the dominant party has induced the complainant to enter the transaction by a legal or equitable wrong. A third party who is put on inquiry in this way as to the risk of misrepresentation or undue influence can avoid constructive notice by explaining, in the absence of the dominant party, to the complainant the nature of the transaction and to recommend that independent legal advice is taken, the third party will also be able to rely upon a certificate from the dominant party's solicitor, stating that they have discussed the consequences of the transaction to the complainant (**Midland Bank v Serter [1995]**.

The leading case (which was actually on misrepresentation but the House of Lords stated that the same rules apply to undue influence) is

Barclays Bank v O'Brien [1993]

Facts: Mrs O'Brien signed a document mortgaging her share of the matrimonial home to Barclays as security for her all husband's business liabilities, present and future. The husband had falsely misrepresented to her that the security was limited to £60,000 and would last only 3 weeks. Barclays prepared the documents and Mrs O'Brien signed them without reading. The bank manager did not explain the documents nor did he recommend she take legal advice. When the husband's business failed the Bank began proceedings to enforce the mortgage against Mrs O'Brien for the full amount of the husband's indebtedness (£154,000). In her defence Mrs O'Brien pleaded her husband's misrepresentation against the bank by way of constructive notice.

Held: her plea (except to the extent of £60,000) succeeded.

CIBC Mortgages v Pitt [1993]

Facts: see earlier for initial facts. Mr Pitt's speculations went disastrously wrong in the stock market crash of October 1987 and the bank sought to enforce the mortgage against Mrs Pitt. In her defence Mrs Pitt pleaded her husband's undue influence against the bank by way of constructive notice.

Held: her plea did not succeed. Unlike **Barclays v O'Brien** where to act as surety was patently not to Mrs O'Brien's advantage, here the facts were different. On the face of it and so far as the bank knew this was a joint loan to both Mr and Mrs Pitt by way of re-mortgage. The bank therefore had no notice of the husband's undue influence.

11.6   Unconscionable bargains

Historically rather similar to undue influence are the associated pleas in equity of 'abuse of confidence' (covered earlier as an aspect of misrepresentation) and of 'unconscionable bargains'. There are very old cases on 'unconscionable bargains' where the court would rescind a contract on the basis that unfair advantage has been taken of a party who was poor, ignorant or weak-minded. The principle has not been applied in a modern case, although there is obiter dicta to support it.

Conclusion   If a contract has been concluded due to either duress or undue influence it is voidable at the option of the innocent party. The contract can be rescinded and the rights to rescission can be lost in the same way as under a misrepresentation in the previous chapter.

Duress - more limited in scope. Usually restricted to threats of physical violence, although economic duress now extends to non-legitimate commercial pressure that takes away one party's freedom to choose whether to contract or not.

Undue Influence - much wider. This looks at the relationship between the parties (usually focusing in on a fiduciary relationship) and questions whether the nature of the relationship takes away one party's rights to choose. The important matter here is whether there is a presumption of undue influence or whether it must be proved.

12   SELF TEST QUESTIONS

12.1   What is the definition of a misrepresentation? (1.1)

12.2   Can silence ever constitute a misrepresentation? (1.2)

12.3   How does a statement of fact differ from a statement of intention or opinion? (1.3)

12.4   Define fraudulent misrepresentation. (2.1)

12.5   If a person is found liable for a negligent misrepresentation under what section of the Misrepresentation Act 1967 can the misrepresentee claim for damages? What tort is also available? (2.2)

12.6   What are the four bars to rescission? (3.2)

12.7   What is the meaning of 'operative mistake'? What are its consequences? (4.1)

12.8   Why was the ruling in **Bell v Lever Bros** not regarded as being an example of operative mistake? (5.3)

12.9   Why is it so hard to prove operative unilateral mistake when the parties are in face-to-face negotiations? (7.2)

12.10   What does *non est factum* mean? What are the consequences of such a claim? (7.3)

12.11   What is the status of a contract that has been entered into as a result of the duress or economic duress of one of the contracting parties? (9)

12.12   What is the definition of duress? (10).

12.13   Describe undue influence (11.1).

12.14   List the five relationships (Class 2A) which as a matter of law raise the presumption of undue influence. (11.3).

12.15   Is it necessary to show manifest disadvantage where actual undue influence has been proved? (11.4).

12.16   What is the remedy that the injured party can seek if he has entered into a contract based on the undue influence of the other party? (11.4).

13   EXAMINATION TYPE QUESTIONS

13.1   Brian and Stella

Brian agrees to buy a computer from Stella.

Explain how the mistakes in each of the following circumstances would affect the contract:

(a)   Brian believes that he is obtaining credit over six months whereas Stella believes that it is a cash sale.

(5 marks)

(b)   Brian believes that he is buying from David and not from Stella.

(5 marks)

(c)   Both Brian and Stella believe that the contract price of £4,000 represents the true value of the computer but, because of a latent defect in its manufacture, the computer is only worth £2,000.

(5 marks)

(d)   Stella offered to sell the computer for £400. Brian believed that a mistake had been made and that £4,000 was intended but, nevertheless, accepted the offer.

(5 marks)

(Total: 20 marks)

13.2   Misrepresentation

(a)   What is a misrepresentation and what effect will it have upon the formation of a contract?

(12 marks)

(b)   Mort completed a proposal form for a life assurance policy. In answer to a question asking what other such proposals he had made he stated that one had been accepted. This was correct, but he omitted to mention that three other proposals had been turned down. Mort has now died and his widow is claiming on the policy.

To what extent is she likely to succeed?

(8 marks)

(Total: 20 marks)

13.3   Duress and undue influence

Define 'duress' and 'undue influence' and explain their effect on a contract.

(10 marks)

14   ANSWERS TO EXAMINATION TYPE QUESTIONS

14.1   Brian and Stella

A mistake in relation to a contract may either make a contract void at common law or voidable in equity. The mistake may be a common mistake, which occurs where both parties are mistaken about the same thing; or a mutual mistake, where the parties are at cross purposes; or a unilateral mistake, where one party only is mistaken usually either as to the nature of a document signed or as to the identity of the other party.

(a)   The contract between Brian and Stella appears to be subject to a mutual mistake; the parties are clearly at cross purposes as Stella believes the sale is a cash sale whilst Brian believes he is obtaining credit over six months. If the mistake were sufficiently fundamental, this would result in no genuine agreement, rendering the contract void. This was the conclusion in **Scriven & Co v Hindley & Co** where X believed he was buying a consignment of oats from Y when in fact it was a consignment of wheat. However, in this case there is agreement about the subject-matter of the contract (a computer); the mistake is merely as to the method of payment. This may not be sufficiently fundamental to render the contract void *ab initio*, but the court may still operate the equitable remedy of rescission **(Grist v Bailey)**.

(b)   This would appear to be a unilateral mistake as to the identity of the other party to the contract. Such a mistake renders the contract void at common law if it can be proved that the identity of the other party is of vital importance. This was established in **Cundy v Lindsay** where the contract was entered into by letter as opposed to face-to-face, and the seller thought he was despatching goods to a customer with whom he had dealt before, whereas in fact he was tricked into despatching them to a rogue, Blenkarn. If Brian has dealt with David before and is contracting other than face-to-face, the situation may well come within **Cundy v Lindsay**.

       If the court does not consider the identity of the other party to be of vital importance, the contract will only be voidable in equity and Brian's position will depend on the availability of the equitable remedy of rescission or, if the contract has not yet been performed, the court's refusal of specific performance. Where the parties contract face-to-face, as in **Lewes v Averay**, it is generally assumed by the court that the injured party intended to contract with the person standing before him and the mistake relates only to the quality/creditworthiness of that party. It would seem that the parties were not contracting face-to-face as it is difficult to see how confusion could have arisen if Stella is a female and David a male, unless the mistake related to whether Stella was an agent of David. If the contract was not entered into face-to-face but Brian had not dealt with David before, this would also seem only to render the contract voidable in equity, being merely a mistake as to the quality/creditworthiness of the other party. This view is supported by the decision in **King's Norton Metal Co Ltd v Edridge, Merrett & Co Ltd**.

(c)   The mistake in this event is a common mistake. Both Brian and Stella are mistaken about the quality of the computer. A common mistake renders a contract void at common law if it is fundamental, such as a mistake as to the existence of the subject-matter of the contract as in **Couturier v Hastie**. However, **Leaf v International Galleries** establishes that a mistake merely as to the quality of the subject-matter of the contract is not generally an operative mistake, even in equity.

(d)   The offer of the computer for £400 by Stella would appear to be a unilateral mistake if the computer is in fact worth £4,000. The mistake has not been induced by Brian but he has taken advantage of the situation. If the contract is a written contract and the contract price has mistakenly been reduced to writing at £400, there being a prior oral agreement for £4,000, the remedy of rectification of the written contract may be available. This would enable Stella to demand £4,000. However, the remedy is discretionary and the court would have to be satisfied that the mistake only occurred in reducing the contract to writing.

       If the mistake is not in the reduction of the contract to writing, the seriousness of the error in the price may still be regarded as amounting to a fundamental mistake such that there can be said to be no true meeting of the minds at the formation of the contract **(Webster v Cecil)**. This would render the contract void.

14.2   Misrepresentation

(a)   Misrepresentation may be defined as an untrue statement of fact made by one party to the contract to the other, which was intended to and did induce the other party to enter the contract. To succeed in a claim for misrepresentation all the elements of the definition must be proved. Thus there must be a statement: mere silence will generally not amount to a misrepresentation. There are exceptions to this rule eg, a half-truth where silence distorts a positive statement, or where a true statement later becomes false and is not corrected: **With v O'Flanagan.**

The statement must be one of fact and not law, opinion or intention. A statement of opinion will not amount to a misrepresentation unless it involves an implicit assertion of facts of which the statement-maker is aware but which is not available to the other party: **Smith v Land & House Property Corporation.** A statement of intention will not amount to a misrepresentation unless the intention was not genuinely held: **Edgington v Fitzmaurice.** Finally, certain latitude is allowed in a tradesman's praising of his wares and an advertising puff will not amount to a representation.

The statement must have induced the other party to enter the contract and there will be no misrepresentation if the other party was not aware of the misrepresentation, knew it was false or did not rely on the statement. However, there is no duty to check that a statement is true and the misrepresentation need not be the sole inducement.

The remedies for misrepresentation depend on the type of misrepresentation which in turn depends on the statement-maker's state of mind when he made the statement. A fraudulent misrepresentation is one where the statement-maker knew that it was false or was reckless as to whether it was true or not. A negligent misrepresentation is one where the statement-maker believed it was true but did not have reasonable grounds for such belief. An innocent misrepresentation is one where the statement-maker believed that it was true and had reasonable grounds for such belief.

The principle remedy for misrepresentation is rescission of the contract which restores the parties to their pre-contractual position. However, the right to rescind may be lost if the innocent party delays in seeking it **(Leaf v International Galleries)**, if he affirms the contract after discovering the misrepresentation, if the parties can no longer be restored (eg, the goods have been destroyed) or if a third party has acquired an interest in the subject-matter of the contract (eg, a building society has a charge on the property as in **Saunders v Anglia Building Society**.) If the misrepresentation was negligent or innocent, the court has the power to order damages in lieu of rescission: Misrepresentation Act 1967.

Damages for additional loss suffered are only available if the statement was made negligently or fraudulently – not if it was made innocently.

(b)   An insurance policy is a special type of contract, a contract *uberrimae fidei* or of utmost good faith. Such contracts occur where one party is in possession of vital information which must be communicated to the other party so that he can assess the advisability of entering the contract. They are subject to different rules in misrepresentation and the general rule that silence will not amount to a misrepresentation does not apply. There is a positive duty on the insured to reveal all material facts to the insurance company. The material facts are those which will influence the insurance company in deciding whether to insure this person for this risk and, if so, what premium to charge. Thus in **London Assurance v Mansel** failure to reveal the fact that he had been refused insurance was a misrepresentation by the insured and entitled the insurance company to rescind the contract.

Thus Mort's failure to reveal the three refusals will amount to a misrepresentation.

A second exception to the general rule that silence does not amount to a misrepresentation is where a half-truth is told eg, where silence distorts a positive statement, as in **Nottingham Brick v Butler** where a solicitor stated that he was unaware of any restrictive covenants on land but failed to say that he had not checked the title deeds where such covenants would be revealed.

Mort's statement that he had been accepted by one insurance company is such a half-truth and thus amounts to a misrepresentation.

14.3   Duress and undue influence

Duress is the use of violence or the threat of violence to induce a party to enter into a contract. It is a common law doctrine which had been interpreted very narrowly to mean actual or threatened physical violence to the person or his immediate family. Threatened physical violence includes the threat of unlawful imprisonment - **Cumming v Ince.** Modern cases have extended the concept to threats (not necessarily physical) to property and threats to break a contract: this is called economic duress. In **Atlas Express v Kafco** the plaintiff refused to perform a contract unless the defendant paid more money. It was held that, in the circumstances, this was economic duress such that the defendant was not then bound when he promised to pay more. There is a narrow line between commercial hard bargaining and duress. It is the particular circumstances of each case to which the court has regard when making the distinction. In **Kafco**, for example, the contract the plaintiff refused to carry out was one for the carriage of goods and he knew, not only that the carriage of the particular goods was of vital importance to the defendant's business but also that the defendant would have been unable to find an alternative carrier in time for delivery.

Undue influence is an equitable doctrine which is an extension of the common law concept of duress. It occurs where one party enters a contract under an influence of mind which prevents him from exercising a free and independent judgement - **Barclays Bank v O'Brien.**

Where a fiduciary relationship exists between the parties the law presumes one party unduly influenced the other: there is no requirement to prove undue influence. Certain fiduciary relationships (eg, parent and child, doctor and patient) as a matter of law raise the presumption of undue influence. Outside these special situations a plaintiff who proves that his relationship with the defendant was a general one of trust and confidence may then rely on the presumption of undue influence in relation to the particular transaction. The presumption of undue influence can be rebutted by the defendant by proof that the plaintiff did in fact exercise a free and independent judgement. The most cogent evidence here is the fact that the plaintiff received impartial legal advice as to the effect of the transaction.

Where no fiduciary relationship exists between the parties it is necessary for the plaintiff to put evidence before the court to prove he was actually under the undue influence of the plaintiff - **CIBC Mortgages v Pitt.**

A contract entered into under either duress or undue influence is voidable at the instance of the party pleading he contracted under duress or undue influence. Where a contract is voidable this means that it can be set aside. A party under presumed undue influence can only set aside the contract if he further shows it was manifestly disadvantageous to him. Since undue influence is an equitable concept there are bars to the remedy of rescission. Thus a party who has affirmed the contract or who has unreasonably delayed cannot rescind; nor can rescission be claimed where the parties cannot be restored to their original positions nor so as to recover property which has been further transferred to third parties unless they had notice of the undue influence. Although duress is a common law, not equitable, doctrine it is very likely that the same bars also apply where a party is seeking to set aside a contract for duress.

6 CONTRACT: TERMS

INTRODUCTION & LEARNING OBJECTIVES

Syllabus area 8a. Contractual terms, including those implied by statute (eg, for the sale of goods). (Ability required 3).

Standard form contracts and exemption clauses. (Ability required 3).

Contracts in restraint of trade. (Ability required 3).

Certainty. (Ability required 3)

Now that the contract has been formed and is valid it is important to look at what its contents are. The contents of the contract are its terms and it is these which will dictate the parties' legal obligations. The terms can include simple things such as price and date of delivery but they can also be complicated references to the passage of title in the goods and the exclusion of liability in the event of a breach of contract.

Terms can be implied into a contract or they can be expressly inserted by either or both of the parties. The most usual example of an examination question on express terms is on exclusion (sometimes known as exemption) clauses. The most usual implied terms are inserted by the Sale of Goods Act 1979.

When you have studied this chapter you should be able to do the following:

- understand the difference between terms and mere representations

- understand the difference between implied and express terms of a contract and how they are inserted into a contract

- have an outline understanding of the terms implied by the Sale of Goods Act 1979 and the Supply of Goods and Services Act 1982

- know the difference between conditions and warranties (and be able to give examples of each)

- understand what an exclusion clause is and know what tests such a clause has to pass before it will be valid both under the common law and under statute.

- understand what a covenant in restraint of trade is and be able to explain the tests which must be satisfied in order for it to be enforced by injunction

1 TERMS OF A CONTRACT

1.1 Introduction

In determining the contents of a contract (ie, the terms) there are a number of areas which need to be considered:

(a) whether a statement made in negotiations has become a term of the contract or not;
(b) the need for certainty of essential terms of the agreement; and
(c) what, if any, terms will be implied into a contract;
(d) the importance of any particular term and what happens if it is broken;
(e) whether a term in a contract excluding or limiting a party's liability for breach is effective.

2   CONTRACTUAL TERMS AND MERE REPRESENTATIONS

2.1   Introduction

A statement, written or oral, made during negotiations leading to a contract, may be a term of the subsequent contract or merely a representation inducing the contract.

It is important to ascertain whether a statement becomes a term of the contract or remains a mere representation because the remedies available to a wronged party will differ depending on whether there is a breach of a contractual term or merely a misrepresentation.

The differences between terms and representations are:

(a)   If the representation is subsequently included in the contract as one of its terms and if it is then later found to be untrue the party misled has remedies for breach of the term, as well as for misrepresentation.

(b)   If, however, the representation does not become a term of the contract, the party misled will have remedies **only** for misrepresentation.

2.2   Intention of the parties

Whether a statement becomes a term of the contract or not depends on the intention of the parties. The test of the parties' intentions is objective and will depend on what was said and the circumstances in which the statement was made. In deciding whether a statement is a term or a representation the following are relevant **guidelines:**

(a)   When the statement was made - the greater the interval of time between making the statement making the contract the more likely that it will be a representation.

(b)   Whether the statement was reduced to writing after it was made - if it was it is more likely to be a term of the contract.

(c)   The importance of the statement to the recipient - eg, where a statement on the quality of the goods being sold is the whole basis upon which the contract is made as far as the buyer is concerned it will be a term.

   Bannerman v White [1861]

   Facts: a buyer of hops asked the seller whether sulphur had been used in the treatment and added that if it had he would not buy. The sellers assured him that sulphur had not been used. Sulphur had been used.

   Held: the court decided that as the use of sulphur was a vital part of the contract, around which the whole deal revolved, it was a term.

(d)   The strength of the statement by the maker - eg, where a party negotiating the contract suggests that the other party should check the accuracy of his assertions before finally concluding the contract eg, suggesting to a potential house-purchaser that a survey should be made and a report of the probable defects in the structure to be given, the statement will probably not be a term.

   However, it has been held to be a term where a forceful or emphatic assertion suggests that a potential buyer need not bother to check its accuracy.

Schawel v Reade [1913]

Facts: Schawel was examining a horse which he was considering buying for stud purposes. The seller stated: 'You need not look for anything, the horse is perfectly sound. If there was anything the matter with the horse I should tell you'. Schawel then ceased his examination. A few days later a price was agreed upon and three weeks later Schawel bought the horse relying on the seller's statement. The horse proved to be unsuitable for stud purposes.

Held: the seller's statement was a contractual term. It was obvious from the words and actions of the parties that it was intended that in the purchase the responsibility for the soundness of the horse should rest upon the vendor.

(e)   Whether the person making the statement had special knowledge or skill - eg, where goods are sold by an expert who guarantees to the buyer that they have stated qualities which, in fact, they lack the statement has been held to be a term of the contract.

Dick Bentley Productions Ltd v Harold Smith (Motors) Ltd [1965]

Facts: Bentley was interested in purchasing a Bentley car with an ascertainable history. The defendant, a car dealer, persuaded Bentley to purchase a car which was described as having a replacement engine and gearbox with only 20,000 miles on the odometer since replacement. The assertion relating to the mileage was false.

Held: the dealer's statements became a term of the contract of sale, for breach of which damages were recoverable. The special skill and knowledge of the car dealer placed him in a stronger position than the purchaser, consequently the court could more easily infer that the statements relating to the condition of the car formed the basis of a contractual term rather than a mere representation.

However, where a layman who does not normally deal in the kind of goods being disposed of makes an assertion to an expert the statement is unlikely to be a term of the contract.

Oscar Chess Ltd v Williams [1957]

Facts: Williams, on selling a car to the plaintiff company of car dealers, asserted that it was a 1948 model. The registration book appeared to confirm this statement, but it had been altered by some previous owner and the car was in fact a 1939 model.

Held: the statement was an innocent misrepresentation but not a term of the contract. The seller, who was not a car dealer with expert knowledge, did not intend to be bound contractually by his statement concerning the age of the vehicle. The dealers should have checked the engine and chassis numbers to verify the date of manufacture.

Conclusion   A representation is something that is said by the offeror in order to induce the offeree to enter into the contract. It only later becomes a term of that contract if it becomes formalised (eg, written down and inserted into a written agreement) or can be said to be a very important part of the contract (for example, a statement on which the other party relies. This is especially the case if the other party is an expert in the relevant matters or has certain information which is critical to the decision making process of the other side).

If what is said is merely a representation and is untrue the innocent party's action is for misrepresentation.

If what is said is not only a representation but also becomes a term of the contract and is untrue the innocent party may sue for misrepresentation and/or breach of contract at his choice.

2.3   Activity

Which of the below would be regarded as terms and which would be merely representations?

(a)   A potential purchaser viewed a property. The owners made several comments about the soundness of the foundations. The sale fell through at the time when the potential purchaser lost her job. One year later the sale was re-activated without any further comments about the foundations being made. It turns out that the foundations were unsound.

(b)   A purchaser of a car wanted to buy a particular model due to its rarity value. It turns out that the car was in fact a much later model.

(c)   When buying diving equipment the purchaser expressed doubt as to whether a particular model of wet suit would withstand conditions in very cold water. The seller was insistent that the suit would be ideal in those conditions and asserted that it was designed specifically with that in mind.

(d)   An art dealer spotted what he considered was a rare painting through the window of someone's private house. He went into the house to enquire if he could buy the painting from the owner and was convinced to buy it when the owner confirmed that the painting was definitely by that particular artist.

2.4   Activity solution

(a)   Mere   (b)   Representation   (c)   Representation (d)   Mere
       representation   and term   and term   representation

3   EXPRESS TERMS

3.1   Introduction

Definition   Express terms may be written or oral or partly written and partly oral. (Normally, an oral contract is as enforceable and as valid as a written contract). Express terms are terms specifically inserted into the contract by either or both of the parties.

3.2   Certainty of terms

An agreement can only be enforced as a contract if it contains, implies or provides for the necessary terms on all essential points. Thus the terms of the contract must be complete and certain of meaning.

King's Motors (Oxford) Ltd v Lax [1969]

Facts: the parties agreed to an option to renew a lease 'at such rental as may be agreed upon between the parties'.

Held: the agreement was void for uncertainty since it was incomplete - the vital term as to amount of rent still being subject to negotiation.

Scammell v Ouston [1941]

Facts: an agreement provided for the balance of the price.... 'on hire purchase terms over a period of two years'.

Held: the words 'hire purchase terms' was considered too imprecise and there was no contract.

It would however be sufficient if the agreement provided that the price under the contract should be the price ruling in an existing market on the completion date or that a dispute over price should be decided by an arbitrator or valuer.

The course of dealing between the parties or the custom of their trade may suffice to indicate the missing term which they intended to adopt but did not express.

Foley v Classique Coaches [1934]

Facts: in a contract to supply the petrol requirements of a bus company, no price was expressed or provided for but, for some time before the dispute, petrol had been supplied at the supplier's standard price to all his customers.

Held: this practice indicated what was to be implied (there was also arbitration on disputes if necessary).

In addition, the Sale of Goods Act 1979 and the Supply of Goods and Services Act 1982 provide that in a contract for the sale of goods or supply of services where the contract is silent on price or how the price is to be fixed, a reasonable price must be paid. Thus, a valid contract will exist even though there is no express term as to price or the method of fixing the price.

The parties may have included meaningless words in their contract; this is particularly likely to happen when they use standard printed conditions not adapted to their transaction. If the words are unnecessary they may be disregarded: **Nicolene v Simmonds [1953]** ('usual conditions of acceptance apply' - but there were none - contract construed without them). If, however, the words used are essential but imprecise then the contract is void.

4   IMPLIED TERMS

Definition   Implied terms are terms which are not expressly included by the parties but which nevertheless are still part of the workings of the contract. They can be implied by:

- the nature of the contract
- business efficacy
- Acts of Parliament
- custom and usage

As a general rule, implied terms bow to the express provisions of the contract. However, some of the statutory implied terms cannot be excluded even by express provision or can only be excluded to a limited extent.

4.1   Terms implicitly required by the nature of the contract

In some situations, for example, employment contracts, many matters are not expressly agreed.

The courts have implied terms which are required by the contractual relationship. These terms are implied into all similar contractual relationships unless excluded or inconsistent with the express terms. They are often called 'terms implied in law'.

In employment contracts there are implied terms expressed as duties of the employee eg, to give honest and faithful service to his employer, and duties of the employer eg, to use reasonable care in providing a safe place of work for his employees. These terms are implied as result of the court deciding the content of these types of contracts generally rather than deciding what the intentions of the parties were in one particular situation.

Liverpool City Council v Irwin [1977]

Facts: the plaintiffs owned a block of flats in which the defendants were tenants. The block was a tower block in which tenants had the right to use the lifts and rubbish chutes, but these frequently did not work. There was no formal agreement and no express undertakings by the plaintiffs.

Held: the nature of the contract implicitly required an obligation on the plaintiffs as landlords to take reasonable care to maintain the common parts (including the lifts and rubbish chutes) in a reasonable state of repair, as, given the provision of the lift, etc, it was necessary to imply some term to cover this. The plaintiffs were in breach of the implied term.

4.2   Terms as are necessary to give business efficacy to the contract

The courts may imply a term where the parties have failed to cover a particular matter which, unless remedied, makes the agreement unworkable. The courts imply a term to implement the parties' presumed intentions, to make the contract workable, ' to give business efficacy' to it.

The test of what will be implied in this way is whether, if an officious bystander had said to the parties, when they were making the contract, 'You agree on this point', both would have replied, 'Oh, of course'.

The Moorcock [1889]

Facts: there was an agreement by a wharf owner to permit a ship owner to unload his ship at the wharf. The ship was damaged when, at low tide, it was grounded on the bottom of the river on a hard ridge.

Held: the court implied a term into the agreement that the river bottom would be reasonably safe.

Such implied terms are based on the presumed but unexpressed intention of the parties. As this will depend on the particular facts of the particular case, these implied terms are often called 'terms implied in fact'.

4.3   Terms implied by Acts of Parliament

Examples are the Sale of Goods Act 1979; the Supply of Goods and Services Act 1982; the Partnership Act 1890; and a number of employment Acts. Many of these implied terms are only effective in the absence of contrary agreement eg, terms in the Partnership Act 1890. Others, however, are automatically included in the contract and cannot be excluded eg, Sale of Goods Act 1979. The most important example here is the Sale of Goods Act 1979. This is discussed in detail later in this chapter.

4.4 Terms implied by custom and usage

Any contract (oral or written) may be deemed to incorporate any relevant custom of the market, trade or locality in which it is made unless the custom is inconsistent with the express terms or the nature of the contract.

A term may be implied on the basis of what the particular parties have done in the past - thus called usage.

4.5 Activity

How will each of the below listed terms be included into a contract?

(a)   A contract for the sale of 15 tractors is written down. The delivery date is to be decided later. The purchaser later faxes through the delivery date.

(b)   When buying a second hand car from a private seller Jimmy fails to ask whether in fact the person selling actually owns the vehicle in question.

(c)   A large property development company lets a business unit on the twelfth floor of a tower block in the city centre. No reference is made to the fact that there are lifts or stairs in the building.

(d)   A holiday company reserves the right to change the destination and date of its customers' destinations.

4.6 Activity solution

(a)   Expressly.

(b)   Impliedly - there is an implied term of ownership in all contracts where one person (being in business or not) sells goods to another (S12 Sale of Goods Act 1979).

(c)   Impliedly - necessary in order to give business efficacy to the contract.

(d)   Expressly.

5 CONDITIONS, WARRANTIES AND INTERMEDIATE TERMS

5.1 Importance of the distinction between conditions and warranties

It has been common practice to classify each term of a contract as a condition or a warranty.

Definition   A **condition** is a **vital term of the contract,** breach of which may be treated by the innocent party as a substantial failure to perform a basic element of the agreement. The innocent party has the choice of either treating the contract as repudiated (or ended) and claiming damages for any loss suffered, or merely claiming damages for the breach.

The individual circumstances of the case will usually indicate quite clearly which of these two alternatives is more appropriate. For example, James may buy a washing machine from Bernard, with the intention of using it in his launderette. If the washing machine is defective, James may wish to treat the contract as repudiated for breach of condition, by refusing to accept the machine and seeking a refund of the purchase price. He may also claim damages for business lost by being unable to hire out the machine to customers. Alternatively, after a complete overhaul by a mechanic, James may decide to affirm the contract, keep the washing machine, but claim damages for the inconvenience, expenses and loss of profits incurred.

Definition **A warranty** is a less important term which is incidental to the main purpose of the contract. Failure to observe it does not cause the whole agreement to collapse: consequently the innocent party may claim damages for its breach but not treat the contract as repudiated.

If the washing machine supplied to James in the example quoted above works but looks shoddy due to damage to the exterior casing caused during delivery by Bernard, a claim for damages may take the form of a reduction in the purchase price, probably by mutual agreement between the two parties.

Compare the following two cases:

Poussard v Spiers [1876]

Facts: a soprano, Madame Poussard, agreed to sing in a series of operas for Spiers. She failed to appear on the opening night and Spiers refused her services for subsequent nights.

It was **held** that the obligation to appear on the opening night was a condition and since Madam Poussard was in breach of this condition Spiers was entitled to treat the contract as at an end and was therefore not himself in breach by refusing her services for the remaining nights.

Bettini v Gye [1876]

Facts: a tenor, Bettini, who agreed to sing in a series of concerts and to attend 6 days of rehearsals beforehand failed to appear for the first 4 rehearsal days. Gye in consequence refused Bettini's services for the balance of the rehearsals and performances.

It was **held** that the obligation to appear for rehearsals was a warranty and therefore Bettini's breach did not entitle Gye to treat the contract as at an end. Gye was accordingly in breach of contract when he refused Bettini's services for the remainder of the contract.

5.2   How the distinction is made

Whether a term is a condition or a warranty depends on a number of factors.

- Statute may declare the category of the term. For example the Sale of Goods Act 1979 implies a term into every contract for the sale of goods to the effect that the seller has a right to sell and the SGA states that the term is a condition.

- The parties may expressly declare that a term is to be a condition, as when for example time is declared to be the essence of the contract. But mere use of the word condition or warranty is not of itself conclusive.

- The court considers, in the light of the circumstances existing when the contract was made, whether the parties regarded the term as an important vital one going to the root of the contract or whether it was a term of lesser importance collateral to the main purpose of the contract. This will be a question of fact in each case. **Bettini v Gye [1876]** and **Poussard v Spiers [1876]** are examples.

5.3   Innominate terms

Over the years the courts have recognised that to classify a term as a condition or a warranty in the light of circumstances obtaining when the contract was made can lead to anomalous results, as for example if a term is classified as a condition then every breach of it, whether in the event serious or not, entitles the other party to terminate the contract.   Thus the courts have recognised an intermediate category of terms (innominate or intermediate terms) which are neither conditions nor warranties. Within this category the courts then consider whether the nature and effect of its breach is to deprive the injured party of substantially the whole benefit of the contract. If this is the effect of breach, sometimes called fundamental breach, then the injured party is entitled to terminate the contract. If the effect of breach is not serious the innocent party may not terminate the contract: he may only claim damages.

The Hansa Nord [1976]

Facts: citrus pulp pellets were sold for £100,000.   One of the conditions of the contract was: 'shipment to be made in good condition'.   On arrival not all the pellets were in good condition, and their market value was reduced by £20,000.   However, even if all the goods had been sound the market value, which had fallen between sale and delivery, was only £86,000.   The buyers rejected the goods which were later sold and eventually re-acquired by the original buyers for £34,000 (and used by them for the original purpose).

Held: on the question of whether the buyers' rejection had been justified, the provision as to shipment in good condition was neither a condition nor a warranty, but an intermediate stipulation. The effect of the breach was not sufficient to justify treating the contract as discharged. The buyers' only remedy was in damages ie, the difference in value of the sound goods and the defective goods.

5.4   Summary

> **Conclusion**   Condition - a vital term, going to very root of the contract. If this is breached the innocent party can claim that the contract is repudiated and/or claim damages.
>
> Warranty - a less critical term. If this is breached the only option that the innocent party has is to claim damages for breach of contract.

An intermediate stipulation is neither a condition nor a warranty at the time the contract is made, but one must consider the effects of a breach of that term. If serious then remedies as if it were a breach of condition should be granted. If less serious then only remedies for breach of warranty can be obtained.

6   SALE OF GOODS ACT 1979 IMPLIED TERMS

6.1   Scope of the Sale of Goods Act 1979

The provisions of the SGA 1979 apply only to a contract for the sale of goods.

> **Definition**   This is defined in the SGA 1979 as a contract whereby the **seller** transfers or agrees to transfer the **property** in **goods** to the **buyer** for a money consideration called the **price**.

6.2   Activity

Annabel agrees to sell her house to Bernard. Is this contract governed by the Sale of Goods Act 1979?

6.3   Activity solution

No: a house is land, not goods.

6.4   Activity

Charles agrees with Diana to swop his CD player for her television.

Is this contract governed by the Sale of Goods Act 1979?

6.5   Activity solution

No: the price must be money (either wholly or partly). This contract (called a contract of exchange or barter) is governed by the Supply of Goods and Services Act 1982.

6.6   Activity

Edward agrees to hire a car from F Rentals Ltd.

Is this contract governed by the Sale of Goods Act 1979?

6.7   Activity solution

No: 'property' in goods means ownership, not possession. This is a contract of hire (governed by the Supply of Goods and Services Act 1982).

6.8   Activity

Gerry takes his car to H Garage plc for its annual service.

Is this contract governed by the Sale of Goods Act 1979?

6.9   Activity solution

No: the main purpose of this contract is the provision of a service (ie, supplying skills and labour), not the sale of goods. The contract is governed by the Supply of Goods and Services Act 1982.

6.10   Implied terms - remedies on breach

The Act sets out in Ss10, 12, 13, 14 and 15 terms which are implied into all contracts of sale of goods, principally to protect the buyer, for example, by implying that goods will be of a certain quality. Each section also labels the implied term as a condition or a warranty. Thus:

(a)   a breach of any of the implied conditions will entitle the innocent party to reject the goods, treat the contract as repudiated and claim any damages he has suffered, although this provision is modified where the buyer is not a consumer and the breach is so slight that it would be unreasonable of him to reject the goods;

(b)   a breach of an implied warranty, on the other hand, will only entitle the innocent party to claim damages.

It is therefore important to note both the terms which are implied and the label given to each term ie, a condition or a warranty.

The SGA 1979 provides that where a contract of sale of goods is subject to a condition to be fulfilled by the seller, the buyer may waive the condition, or may elect to treat the breach of the condition as a breach of warranty and not as a ground for treating the contract as repudiated. Thus the buyer need not treat the contract as repudiated for breach of condition. He may elect to waive the breach entirely or to treat it as a breach of warranty and sue for damages only.

Even though the seller is in breach of condition, the buyer loses his right to repudiate the contract once he has accepted the goods. Thus once the buyer has accepted the goods he can only treat a breach of condition as a breach of warranty ie, he can only sue for damages, he cannot reject the goods. Under the Sale of Goods Act 1979 the buyer is deemed to have accepted the goods:

(a)   when he intimates to the seller that he has accepted them. *Note:* however, where he accepts only some of the goods, he does not lose his right to reject the rest; or

(b)   when the goods have been delivered to him and he performs any act in relation to them which is inconsistent with the seller's ownership. However, where goods are delivered which the buyer has not previously examined, he is not deemed to have accepted them unless and until he has had a reasonable opportunity of examining them to see if they conform with the contract. Unless otherwise agreed, when the seller tenders delivery of the goods he must on request give the buyer a reasonable opportunity of examining the goods: S34 SGA 1979; or

(c)   when, after the lapse of a reasonable time, he retains the goods without intimating to the seller that he rejects them: S35 SGA 1979.

Bernstein v Pamsons Motors [1987]

Facts: Mr Bernstein bought a new Nissan motor car which unknown to him had a blockage in the lubrication system at the time of delivery. This manifested itself three weeks later when after 140 miles the engine seized up. Mr Bernstein wished to repudiate the contract (ie, return the car and recover his money) on the basis that the car was not of merchantable quality nor fit for its purpose.

Held: the car was not of merchantable quality nor fit for its purpose therefore the seller was in breach of the conditions implied by S14(2) and S14(3). However, Mr Bernstein could not repudiate the contract: he was deemed to have accepted the goods because a reasonable time had elapsed. 3 weeks was more than a reasonable time to try out the goods.

Note: although Mr Bernstein was unable to repudiate the contract he was nevertheless able to claim damages.

6.11   Terms as to time

Stipulations as to **time of payment** are **not** deemed to be **of the essence** of a contract of sale (ie, are not treated as **conditions**) **unless** a different intention appears from its terms: S10 Thus a seller cannot generally repudiate a sale or even an agreement to sell merely because the buyer has not paid for the goods by a stipulated date. Whether a stipulation as to time of payment is of the essence of the contract, allowing repudiation of the contract if breached, depends on the terms of the contract: S10. The safe course is to say **time** of payment **shall be of the essence,** in explicit words, if that is the intention.

Other stipulations as to time, such as dates of shipment, transfer or delivery, are normally treated as **conditions**, at any rate in **commercial** contracts, where time is likely to be an important factor. The approach is fundamentally one of treating a time stipulation as part of the essential description of the goods, so that it is governed by the rule as to implied conditions in relation to description as found in S13 SGA 1979.

A stipulation as to time may be waived, so that thereafter (for example) a buyer cannot insist upon a delivery date specified in the contract. However, on giving reasonable notice, the buyer can once again make time of the essence in the contract.

6.12   Implied terms: title - S12 SGA 1979

At present, whatever a contract may say, the seller is **deemed to undertake**:

(a)   as a **condition**, that he has a **right to sell** the goods; or in the case of an agreement to sell, that, when the property is to pass, he will have a right to sell then: S12(1) SGA 1979; and

(b)   as a **warranty**, that the goods are and will remain **free from any charge or encumbrance** not disclosed to the buyer before the contract is made, and that the buyer will enjoy **quiet possession** of them: S12(2) SGA 1979.

The **condition** that the seller has **a right to sell** is most useful to a buyer when a seller turns out not to have been the true owner of the goods.

Rowland v Divall [1923]

Facts: a plaintiff who had bought, and for some months used, a car, then discovered that it had been stolen and returned it to the actual owner. *(Note:* the law requires him to return it to the true owner).

Held: in an action against the seller, the plaintiff recovered the full purchase price as being money paid on a consideration which had wholly failed. The defendant's argument that the plaintiff had accepted the goods and so could only sue for damages as if it were a breach of warranty was rejected. The defendant's argument that the plaintiff had received a benefit (the several months use of the car) also failed.

The S12(1) condition may also be used where a trader buys goods which cannot be marketed in their existing form because they would infringe a patent. The trader can rely on the seller's inadequate title and either reject the goods or claim damages for their reduced value.

Niblett v Confectioners' Materials Co. [1921]

Facts: tins of condensed milk bearing labels which contravened Nestle's trade mark were sold to a trader. They had to be relabelled before resale by him.

Held: breach of S12(1).

If at the time of the contract the seller lacked the right to sell but later acquired it, so that the buyer eventually acquires good title, the buyer loses the right to repudiate the contract for breach of condition as there is no longer a total failure of consideration. He can, however, still claim damages, not least for any expenses which he may reasonably have undertaken to establish the seller's title upon which he relies. He is not, of course, obliged to assist the seller in this way.

The **warranty** of **quiet possession** is rarely invoked in the courts.

Microbeads AG v Vinhurst Road Markings Ltd [1975]

Facts: a seller sold an apparatus for marking roads to a buyer against whom a third party took steps to prevent him using it, on the ground that it infringed a patent granted to the third party.

Held: the seller was held in breach of the warranty of quiet possession even though the third party's specification for the patent was not published until after the sale.

6.13   Implied terms: description - S13 SGA 1979

(a)   **Introduction**

In a **sale by description** the contract includes some description of the goods and the buyer contracts in reliance on that description. If it is a sale by description there is an implied **condition** that the goods **correspond** with the **description.**

(b)   **What is a sale by description?**

Most sales involve some description, if only to identify the goods.

- Where the buyer has not seen the goods, the contract is necessarily a sale by description.

- A sale is not prevented from being a sale by description only because, being exposed for sale or hire, the goods are selected by the buyer: S13(3) SGA 1979.

   Beale v Taylor [1967]

   Facts: a car was described as 'a Herald 1200' in an advertisement and had a plate 'Herald 1200' on it. The buyer saw the car and agreed to buy it. It transpired that the car was only partly a 'Herald 1200': part of another, older, model had been welded on to it.

   Held: this was a sale by description notwithstanding the buyer had seen the car. Since the car was not a 'Herald 1200' the condition of compliance with description had been breached.

- Where there is uncertainty about the status of a description the test is: did the buyer rely on it? Was it used to identify the thing sold or was it merely collateral?

   Varley v Whipp [1900]

   Facts: the seller described a second-hand reaping machine, which the buyer had not seen, as 'new the previous year'.

   Held: the phrase formed part of the description.

   Harlingdon Ltd v Hull Fine Art [1990]

   Point of law: what is a 'sale by description' such that S13 SGA 1979 will then apply?

   Facts: D, who had 2 paintings for sale which were described in an auction catalogue as being by Gabriele Münter, telephoned P to see if P was interested in buying them. When P came to examine the paintings D told him that he did not know much about the paintings and he had never heard of Gabriele Münter. P examined the paintings, asked no further questions about their provenance and bought one for £6,000. The paintings were later discovered to be a fake and P wished to repudiate the contract under S13 SGA 1979 for breach of implied condition that the goods supplied shall correspond with the description.

   Held: S13 implies such a condition only when the sale is by description. This was not a sale by description since P placed no reliance on the description.

- A statement which is part of a written advertisement is more likely to be treated as part of the description than one which is made orally in the presence of the buyer.

- The buyer cannot usually rely on S13(3), if he sees the goods before making the contract **and** it is obvious to him that the description is inaccurate, for he could not then claim he had relied on the description.

(c)   Why is it important?

In a sale of goods by description, there is an implied **condition** that the **goods correspond with the description:** S13 SGA 1979.

Re Moore and Co & Landauer and Co [1921]

Facts: a contract provided for the sale of a consignment of 3,000 tins of fruit packed in cases of 30 tins each, but some of the tins were actually packed in cases of 24 tins.

Held: the buyer was allowed by S13 to reject the whole consignment.

Arcos Ltd v EA Ronaasen [1933]

Facts: a buyer ordered a quantity of timber for the purpose of making cement barrels and the contract specified it should be of half an inch thickness. Most of what was delivered was nearer 9/16" thickness than half an inch though this in no way impaired its usefulness for the intended purpose.

Held: the buyer was entitled to reject all the timber.

6.14   Implied terms: satisfactory quality and fitness for purpose - S14 SGA 1979

(a)   Introduction

The most important of the conditions implied by the SGA 1979, though applying only where the seller supplies goods **in the course of a business**, are in S14. The two conditions are:

(i)   that the goods **supplied** are of a **satisfactory quality** except in respect of:

- defects specifically drawn to the buyer's attention before the contract is made; and

- defects which any examination actually carried out by the buyer before the contract ought to reveal: S14(2) SGA 1979. The buyer is not obliged to make any examination at all and therefore, the more detailed the examination, the more the buyer restricts his rights.

(ii)   in a case where the buyer, expressly or by implication, makes known to the seller any particular purpose for which the goods are being bought, that the goods **supplied are reasonably fit for the purpose,** whether or not it is a purpose for which such goods are commonly supplied, except where either the buyer does not rely, or it is unreasonable for him to rely, on the skill or judgement of the seller: S14(3) SGA 1979.

(b)   **'Supplied/not supplied' is wider than 'sold'**

It is not enough if the goods contracted for are in themselves sound but are so mixed with other contaminating matter as to prevent them being used.

Wilson v Rickett Cockerell and Co Ltd [1954]

Facts: there was detonator in a sack of coalite.

Held: goods **supplied** were not of merchantable quality.

(c)   **In the course of business**

The S14 terms are only implied into contracts made in the course of a business. 'Business' is defined in S61 SGA 1979 as including a profession and the activities of any government department or local or public authority. Similar terminology (in the course of business) is used in the Unfair Contract Terms Act 1977 and has been interpreted to mean that there must be some regularity of dealing in those kinds of goods or the transaction must be an integral part of the business. Thus, for example, an accountant selling his stereo would not be selling in the course of business. However, S14 SGA 1979 makes it clear that where a private person sells through a professional agent eg, an auctioneer, he sells in the course of business unless the buyer knew the seller was a private person or reasonable notice was given to the seller of this fact.

(d)   **Satisfactory quality: S14(2)**

> **Definition**   Goods are of **satisfactory quality** if they meet the standard that a reasonable person would regard as satisfactory, taking account of any description of the goods, the price (if relevant) and all other relevant circumstances.

The quality of goods include their state and condition and the following (among others) are, in appropriate cases, aspects of the quality of goods:

(i)   fitness for all the purposes for which goods of the kind in question are commonly supplied;

(ii)   appearance and finish;

(iii)   freedom from minor defects;

(iv)   safety; and

(v)   durability.

Particular note should be made of:

* any description applied to them;
* the price, if relevant; and
* all other relevant circumstances: S14(6) SGA 1979.

Thus, a buyer must not expect very cheap goods to be of the same quality as more expensive ones. Other relevant considerations might be that the goods are secondhand, or were made or acquired at great speed to comply with the buyer's special request. Goods used in the way or ways in which goods of that class are normally used and which do not work properly or fail after an unreasonably short time or which are unsafe or injurious are clearly not of satisfactory quality. So too are goods which though originally sound are damaged through having been badly packed by the seller with the knowledge of the kind of journey they would have to make. They are defective in quality notwithstanding that the damage occurs after the buyer has taken them away.

(e)   **Fitness for purpose S14(3)**

As to whether goods are as fit for the purpose(s) that goods of that kind are commonly supplied is an aspect as to whether they are of satisfactory quality. However, where the buyer may explain to the seller a **particular** purpose for which he requires the goods, then if the seller contracts with him, he is in general liable under S14(3) if the goods are not fit for that purpose.

Griffiths v Peter Conway Ltd [1939]

Facts: the buyer was allergic to a Harris tweed coat which was perfectly fit for a normal person.

Held: there was held to be no breach of condition of fitness for purpose as the buyer had not told the seller of the special circumstances (ie her sensitivity to such fabric).

If the buyer does rely on the seller's judgement, it is unlikely that a court will find it was unreasonable for him to do so, even if both parties trade in the same business. Even a retail shopkeeper can be relied on in this way since he is expected to select his stock with skill and judgement. It is not necessary that the buyer rely **exclusively** on the seller's skill and judgement, provided that the matter complained of arises from that aspect of the goods for which the buyer did rely on the seller.

(f)   **Comparing: S14(2) & S14(3)**

S14(2) gives the buyer protection against shoddy goods; S14(3) gives him protection against unsuitable goods. Sometimes, however both are available. They are invaluable in the field of consumer protection since liability is strict. The shopkeeper does not have to be shown to be at fault.

6.15   Activity

B buys a car from S, an accountant. The next day the car breaks down and B discovers that the engine is completely worn out. Can B return the car to S and recover his money on the basis of breach of either S14(2) or S14(3) SGA 1979?

6.16   Activity solution

No. This is a private sale (presumably) and therefore S14(2) and S14(3) do not apply to protect the buyer. Thus the position is, at common law, caveat emptor ('let the buyer beware').

6.17   Implied terms: sales by sample -S15 SGA 1979

(a)   **Introduction**

[Definition]   A sale by **sample** occurs when the buyer is given the opportunity of examining a small part only of the goods to be bought, but such as to be typical of the whole, in this context usually called the **bulk** of the goods.

Thus, corn, toys, pianos or parrots might all be sold by sample if the bulk of the goods was large enough to justify the method. A contract of sale is by sample if, and only if, there is a term in the contract, express or implied, to that effect: S15 SGA 1979.

A contract of sale is not by sample merely because part of the goods was shown to the buyer during the negotiations preceding the contract: both parties must accept as a contract term that the sale is by sample. Trade usage may, of course, raise the necessary presumption without any express agreement to that effect but if the contract is written it will normally be treated as a sale by sample only if stated to be so.

(b)   **Why is it important?**

In a contract for sale by sample there are implied conditions:

(i)   that the bulk shall correspond with the sample in quality;

(ii)   that the buyer shall have a reasonable opportunity of comparing the bulk with the sample; and

(iii) that the goods shall be free from any defect rendering them unsatisfactory, which would not be apparent on reasonable examination of the sample: S15 SGA 1979.

The test is one of **'reasonable examination'** of the sample and not one of thorough examination.

Godley v Perry [1960]

Facts: a boy of six bought a catapult from the defendant's newsagency shop and damaged his eye when it broke in his hands as a result of having been indifferently manufactured. The catapult was part of a quantity bought by sample from a wholesaler and the defendant's wife had tested the sample beforehand by pulling back its elastic.

Held: while the defendant was liable to the boy in damages for the catapult being neither fit for its purpose nor of satisfactory quality (S14(2);(3)), the defendant could also himself claim against the wholesaler because the defect of the goods could not be discovered by reasonable examination of the sample (S15).

'Reasonableness' is the statutory yardstick. The Act does not even speak of carrying out 'practicable' tests on the goods concerned, but of 'reasonable examination'.

If the bulk does not correspond with the sample, the buyer is not prevented from rejecting the bulk merely because he has made payment in full. Whenever the bulk does not correspond with the sample, the buyer can either reject the whole or retain the whole, or retain some of the goods and reject the rest.

(c)   **Sale by description and sample**

If a sale is both by description and by sample it must satisfy the requirements appropriate for each: S13. Thus, a contract to sell 'foreign refined rape oil, warranted only equal to sample', was broken when the seller delivered oil corresponding to the sample, but not answering to the description 'foreign refined rape oil': **Nichol v Godts [1854]**

Conclusion   In a sale by sample the bulk must correspond with the sample in quality, the buyer has the opportunity to compare the bulk and the sample and the bulk has no defect that was not apparent in the sample.

6.18   Modifications in non-consumer contracts, in respect of remedies for breach of conditions imposed by Sections 13, 14 & 15 SGA 1979

The terms implied into contracts for the sale of goods by sections **13, 14 & 15** SGA 1979 are all **conditions**. Normally, if breached, the buyer would always be allowed to treat the contract as discharged, reject the goods and claim damages. However, where the buyer is a **non-consumer** ie, he is not acting in the course of his business, he will be unable to treat the contract as discharged and reject the goods if the breach is so slight that it would be unreasonable for him to reject them. He will only be able to claim damages.

6.19   Conclusion

S12, S13, S14(2), S14(3) and S15 SGA 1979 give a buyer of goods and very high level of protection against unscrupulous sellers.

S12, S13 and S15 imply terms whether the seller is a business or a private seller. S14(2) and S14(3) imply terms only where the seller sells in the course of a business. There is therefore no statutory protection as to quality or fitness for purpose where a buyer buys from a private seller: in this situation the common law rule caveat emptor (let the buyer beware) applies.

6.20   Activity

Rosemary purchased a second-hand computer for her business from a private seller. She bought it in a telephone conversation having seen an advertisement for a 'XXX 123 model'. Rosemary already used XXX 123 models and was delighted to acquire another. A short while after the computer was delivered it broke down and the engineer discovered that it was a WWW 789 model that was now obsolete. What rights does Rosemary have?

6.21   Activity solution

This would appear to be a sale by description. There is an implied condition, from S13 SGA 1979, that goods sold by description shall correspond to that description. The breach of this condition gives Rosemary the right to terminate the contract and recover the purchase price. Since Rosemary bought from a private seller neither S14(2) merchantable quality nor S14(3) fitness for purpose apply.

7   SUPPLY OF GOODS AND SERVICES ACT 1982 IMPLIED TERMS

7.1   Scope of the Supply of Goods and Services Act 1982

This Act governs contracts of hire, contracts of exchange, contracts for work and labour and contracts for the supply of a service.

7.2   Part I of the SGSA

(a)   **Contracts for the transfer of goods**

> **Definition**   'Contracts for the transfer of goods' includes contracts by way of exchange and contracts for work and materials.

S2 implies undertakings as to **title** similar to those in S12 Sale of Goods Act 1979.

S3 implies terms where the transfer is by **description** and S5 implies terms where the transfer is by **sample** similar to those in Ss13 & 15 Sale of Goods Act 1979.

S4 implies undertakings as to **satisfactory quality** and **fitness for purpose** similar to those in S14 Sale of Goods Act 1979.

(b)   **Contracts for the hire of goods**

S7 implies undertakings as to **title** similar to those in S12 Sale of Goods Act 1979 ie, that the hirer or bailor has the right to transfer possession of the goods to the bailee.

S8 implies terms where the hire is by **description** and S10 implies terms where the hire is by **sample** similar to those in Ss13 & 15 Sale of Goods Act 1979.

S9 implies undertakings as to **satisfactory quality** and **fitness for purpose** similar to those in S14 Sale of Goods Act 1979.

7.3   Activity

Define satisfactory quality.

7.4   Activity solution

Goods are of a satisfactory quality if they meet the standard that a reasonable person would regard as satisfactory, taking account of any description of the goods, the price (if relevant) and all other relevant circumstances.

7.5   Part II of the SGSA 1982

(a)   **Introduction**

This part of the Act deals with contracts for the supply of services which have been the subject of much complaint over the last twenty years, particularly about the quality of services, delay in performance and cost. The problems arise because in many service industries the consumer has little idea of what is involved in providing the service and is, therefore, not in a good position to judge whether a good service has been provided or whether a reasonable charge made. In addition, there is the added problem that many people who provide services eg, accountants, do not quote the price for providing the service at the commencement of the contract.

The service industries have expanded greatly and a review of the complaints made by the National Consumer Council highlighted these areas of complaint. The Act therefore attempts to codify the existing law and take into account the recommendations made by the National Consumer Council, in particular, to deal with the three main areas of complaint of quality, delay and cost.

The Act covers 'contracts for the supply of a service' under which a person 'the supplier' agrees to carry out a service. The Act does not cover contracts of employment, apprenticeship, services of an advocate in a court or tribunal or of a company director to his company.

(b)   **Implied terms**

S13 implies a term into a contract for the supply of a service where the supplier is acting in the course of business, that the supplier will carry out the service with **reasonable care and skill**.

S14 implies a term into a contract for the supply of a service where the supplier is acting in the course of business where the **time** for the service to be carried out is not fixed by the contract, nor left to be fixed in a manner agreed by the parties nor by a course of dealing, that the supplier will carry out the service within a **reasonable time**.

S15 implies a term into a contract for the supply of a service where the **consideration** for the service is not determined by the contract, nor left to be determined in a manner agreed by the parties nor a course of dealings, that the party contracting with the supplier will pay a **reasonable charge.**

Conclusion   The Supply of Goods and Services Act 1982 implies similar terms to those in the Sale of Goods Act for contracts of hire, contracts for work and materials, contracts by way of exchange. In contracts for the supply of a service, the SGSA implies three terms as to reasonable care and skill, reasonable time and reasonable charge.

8   EXCLUSION CLAUSES

8.1   Definition and effect

The term **exclusion clause** (or exemption clause) is applied both to clauses which totally exclude one party from the liability which would otherwise arise from some breach of contract such as the supply of goods of inferior quality, and to clauses which restrict liability in some way or offer some dubious 'guarantee' in place of normal liability for breach of contract. Such clauses used to be very common in printed contracts and conditions of sale put forward by manufacturers, distributors or carriers of goods.

The tendency of modern statutes is to prevent the use of exclusion clauses, especially in dealing with private citizens who frequently do not read or do not understand the effect of the printed document put before them for acceptance.

8.2   Applicability and validity of exclusion clauses

In order to be valid the exclusion clause must pass two separate tests:

(a)   The common law test. This test is broken down into two sub-parts:

- the clause must be incorporated into the contract and not added after the contract is complete

- the clause must be clear and precise; any vagueness will be construed against the party who is attempting to rely on it

(b)   The statutory test laid down by The Unfair Contract Terms Act 1977 (often known as UCTA).

It is important to be aware of these two tests when answering examination questions. It is also important to be aware that if the exclusion clause does not pass the first test it need not be subjected to the rigours of UCTA.

8.3   The common law test - incorporation into the contract

It must be shown that the party who is to be bound by the clause did in fact agree to it.

If he **signed a contractual** document in which the clause is included he will generally be treated as having agreed to it even if he did not read the document.

L'Estrange v Graucob [1934]

Facts: the proprietress of a cafe bought a cigarette vending machine and signed a contract of sale, which she did not read, which contained a clause. **'Any express or implied condition statement or warranty statutory or otherwise not stated herein is hereby excluded'.** The machine was defective.

Held: she was unable to recover the price or obtain damages as she was bound by the clause as she had signed the contract.

However, a signatory is not bound by an exclusion or limiting clause where his signature to the document was induced by fraud or misrepresentation by the other party, or his agent.

Curtis v Chemical Cleaning Co [1951]

Facts: the plaintiff took a white satin wedding dress to the defendants for cleaning. She was asked to sign a document which contained a clause: **'that the dress is accepted on condition that the company is not liable for any damage howsoever arising'** but, before she signed, she was told that the effect of the document which she was about to sign was to exclude liability for damage to beads or sequins. Without reading all the terms of the document the plaintiff then signed as she was asked. The dress was stained due to the negligence of the defendants.

Held: the defendants were liable and could not rely on the exclusion clause because of the misrepresentation as to the extent of the exemption clause.

If the document was not signed (as most contracts will not be) then the offeree is not bound if it can be shown that he did not know that the document contained (or incorporated by reference) terms of the contract or that reasonable notice of those terms was not given to him eg, by stating where they could be read. Most of the 'railway ticket' case law is on the application of this principle.

An exclusion clause cannot be introduced into a contract **after** it has been made unless the other party agrees. Examples include the following cases:

Chapelton v Barry UDC [1940]

Facts: C hired a deckchair. The chairs were stacked beside a notice which said **'Hire of Chairs 2d for 3 hours'.** He paid 2d and received a ticket which was, in effect, a receipt, on the back of which, unknown to him, were certain exemption provisions. The chair collapsed and C was injured.

Held: the defendants could not rely on the exemption clause because the contract was complete when the chair attendant accepted the money and up to that point there was no indication of any special terms. The ticket merely acted as a receipt after the contract had been completed.

Olley v Marlborough Court [1949]

Facts: a notice in a hotel room excluded liability for loss or damage to guests' property.

Held: this was ineffective because the contract for accommodation had been made at the reception desk.

Thornton v Shoe Lane Parking [1971]

Facts: a clause on the back of the ticket produced by a machine at the entrance to a car park with an automatic barrier attempted to exclude liability.

Held: it was not a term of the contract. The contract was made when the offer by the car park was accepted by the driver activating the machine. The ticket was produced after acceptance.

However, when there has been a previous consistent course of dealings between the parties on terms which include a similar exemption clause, this might constitute notice of its existence in a later contract even though express notice in the later contract was not given prior to the contract being made.

J Spurling Ltd v Bradshaw [1966]

Facts: the defendant had dealt with the plaintiff for a number of years. On the contract in question he had delivered four full barrels to the plaintiff to store. As usual, he later received a document which both acknowledged receipt and contained a clause excluding liability for negligence by the plaintiff. The barrels were empty when he collected them. The defendant refused to pay and the plaintiff sued.

Held: the exclusion clause had been incorporated into the contract through previous course of dealings whereby he had been sent copies of documents containing the clause, even though he had never read the clause.

Notice though that in **Hollier v Rambler Motors [1972]** it was stated that merely three or four deals over a period of five years was insufficient to constitute a course of dealing.

8.4   Common law test - construction of the clause

The party relying on an exemption clause to relieve him from some or all of the consequences flowing from his breach of contract must prove that it was a term which, when properly construed, covered the loss or damage suffered by the other party.

Andrew Bros (Bournemouth) Ltd v Singer & Co Ltd [1934]

Facts: a contract for sale of 'new' cars contained a clause exempting the seller from liability for breach of all terms implied by common law, statute or otherwise. One of the cars was not new.

Held: the exemption clause did not protect the seller because there had been a breach of an express term.

If there is any doubt as to the clause's meaning and scope, the ambiguity will be resolved by interpreting the clause in a manner restricting the interests of the party who inserted it into the contract and who is now seeking to rely on it as a protection against his legal liability. This is called the **contra proferentem rule**

Hollier v Rambler Motors [1972]

Facts: a contract contained a clause excluding a garage for damage to cars caused by fire (the car was damaged by fire due to the negligence of a garage employee). This was ambiguous as it could mean either fire damage caused without negligence or fire damage caused by the garage's negligence.

Held: the court interpreted it in the narrower sense ie, only exempting liability for non-negligent damage and the garage was therefore liable as the liability for broader negligence was not covered.

A case law example of a clause which passed the common law test of construction is the House of Lords decision in:

Photo Productions Ltd v Securicor [1980]

Facts: the plaintiff, a company which owned a factory, entered into a contract with the defendant, a security company, by which the defendant was to provide security services at the factory, including night patrols. While carrying out a night patrol at the factory an employee of the defendant deliberately lit a fire and as a result the factory and stock inside, together valued at £615,000, were completely destroyed. The plaintiff sued the defendant for breach of contract and in their defence the defendant pleaded an exemption clause the relevant wording of which was:'...under no circumstances shall [Securicor] be responsible for any injurious act or default by any employee of [Securicor] unless such act or default could have been foreseen and avoided by the exercise of due diligence on the part of [Securicor] as his employer...' No negligence was alleged against the defendant for employing the employee.

The House of Lords **held:** even such a fundamental breach could be excluded and the exemption clause was clear and unambiguous and protected the defendant from liability.

Note: the facts of this case (and all the previously cited cases) arose before UCTA 1977 became law.

8.5 Unfair Contract Terms Act 1977

This Act relates to contracts made in the course of business on or after 1 February 1978 and provides the most important limitations on the validity of exemption clauses. If the clause passes the common law test it must still satisfy this statutory test.

The Act restricts the extent to which a person can exclude or limit his liability for negligence for breach of contract; and for misrepresentation

(a)   **Liability for negligence: S2**

Negligence includes any express or implied term of a contract to take reasonable care and the common law duty in the tort of negligence to take reasonable care.

The Act provides that:

* A person **in business cannot** exclude or restrict liability for **death or personal injury** resulting from negligence, by contract or any notice: S2 UCTA 1977, (ie, a total prohibition on such terms).

* A person **in business cannot** exclude or restrict liability for **negligence** causing loss **other than death or personal injury** unless it is reasonable: S2 UCTA 1977, (ie, provisions subject to requirement of reasonableness)

(b)   **Liability for breach of the SGA 1979 terms implied by S12, 13, 14 and 15: S6 UCTA 1977**

* Any exclusion of the S12 SGA 1979 implied term as to title is void - S6(1) UCTA 1977.

* The SGA 1979 implied terms as to description (S13), satisfactory quality (S14(2)), fitness for purpose (S14(3)), and sample (S15).

    (i)   cannot be excluded or restricted by reference to a contract term, as against a UCTA 1977 person dealing as a consumer - S6(2).

    (ii)   as against any other person, such liability can only be excluded or restricted in so far as the term satisfies the requirement of reasonableness - S6(3) UCTA 1977.

(*Note:* unlike most of UCTA 1977, S6 can apply even where it is a non-business attempting to exclude liability.)

(*Note:* S6 also applies, in the same way, to the equivalent terms implied by the SGSA 1982.)

(c)   Liability for other breaches of contract

Any term in a **standard term** contract or in any **consumer** contract purporting to exclude or restrict liability for **breach** is effective only if it is reasonable: S3 UCTA 1977.

(d)   Liability for misrepresentation

S3 Misrepresentation Act 1967 (as inserted by UCTA) states that if a contract contains a term which would exclude or restrict liability for pre-contractual misrepresentations that term shall have no effect except in so far as it satisfies the requirement of reasonableness.

The following definitions are contained in the UCTA 1977.

(a)   Standard term contracts

Standard term contracts arise where the exemption clause is contained in a contract setting out in writing that party's standard terms of business.

(b)   Consumer contracts: S12 UCTA 1977

A party deals as a consumer in relation to another party if:

- he neither makes the contract in the course of a business nor holds himself out as doing so;

- the other party does make the contract in the course of a business; and

- the goods (if any) passing under or in pursuance of the contract are of a type ordinarily supplied for private use or consumption.

It is for those claiming that a party does not deal as a consumer to show that he does not.

(c)   The requirement of reasonableness: Sch 2 UCTA 1977

The burden of proving reasonableness is on the party wishing to rely on the clause. To be reasonable the term must be a fair and reasonable one to be included having regard to the circumstances which were, or ought reasonably to have been, known to or in the contemplation of the parties when the contract was made.

By way of supplement to the test, Sch2 UCTA 1977 lists five **guidelines** indicating which matters in particular are to be taken into account. These are:

(1)   the strength of the bargaining positions of the parties relative to each other, taking into account (among other things) alternative means of supplying the buyer's requirements;

(2)   whether the buyer received an inducement to agree to the term, or in accepting it had an opportunity of making a similar contract lacking such a term with other persons;

(3)   whether the buyer knew or ought to have known of the existence and the extent of the term, having regard to trade custom and any previous course of dealing between the parties;

(4)   whether it was reasonable to expect when the contract was made that it would be practical for the buyer to comply with a condition such that liability of the seller would be excluded or restricted if he did not; and

(5)   whether the goods were manufactured, processed or adapted to the special order of the customer.

These guidelines are specifically applied by UCTA 1977 to ascertain reasonableness in the context of contracts for the sale of goods and other transfers of goods eg, hire, of exchange or for work and materials).   However, they are also used when ascertaining the reasonableness of exemption or limitation clauses in relation to other breaches of contract.

Where the clause is attempting to limit (rather than exclude) liability the courts must have regard to the resources which that party could expect to be available to him for the purpose of meeting the liability should it arise and how far it was open to him to cover himself by insurance.

8.6   Activity

Will the following exclusion clauses be valid or invalid?

(a)   Sharon buys a fire extinguisher and within a week receives the guarantee for the product. On the guarantee there is a clear exclusion clause.

(b)   Dominic enters a car park. At the entrance, before he buys his ticket, there is a clear sign excluding all liability for injury done to any of the car park's users by falling masonry from nearby building work.

(c)   Lola gets on a train without a ticket. She buys one on the train and the conductor informs her that the train has had to change destinations due to some signalling work. He explains to her that the terms and conditions of travel exclude British Rail from liability for any resulting breach of contract and that these can be seen at any railway station.

(d)   Company A has been dealing with Company B for two years. Each time the contract has included an exclusion clause, exempting Company B from liability for delay in shipping the products to Company A. On this occasion the contract has mistakenly omitted the clause and the goods are delayed due to the closure of the Suez Canel. Company B attempts to exclude liability.

8.7   Activity solution

(a)   Invalid - not incorporated at common law
(b)   Void - under S2 UCTA 1977
(c)   Valid - if reasonable under S3 UCTA 1977
(d)   Valid

9   CONTRACTS IN RESTRAINT OF TRADE

9.1   Introduction

> [Definition] Restraint of trade exists where a contract imposes on a person a restriction wholly or in part from carrying on his trade, business, profession or occupation as he wishes. Note that *trade* is not here limited to the usual sense of the word. (There are, however, certain types of commercial contract such as sole agency agreements or restrictions on the use of business premises imposed on a tenant under a lease, which the law treats as inherently reasonable and so outside the scope of the rules.)

Three types of contract in restraint of trade are:

(a)   Where an employer requires his employer to agree not to solicit his customers or use his trade secrets after leaving his employment, or to enter the employment of a competitor.

(b)   Where the vendor of a business, including goodwill, covenants with the purchaser that he will not carry on a competing business; the same principle applies to a partner retiring from a partnership.

(c)   Where a person enters into a long-term agreement with another to purchase all his supplies from that person (a **solus agreement**) (often found between petrol companies and petrol station proprietors).

In all these cases, the restraint of trade clause is part of a larger contract. These clauses are sometimes known as 'restrictive covenants':

•   In an employer/employee agreement there is an employment contract whereby the employer agrees to pay the employee who agrees to work and one clause in the contract is a promise by the employee not to enter employment of a competitor after he leaves his current employment

•   In a vendor/purchaser agreement there is a contract for the sale of a business (ie, the seller will transfer the business plus goodwill to the buyer who will pay). One of the terms of the contract is that the seller promises not to continue carrying on the business he is selling as this would mean that the goodwill for which the buyer is paying is of no value.

•   In a solus agreement the petrol company usually leases a garage to the proprietor, who pays rent and promises to buy all his supplies from the petrol company.

In all these cases it is only the validity of the restraint of trade clause which is generally in question (not the rest of the contract).

The general rule is that these clauses are contrary to public policy and therefore void at common law. However it may be enforceable if the person attempting to rely on it can prove that it is reasonable. The restraint is reasonable if:

(a)   It is imposed to **protect a legitimate interest** of a party to the contract; and

(b)   As between the parties it is a reasonable safeguard of that interest (ie, it is **no wider than necessary** to protect that interest); and

(c)   It **is reasonable in the interest of the public** (ie, it is not prejudicial to the public interest).

These rules have a long history and the law as developed by precedent in decided cases has somewhat changed with business practice. On the whole the scope of the rules against restraint of trade has tended to widen, and the trend continues.

9.2 Legitimate interest to protect

In each case of this kind the first step is to identify and define the interest which is to be protected. The tests are applied particularly strictly to restrictions imposed by employers on their employees since the bargaining strength of the parties may be unequal. The employer is not allowed to use a restraint of trade clause merely to prevent a former employee from competing with him, from obtaining other employment or from using personal skills or generally available knowledge acquired during the course of employment. The two interests which are legitimate interests to protect are **trade secrets** and **client connections.**

Trade secrets

An employer is entitled to protect his proprietary interest by restraining his former employee from using knowledge gained during employment of a secret manufacturing process.

Forster & Son Ltd v Suggett [1918]

Facts: Suggett, who was employed as works engineer, covenanted with his employers that for five years after leaving his present employment he would not engage in the manufacture of glass bottles, or any business connected with glass-making, these two activities being the main activities carried on by the plaintiff company. An action was brought to restrain a breach of this promise.

Held: since the defendant had acquired knowledge of secret processes used by the plaintiff company, the restraint clause imposed on him was both reasonable and enforceable to restrain his violation of that covenant.

Client connections

An employer is entitled to prevent employees from using confidential relationships. An employee's close and regular contact with his employer's business customers may cause them to place confidence in his skill and judgement, with the result that they would probably transfer their custom to him if he set himself up in business or went to work for a competitor in the same area. This kind of contract has been enforced in cases where the employees acted in a variety of occupations: as a milk roundsman, a dressmaker, a tailor, a garage mechanic, an electrical engineer, a solicitor's clerk.

Fitch v Dewes [1921]

Facts: Dewes, a solicitor's managing clerk, promised that, on termination of his employment with Fitch, he would not **be engaged or manage or be concerned in the office, profession, or business of a solicitor within a radius of seven miles of the Town Hall of Tamworth.** Whilst with Fitch, Dewes dealt with the affairs of almost half of his employer's clients. An action was brought to restrain a breach of this restrictive covenant.

Held: although there was no time limit to the covenant, making it lifelong, it was nonetheless reasonable and enforceable in the circumstances since it conferred a necessary protection on Fitch's business, as Dewes had been in a position to have influence over the clients.

9.3 No wider than necessary

The next question is whether the restraint imposed is reasonable in **scope, geographical extent** and **duration.** If it is excessive it will not be upheld.

The wider the area stipulated, or the longer the period during which it will continue, the greater the burden on the employer to justify its reasonableness.

The court must balance the restrictions relating to area and time against each other when ascertaining the acceptability of any covenant in restraint of trade. The greater the area covered, the shorter the time limit must be, and vice versa.

An employer may impose a world-wide restraint over the employee's competitive activities if the business is conducted over such a wide area, provided the employee's influence over clients is also world-wide. By way of contrast, a restraint in the contract of employment of the manager of a butcher's shop covering an area of only five miles may be too wide where customers are drawn from a two mile radius.

The complete absence of any time limit will not necessarily invalidate a restraint if the area covered is reasonable (as in the case of **Fitch v Dewes** which clearly illustrates this point) but it increases the difficulty of convincing the court that it should be upheld. You should however realise that the tendency of the courts in modern cases is to allow only a short time limit since the present view with the majority of employees (particularly with regard to client connections) is that the employee's influence is largely ephemeral.

Restraint clauses agreed upon by the vendor and purchaser of a business are more readily upheld by the court as being reasonable than covenants embodied in contracts of employment. The parties are of equal bargaining strength and the risk of one party insisting on terms that protect his interests unfairly at the expense of the other party is a much less likely occurrence than in contracts of employment.

Two case law examples which can be contrasted are

Nordenfelt v Maxim-Nordenfelt Guns & Ammunition Co Ltd [1894]

Facts: Nordenfelt, a manufacturer of quick-firing guns and other implements of war, sold his business and promised the respondent company that for the next twenty-five years he would not engage in the manufacture of guns or any other business competing with, or likely to compete with, that of the respondent company. An injunction was sought to prevent a breach of this covenant.

Held: the covenant restraining competition by Nordenfelt in relation to the manufacture of guns was reasonable in scope as between the contracting parties since the business sold was concerned with the manufacture of identical products. This part of the covenant was also reasonable in the interests of the public, since the country's trade was increased by exploiting the business and inventions of a foreign national.

The last part of the covenant, which prevented Nordenfelt from being concerned with any other business competing with, or likely to compete with, the company's activities, was wider than was necessary to protect the proprietary interest purchased by the company, and consequently it was void.

British Reinforced Concrete v Schelff [1921]

S, who ran a small local business for the sale of road reinforcements, sold it to the plaintiff company, a large nationwide company which manufactured and sold road reinforcements. In the contract of sale S covenanted that he would not for three years ...'be concerned in ... the business of the manufacture or sale of road reinforcements in any part of the United Kingdom'.

Held: the covenant was too wide for two reasons. First: the scope of the restraint was too wide in that it sought to restrain **manufacture** whereas his business was purely **sale.** Second, the area of the restraint was too wide since it applied to the whole of the UK whereas his business operated only in a local area.

9.4   Reasonable in the interest of the public

What is judged reasonable between the parties will usually pass the test of not being prejudicial to the public interest.   In **petrol solus** cases the petrol company usually provides substantial consideration in the form of a money payment to purchase exclusivity, which is a legitimate interest, and seeks to impose the restriction to protect that interest.   The cases on **petrol solus** agreements decided in the last fifteen years, however, have been concerned more especially with protecting the public interest in free competition

Petrofina v Martin [1966]

Facts: there was a limitation of a petrol station to one source of supply for twelve years.

Held: this was excessive.

Esso v Harper's Garage [1968]

Facts: Harper's Garage agreed to buy all of its fuel from Esso and to operate its petrol stations in accordance with Esso's plans.   In return Esso granted a rebate on the price of fuel paid by Harper's Garage.   The contract stated that the arrangements were to operate for 4 years on one garage and 21 years on another.

Held: the common law doctrine of restraint of trade did apply.   This was a 'tying agreement' and although reasonable in the interests of the parties it might be considered excessive in the wider context of the public interest if it is endured for an excessive period.   The 4 year contract was upheld.   The 21 year contract was held to be void.

9.5   Severance

Where any part of the covenant offends against the common law the whole covenant, as a general rule, is void.   Thus in **BRC v Schelff,** for example, S could set up a new business exactly the same as the one he had sold.   The court will not rewrite a clause so as to make it acceptable.

Sometimes, however, it may be possible to sever void restraints from valid restraints.   The court will do this if it can *delete* a restraint: this is called the blue pencil test.   Severance will therefore usually only be possible if the covenant seeks to restrict a series of different activities.   The blue pencil test was satisfied in **Nordenfelt v Maxim Nordenfelt** where the court accordingly deleted the last part of the covenant.

> **Definition**   The 'blue pencil test' permits the court to delete offending portions of restraints only if the remainder can be enforced without being rewritten.

9.6   Attempted evasion

The parties are not permitted to evade the rules against restraint of trade by indirect means.

Bull v Pitney Bowes [1966]

Facts: an employer made it a condition of entitlement to retirement pension that employees should not, after retirement, engage in any activity in competition with them.

Held: this was the equivalent to a restraint of trade, contrary to public interest and void.

Kores Manufacturing Co v Kolok Manufacturing Co [1959]

Facts: an agreement was made between two employers, who carried on similar businesses, that neither would employ any person who had been an employee of the other during the previous five years.

Held: this was contrary to public interest and void.

10 SELF TEST QUESTIONS

10.1 What is the importance of the difference between a representation and a term? (2.1)

10.2 What were the facts in the case of **Dick Bentley Productions Ltd v Harold Smith (Motors) Ltd?** (2.2)

10.3 What are the 2 situations where the courts will imply terms into a contract? (4.1 and 4.2)

10.4 What are the differences between conditions and warranties? (5.1)

10.5 Rationalise the distinction between **Bettini v Gye** and **Poussard v Spiers** (5.1)

10.6 What conditions and what warranties does S12 SGA 1979 imply? (6.12)

10.7 What is a sale by description? (6.13)

10.8 Does S14 SGA 1979 apply to private sales? (6.14)

10.9 Define satisfactory quality (6.14)

10.10 Distinguish S14(2) and S14(3) SGA 1979 (6.14)

10.11 Which Act implies terms into a contract between an auditor and the company he is auditing? (7.5)

10.12 What is the purpose of an exclusion clause? (8.1)

10.13 If a contract is signed when will an exclusion clause contained in that contract not be valid at common law? (8.3)

10.14 What is the *contra proferentem* rule? (8.4)

10.15 Define a consumer transaction for the purposes of UCTA 1977 (8.5)

10.16 When considering whether a covenant in restraint of trade is reasonable in the interests of the parties, what 3 factors does the court consider? (9.3).

10.17 What is the blue pencil test? (9.5).

11 EXAMINATION TYPE QUESTIONS

11.1 A holiday tour operator

A holiday tour operator has recently been obliged to pay compensation to a number of clients whose holidays did not conform to what had been promised in his brochures. The operator now wishes to amend his contracts in order to exclude or limit such claims as far as possible.

You are required:

(a) to explain how this may be done to satisfy common law requirements;

(12 marks)

(b) to detail any statutory restrictions which must be taken into account.

(8 marks)

(Total: 20 marks)

11.2   F and W - Toaster

(a)   Explain the conditions and warranties implied into contracts for the sale of goods by the Sale of Goods Act 1979.

(12 marks)

(b)   F purchased an electric toaster from a shop owned by W. A week later, while she was using the toaster, she suffered a relatively severe electric shock and the toaster ceased to function. F took the toaster back to the shop and demanded a refund of her money from W. W informed her she should complain to the manufacturers as the shop was not responsible for a manufacturing fault.

After F had left the shop, W looked at the conditions of sale which he had agreed with the manufacturers of the toaster. He discovered the agreement included a clause which excluded the manufacturers from liability for any express or implied conditions or warranties concerning the quality and fitness of the toasters they had supplied to him.

Advise F and W in the law of contract.

(8 marks)

(Total: 20 marks)

11.3   Restraint of trade

Explain the main types of contracts in restraint of trade which may exist, stating in each case the rules determining validity.

(20 marks)

12   ANSWERS TO EXAMINATION TYPE QUESTIONS

12.1   A holiday tour operator

(a)   The tour operator wishes to introduce an exemption clause which either totally exempts him from liability or restricts his liability for breach, negligence or misrepresentation. Such clauses are common in contracts for the sale of goods or services. To ensure that such clauses are effective the tour operator must take care that the following matters are covered:

(i)   The clause must be part of the contract – it is important that he ensures that the clause is incorporated into the contract to become a term. If it is not a term, the client will not be bound by it. If the contract is in writing and signed by the client, then if the clause is part of the signed contract, the client will have difficulty denying that it is a term: **L'Estrange v F Graucob Ltd**. However, even where the clause is in a signed contract it may not be binding on the client if his signature was obtained by fraud or misrepresentation: **Curtis v Chemical Cleaning & Dyeing Co**. If the contract is not a signed one, a term may still be incorporated by giving notice to the client before the contract is made. Such notice may be by a notice on the wall or counter in the shop or on any document, such as in a brochure.

However, in this case the client must have been given reasonable notice of the term on which the tour operator intended to contract before the contract was made. A clause on the back of a document handed to the client after the contract was made is not sufficient: **Thornton v Shoe Lane Parking Ltd**. Thus the tour operator must be aware of the exact moment the contract is made (when the offer is accepted) and ensure that notice of the term is given before then. Notice on the receipt or invoice would therefore not usually be sufficient. A term in such a document may, however, become a term in a later contract with the same client as a previous course of dealing may result in a client being deemed to have notice of the term from past dealings: **J Spurling Ltd v Bradshaw**.

(ii)   The clause must cover the event which occurs – the party relying on the exemption clause to relieve him of all or part of the liability must prove that the term when properly construed covered the loss or damage suffered by the other party. Thus a clause excluding liability for negligence will not operate to exclude liability for breach of contract. Most exemption clauses are very widely drafted to cover all possible eventualities. If there is any doubt as to the meaning or scope, the ambiguity will be resolved by interpreting it against the person relying on it (ie, the tour operator). This is known as the *contra proferentem* rule. In **Hollier v Rambler Motors** a contract exempting a garage from liability for damage to cars by fire was ambiguous in that it could have covered only non-negligent fire or both non-negligent and negligent fire. It was interpreted to include non-negligent fire only.

(b)   The Unfair Contract Terms Act 1977 restricts the validity of exemption clauses in contracts made in the course of business. *S2* provides that a person in business cannot exclude or restrict liability for death or personal injury due to negligence. It also provides that a person in business cannot exclude or limit liability for negligence causing other loss unless it is reasonable. *S3* deals with standard term contracts, where one party deals on the other party's written standard terms of business, and consumer contracts, where one party acts in the course of business and the other party does not (ie, acts as a consumer). In these types of contracts any term purporting to exclude or limit liability for breach of contract is effective only if it is reasonable. The burden of proving reasonableness is on the party seeking to rely on the clause. To be reasonable, the term must be a fair and reasonable one to be included, having regard to the circumstances which were, or ought reasonably to have been, known to or in the contemplation of the parties when the contract was made. Where the contract attempts to limit rather than exclude liability, the courts must also have regard to the resources which the party could expect to have available to meet the liability and the availability of insurance.

Where the clause attempts to limit or exclude liability for misrepresentation, S3 Misrepresentation Act 1967, as amended by the Unfair Contract Terms Act 1977, requires the test of reasonableness as set out above to be satisfied.

12.2   F and W - Toaster

(a)   The conditions and warranties implied into contracts for the sale of goods are set down in Ss12 – 15 Sale of Goods Act 1979.

S12 provides there is an implied condition that the seller has the right to sell the goods. This means the seller must be the owner of the goods (**Rowland v Divall**). However, it also covers sellers who are owners of the goods who sell in the infringement of a third party trademark or other right (**Niblett v Confectioner's Material Co**).

S12 also provides there is an implied warranty that goods will be free from any charge or other encumbrance not revealed to the buyer and that the purchaser will enjoy quiet possession.

S13 sets down an implied condition that, in the case of a sale by description, the goods shall correspond with the description. Most sales of goods are sales by description and this can be so even though the goods are examined by the buyer at the time of purchase (**Beale v Taylor**).

S14(2) implies a condition that the goods will be of satisfactory quality. The Act defines satisfactory quality as meaning the goods must meet the standard that a reasonable person would regard as satisfactory, taking account of any description of the goods, the price (if relevant) and all the other relevant circumstances. However, the section only operates if the seller is selling in the course of a business and does not operate in any case where the defects have been drawn to the buyer's attention or **if** the buyer examined the goods for defects which his particular examination should have revealed.

S14(3) implies a condition that goods are fit for the purpose sold where the buyer has made known, expressly or by implication, the purpose for which the goods are bought. Once again the section does not operate unless the seller is selling in the course of a business, and in any event will not operate where it is not reasonable to rely on the seller's skill and judgement or the buyer does not, in fact, rely upon it.

Finally, S15 implies certain conditions in the case of a sale by sample. Namely:

(i)   the bulk of the goods should correspond with the sample in quality and description;

(ii)   that the buyer should have a reasonable opportunity of comparing the bulk with the sample; and

(iii)   that the goods are free from any defect rendering them unsatisfactory, not apparent from a reasonable examination of the goods.

(b)   **F v W**. F has no action in the law of contract against the manufacturer - she does not have a contract with the manufacturer.

F is advised that she may have a claim in contract against W on the basis of breach of the terms implied by the Sale of Goods Act 1979. As the toaster has ceased to function after a week it is not of satisfactory quality within S14(2). The section clearly applies to F's situation as the seller is selling in the course of a business. The fact that W is not in any way at fault does not relieve him from liability as liability under the SGA 1979 is strict.

The term implied by S14(2) is a condition and therefore F prima facie has the right to repudiate the contract and recover her money.

However, it may be that F has lost her right to reject the toaster by virtue of S35 SGA 1979. A buyer cannot reject goods once they have been accepted and this section states that a person is deemed to have accepted goods when, after the lapse of a reasonable time, he retains the goods without intimating to the seller that he rejects them. In **Bernstein v Pamsons Motors** it was explained that 'reasonable time' meant enough time to try out the goods generally. It may be that the court considers a week more than long enough to try out a toaster. If this is so F cannot return the toaster to the shop and reclaim her money: her sole remedy is for damages to cover the cost of any repairs. In any event she will also have a claim in damages for the electric shock suffered.

(***Tutorial note:*** any exclusion clause in the contract between F and W would be void by virtue of S6(2) UCTA 1977 since F is dealing as a consumer.)

W v manufacturer

W's claim is against the manufacturer, again for breach of the term implied by S14 SGA 1979.

As to the validity of the exclusion clause, the clause clearly fulfils the common law tests of incorporation into the contract and aptness of wording. Since the contract between W and the manufacturer is not a consumer transaction it will be valid if the manufacturer can prove that it is reasonable - S6(3) Unfair Contract Terms Act 1977. This involves the courts weighing up a number of factors ie, the price and the bargaining position of the parties. Also of significance is the degree of knowledge of the exemption clause, and it is therefore necessary to question why W has only just discovered its existence. This could be a factor in his favour on finding the clause is unreasonable.

Again W's claim could be to repudiate the contract and/or to claim damages. It is unlikely that he is deemed to have accepted the goods because S34 and S35 SGA 1979 states that a buyer is not deemed to have accepted goods by treating them as his own (eg, re-selling) until and unless he has had a reasonable opportunity of examining them: this is not normally the case where goods are packaged for immediate re-sale.

*(**Tutorial note:** S35 SGA 1979 has been very much criticised by consumer associations because of the way it operates to limit the remedies of the 'man on the street'.)*

12.3   Restraint of trade

A contract in restraint of trade is one where a party to the agreement restricts the future contractual relations of the other party in some way. Such agreements are *prima facie* void, being against public policy. Restraint of trade features in agreements between employer and employee whereby an employee's future right to enter the employment of another is restricted; between vendors and purchasers of a business, whereby a vendor agrees to restrict his rights to act in competition with the purchaser. They also arise in the provision of management services within the entertainment industry; between suppliers and retailers, as well as between groups of suppliers. The rules determining the validity of such restraint clauses in each sphere are as follows:

(a)   **Contracts of employment**

In order to rebut the presumption that the restraint clause is void it is necessary to establish that the clause is reasonable from the point of view of the public interest and reasonable as that between the parties. Reasonableness in the public interest can only be established if the clause is used to protect either trade secrets or business connections. In the case of the latter it is necessary to show some contact with clients or customers of the employer (**Cornwall v Hawkins**) (milkman) but this employee need not hold a prestigious position in the business (eg, **Fitch v Dewes**) (articled clerk in a firm of solicitors). If the clause is reasonable from the point of view of the public interest, it is then necessary to prove it is reasonable as between the parties. This depends largely on the area and duration of the restraint. The area must not extend beyond that in which the employer's business operates and, in relation to business connections, a restraint of more than three years is rarely permissible.

(b)   **Contracts between vendor and purchaser of business**

Once again, the validity of such a restraint clause depends on reasonableness. The clause will be reasonable from the point of view of the public interest if it is to protect a genuine

employment, this depends upon the area and duration of the restraint **(Nordenfelt v Maxim Nordenfelt Guns and Ammunition Co)**. If the business is genuinely a 'worldwide' business, the area of restraint can, as in the Nordenfelt case, be the whole world. The duration of the restraint depends upon the nature of the business.

(c)   **Contracts between suppliers and retailers**

Retailers often enter into 'solus agreements' whereby they agree to buy only from a particular supplier, in return for a mortgage for example. The validity of such agreements is once again determined by the criteria of reasonableness **(Esso Petroleum v Harper's Garage)** and depends upon such factors as the duration of the restraint and the benefits received by the retailer in return for agreeing to the restriction. The reasonableness from the point of view of the public interest is justified by the need to promote price competition in certain areas of commerce.

7 CONTRACT: DISCHARGE

INTRODUCTION & LEARNING OBJECTIVES

Syllabus area 8a. Discharge of contract (by performance, frustration, agreement and breach). (Ability required 3).

This chapter examines the termination of a contract. To discharge a contract is to end it. If a contract has been discharged neither party has further obligations under it..

Discharge of a contract is a popular examination area and the main questions that are asked tend to be in the areas of:

(a)   performance of a contract
(b)   frustration.

When you have studied this chapter you should be able to do the following:

- Understand the various ways in which a contract can be discharged.

- Know what performance of a contract is; understand the general common law rule of performance and the common law and equitable exceptions to that rule.

- Understand discharge by agreement (and in particular how this overlaps with your understanding of your notes on consideration).

- Recognise when a contract has been discharged by breach (known as 'accepting' the breach).

- Understand discharge by frustration and when an apparent frustrating act will not give rise to the end of the contract.

---

1   METHODS OF DISCHARGE

A contract imposes obligations on the parties from which they may be discharged in various ways:

(a)   **Performance.** When a party has done what is required of him under the contract he no longer has any obligations under it.

(b)   **Agreement.** The parties may agree to terminate unfulfilled obligations. That agreement must itself be a contract subject to the usual rules, especially consideration.

(c)   **Breach.** If one party commits a breach of contract the other may in some cases, at his option, elect to treat the contract as at an end with the result that his own obligations are discharged. He is accepting that the other's repudiatory breach terminates the contract.

> **Definition**   Breach of contract is the inexcusable failure by a party to a contract to fulfil some or all of his obligations under it.

(d)   **Frustration.** In certain cases a contract which becomes impossible to perform is thereby discharged.

2   PERFORMANCE

2.1   General Rule

The general rule is that a contract is discharged by performance only when both parties have complied **fully and exactly** with the terms of the contract

Re Moore & Landauer [1927]

Facts: contract for tinned fruit to be delivered packed in cases of thirty tins each. The correct number of tins was delivered but in cases varying between twenty four and thirty tins each.

Held: the contract was not performed even though the market value was the same. The buyer could reject all the goods and not pay.

From this general rule it has sometimes been held that if a single price has been agreed for performance of the contract no part of the price is payable unless and until the entire contract has been exactly performed.

Cutter v Powell [1795]

Facts: the defendants agreed to pay Cutter thirty guineas 'provided he proceeds, continues and does his duty as second mate' on a voyage from Kingston, Jamaica, to Liverpool. Cutter began the journey but died when the ship was about three week's sail from Liverpool. His administrator sought to recover a proportion of the agreed wage in respect of that part of the journey for which Cutter had acted as second mate.

Held: she was unable to succeed as Cutter had not performed his part of the contract. (But note that nowadays the doctrine of frustration would apply to the contract).

2.2   Exceptions

The general rule that performance must be complete, accurate and exact to be effective could lead to injustice (as in **Cutter v Powell** above). It is subject to exceptions some of which have been imposed by the common law and some by equity to make the rule fairer.

2.3   Severable or divisible contracts

Cutter v Powell is an example of an 'entire' contract. However, some contracts may be treated as divisible into distinct and separate obligations eg, a contract for a number of separate consignments of goods. Whether a contract is 'entire' or severable will depend on construction of the contract and the intention of the parties.

The parties may be deemed to have intended to divide their contract into two or more separate contracts, in which case each individual contract may be discharged separately. For example, in a contract to deliver a consignment of goods by instalments, the buyer may agree to pay for each instalment when delivered.

If the first instalment delivered conforms with the terms of the contract, the buyer cannot refuse to pay for it on the grounds that the second delivery is defective in some respect, although payment for the second instalment may be validly refused. Such contracts are called **severable** or **divisible contracts**.

2.4   Performance prevented by one party

One party may be prevented from fully carrying out his contractual duties because of some act or omission by the other party which effectively prevents the contract being duly performed as anticipated. In such cases the party partially implementing the agreed terms may sue on a *quantum meruit*, or for damages for breach of contract, in order to recover compensation for the amount of work actually completed.

Definition   *Quantum meruit* is a claim for the value of work done or services rendered, rather than for the contract price. The words literally mean 'as much as is merited'.

Planché v Colburn [1831]

Facts: Planché agreed to write a book for a series of books to be published by Colburn, but the series was discontinued before completion of the work by the author.

Held: the original contract had been discharged by the defendant's breach, but reasonable remuneration was recoverable on a *quantum meruit* basis, independently of the original contract.

2.5   Acceptance of partial performance

Where a party accepts the benefit conferred on him by the other party's partial performance, the court may infer a promise to pay for the benefit received and grant the other party a right to recover a reasonable price on a *quantum meruit* claim.

For example, a seller may agree to deliver forty bottles of a specified wine to a buyer. If only twenty bottles are tendered, the buyer may refuse to accept delivery; but if he accepts the twenty bottles he must pay a reasonable price for them. However, if he had no choice but to accept partial performance, then no payment can be claimed.

Sumpter v Hedges [1898]

Facts: Sumpter contracted to erect buildings on Hedges' land, but abandoned the work when it was only partially completed. Hedges took possession of the land and buildings and completed the work himself, using materials which Sumpter had left behind. Sumpter sued on a *quantum meruit* to recover compensation for the value of the work done prior to his abandonment of the job.

Held: Sumpter could not recover a reasonable price for his work. It could not be presumed from his conduct that Hedges voluntarily accepted partial performance. He had no other option open to him than to accept the half-completed buildings and finish the work himself, or employ another builder to do so. (However, Sumpter was allowed to recover the value of the materials used, because it was open to Hedges to choose whether or not to use those particular materials in completing the building.)

2.6   Substantial performance

A party who has substantially performed his contractual duties in the manner stipulated may recover the agreed price, less a deduction by way of a claim for damages in respect of duties not properly executed. This is an equitable exception to the rule of full performance.

Hoenig v Isaacs [1952]

Facts: the plaintiff, an interior decorator, agreed to decorate and furnish the defendant's flat for a sum of £750 payable 'as the work proceeds and balance on completion'. When the job was done the defendant moved in but complained of faulty design and bad workmanship and would not pay the £350 balance.

Held: in a contract for work and labour for a lump sum the employer cannot repudiate liability on the ground that the work, when substantially performed and when he has taken the enjoyment of it, is in some respects not in accordance with the contract. The term that required completion was not a condition; hence, defendant should pay for the work less a sum in damages for breach of warranty.

If the defects are so extensive that it cannot be said that the contract has been substantially performed, then no part of the contract price can be recovered.

Bolton v Mahadeva [1972]

Facts: the plaintiff agreed to install central heating in the defendant's house for £560. His work was defective: the system did not produce adequate heat, and it gave off fumes. It would have cost £174 to put the defects right.

Held: the plumber could not recover £560 less £174 - he could not rely on the doctrine of substantial performance.

The doctrine of substantial performance raises the question of the distinction between conditions and warranties. All terms which are conditions must be strictly performed. No breach of warranty justifies non-performance by the other party. In respect of 'intermediate' terms, the test of substantial performance is whether the party has received substantially the whole benefit as intended under the contract.

If the party abandons the contract the doctrine cannot be relied upon. It is an equitable doctrine and to abandon work in this way would be unfair.

2.7   Time for performance

When a contract does not specify the time of performance of the obligations, they must be performed within a reasonable time.

When a contract does specify the time of performance of the obligations, the question arises as to whether 'time is of the essence', ie, a condition of the contract. In such cases, if there is a delay in performance the injured party may treat this delay as breach of condition and pay nothing (and also refuse to accept late performance if offered).

The parties may expressly agree in their contract that time shall be of the essence. Even if they do not so provide and there is delay, the injured party may then make time of the essence of the contract by serving a notice requiring performance within a specified but reasonable additional period.

Charles Rickards Ltd v Oppenheim [1950]

Facts: the contract was for delivery of a custom-built Rolls Royce car within seven months; the buyer agreed to wait three months more and then gave four weeks' notice to complete.

Held: at the expiry of his notice he could cancel the order as by serving notice he had made time of the essence, although he could not have done so immediately the original delivery period expired (as he had waived his right).

In absence of any such explicit provision the question of whether time is to be treated as of the essence depends on the nature of the contract, eg:

(a)   In commercial contracts and any others where lapse in time could materially affect the value of the subject matter, time is of the essence unless there is evidence to the contrary.

(b)   In contracts where specific performance might be ordered, the court (applying equitable principles) will be inclined to treat the time of performance as not of the essence. In particular, time is not of the essence in completion of the sale of land, ie, if the vendor fails to effect a transfer of the land at the agreed date he may hold the purchaser to accepting it at a later date (unless, of course, time has been made of the essence - see above). The purchaser must satisfy himself with his action for damages.

Definition   Specific performance is an equitable remedy whereby the court orders a person to complete his obligations under a contract. It is usually only available in contracts for the transfer of land or goods (not work or services).

Time for payment of the contract price is not of the essence unless so agreed.

2.8   Tender of performance

Where the promise/obligation is to **do something other than pay money** then if the party tenders performance but the other refuses it, the party tendering is discharged from further obligations and is entitled to damages for breach, provided that the tender is in exact conformity with the agreed terms., giving the other party reasonable opportunity of examining the performance tendered, eg, goods tendered, to ascertain that it confirms with the contract.

Where the promise/obligation is **to pay money** the exact amount must be tendered in legal currency. Refusal of tender does not discharge the obligation to pay, but merely enables the debtor, if sued, to plead the defence that he had tendered performance. If he is sued for the debt he may pay the money into court. This will not operate as a defence but the creditor will be awarded only the amount of the debt owed, with no interest or costs adds on, and he will have to pay the debtor's costs of the action.

Payment by cheque is not good tender if the creditor objects. If accepted, a cheque is a discharge of the debt only when it is honoured. Payment of a lesser sum is not discharge of liability to pay a larger amount unless it is made before the due date or by a third party.

Payment by post is effective only if and when the remittance reaches the creditor, unless he has requested that it be posted to him and the debtor has taken reasonable care (the risk of loss in the post is then on the creditor).

3   AGREEMENT

3.1   By condition subsequent

The original contract may itself contain some terms ('conditions') providing for discharge. As this procedure is part of the original contract, no new consideration is required for its application, eg, a contract for the sale of land may contain a **condition precedent** by which the contract **does not become effective unless and until** specified planning permission is obtained. If it is refused the contract is discharged.

Alternatively, a contract may provide that it shall be **terminated on the happening of some event**, eg, a contract of employment is usually terminable by notice given by one party to another; a contract made by a company promoter may be expressed to terminate automatically if the company is not formed or fails to adopt the contract by a certain date. In such cases the contract is in force until terminated by the **condition subsequent**.

Definition   A condition precedent is a term of a contract preventing its taking effect unless a specified event occurs or a specified act is performed (eg, signing a contract of service).

Definition   A condition subsequent is a term of a contract permitting its discharge on the happening of a specified event or performance of a specified act (eg, giving notice of termination of employment).

3.2   By a new agreement

The parties may agree to discharge (ie, end) the contract. This agreement will be binding only if it is under seal or supported by consideration. The discharge may be **bilateral** or **unilateral**:

(a)   **Bilateral discharge**

Discharge will be **bilateral** where both parties still have contractual obligations to perform. Any agreement to discharge the contract relieves both parties from further performance. Each party's promise to release the other party from further performance is his consideration for the release from his own obligations.

(b)   **Unilateral discharge**

Discharge will be **unilateral** where one party has performed all his obligations but the other has not. Any promise by the party who has performed his obligation to release the other ('accord') will not be binding on him unless the other party has given consideration ('satisfaction') or the agreement to discharge is made by deed.

Where fresh consideration is given (eg, a cancellation fee) there is 'accord', ie, agreement by which the obligation is discharged, and 'satisfaction', ie, the consideration which makes the agreement effective.

The parties may agree to discharge the original contract and substitute a new one in its place (novation) eg, a contract to supply a colour television replaced by a contract to supply a radio. They may agree to vary the original contract, eg, a contract to deliver a carpet in January is varied by extending the delivery date to March.

3.3   Activity

Look back at your notes on consideration as a pre-requisite to the formation of a contract. What are the similarities between certain aspects of those notes and the rules set out above on discharge of a contract by a new agreement?

3.4   Activity solution

As with consideration an agreement to end a contract must be *bilateral* in that each party's promise to release the other party from his obligations is consideration for the release from his own obligations. This is identical to the exchange of consideration necessary to validly create a contract.

Equally the parties can agree to end/discharge one contract by agreeing to replace it with another one (this is sometimes known as a 'novation'). Such an agreement requires new consideration or, as it was called in the chapter on consideration, 'accord and satisfaction'.

4   BREACH

4.1   Discharge by acceptance of breach

Definition   A breach of contract occurs:

(a)   when a party fails to perform an obligation under the contract **(actual breach)**; or

(b)   when, before the time fixed to perform an obligation, a party shows an intention not to perform **(anticipatory breach).**

If one party commits a breach of condition, or a substantial breach of an intermediate term, or totally renounces the contract, the breach does not automatically terminate the contract but the other party may then at his option:

(a)   treat the contract as terminated (discharged) and claim damages for any loss suffered; or

(b)   treat the contract as operative and claim damages for any loss suffered.

In case (a) their outstanding obligations are discharged by the breach followed by the election to terminate, but in case (b) the parties continue to be bound by the contract since the contract remains in existence

A breach of warranty will not entitle the innocent party to treat the contract as discharged, ie, treat his outstanding obligations as discharged by the breach: he may claim damages only.

Poussard v Spiers [1876]

Facts: P agreed to perform in an operetta staged by S on the opening night and for such further time as the production should run. She failed to appear on opening night, but returned later in the run to be told by S that she had been replaced.

Held: her failure to appear on the first night broke a condition of the contract and entitled S to treat the contract as discharged.

Bettini v Gye [1876]

Facts: B turned up late for rehearsals which he had contracted to attend before a concert tour. He would have been available and competent to perform on the tour, but was dismissed on the grounds of his lateness for rehearsals.

Held: failure to attend rehearsals was only a breach of warranty. G had not therefore acted properly in dismissing B, and was himself in breach of contract in doing so.

4.2   Actual breach

Definition   This occurs where one party is in breach of a condition or improperly repudiates (ends) the contract, (see **Bettini v Gye** above), or if he makes it impossible to perform during his own performance of it or where he prevents completion of the contract by the other party during performance.

If the contract is an entire one in which the obligations are interdependent or concurrent, then the contract is discharged by such a breach, eg, purchase of an item which does not work. Breach of condition by seller discharges the buyer from his duty to pay.

If the contract is a divisible one, or if the obligations are independent of each other, then the innocent party's only remedy is to sue for damages for the breach; he cannot treat himself as discharged from his own contractual obligations by the other party's breach of performance:

If the innocent party does have the right to treat himself as discharged from his contractual obligations and wishes to exercise that right, he must, as a general rule, communicate that decision to the party in breach for otherwise silence may be construed as evidence that he waives his right to treat himself as discharged.

4.3   Anticipatory breach

Definition   A contract is discharged by anticipatory breach when one party expressly or impliedly repudiates the obligations imposed on him by the contract before the arrival of the time fixed for performance.

In any such case the injured party has a choice of action:

(a)   He can, by notifying the other party of his decision accept the repudiation and treat the contract as immediately discharged and even commence proceedings for breach before the time has arrived. This is known as 'accepting' the breach.

Thus the party repudiating the contract may be sued immediately for breach of contract even though the date has not yet arrived for the repudiating party to perform his obligations under the contract.

Hochester v De La Tour [1853]

Facts: the defendant, who had agreed to engage the plaintiff as a courier as from 1 June 1852, wrote a letter on 11 May repudiating the contract of employment. On 22 May the plaintiff brought an action claiming damages for breach of contract.

Held: damages were recoverable. It was not necessary to wait until 1 June 1852, the date when his duties as courier were to begin, before suing for breach of contract.

(b)   Alternatively, he can affirm the contract in the hope that performance will be rendered. In this case he must wait until the time for performance arrives before he can sue.

In this case the party in default can escape liability if he in fact performs the contract at the due date or if his obligation to do so is meanwhile discharged, eg, by frustration.

Definition   Frustration is the discharge of a contract by unforeseen events rendering it impossible or pointless to perform.

Avery v Bowden [1855]

Facts: the charterers of a ship declared in advance that they did not require her; the ship owners refused to accept the repudiation and affirmed the contract by sending the ship to the port of loading (Odessa). However before she arrived there the contract was frustrated by the outbreak of the Crimean War, as civilian shipping was barred from the theatre of war. The owners now sued.

Held: the contract had not been discharged by the breach because the owners had not accepted the breach; but the frustrating event discharged it rendering the ship owners unable to sue for breach.

Generally the innocent party is under a duty to mitigate the loss from a breach of contract (ie, take such steps as are reasonable to reduce or contain the loss suffered). However, it would appear that where there is an anticipatory breach and the innocent party elects to affirm the contract and perform his obligations there is no duty to mitigate the resultant loss.

White & Carter v MacGregor [1961]

Facts: W and C agreed to advertise M's garage business for three years on plates attached to their litter bins. M repudiated the agreement the very day it was made. W and C affirmed the contract, prepared the plates and displayed them as required by the contract. They then claimed full payment.

Held: they could claim the full contract amount. If they had abandoned the contract on the day M cancelled they would not have been able to claim full payment in compensation as they would have been obliged to mitigate their loss, eg, by seeking alternative clients to hire the advertising space.

This case was decided by a bare majority in the House of Lords: the two Law Lords in the minority giving strong dissenting speeches. The decision has been the subject of much criticism (both by academics, practitioners and the judiciary) along the lines that, although the appellants were not bound to mitigate their loss, surely the law should not allow them to inflate their loss, deliberately and unreasonably, and then recover that amount from the respondent?

Conclusion	Where one party commits a repudiatory breach of contract the other party has a choice

(a)   he may accept that the breach discharges the contract. He is then released from his obligations and can sue the other party for damages.

(b)   or he may affirm the contract and treat it as continuing.

Where the repudiatory breach is anticipatory he may exercise his choice immediately: he is not required to wait for the date of performance to arrive.

5   FRUSTRATION

5.1   Introduction

The general rule is that, unless otherwise agreed, a party who fails to perform his contractual obligations is in breach of contract and liable for damages. This is the position whatever the reason given in excuse.

Paradine v Jane [1647]

Facts a tenant was sued for rent of premises of which he had been dispossessed for three years by the King's enemies.

Held: he was nevertheless liable for the rent.

The doctrine of frustration was developed to mitigate the severity of this rule where performance of a contract subsequently becomes impossible through the happening of a supervening event which occurred through the fault of neither party. Later cases have extended the doctrine beyond strict 'impossibility' to situations where circumstances have so changed that performance would now be so radically different as to destroy the commercial purpose of the contract.

If a contract is frustrated it is automatically discharged with the result that both parties are lawfully excused from further performance.

The doctrine is narrowly applied and the following cases show the limits of the doctrine.

[Definition]   A contract is frustrated where, although possible to perform when made, it subsequently becomes 'impossible' through the happening of a supervening event which was the fault of neither party.

5.2   Application of the doctrine

Frustration has been held to apply in the following circumstances:

(a)   **Destruction of the subject matter**

Taylor v Caldwell [1863]

Facts: the plaintiffs entered into an agreement with the defendants for the hire of a certain music hall for the purpose of giving a series of concerts. Before the series was due to begin the hall was destroyed by accidental fire.

Held: the plaintiffs could not recover damages. The destruction of the hall excused both parties from the performance of their promises.

Destruction of the essential object need not be complete; it suffices if the damage is so extensive that the commercial purpose of the agreement is thwarted.

(b)   **Non-occurrence of the event on which the contract was based**

Krell v Henry [1903]

Facts: Henry hired a room from Krell for two days. Both parties knew that the room would be used as a position from which to view the coronation procession of Edward VII, but the contract itself made no reference to that intended use. The King's illness caused a postponement of the procession.

Held: the contract was frustrated. Henry was excused from paying rent for the room. The necessary inference to be drawn from circumstances surrounding conclusion of the contract was that the holding of the procession on the dates planned was regarded by both parties as basic to performance of the contract.

Herne Bay Steamboat Co v Hutton [1903]

Facts: the plaintiff company agreed to hire out a steamboat to the defendant for a fee of £250 for a period of two days, for the purpose of taking passengers to Spithead to cruise round the fleet and see the naval review on the occasion of Edward VII's coronation. The review was cancelled, but the boat could still have been used to cruise round the assembled fleet. The defendant refused to use the boat or pay the balance of the agreed fee still outstanding, and the plaintiff company sued for payment.

Held: the plaintiff company was entitled to sue. The contract was not frustrated. The holding of the naval review was not the only event upon which the intended use of the boat was dependent. The other object of the contract was to cruise around the fleet and this remained capable of fulfilment.

(c)   **Incapacity where the contract requires personal performance**

A prime example of a contract of personal service is the contract of employment and such a contract is always frustrated by the death of the employee. The position is the same where illness or injury renders him **permanently** incapable of performing the contract.

Where the illness (or other incapacity such as internment, conscription and, possibly, imprisonment) is temporary much depends on whether resumed performance after the incapacity would be radically different commercially from what was envisaged by the contract.

A factor relevant here is the probable length of the contract. For example a day's illness would not frustrate a contract of employment of no fixed duration whereas in

Robinson v Davison [1871]

Facts: a pianist was engaged to give a concert on a particular date. She became ill and was incapable of appearing.

It was **held** that the contract was frustrated.

Hare v Murphy Bros [1974]

Facts: an employee was sent to prison for twelve months.

Held: his contract of employment was frustrated, though it has also been argued since that such a sentence, being caused by the actions of the employee would negate the doctrine of frustration because the event is self-induced.

Another factor of possible relevance is the importance to the organisation that the particular worker does the particular job. This 'key worker' factor was relevant in

Condor v The Barron Knights [1966]

Facts: the drummer in a pop group ordinarily employed for seven nights a week was advised by his doctor not to work for more than four nights.

Held: his contract had been frustrated because it was not commercially feasible to employ a second part-time drummer.

The courts and tribunals dealing with contracts of employment are today very reluctant to find frustration of the contract because in doing so they would deprive the employee of his right to claim unfair dismissal.

(d)   **Impossibility caused by some change in the law or by action taken under statutory authority**

Re Shipton, Anderson & Co [1915]

Facts: could a contract for the sale of wheat stored in a warehouse be frustrated when the government requisitioned it under its emergency wartime powers?

Held: yes it could. The war was a 'supervening event' which over-rode the original contract.

(e)   **On an extensive interruption which alters performance**

An extensive interruption to performance may make any further execution of the contract fundamentally impracticable or essentially different to performance as originally contemplated by the contracting parties.

Metropolitan Water Board v Dick Kerr & Co Ltd [1918]

Facts: Kerr & Co agreed to construct a reservoir for the water board within a period of six years, subject to an extension of time if the work should be unduly delayed or impeded **however occasioned.** During the First World War the Minister of Munitions ordered work to stop and the plant to be sold.

Held: although the event that occurred was literally within the delay clause and seemingly precluded frustration, nonetheless the contract has been frustrated. The interruption to the work was of such a character and duration that it vitally and fundamentally changed the conditions of the contract. If performance was resumed it would be essentially different to the type of performance as originally envisaged.

5.3   When frustration will not apply

A contract is not frustrated:

(a)   If it merely becomes more difficult or expensive to perform in a different way.

Tsakiroglou v Obleé Thorl [1960]

Facts: a contract was entered into for the sale of groundnuts. The contract price included shipment from the Sudan to Hambourg in Germany. The seller costed the contract on the basis of the shortest shipping route (via the Suez Canal) although this was not an express term of the contract nor would the court allow it to be an implied term. After the making of the contract the Suez Canal was unexpectedly closed. As this would have meant a 2½ times longer journey around the Cape of Good Hope the seller alleged that the contract was discharged by frustration.

Held: the contract was not impossible to perform it was merely more expensive for the seller and therefore not frustrated.

Davis Contractors v Fareham UDC [1956]

Facts: the plaintiff contracted to build a number of houses for the defendant for £94,000 over a specified period. Due to labour shortages it took much longer and cost the plaintiff £110,000. They pleaded that the contract had been frustrated and were therefore entitled to claim on a *quantum meruit* basis for the benefit conferred.

Held: undue delay which caused extra expense did not amount to frustration.

(b)   If one party has expressly undertaken that he will do something which he later finds he cannot achieve - **Cassidy v Osuustukkukauppa [1957]**

(c)   If one party by his own choice induces impossibility which could have been avoided; 'self-induced' frustration is not frustration.

Maritime National Fish v Ocean Trawlers [1935]

Facts: a contract for hire of a trawler which required a trawler licence was claimed to be frustrated when the owner obtained insufficient trawler licences for all its boats and failed to allocate one to the trawler which had been hired.

Held: the contract was not frustrated. The person claiming the frustration had caused the event himself and so could not rely upon the doctrine. The owner remained liable to the hirer.

5.4 Effects of frustration

The position of the parties is governed by the Law Reform (Frustrated Contracts) Act 1943:

(a) All sums paid under the contract must be repaid. Any sums payable (whether overdue or due in the future) cease to be payable.

(b) If one party has incurred expenses under the contract he can deduct them from any sums which have to be repaid under paragraph (a), or claim them from any overdue sums, but if there are no such sums, he cannot recover such expenses from the other party.

(c) Where one party has received some benefit under the contract, he must pay for that benefit.

(d) The Act does not cover:

- contracts which themselves contain a provision to meet the possibility of frustration;

- shipping contracts;

- contracts for insurance; or

- contracts for the sale of specific goods which have perished before the property in the goods have passed to the buyer (covered later in Sale of Goods)

6 SELF TEST QUESTIONS

6.1 What are the four ways in which a contract can be discharged? (1).

6.2 What is the general rule about the performance of a contract? (2.1).

6.3 When can a party to a severable contract who has not completed the whole contract claim payment? (2.3).

6.4 Is the doctrine of substantial performance a common law or an equitable doctrine? (2.6).

6.5 Give an example of a contract where 'time will be of the essence'. (2.7).

6.6 What is 'bilateral discharge' of a contract? (3.2).

6.7 Will a breach of warranty ever entitle the innocent party to 'accept' the breach and end the contract? (4.1).

6.8 Define frustration (5.1).

6.9 What was decided in the case of **Herne Bay Steamboat Co v Hutton?** (5.2).

6.10   What is the position of a party who has incurred expenses under a frustrated contract? (5.4).

7   EXAMINATION TYPE QUESTIONS

7.1   E's series of concerts

(a)   In what circumstances will a contract be discharged through frustration?

(12 marks)

(b)   D engages E to sing in a series of concerts.

In each of the following situations what is the legal position if, before the first concert can take place:

(i)   the theatre in which the concerts are to be held is seriously damaged by fire and the concerts are cancelled;

(ii)   E is found guilty of drug smuggling and sent to prison for two years?

(8 marks)

(Total: 20 marks)

7.2   Seville publications plc

Seville Publications plc agree to pay Leporello £20,000 for writing a biography they would like to publish. They agree a time-scale for the writing of the book and an immediate advance of £5,000 to Leporello. No formal contract is drawn up but Seville write to Leporello and say 'As arranged at our meeting, we confirm that you are to write for us a biography of the late Don Giovanni called 'The Catalogue Song' for a fee of £20,000. We enclose a cheque for £5,000 by way of advance as agreed.'

Leporello begins work and three months later, when he has written 50,000 words, the publishers tell him that they have had a change of company policy and no longer intend to publish biographies. They ask for the return of the £5,000 advance.

Advise Leporello.

(12 marks)

8   ANSWERS TO EXAMINATION TYPE QUESTIONS

8.1   E's series of concerts

(a)   Frustration occurs when a contract becomes impossible to perform at some stage after the contract has been made. However, the courts are unwilling to recognise anything but the most fundamental of changes as giving rise to impossibility and will not regard the event as frustrating if the supervening impossibility is due to the fault of a party to the contract. The following are the main examples of frustrating events:

(i)   Destruction of the subject matter of the contract. In **Taylor v Caldwell** a hall which was to be hired for three days burnt down before the hire period began. This was held to be a frustrating event.

(ii)   The non-occurrence of an essential event. In **Krell v Henry,** the balcony overlooking the route of the coronation procession to Westminster Abbey was let out for the coronation day. The court held the doctrine of frustration occurred when the coronation was cancelled rendering the hiring of the balcony totally pointless. However, if there is some point to the contract remaining, the non-occurrence of an important event will not cause frustration. The dispute in **Herne Bay Steamboat Co. v Hutton** arose out of the same cancellation of the coronation ceremony. This meant the newly crowned king could not review the British fleet. The plaintiffs had agreed to take people out in boats for the dual purpose of seeing the assembled British fleet and seeing the king reviewing the fleet. As it was still possible to see the assembled British fleet some purpose remained and the contract was not frustrated.

(iii)   Government interference through making contracts illegal or through the requisitioning of tools in wartime situations: **Avery v Bowden**.

(iv)   Death or personal non-availability in a contract of personal services. In the case of non-availability the length of absence is relevant to whether the doctrine applies. It is only where absence makes performance of the contract impossible or radically different will illness or other non-availability amount to frustration. In very specialised contracts of personal services such as that of a drummer in a pop group **(Condor v Barron Knights)** even very limited absences through illness will frustrate the contract.

(b)   (i)   Depending on the precise circumstances this situation will either give rise to a breach of contract on the part of D in which case he will be liable to pay damages to E or he will be able to rely on the doctrine of frustration. In the latter event D will be discharged from his duty to engage E, but will have to pay any expenses etc that E may have incurred prior to the frustrating event: Law Reform (Frustrated Contracts) Act 1943. There will only be a frustrating event if the theatre is essential to the performance of the contract as in **Taylor v Caldwell** (see (a)). This will only be the case if there is absolutely nowhere else for the concerts to be held. If there are other premises available, even if these are much more expensive to hire, the fact the contract becomes more difficult and expensive to perform is not a frustrating event: **Tsakiroglou v Obleé Thorl.**

(ii)   E may be liable for breach of contract on the basis of non-performance of the contract. E may try to claim frustration on the grounds of personal non-availability. However, as he has been held guilty of drug smuggling which has led to his non-availability, this would seem to be a case of self-induced frustration which does not discharge E from the contract.

8.2   Seville publications plc

The basic common law rule is that a contract is not discharged by partial performance; and that one who had not fully and perfectly fulfilled his contractual obligations cannot claim any payment for the part of the work he had completed. The authority for this basic proposition is **Cutter v Powell**. In that case, the widow of a seaman failed to recover even a proportion of the fee he was to have been paid for completing a voyage, he having died at sea.

This strict and sometimes unfair rule has been modified by a number of exceptions. For example, the widow in **Cutter v Powell** would now recover, under the doctrine of frustration of contract, a reasonable sum on a *quantum meruit* basis, to reflect the value of the benefit conferred by the proportion of the work actually completed by her husband. A similar approach is adopted where the contract has not been frustrated, but its completion has been prevented by the other party. Thus, in **Planché v Colburn,** an author was commissioned to write a series of articles for publication by instalments in a periodical. He undertook a substantial amount of work, only to be told by the publishers that they had decided to discontinue publication. They declined to pay him anything, on the basis that he had not completed the agreed work, although the reason for this was that they had stopped him. The court awarded him a reasonable sum for work done on the *quantum meruit* ('as much as it deserves') basis.

The facts outlined in the question are indistinguishable in substance from those in **Planché v Colburn.** Leporello should be advised accordingly. He should retain the £5,000 deposit pending negotiations upon what would be a reasonable payment for the work done. If he proposed to write, say, no less that 100,000 words and he has written 50,000, together with his planning and preparation, he has probably completed more than half the work; and on the basis of the contract price he should receive more than half of the £20,000 agreed. He should negotiate on these lines; but if litigation is necessary to enforce his claim, he should bear in mind that the court will award what it considers to be a reasonable sum for the work done and will not be bound to adhere to proportion of the contract price.

Leporello might have in mind continuing work, finishing the book and demanding full payment. In **White & Carter (Councils) Ltd v McGregor** a similar approach in the case of an advertising contract succeeded: the court held that there was no need for the plaintiff to mitigate his loss in the case of such anticipatory breach of contract. The plaintiff completed the contract and recovered the full price. However, the **White & Carter** case seems to be an unusual decision based upon unusual facts; and it was made clear in **Clea Shipping v Bulk Oil** that the court will not automatically allow the full amount in such cases. Probably, Leporello should mitigate his loss by ceasing to write, at least until he has taken steps to try to arrange for another publisher to take the book. If he continues to write the book, he cannot, as the law stands, be sure of any damages for the work done by him after the publisher's breach of contract.

8 CONTRACT: REMEDIES FOR BREACH

INTRODUCTION & LEARNING OBJECTIVES

Syllabus area 8a. Remedies for breach. (Ability required 3).

The preceding chapters considered whether or not a contract has been breached. This chapter considers the remedies available for breach of contract comprising monetary remedies (eg, damages and an action for the price) and, where a monetary remedy would be inadequate, the court orders of specific performance and injunction.

An examination question in this area may require knowledge of the calculation of damages as an adjunct to a question on a main topic area. Equally there have been essay questions in the past which have required a detailed discussion about the assessment of damages or the availability of the equitable remedies.

This chapter also covers limitation of action and the doctrine of privity of contract.

When you have studied this chapter you should be able to do the following:

- Understand the aim of damages for breach of contract and recognise the difference between liquidated damages clauses and penalty clauses.

- Explain the two main questions that arise in the calculation of damages: remoteness of damage and the measure of damages.

- List the different types of equitable remedy.

- Explain when each type of remedy is applicable and what the aim of the particular type of remedy is.

- Be able to state when contractual actions become statute barred.

- Understand that in general the doctrine of privity allows only those who are party to a contract to sue and be sued on it.

---

1 SUMMARY OF REMEDIES

In appropriate cases the party who has suffered a breach of contract may have any of the following remedies:

(a) damages;
(b) action for price;
(c) specific performance;
(d) injunction;
(e) quantum merit;

2   DAMAGES

2.1   Aim of damages

The aim of damages in contract is to put the injured party into the position he would have been in if the contract had been properly performed - often referred to as *bargain loss*. Thus in a contract for the sale of goods where the seller has failed to deliver goods, the buyer's measure of damages will be the difference between the agreed contract price and the price the buyer needed to pay in order to get the goods elsewhere, ie, the prevailing market price.

Damages are compensatory; they are not usually intended to be punitive. Thus damages are not usually affected by the motive or intention behind the breach of contract - whether good or bad.

2.2   Liquidated damages and penalty clauses

The parties may agree a sum to be paid in the event of breach or may not discuss it at all.

(a)   Where the contract does not make any provision for damages the court will determine the damages payable on the basis of the principles set out in paras 3 and 4. They are **unliquidated damages.**

(b)   Where a contract provides for the payment of a fixed sum on breach, it may either be a **liquidated damages clause** or a **penalty clause.** It is crucial to differentiate these as the results are different.

> Definition   **Liquidated damages**: if the clause is a **genuine attempt at estimating the loss** in advance of the breach it is a **liquidated damages clause** and will be valid and **enforceable** by either party to the contract. Thus, if the actual damages suffered by the innocent party are greater than the damages provided for, he can only claim the liquidated amount.

Cellulose Acetate Silk Co v Widnes Foundry [1933]

Facts: a contract for the building of a factory contained a clause providing for payment of a fixed sum in compensation for each day's delay in completion of the work. The work was finished late and the plaintiffs suffered losses considerably greater than those envisaged when the contract was made.

Held: the plaintiffs were entitled only to the contract rate of damages: that figure had represented a genuine estimate of loss when it was inserted in the contract.

> Definition   **Penalty clauses**: where the clause is expressed to force a party to perform his obligations under the contract, it will be *penal*, and the clause will be of **no effect** (ie, the person will have to prove the loss suffered and the damages will be unliquidated damages assessed in accordance with the rules set out in paras 3 and 4).

Whether a clause is a penalty or for liquidated damages is a question of construction of the contract; certainly the name that the contract gives to the clause is not conclusive.

2.3   Guidelines for construing the clauses

Dunlop Pneumatic Tyre Co v New Garage [1915]

Facts: the plaintiff supplied tyres to the defendants. The defendants agreed that for any of a number of breaches they would pay Dunlop £5 per tyre sold in breach. The defendants sold tyres at below the listed price, which was one of the breaches mentioned in the contract.

Held: the stipulated sum was for liquidated damages. The figure of £5 was a rough and ready estimate of the possible loss which the plaintiffs might suffer. Moreover, although the sum was payable on the happening of a number of different types of breach, the range of breaches was very limited. They were all fairly trivial.

Certain guidelines were laid down in the case to help the court construe penalty clauses. The guidelines suggest that there is a presumption that a clause is penal:

(a)   if the sum stipulated is extravagant and unconscionable;

(b)   if one sum is payable on the occurrence of one or more breaches; some trifling, others serious; or

(c)   if it is a sum payable for a breach, where the breach is non-payment of money, and the sum stipulated is larger than the non-payment.

However, a penalty is not necessarily penal merely because the stipulated sum is more than the loss actually suffered. As long as the stipulated figure is a genuine attempt to pre-estimate the loss it will be permissible. These are only presumptions and can be rebutted by evidence to the contrary.

The burden of proof is on the party alleging that the clause is a penalty.

3   UNLIQUIDATED DAMAGES

3.1   Calculation of unliquidated damages

Damages is the common law remedy and is available as of right for every breach of contract.

Two questions arise when the court is assessing a claim for unliquidated damages:

(a)   What losses should be included in the claim? - remoteness of damage.
(b)   What level of damages will compensate the party claiming? - measure of damages.

3.2   Remoteness of damage

The basic rule is that damages are awarded to put the innocent party in the same position that he would have been in had the contract been properly performed. Thus damages are awarded for loss of bargain. However, some losses, albeit flowing from the breach, are nevertheless too remote and not recoverable.

Consider, for example, the following situation. A builder agrees to build a factory by a certain date. If erection of a new factory is delayed, the manufacturer may lose profits on his trade for the period of delay; he may have to buy products (which he could have made) in order to fulfil contracts to supply customers; he may have to pay interest charges on capital invested in raw materials which he cannot use or pay wages to employees for whom he has no work. Which of these indirect losses and expenses (loosely called **consequential loss**) can he recover from the builder as damages for breach of contract in failing to complete the factory on time?

Hadley v Baxendale [1854]

Facts: a carrier was given a mill-shaft to deliver to a plant manufacturer as a model for making a new shaft. The carrier delayed in delivery and, unknown to him, the mill stood idle during the period of delay.

Held: he was not liable for the loss of profit and the rule was formulated as follows: **the loss should be such as may fairly and reasonably be considered either arising naturally, ie, according to the usual course of things, from the breach of contract, or such as may reasonably be supposed to have been in the contemplation of both parties at the time they made the contract as the probable result of the breach of it.**

So there are two types of loss for which damages may be recovered:

(a)   that which arises naturally in the usual course of things - **general damages;** sometimes known as 'normal loss'; and

(b)   that which does not occur naturally in the usual course of things but both parties could foresee, when the contract was made, as the likely result of breach - **special damages**; sometimes known as 'abnormal loss'.

3.3   Hadley v Baxendale applied

Both branches of the rule arising from the case of **Hadley v Baxendale** are based on a test of foresight and probability. In the first branch the test is what would an outsider with no special knowledge of the circumstances regard as the likely consequence of a breach.

In **Hadley v Baxendale** it was held that without inside knowledge the carrier could not be expected to realise that delay on his part would keep the mill idle (in many cases mill owners were likely to have a spare shaft to use in an emergency).

The second branch of the rule starts from the special knowledge (if any) which the parties possessed when they made their contract and asks what with that knowledge, should reasonably have been foreseen as the likely loss resulting from breach.

The rule in **Hadley v Baxendale** has been considered and approved in many cases.

Victoria Laundry v Newman Industries [1949]

Facts: a laundry required a new boiler to enlarge its plant. There was delay in delivery of the boiler and as a result the laundry lost:

(a)   a normal trading profit from delay in bringing the new plant into use; and
(b)   an extra large profit on certain government contracts.

Held: the boiler manufacturer was held liable for the loss of normal profits; under the first branch of the rule, he or anyone else would know that an industrial boiler was essential to the operation of the plant, and, therefore, to earning normal profits from it. He was not liable for the loss of profit on the government contracts, of which he had no information. (If, of course, he had known of them he would have been liable under the second branch of the rule.)

The Heron II [1969]

Facts: a vessel was chartered for a voyage from Contanza to Basrah for the carriage of sugar. She deviated to Berhera to load livestock for the shipowner. If she had not deviated, she would have arrived at Basrah ten days earlier than she in fact did. The charterers claimed damages for the difference between the market value of the sugar at the due date of delivery and at the actual date of delivery.

Held: their claim should succeed. Although the shipowner did not know what the charterers intended to do with the sugar, they knew that there was a market for sugar in Basrah. They must have at least realised that it was not unlikely that the sugar would be sold there on arrival, and that in any ordinary market process were apt to fluctuate daily. It was an even chance that the fluctuation would be downwards. The loss was of a kind which the shipowner, when they made the contract, ought to have realised was liable to result from a breach causing delay in delivery.

Where parties contemplate the type of damage which may follow a breach of contract they will be liable for damage of that type even where its extent was not foreseen.

H Parsons Livestock v Uttley Ingham & Co [1978]

Facts: D had supplied a 'feed storage hopper' to P, who was a pig breeder and who needed the hopper to store nuts for his pigs. The hopper proved defective, the nuts went mouldy and a number of pigs died from a rare stomach disease as a result of eating those nuts. P claimed:

(a)   damages for the death of the pigs, and also for
(b)   consequent financial loss from lost sales, etc.

Held: that damages under (a) were recoverable, because the parties would have contemplated at least a 'serious possibility' of some harm coming to the pigs if the hopper failed to keep the pigs' food in a satisfactory condition; it was not relevant that the parties would not have foreseen the extent of the harm (ie, a fatal stomach disease). Damages under (b) were not recoverable being too remote under the guidelines of **Hadley v Baxendale**.

Recovery of damages in contract is usually for financial loss (eg, loss of profits) but other types of loss are also recoverable eg, personal injury and property damage. In an appropriate case damages can be recovered for mental distress and loss of enjoyment.

Jarvis v Swan's Tours Ltd [1973]

Facts: the defendant's winter sports holiday brochure represented various facilities available at a ski-resort. On the basis of these representations, the plaintiff booked a holiday. The advertised facilities were not available and the plaintiff was very disappointed. The plaintiff claimed damages for breach of contract to provide the holiday promised.

Held: the plaintiff was entitled to compensation for loss of entertainment and enjoyment. Damages for mental stress can be recovered in an action for breach of contract in a proper case. This was such a case, since the parties contemplated that on breach there might be mental inconveniences eg, frustration, annoyance and disappointment.

| Conclusion | If the loss is a normal loss it is recoverable. However where the loss is abnormal it is not recoverable unless the parties knew of it, or ought reasonably to have known of it, at the time the contract is made. |

4   MEASURE OF DAMAGES

4.1   General

| Definition | The measure of damages is the amount which will, so far as money can, put the plaintiff in the position in which he would have been had the contract been performed. |

Thus for example if a buyer bought goods for £50 which the seller refused to deliver, the buyer's damages would be the cost to him of acquiring the same goods from someone else. So if he had to pay £60 his damages would be £10 (plus the £50 if he had already paid that to the seller). If a buyer refused to accept goods the seller's loss will be the difference between the contract price and the price he can actually sell for.

If the plaintiff has suffered no actual loss he will be awarded only nominal damages.

Surrey County Council v Bredero Homes Ltd [1993]

Facts: SCC sold some land to BH and in the contract of sale BH covenanted to build no more than 72 houses on the plot. In deliberate breach of contract BH built 77 houses. SCC claimed damages equal to the profit BH had made on the extra houses.

The Court of Appeal **held** that the remedy at common law for breach of contract was the award of damages to compensate the innocent party for his loss: it was not to transfer to him any benefit which the wrongdoer had gained by his breach of contract. Since SCC had not suffered any loss, it followed that the damages recoverable had to be nominal.

4.2   Difficulties of evaluation

The court's inability to evaluate the plaintiff's losses with mathematical accuracy is not sufficient reason for refusing to grant any compensation at all, even though the assessment of damages is almost a matter of guesswork.

Chaplin v Hicks [1911]

Facts: Chaplin agreed with Hicks, a theatrical manager, to attend an interview at which twelve girls would be chosen from fifty contestants to work in the theatre. Hick's failure to give Chaplin sufficient notice of the interview prevented her attendance. She claimed damages for loss of her chance of being selected. The defendant contended that Miss Chaplin was entitled to nominal damages only since it was impossible to determine objectively whether she would have been chosen.

Held: although assessment of her loss was problematic, since it could not be determined whether Chaplin would have been chosen, the plaintiff should nonetheless receive some compensation. Damages of £100 were awarded.

4.3   Taxation

Sometimes the court will take into account the effect of taxation. This is particularly important in an action for wrongful dismissal where an employee is claiming loss of earnings. His actual loss will not be his gross pay but his net pay after taxation. This is sometimes called the **BTC v Gourlay [1956]** principle.

4.4   Mitigation

A duty is imposed upon a plaintiff to take all reasonable steps to mitigate any loss caused to him by the defendant's breach of contract. Compensation will not be awarded for any damage incurred which the plaintiff had a reasonable opportunity to avoid.

Brace v Calder [1895]

Facts: Brace was employed by a partnership for a fixed period of two years, but after only five months the partnership was dissolved thereby prematurely terminating his contract of employment. He was offered identical employment with a reconstituted partnership which was immediately formed to replace the previous one. He refused the offer and sued for wages he would have earned had his job continued for the agreed two year period.

Held: Brace had not mitigated the loss he suffered by his employer's breach of contract, thus he could only recover nominal damages.

If there is an anticipatory breach as in **White & Carter v MacGregor [1961]** it may be that if the innocent party elects to treat the contract as operative he is under no duty to mitigate his loss and may continue with his own performance.

4.5   The available market rule

This special rule applies to contracts for the sale of goods where the breach is either the buyer wrongfully refusing to accept the goods or the seller wrongfully refusing to deliver the goods. By S51 Sale of Goods Act 1979, if an available market exists, the damages are deemed to be the difference between the contract price and the available market price as at the date of breach. An available market exists where goods of that type can be freely bought or sold at prices fixed by supply and demand.

4.6   Activity

S agrees to sell 100 barrels of crude oil to B at £20 per barrel, delivery on 1 May. S refuses to deliver and B buys oil elsewhere at £25 per barrel. The 'spot' price (ie, available market price) for crude on 1 May is £22 per barrel.

What is B's measure of damages?

4.7   Activity solution

£200.

4.8   Date of assessment of damages

In most cases the loss must be assessed as at the date of the breach, and may include a claim for pre-contract expenditure reasonably incurred in anticipation of performance.

Conclusion   When calculating the amount of damages to be awarded the court will award an amount which, as far as possible, puts the injured party into the position that he would have been in had the contract been properly performed. Factors include:

- financial loss will be recovered but damages can also be awarded for stress, inconvenience and frustration

- even if the award cannot be mathematically calculated the court will award damages by the process of estimating the loss

- usually losses are assessed as at the date of the breach

- the party who suffered loss is under a duty to mitigate their loss and the damages awarded will reflect this.

5   ACTION FOR THE PRICE

Where the breach of contract is non-payment of the price the seller sues for the price. This is an action for a liquidated sum - no question of remoteness or quantum arising. There is also no duty to mitigate: **White & Carter Council v McGregor (1961)**.

6   SPECIFIC PERFORMANCE

This is an equitable remedy whereby the court orders the defendant to carry out his obligations under the contract. Like other equitable remedies it is at the discretion of the court to grant it and cannot be obtained as of right (contrast damages which is a common law remedy and is awarded as of right). It therefore follows that it is only given where it is just and equitable to do so. The main principles which determine when specific performance is ordered or refused are:

(a)   Where damages are an adequate remedy, specific performance will not be ordered. On a sale of goods (unless they are unique) or an agreement to lend money, damages is an adequate remedy for the extra cost if the plaintiff can obtain similar goods or money elsewhere. By contrast, specific performance will often be ordered on a contract for sale of land: each piece of the earth's surface is unique.

(b)   Where the court could not adequately supervise the performance of the contract and decide if it was being properly done (in detail) it refuses to order specific performance. Contracts for construction of buildings fall under this head.

(c)   Specific performance will not be given where it would cause undue hardship. Thus specific performance will not be ordered of a contract of personal services, such as an employment contract, on the basis that it is contrary to public policy to compel an unwilling party to maintain continuous personal relations with another (also it would require constant supervision).

(d)   The remedy will only be given on the basis of mutuality, ie, the remedy will only be granted if both parties could, if necessary, seek the protection of the court. For this reason an infant cannot obtain an order for specific performance since the court would not be able to enforce such an order against him.

   Definition   An infant, or minor, is a person under eighteen years of age. Infants have only limited power to contract in English law.

(e)   Specific performance will not be given to a party who has acted unfairly or improperly. This is expressed by the maxim "He who comes to Equity must come with clean hands".

(f)   As will all equitable remedies, a party who wishes for specific performance must act promptly - "Delay defeats the Equities".

7   INJUNCTION

This is also an equitable remedy and is granted on the same principles as specific performance.

Definition   An **injunction** is an order of the court which either requires a person to do something (mandatory injunction) or prohibits a person from doing something (prohibitory injunction).

The court will grant an injunction to restrain a party from committing a breach of contract. Although it is said that an injunction will only be granted to enforce a negative stipulation in a contract it may be extended to cases where a negative term may be inferred.

Metropolitan Electric Supply v Ginder [1901]

Facts: the contract obliged the defendant to take all his electricity from the plaintiff; the obligation was in substance not to take electricity from another supplier.

Held: an injunction to that effect was issued.

An injunction will not be granted if it would have the effect of requiring specific performance in circumstances where the latter would be refused.

Page One Records Ltd v Britton [1967]

Facts: the Troggs (a pop group) agreed to employ P as their manager for five years and not to employ any other manager. The Troggs dismissed P, who consequently sought an injunction to restrain them from employing any other manager.

Held: the injunction was refused because if denied the services of another manager, the Troggs would in effect have had to employ P, since they could not do without a manager.

However, an injunction may be granted in circumstances such as the following:

Warner Brothers Pictures Inc v Nelson [1936]

Facts: the film star, Bette Davis (really Miss Nelson) entered into a contract with the plaintiffs, initially for a term of one year, but giving the plaintiffs the option of extending it, whereby she agreed that she would not undertake other film work without obtaining their written consent. The plaintiff sought an injunction to restrain her from doing film work for another company in breach of this agreement.

Held: the injunction would be granted since she could still earn her living as an actress, in other ways.

An injunction will be granted only where it is 'just and convenient to do so', and, if it is inappropriate, the court can award damages in lieu of the injunction.

8   QUANTUM MERUIT

Quantum meruit means 'as much as it is worth'. It is not a claim for damages under a contract, but an award to compensate a person in some circumstances where a contract either never existed or subsequently ceased to exist. The plaintiff can be rewarded for his work or his goods as much as they are worth in the sense of a reasonable value.

Planché v Colburn [1831]

Facts: the plaintiff agreed to write a series of articles for *The Juvenile Library* on costume and ancient armour, to be published by instalments. When the work was partly completed, the defendants abandoned the series.

Held: the plaintiff recovered reasonable remuneration for the work which he had completed, on a *quantum meruit* basis. In such a case, where the defendant unjustifiably prevents completion of the contract the plaintiff can recover either damages (for breach of contract) or on a *quantum meruit*. (This case was previously outlined in the notes on performance of a contract).

Other applications of *quantum meruit* are:

(a)   Where minors or drunken persons are supplied with necessaries, the supplier can recover a reasonable price.

(b)   Where the plaintiff has performed services under a void contract.

> **Craven-Ellis v Cannons Ltd [1936]**
>
> **Facts:** a managing director's contract was unauthorised and void but he nevertheless served under it.
>
> **Held:** he recovered a reasonable sum for work done for the company.

(c)   Where a contract does not fix a precise sum the court will fix a reasonable sum on a *quantum meruit* basis.

9   LIMITATION OF ACTIONS

The Limitation Act 1980 provides that any action on a contract is 'barred' if not brought within the requisite period. Normally 'time runs' from the date on which the breach occurred. In the case of **simple contracts** the limitation period is **six years** and in the case of **contracts by deed, twelve years**. If the claim includes damages for personal injuries or death, however, the period is normally reduced to three years (however, the Act provides that the three year period can be extended by the court if the injury does not become apparent within the period).

There are three instances where the limitation period may be extended:

(a)   Where the plaintiff is an infant or of unsound mind when the cause of action accrued, time does not begin to run until the disability ceases.

(b)   Where the cause of action is concealed by the defendant's fraud, time does not begin to run until such moment as the plaintiff should, with reasonable diligence, have discovered the breach.

(c)   Where the defendant makes some acknowledgement in writing of his liability or makes a payment towards it, then time begins to run afresh from the date of such acknowledgement or payment. However, such acknowledgement or part payment made after the limitation period has expired will not start time running again. This rule applies only to claims for liquidated damages.

The Limitation Act 1980 only applies to common law remedies. In equity there is a more flexible doctrine known as **laches** (pronounced 'laitches') which requires the plaintiff to bring his action within a reasonable time depending on all the circumstances.

10   PRIVITY OF CONTRACT

10.1   The doctrine of privity

> *Definition*   A contract creates a personal obligation and only the original contracting parties can acquire enforceable rights or be subject to legal liabilities under it.

Dunlop Pneumatic Tyre Co v Selfridge [1915]

Facts: D made and sold tyres to a distributor on condition that he would not resell the tyres at less than the list price (the Resale Prices Act 1976 would now invalidate such terms) nor resell them to a retailer without imposing the same conditions about retail price. The distributor resold to S who offered the tyres to the public at less than D's list price.

Held: D could not enforce the contract between the distributor and S because D was not a party to it.

10.2   Consideration must move from the promisee

The doctrine of privity of contract is closely related to, but not the same as, the rule which requires consideration to be provided by each party to the contract. (This rule was covered in the chapter 'Contract: Consideration'). Often both matters will be relevant in the same examination question.

Tweddle v Atkinson [1861]

Facts: Tweddle was to marry G's daughter. G exchanged promises with Tweddle's father that they would each give a sum of money to Tweddle when the marriage had been formalised. G later died, not having made the payment, and Tweddle sued his estate for the money.

Held: Tweddle had provided no consideration for G's promise nor was he a party to the original contract. As a result of both reasons he had no enforceable rights under the contract.

There is one decisive method of ensuring that any benefit conferred by the terms of a contract will be legally enforceable at the instance of the person intended to benefit, that is, by joining him as a party to a contract under seal. To meet the requirements of the doctrine of privity, the intended beneficiary is now a party to the contract, and further, his failure to provide consideration will not bar any attempt to enforce the agreement since it is a specialty contract which need not be supported by consideration.

10.3   Exceptions and limitations to the doctrine of privity

There are a number of exceptions to the general rule of privity:

(a)   **Trusts**

   A third party to a contract, intended by the parties to be granted a benefit by the terms of the agreement, may be able to enforce his right to that benefit by establishing that the contract created a trust in his favour.

   In its simplest form a trust may be described as follows: a person called the settlor transfers his title in property, real or personal, to another person called a trustee to hold on trust for a beneficiary named by the settlor. The trustee is accountable to the beneficiary for benefits received in relation to the property. Usually the beneficiary does not provide any consideration in return for the benefit received under the trust, nor is he usually a party to the arrangement creating it, but if the trustee fails to discharge his duties by misappropriating trust money to his own use, then the beneficiary may sue the trustee for breach of trust and recover the money improperly used.

   A contract and a trust are separate legal concepts, but a third party may attempt to secure relief in equity and enforce the terms of a contract to which he is not a party in order to receive any benefit contemplated by the agreement, by establishing that it also gave rise to a trust in his favour.

   In order to ascertain whether a contract has created a trust, the following criteria must be satisfied:

   (i)   There must be clear proof of an intention by the parties to a contract to create equitable rights by way of trust in favour of a third party named by them, even though it is unnecessary to use any special form of wording.

(ii) There should be appropriation by parties to the contract of definite property for some purpose defined by them, which includes conferring some benefit in relation to that property on a third party.

The courts are, however, slow to imply that contracting parties have created a trust. The mere fact that the parties intend to benefit a third party will not be sufficient, and if the parties retain freedom to alter their agreement there can be no trust.

(b) Land Law

(i) Restrictive covenants

There are important exceptions to the privity doctrine operating in the realm of land law. For example, if Albert is the owner of a plot of building land adjoining his own residence then on selling the servient land he may not wish it to be used in a manner that will spoil enjoyment of his house and perhaps alter the character of the neighbourhood. Any restrictive covenant which limits the purpose for which the land may be used is binding not only against the original purchaser, but also against any other person to whom the land is later transferred, even though the transferee was not a party to the original agreement, provided that the purchaser bought the land with notice of the covenant and that the vendor retains some proprietary interest which will be protected by enforcement of the covenant.

The benefit of the restrictive covenant can be expressly assigned to each purchaser of the dominant land when the land is conveyed to him. The burden of a restrictive covenant passes to the purchaser of servient land with notice of the covenant's existence, provided that it is negative in substance and does not require the expenditure of money.

(ii) Leases

The assignee of a lease takes it with the benefits of, and subject to the burdens of, the assignor. Although there is no contract between the lessor and the assignee there is, under land law, 'privity of estate' and the assignee may therefore sue and be sued by the lessor.

Suppose for example that L leases a flat to R for 99 years and the lease contract provides, amongst other things, that R must pay ground rent of £75 per annum and that L must keep the common part stairways clean. Some years later R sells the lease to E. Despite there being no contract between L and E, L may sue E for the ground rent and E may sue L if he fails to keep the stairways clean.

(c) Statutory exceptions

There are a number of important exceptions to the doctrine of privity provided by Statute, but these are piecemeal qualifications which only remedy some of the more blatantly inconvenient aspects of the privity doctrine. Examples are given below:

(i) **S11 Married Women's Property Act 1882** provides that where a husband has taken out a life insurance policy, expressed to be in favour of his wife and children as beneficiaries, an enforceable trust is created.

(ii) **Road Traffic Act 1972** confers rights upon those injured by a motor vehicle to proceed, in some cases, directly against the insurance company, instead of the car owner.

(iii)   The **Bills of Exchange Act 1882** provides a number of exceptions to the doctrine of privity in relation to negotiable instruments. This topic is dealt with separately.

(d)   **Agency**

In most cases of agency, there is no real exception to the doctrine of privity. Where an agent enters into a contract with a third party on behalf of his principal, the two parties to the contract are the principal and the third party. The agent has no rights or obligations under the contract.

There is, however, one situation where there is a genuine exception to the privity rule: an agent may negotiate a contract without disclosing either the existence or the identity of the principal for whom he is acting. Even at common law the undisclosed principal, although not party to the discussions leading to the conclusion of the contract, has the right to sue and enforce the contractual obligations negotiated for his benefit against the other contracting party. He is also bound by burdens imposed by the contract. The other contract party may sue either the agent or the principal.

(e)   **Collateral contracts**

The court may find a collateral contract, for example, where there is a contract between A and B which in some way relates to C although C is not a party. There may be another contract between A and C on which C can sue.

Shanklin Pier Ltd v Detel Products Ltd [1951]

Facts: the plaintiffs owned a pier which needed painting. They were told by the defendants that the paint which they manufactured would last for seven to ten years. The plaintiffs employed a contractor to paint the pier and told him to use paint manufactured by the defendants. The contractor purchased the paint from the defendants and painted the pier with it. After three months it began to flake. The plaintiffs sued the defendants, who argued that the plaintiffs were not a party to the contract under which the paint was sold.

Held: that there was a separate contract between the plaintiffs and the defendants, which contained a promise by the defendants that the paint would last for seven to ten years. The plaintiffs had provided consideration by requiring the contractor to use the paint.

(f)   **Assignment - voluntary assignment of rights (benefits)**

Assignment is not in the syllabus as a topic in its own right, but it is examinable in the context of privity of contract, and this is covered below.

A person entitled to the benefit of a contract may assign it (ie, transfer it) to a third party, who will then be entitled to sue the other party to the contract. For example, if A and B make a contract under which A supplies goods to B who will pay A £500 then A's right to receive the £500 may be assigned to C who then has the right to sue B for the money. Compare this with the situation where A and B have a similar contract except that the payment by B was to be to C and not to A. C could not sue for the money as he is not party to the contract (there is no privity of contract).

Most contractual rights can be assigned unless otherwise agreed. However, the following cannot be assigned:

(a)   rights which are personal eg, an employer cannot assign his right to his employees' services; and

(b)   where public policy would forbid it eg, salaries and pensions of public office, financial payments in matrimonial proceedings, a bare right of action (ie, to sue).

The right to receive payment of a debt, like the benefit of any other contract, may be transferred or assigned. To remove difficulties of earlier procedure, S136 Law of Property Act 1925 gives a statutory right to assign provided that:

(a)   the assignment is in writing;

(b)   written notice is given to the debtor; and

(c)   the assignment is absolute (ie, of the whole debt).

If these conditions are satisfied then the assignee can sue in his own name to enforce payment of the debt, and his receipt discharges the debtor from his liability to the original creditor.

Where these conditions are not wholly satisfied or where the assignment is not of a debt owing at common law but of an equitable right eg, under a trust, the assignee must sue in the name of the original creditor or owner to whom in law the debt is still due.

Even the statutory assignment procedure is inadequate for some commercial needs. There major disadvantages arises from the doctrine of **nemo dat.** The transferor of a debt can only give to his transferee the same title to the debt as he has - nothing more. Thus, if the assignor's title is defective, so is that of the assignee.

For example, suppose P sells a car to D for £600 the money to be paid in a month's time and P then assigns the debt (ie, the right to claim the £600 from D) to Q. D now discovers that the car is defective and had in consequence a counterclaim against P for £100. The effect of the nemo dat rule is that Q owns a debt only worth £500. The assignment is said to be 'subject to equities' ie, subject to any rights of set-off or counterclaim that the debtor may have against the original creditor. In short: Q obtained no better rights to the debt than P had.

(g)   **Assignment by operation of law - involuntary assignment of rights and duties**

When a person dies, the law automatically transfers his rights and duties to his personal representative (whether executor or administrator).

Beswick v Beswick [1968]

Facts: by written agreement, Peter Beswick a coal merchant, sold his business to his nephew, John Beswick. In return John promised to pay £6.50 to Peter during his lifetime and thereafter a payment of £5 per week to his widow. On Peter's death his widow became administratrix of his estate. John made only one payment of £5 and refused to make further payments. The widow sued John for arrears and specific performance of the contract in her capacity as administratrix.

Held: John's failure to pay the annuity did not result in any loss to the deceased's estate; nevertheless the administratrix, standing in the shoes of the deceased and taking over his rights in relation to the contract, could enforce it by way of specific performance.

Note:

(i)   The widow could not sue in her personal capacity to enforce the contractual promise to pay the annuity since she was not a party to the agreement. If someone other than the widow had been appointed administrator, her only remedy would have been through an action by the administrator on her behalf, with accountability to her for any benefit secured as the result of a successful action.

(ii)   The Court of Appeal held that under the contract between Peter and his nephew a trust had not been created in the widow's favour, enforceable by her personally so that she could claim payment of the promised annuity. The issue was not even raised in the House of Lords.

The same involuntary assignment occurs of a bankrupt's rights and duties to his trustee in bankruptcy.

11   SELF TEST QUESTIONS

11.1   What is the aim of damages? (2.1)

11.2   Where a contract provides a clause which is a genuine attempt at estimating the loss what is this clause known as? (2.2)

11.3   What is the name of the case which set out the guidelines for making the distinction between a liquidated damages clause and a penalty clause? (2.3)

11.4   Is damages a common law or an equitable remedy?(3.1)

11.5   State the rule in **Hadley v Baxendale**? (3.2)

11.6   Identify the 2 limbs of the rule in **Hadley v Baxendale** (3.2)

11.7   If a person cannot show actual loss as a result of a breach of contract what sort of damages will the court award? (4.1)

11.8   What is the **BTC v Gourlay** principle? (4.3)

11.9   Apart from damages, what other monetary remedy is available for breach of contract? (5)

11.10   What equitable remedy will order the defendant to carry out the terms of the contract? (6)

11.11   Why will specific performance not be given of a contract of employment? (6)

11.12   What is the limitation period in the case of simple contracts? (9)

11.13   State the doctrine of privity of contract. (10.1)

11.14   Name the leading illustrative case in the doctrine of privity of contract. (10.1)

11.15   Give two situations whereby a person may sue to take the benefit of a contract of insurance even though he is not party to it. (10.3)

11.16   Explain the ratio decidendi of **Beswick v Beswick.** (10.3)

12   EXAMINATION TYPE QUESTIONS

12.1   Definitions of remedies

Explain the meaning (in contract law) of:

(a)   Liquidated damages clauses;

(5 marks)

(b)   Penalty clauses;

(5 marks)

(c)   Mitigation of loss; and

(5 marks)

(d)   The rule in Hadley v Baxendale.

(5 marks)

(Total: 20 marks)

12.2   Breach of contract

Explain the principles which apply to determine:

(a)   the validity of a contractual clause providing for damages payable in the event of breach; and

(10 marks)

(b)   the amount of damages awarded by a court following a breach of contract.

(10 marks)

(Total: 20 marks)

13   ANSWERS TO EXAMINATION TYPE QUESTIONS

13.1   Definitions of remedies

(a)   Liquidated damages are damages agreed by the parties to a contract when the contract is made as a genuine pre-estimate of the loss likely to be incurred if there is a breach of contract. Here, the parties have fixed the appropriate figure in advance. This is in contrast to unliquidated damages, which are fixed by the court. Whereas damages in contract may be either liquidated or unliquidated according to the terms of the contract, damages in tort are always unliquidated.

An example of liquidated damages would be a reduction in price of £X per day during which there is a delay in building work after the agreed completion date, if the £X is in fact a genuine (though not necessarily absolutely accurate) estimate of the actual loss should delay occur.

(b)   A penalty is not a genuine pre-estimate of loss but a penal provision which attempts to frighten one of the parties so that he performs the contract. Very large sums greatly in excess of the actual loss will be so construed. While liquidated damages clauses are enforced by the courts, penalties are not. The court's view of the matter, and not the description in the contract, decides whether a clause amounts to a penalty or liquidated damages.

(c)   Mitigation of loss, sometimes called mitigation of damages, is what the court expects of the party injured by a breach of contract. He must take reasonable steps to minimise the loss he suffers. If my garage does not deliver my new car I should buy one elsewhere and not wait for months until the price rises and I have to pay more. The damages I get for the breach will be restricted to what my loss would have been had I acted reasonably promptly. In **Brace v Calder** an employee failed to mitigate his loss by refusing to take up an offer of renewed employment and he was restricted to nominal damages: he could not simply sit back and claim loss of earnings for the whole of the remainder of his broken service agreement.

(d) **Hadley v Baxendale** is the leading case on remoteness of damages in contract law. Damages are restricted to such loss as:

(i) arises naturally from the breach; or

(ii) were in contemplation of the parties when they made the contract.

Thus, in the case itself, a carrier was not liable for loss of mill profit caused by his delay in carrying the only shaft. He did not know it was the only one and that the mill would be made idle. Thus, only reasonably foreseeable losses or prospective losses of which the defendant is aware will be covered by an award of damages: **Victoria Laundry v Newman** where a boiler was not fitted to laundry on time. The defendants were liable only for normal loss of profits and not for losses on special government contracts of which they as contractors knew nothing.

13.2 Breach of contract

(a) The general rule of freedom of contract means that parties are free to contract on whatever terms they choose and the terms so agreed will be binding on both parties in the absence of vitiating factors. This will include a term setting out damages payable in the event of breach of contract.

The aim of damages, the principal remedy for breach of contract, is to compensate the innocent party for the loss suffered by the breach and not to punish the guilty party for his behaviour. Thus they are compensatory and not punitive.

Where the contract provides for damages payable on breach it will be interpreted as a liquidated damages clause if it is a genuine attempt to estimate the loss likely to be suffered in the event of breach. In this case the innocent party may enforce the clause and claim the damages stipulated without reference to the actual loss he has suffered.

However, where the clause is expressed *in terrorem* ie, is an attempt to punish a party who breaches the contract and thus force him to perform his obligations, it will be interpreted as a penalty clause and be unenforceable. In this case the innocent party will be able to claim damages for the breach but they will be unliquidated damages and be calculated by the court in accordance with the principles set out in (b) below.

Whether the clause is a liquidated damages clause or a penalty clause depends on construction of the contract and the title used by the parties is not conclusive. In **Dunlop Tyre Co. v New Garage** the court laid down guidelines in the form of presumptions to assist in determining the matter. There is a presumption that the clause is penal if the sum stipulated is extravagant compared with the possible loss which could be suffered, or if one sum is payable on the occurrence of several breaches, or where the breach is non-payment of money and a larger sum is then payable. These are presumptions only and can be rebutted by evidence to show a genuine attempt to estimate loss.

(b) The court will assess damages where, although the contract stipulates a sum payable on breach, the clause has been interpreted as a penalty clause or where the contract makes no provision as to what should happen if there is a breach. These are called unliquidated damages and two questions arise in assessing them – firstly, what damage should be included (remoteness of damage) and, secondly, what level of damages will compensate the party claiming (measure of damage).

Remoteness of damage is concerned with determining the loss suffered by the innocent party for which the guilty party should compensate him. The rules to determine this were laid down in **Hadley v Baxendale** which set out two types of loss for which damages may be recovered. General damages cover losses which arise naturally from the breach and special damages cover losses due to special circumstances but which are reasonably contemplated by both parties when the contract was made. These rules were applied and illustrated in **Victoria Laundry v Newman Industries** in which the defendant contracted to deliver a new boiler to the plaintiff laundry by a certain date but failed to deliver on the due date. As a result of the breach, during the period of delay the laundry lost its normal trading profit and a particularly lucrative contract with the National Health Service. It was held that damages would be payable for the normal trading profit as general damages as these arose naturally from the breach. However, the damages for the loss of the particular contract were not general damages and were recoverable only if they had been in the contemplation of both parties at the time the contract was made. As the defendant was not aware that such a contract was being negotiated, this loss could not be claimed.

The question of measure of damages is concerned with the attempt to ascertain what amount of money will put the plaintiff in the same position as he would have been in if the contract had been performed. It will include damages to cover financial loss, damage to property, personal injury and, although the courts have been reluctant in the past to award damages to cover mental distress and discomfort, it is clear that these can now be claimed: **Jarvis v Swan's Tours Ltd** where damages were awarded for mental distress caused by lack of holiday facilities promised in the contract.

In a contract for the sale of goods the Sale of Goods Act 1979 codifies the rules and the damages awarded for non-delivery by the seller or non-acceptance by the buyer will depend on whether or not there is an available market. Where there is one, the measure of damages is the difference between the contract price and the market price at the contract time of delivery or acceptance.

Finally, in assessing the measure of damages, the court may reduce the amount if it finds that the innocent party has failed to mitigate his loss. The court will not award damages to compensate him for loss suffered which he could have avoided by taking reasonable steps. Thus, in **Brace v Calder** an employee's failure to mitigate his loss when his employer wrongfully terminated a fixed term contract resulted in a reduction of damages.

9 AGENCY

INTRODUCTION & LEARNING OBJECTIVES

Syllabus area 8b. Legal relationships between the parties to agency agreements with special reference to the authority of persons to act on behalf of others, particularly in companies and partnerships. (Ability required 3).

An agent is a person empowered by a principal to enter into legal relations with a third party on the principal's behalf. In this chapter consideration will be given to how an agency relationship is created and terminated, the authority and liability of an agent and the relationship between the principal and the agent.

When you have studied this chapter you should be able to do the following:

- Explain how an agency can be created.

- Distinguish between the different types of authority of an agent.

- Explain the rights, duties and liabilities of agent and principal.

- Explain how an agency can be terminated.

- Apply agency rules to the special situation within companies.

- Explain how agency operates in partnerships.

1 WHAT IS AGENCY

1.1 Introduction

 Agency is the relationship which arises when one person, the agent (A), is authorised to act as the representative of another, the principal (P), and to effect the principal's legal rights and obligations

The agent is the instrument for entering into legal relations between his principal and the third party. As long as the agent acts within the scope of the authority delegated to him the principal is bound by the transactions made by the agent with the third party.

1.2 Agency and contracts

Although agents may commit their principals in a variety of ways (eg, a principal may be liable for torts such as negligence committed by his agent in the course of his agency), the following discussion is limited to agents entering into contracts on behalf of their principals. The contract is made between the principal and third party and generally the agent has no rights or liabilities on the contract.

As the contract is between the principal and the third party the principal must have capacity to make the contract but the agent need not. A contract which would not bind an infant if he made it himself will not be binding on him merely because it is made through an adult agent. But, an infant could contract as an agent for an adult principal who would be bound by it. The agent's own contractual capacity will determine his personal liability on any contract of agency and on the contract with the third party.

2 FORMATION OF AN AGENCY

2.1 Introduction

In deciding whether one person has acted as an agent for another (the principal) and affected that principal's legal position it is necessary to consider whether an agency has been created and whether the agent has acted within the scope of his authority.

> **Definition** An agency may be created by agreement, (express or implied), between the principal and agent or by ratification; or, in the absence of any agreement, by estoppel, or by necessity.

The terms used to describe an agent's authority are derived to a degree from the way in which the agency is created. However, there is an overlap of types of authority and some disagreement as to the terms used to describe the different types of authority. The five ways in which an agency may be created are set out in the paragraphs below. The terminology used to describe the agent's authority is discussed later in the chapter.

2.2 Formation by express agreement

> **Definition** The principal expressly appoints the agent to act for him.

Apart from one exception, no formality is required. The appointment may be oral, in writing or by deed. The one exception is that if the agent is to be empowered to execute deeds on behalf of the principal his appointment must be by deed and is referred to as a **power of attorney**. The agreement appointing the agent will usually set out the extent of the agent's authority (express authority) although this may be extended by implication (implied or usual authority) or by estoppel (apparent/ostensible authority).

The agreement may, but will not necessarily, be a contract. If the appointment is by contract all the rules of contract will apply to its formation and termination. An agreement will not be a contract where, for example, no consideration is paid to the agent.

2.3 Formation by implied agreement

> **Definition** Even where there is no express agreement whereby the principal appoints the agent an agreement may be implied from their conduct towards each other or their relationship.

Where one person (the principal) places another in a position in which it would usually be accepted, either by general custom or by the custom in a particular trade, that the person in that position would have the authority to act for the principal, that person will be impliedly appointed to act as agent for the principal. For example, an auctioneer of land will become the agent for the buyer when he accepts the buyer's bid by banging the hammer. The auctioneer will have been expressly appointed by the seller. On the fall of the hammer he will also become the agent of the buyer for the purpose of signing the memorandum of sale and purchase. When he signs, both parties are bound.

The agency is derived from the implied mutual consent of the principal and agent to an agency relationship. This should not be confused with agency by estoppel which is created by representations by the principal to a third party that a person is his agent, and the third party relies on it (see below).

A relationship which is described in some texts as an example of agency by implied agreement is cohabitation of a man and a woman. Such cohabitation, whether the man and woman are married or just 'living together', carries the implication that the woman has the authority to pledge the man's credit (ie, order goods for which he will be liable for payment) for domestic necessaries suitable for his lifestyle. Necessaries include food, household items, and clothes for himself and their children which are appropriate to the couple's lifestyle even if beyond the man's means. Expensive items inappropriate to their lifestyle are not necessaries. The implication arises only where they are living together and may be rebutted:

- if the goods are not necessaries in that the woman already had sufficient supply of them or had sufficient allowance with which to buy them;

- by warning third parties not to supply goods on credit;

- by forbidding the woman to pledge his credit: this will end her 'implied authority' (however, if the man in the past has paid for goods ordered by the woman he will have to give notice to the people he has paid previously (ie, the third parties) to end her apparent or ostensible authority (see below)).

2.4   Formation by ratification

Meaning of ratification

A person may purport to enter into a contract as an agent although he has no authority to do so either because no agency exists or because he is acting beyond the scope of his authority. If the principal so chooses he may adopt the contract: this is called ratification.

Effect of ratification

Ratification operates retrospectively ie, once it occurs the effect is as if the purported agent had had authority at the date he purported to make the contract. This principle, which can have startling results, was established in **Bolton Partners v Lambert [1888]** and has since been followed in **Presentaciones Musicales SA v Secunda [1994].**

Bolton Partners v Lambert [1889]

Facts: A was an agent of Bolton Partners and purported to accept an offer from Lamber. A, however, was acting beyond the scope of his authority in so doing. Lambert then withdrew his offer (remember the rule of offer and acceptance that an offer can be revoked at any time before acceptance). Bolton Partners then ratified A's unauthorised acceptance.

Held: The ratification of Bolton Partners dated back to the date of A's purported acceptance. Thus A's purported acceptance has full legal effect as from the time of A's act. Accordingly Lambert's revocation, being after acceptance, was too late.

Presentaciones Musicales SA v Secunda [1994]

Facts: In 1988 solicitors to PMSA, but acting without authority, started legal action against Secunda by issuing a writ. In 1991 PMSA ratified what the solicitors had done.

Held: The 1991 ratification meant that the writ was backdated to 1988 and thus Secunda's argument that the action had become statute-barred on expiry of the limitation period in 1990 failed.

There are some limitations on this retrospective effect of ratification. Thus in **Warehousing & Forwarding Co of East Africa v Jafferali [1964]** an offer was validly revoked despite the principal's subsequent ratification of the agent's earlier acceptance because the 'acceptance' had been made expressly subject to ratification (and therefore, not being unconditional, was not in law an acceptance at all). In **Bird v Jones [1850]** ratification was held ineffective to divest an outside party of rights which had in the meantime vested in him.

Where ratification is effective it not only validates the contract which the agent has made but also relieves him from any liability to the principal for acting beyond his authority and also relieves him from any liability to the third party for breach of warranty of authority. It will not confer authority on the agent for future transactions.

Conditions for ratification. The doctrine has been criticised (mainly because of the possible oppressive effect on the third party) and ratification is therefore only possible under the following conditions:

(a) The agent, in making the contract, must purport to act as an agent and must name or clearly identify his principal. For example in

Keighley, Maxsted v Durant [1901]

An agent purchased wheat at a price which was higher than that which he had been authorised to pay. The agent had not revealed that he was acting as an agent when he bought the wheat and because of this the House of Lords held that the principal was not liable for breach of contract when he refused to accept delivery of the wheat, even though he had purported to ratify the contract of sale.

(b) The principal must be in existence and competent to contract when the contract is made and ratified

Kelner v Baxter [1866]

Facts: the plaintiff sold wine to the defendant who purported to act as agent for a company which was about to be formed. When it was formed, the company attempted to ratify the contract made by the defendant.

Held: the company could not do so, since it was not in existence when the contract was made.

(c) At the time of ratification the principal must either have full knowledge of what has been done on his behalf or be willing to adopt the agent's acts whatever they might prove to be.

(d) The principal cannot ratify the contract in part only. Any such attempt will operate as ratification of the whole contract.

(e) The principal must ratify in time, either before the time fixed for performance of the contract or, if no time is fixed, within a reasonable time.

(f) The principal must signify his intention to ratify. This may be by express affirmation of the contract; it may be by conduct although mere inactivity is insufficient.

Cornwal v Wilson [1750]

Facts: the agent bought some goods in excess of the price authorised by the principal. The principal objected to the purchase but sold some of the goods.

It was **held** that he had ratified the unauthorised act by selling the goods.

The principal cannot, of course, ratify a void or illegal contract.

2.5   Formation by estoppel

> **Definition**   Estoppel is the doctrine which 'estops', or prevents, a person from denying representations he has made to others either by word or conduct.

It has been discussed in relation to contracts generally earlier in the studytext. In the law of agency it arises when a person (the principal) by words or conduct holds out another as having authority to make contracts on his behalf (ie, to act as his agent). The principal is estopped or prevented from denying that the person has this authority and is bound by such contracts as if he had expressly authorised them.

The authority which the agent appears to have rests on the representations (or 'holding out') by the principal that the agent has authority and is called **apparent** or **ostensible** authority. There is not necessarily any agreement between the principal and agent and the agent need not be, although he generally is, aware of the existence of the representation.

The doctrine operates:

- Where a person allows another who is not his agent at all to appear (ie, holds him out) as his agent. For example, P tells C that he has taken A into partnership and A orders goods from C for the firm. P will be liable for the goods even if the firm is a sham. Another example is where a board of directors of a company allow one of the directors to act as a managing director even though he has not been properly appointed. A managing director will usually have extensive actual authority to act as agent for the company. By allowing the person to act as managing director the board will be estopped from denying he has the usual authority of a managing director.

- Where a principal fails to notify third parties who have dealt with his agent that the agent's authority has been terminated - as in the examples above where the wife continues to pledge her husband's credit after he has forbidden her to do so.

- Where the principal allows his agent to appear to have (or 'holds him out' as having) more authority than he actually has by agreement. This can be done by appointing someone to a position which usually carries with it the authority to make certain contracts but specifically forbidding him to make such contracts. For example, appointing a person as managing director of a large company and forbidding him to enter into contracts of more than £100 without the board's consent. If he orders goods worth £1,000 the board may be estopped from denying his apparent authority as it is usually within such a managing director's authority to make such contracts for the company.

To create apparent or ostensible authority by estoppel there must be a **representation**:

- express or implied from **conduct**

- by the **principal**

- to a **third party** who **relied** on it

- that the **agent has authority** to enter into a contract on behalf of the principal of a kind within the scope of the apparent authority.

This analysis of the relevant principles was set down in the following case.

Freeman and Lockyer v Buckhurst Park Properties [1964]

Facts: Kapoor, a property developer, and Hoon, formed a private company which purchased Buckhurst Park Estate. The board of directors consisted of Kapoor and Hoon and a nominee of each. The company's articles gave the company power to appoint a managing director but none was appointed. Kapoor, however, acted as such with the board's knowledge and consent. He instructed the plaintiffs, a firm of architects, to do work for the company which was completed. The company refused to pay, claiming that Kapoor had no authority to bind the company to this type of transaction.

Held: Kapoor had been held out as having apparent authority to enter into this transaction by those having actual authority to commit the company in this way, ie, the board. The company was therefore estopped from denying to anyone who had entered into a contract with him in reliance upon such apparent authority that he had authority to contract on behalf of the company.

2.6   Formation by necessity

If one person, A, is entrusted with another's property and an emergency arises requiring action to preserve that property then the person holding the property may take the necessary action on behalf of the owner. Because of the necessity such authority is implied.

G N Railway v Swaffield [1874]

Facts: a horse was sent by rail and on its arrival at its destination there was no one to collect it. The railway incurred the expense of stabling the horse for the night, and sought to recover the stabling costs from the owner.

Held: the railway was an agent of necessity which had implied authority to incur the expense in question, and also therefore the right to recover expenses.

Agency of necessity is confined within narrow limits. All four of the following conditions must be satisfied.

(a)   P's property is entrusted to 'A'. It seems that there is no agency of necessity where a person who has no existing responsibility for the other's property takes charge of it. The most usual examples of agency of necessity are perishable goods entrusted to a carrier such as a ship or railway company.

(b)   An emergency arises, making it necessary for 'A' to act in the way he did.

Prager v Blatspiel [1924]

Facts: A bought skins as agent for P but was unable to send them to P because of prevailing war conditions. A was unable to communicate with P and he sold the skins before the end of the war.

Held: A was not an agent of necessity. There was no emergency necessitating action: he could have stored the skins until the end of the war.

(c)   'A' is unable to communicate with 'P' to obtain his instructions.

Springer v GWR [1921]

Facts: a consignment of fruit was found by the carrier to be going bad. The carrier sold the consignment locally instead of delivering it to its destination.

Held: the carrier was not an agent of necessity because he could have obtained new instructions from the true owner.

(d)   The action 'A' took was in good faith in the sense of being in P's interests and not merely for A's own convenience - **GNR v Swaffield [1974]**.

Conclusion An agency can be formed by either express or implied agreement, under the doctrine of estoppel, by ratification or for reasons of necessity.

2.7   Activity

Petra authorised her agent Anton to buy curtain fabric at a specific price. However, Anton bought the fabric from Tilly even though it was at a higher price. Anton bought the fabric in his own name and Tilly was not aware that Anton was acting as an agent. Anton however did intend to buy the fabric for Petra. Petra agreed to take delivery of the fabric and then decided not to. Is Petra obliged to take delivery of the fabric?

2.8   Activity solution

Petra is not liable to Tilly and not obliged to take delivery of the fabric as Petra could not ratify Anton's contract with Tilly as Tilly was not aware that Petra existed.

3   THE AUTHORITY OF AN AGENT

3.1   Introduction

The ability of the agent to bind the principal depends on his having the authority to act, which can be created in any of the ways set out above. As long as the agent acts within the scope of his authority the principal will be bound.

3.2   Actual authority

Definition Actual authority is the authority which the principal has agreed the agent shall have.

It can be:

(a)   **Express actual authority** - ie, expressly given by the principal.

(b)   **Implied actual authority** - ie, impliedly given by the principal either:

(i)   to do everything necessarily and ordinarily incidental to the carrying out of the activity expressly authorised (called **implied** or sometimes **incidental authority**); or

(ii)   to do whatever an agent in that trade, profession or business would usually have the authority to do (called **usual authority**), eg, a managing director of a company has usual authority to act for a company in all commercial matters connected with managing the business.

Note: actual authority (express or implied) cannot exist to do an act which has been forbidden by the principal.

3.3   Apparent or ostensible authority

> **Definition** Apparent or ostensible authority is the authority of an agent as it appears to others, based on representations by the principal (ie, by estoppel), to the third party.

3.4   Usual authority

Although the terminology set out above is widely accepted there are difficulties, particularly with the term 'usual authority', which can be used in three different senses:

(a)   As a form of implied authority as above eg, when a board of directors of a company appoints a managing director they impliedly agree that he shall have the usual authority of a managing director.

(b)   As a form of apparent authority as in the example given above, where a board of directors appoint a managing director but specifically limit his authority to ordering goods worth £100 or less and requiring him to ask the board's approval on any orders above £100. If he orders goods worth £1,000 without the board's approval the company may still be liable to pay for them if £1,000 orders are within the usual authority of a managing director and the board has not given notice of the limits on the authority of their managing director. Because of the board's limitation the usual authority here cannot be implied; it can only be apparent.

(c)   As an independent type of authority where an **undisclosed principal** is bound by a contract made by an agent which is a type of contract which an agent in such a position would usually have the authority to make but in fact his authority has been withdrawn. The leading case is **Watteau v Fenwick [1891].**

Facts: in this case Humble owned a hotel which he sold to Fenwick who employed Humble as manager. Humble's name remained over the door of the hotel. Fenwick specifically forbade Humble from ordering cigars on credit. However, Humble did order cigars from Watteau on credit. Watteau gave credit to Humble and had never heard of Fenwick. It was usual to supply cigars to such hotels. Watteau discovered Fenwick's existence and sued him for the price of the cigars.

Held: the real principal Fenwick was liable for all acts of his agent, Humble, which were within the authority usually conferred on an agent of that particular kind, even though Humble had never been held out by Fenwick as his agent and the actual authority given to Humble by Fenwick had been exceeded.

In this type of case it cannot be said that the agent had actual authority, in view of the specific limitations. Nor can it be said that he has apparent authority as the principal was undisclosed and could not have made representations.

3.5   Actual and apparent authority

Recent discussions, such as that in **Freeman & Lockyer v Buckhurst Park Properties** above, state the principles of agency based on actual and apparent authority. In that case Diplock LJ in restating the agency principle said:

"It is necessary at the outset to distinguish between an 'actual' authority of an agent on the one hand, and an 'apparent' or 'ostensible' authority on the other. Actual and apparent authority are quite independent of one another. Generally, they coexist and coincide, but either may exist without the other and their relative scopes may be different."

An agent's apparent authority may be greater than his actual authority, eg, where restrictions have been placed on his authority, eg, as managing director of a company, but the principal has not notified third parties of these restrictions. His actual authority may exceed his apparent authority, eg, where the principal specifically gives him more authority than an agent in his position would usually have, but third parties are unaware of this.

> **Conclusion** An agent may have actual authority which has either been expressed or implied or alternatively his authority may be apparent or ostensible.

3.6 Agent acting without authority

If an agent acts without any authority (actual, apparent or possibly usual authority in the sense established by **Watteau v Fenwick**) and purports to negotiate a contract on behalf of an alleged principal with a third party:

(a)   the alleged principal will not be bound;

(b)   there is no contract between the agent and the third party as the third party did not intend to contract with the agent personally;

(c)   the agent will have impliedly warranted to the third party that he had authority and he will be liable to the third party for breach of warranty of authority.

If an agent acts in excess of his actual authority the principal will be bound if he has acted within his apparent authority (or possibly usual authority in the sense established by **Watteau v Fenwick**) but the agent may be liable to the principal for breach of their agreement.

4 LIABILITY OF AGENT AND PRINCIPAL TO THIRD PARTIES ON THE CONTRACT

4.1 Introduction

When ascertaining the liability of an agent or his principal it is important to distinguish between situations where the principal is disclosed and situations where the principal is not disclosed.

4.2 Principal disclosed

In the normal case the agent discloses to the third party that he is acting as an agent for a named principal or at least for some principal even if not named. The general rule is that the agent is not then liable on the contract nor can he enforce it. The contract is between the principal and the third party.

There are however certain exceptions:

(a)   The agent may in signing the contract for his principal accept personal liability. In particular the agent is liable on a deed or bill of exchange if he signs it in his own name.

(b)   Where by custom of the trade the agent is liable.

(c)   If the agent purports to act for a named principal who does not exist ie, is fictitious.

(d)   If the agent, when required, refuses to disclose the identity of the principal.

(e)   If a person purports to act on behalf of a company which is not yet incorporated - S36C Companies Act 1985.

Where the agent purports to act for an unnamed principal he can subsequently declare himself the true principal if it is consistent with the description of the supposed unnamed principal and the third party cannot show that he was not willing to contract with the agent.

4.3   Principal not disclosed (the doctrine of the undisclosed principal)

The agent may, of course, make a contract without disclosing that he has a principal for whom he is acting. The agent will then appear to be the principal. When the other party discovers the true position he may at his option hold the agent bound by the contract or treat the principal as bound. However, if he obtains judgement against one then he is barred from suing the other.

The undisclosed principal can usually intervene and claim against the third party provided:

(a)   The terms of the contract are consistent with agency.

Humble v Hunter [1948]

Facts: an agent entered into a contract to charter his principal's ship and signed as **owner.**

Held: this was not consistent with him acting as an agent and the principal could not sue on the contract.

(b)   The agent had the authority to act for the principal when he made the contract.

(c)   The third party cannot show that he had wanted to deal with the agent and no-one else, eg, the agent was well known as possessing certain skills which were necessary for performance of the contract. This is similar to the rules on unilateral mistake of identity in contract law.

If the principal does intervene and claims against the third party he thereby makes himself liable. The agent remains liable to be sued and entitled to sue on the contract.

Conclusion   If an agent discloses that he is an agent then generally the agent is not liable on the contract. If an agent does not disclose that he has a principal then the third party has a choice: he may sue either the principal or the agent on the contract, but not both.

5   RELATIONSHIP BETWEEN PRINCIPAL AND AGENT

5.1   Introduction

Agency is a relationship between the principal and the agent. This may be a contractual relationship and the rights and duties of agent and principal will depend on the terms of the contract. However, where there is no contract (eg, agent undertakes to act without pay, ie, consideration by the principal) or where there is a contract but the terms are not clear the rights and duties of agent and principal will be implied by the common law. These general rules are set out below as the common law duties of the agent and the common law duties of the principal.

5.2   Duties of an agent to his principal

(a)   To perform the agency by obeying his principal's lawful instructions - unless he is acting gratuitously, an agent is liable in damages if he fails to carry out his instructions.

Turpin v Bilton [1843]

Facts: an insurance broker, in return for a fee, agreed to arrange insurance for P's ship. He failed to do so. The ship was lost at sea.

Held: the broker had failed to perform the agency and was liable to P in damages for the loss.

Note that an agent will not be liable if he fails to perform an act which is illegal or void.

(b)   To perform the agency with reasonable care and skill. What is reasonable will depend on the circumstances. In general a professional and paid agent would be expected to show a greater degree of care and skill than an unpaid amateur.

(c)   To render an account when required (monetary and factual).

(d)   To act personally and not to delegate his authority, except:

     (i)   when expressly or impliedly authorised by the principal to delegate;
     (ii)   where delegation is customary;
     (iii)   in case of necessity; or
     (iv)   where the acts delegated are purely ministerial eg, simple clerical tasks.

(e)   To act in good faith - the fiduciary duty.

5.3   The fiduciary duty

This duty has a number of different, but overlapping, aspects:

- An agent must not allow his personal interests to conflict with those of his principal.

  An agent who sells his own property to his principal (or vice versa) breaches this duty.

  Armstrong v Jackson [1917]

  Facts: a stockbroker, who was appointed to buy shares for his principal, sold the principal his own shares without disclosing this fact.

  It was **held** that this was a breach of fiduciary duty and the principal could avoid the contract and recover his money.

- An agent must not make a secret profit. Thus, for example, he must disclose to his principal the receipt of any gift or commission. Where the secret profit takes the form of a payment from a third party who is aware that he is dealing with an agent, it is called a 'bribe'.

- An agent must maintain confidentiality about his principal's affairs.

5.4   Remedies for breach of duty

- Every breach of duty is a breach of the agency agreement and renders the agent liable in damages to the principal for any loss. See for example **Turpin v Bilton [1843].**

  The principal may have an action for damages against the third party where he is party to the breach and the breach is fraudulent (as is the case with a bribe).

- Where the breach is serious (as is always the situation where the agent is dishonest) the principal may dismiss the agent and refuse to pay him his remuneration.

Boston Deep Sea Fishing v Ansell [1888]

Facts: A (a manager director of a company) agreed with suppliers that he would receive a commission on any of their goods which he arranged for the company to order.

Held: the company was entitled to dismiss him (and to recover the commissions from him.)

- The principal may recover any benefit from the agent. See **Boston Deep Sea Fishing v Ansell [1888]**.

- Where the agent sells his own property to the principal (or vice versa) the principal may avoid the contract. See **Armstrong v Jackson [1917]**.

- Where the third party is fraudulently party to the breach (as is the case with a bribe) the principal may avoid the contract with the third party.

- Both to receive and to offer a bribe is a criminal offence. Thus in this situation the principal could report the matter to the authorities for the purpose of prosecution.

5.5 Activity

Alf has been appointed to buy cars on behalf of Pat. Unknown to Pat, Alf enters into an arrangement with Tom that Tom will pay Alf a secret £100 commission on every car Alf buys from him.

Advise Pat.

5.6 Activity solution

Alf is in breach of fiduciary duty in that he has made a secret profit in the form of a bribe. Pat may take any or all of the following actions:

(a)   he may dismiss Alf

(b)   he may refuse to pay Alf his remuneration

(c)   he may recover any bribe from Alf

(d)   he may sue Alf or Tom for any loss

(e)   he may avoid any contract with Tom

(f)   he may report both Alf and Tom to the police with a view to a criminal prosecution for corruption.

5.7 Duties of a principal to his agent

The principal is under a duty to indemnify the agent for all acts performed, expenses incurred and liability arising from the proper performance by the agent of his duties.

The other duty of the principal is to pay the agent his agreed remuneration. The case law on this duty relates almost entirely to claims by estate agents for their commission on the sale of property. Where the sale goes through to a purchaser found by the estate agent there is usually no difficulty. He has performed his duty and is clearly entitled to commission out of the proceeds of the sale.

However, an estate agent is not entitled to commission unless a purchaser introduced by him signs a contract and completes the purchase or the agent's appointment states in explicit terms that the mere introduction of a person willing to purchase is sufficient and he introduces such a person. The presumption is that commission is to be payable only on completion of the sale and very clear words are needed to establish entitlement for anything else.

If, however, the house owner signs the contract and then refuses to complete the sale the agent is usually entitled to commission. It is not his fault if the sale is not completed.

If the property is sold by the owner direct or through some other agent, the agent's rights depend on the terms of his appointment. The words **sole agent** do not prevent the owner from selling direct (and not paying commission to the agent as compensation) but they do preclude appointing another agent.

5.8   Activity

An agent is to purchase a yacht for his principal but instead buys a yacht for himself and resells it to his principal at a profit.

What is this an example of and how would the courts deal with it?

5.9   Activity solution

This is an example of a **secret profit** and the profit would have to be given back to the principal. (*Note*: the fact of this activity closely follow those of a decided case - **Lucifero v Castel**). It is also likely that this conflict of interest, being dishonesty, would also enable the principal to dismiss the agent, refuse to pay him his remuneration and to avoid the contract.

6   TERMINATION OF AGENCY

6.1   Ways of terminating agency

A contract of agency may be terminated in the same way as any other contract, by performance, agreement, breach or frustration. In addition, there are certain rules which apply to termination of agency.

6.2   Termination by complete performance

Termination can be by complete performance: in an agency for a particular transaction where the agent completes the transaction; or by expiration of time where the agency was for a fixed period and the period expires.

6.3   Termination by unilateral revocation or renunciation

Termination can be by unilateral revocation (by the principal) or renunciation (by the agent). If the principal and agent are contractually bound there may be an action for breach of contract if the terms of the contract eg, as to notice are not followed. The revocation or renunciation will terminate the agency even if there is a breach of contract, unless the agency is one which is irrevocable.

[Definition]   (i)   **where the agent's authority is coupled with an interest it is irrevocable** during the subsistence of that interest because the agency has been created to protect that interest eg, X owes Y money and appoints Y as his agent to sell some of X's property to pay the debt;

            (ii)   **where the agent has started to perform his duties and incurred liabilities** eg, to pay a third party, the agency is irrevocable in that the agent is entitled to be reimbursed for the payments due to the third party even if the principal forbids them;

(iii) **in certain cases statute provides that the agent's authority cannot be revoked** eg, Powers of Attorney Act 1971 provides that certain powers of attorney are irrevocable while the donee of the power retains an interest to be protected.

6.4 Operation of law

Agency will be terminated by operation of law in the following ways:

(a) Death of the agent or principal, even if the agent is unaware of the principal's death.

(b) Insanity of the agent or principal. However, the Enduring Powers of Attorney Act 1985 provides that powers of attorney created in the manner prescribed by the Act may endure after the donor becomes insane.

(c) Bankruptcy of the principal and of the agent if it makes the agent unfit to carry out his duties.

(d) Frustration eg, where the agency becomes unlawful because the principal becomes an enemy alien, or military service makes it impossible for the agent to perform his duties.

6.5 The effect of termination

Termination of agency ends the agent's actual authority. However, he may still appear to have authority to third parties who have not had notice of the termination of his actual authority. The principal will be bound by acts of the agent within this apparent/ostensible authority unless the agent's authority was terminated by the death or bankruptcy of the principal. There are conflicting cases on termination by insanity.

6.6 Activity

J lends money to F on condition that F gives him the authority to sell an item of J's property in order to repay the loan. Can F revoke the authority before the loan is paid?

6.7 Activity solution

The authorisation was coupled with an interest and therefore the authority cannot be revoked until the loan has been repaid.

7 AGENCY AND COMPANIES

7.1 Introduction

As a company is an artificial legal entity it must act through humans. As with the general law of agency the company will only be bound by the acts of its human agents where those agents are acting within their authority, actual or apparent.

The company (acting through its board) may give an agent actual authority or an agent may have apparent authority because of representations made by the board on the company's behalf.

Two particular ways in which a representation may be made are now further considered. These are special adaptions of the normal rules of agency.

7.2   Authority by virtue of appointment to a particular office

Certain officers of a company have power to bind the company in contract by virtue of their appointment to a particular office or position. Their resulting authority is variously termed implied, apparent, ostensible or usual. In conformity with the general rules of agency this paragraph will use the term 'usual' authority.

The position of a managing director carries usual authority to bind the company in all contracts of a commercial nature such as the ordering of goods for the company's factory and the borrowing of money.

The position of company secretary carries usual authority to bind the company in all contracts of an administrative nature such as engagement of office staff, purchase of office equipment and hiring of cars - **Panorama Developments v Fidelis Furnishing Fabrics [1971]**. This leading case is considered further in company law.

The position of director (not being a 'special' position like managing director or finance director) carries no authority by virtue of the office - **Freeman & Lockyer v Buckhurst Park Properties**.

7.3   Authority by virtue of holding out

This is very close to agency by estoppel and arises where the board has allowed a director to act as if he were managing director. The company is then estopped from denying to third parties who, relying on the board's representation, believed the director was managing director and therefore had authority usual to that position. The leading case on this doctrine of holding out - **Freeman & Lockyer v Buckhurst Park Properties** is also considered further in company law.

8   AGENCY AND PARTNERSHIPS

8.1   Partnerships as unincorporated associations

> *(Definition)*   A partnership is the relation which subsists between persons carrying on a business in common with a view to profit.

A partnership is simply an interpersonal relationship between partners. Although the partnership is often referred to as a firm there is no question of the firm being a corporate body as a person distinct from the partners. The partnership is an unincorporated association of the natural persons who are the partners. The law recognises that these people have formed an association. The importance of this recognition is that the acts of one member of the association may make the other members liable. Thus, if one partner enters into a contract his co-partners may be liable on it.

8.2   Liability of partners

The importance of the difference between a company and a partnership is that the partnership (the firm) is not a separate legal person. Thus, if the **firm** owes a creditor money he is entitled to be paid and if the firm's assets are insufficient the partners are personally liable to the extent of their own personal wealth (ie, they could be made bankrupt if they have insufficient personal money to pay the debt - there is no limit on their liability to the creditors (unless it is a limited partnership which is rare).

8.3   Formation of a partnership

No formality is required to create a partnership.

A relationship between two or more people will be a partnership whether or not they intended it to be (with the result that each may be liable for the other's acts) if it falls within the definition of a partnership in S1 Partnership Act 1890 which states that a partnership is the relation which subsists between persons carrying on a business in common with a view of profit. An entitlement to a share of the profits is evidence that the recipient is a partner, but the entire relationship must be examined and if it comes within the definition the recipient is a partner.

One can therefore be a partner unintentionally (by mistake).

8.4   Good faith

Partnership is by its nature a relationship of extreme good faith *(uberrimae fides)*. In their dealings with each other and in the exercise of their rights partners must observe this principle, though it is not stated in the Act.

Partners are bound to render true accounts and **full information** of all things affecting the partnership to any partner or to his legal representatives.

Every partner must **account** to the firm for any **benefit** derived by him without the consent of the other partners from any **transaction concerning the partnership** or from any use by him of the **partnership property name or business connection.** This rule applies to transactions undertaken after dissolution of a partnership by death of a partner and before its affairs have been wound up.

If a partner without the consent of the other partners carries on **any business of the same nature as and competing with** that of the firm, he must account for, and pay over to the firm, all profits made by him in that business.

Note: the similarities of these duties with those of an agent to his principal.

8.5   Partnership agreement

Subject to the overriding principle of good faith, partners may fix and vary their mutual rights and obligations by agreement as they see fit. The agreement may be express or implied by conduct. In the absence of agreements to the contrary, the Partnership Act implies terms which regulate the rights and obligations of partners for example that all partners shall profit equally and have an equal say in the management of the business.

8.6   Partners as agents

As discussed above there are two important differences between companies and partnerships which you should understand when considering agency in partnerships.

(i)   the partnership (firm) is not a separate artificial legal entity, it is merely an association of human legal persons;

(ii)   the partners are, usually, both owners and managers of the business and there is no split as there often is in companies.

The consequence of these two differences is that, generally, each partner will take part in the decisions made about the firm's business and will be bound by those decisions. The partnership as a whole is the principal. Each partner is part of the principal. Each partner will also deal with outsiders on behalf of the partnership. When so acting he is an agent of the firm (the principal) of which he is also part.

Conclusion Thus a partner is an agent of the firm and of the other partners. They may, therefore, be bound by contracts which he makes. On similar principles they may also be liable for his torts, misappropriations of property and certain other acts.

But the power of a partner thus to impose liability on his fellow partners (and of course on himself) is not unlimited. For each type of liability restricting conditions are laid down by the Act.

The Partnership Act 1890 makes specific provision as to the manner in which partners may bind their co-partners. The provisions in that Act which have been supplemented by case law are set out below.

8.7   Contract

By S5 PA 1890:

'Every partner is an agent of the firm and his other partners for the purpose of the business of the partnership; and the acts of every partner who does any act for carrying on in the usual way business of the kind carried on by the firm of which he is a member bind the firm and his partners, unless the partner so acting has in fact no authority to act for the firm in the particular manner, and the person with whom he is dealing either knows that he has no authority, or does not know or believe him to be a partner.'

8.8   Partner's authority

The extent of the partner's authority as an agent of the firm in making contracts can be expressed in four propositions:

(a)   subject to (c) and (d) below a partner has **apparent authority** to enter into contracts for carrying on the business of the firm in the usual way and in the firm's name and third parties may deal with him on that basis;

(b)   his **actual authority** may be more or less than his apparent authority. Actual authority is what the other partners have conferred on him expressly or by implication.

(c)   a **restriction** which seeks to set actual authority at less than apparent authority is only effective if the person with whom the partner is dealing either knows of the restriction or is unaware that he is a partner;

(d)   an **extension** of actual authority beyond the normal limits of apparent authority may be effected either by:

(i)   **express authorisation** given by the other partners; or

(ii)   by their **holding out** or representing that he has greater authority than he has in fact been given: S14 PA 1890. Holding out usually occurs where the other partners acquiesce in a partner repeatedly exceeding his actual authority.

It is difficult, however, to reconcile proposition (c) with the decision in **Watteau v Fenwick** because in that case the person dealing with the agent believed that the agent was acting for himself and was unaware that he had a principal. This conflicts with the final words of S5 quoted above, but this is a case on general agency principles and not partnership as such.

8.9   Activity

What is the point of law from **Watteau v Fenwick**?

8.10 Activity solution

If a principal allows an agent to appear to be acting for himself than the agent may have all the usual powers of a person in that position, even if this usual authority exceeds the agent's actual authority.

8.11 The apparent authority of a partner

The effect of the analysis above is that the apparent authority of the partner is the starting point or baseline. Having determined what is the apparent authority (also called usual, normal or ostensible authority) one has to consider whether it has been effectually increased or reduced and whether the contract is within the limits of authority thus determined.

Apparent authority of a partner is limited to contracts for the purposes of **business of the kind** carried on by the firm. But the test is an external one ie, what does the 'outside world in general' regard as within the scope of the business.

Mercantile Credit Co v Garrod [1962]

Facts: Garrod and a partner were garage proprietors, effecting car repairs and letting lock-up garages. The partner unilaterally pledged the firm's credit in motor dealing contracts.

Held: sale of cars (expressly excluded from the firm's business by the partnership agreement) was held to be business of the kind usually carried on by garage firms generally. The firm was therefore bound.

A partner's apparent authority is also confined to what he does in the firm name or expressly on its behalf: S6. If a partner purports to act for himself alone the firm will not be bound.

8.12 Business in the usual way

The test of what is carrying on the firm's business *in the usual way* has been developed into a list of transactions which are or are not within the limits of a partner's apparent authority. The general test is one of normal practice - which is not the same for all firms nor for all types of business. If one appoints an agent for business purposes that is an implied authorisation to do acts which are usually or normally done in the transaction of the relevant type of business. If one appoints a manager of a public house he has apparent authority to make those trade purchases of goods which are usually made by those who are in charge of a public house: **Watteau v Fenwick.**

Case law has distinguished between trading (commercial) partnerships and non-trading (professional) partnerships.

A trading or **commercial firm** has been rather narrowly interpreted as excluding firms which do not buy or sell goods in the course of their business. Thus the business of auctioneers (**Wheatley v Smithers [1907]**) and of cinema proprietors (**Higgins v Beauchamp [1914]**) is non-commercial for this purpose.

8.13 Apparent authority for all types of partnership

Partners in **any** firm (ie, commercial or professional) will have apparent authority to:

(a)   sell any goods or personal chattels of the firm;
(b)   buy goods of a kind necessary or usual in the business;
(c)   receive payment of sums owing to the firm and to issue receipts;
(d)   engage employees for the purpose of the firm's business;
(e)   employ a solicitor to defend an action against the firm or recover a debt.

8.14   Apparent authority in a commercial firm

Partners in a commercial or trading firm have the additional apparent authority to:

(a)   draw, accept, indorse, etc, bills of exchange and other negotiable instruments in the name of the firm;

(b)   borrow money on the credit of the firm and for that purpose pledge as security:

   (i)   goods or personal chattels of the firm; and

   (ii)   its real property by deposit of title deeds as an equitable mortgage.

8.15   Matters not covered by apparent authority

There are certain acts which are always outside the apparent authority of any partner and which must be expressly authorised by all the partners in order to bind the firm. These include:

(a)   execution of a **deed under seal**. For this the partner must have a power of attorney under seal from the other partners;

(b)   giving a **guarantee** on behalf of the firm (unless it is the custom of the trade);

(c)   **accepting shares** of a company, even if fully paid, in satisfaction of sums owing to the firm;

(d)   submitting a dispute to **arbitration**.

8.16   Sleeping partner

A **sleeping partner** is by reason of his status not ordinarily concerned in making contracts for the firm. He is liable for contracts made by an active partner in the exercise of his apparent authority: **Mercantile Credit v Garrod** (see above).

9   CHAPTER SUMMARY

Agency is the relationship whereby one person, the agent, is recognised in law as having the authority to act for the other, the principal, and alter his legal rights and duties. Unlike human persons a company must necessarily act through agents in order to make contracts. In partnerships the PA 1890 deems every partner an agent of each and every partner and of the firm.

In all situations the principal is bound to the third party only where the agent acts within his authority.

In all situations the agent will owe duties to his principal. These duties are both contractual and fiduciary. With partnerships and commercial agents the common law duties have been largely subsumed by statute.

10   POSTSCRIPT: COMMERCIAL AGENTS

10.1   Introduction

In early 1994 the Commercial Agents (Council Directive) Regulations 1993 - made in response to an EC directive - came into operation. The Regulations radically add to the common law duties which a principal owes to a commercial agent and vice versa.

10.2   Who is a commercial agent?

Definition   A self-employed intermediary who has continuing authority to negotiate the sale or purchase of goods on behalf of another person (the principal), or to negotiate and conclude the sale and purchase of goods on behalf of and in the name of that principal.

(Note:

- 'self employed' excludes employees, partners and directors

- 'continuing' excludes an agent who is appointed for a one-off transaction

- 'goods' excludes land and services*)*

10.3   Main provisions of the Regulations

(a)   **Written statement**.

Either side has the right to receive from the other, on request, a signed written document setting out the full terms of the agency contract.

(b)   **Commission**

The Regulations impose detailed duties as to when, where and in what circumstances commission is payable including in particular the duty of the principal to supply written information, so as to enable the agent to check the amount, not later than the end of the month following the quarter in which the commission became due.

(c)   **Termination**

(i)   If the agency is for an indefinite duration the agent has a right to the following minimum notice periods.

- one month for any termination during the first year

- two months for any termination in the second year

- three months for any termination in the third or subsequent years

(ii)   The agent has a right to compensation if his agency is ended

- by the principal (otherwise than for breach of duty by the agent)

- by the agent because of breach of duty by the principal (this is similar to constructive dismissal in employment law)

- because of the agent's age, illness or other incapacity in consequence of which he cannot reasonably be required to continue his activities.

If the agent is to claim compensation, he has a maximum of one year following termination in which to do so.

(d)   **Restraint of trade**

The Regulations permit a principal to restrict the agent's right to compete after the termination of the agency provided the restrictions

(i)   are in writing

(ii)   are related to the geographical areas of the agency or the group of customers of the agency

(iii)   operate for no more than two years following termination of the agency, and

(iv)   are reasonable under the general law (see covenants in restraint of trade).

11   SELF TEST QUESTIONS

11.1   What is agency? (1.1)

11.2   What are the five ways in which an agency may be created? (2.2 to 2.6)

11.3   What are the conditions necessary for ratification of a contract made by an agent? (2.4)

11.4   What is the doctrine of estoppel in agency law? (2.5)

11.5   What is actual authority? (3.2)

11.6   What is apparent authority? (3.3)

11.7   What is the effect of an agent acting without authority? (3.6)

11.8   What is the liability of an agent if he discloses a principal but does not name the principal? (4.2)

11.9   What are a principal's rights where an agent has received a bribe? (5.6)

11.10   What are the duties of a principal to his agent? (5.7)

11.11   How is the agency relationship terminated? (6)

11.12   What is the usual authority of a company secretary? (7.2)

11.13   What is the doctrine of holding out in relation to companies? (7.3)

11.14   What is a partnership? (8.1)

11.15   State S5 Partnership Act 1890 (8.7)

11.16   Define a commercial agent (10.2)

12   EXAMINATION TYPE QUESTIONS

12.1   Agency definitions

Explain, with illustrations, the meaning of the following terms used in the context of principal and agent:

(a)   breach of warranty of authority;

(5 marks)

(b)   ratification;

(5 marks)

(c)   apparent authority; and

(5 marks)

(d)   estoppel.

(5 marks)

(Total: 20 marks)

12.2   K and L partnership

(a)   Explain the various forms which the authority of an agent can take. How can this authority be terminated?

(12 marks)

(b)   K and L are partners in a business.

What is the legal position if:

(i)   They appoint M to buy goods on behalf of the business. They later become dissatisfied with M's work and write to him on 1 September telling him he is to cease acting on their behalf. On 7 September M purchases goods from N, and N invoices K and L for the goods;

(ii)   K, pretending to act on behalf of the business, borrows a large sum of money from the bank and disappears with the money?

(8 marks)

(Total: 20 marks)

12.3   Pataball Ltd

Pataball Ltd has recently been incorporated and intends to manufacture sports equipment. It employs Albert to purchase raw materials and Arthur to sell the finished product.

Explain:

(a)   how Pataball Ltd may acquire rights or incur liabilities when Albert makes a contract which was not previously authorised; and

(10 marks)

(b)   when Arthur may be held personally liable for a contract entered into on behalf of Pataball Ltd.

(10 marks)

(Total: 20 marks)

13 ANSWERS TO EXAMINATION TYPE QUESTIONS

13.1 Agency definitions

(a) An agent has power to make contracts between his principal and third parties because he is authorised to do so by the principal. If he is so authorised and keeps within the limits of his authority, the agent is not usually himself liable on the contract he makes – the contractual relationship is between the principal and the third party and the agent is merely the instrument through whom the contract is made.

However, anyone who says he is an agent when he is not, or, being an agent, exceeds his authority, is said to be in breach of warranty of authority. The third party cannot then sue the principal or supposed principal, but the agent is personally liable for breach of warranty of authority.

(b) Ratification arises when the principal ratifies so as to make valid an act performed by an agent on his behalf but either without authority or in excess of it. This may not be done unless the following conditions are fulfilled.

(i) the agent must have contracted expressly as an agent, naming the principal or making identification of the principal possible;

(ii) the principal must be in existence and capable of making the contract when it is made. It is too late if the principal later acquires contractual capacity. The best example of this is the case of **Kelner v Baxter.** In this case a company promoter agreed to buy wine for a hotel company which was in the process of being formed but did not then exist. It was held that the company when it was formed could not ratify the contract. Moreover, the promoter remained personally liable (for breach of warranty of authority) and had to pay for the wine himself;

(iii) the principal must at the time of ratification know all the facts or be prepared to ratify whatever his 'agent' has done, whether he knows the extent of it or not;

(iv) the whole of the agreement must be ratified. It is impossible to ratify in part.

(v) ratification must be within a reasonable time;

(vi) the principal must signify his intention to ratify: mere inactivity is not ratification.

(c) Apparent authority links closely with the estoppel aspect mentioned in (d) below. An agent may do what is normal for one in his position unless restricted by his agreement with his principal; he has an implied agreement to this effect.

To avoid the problem of an agent acting in the absence of authority of exceeding his authority, the principal should give notice to any third party of whose existence he is aware that the authority is restricted or has been withdrawn.

What could be an implied agreement (internally) between principal and agent can (externally) work an estoppel precluding the principal from denying that his agent has authority, unless he can show that the third party knew of the restriction placed on the agent's authority. This applies even if the agent has been held out as authorised to do something in excess of what is usual: usual authority can be extended by estoppel in this way.

(d) If the principal by words or conduct had made a statement of fact as to the agent's authority, a third party who acts on the statement may sue the principal on the footing that he is estopped (precluded) from going back on the statement. Estoppel can (as explained) extend an agent's authority to cover matters which an outsider cannot normally assume to be within the agent's authority. Estoppel is also important in determining whether there is an agency at all. If a person holds out another as his agent (by words or by conduct) he will be estopped from denying the agency as against anyone who has entered upon the holding out.

13.2   K and L partnership

(a)   Agency is the relationship which arises when one person, the agent, is recognised as being able to effect another person's, the principal's, legal rights and duties.

The terminology to describe an agent's authority is confused. However, in the case of **Freeman & Lockyer v Buckhurst Park Properties Ltd** the types of authority of an agent were reviewed. The agent's authority can be actual or apparent.

An agent's actual authority is the authority which has been agreed between himself and his principal. Thus, when he is appointed as agent he may be given express authority to do certain things on behalf of the principal. In addition, by virtue of the position he holds, he may have implied authority to do certain things. Thus, if he is appointed as sales manager of a business he will have the actual authority to do those things he is expressly told he can do. In addition he will be able to assume that he has authority to do other things which a person in his position would normally have the authority to do. What he is entitled to assume he has the authority to do will depend on the custom of the particular trade or business. Obviously if he is expressly told that this implied authority is limited then his actual authority will be so limited.

An agent's apparent authority is the authority which outsiders are entitled to assume he has. His apparent authority may be greater than his actual authority. An agent's apparent authority will depend on a holding out by the principal appointing a person to a position which usually carries with it certain authority. The outsider is entitled to assume that the agent has the usual authority of a person occupying that position. If, in fact, the agent has been told there are restrictions on this usual authority the outsider will not be affected by these restrictions unless he has notice of them. What is within the usual authority of an agent will depend on the custom of the particular trade or business.

An agent's actual authority can be terminated by:

(i)   agreement of the agent and principal

(ii)   complete performance of his duties or expiry of the term if the agency was for a fixed term

(iii)   act of one of the partners – revocation of authority by the principal or renunciation of authority by the Agent. (There may be a breach of contract).

(iv)   death of the agent or principal

(v)   insanity of the agent or principal

(vi)   bankruptcy of the principal and the agent if it makes the agent unfit to act

(vii)   frustration.

Even though an agent's actual authority has been terminated, his apparent authority may continue unless notice is given to third parties that the principal is no longer authorising the agent to act for him.

(b)   (i)   K and L have appointed M as their agent. He will have the actual authority to buy goods on their behalf. However, by notice they can revoke this authority. Whether in so revoking there is a breach of contract will depend on the terms of the original agreement between K and L and M. The letter of 1 September revokes M's actual authority. However, his apparent authority may continue unless K and L give notice of the termination of his actual authority. Whether K and L are liable on the contract made by M on 7 September will depend on whether N can argue that he was entitled to assume that M was still acting as agent for K and L ie, had notice been sent to him of the termination of M's authority, and was the contract of a type which would usually come within the authority of a person in M's position.

                 K and L as partners are joint principals and both are equally liable on the contracts made by M if N is successful in pleading that they came within M's apparent authority.

      (ii)   Under the Partnership Act 1890 partners are deemed to be agents of the firm and their co-partners and will bind them by acts done for a purpose apparently connected with the ordinary business of the firm. It would appear from the facts of the question that this is a trading partnership and, therefore, an individual partner will have the apparent authority to borrow on behalf of the firm. Whether this particular loan would come within the apparent authority of K as a partner in this firm will depend on the size of the loan and the business. Should the size of the loan put the bank on notice? In addition, one would need to know whether there were any restrictions on K's actual authority to bind the firm on loans made by him and whether the bank was aware of such restrictions. L could be made liable to repay the whole amount. He in turn could seek to recover the money from K if he can find him.

13.3   Pataball Ltd

Albert and Arthur are employed to negotiate contracts on behalf of Pataball Ltd; in this capacity they would be acting as agents of the company. In agency the acts of the agent will bind the principal providing the agent has authority to act.

(a)   Pataball may acquire rights as a result of Albert's negotiations if it decides to retrospectively ratify his unauthorised action. Ratification is only possible if Pataball had contractual capacity and was in existence when the contract was entered into.

        A principal is bound if the agent had authority to act. In this case Pataball would be liable if Albert acted within the scope of his usual or apparent authority. Usual authority is the authority vested in a person by virtue of his position. If it is usual for an agent of Albert's type to have certain powers, then a person dealing with Albert can assume that he has those powers, unless any restriction is known or suspected. Thus, in **Watteau v Fenwick** a company was liable for the unauthorised act of its agent because the third party had contracted with the agent in good faith and had no reason to suspect that the authority was restricted.

        Apparent authority occurs when the principal gives the third party the impression that the agent has authority. If that is the case the principal cannot subsequently deny the agent's authority. Thus, in **Hely-Hutchinson v Brayhead Ltd** the company had honoured unauthorised contracts negotiated by its chairman. It was held that the company could not then refuse to accept a subsequent unauthorised contract.

        Finally, Albert may acquire authority by necessity if an emergency arises which requires immediate action. If Albert, unable to contact Pataball, acted in good faith in Pataball's interest the company would be bound even though it gave no express authority.

(b)   The general rule is that an agent can neither sue, nor be sued on a contract concluded between his principal and a third party. However, in exceptional circumstances Arthur may be held liable.

If Arthur's conduct fails to reveal that he is an agent, so that the third party believes that he is dealing with Arthur as a principal, the third party would have the option of holding either Pataball or Arthur liable. If he actually sues one, he cannot later sue the other.

If Arthur signs the contract in his own name without indicating that he does so merely as an agent a court may not accept evidence that he was acting as an agent.

Furthermore, if Arthur warrants that he has authority which he does not in fact possess, a third party who relies on such warranty can sue him for breach of warranty of authority.

Finally, if Arthur is a *del credere* agent he may be liable to the third party. A *del credere* agent is usually a broker who has implied authority to contract on behalf of his principal. The special feature of this type of agency is that the agent agrees, in return for a commission, to guarantee payment of the price.

10 TORT: GENERAL PRINCIPLES

INTRODUCTION & LEARNING OBJECTIVES

Syllabus area 8c. Basic concepts. (Ability required 3).
Vicarious liability. (Ability required 3).
Defences in tort. (Ability required 3).
Remedies. (Ability required 3).

This chapter is designed to introduce students to the law of torts. In particular the area of vicarious liability is explained whereby someone other than the person who committed the tort might be liable.

This chapter will also consider the general defences to a tort that might be available if it is proved that a tort has been committed. Exemption clauses, limitation of action, death and remedies will also be considered.

When you have studied this chapter you should be able to do the following:

- Understand the concept of vicarious liability, and apply it in detail to employers and employees.

- Be aware of all the general defences and be able to describe 'volenti' and 'contributory negligence' in detail.

- Understand the effect the Unfair Contract Terms Act 1977 has on notices purporting to exempt a business from liability in negligence.

- Recognise who can sue in tort should the victim of the tort die.

- Outline the remedies of damages and injunction.

---

1 GENERAL PRINCIPLES

1.1 Introduction

The word 'tort' is derived from Norman French and means harm or wrong. The plaintiff's claim, generally, is that he has suffered loss eg, personal injury or damage to property, as a result of a wrong which was done to him by the defendant and the defendant should pay him money compensation (damages) for the loss suffered. In certain circumstances the plaintiff may also ask the court to order the defendant not to cause him harm (ie, grant an injunction).

1.2 Law of torts

The law of torts is the set of rules which determine when one person must pay another person compensation for harm wrongfully caused. It is basically common law, based on the decisions of the courts and covers a wide range of situations. Over the years a number of 'torts' have been recognised and rules established for determining whether the plaintiff's action will succeed or not. However, the law of torts is a developing field of law in that the rules relating to established torts develop and there is scope for the development of new torts.

1.3   What is a tort?

Definition   A 'tort' can be defined as a breach of a legal duty or infringement of a legal right arising independently of contract which gives rise to a claim for unliquidated damages.

*   Breach of legal duty or infringement of legal right - there is no liability in tort unless the law recognises that a legal duty or right exists which has been breached.

*   Arising independently of contract - no contractual relationship need exist for a claim to be made.

*   Claim for unliquidated damages - the compensation to be paid for the loss suffered is not a set amount, but is determined by the court.

1.4   Different torts

There are numerous different torts - all with different ingredients. The three torts of relevance to your examination are:

*   the tort of negligence - a creation of the common law;

*   the tort, breach of statutory duty - a creation of the common law but which, as its name suggests, depends for its detail on legislation;

*   the tort created by the Consumer Protection Act 1987 - called a 'statutory' tort - in relation to unsafe goods.

2   LIABILITY IN TORT

2.1   Who is liable?

The person who committed the tort (the tortfeasor) is always liable because it was his wrongful act. The injured person can always sue him. His liability is said to be personal. In certain circumstances the injured person may sue someone else, even though he took no part in the wrongful act: he is said to be vicariously liable.

Definition   Vicarious liability is the principle whereby a person is deemed liable for a tort committed by another.

Vicarious liability can arise in a number of circumstances.

*   By Ss10-12 Partnership Act 1890, **partners** are jointly and severally liable for the torts of other partners if the tort was committed in the ordinary course of the firm's business or if it was committed with the authority of the other partners.

*   A **principal** will be liable for the torts of his **agent** committed within the scope of his actual or apparent authority.

*   An **employer** may be vicariously liable for torts committed by his **employees.**

    This is the situation in which vicarious liability is examined in detail.

3   VICARIOUS LIABILITY OF AN EMPLOYER

3.1   Conditions

An employer will be liable for a tort of a worker if it is shown that:

(a)   he is an **employee** (under a contract of service) and not an independent contractor (under a contract for services); and

(b)   the tort was committed by the employee **in the course of his employment**, and not whilst the employee was on a 'frolic of his own'.

The first condition, that the worker must be an employee, is covered in detail in the chapter 'Employment: the contract of employment'.

3.2   Course of employment

Unless the employer has expressly authorised the conduct, he is vicariously liable only for those torts committed by his employee 'in the course of his employment'. In determining this difficult question, the courts pay regard to several factors.

•   A distinction is drawn between a wrongful way of doing something which the employee is authorised to do, and an act which the servant is not authorised to perform at all.

Limpus v London General Omnibus Co [1862]

Facts: the defendants' **driver** was forbidden to race with or obstruct other buses. He disobeyed these instructions and the plaintiff was injured.

Held: the company were held to be vicariously liable for his tort since he had merely done what he was authorised to do albeit in an improper and unauthorised manner.

Beard v London General Omnibus Co [1900]

Facts: a bus conductor, on his own initiative, turned round a bus at a terminus and negligently injured a third party.

Held: he was not acting within the course of his employment as it was not his job to drive buses, merely to act as conductor. He was on a frolic of his own.

Century Insurance Co Ltd v Northern Ireland Transport Board [1942]

Facts: the employers of a petrol-tanker driver were sued in tort when he, while transferring petrol, discarded a match after lighting a cigarette, thereby causing a violent explosion.

Held: his carelessness was held to be an unauthorised mode of doing that which he was employed to do. It therefore occurred 'in the course' of his employment. The employers were vicariously liable.

Warren v Henly's Ltd [1948]

Facts: the defendant's employee, a petrol attendant, wrongly accused the plaintiff of trying to drive away without paying. He used language threatening violence and the plaintiff paid the bill, called the police and told the defendant's employee that he would be reported to the defendant. The defendant's employee then assaulted and injured the plaintiff, who sued the defendant.

Held: the defendant was not liable since the acts were not of the class which the employee was authorised to perform; they were acts of personal vengeance. He was on a frolic of his own.

Twine v Bean's Express [1944]

Facts: a van driver was instructed not to give lifts. He did so, and the passenger was injured in a crash.

Held: 'in driving his van along a proper route he was acting within the scope of his employment whereas ... the other thing he was doing simultaneously was something totally outside the scope of his employment, namely giving a lift to a person who had no right whatsoever to be there ...' The employers were not vicariously liable.

Rose v Plenty [1976]

Facts: a milkman was prohibited from giving lifts on a milk float. However, he used a boy to help with weekend deliveries of milk, and this boy was injured.

Held: the defendant company was held vicariously liable because, despite its prohibition, the boy was on the milk float for the purpose of furthering the defendant's business, and this distinguished this case from **Twine v Bean's Express**.

- Even where an employee is acting fraudulently for his own personal gain this does not necessarily mean he is on a frolic of his own.

Lloyd v Grace, Smith & Co [1912]

Facts: the defendants, a firm of solicitors, employed a clerk to supervise conveyancing. The clerk tricked a client of the firm into signing documents which conveyed her property to himself. The clerk then sold the property and spent the money. The client sued the firm.

Held: the clerk was doing what he was employed to do, conveyancing, albeit in a fraudulent manner. The firm was vicariously liable.

Summary: it is not always easy to predict the court's decision as to 'course of employment' or 'frolic of employee's own'. The cases abound with fine line distinctions.

3.3   Indemnity

Where an employer is sued and pays the damages under the vicarious liability principle he has a right of full indemnity against the employee.

Lister v Romford Ice and Cold Storage Co Ltd [1957]

Facts: a company employed S to drive a lorry and he negligently injured his father who also worked for the company. The employer was held vicariously liable to the father; it paid him compensation and then sued S, the actual tortfeasor, for re-imbursement.

Held: it was entitled to a full re-imbursement.

3.4   Borrowed employees

A particular problem arises where an employee who is on secondment commits a tort. In the **Mersey Docks** case the House of Lords stated that there is a presumption that the permanent employer remains vicariously liable but that this presumption can be rebutted (with the result that the temporary employer becomes vicariously liable) if it can be shown that the temporary employer controls not only when and where the work is done but also **how** it is done.

Mersey Docks & Harbour Board v Coggins and Griffiths [1947]

Facts: an employee was employed by MDHB as a crane driver. MDHB entered into a contract with Coggins to hire a driver and a crane to Coggins. It was further agreed in the contract that the driver would be regarded as the employee of Coggins. Coggins told the crane driver what they required to be done but did not attempt to instruct him how to operate his crane. In doing the job for Coggins the crane driver injured X when he operated his crane negligently.

Held: the permanent (or general) employer, MDHB, was vicariously liable for the tort: the presumption had not been rebutted.

3.5   Independent contractors

An employer is never vicariously liable for the torts of independent contractors. The employer may, however, be personally liable in tort if he is in breach of his own **primary duty**, which may arise in three forms:

(a)   **Authorisation**

A person will be liable as a joint tortfeasor if he authorises or procures another to commit a tortious act.

Definition   A tortfeasor is a person who commits a tort.

Ellis v Sheffield Gas Consumers Co [1853]

Facts: the defendant company engaged an independent contractor to excavate a street which constituted an actionable nuisance.

Held: it was held liable.

(b)   **Non-delegable duties**

If a person is under a duty to ensure that care is taken, the fact that he has engaged an independent contractor is immaterial. Examples are:

(i)   where a strict personal liability is imposed on the employer eg, to install safe factory machinery, he cannot escape liability because he delegated the task to someone else:

Wilson & Clyde Coal v English [1938]

Facts: the employer engaged an independent contractor to design and ensure a safe system of work at the workplace. The independent contractor failed to carry out this task properly and an employee was crushed by some haulage plant.

Held: the employer was nevertheless liable to the employee because the duty to provide a safe system of work is a personal duty and although the employer can delegate the task he cannot delegate the responsibility.

(ii)   where the work is especially hazardous:

Honeywill and Stein v Larkin Bros [1934]

Facts: the plaintiff engaged a photographer to take photographs of the interior of a theatre using naked magnesium flames as flashlight. This resulted in damage by fire to the theatre.

Held: the plaintiff was liable for this very dangerous activity.

(iii)   torts of strict liability.

(iv)   operations on the highway.

(c)   **Personal negligence of employer**

The employer will be in breach of his own duty if he carelessly fails to engage a competent independent contractor, or if he fails to instruct him properly.

3.6   Activity

A fur coat is stolen by an employee of a cleaning firm whilst entrusted to the firm for cleaning. Would the employer be liable?

3.7   Activity solution

As in **Lloyd v Grace, Smith and Co** the employee was acting within the course of his employment and therefore the employer would be vicariously liable.

Conclusion   Where an employee commits a tort the injured party may be able to sue two persons: the employee who will be personally liable and the employer who will be vicariously liable if the employee was acting within the scope of his employment.

4   GENERAL DEFENCES

4.1   Introduction

The plaintiff must first prove that the defendant has committed a tort. The defendant's first line of argument will therefore be that no tort was committed eg, he was not negligent. Only if the plaintiff proves that the defendant committed a tort need the defendant actually plead a defence.

There are particular defences for particular torts eg, in an action for defamation the defendant may seek to rely on the defence of justification (ie, that the statement was substantially true). Apart from specific defences there are a number of general defences available in most tort actions.

4.2   Volenti non fit injuria

Definition   "to he who consents no injury is done".

In this defence (sometimes simply called 'consent') the defendant is claiming that the plaintiff was aware of risk of harm and consented to that risk.

For example, a patient under the surgeon's knife has consented to the operation. Another example arises in sport whereby every participant, in for example, a rugby game, is taken to consent to injuries in the course of a fair tackle.

A recent example of the defence of volenti is

Morris v Murray [1990]

Facts: Morris and Murray went on a drinking spree. (Murray had consumed the equivalent of 17 whiskies.) Murray then invited Morris to go for a joyride in Murray's light aircraft. They drove to the airfield for take-off. The aircraft, piloted by Murray, took off downwind and uphill in conditions of poor visibility, low cloud and drizzle when other flying at the aerodrome had been suspended. The aircraft only just managed to get airborne and crashed soon after. Murray was killed and Morris was badly injured. Morris sued Murray in the tort of negligence and Murray raised the defence of volenti.

Held: the defence succeeded: Morris willingly embarked on a flight with a pilot whom he knew to be drunk at the outset. The effect of the defence was to defeat totally Morris' action for negligence.

The defence has two aspects (i) that the plaintiff knew of the risk of injury, and (ii) that he consented to run the risk of injury. There cannot of course be consent without knowledge, but knowledge by itself is not sufficient. Consent may be express or implied (and the latter may arise from the actions of the parties) but whichever it is the consent must have been freely given and not obtained under economic, social or even moral pressure.

- **Employment cases**

  The courts are unwilling to allow an employer to raise the defence of volenti against an employee unless there are exceptional circumstances.

  An employee does not consent to the risk if he complains of it and, sometimes, even if he does not.

  ### Baker v James [1921]

  Facts: an employee had complained of a mechanical defect in the car provided for his use, but continued to use it. He was subsequently injured.

  Held: he had not consented to the risk.

  ### Bowater v Rowley Regis Corporation [1944]

  Facts: the employer ordered B to take out a horse which both knew was unsafe. B complied with the order because he was in fear of losing his job if he did not, B was injured.

  Held: the employer's defence of volenti failed because B's consent was not freely given.

  ### Smith v Charles Baker [1891]

  Facts: a workman at a quarry worked under a crane which he knew was swinging loads of stone over his head. He had never expressly objected to the risk. Some stone fell, injuring him.

  Held: his silence was not consent

An exceptional employment case where the defence succeeded is

Bolt v WM Moss

Facts: a workman was expressly warned of the danger of standing on a painters' scaffold whilst it was being moved. Nevertheless he persisted in so doing and in consequence fell off and was injured.

Held: in these circumstances the employer could successfully raise the defence of volenti.

- **Strict liability**

The defence is never available as a defence to strict liability, such as the absolute duty to fence dangerous machinery under the Factories Act 1961.

- **Rescue cases**

There is no true consent in what are called the 'rescue cases', where a risk of injury is created by a wrongful act of the defendant and the plaintiff exposes himself to the risk to save others.

Baker v Hopkins [1959]

Facts: a doctor went down a well full of noxious fumes to treat workmen overcome by them.

Held: although the doctor knew of the risks he did not freely assent to them, he acted out of a sense of duty.

- **Road Traffic Acts**

The road traffic legislation specifically disallows a motor vehicle driver from raising the defence of volenti when sued by his passenger.

4.3   Inevitable accident

Definition   This is an accident which could not have been foreseen nor avoided by any reasonable precautions.

This is strictly not a defence, rather a plea to the effect that no tort has been **committed**. It is not available as a defence in torts of strict liability where fault is immaterial.

4.4   Act of God

Definition   This is a natural disaster, such as floods or lightning, which could neither have been foreseen nor prevented by any reasonable precautions.

This can be pleaded as a defence if appropriate, even in torts of strict liability.

4.5   Necessity

The defendant may avoid liability if his action was essential to prevent a greater loss or injury to the community.

Dewey v White [1827]

Facts: a building was destroyed because it had been damaged by fire and was threatening to collapse on the highway.

Held: the owner could not succeed against those who had demolished the building. They acted out of necessity.

This defence is strictly applied.

Ward v London County Council [1938]

Facts: a fire engine went through a red light, injuring the plaintiff.

Held: the defendants were held vicariously liable for this tort since, although the fire engine was attending a fire, the risk taken was great and possibly not essential to avoid greater loss.

4.6   Defence of person/property

A person may use a reasonable degree of force to protect himself or any other person against any unlawful use of force. Such force must be both necessary and proportionate to the harm to be prevented.

A person may also use reasonable force to defend land or property in his possession against any person committing or threatening to commit a tortious act against that property.

4.7   Statutory authority

Definition   Statutory authority is a plea to the effect that the defendant had the backing of statute to perform the act complained of.

Where the authority is **absolute** (ie, where the law compels the defendant to act in that way) he has no liability.

Vaughan v Taff Vale Railway [1890]

Facts: the defendant railway company had a statutory obligation to run a passenger rail service on a particular route. The state of technology at the time made it inevitable that sparks and cinders would escape from the railway engine. The plaintiff's crops, which were near the line, were damaged by fire from cinders.

Held: the railway company would have been breaking the law if it failed to run trains on the line. They had statutory authority to do so, and no liability.

However, modern statutes generally require persons acting under their authority to do so reasonably: their authority is therefore **conditional**. If injury arises from unreasonable exercise of conditional authority, liability will arise.

4.8   Contributory negligence

At common law, the plaintiff recovered nothing if he was guilty of any negligence which contributed to the cause of his injury. It was, therefore, a complete defence. The Law Reform (Contributory Negligence) Act 1945 reformed the law so that contributory negligence no longer absolves the defendant but merely reduces the damages which he has to pay.

In essence the defendant alleges by this defence that the plaintiff contributed, by his own negligence, to the extent of his injuries. The effect is that the court will reduce the plaintiff's damages by a percentage to reflect his contributory negligence. Although seen as a partial defence it is possible for contributory negligence to be held to be 100% and therefore reducing damages to zero - **Jayes v IMI (Kynoch) Ltd**.

The following covers particular aspects of this defence.

- **Specific risk**

  The injury of which the plaintiff complains must at least in part result from that specific risk to which, by his negligence, the plaintiff exposed himself.

  Jones v Livox Quarries Ltd [1952]

  Facts: the plaintiff rode on the back of the defendant's vehicle, thereby exposing himself not only to the risk of falling off, but also to being injured if a third party collided with the vehicle.

  Held: he was held to have been contributorily negligent, but would not, apparently, have been contributorily negligent if, while riding on the vehicle, he had been shot by a negligent sportsman, as that injury would be entirely foreign to the risk to which he exposed himself.

- **Contribution to injury**

  The plaintiff must have contributed to his injury ie, causation is relevant.

  Note that causation relates to the injury, **not** to the accident. Therefore, a plaintiff may be contributorily negligent even though his conduct in no way contributed to the cause of the accident, as long as his conduct contributed to the extent of injuries. For example, failure to wear a seatbelt would be an act of contributory negligence in a claim for damages in a motor accident case, even though the failure did not contribute to the cause of the accident.

- **Fault**

  The plaintiff must have been at fault. It is sufficient to show he failed to take reasonable precautions to avoid a risk he could foresee. However, if the defendant's negligence puts the plaintiff in a position of imminent danger, reasonable conduct by the plaintiff in these circumstances does not amount to contributory negligence even though such conduct may actually be harmful.

  Jones v Boyce [1816]

  Facts: the plaintiff was a passenger on the top of the defendant's bus, and because of negligent maintenance the bus was in danger of turning over. The plaintiff, realising this, jumped out and broke his leg. In fact the bus did not turn over and the plaintiff would not have been injured had he remained on board.

  Held: he was nevertheless entitled to recover damages since, when faced with imminent danger, he had acted as a reasonable and prudent man.

- **Young children and other vulnerable persons**

  Contributory negligence is difficult to establish. See later for example, the express provision in the Occupiers Liability Act 1957 that an occupier must expect children to be less careful than adults.

- **Strict liability**

  Unlike volenti, contributory negligence is available even when strict liability is imposed. See later, for example, **Uddin v Portland Cement**.

4.9   Activity

A employee of a local council drives a refuse truck that he has frequently complained is unsafe. However he has agreed to drive it under threat of dismissal should he refuse. Would the defence of *volenti non fit injuria* be valid in these circumstances?

4.10   Activity solution

No as the employee only consented to the risks under duress. (This problem is based on the facts of a decided case - **Bowater v Rowley Regis Corporation.**)

4.11   Activity

Peter was riding his moped without a crash helmet when he was hit by a car. The car driver was responsible for the accident. Peter suffered head injuries and it was shown that these would not have been so severe if he had been wearing the helmet. What effect would this have on the car driver's liability?

4.12   Activity solution

The car driver was responsible for the accident and therefore liable whether or not Peter was wearing a crash helmet. However Peter's carelessness in not wearing a helmet would be seen to be contributory negligence and the damages awarded would be likely to be reduced.

5   EXEMPTION NOTICES

With regard to business liability the Unfair Contract Terms Act 1977 provides that a notice excluding liability for negligence causing

- death or personal injury is void.
- other loss is valid only if it passes the test of reasonableness.

  Other loss is, for example, property damage and economic loss.

  An example of the application of the reasonableness test arose in

  Smith v Eric S Bush [1989]

  Facts: Mrs S proposed to buy a house for £18,000 on mortgage from the Abbey National Building Society.

  ANBS instructed surveyors, ESB, to do a valuation report which was done without reasonable care and valued the house for more than its true worth. Mrs S paid ANBS a fee to cover the cost of the report. A copy of the report was given to Mrs S by ANBS. The report contained a disclaimer of liability for negligence.

  Held: by the House of Lords

  (i)   ESB owed Mrs S a duty of care in the tort of negligence and had breached their duty of care which caused loss to Mrs S;

(ii)   the disclaimer was subject to the 'reasonableness' test of S2(2) UCTA 1977;

(iii)   in the circumstances the disclaimer was not reasonable taking into account

- unequal bargaining power: Mrs S had no choice but to accept the surveyor appointed by the society

- alternative source of advice: Mrs S was a young first time buyer at the bottom end of the market. It was unreasonable to expect her to pay twice for the same service.

- difficulty of task: valuation is at the lower end of a surveyor's field of professional expertise.

- insurance: it is easy and usual for professional men to insure.

Obiter dicta: disclaimer might be reasonable when large sums of money are at stake eg, with industrial property.

'Negligence' includes not only the tort of negligence but also occupiers liability.

6   LIMITATION

Under the Limitation Act 1980 the limitation period is six years and time begins to run from when the injury (ie, the tort) occurred. There are two main modifications to this basic six year period.

- An action for personal injury must be brought within 3 years of the injury occurring or within 3 years of when it manifested itself, whichever later.

- An action for latent property damage must be brought within 6 years of the injury or within 6 years of when the plaintiff with due diligence ought to have discovered it, whichever later, subject to an overall longstop period of 15 years from when the injury occurred.

7   DEATH

7.1   Death of the injured party

Causing death is not itself a tort (although it may be a crime). However, if the deceased had grounds of action for the act which caused his death, it does not die with him, but may be enforced by his personal representatives. In addition, dependants of the deceased who have lost their means of support by his death have a separate claim for their loss against the wrongdoer: Fatal Accidents Act 1976.

The one exception is the tort of defamation. Here an action cannot be begun or continued on behalf of a dead person whether by his estate or his dependants.

7.2   Death of the tortfeasor

This makes no difference: the action is brought or continued against his estate as if he were still alive.

8   REMEDIES

8.1   Damages

The usual remedy is **unliquidated damages** (ie, which cannot be predetermined by the parties):

- **Compensatory damages**

    Generally the amount of damages awarded by the court is based on the principle of compensating the plaintiff for the loss he has suffered: the basis of assessment in the law of tort is to put the plaintiff in the position he would have been had the tort not occurred. Tort rules on remoteness are different from contract rules and are covered in relation to the tort of negligence in the next chapter.

    The damages can be:

    (a)   **General damages**

           Which the court will assess as compensation for losses which cannot be positively quantified eg, for pain and suffering.

    (b)   **Special damages**

           Which the plaintiff can positively prove eg, medical expenses or loss of earnings during incapacity.

- **Nominal damages**

    These are awarded in torts actionable *per se* where the plaintiff's right has been infringed but he has suffered no actual loss eg, £5 damages for trespass to land without any damage done.

- **Contemptuous damages**

    These are awarded where the plaintiff has proved his case and the court must therefore find in his favour but the court is of the view that the plaintiff should not have brought the court action - eg, 1p damages for trespass to land without any damage done.

    The difference between the examples given of contemptuous and nominal damages could be that in the case where nominal damages were awarded there had been trespass on several occasions and the plaintiff brought the action principally to obtain an injunction to prevent it happening in future. In the case where contemptuous damages were awarded there had been trespass on only one occasion with no likelihood of repetition. Technically the defendant had committed the tort of trespass but the court considers that the case was not properly brought as nothing was gained by doing so.

- **Exemplary damages**

    These are awarded to punish the defendant for his conduct and deter others from similar conduct. These damages are rarely awarded and are restricted to three cases:

    (a)   for oppressive, arbitrary acts of public officials;

    (b)   for acts which were calculated to make a profit for the defendant (eg, publishing of defamatory material which will sell books or newspapers); and

    (c)   where certified by statute.

8.2   Injunctions

[Definition]   An injunction is an equitable remedy, granted at the discretion of the court. It is an order of the court to a person to do something or to desist from doing something.

There are four types of injunction:

(a)   **Prohibitory** - an order to restrain the defendant from committing or repeating a tortious act (eg, to cease a nuisance).

(b)   **Mandatory** - an order requiring the defendant to perform a positive act to put an end to some wrongful state of affairs (eg, to depart from land on which he is trespassing).

(c)   **Perpetual** - awarded after the trial and permanently binding on the defendant.

(d)   **Interlocutory** - granted to be effective only until the time of the hearing, but only in certain circumstances (eg, to cease an alleged nuisance until the case is finally determined).

Injunctions would be appropriate, for example, to prevent further publication of a defamatory statement, or further nuisance.

9   SELF TEST QUESTIONS

9.1   What is vicarious liability? (2.1)

9.2   If an employer is to be vicariously liable for the torts of his worker what two matters must be proved? (3.1)

9.3   Is an employer vicariously liable for torts committed by his workers who are independent contractors? (3.5)

9.4   Translate *volenti non fit injuria* (4.2)

9.5   What are the two elements of the defence of volenti? (4.2)

9.6   Is the defence of volenti available to a tort which is one of strict liability? (4.2)

9.7   What is the effect of a successful plea of contributory negligence? (4.8)

9.8   Describe the effect that UCTA 1977 has on disclaimers of liability for negligence (5)

9.9   What is the limitation period for an action in tort for personal injury? (6)

9.10   Identify the two sets of persons who can sue where the victim of the tort dies as a result of the tort (7.1)

9.11   What are special damages? (8.1)

10   EXAMINATION TYPE QUESTION

10.1   Defence to tort

(a)   Explain the meaning and effect of the following defences which may be put forward to an action in tort:

(i)   consent;

(4 marks)

(ii)   contributory negligence; and

(4 marks)

(iii)   statutory authority.

(4 marks)

(b)   What remedies may follow a successful tort action?

(8 marks)

(Total: 20 marks)

11   ANSWER TO EXAMINATION TYPE QUESTION

11.1   Defence to tort

(a)   (i)   The defence of consent is often termed *volenti non fit injuria* meaning a person who willingly agrees to suffer damage or accept risks cannot later complain of injury. Before the defence operates it is necessary to prove there is express or implied consent to injury/damage or the risk thereof. The consent will be express where, for example, it is a term of the contract. It may be implied, for instance when a person participates in a sporting event of a hazardous nature eg, rugby.

There are a number of situations where, as a matter of policy, the defence does not operate. Firstly, where an employee is injured in the course of employment he will not normally be taken to have consented to the risk, unless it is in the nature of a task which is obviously dangerous. ***Smith v Charles Baker and Sons*** establishes that mere acquiescence is not enough. Furthermore the strict liability requirements eg, fencing of the **Factories Acts** are exempted from the general rules about the use of consent as a defence. Secondly, a person who volunteers for a rescue attempt and is injured will not be taken to have consented, unless there was no immediate danger requiring intervention **(Haynes v Harwood).**

(ii)   Contributory negligence, in contrast to consent, is only a partial defence and as such does not totally negate liability.   The effect of raising the defence of contributory negligence is normally to reduce the amount of damages payable in proportion to the percentage of fault on the part of the plaintiff. It is possible, however, for contributory negligence to be 100% but at the same time for the defendant's liability to be established. In this event no damages will be awarded. The method of reducing damages for contributory negligence is laid down by the Law Reform (Contributory Negligence) Act 1945.

(iii)   The defence of statutory authority arises where the actions of the defendant would, but for the statute, amount to a tort. Such statutory authority is also a statutory indemnity, taking away all legal remedies provided by the law of tort, except if the statute provides otherwise. Many statutes in fact provide for compensation. The courts, however, tend to restrict the availability of the defence. An example of this is seen in **Pride of Derby and Derbyshire Angling Association Ltd v British Celanese Ltd** where the defendants admitted to polluting the plaintiff's fishery by discharging into it insufficiently treated sewage, but claimed under a certain Act of

Parliament it was under a duty to provide a sewage system and this was the only way of doing so given increases in the population in the relevant area. The court held it was not inevitable that carrying out the duty should cause a nuisance and that in any case the Act did not on its true construction authorise the commission of a nuisance.

(b)   The common law remedy for tort is damages. The aim of damages is to compensate the plaintiff so as to put him/her in the position he/she would have been in had the tort not been committed. Damages are available not only for the recovery of property and financial loss but also for personal injury but here the quantification of damages is more complex eg, assessment of such heads as loss of life, pain and suffering. The equitable remedy of an injunction may also be available where damages are not adequate. Injunctions are either prohibitory or mandatory. A prohibitory injunction is an order restraining the defendant from continuing or repeating an injurious act eg, trespass to land. A mandatory injunction is an order requiring the defendant to do a positive act for the purpose of putting an end to a wrongful state of things created by him eg, to pull down a building already erected to reverse obstruction of the plaintiff's light.

11 TORT: NEGLIGENCE

INTRODUCTION & LEARNING OBJECTIVES

Syllabus area 8c. The basic concepts of negligence in order to assess and guard against negligence with special reference to professional advice, product liability, industrial accidents and dangerous premises. (Ability required 3).

Strict liability. (Ability required 3).

The tort of negligence is a developing area of the law and has become the most common tort. As a tort negligence is the breach of a legal duty to take care which results in damage undesired by the defendant to the plaintiff. In order to establish negligence the plaintiff must prove that the defendant owed the plaintiff a duty of care, that there was a breach of that duty and that the plaintiff thereby suffered loss or damage.

In this chapter each of these three areas, duty of care, breach of duty and damage will be considered. This area of the law is still developing and is therefore very dependant upon case law.

Once the general tort of negligence has been considered then three particular areas of application of the tort, together with the statutory torts, will be examined. These are product liability, dangerous premises and industrial accidents.

When you have studied this chapter you should be able to do the following:

- Discuss the case law surrounding duty of care.
- Discuss the rules regarding breach of duty of care.
- Discuss the tests set out by the courts regarding damage resulting from a breach.
- Apply the case law and statute law to product liability and occupiers' liability and injuries at work.

---

1   DUTY OF CARE

1.1   To whom is it owed? - the 'neighbour principle'

"You must take reasonable care to avoid acts or omissions which you can reasonably foresee would be likely to injure your neighbour. Who then is my neighbour? The answer seems to be persons who are so closely and directly affected by my act that I ought reasonably to have them in contemplation as being so affected when I am directing my mind to the acts or omissions which are called in question". Lord Atkin in **Donoghue v Stevenson**.

Donoghue v Stevenson [1932]

Facts: Mrs Donoghue went to a cafe with a friend. The friend bought her a bottle of ginger beer which Mrs Donoghue drank and then discovered that there was a decomposed snail in the bottom of the opaque bottle. Mrs Donoghue found this sight so upsetting that she suffered physical illness.

She sued the manufacturer, claiming that they were under a duty to see that such outside bodies did not get into the beer.

Held: there was a duty on behalf of the manufacturer to take reasonable care in the manufacture of products. The manufacturer owes a duty to the consumer to take reasonable care to prevent injury.

Note that the word 'reasonable' appears twice in the quoted passage from Lord Atkin's judgement. In general, it denotes the objective standard of an ordinary person (as distinct from any personal standard of the individual involved).

Conclusion The importance of the neighbour principle is that it can impose a duty of care towards persons with whom the party at fault has no contractual relationship and of whose identity he was previously unaware.

In **Donoghue's case**, the soft-drink manufacturer was held to owe a duty of care towards **any person** who might consume his product. This was because he could foresee that if he put his product on the market in an impure state and in closed and opaque container, injury to the consumer was likely to result.

1.2   Restrictions

The principle underlies the considerable extension of the tort of negligence in recent times. There are, however, exceptions to it and limitations on it.

The court is not prepared to find a duty of care exists in all situations. Thus, there are situations where the plaintiff has suffered damage as a consequence of the defendant's behaviour but the courts are not willing to impose liability on the defendant. Although the plaintiff has suffered loss, or the defendant acted unreasonably, or the defendant's behaviour caused the plaintiff loss, the court refuses to impose liability on the defendant on the ground that the defendant did not owe the plaintiff a duty of care. There are two areas where such difficulties have arisen.

- **Negligent misstatement**

  The law has been reluctant to impose a duty of care in the making of statements as opposed to the doing or failing to do physical acts. In **Donoghue v Stevenson** damage was caused by a negligent omission (failure to check that there was no extraneous matter in the ginger beer). It was thought until 1964 that there was no liability for loss caused by the production of inaccurate information through lack of care. This last has been a 'growth area' in law and is generally called professional negligence.

- **Damage other than physical damage**

  The law has been reluctant to impose a duty of care to avoid causing loss other than physical damage to person or property. Strict limits have been imposed in determining liability when the plaintiff suffers psychological damage or 'nervous shock'.

We shall deal with each of these particular problem areas in turn.

1.3   Negligent misstatement causing economic loss

In **Hedley Byrne**, the House of Lords created a new duty-situation by recognising liability for negligent **statements** causing **economic** loss made in circumstances where there exists a **special relationship** between the parties. Previously, damages for pecuniary loss were recoverable only if the loss arose from a wilful or reckless false statement ie, the tort of deceit.

Hedley Byrne & Co Ltd v Heller & Partners Ltd [1963]

Facts: the appellants were advertising agents and the respondents were merchant bankers.   The appellants had a client called Easipower Ltd who were customers of the respondents.

The appellants had contracted to place orders for advertising Easipower's products on television and in newspapers and since this involved giving Easipower credit, they asked the respondents, who were Easipower's bankers, for a reference as to the creditworthiness of Easipower.

Heller gave favourable references (but stipulated that the information was given **without responsibility** on their part).   Relying on this information, the plaintiffs extended credit to Easipower and lost over £17,000 when the latter, soon after, went into liquidation.   The plaintiffs sued Easipower's bankers for negligence.

Held*:* the respondents' disclaimer was adequate to exclude the assumption by them of the legal duty of care, but, in the absence of the disclaimer, the circumstances would have given rise to a duty of care in spite of the absence of a contract or fiduciary relationship.   Thus, but for the disclaimer, the bank was liable on its misleading statement.   *(Note:* nowadays the disclaimer might be invalidated under UCTA 1977).

For an action for a negligent misstatement, there must be a special relationship between the parties which has been established in an appropriate context

In **Hedley Byrne** Lord Morris expounded the formulation of a **special relationship** in these terms:

"... it should now be regarded as settled that if someone possessed of a special skill undertakes, quite irrespective of contract, to apply that skill for the assistance of another person who relies on such skill, a duty of care will arise ...

... furthermore, if, in a sphere in which a person is so placed that others could reasonably rely on his judgement or his skill or his liability to make careful enquiry, a person takes it on himself to give information or advice to be passed on to another person who, as he knows or should know, will place reliance on it, then a duty of care will arise ..."

The concept of 'special relationship' has now been redefined by the House of Lords in the leading case of

Caparo Industries plc v Dickman and others [1990]

Facts: in this case Caparo owned shares in F plc and after receiving the audited accounts which showed a profit for the year it purchased more shares in F plc and then made a successful takeover bid for F plc.   After the take-over Caparo sued the auditors alleging that the accounts were misleading in that they showed a profit when in fact there had been a loss.   The House of Lords in determining the existence and scope of the duty of care recognised the difficulty in setting a single general principle which could be applied to every situation.   However, it did set out three criteria which must be fulfilled to give rise to a duty of care.

The first criterion is foreseeability of damage.   This appears to be the standard test of foreseeability in the tort of negligence.

The second criterion is proximity.   The court accepted that it was difficult to precisely define proximity.   It is clear that there are circumstances where, although damage is foreseeable, there will be no duty of care because there is insufficient proximity.   The court is anxious to differentiate between the situation where an expert advises a known person who relies on the statement for a known purpose (as in **Hedley Byrne**) and the situation where a statement made by an expert is generally made available and could foreseeably be relied on for a number of purposes of which the statement maker had no reason to know. If a duty of care were owed in the second situation to anyone who read the statement this would create for the statement maker 'liability in an indeterminate amount for an indeterminate time to an indeterminate class' or, looking at it the other way, would give the general public an entitlement to use expert knowledge, unknown to the expert, for its own purposes and hold him liable if it were wrong. Thus, the second criteria of proximity limits the duty to circumstances where the defendant knew the statement would be communicated to the plaintiff either as an individual or a member of an identifiable class in respect of transactions of a particular kind and that the plaintiff would rely on the statement in considering whether to undertake that particular kind of transaction. Thus, one must look at the purpose for which the statement was made, the statement maker's knowledge of the person relying on the statement and the type of transaction in which it was used.

The third criterion is whether it is just and reasonable that a duty of care should be imposed in the sense that to impose liability is not contrary to public policy. Again the court acknowledged that it was difficult to set out precisely a definition of this.

Held: applying these criteria the court held that **auditors of a public company owe no duty of care to the public at large** who rely on the accounts when purchasing shares in the company nor was any duty owed to existing individual shareholders who purchased additional shares as they are in no better position than a member of the public.

There are numerous cases which illustrate the **Caparo** 3-fold test for the existence of a special relationship.

A1 Saudi Banque v Clarke Pixley [1989]

Facts: in reliance on accounts audited by Clarke Pixley, A1 Saudi Banque loaned money to a company called Gallic Credit International Ltd. Later Gallic went into insolvent liquidation with an estimated deficiency of £8.6m. It was alleged that Gallic's accounts had been negligently audited. So A1 Saudi Banque (and other lenders) sued Clarke Pixley in the tort of negligence.

It was **held** that auditors owe no duty of care to a bank which lends money, regardless of whether the bank is an existing creditor making further advances or was only a potential creditor making new advances, because in such circumstances there is no proximity between existing or potential creditors of a company and its auditors. Accordingly A1 Saudi Banque failed in their action against Clarke Pixley.

Esso Petroleum v Mardon [1976]

Facts: during pre-contractual negotiations for the 3 year lease of a petrol filling station L (an expert with over 40 years experience acting on behalf of Esso) forecast the throughput of the station by the third year as 200,000 gallons. Mr Mardon suggested that 100,000 gallons might be more realistic but his doubts were quelled by L's expertise and experience and Mardon took the lease. In the event the throughput in the third year was only 86,000 gallons and Mr Mardon lost all his capital. Esso sued Mr Mardon for arrears of rent and Mr Mardon counterclaimed for damages in the tort of negligence.

It was **held** the action in tort for negligent mis-statement succeeded. A duty of care existed because there was a special relationship between the parties based on proximity and reasonable foreseeability. (Breach of duty and resultant loss were also proved.)

Also see the House of Lords decision in **Smith v Bush [1989]**.

In **Caparo** the House of Lords was of the opinion, obiter:

- that a duty of care might be owed to the shareholders as a body (in effect meaning a duty of care would be owed to the company): the purpose of the statutory audit report is to provide the general meeting with an independent view as to the truth and fairness of the accounts prepared by the directors so that the general meeting can reward (or otherwise) the directors - thus the proximity test would be established.

- that if during the audit the auditor was told that a particular person intended to rely on the accounts for a stated purpose, the auditors would owe a duty of care to that person in respect of that purpose. This dicta appears to have been applied in **Morgan Crucible v Hill Samuel [1991]** but distinguished in **James McNaughten Paper v Hicks Anderson [1991]**.

Morgan Crucible v Hill Samuel [1991]

Facts: MC made a bid for First Castle Electronics plc which then issued circulars containing profit records and forecasts recommending its shareholders not to accept the bid. The circulars expressly referred to the 1984 and 1985 audited accounts. Eventually MC increased its bid and, on the FCE board recommending acceptance, MC's bid succeeded. Subsequently MC discovered that the accounts and the profit forecasts grossly overstated FCE's profits and that FCE was worthless and had it known the true facts it would never have made the bid, let alone increased it. So MC sued FCE's merchant bank, directors and accountants in the tort of negligence in respect of circulars issued after the bid was first made.

The question before the Court of Appeal: is the action bound to fail because lack of proximity denies the existence of a duty of care?

Held: that the action is not bound to fail. **Caparo** could be distinguished because here it is alleged the plaintiffs knew MC would rely on the circulars for the particular purpose of deciding whether or not to make an increased bid and intended that they should. Thus there might be proximity.

Note: the full trial of the action was never heard: this was an interlocutory proceeding to decide whether there was any cause of action. (In legal procedures a case can be 'struck out' before it comes to trial if, on the facts alleged, there is no law on which the plaintiff could possibly succeed.) Presumably the parties eventually settled out of court.

James McNaughten Paper v Hicks Anderson [1991]

Facts: JMP entered into negotiations with MK Paper for an agreed take-over of MK. The chairman of MK asked its accountants, HA, to prepare draft accounts as quickly as possible for use in the negotiations. The accounts when prepared were shown by MK to JMP. After the take-over was completed JMP discovered certain discrepancies in the accounts. JMP brought an action against MK's accountants in the tort of negligence.

Held: that no duty of care was owed because of lack of proximity between JMP and HA. The prime reasons for lack of proximity included:

- the accounts were produced for MK's use in negotiations not for JMP's; and
- draft accounts are not intended to be relied on as if they were final accounts.

A further recent example is

Spring v Guardian Assurance [1994]

Facts: Guardian Assurance gave an unfavourable reference about their employee, Spring, to his potential new employer. Because of the reference Spring did not get the new job.

Held: by the House of Lords (reversing the Court of Appeal) that an employer owes a duty of care in the tort of negligence to the subject of a reference.

Note: the House of Lords recognised, obiter, that a duty of care might be owed to the recipient of the reference.

An example of public policy consideration which negatives the duty is the well established principle that solicitors, barristers, judges, juries and witnesses are absolutely immune from proceedings in respect of acts etc done in court - **Rondel v Worsley [1969]**. There is no duty of care recognised.

1.4   Nervous shock

Another area where for a long period the courts showed a marked reluctance to allow a duty of care is where a person is responsible for a horrifying event (such as a major accident) which others see and hear and as a result suffer psychiatric illness. Case law (the leading case is **Alcock v Chief Constable of South Yorkshire [1991]**) now shows that nervous shock caused to persons who are active participants in the peril is treated differently from nervous shock caused to persons, such as bystanders, who are not actively involved. The law is ready to admit that the causer of the peril owes a duty of care to active participants but much less ready in the case of bystanders.

(a)   **Case law - active participants**

Chadwick v BRB [1967] - the 'Lewisham' train disaster

Facts: British Rail (negligently) caused a train crash. Chadwick (a doctor) who helped to rescue the dead and dying from the disaster suffered nervous shock because of what he had seen.

Held: BRB owed him, a rescuer, a duty of care.

Dulieu v White [1901]

Facts: the plaintiff suffered nervous shock when the defendant (negligently) drove his vehicle straight towards her at great speed. *(note:* he did not actually hit her so there was no physical injury).

Held: the defendant owed her, a person put in fear of her own safety, a duty of care.

Dooley v Cammell Laird [1951]

Facts: the defendant employer (negligently) provided the plaintiff employee with a defective crane and as he was operating the crane the cable broke allowing the load to fall down into the hold of a ship where his work-mates were working. The fear of injury to his work-mates caused the plaintiff to suffer nervous shock.

Held: he was owed a duty of care by his employer.

(b)   **Case law - those who are not active participants**

In respect of this category of persons who suffer nervous shock the House of Lords in **Alcock v Chief Constable of South Yorkshire [1991]** explained the neighbour principle as a two fold test.

- reasonable foreseeability: it is reasonably foreseeable that the plaintiff will suffer nervous shock where he has a close tie of love and affection with the primary victim of the horrifying event. A close tie of love and affection is rebuttably presumed between husband and wife; parent and child; and fiancé and fiancée.

Bourhill v Young [1942]

Facts: the plaintiff, a pregnant fishwife, suffered nervous shock when, on getting off a tram, she heard a motor vehicle accident and when she saw blood on the road afterwards.

Held: she was owed no duty of care: she was a mere onlooker and a stranger to the victims of the accident and it was therefore not reasonably foreseeable that she would suffer nervous shock.

- proximity in time and space: there will be proximity where the plaintiff sees or hears the accident or its immediate aftermath directly with his own unaided senses.

Alcock v Chief Constable of South Yorkshire [1991]: the 'Hillsborough' disaster

Facts: a large number of spectators at a football match were killed or injured by crushing when too many people were allowed onto the terraces at one end of the ground. Mrs Copoc saw the event as it was broadcast on live television and was later informed that her son was dead. As a result she suffered nervous shock.

Held: she was not owed a duty of care because she had not seen or heard the accident directly: there was no proximity in time and space.

Note: this was a 'test' case in which there were a number of plaintiffs. The defendant was the police officer in charge of crowd control at the ground. He admitted breach of duty and resultant loss: the case was litigated solely on duty of care as a preliminary point. We shall refer back to this case later to consider some of the other plaintiffs.

McLoughlin v O'Brian [1982]

Facts: the primary victims of the accident caused by the respondent's negligence were the husband and two children of the appellant, who were injured, and another child of hers who was killed. At the time of the accident the appellant was some two miles away but she was taken about an hour later to the hospital where the injured were being treated and saw them in more or less the state in which they had been brought in. As a result of what she saw she suffered nervous shock.

Held: she was owed a duty of care since she satisfied the necessary criteria: she was a close relative, she had witnessed the immediate aftermath and she had witnessed this with her own unaided senses.

Contrast this with another plaintiff in the Hillsborough disaster:

Alcock v Chief Constable of South Yorkshire [1991]

Facts: Robert Alcock saw gruesome scenes in the makeshift mortuary when he identified, some 8 hours after the disaster happened, the dead body of his brother. As a result of this he suffered nervous shock.

Held: he was not owed a duty of care for two reasons. First: since he was unable to prove he had a close tie of love and affection with his brother it was not reasonably foreseeable he would suffer nervous shock. Second: there was no proximity in time - although he saw the aftermath this, being 8 hours later, was not sufficiently immediate.

The latest case on nervous shock, which follows the two fold test for bystanders established in **Alcock** is

McFarlane v EE Caledonia Ltd [1993] - the 'Piper Alpha' disaster

Facts: due to the negligence of the defendant a series of massive explosions occurred on an oil rig and in the ensuing fire 164 men were killed. The plaintiff was on a support vessel (at times between 100 and 550 metres away) and suffered nervous shock as a result of what he saw.

Held: he was owed no duty of care as he had no close relationship with the victims of the disaster. *Note:* the plaintiff was not a rescuer, he was merely a witness, albeit unwilling, to the disaster.

1.5   Activity

What three things must the plaintiff prove in order to succeed in the tort of negligence?

1.6   Activity solution

(1)   that the defendant owes him a duty of care, and
(2)   that the defendant has breached his duty of care, and
(3)   and as a result the plaintiff has suffered loss

2   BREACH OF DUTY OF CARE

2.1   Introduction

The second element of negligence is that there has been a **breach of that duty of care**.

'Negligence is the omission to do something which a reasonable man, guided upon the considerations which ordinarily regulate the conduct of human affairs, would do, or doing something which a prudent and reasonable man would not do.'

The plaintiff generally must show that the defendant failed to take the degree of care which a 'reasonable man' would have taken in the circumstances.

2.2   The standard of care

The reasonable man is sometimes described as 'the man in the street' or 'the man on the Clapham omnibus'.

There are some general rules on the standard applied to determine whether a person has acted as a 'reasonable man'.

- **Professional man**

  The reasonable man is not expected to be skilled in any particular trade or profession. However, if he acts or purports to act in a professional capacity he must show the care and skill of an ordinary man of that profession.

  The skill of an ordinary man of that profession will depend on the profession and the standards and practices existing at the time ie, not those applied with more advanced knowledge.

  Roe v Minister of Health [1954]

  Facts: the plaintiff was injured when contaminated anaesthetic was administered to him during an operation. This contamination occurred because of invisible cracks in the container, the possibility of which was not known to the medical profession at that time.

  Held: the defendant was not liable in negligence as his behaviour was to be judged in the light of medical knowledge current at the time of the incident.

- **Amateur**

  An amateur who undertakes the job of an expert will be judged by expert standards.

  Nettleship v Weston [1971]

  Facts: a learner driver was in a collision.

  Held: the standard of care required was that of a reasonable driver, and not that of a reasonable learner driver.

- **Accountants**

  The standard used to judge whether accountants have exercised sufficient care and skill in their work will depend on the actual work undertaken, and:

  (a)   any statutory provisions or professional codes or guidelines setting out what the accountant must do or not do in carrying out that particular work. In audit work there are a number of such professional standards. Failure to follow any such provision or code would be evidence of failure to meet the required standard - **Twomax v Dickson [1983]**; and

  (b)   general practice and knowledge of the profession as a whole. This will include any professional code but will also cover areas where there is no such agreed code or where the code itself is outmoded or not followed.

  In **JEB Fasteners v Marks Bloom [1982]** there were various allegations of negligence:

  (a)   Various sales were omitted - there was no justification for the omission and the accountants were in breach of their duty.

(b)   Various purchases were omitted - this was due to the failure of the accountants in delaying making enquiries and failing to make exhaustive enquiries and they were, therefore, in breach of their duty.

(c)   Various expenses were understated - the individual items were small but there were a number of them, and given that it is accepted that there will be some small errors in even the most carefully audited accounts the accountants were not found to be in breach of their duty in making these errors.

(d)   The stock was wrongly described and consequently overvalued - on this the accountants had not followed normal accountancy practice nor had they shown this on the accounts. They were, therefore, in breach of their duty. This was the major finding of negligence as it most drastically affected the true financial position of the company.

In deciding whether **particular conduct** meets the reasonable man standard of care required the court will consider a number of factors.

- **Likelihood that injury will result**

   The plaintiff must show not only that the occurrence was foreseeable but also that there was a reasonable probability of injury to persons or property.

   Bolton v Stone [1951]

   Facts: a passer-by was injured by a cricket ball.

   Held: the likelihood of injury to passers-by was so slight that the defendant cricket club was not negligent in allowing cricket to be played on that particular ground.

   Hilder v Associated Portland Cement Manufacturers Ltd [1961]

   Facts: the plaintiff was riding his motorcycle along a road that ran by a piece of open land occupied by the defendants. The defendants allowed children to play football there, and a ball was kicked into the road causing the plaintiff to have an accident.

   Held: the likelihood of injury to passers-by was much greater than in **Bolton v Stone** and, therefore, the defendants would be liable in negligence for allowing football to be played without adequate precautions.

- **Known susceptibility of people exposed to the risk**

   It is a breach of duty to fail to take extra precautions to avoid injury to a person who is abnormally vulnerable if the infirmity is known.

   Paris v Stepney Borough Council [1951]

   Facts: P was blind in one eye. He was employed as a motor mechanic and was not provided with safety goggles. He was injured, in the course of his employment, damaging his good eye.

   Held: the employers should have taken special care to prevent damage to his good eye. By failing to do so they had fallen short of the standard of care expected of them, and were liable to compensate P for his injuries.

- **Balance risk against end to be achieved**

  In **Watt v Hertfordshire County Council [1954]**, the defendant was not negligent in requiring plaintiff fireman to take an abnormal risk in order to save life and limb.

- **Practicability of precautions**

  In **Latimer v AEC Ltd [1952]**, Denning, LJ observed that:

  'In every case of foreseeable risk it is a question of balancing the risk against the measure necessary for eliminating it.'

  The House of Lords agreed that the risk of the defendants' slippery factory floor did not justify or require so expensive a step as closing the factory down.

2.3   Res ipsa loquitur

In general, the burden of proving breach of duty rests on the plaintiff. However, there may be cases where the facts speak for themselves *(res ipsa loquitur)* and raise a presumption of negligence. In this situation the burden of proof shifts to the defendant to prove he did exercise reasonable care.

In **Scott v London and St Katherine Docks Co [1865]** *res ipsa loquitur* was defined as follows:

'There must be reasonable evidence of negligence. But where the thing is shown to be under the management of the defendant or his servants, and the accident is such as in the ordinary course of things does not happen if those who have the management use proper care, it affords reasonable evidence, in the absence of explanation by the defendants, that the accident arose from want of care.'

Thus, if the plaintiff relies on this principle he must show that:

(a)   Harm was caused by something under the control of the defendant:

Easson v LNER [1944]

Facts: a child fell out of the open door of a railway carriage at a point seven miles from the last stop; at this stage the railway company had no control over the doors, ie, a passenger might have opened the door after the train left the station.

Held: res ipsa loquitur did not apply

(b)   The accident is one which would not have happened if reasonable care had been taken.

Ward v Tesco Stores [1976]

Facts: Mrs Ward slipped on some spilt yoghurt on the floor of a supermarket. (She was unable to show how long the yoghurt remained on the floor.)

Held: the yoghurt would not have been on the floor if Tesco had cleaned it up. Therefore res ipsa loquitur applied with the result that the burden of proof shifted to Tesco to show that the yoghurt had been there only a short time. As they were unable to prove how long it had been there, they had failed to discharge the burden of proof.

Conclusion | Unless the doctrine of res ipsa loquitur applies it is for the plaintiff to prove that the defendant did not exercise the degree of care of a reasonable man in the circumstances.

3   RESULTANT LOSS

3.1   Introduction

In negligence there is no liability unless damage is shown to have resulted from the breach of the duty of care. The plaintiff must establish a causal link between the defendant's conduct and the damage which he has incurred.

The defendant's conduct must have been an effective **cause** of the plaintiff's loss.

Once causation has been proved the plaintiff must then prove that the loss is not too remote.

3.2   Cause of loss

The test used to describe liability is referred to as the 'but for' test. If the plaintiff's loss would not have occurred **but for** the defendants conduct then the defendant has caused the loss. If, however, the plaintiff would have suffered the loss regardless of the defendant's conduct then he has not caused the loss.

McWilliams v Sir William Arrol Ltd [1962]

Facts: an experienced steel erector fell 70 feet to his death. His employers had not provided him with safety harness, but at the trial there was evidence that he would not have worn one even if it had been made available.

Held: the employers were not liable. The **cause** of the injury was not the employer's breach but the employee's failure to wear the safety harness.

A further aspect of causation arises when there is a series of events which lead eventually to the loss. If there is a novus actus interveniens (new factor intervening) there is a break in the chain of causation. Generally, therefore, a defendant is not liable for the end result of a series of events which he started if there were intervening acts (by the plaintiff or by a third party) over which he had no control.

The alleged novus actus interveniens must be one which the intervening party had a freedom to do or not do.

Scott v Shepherd [1773]

Facts: the defendant threw a lighted squib onto a stall in a market. A bystander picked it up and threw it and it was picked up again and thrown in an attempt to avoid it exploding. Unfortunately, it hit the plaintiff who was injured.

Held: the defendant was liable since he intended that someone should be hurt or frightened, and the intervening acts were those of men acting in sudden and excusable fear for their own safety.

Haynes v Harwood [1935]

Facts: the defendant left his horse and cart in the street and some children threw a stone, causing the horse to bolt. The plaintiff, a policeman, saw this and was injured whilst trying to stop the horse.

Held: it was held that the act of the children was not a *novus actus interveniens* since it was precisely the sort of consequence that would follow from negligently leaving a horse unattended. The plaintiff's act in attempting a rescue was also not a *novus actus interveniens*.

3.3   Remoteness of damage

The court will have to determine the extent of the loss for which the plaintiff is entitled to recover damages. The defendant will not be liable for damage which, legally, is too remote a consequence of his conduct.

Whether the damage is too remote or not depends on the 'reasonable foreseeability' test. A loss is not too remote if a reasonable man would have foreseen the *type* of injury, loss or damage.

The Wagon Mound (No.1) [1961]

Facts: due to the defendants' negligence, oil was spilled overboard and accumulated around the plaintiff's wharf. Somehow, the oil ignited and the wharf suffered fire damage.

Held: the defendants were held not liable since, while damage to the wharf by oil pollution was foreseeable, damage by fire was not.

- Provided the type (or kind) of damage is reasonably foreseeable it is not necessary to foresee the exact *way* in which it happened nor the seriousness of its *extent*.

Hughes v Lord Advocate [1963]

Facts: the defendants left a manhole open with a hut covering it, and surrounded by paraffin lamps. The plaintiff, a boy aged eight, took one of the lamps into the shelter, and was playing with it when he tripped and dropped the lamp. He was badly burned when the lamp exploded.

Held: although the precise sequence of events causing the harm could not be foreseen, it was foreseeable that the lamps might cause burning and therefore the defendants were liable.

- Where *some* personal injury can be reasonably foreseen the defendant is liable for its *full extent* even though this may be due to the physical weakness of the plaintiff. This is called the 'thin skull rule' ie, a defendant must take his victim as he finds him.

Smith v Leech Braine [1962]

Facts: S was employed in a metal smelting foundry. His employer failed to provide protective clothing and S's lip was burnt by a small splash of molten metal. Unknown to all parties S was suffering from a dormant malignant cancerous condition. The burn activated the cancer and S died.

Held: the employer was liable for S's death under the thin skull rule.

- Except in cases of negligent mis-statement *pure* economic loss is too remote. Pure economic loss is economic loss which is not consequent on physical damage.

Spartan Steel and Alloys Ltd v Martin & Co Ltd [1973]

Facts: in excavating a trench in a public road workmen damaged an electric cable (belonging to the local electricity company) which they knew lay under the road and which supplied power to the plaintiff's factory. As a result of the interruption of power supply one batch of molten metal in furnaces was spoilt and the factory was out of action for fourteen hours.

Held: damages would be awarded for the value of the spoilt metal and the loss of profit allocated to that melt. But the plaintiff's claim for loss of profits for the entire period of interruption of their operations was dismissed on the ground that this pure economic loss was too remote.

Simaan General Contracting Co v Pilkington Glass Ltd [1988]

Facts: a claim for economic loss was made by contractors against sub-contractors, made because the goods supplied by the sub-contractors were not up to specification.

Held: the House of Lords dismissed the claim. In the judgement it was emphasised that the situations which could give rise to a claim for pure economic loss were limited.

4   NEGLIGENCE IN PARTICULAR CIRCUMSTANCES

4.1   Introduction

In the next section we shall deal with negligence in the particular circumstances of:

(a)   dangerous goods (product liability)
(b)   dangerous premises (occupiers liability)
(c)   industrial accidents (injury at work)

In some of these areas the common law rules of negligence have been added to or codified by statutory provisions.

4.2   Activity

What are the three essential elements of the tort of negligence?

4.3   Activity solution

(1)   duty of care
(2)   breach of duty
(3)   resultant loss

5   PRODUCT LIABILITY

5.1   Civil liability

Liability for products involves a mixture of approaches, both civil and criminal.

Civil liability includes:

(a)   **Possible breach of contract**

Under the Sale of Goods Act 1979 there is a breach of the implied term if products prove defective. This contract-based strict liability covers goods which are not of merchantable quality (S14(2)) and not fit for their purpose (S14(3)). Here, liability would be established not only if they are defective in the sense of danger but also if they are of 'bad quality'. Remember also that in the law of contract pure economic loss is recoverable.

(b)   **Possible liability in tort**

       (i)   for negligence - (see above and below).

       (ii)   for breach of statutory duty - (see next chapter).

       (iii)   Liability under Consumer Protection Act (1987) - Part I for defective goods (see below).

5.2   Criminal liability

Criminal liability is covered by Part II Consumer Protection Act (1987) for unsafe goods (see below). There may also be criminal liability under other statutory provisions.

5.3   The elements of the tort of negligence

The basic elements which the plaintiff needs to prove to establish liability for product liability in the tort of negligence are:

(a)   A duty of care owed by the defendant to the plaintiff.
(b)   The duty of care was breached.
(c)   The plaintiff suffered damage as a result of the breach of duty of care, which was not too remote.

5.4   The duty of care

Prior to 1932 a duty only existed if either the thing causing the damage was of a class of dangerous things or if it was dangerous for some reason known to the defendant. However, the duty of care owed by manufacturers was set out by the House of Lords in the case of **Donoghue v Stevenson** (snail in ginger beer bottle) where Lord Atkin described the 'narrow principle' of manufacturer's negligence in terms that:

"A **manufacturer of products,** which he **sells** in such a form as to show that he intends them to reach the **ultimate consumer** in the form in which they left him **with no reasonable possibility of intermediate examination,** and with the knowledge that the absence of reasonable care **in the preparation or putting up** of the products will result in an injury to the consumer's **life or property,** owes a duty to the consumer **to take that reasonable care**" (emphasis added).

This classic statement of the liability of manufacturers in negligence (which is independent of any right of action in contract), has been extended in several respects by subsequent case law.

The principle has been extended beyond the manufacturer so that it can encompass anyone in the chain of distribution, from manufacturer through assembler, distributors and may include repairers.

Stennett v Hancock & Peters [1939]

Facts: the plaintiff was injured when part of the wheel of D1's lorry fell off and hit him as he was walking on the pavement. The wheel had just been repaired by D2 and D1 had not checked the work.

Held: D2 as the repairer should be liable, but D1 was not liable since he was entitled to assume the wheel was properly assembled.

Andrews v Hopkinson [1957]

Facts: the defendant sold an eighteen-year-old car to a finance company which was providing HP for the plaintiff, the person who had agreed to buy the car from the defendant. The defendant had not checked the car, and it had a defective steering mechanism which caused the plaintiff to have an accident. The plaintiff sued the defendant in tort (remember there was no contract between the plaintiff and the defendant).

Held: the defendant was held liable since he was a supplier, and should have known that the car was likely to be dangerous.

Thus, the ultimate retailer may, therefore, find himself both liable in contract to the buyer and also in tort. The kind of liability will be different in that it will involve strict liability under S14 Sale of Goods Act but in tort, negligence on the part of the retailer must be proved.

5.5   Breach of duty of care

As a general rule the plaintiff must show that the defendant failed to take the degree of care which a 'reasonable man' would have taken in the circumstances.

Fault (ie, lack of reasonable care) may arise in a variety of ways:

- Miscarriage in the production and assembly process. The manufacturer may fail to take reasonable care to ensure that foreign substances do not find their way into the product or the manufacturer may use weak or unsuitable materials. The product may alternatively be poorly assembled or constructed.

- Inadequate warnings or directions for use. A failure to warn adequately or give directions will lead to liability in some circumstances but is dependant on a number of factors:

  (a)   likelihood and scale of danger;
  (b)   cost and practicability of warning;
  (c)   whether the danger is obvious or latent.

- In deciding whether the defendant has been negligent the courts will take into consideration (although these may not be decisive), the safety record of the product, industry standards and practices. Moreover, the manufacturer may argue that the product was not defective when put into circulation, it had been interfered with or it should have been inspected or tested before use or sale or finally it has been misused (eg, article was either put to a different use from that which was intended).

5.6   Resultant loss

In negligence there is no liability unless damage is shown to have resulted from the breach of the duty of care. The plaintiff must establish a causal link between the defendant's conduct and the damage which he has incurred.

The defendant's conduct must have been an effective **cause** of the plaintiff's loss.

Any loss claimed for must not be too remote. Actual harm must be caused to the plaintiff or his property other than the thing itself. Thus, a product not working may mean it is not fit for its purpose but there is no liability in negligence.

If a manufacturer produces and sells a thing which is defective, rendering it dangerous to people or property, the manufacturer will be liable for any injury to persons or property caused by it. However, if the manufacturer produces and sells a thing which is merely defective in quality even to the extent that it is useless, the manufacturer's liability is in contract only and he will not be liable to persons who, having no contract with him, suffer purely economic loss due to the defect - **Simaan General Contracting v Pilkington [1988].**

6 CONSUMER PROTECTION ACT 1987 - PRODUCT LIABILITY - PART I

6.1 Introduction

Part I of the Consumer Protection Act 1987 came into force on 1 March 1988. It was enacted to implement the provisions in an EC Directive - the 'product liability directive' to harmonise the laws on product liability.

Part I imposes **strict** civil liability on certain people (although there are also statutory defences) which they cannot exclude or limit, for damage caused by defective products. It is intended to fill a gap in the law to protect consumers who cannot claim breach of contract (because the person damaged did not buy it) or negligence (because the producer cannot be shown to have been negligent). However the common law claims are preserved – see above.

6.2 Liability

Where any damage is caused wholly or partly by a defect in a product **primary** liability rests with:

(a)   the producer (the manufacturer or in the case of minerals the person who abstracted it or where the essential characteristics of a product are attributable to an industrial or other process (eg, canned vegetables) the person who carried out that process);

(b)   any person who by putting his name or brand or trade mark on the product holds himself out as being the producer;

(c)   any person who imported the product from outside the EC.

Secondary liability lies on the supplier of the product, or the person who supplied the product to him, if he has been requested to identify the producer, own-brander or importer, and fails to do so. Thus, he may avoid liability by disclosing on request the name of his supplier. The purpose of this provision is to ensure as far as possible the product is traced back to the producer or other person who is primarily liable. This secondary responsibility also applies to an assembler who uses unsafe parts. Thus, a car manufacturer who uses another's components which are unsafe will only be liable as a supplier of the finished product. A supplier is only liable where he makes a supply in the course of business.

6.3 Products

S1 defines 'product' widely to include any goods, electricity, component parts and raw materials which have been abstracted (eg, minerals) or agricultural products which have been subject to an industrial or other process (the Act does not impose liability in respect of game or agricultural produce which has not undergone any industrial process. 'Industrial process' is not defined in the Act and could give rise to problems.).

'Goods' is defined as including substances, growing crops and things attached to the land, ships, aircraft or vehicles. Aircraft includes gliders, balloons and hovercraft. Ships include boats and any other vessel used in navigation.

Buildings are not products but a supplier of bricks, cement, etc will be liable as supplier of the constituent parts.

Problems could arise in this area. Are organs or blood goods? Is a computer program goods?

6.4   Defective

S3 provides that there is a defect in a product if its safety is not such as people generally are entitled to expect.   Lack of safety includes risk of damage to property, death or personal injury.   In determining the standard of safety which people are generally entitled to expect, regard must be paid to:

(a)   the manner in which the product is marketed;
(b)   instructions or warnings as to its use;
(c)   what might reasonably be expected to be done with it; and
(d)   the time when the product was supplied by its producer.

Exactly how the courts will apply these factors is as yet unknown. The first three seem to be fairly clear and the fourth criterion presumably means that the product will be judged by the safety standards at the time it was first supplied and not later more stringent standards eg, a car brought out in 1970 should not be judged by the safety aspects of a 1991 car.

It should be noted that liability is strict. The defendant cannot plead he took all reasonable care. Once it is shown that the product was unsafe when it was supplied (subject to S4 defences below) the defendant is liable.

Conclusion   In comparison with the tort of negligence there is a shift of emphasis from the nature of the defendant's conduct or lack of it to the nature of the product. Was it unsafe when marketed?

6.5   Damage

S5 defines the damage which will give rise to liability to include death, personal injury, loss or damage to any property including land. It does **not** include:

(a)   loss or damage to the product itself;

(b)   loss or damage to property which is not ordinarily intended for private use, occupation or consumption and was not actually privately used by the persons suffering the loss or damage. Thus for damage to property by reason of defective products, in a commercial context, the common law alone will still apply;

(c)   loss or damage to property of £275 or less.

6.6   Exclusion/limitation clauses

S8 provides that liability under the Act cannot be excluded or limited.

6.7   Defences

Although liability is strict, S4 provides the following defences:

(a)   the defect is attributable to compliance with any requirement imposed by EC obligations;

(b)   the defendant did not supply the product;

(c)   the defendant did not supply in the course of business nor with a view of profit;

(d)   the defect did not exist in the product at the relevant time (the time it was supplied);

(e)   the state of scientific and technical knowledge at the relevant time was not such that the producer of such products might be expected to have discovered the defect. This defence, which is controversial, is sometimes called the 'state of the art' or 'development risks' defence. It is controversial because, in the view of many, it drives a coach and horses through the concept of strict liability;

(f)   the product was comprised in another product and the defect was wholly attributable to the design of the other product or compliance with instructions given by the manufacturer of the other product.

6.8   Limitation period

The period of limitation within which a claim must be brought is normally ten years (three years for personal injury) from the date when the right of action 'accrued'. The right of action accrues (or arises) at the time at which the loss or damage occurred, which is deemed to be at the earliest time at which the person had knowledge of the material facts of loss or damage given the facts observable by him alone or with expert advice which it is reasonable for him to seek.

6.9   Problems with Consumer Protection Act 1987 - Part I

The Consumer Protection Act 1987 Part I is likely to supersede negligence-based liability in importance in the area of consumer safety but the Act does not prevent action being brought simultaneously for negligence.

There are some situations where the Act will not apply for defective products and therefore negligence may be the only avenue of redress available, namely:

(a)   products supplied before 1 March 1988;

(b)   any game or agricultural product which has not undergone an industrial process;

(c)   where a product causes property damage below £275 or the property damaged is of a type not ordinarily used for private use, occupation or consumption;

(d)   things not seen to be products. Examples might be computer software or blood and organs;

(e)   the goods were not supplied for business or profit.

6.10   Consumer Protection Act 1987 - Consumer Safety - Part II

The Consumer Protection Act 1987 (Part II) replaces the Consumer Safety Act 1978 and came into force on 1 October 1987. Under the Consumer Safety Act 1978 the Secretary of State had power to make regulations to ensure that goods were safe and that appropriate information was supplied to the consumer. This system of control was slow to respond to newly discovered dangers. Thus the Consumer Protection Act imposes a general duty to ensure that goods comply with general safety requirements and failure to do so is a criminal offence. In addition it empowers the Secretary of State to make more specific regulations and failure to comply with any such regulation is also an offence.

7   DANGEROUS PREMISES: OCCUPIERS LIABILITY

7.1   Statutory provisions for liability

The occupier, landlord or builder of premises may be liable if a person suffers personal injury or damage to his property while in the premises. Three statutes make provisions for liability for dangerous premises.

(a)   **Occupiers Liability Act 1957**

(b)   **Occupiers Liability Act 1984**

Both these statutes impose a duty of care on **occupiers** (note the definition below) of **premises** (note the definition below) towards people in the premises. The basic difference between the two Acts is that the 1957 Act imposes a duty towards **lawful visitors** and the 1984 Act imposes a duty towards **trespassers** and others who are not lawful visitors.

The OLA 1957 codified, with amendments, the common law tort of negligence as far as it related to occupiers liability to lawful visitors. In 1984 the OLA 1984 was enacted with the equivalent aim of codification.

(c)   **Defective Premises Act 1972**

This Act imposes a duty of care on people who erect, convert or enlarge dwellings and a duty of care on landlords of dwellings. This Act is rarely examined.

7.2   Occupier's liability

An **occupier** of **premises** owes a duty of care to people who come onto them.

[Definition]   An 'occupier' is any person who has control of the premises.

He may not necessarily be the owner and there may be more than one occupier at any one time.

Wheat v E Lacon and Co Ltd [1966]

Facts: the plaintiff's husband was killed when he fell down an unlit staircase which had an inadequate handrail. The staircase was in a public house owned by the respondents, a brewery, and run by a Mr Richardson. His wife used their first floor flat in the pub to take in summer guests, of whom the plaintiff and her husband were two.

Held: both the brewery and the Richardsons were 'occupiers'. However, there was no evidence of negligence and so they had no liability under the Act.

[Definition]   'Premises' includes land, buildings and fixed or moveable structures.

7.3   Lawful visitors - Occupiers' Liability Act 1957

[Definition]   Lawful visitors include people who have express or implied permission to enter (eg, door-to-door salesmen) and people who have a legal right to enter (eg, an inspector of factories).

The common duty of care is a duty to take such care as in all the circumstances of the case is reasonable to see that the visitor will be reasonably safe in using the premises for the purpose for which he is invited or permitted by the occupier to be there. (S2 Occupiers' Liability Act 1957). His duty includes care to ensure that the visitors and their property are reasonably safe.

In particular:

(a)   An occupier must be prepared for children to be less careful than adults (although he may assume that very young children will be properly supervised).

(b)   An occupier may expect that a person in the exercise of his calling will appreciate and take precautions against any special risks ordinarily incidental to that calling so far as the occupier leaves him free to do so (S2(3)(b)).

Christmas v General Cleaning Contractors Ltd [1952]

Facts: a window cleaner was injured when cleaning the defendants' windows, one of which was defective and caused him to fall.

Held: he had no cause of action against the occupier, since the occupier is concerned that the windows are safe for his guests, not for a window cleaner to hold on to. A defective window is a special risk, but one which is ordinarily incidental to the calling of a window cleaner, and so he must take care for himself, and not expect the occupier to do so.

7.4   Duty under the Act

The duty imposed by the Act may be discharged by:

(a)   making the premises reasonably safe;

(b)   warning visitors of the danger provided the warning is adequate to enable the visitor to be reasonably safe – whether the warning is adequate will depend on the warning given and the danger.

The occupier will not be liable if he can show that:

(a)   the visitor's injury was caused by the defective work of an independent contractor if the occupier had reasonably entrusted him with the work and had taken reasonable steps to ensure he was competent and that the work had been properly done;

(b)   the visitor willingly consented to the risk, eg ignored a warning (the occupier may also be able to argue contributory negligence on the part of the visitor).

7.5   Trespassers and others

The 1957 Act only covered the occupier's liability to lawful visitors. His liability to other people, trespassers or others who fall outside the definition of lawful visitor, such as those using a right of way, were governed by common law.

In the leading case of **British Railway Board v Herrington**, the House of Lords held that an occupier owed a duty of care to a trespasser. The standard of care was lower than the common duty of care, the occupier being required merely to act with 'common humanity'.

BRB v Herrington [1972]

Facts: a BRB electrified railway line came alongside a children's playground. Although BRB had fencing along the line it was broken in places and children climbed through from the playground. BRB knew this. A child who had climbed through the fence was seriously injured.

Held: where an occupier knows that there are trespassers on his land or knows of circumstances that make it likely that trespassers will come onto his land and also knows of physical facts in relation to the state of the land or some activity carried out on it which would constitute a serious danger to such trespassers he is under a duty to take reasonable steps to enable them to avoid the danger. BRB were in breach of their duty to the child.

7.6   Duty under the Act

The Occupiers' Liability Act 1984 (which in effect codified the common law as established in **BRB v Herrington**) provides that an occupier of premises owes a duty if:

(a)   he is aware of the danger or has reasonable grounds to believe that it exists;

(b)   he knows or should know that someone is in (or may come into) the vicinity of the danger; and

(c)   the risk is one against which he may reasonably be expected to offer that person some protection.

The duty he owes is to take such care as is reasonable in all the circumstances to see that the person to whom the duty is owed does not suffer injury (ie, personal injury or death and not damage to property) on the premises by reason of the danger concerned. The duty may, in appropriate cases, be discharged by taking reasonable steps to give warning of the danger or to discourage people from incurring the risk. No duty is owed to any person in respect of risks willingly accepted by him.

7.7   Defective Premises Act 1972

The DPA 1972 imposes on **persons who undertake work** of building converting or enlarging **dwellings** such duties:

(a)   to see that the work is done in a workmanlike and professional manner;
(b)   to use proper materials;
(c)   that the completed dwelling will be fit for human habitation.

The **duty** is **owed by** the builder, surveyor, architect, engineer and a developer or local authority who arranges for the provision of the dwelling.

The **duty is owed to** the person who ordered the work and every person who acquires a legal or equitable interest in the dwelling. Note that the duty is owed in respect of dwellings only.

Definition   Dwellings are buildings used or capable of use as a residence by one or more households.

Thus an owner or a tenant of a house or flat would be owed a duty under this section. It is relevant where, for example, problems suffered result from inherent defects in the design or construction of the building.

The Act only relates to work commenced after 1 January 1974 (the date the Act came into force). Thus it will not cover older buildings or conversions. (In assessing the limitation period, time runs from the date of completion of the works.)

The DPA 1972 provides that where **premises** are let under a **tenancy** which puts on the landlord an obligation to the tenant for the maintenance or repair of the premises, the **landlord** owes to all persons who might reasonably be expected to be affected by defects in the state of the premises a duty to take such care as is reasonable in all the circumstances to see that they are **reasonably safe** from **personal injury or from damage** to their property caused by a **relevant defect**.

The duty is owed to the tenant or licensee of the premises and all persons who might reasonably be expected to be affected eg, his family or guests.

The duty is owed by a landlord who has repairing obligations. Such obligations may be expressly stated in the lease or implied either because the landlord reserves the right to enter and do repairs or under the Housing Act 1985 which imposes repairing obligations on landlords in tenancies of less than seven years.

Definition | **Relevant defect** is a defect in the premises resulting from an act or omission of the landlord which constitutes a breach of his repairing obligations or which would do so if he had notice of the defect.

Definition | **Premises** are not defined in the Act but have given a wide interpretation to include 'the whole letting, land and building'. (In **Smith v Bradford Metropolitan Council** the landlord was held liable to a tenant who was injured when a concrete patio in the garden gave way.)

Definition | **Personal injury** has a wide definition and includes any disease and any impairment of a person's physical or mental condition.

Conclusion | The duties under the DPA cannot be excluded or restricted. No remedy is given in the Act for breach of either duty. A person who suffered would therefore sue for breach of statutory duty.

8   INDUSTRIAL ACCIDENTS

8.1   Introduction

An employee who is injured at work may be able to sue his employer in contract or in tort.

An employee's action in contract would be for breach of a term that the employer will provide a safe system of work. Even if there is no express term there is a term implied at common law that the employer will take reasonable care for the safety of his employees.

An employee (or other person injured at a workplace) can sue in tort for:

(a)   negligence;
(b)   breach of statutory duty;
(c)   trespass to person or property.

8.2   Negligence - basic principles apply

The normal rules of negligence apply and the person claiming will have to show that:

(a)   a duty was owed;
(b)   it was breached;
(c)   the damage he suffered was caused by the breach.

The employer may then have a defence. If not the court will have to assess the damages to be awarded to the plaintiff.

8.3   The duty owed

The common law duty of care owed by an employer to his employees was set out in the leading case of **Wilson and Clyde Coal Company Ltd v English [1938]**

Facts: the plaintiff was injured by being crushed by the haulage plant in the defendant's mine.

Held: the defendants argued that they had fulfilled their duty by appointing a qualified manager but the House of Lords rejected their argument and held that the employer owed a personal non-delegable duty to take reasonable care for the safety of his employees.

- **A competent staff of workers**

   The employer must select his workers with care and ensure that they have sufficient skill and experience to do the particular work they have been engaged to do without causing injury to other employees.

   If the employer knows that an employee has tendencies for violent horseplay or actual assault he has a duty to take precautions to ensure that other employees are not injured.

   Hudson v Ridge Manufacturing Co Ltd [1957]

   Facts: an employee was injured as the result of a practical joke played by a fellow employee. The employers knew of the employee's propensity for horseplay.

   Held: the employers were held liable for breach of their personal duty to provide competent staff.

- **Adequate premises**

   The employer must take reasonable care to maintain the premises and access to it in proper safe condition.

   Latimer v AEC [1952]

   Facts: a factory floor was flooded after a heavy rainstorm. The water mixed with the oil on the floor and made it very slippery. The employer dried the floor and spread sawdust over it. Nevertheless, some small slippery patches remained. Latimer slipped and was injured.

   Held: he sued for negligence but lost as it was held that the employer had taken reasonable care in the circumstances. There was no duty on the employer to close the factory until they had cleaned the floor.

   Certain standards are required by the Factories Act 1961, Offices, Shops and Railway Premises Act 1963 and the Health and Safety at Work Act 1974. However, note that many of these merely require 'reasonable' provision of eg, lighting.

- **Adequate equipment**

   The employer must ensure that machinery is properly maintained and that, where necessary, protective clothing, safety devices such as metal hats, goggles, safety belts etc, are provided and available for use.

The employer will not be liable if the employee has disregarded safety precautions which are available provided the employer has done his best to see that such precautions are observed.

Bux v Slough Metals Ltd [1973]

Facts: the employers supplied goggles in line with safety regulations. However, they had taken no steps to ensure that they were worn even though they knew that, to a large extent, the employees were not using them. Bux was not wearing goggles and was injured when molten metal splashed in his eyes.

Held: the employers were held in breach of their duty and they had not taken steps to ensure the goggles were worn. (Note the employee's damages were reduced 40% because of contributory negligence.)

James v Hepworth & Grandage Ltd [1967]

Facts: the employers put up notices stating safety spats should be worn and explaining how to obtain to and use them. James could not read and was injured when not wearing safety spats.

Held: however, the employers were not in breach of their duty as there was no reason for them to believe he could not read and no duty to find out whether he could. (If the employers had known James could not read they might have been liable.)

At common law an employer who bought standard equipment from a reputable supplier was not liable for latent defects which caused injury to employees. However, the Employers Liability (Defective Equipment) Act 1969 provides that where an employee suffers personal injury in the course of his employment in consequence of a defect in equipment provided by the employer and the defect is attributable wholly or partly to the fault of a third party, the injury shall be deemed to be also attributable to the employer's negligence. Thus the employee can sue the employer who will be liable without proof of fault on his part but on fault of the third party. The employer can then seek a contribution from the third party.

- **A proper system and effective supervision**

The employer must ensure that there is a safe system of work commensurate with the risk involved in the job. This will include providing safety equipment and ensuring it is used. In addition it will include warning of dangers and giving instructions, training and supervision where necessary. Thus new, inexperienced employees will require more instruction, supervision etc, than experienced employees. It will also include ensuring that there are sufficient numbers of employees to carry out the work without danger.

Hardaker v Huby [1962]

Facts: an employer caused injury because he had not provided an assistant to help a man carry a bath upstairs.

Held: the employer was liable.

It will also include ensuring that there is adequate co-ordination where necessary to ensure the safety of employees.

Sword v Cameron [1839]

Facts: employees were injured by blasting in a quarry because of lack of co-ordination in giving them enough time to leave the area before the blasting was done.

Held: the employer was liable.

The duty will also be breached if the employee suffers mental injury. In **Walker v Northumberland County Council (1995)**, the Council was held liable where the plaintiff social worker suffered a nervous breakdown due to pressures of work arising from inadequate assistance after the plaintiff had requested such assistance.

The duty is owed to the employee at work and not, for example, if he goes off to do work not required or expected of him although it will include work which might reasonably be expected of him. It will not include travel to and from work but will cover journeys between places of work.

In the case of loaned employees the borrower may be liable if he has a right of control over what the borrowed employee does and the method of doing it.

8.4   When is the duty breached – the standard required

The duty is similar to the duty of care in negligence generally but expressed in terms appropriate to the relationship of employee and employer. The duty is not absolute and is fulfilled if the employer takes reasonable care. The duty is not to subject an employee to any risk which the employer can reasonably foresee and which he can guard against by any measure, the convenience and expense of which are not entirely disproportionate to the risk involved. Thus the court will:

(a)   assess whether the risk was reasonably foreseeable as opposed to wholly exceptional or unique;

(b)   balance

　　(i)   the likelihood that injury will result from the risk and the seriousness of any injury which might result

　　against

　　(ii)   the practicability of precautions necessary to avoid the risk (**Latimer v AEC Ltd** above);

(c)   take into account the known susceptibility of people exposed to the risk. He should take special care where the employee is known to be at extra risk. However, again the standard is reasonable on the basis of what is known, the likelihood of injury and the seriousness of any such injury.

(d)   acknowledge that the general practice in the particular business or industry in question is relevant. Any official or trade guidelines and statutory safety provisions are relevant in deciding whether the employer acted reasonably.

Although the employee must generally prove the duty, the breach and that damages flowed from the breach, the plea of *res ipsa loquitur* is open to him in circumstances where the facts speak for themselves eg, where a crane rest collapsed, and the burden to disprove negligence shifts to the employer.

If an employee is sent to work at the place of a third party the employer will still owe him a duty of care but it will differ according to the circumstances. Thus an employer who sends his employee to do cleaning work at various premises will not have to visit them all to ensure that they are safe.

8.5   Damage has been caused by the breach of duty

The plaintiff employee must also show that the damage he suffered was caused by the employer's breach of duty. This is as relevant in negligence causing industrial accidents as in any other type of negligence. See **McWilliams v Sir William Arrol [1962]**

9   CHAPTER SUMMARY

Much of this chapter has been concerned with the case law that surrounds the tort of negligence.

The three main areas of case law are to do with proof of the three necessary elements in order to establish negligence. These are that a duty of care is owed, that duty has been breached by the defendant and that damage to the plaintiff was as a result of that breach.

The tort of negligence is also relevant in three specific practical areas regarding product liability, dangerous premises and industrial accidents.

10   SELF TEST QUESTIONS

10.1   In **Caparo Industries v Dickman** what 3 factors were held relevant to the establishment of a duty of care? (1.3)

10.2   What does *res ipsa loquitur* mean? (2.3)

10.3   What is the test for remoteness in tort? (3.3)

10.4   Which Act of Parliament deals with liability for unsafe goods? (6.1)

10.5   Which statute covers liability towards lawful visitors? (7.1)

10.6   What is an occupier? (7.2)

11   EXAMINATION TYPE QUESTIONS

11.1   Negligence/vicarious liability

(a)   Define the tort of negligence. What must the plaintiff prove in order to succeed in an action for negligence?

(5 marks)

(b)   What is vicarious liability? Illustrate your answer by specific examples.

(5 marks)

(Total: 10 marks)

11.2   Inaccurate statements

Discuss the liability in tort of the maker of a statement which causes loss to a person who has relied on its accuracy, where the statement proves to have been, in fact, inaccurate.

(20 marks)

12   ANSWERS TO EXAMINATION TYPE QUESTIONS

12.1   Negligence/vicarious liability

(a)   Negligence is the breach of a legal duty of care which results in damage to the plaintiff.

In negligence the plaintiff has to prove, firstly, that the defendant owed him a duty of care. Such a duty is owed at common law to a neighbour, who was defined in **Donoghue v Stevenson** as: a person who would be so closely affected by the acts or omissions of the defendant that he ought to have him in contemplation when directing his mind to the acts or omissions in question.

Secondly, the plaintiff must prove that the defendant was in breach of that duty of care. The standard expected is that of a reasonable member of the class to which the defendant belonged. Thus, in an action against a doctor who is a general practitioner, it would be that of a reasonable general practitioner and not that of a specialist.

Thirdly, the plaintiff must show that the damage which he has suffered is the result of the act or omission of the defendant.

(b)   Vicarious liability is liability for the torts of others. A person who is negligent will be liable to the person who has suffered loss as result of his negligence. However, others may also be liable to the person who suffered loss if a relationship is established which is recognised as creating vicarious liability. These include the following:

(i)   Partners are liable for the torts of their co-partners.

(ii)   Employers are liable for some torts committed by their employees. Employers are not vicariously liable for the torts committed by independent contractors. It is sometimes difficult to establish whether a person is an employee or an independent contractor. However, a person who is employed on a contract of service which stipulates holidays, sick pay, hours of work and periodic payment eg, monthly, will be an employee. An employer will only be liable for torts committed by employees in the course of their employment ie, torts committed while undertaking tasks which they have been employed to do, even if they undertake these tasks negligently.

12.2   Inaccurate statements

Until 1963, although there was liability in the tort of negligence for physical injury resulting from carelessly made statements, it was thought that there was no liability for financial loss caused as the result of a statement which was inaccurate. However, in the case of **Hedley Byrne v Heller** the court stated that there would be liability if there was a special relationship in which a person reasonably relied on a statement made by an expert and suffered loss as a result of that reliance, provided there was no effective disclaimer by the maker of the statement.

In **Hedley Byrne** a bank gave a reference as to the creditworthiness of one of its customers to an advertising agency. There was no contract between the bank and the agency as the agency provided no consideration for the reference. The reference was incorrect as it stated that the customer was creditworthy when he was not. However, the bank had included in the reference a statement that it would not accept any liability for the actual creditworthiness of the customer. This was sufficient to result in the bank not being liable to the agency. The court did state that, but for the disclaimer, the bank would have been liable. It then set out the situation in which it considered that a person could be liable for loss suffered as a result of making inaccurate statements.

There have been many cases since **Hedley Byrne** and different courts have approached the problem in different ways depending on the circumstances involved.

However, the principles set out in **Hedley Byrne** are still applied. These are as follows.

There must be a special relationship. No definitive limits have been set on what constitutes a special relationship and there has been much discussion on whether the person making the statement must be a professional. Most cases are about professionals eg, solicitors, accountants and surveyors. However, in **Esso Petroleum v Mardon** a businessman was held to owe a duty of care. There has also been much discussion on exactly how far the duty extends ie, does it extend to people who are not specifically known to the maker of the statement. It would appear that a special relationship will exist where a person with special knowledge or skill makes a statement which he knows or ought to know people will rely on ie, the maker need not actually know the person who does rely on it provided he is aware of the likelihood of such reliance. This point is still far from clear.

In **Caparo Industries Plc v Dickman and others** the House of Lords held that the three criteria for the imposition of a duty of care are foreseeability of damage, proximity of relationship and the reasonableness of imposing a duty.

The person must have relied on the statement. In **JEB Fasteners v Marks Bloom** accountants prepared accounts of a company which was the target of a takeover by another company. The bidding company read the accounts but, although they were suspicious about them, decided to acquire the company anyway because they wanted to acquire the services of two directors of the target company. They acquired the company which then failed. The accounts had been negligently prepared and the accountants were aware that the target company was seeking finance, although not necessarily aware of the actual company. However, they were not liable to the bidding company for the loss suffered because the court found that the bidding company had not relied on the accounts.

In **Hedley Byrne** the bank was not liable because it disclaimed responsibility. However, this case was based on facts before the Unfair Contract Terms Act 1977 came into force. This Act limits the ability of a person to limit or exclude his liability for loss suffered to others as a result of his negligence. There have been several cases, most involving surveyors preparing reports for building societies which were shown to purchasers who relied on them. The reports had disclaimers on them but in most cases these have proved ineffective to escape liability.

The person making the statement must have been negligent ie, been in breach of their duty of care. The test of breach of duty is whether the maker took the care which a reasonable man in his position would have taken. If the person is an expert then he will be judged by the standards of expertise of his professional or calling. It would appear that the standard will be that of the post occupied by the person not his own personal expertise. Thus, a trainee will be judged by the standard of a fully qualified person if he is carrying out such work.

Finally, the person who relied on the statement must have suffered loss. It would appear that this is basically the same point as that of showing that the person did rely on the statement.

12 TORT: OTHER TORTS

INTRODUCTION & LEARNING OBJECTIVES

Syllabus area 8c. Basic concepts. (Ability required 3).
Strict liability. (Ability required 3).
Breach of statutory duty. (Ability required 3).

In this chapter the remaining torts of breach of statutory duty, trespass, deceit and defamation will be considered.

When you have studied this chapter you should be able to do the following:

- Understand the concept of the tort breach of statutory duty.

- Be able to apply breach of statutory duty in the context of the strict liability provisions of the Factories Act 1961.

- Be able to recognise in outline the torts of trespass, deceit and defamation.

---

1   BREACH OF STATUTORY DUTY

1.1   Introduction

> **Definition**   Breach of statutory duty is a breach of a duty imposed on some person or body by legislation.

The person or body in breach of the statutory duty may be liable to a criminal penalty and also may be liable in tort to pay damages to the person injured by the breach.

It is important to note that not every statutory provision creates a duty. Statute may give a person or body a power or discretion to act. The negligent exercise of the power may give rise to an action for negligence. However, the tort of breach of statutory duty is only applicable to statutory provisions which impose a duty. Most actions for breach of statutory duty are taken in respect of statutes dealing with safety at work.

1.2   Three essential elements

In order to bring a civil action in tort for breach of statutory duty the plaintiff must prove three matters

(a)   The existence of legislation which imposes a duty on the defendant which the defendant has broken.

The legislation could be a statute eg, the Factories Act 1961 and the Office, Shops and Railway Premises Act 1963, or it could be delegated legislation, eg, regulations made under the Health and Safety at Work Act 1974. It is important to note whether the particular legislation imposes strict liability or merely a duty to take reasonable care.

(b)   The legislation contemplates civil liability.

Some pieces of legislation expressly state they allow civil liability, eg, some of the regulations made under the Health and Safety at Work Act 1974; others expressly state they create criminal liability only and not civil liability, (eg, the Health and Safety at Work Act 1974); whilst others expressly state they create criminal liability and are silent on whether or not they allow civil liability. In this last situation the court will look at the entire context of the statute to decide whether Parliament contemplated civil proceedings. Case law shows that this is the situation with the Factories Act 1961 and the Office, Shops and Railways Act 1963.

(c)   What happened was within the 'mischief' which the legislation was intended to prevent.

Gorris v Scott [1874]

Facts: the defendant shipowner agreed to take the plaintiff's sheep from Hamburg to Newcastle. A statute required that animals be kept in separate pens when being transported by sea in order to prevent the spread of infectious diseases. The sheep were not penned and were swept overboard. The plaintiff sued the defendant for breach of statutory duty.

Held: the defendant was not liable because the loss suffered by the plaintiff was not of a kind that the statute was intended to prevent.

See also **Close v Steel Company of Wales [1961]**

This tort is now examined more closely in the context of the Factories Act 1961 and the Office Shops and Railway Premises Act 1963.

1.3   Factories Act 1961

The FA 1961 contains a number of provisions dealing with health and safety in factories. There is a general duty to ensure factories are safe so far as is reasonably practicable eg, to keep passageways clear. However, it is the specific strict liability provisions relating to the fencing of dangerous machinery which are of most importance in your examination and are now covered in detail.

The FA 1961 imposes an absolute duty on the occupier of a factory to fence securely (i) all prime movers, (ii) all transmission machinery, and (iii) every dangerous part of a machine

- the duty is imposed on the **occupier** of a **factory.**

    The occupier is the person who has control over the state of the factory and/or the activities carried on there. This will inevitably include the employer. A factory is defined by the FA 1961 to include not only a place where things are manufactured but also where things are processed or packaged including a slaughterhouse and filmset and premises ancillary to a factory.

- the duty is an **absolute** duty to fence securely.

    This means strict liability. Thus if there is a dangerous machine there **must** be a secure guard on it. In **Frost v John Summers** the employer unsuccessfully argued that to put a guard on his dangerous machine would make it unusable.

    The guard must be secure. It is not secure if an employee can remove it or circumvent it. The guard must be kept in position at all times when the machine is in operation: it may, however, be removed for maintenance and repair.

- the duty is owed to every person employed or working on the premises and even though they have no business to be near the machine.

Uddin v Associated Portland Cement [1965]

Facts: the plaintiff, an employee, climbed up onto the rafters of a factory to catch a pigeon. As he leaned across a dangerous unfenced revolving shaft his clothing became entangled and he was seriously injured.

Held: his action against his employer for breach of statutory duty succeeded. (*Note:* his damages were reduced on account of his contributory negligence)

- the purpose of the fencing provisions is to prevent persons becoming entangled in the machine's moving parts. It does not extend to protection from crushing between two machines or between the machine and some other structure such as a wall nor to protection from pieces of the machine breaking off and flying out.

Close v Steel Company of Wales [1961]

Facts: an unfenced drill shattered and the bit entered the operator's eye.

Held: the operator failed in his action for breach of duty because what happened was not within the mischief that the FA 1961 fencing provisions were intended to prevent. (*Note:* he succeeded in an action in the tort of negligence)

1.4   Office, Shops and Railway Premises Act 1963

Like the Factories Act 1961 this Act imposes an absolute duty to fence dangerous machinery and other duties relating to safety in such premises.

1.5   Activity

Wilma is injured at work due to the failure of her employer to comply with a provision contained in the Health and Safety at Work Act 1974.

Can she sue her employer for damages for breach of statutory duty?

1.6   Activity solution

No. The HSWA 1974 specifically disallows civil proceedings in respect of its breach.

2   TRESPASS

2.1   Introduction

Definition   Trespass is a direct and unjustifiable interference with the 'person', 'land' or 'goods' of another person.

All three kinds of trespass are actionable *per se* (in themselves) ie, the plaintiff can sue even if he has not suffered any damage or loss. However the plaintiff must prove that the defendant acted intentionally (as opposed to merely negligently).

2.2   Trespass to the person

There are three torts which constitute trespass to the person.

(a)   **Battery** - the intentional application of unlawful physical force to another person. Actual bodily contact is not essential. Throwing water or spitting at someone would be a battery. However, merely touching a person to attract their attention or inadvertently bumping in to someone eg, on the train, is not a battery.

(b)   **Assault** - the causing of reasonable fear of the infliction of a battery. Thus pointing a gun at someone, threatening to shoot, would be an assault.

(c)   **False imprisonment** - the unauthorised detention of a person. Any such detention may amount to false imprisonment eg, an employer preventing an employee from leaving the premises until he has answered questions because the employer suspects him of theft. There may be false imprisonment even though the employee is unaware that he is being prevented from leaving, for example security guards are stationed outside the door but he does not know this. The person must be detained in a way which prevents them from leaving. Thus merely requiring someone to leave by an alternative exit is not false imprisonment. Finally the detention must be unauthorised. Thus a police officer arresting someone under a warrant is properly authorised and therefore is not liable.

2.3   Trespass to land

Definition   This is the unjustifiable interference with the possession of land.

Land includes buildings, subsoil and the air space above the surface (although aircraft have a statutory right to fly in the airspace subject to safety conditions and height requirements).

Unjustifiable interference includes:

(a)   bringing something into direct contact with the land. Thus putting a ladder against another person's wall will amount to a trespass but blowing smoke into another person's air space will be too indirect (although it may be actionable as a private nuisance);

(b)   going onto the land without consent, which may be express or implied (eg, the postman), or lawful authority (eg, police with a search warrant);

(c)   going onto land with consent but remaining after the consent has been withdrawn. However, if the consent is given by contract eg, paying to go to the cinema, the consent so granted cannot generally be revoked until the contract has been completed (the end of the movie);

(d)   going onto land with consent for a particular purpose and doing something which is not allowed eg, going to the theatre to see a play and wandering into the restricted areas backstage.

The tort is committed against the person in possession so that, for example, a tenant may sue an intruder for trespass. It is actionable *per se* ie, the plaintiff need not prove that he has suffered damage, merely that there has been a trespass. The remedies will be damages or an injunction to prevent reoccurrence.

2.4   Trespass to goods

The Torts (Interference with Goods) Act 1977 provides that wrongful interference with goods means:

(a)   the wrongful interference with the possession of goods such as moving, removing, damaging or destroying them. Actual physical contact is not necessary so that throwing a stone through a window would be trespass to goods. The person in possession may sue and it is actionable *per se* ie, the plaintiff need not prove that he has suffered damage, merely that, for example, the goods have been removed from his possession;

(b)   **conversion** - which is any act which constitutes an unjustifiable denial of another's title to goods. Thus only the owner of goods may sue for conversion. Thus taking goods belonging to another or refusing to return them is conversion if it is done in a way which constitutes a denial that the other person owns it eg, selling, pawning or destroying the goods. Merely taking goods of another with no such denial is a trespass. If a bank collects the proceeds of a cheque for a person who is not entitled to the money it may be sued in conversion by the rightful owner.

2.5   Activity

If an auctioneer sells James' goods without his permission believing that the goods belonged to Andrew what, if any, tort has been committed?

2.6   Activity solution

The tort of conversion in dealing in the goods in such a way as to deny James' title to them.

3   TORT OF DECEIT

Definition   a statement made knowing it is untrue or with recklessness as to its truth or falsity and with the intention of causing financial loss to the defendant.

This tort is of relevance to a damages claim as an alternative to rescission for fraudulent misrepresentation in the law of contract.

4   DEFAMATION

4.1

Definition   the publication of a defamatory statement about another living person without lawful justification.

A **defamatory** statement is one which lowers a person's reputation in the minds of right-thinking members of society or which exposes him to hatred, ridicule or contempt.

A defamatory **statement** may be in the form of a libel or in the form of slander.

Definition   libel is a defamatory statement in permanent form eg, writing in a book or newspaper; a picture; a statue; anything broadcast whether radio, television or film.

Definition   slander is a defamatory statement in transient form eg, the spoken word.

4.2   Lawful justification

The defendant can escape liability if he can prove any one or more of the following defences.

- **Truth**

- **Fair comment** on a matter of public interest. This would include such things as film reviews. The comment must be fair ie, without malice.

- **Absolute privilege.** Statements which attract this defence are speeches in Parliament and statements in any court together with verbatim newspaper and television etc reports.

- **Qualified privilege.** Statements which attract this defence include statements at public meetings and an employer's reference for an employee. This defence cannot be relied on if the statement was made maliciously.

- Offer of amends or suitable **apology and correction.**

4.3   Activity

Edward has failed to obtain a new job and was told that this was because of a bad reference from his ex-employer. On the basis that the reference was untrue is it likely that Edward can sue his ex-employer in

(a)   tort of negligence?
(b)   tort of defamation?

4.4   Activity solution

(a)   Yes: duty of care owed - **Spring v Guardian Assurance [1994]** but Edward must prove the employer gave the reference without reasonable care.

(b)   Yes, but if his employer made the statement without malice his employer will not be liable on the basis of qualified privilege.

5   SELF TEST QUESTIONS

5.1   What is breach of statutory duty? (1.1)

5.2   When can an action in tort be brought for breach of statutory duty? (1.2)

5.3   Can an action in tort be brought for breach of the Health and Safety at Work Act? (1.2, 1.5)

5.4   Can an action in tort be brought for breach of regulations made under the HSWA 1974? (1.2)

5.5   Explain what is meant by strict liability (1.3)

5.6   What are the three types of trespass? (2.1)

5.7   Define the tort of defamation (4.1)

5.8   List the five special defences available to the tort of defamation (4.2)

6   EXAMINATION TYPE QUESTION

6.1   Injury at work

(a)   An employee, who has been injured at work, may seek compensation from his employer by an action in negligence.

What must the employee prove to succeed in such action?   **(12 marks)**

(b)   To what extent will the employee's action differ if he claims that there has been a breach of safety regulations?   **(8 marks)**

(Total: 20 marks)

7   EXAMINATION TYPE ANSWER

7.1   Injury at work

(a)   In order to succeed in an action in the tort of negligence against his employer the injured employee must prove (i) that the employer owes him a duty of care, and (ii) that the employer has breached his duty of care, and (iii) that as a result the employee has suffered loss which is not too remote.

Duty of care

Under the neighbour principle established by **Donoghue v Stevenson** an employer owes a duty of care to his employees in relation to their health and safety at work. In particular an employer owes a duty to provide safe plant **(Bradford v Robinson)**, safe premises **(Latimer v AEC)**, a safe system of work **(Smith v Charles Baker)**, safety equipment **(Paris v Stepney Borough Council** and **McWilliams v Sir William Arrol)** and reasonably competent fellow employees **(Hudson v Ridge Manufacturing)**.

The duty at common law is owed personally by the employer to his employees, and he does not escape that duty by showing that he has delegated the performance to some competent person. In **Williams and Clyde Coal Co. v English,** the employer was compelled by law to employ a colliery agent who was responsible for safety in the mine. Nonetheless, when the accident occurred the employer was held liable. Thus it can never be a defence for an employer to show that he has assigned the responsibility of securing and maintaining health and safety precautions to a safety officer or other person. He can delegate the performance but not the responsibility.

Breach of duty

The standard of care which must be exercised by the employer is 'the care which an ordinary prudent employer would take in all the circumstances'. The employer does not give an absolute guarantee of health and safety, he must take **reasonable** care, and he therefore will be liable only if there is some lack of care on his part or in failing to foresee something which was reasonably foreseeable. In **Latimer v AEC** oil had spread over the factory floor because of flooding. When an employee slipped and injured himself on a small patch of oil which still remained on the floor the employer was not liable because he had taken reasonable steps to clear up the oil (eg, by using all available sawdust). If the particular employee has a disability known to the employer or he is a young or inexperienced employee the standard of care to be expected is higher than would otherwise be the case - **Paris v Stepney Borough Council.** Thus with experienced employees the employer's duty would be discharged by merely providing safety equipment together with instructions for its use, but with inexperienced more vulnerable employees the employer would be expected to go further and exhort them to use it.

Ordinarily it will be for the employee to provide that the employer was in breach of duty. However, there are two possible modifications to this. First if the maxim 'res ipsa loquitur' (the thing speaks for itself) applies. This will be the case where, the safety of the workplace being within the control of the employer, the accident is such as would not ordinarily have happened if the employer had taken reasonable care. In this situation the burden of proof is shifted to the defendant employer who will only escape liability if he can show he did take reasonable care. Second, in relation to accidents caused by the provision of defective plant and equipment the employee is not obliged to prove the defect was the fault of the employer because the Employers' Liability (Defective Equipment) Act 1969 deems the employer in breach of duty even though the injury was caused by a manufacturing defect.

Loss

The employee must prove that it was the employer's breach of duty which **caused** the loss claimed. In **McWilliams v Sir William Arrol** an employer admitted breach of duty by failing to provide a safety harness for an employee who was employed as a steeplejack. But he was not liable because evidence showed that the employee (who fell to his death) would not have used the safety harness even had it been provided.

The employee must prove that the resultant loss is not too remote. It will not be too remote where a reasonable man would foresee the type of damage which occurred: it is not necessary to foresee the exact way in which it occurred nor its extent. Thus under the thin skull rule an employer whom it was held could reasonably foresee that an employee employed to stir vats of molten metal would suffer a burn from a splash if not provided with protective clothing was fully liable for that employee's death caused by the burns activation of a dormant malignant cancerous condition - **Smith v Leech Braine.** Since some personal injury was reasonably foreseeable it did not matter that its extent was more devastating due to the susceptible state of health of the particular employee.

(b)   Where an employee has been injured because of breach of safety regulations his action is in tort for breach of statutory duty.

In order to succeed in this tort the employee must prove (i) the existence of an Act of Parliament or other legislation which imposes a duty on the employer and that legislation has been broken, and (ii) the legislation contemplates civil liability (as opposed to solely creating a criminal offence), and (iii) the accident which happened was within the 'mischief' which the legislation was intended to prevent.

An example is the Factories Act 1961. This Act imposes an absolute duty on the occupier of a factory to fence securely dangerous machinery. Case law shows that this Act contemplates civil liability. The mischief that the Act was designed to prevent is that of preventing employees becoming entangled in moving parts of machines. Thus in **Close v Steel Company of Wales** an employee had no action for breach of the Act's fencing requirements because his injury occurred by means of a piece of the machine flying out and hitting him, not by him becoming caught up in the machine.

The main differences between an action for negligence and an action for breach of statutory duty will largely arise from the precise wording of the particular piece of legislation. As shown above all employers owe a duty of care in the tort of negligence whereas under the Factories Act it is only employers who are occupiers of factories who are within the ambit of the Act. In the tort of negligence the duty is broken only where the employer fails to exercise reasonable care, whereas under the Factories Act it is an absolute duty to fence securely: there would therefore be a breach of the Act if the dangerous machine is unfenced however much care the employer took.

13 EMPLOYMENT: THE CONTRACT OF EMPLOYMENT

INTRODUCTION & LEARNING OBJECTIVES

Syllabus area 8d. The contract of employment:
Engagement. (Ability required 3.)
Terms (including wages). (Ability required 3.)
Health and safety requirements. (Ability required 3.)

Historically, employment law was called the law of master and servant and the relationship between them was one of servitude: the servant serving his master. The concepts have changed and the master is now called the employer and the servant called the employee, and their relationship is generally seen as one based on contract. Until recently there was very little statutory or judicial intervention into this relationship. The generally accepted view was that the parties were and should be free to enter into contracts on whatever terms they chose. Since the mid 1960s a number of statutes have been enacted which affect the employment relationship. Largely as a result of these statutory changes there have been many more judicial decisions which also affect the way in which the relationship is seen.

Employment law is concerned with the law relating to individual contracts of employment (ie, the law which affects employees). It is not generally concerned with the law relating to the self-employed which is largely governed by consumer or commercial law. However, the law is not consistent and some provisions do affect both employees and the self-employed. Thus we first turn to the important distinction between these two types of employment and then consider the employment contract itself.

When you have studied this chapter you should be able to do the following:

- Distinguish between a contract of service and a contract for services and understand the importance of the distinction.

- Understand the concept of a contract of employment and its express terms.

- Discuss the terms implied into employment contracts in common law and the duties of employer and employee.

- Discuss the terms implied into employment contracts from sources other than common law.

---

1 TYPES OF CONTRACT

1.1 Introduction

There are two types of working relationship.

A shop assistant who works for a large department store from 9 to 5 Monday to Friday, with specific holidays and wages will be an employee of the store.

An electrician who runs his own business and comes in to do a one off rewiring job for the department store is not an employee of the store. He is self-employed.

The legal distinctions between these two types of working relationship are important. In legal terminology, the shop assistant is an **employee** under a contract **of service** and the electrician is an **independent contractor** under a contract **for services.**

1.2   Importance of distinction

The **difference is important** for a variety of reasons, the most important are:

(a)   only employees are afforded protection under employment protection legislation;

(b)   only employees have implied into their contract certain common law duties of employer and employee;

(c)   only employees can make their employers vicariously liable for their torts;

(d)   only employees are given preferential rights to what they are owed on the insolvency of the employers;

(e)   only employees are entitled to certain state benefits such as unemployment benefit, industrial injury benefit, statutory sick pay, and statutory maternity pay;

(f)   employees' tax is deducted through PAYE assessed under Schedule E. Independent contractors are assessed under Schedule D and are themselves responsible for payment of tax.

(g)   an employer must pay National Insurance contributions in respect of every employee, but not in respect of independent contractors. Further, every employee must also pay an 'employees' contribution and this must be deducted from his wages by the employer. Independent contractors pay a 'self-employed' contribution and is himself responsible for payment.

The two examples given above are fairly clear cut ones. However it is not always easy to determine whether a person is an employee or an independent contractor, and the courts have developed a number of tests to make the distinction.

1.3   The 'control' test

The sole test which was used until about the 1940/50s to determine whether a person was an employee or an independent contractor was the 'control' test. This was set out in **Yewens v Noakes [1880]** 'a servant is a person subject to the command of his master as to the manner in which he shall do his work'.

Thus a person was an employee if the employer could tell him not only what to do but how to do it. Most of the cases in which this test was applied as the sole test were cases concerning the possibility of vicarious liability. See for example **Mersey Docks & Harbour Board v Coggins & Griffiths [1947].** The test was based on the fact that in an agricultural or early industrial society the employer did have more knowledge and skill than the employees.

However, with developing technology and specialisation the control test became inappropriate as employers would hire people for particular skills eg, a chemical engineer, which the employer did not have sufficient knowledge or skill to instruct the manner in which they carried out their work.

Therefore several other tests have been developed. There is now no single test and the operation of the various tests is far from satisfactory.

1.4   The integration test

This test provides that under a contract **of service** the work done is an **integral** part of the business whereas under a contract **for services** the work done is not integrated into it but only **accessory** to it and is being done by the worker as a person in business on his own account.

Cassidy v Minister of Health [1951]

Facts: was a doctor in a hospital an employee of the hospital or an independent contractor?

Held: although the hospital did not control the manner of his work he was nevertheless an employee because he was part of the institution of the hospital.

Beloff v Pressdam [1973]

Facts: B was a regular contributor to a newspaper. She had no regular hours, wrote for other newspapers and journals, and had leave to write books. However, she wrote regularly for this newspaper, including leaders and was an active member of the editorial staff, attending regular meetings and taking part in editorial decisions. Was she an employee?

Held: she was an employee: her work was an integral part of the business.

However the test is not satisfactory because it is sometimes difficult to ascertain what is integral and what is accessory and it does not deal with certain cases, for example, the worker who provides his own equipment.

1.5   The economic reality test

This is also sometimes called the multiple test. It looks at the economic reality behind the relationship.

Ready Mixed Concrete v Ministry of Pensions [1968]

Facts: the driver of a lorry had a contract with a company under which he drove his lorry only on company business, obeyed instructions of the foreman and wore company colours. He provided his own lorry which he had obtained from the company on hire purchase and was painted company colours. He could employ a substitute driver. He was paid on the basis of mileage and quantity of goods delivered. He paid the expenses of repair and maintenance of the lorry and his own national insurance and income tax. The Minister of Pensions claimed that he was an employee and the company had therefore to make the employer's insurance contributions.

Held: although the employer exercised some control over his work, the other factors were not consistent with there being a contract of service. In particular the fact that he owned his own equipment and was operating at his own financial risk to a degree (ie, was **'a small businessman'**) meant that he was an independent contractor.

Market Investigations Ltd v Minister of Social Security [1969]

Facts: a market research interviewer worked on and off under a series of contracts whereby she interviewed for a company in accordance with interview instructions issued by the company. She had to complete the work within a specified period but otherwise had no specified hours of work. There was no provision for holiday or sick pay and she was free to work for others while working for the company.

Held: the company did have some control over the manner in which she did her work and that the terms of the contract were consistent with a contract of service. The court emphasised that she did not provide her own tools and took no risk. She was therefore not **'in business on her own account'** and was an employee not an independent contractor. The court also emphasised that there was **'no exhaustive test compiled, nor strict rules laid down'** as to the factors which identified a contract of service.

A list of factors which will be considered include:

(a)   degree of control by the 'employer' - still a relevant factor;

(b)   degree to which the worker risks loss/stands to gain from profit;

(c)   ownership of tools and equipment;

(d)   degree to which the worker's work is an integral part of the business;

(e)   regularity and method of payment;

(f)   regularity of hours;

(g)   whether there is a mutuality of obligations – ie, is the employer under a duty to provide work and the worker under a duty to accept it;

(h)   ability to provide a substitute (ie, ability to delegate the performance of the contract);

(i)   the terms used by the parties - although it is a factor to be considered, it is not decisive. The court will consider the substance not the form, and will not be persuaded by a label which is clearly inconsistent with the facts of the relationship.

The court will weigh up the factors, giving such weight to each factor as is warranted in the circumstances.

> **Conclusion**   No one test is really capable of determining employee status therefore all of the above factors will be considered.

Note that the amount of work done is not a deciding factor. Thus a person who works part-time can be an employee or an independent contractor depending on which side of the line he or she falls on the above tests.

1.6   Temporary or casual workers

There are real problems in determining the status of **temporary or casual workers**.

O'Kelly v Trusthouse Forte [1983]

Facts: a wine waiter was called a **'regular casual'** because he was given work when it was required in the banqueting hall. He had no other employment and it was generally accepted that he would be offered work in preference to others when work was available, and that he would accept such work when offered.

Held: he was an independent contractor because there was **'no mutuality of obligation'** in that the company was under no duty to offer him work and he was under no duty to accept it. However when at work he wore a company uniform, did not use his own equipment, did not share in the profit and had no investment in the business (aside from his time as a waiter).

Contrast this with **Market Investigations Ltd v Minister of Social Security [1969]** above where the interviewer was also a **'temporary worker'**.

1.7   Homeworkers or outworkers

There are also problems with **homeworkers** or **outworkers** (ie, people who work at home not at the employer's premises.) Generally such people will be paid by the number of pieces they produce and will supply their own equipment. Their position is ambiguous and many consider themselves to be self-employed (ie, independent contractors), but the law does not always take this view.

Nethermere v Taverna & Gardiner [1984]

Facts: two women who sewed trousers at home let the company know when to deliver the material and collect the finished garments. They rarely refused work but did give warning if they did not want it eg, going on holiday. They submitted time sheets and were paid the same rate as the workers in the factory. The company relied on the work they produced. The company provided the machines.

Held: they were employees because by the giving and taking of work regularly over a continuous period of time they had built up a mutuality of obligation (ie, the company to provide work and the women to accept it).

1.8   Activity

James employs a marketing advisor Andrew. Andrew pays his own income tax and national insurance contribution and works an agreed number of hours each week but at times of his own choosing. Andrew also works for other employers provided that they are not competitors of James. What factors would need to be considered in order to decide whether Andrew's contract was one of service or for services?

1.9   Activity solution

(a)   Level of James's control over Andrew despite Andrew being free to work at whatever times he pleases.

(b)   Any financial risk that Andrew bears.

(c)   Whether Andrew provides any equipment or materials for their job.

(d)   The way in which James and Andrew view the contract. (The tax and national insurance position is evidence they view it as a contract for services).

(e)   Is James under an obligation to provide work for Andrew?

2   FORMATION OF THE CONTRACT OF EMPLOYMENT

2.1   Introduction

The employment relationship is a contractual one. The basic rules of contract will apply. There must be offer and acceptance, intention to create legal relations and consideration. Usually the offer comes from the employer and the acceptance from the employee: the consideration provided by the employer is his promise to pay the employee and the consideration of the employee is his promise to work for the employer.

Both parties must have capacity to contract. Generally an employment contract is binding on a minor only if it is on the whole for his benefit. The minimum age at which a minor may be employed is 13 and there are also statutory restrictions of employing children under 16.

Generally the contract may take any form. It can be oral or in writing, express or implied. Certain contracts eg, apprentices or seamen, must be in writing. There is also a duty on employers to provide a written statement of particulars.

The vitiating factors of mistake, misrepresentation, duress, undue influence and illegality will also apply to employment contracts. In a number of cases attempts by the employer and employee to evade the payment of tax rendered the contract void for illegality. If the contract is void the employee will have no right to claim wages, redundancy, unfair dismissal etc.

Finally the contract may be discharged by performance, agreement, frustration and breach. The remedies available will include the usual contractual remedies plus the statutory remedies of unfair dismissal and redundancy.

2.2   Express terms of the contract

The employment contract like any other will include terms **expressly** agreed between the parties.

2.3   Activity

What are the sort of terms that you think might be expressly included in a contract of employment?

2.4   Activity solution

(a)   pay and other benefits - rate and date/period paid;

(b)   holiday leave/pay;

(c)   sick leave/pay;

(d)   length of notice to terminate;

(e)   work to be done by employee.

2.5   Implied terms

Common law also **implies terms** into employment contracts. These are by way of duties of the employee and employer.

Terms may be implied by **custom and practice** of the trade or by usage over a period of time. Many employees will therefore have terms incorporated into their contracts of employment from **collective agreements** between the union and the employer.

2.6   Statutory provisions

Statute has impinged greatly on the ability of the employer and employee to set their own terms. The statutes were enacted partially in recognition of the employer's superior bargaining power to give some protection to the employee, partially to bring UK law into line with EC law and partially through measures which apply to many situations to prevent discrimination.

(a)   The Equal Pay Act 1970 implies terms ie, that persons have the same conditions of employment irrespective of sex or marital status.

(b)   The Sex Discrimination Act 1975 prohibits discrimination on the basis of sex; the Race Relations Act 1976 prohibits discrimination on the basis of race; and the Trade Union and Labour Relations Act 1992 prohibits discrimination on grounds of a membership of a trade union; and the Employment Protection (Consolidation) Act 1978 prohibits discrimination on grounds of health and safety complaints.

(c)   Various statutes, in particular the Factories Act 1961, the Offices, Shops and Railway Premises Act 1963 and the Health and Safety at Work Act 1974 impose safety standards on employers and on employees.

(d)   The Employment Protection (Consolidation) Act 1978 gives employees certain rights. The most important rights are a right not to be unfairly dismissed and a right to a redundancy payment if made redundant. However there are certain other rights such as a minimum period of notice to terminate the contract, time off in certain circumstances and the right to guarantee payments.

(e)   The Wages Act 1986 makes provision in respect of the manner of payment of wages and deductions.

The Equal Pay Act 1970 actually implies a term into an employee's contract. The other statutory provisions do not imply terms but give the employee rights which have the effect of making provisions in contracts invalid because they contravene the rights given or giving the employee a statutory right to make a claim over and above the provisions in his or her contract.

3   WRITTEN PARTICULARS OF EMPLOYMENT

3.1   Timing and content

S1 Employment Protection (Consolidation) Act 1978 requires an employer to provide employees with a written statement of certain particulars of their employment within two months of the commencement of employment. The aim of the provision is to ensure that the employee knows what the employer believes to be his legal rights under the contract.

The statement must contain the following information:

(a)   names of the employer and employee;

(b)   the date on which the employment began and the date on which the employee's period of continuous employment began, taking into account any employment with a previous employer which counts towards that period. (This is important for the employee to calculate his entitlement to many of the statutory rights.);

(c)   scale or rate of pay or method of calculating it, for example rates for piece work or overtime;

(d)   intervals of pay - weekly, monthly etc;

(e)   hours of work;

(f)   holidays and holiday pay;

(g)   sick pay/leave;

(h)   pension and pension schemes and whether a contracting out certificate in respect of the State Pension Scheme is in force;

(i)   job title or brief description of work;

(j)   place or places of work;

(k)   any collective agreement affecting the employment;

(l)   length of notice required by employer and employee to terminate a contract (or if the employment is to be temporary or for a fixed term, the date it is to end);

(m)   details of any disciplinary or grievance procedure, specifying the person to whom the employee can apply if he has a grievance generally or is dissatisfied with any disciplinary decision relating to him and any further steps which follow from his application eg, an appeal procedure if the employee is not satisfied.

Any change in the particulars must be notified by written statement within one month.

3.2   Purpose of written statement

The statement is not the contract itself unless both the employer and employee acknowledge that it is such, for example if it is called a contract and both parties sign it. The statement is prepared by the employer and it is therefore generally seen by the courts as a unilateral declaration by the employer of his view of the terms. It is strong **prima facie** evidence of the terms but by no means conclusive and the court will allow evidence to determine what the terms are.

If an employer fails to provide a written statement or the statement is incomplete the employee can complain to an industrial tribunal which can determine the terms which ought to have been included. It must attempt to discover what the parties in fact agreed. The effect of the determination is that the employer is deemed to have supplied a statement in the correct form. The tribunal cannot then enforce the terms. Because the remedy is so limited applications on their own are rare. Generally the application will be coupled with one for unfair dismissal or redundancy.

3.3   Employees to whom statement need not be given

The written statement need not be given to the following categories of employees:

(a)   Part-time employees ie, where the normal working hours are less than 8 hours each week.

(b)   Where the employment continues for less than one month.

No statement need be given in respect of disciplinary procedures if at the start of employment there are fewer than twenty employees. However, details of grievance procedures must be given.

Conclusion   The written statement is an expression of the employer's view of the terms of the employment contract.

4   TERMS IMPLIED BY THE COURTS

4.1   Introduction

As in other contracts, if there is a gap in what the parties have expressly agreed in an employment contract the common law may imply a term. Thus, the law has implied terms into employment contracts to give effect to the presumed but unexpressed intentions of the parties using the 'officious bystander' or 'business efficacy' test. These implied terms are sometimes called terms implied in fact.

There are also terms implied in law which arise from the nature of the employment relationship. The employment relationship is based on one of obedience by the employee and managerial prerogative of the employer. This produced a set of implied terms which were fairly standard. They are generally listed as duties of the employee and of the employer and are called the common law implied terms. However recent developments have meant that it is no longer easy to set out a standard set of implied terms.

Frequently the question of terms of a contract arises when an employee claims unfair dismissal alleging that the employer is in breach of contract eg, the employer has been rude to the employee (constructive dismissal). The Industrial Tribunal must decide what the terms are and whether the employer is in breach. As each Tribunal decides the case on its facts there are a variety of decisions on behaviour which amounts to constructive dismissal. As these decisions must relate to contractual obligations there is also variety in the precise contractual obligations found by the Tribunals.

Thus, the standard implied terms are now less easy to list under set headings and various books may list them differently. However, common law implied terms still clearly exist, regardless of how they are labelled, which are still expressed as duties of the employee and employer.

If an employee is in breach of his contract (including breach of an implied term) the employer may sue him for damages to recover any loss. Moreover, if the employee commits a very serious breach of contract the employer may elect to treat the contract as discharged ie, he may dismiss him without notice (called summary dismissal).

The same principles apply when an employer breaches his duties. When an employer commits a serious breach such that the employee is entitled to treat the contract as discharged the effect is that the employee resigns and is treated as having been constructively dismissed.

4.2   Duties of the employee

(a)   **Duty to obey lawful and reasonable orders**

Pepper v Webb [1968]

Facts: a gardener refused to plant the plants where instructed by the employer.

Held: he was in breach of the duty of obedience and this, coupled with the fact that he was rude and surly, justified summary dismissal.

The order must be **lawful**. The employee need not obey an order which would result in the commission of a criminal offence.

Gregory v Ford [1951]

Facts: an employee refused to drive a vehicle which was not covered by third party insurance.

Held: this was not a breach of duty.

The employee is not obliged to do work which is clearly not within his contract of employment. An order to work at another place will not be lawful unless there is a term that the employer has the right to transfer the employee. Where there is no express term the courts have been prepared to imply a reasonable term depending on the facts of the particular contract..

O'Brien v Associated Fire Alarms [1968]

Facts: an employee in Liverpool was ordered to work some distance away in Barrow.

Held: this was not lawful as it was not within the contract.

Jones v Associated Tunnelling [1981]

Facts: an employee was ordered to work at another plant within travelling distance of the employee's home.

Held: this was within the terms of the contract, as the court was prepared to imply a term that the employer had a right to transfer the employee to another place of work 'within reasonable distance'.

Cresswell v Inland Revenue [1984]

Facts: the employee was given an order to adapt to new work methods (computerised systems) was valid.

Held: this was a lawful instruction which should be obeyed.

The order must be **reasonable**. In the 19th century a single act of disobedience was sufficient to justify instant (summary) dismissal.

Turner v Mason [1845]

Facts: an employee was ordered to obey an order not to visit a sick mother.

Held: this was a reasonable order and breach of it entitled the employer to dismiss the employee.

What is reasonable changes with changing social standards.

Law v London Chronicle [1959]

Facts: L, a secretary was attending a meeting between her immediate superior and the managing director of the company. The managing director severely criticised her immediate superior and he walked out of the meeting calling on L to leave with him. L did so although the managing director ordered her to stay.

Held: in the circumstances this isolated act of disobedience was not sufficient to justify summary dismissal.

(b)   **Duty of mutual co-operation (or the duty to perform the work in a reasonable manner)**

The duty of the employer to give, and employee to obey, lawful instructions is now often expressed as the duty of mutual co-operation, the duty of mutual respect or the duty of mutual trust and confidence, highlighting the changing social conditions and the greater emphasis on mutuality of obligations. Two things flow from this change. First, the courts have begun to imply a term that the employer must not act in a manner calculated to damage the mutual trust and confidence and this is taken into account in considering the reasonableness of the order. Secondly, the courts have interpreted the duty to obey lawful and reasonable orders as a duty not to frustrate the commercial objectives of the employer.

Pepper v Webb [1968]

Facts: the gardener was extremely surly and rude (he swore at the employer, Mrs Webb)

Held: he was in breach of an implied duty to act in a reasonable manner, and this, coupled with the fact that he refused to obey orders, justified summary dismissal.

Secretary of State for Employment v ASLEF [1972]

Facts: railway workers 'worked to rule' ie, obeyed the British Rail rule book to the letter. This resulted in considerable delays in the train service.

Held: there was an implied term that each employee in obeying instructions would not do so in a wholly unreasonable way which had the effect of disrupting the service he was there to provide.

(c)   **Duty to exercise reasonable care and skill**

The employee must act with reasonable care in performing his duties. The standard of care will depend on the circumstances. It is generally accepted that a single act of negligence, unless it is gross negligence, will not justify summary dismissal. There are certain occupations such as airline pilots where a single act of negligence in performing essential duties may warrant dismissal.

The employee must exercise the skill he claims to have.

Harmer v Cornelius [1858]

Facts: a person given a job as a scene painter impliedly represented he was competent to do the job. However he was not competent.

Held: he was in breach of duty.

An extension of this duty of care is a duty to indemnify the employer for any damages which he has had to pay as a result of his vicarious liability for the employee's negligence.

Lister v Romford Ice & Cold Storage Co Ltd [1957]

Facts: an employee negligently drove a lorry into another employee who then sued the employer.

Held: the employer's insurance company through its right of subrogation, in turn sued the employee-driver who was held liable to pay. (In fact this right of indemnity is rarely enforced because the employer is insured and the insurance companies have generally agreed not to pursue this line.)

(d)   **Duty of good faith - a duty to give honest and faithful service**

This rather vague term also called the duty of fidelity covers a number of obligations and based on the concept that the employment relationship is one of mutual trust and confidence.

*   **Misappropriation of property/accounting for secret profits**

    The employee cannot use the employer's property as his own.

    Sinclair v Neighbour [1967]

    Facts: money was illicitly borrowed from the till.

    Held: this was a breach of duty sufficient to warrant dismissal even though the employee intended to return it.

    The employee must account to his employer for any money or property (secret profit) which he receives in the course of his employment.

    Boston Deep Sea Fishing & Ice Co v Ansell [1888]

    Facts: a managing director received a commission from suppliers to his company on each sale made. The company dismissed him.

    Held: he was in breach of his duty and therefore lawfully dismissed and liable to account for the profit made.

*   **Duty not to compete with his employer's business**

    The employee may do other work in his own time. However the law imposes a duty not to do spare time work which competes with his employer's and may cause him damage.

Hivac Ltd v Park Royal Scientific Instruments Ltd [1946]

Facts: two employees of a company which manufactured sophisticated components for hearing aids worked on weekends for a rival company.

Held: the court granted an injunction restraining them from breaching their duty even though there was no evidence of misuse of confidential information. The manner of making the devices was secret and there was a real risk that there might be a transfer of such information.

Nova Plastics Ltd v Froggatt [1982]

Facts: an odd job man worked for a competitor in his spare time.

Held: he was not in breach of contract.

The dividing line is not clear but the test is probably whether the employee's spare time work results in a real danger of causing loss to the employer.

Note that if the employer wishes to restrain his employee from working for a competitor after leaving his employment he must obtain a promise from the employee to that effect. (See covenants in restraint of trade.)

- **Duty not to disclose trade secrets or misuse confidential information**

Many contracts will have an express term covering this area. However, even if there is no such express term, an employee must not disclose trade secrets to a third party nor misuse confidential information he has acquired in the course of his employment. This implied duty may continue after employment has ceased - **Faccenda Chicken v Fowler [1986]**. Clearly an employee who uses or sells secret processes such as chemical formulae or photocopies list of customers and sells them or uses them for his own purposes will be in breach.

Where a person invents or writes something as part of his employment the right to the patent or copyright will generally belong to his employer.

British Syphon v Homewood [1956]

Facts: a Syphon was designed by an employee at the request of the employer but patented in the employee's name.

Held: it belonged to the employer.

If it is produced outside work but the employee allows the employer to use it, the patent or copyright will belong to the employee. However, even if the employer is entitled to the invention, the employee may claim compensation if his employer has given him inadequate reward or it was of outstanding benefit.

The duty of confidentiality does not extend to information which there is a public duty to disclose, such as unlawful acts of the employer.

The real problem arises in drawing a line between trade secrets/confidential information and general knowledge and skill acquired by the employee in the course of his employment.

(e)   **Duty to render personal service**

4.3   Duties of the employer

The definition of these duties is also in a state of change. They include the following areas.

(a)   **Duty to pay reasonable remuneration**

In practice this implied duty rarely arises since most contracts of employment contain an express term regarding pay.

The employer is obliged to pay remuneration (whether under an express or implied term) even though there may be no work available.

(b)   **Duty to indemnify the employee**

The employer must indemnify his employee where the employee has incurred a legal liability whilst acting on the employer's behalf except where:

(a)   the employee knew he was committing an unlawful act;

(b)   the employee knew the employer had no right to give the order.

(c)   **Duty to take reasonable care for the health and safety of his employees**

There is a general common law duty to provide safe plant and equipment, a safe system of work and competent staff. The standard of care required is the same as in the tort of negligence.

(d)   **Duty to give reasonable notice of termination of employment**

In practice this implied duty rarely arises since most contracts of employment contain express provision stating the exact length of notice or stating that the contract is to be for a fixed term.

(e)   **Duty of mutual co-operation, duty of mutual trust and confidence, duty of mutual respect**

These duties have already been discussed in respect of employees' duties. There is a developing concept of mutuality of obligation which reflects changing social conditions. The employer has a duty not to behave in a manner calculated to damage the relationship of trust and confidence.

Wares v Caithness Leather Products [1974]

Facts: an employer abusively reprimanded a woman employee in foul language.

Held: he had broken the contract of employment.

4.4   Provision of work

There is no general common law duty to provide work. However, such a term may be implied, under the business efficacy test, where the particular circumstances show that failure to provide work would deprive the employee of a benefit contemplated by the contract. For example:

•   if the contract expressly provides for remuneration on a piecework or commission basis it may be possible to imply a duty on the employer to provide sufficient work to enable the employee to earn a reasonable sum.

Turner v Goldsmith [1891]

Facts: G, a shirt manufacturer, expressly agreed to employ T as a travelling salesman for 5 years on a commission basis. After 2 years G failed to supply shirts.

Held: T was entitled to damages for breach of contract based on the commission he would have earned in the remaining 3 years.

- where the contract contemplates an opportunity of publicity as well as salary eg, an actor - **Herbert Clayton and Jack Waller Ltd v Oliver [1930]**

- where the employee is appointed to a particular office and lack of work would deprive him of status.

Collier v Sunday Referee [1940]

Facts: C was appointed to the post of sub-editor and SR later abolished that position.

Held: SR was in breach of contract (even though he continued to pay C).

4.5   Sick pay

There is no common law duty on the employer to pay an employee who is absent from work through sickness or injury.

4.6   Holidays and holiday pay

There is no common law duty on an employer to allow an employee a holiday (whether or not the so-called 'statutory' or 'public' holidays).

4.7   References

There is no common law duty on the employer to provide a reference but if he does so

(i)   the employee may have an action in the tort of defamation where the reference is derogatory subject to the defences of truth and qualified privilege.

(ii)   the employee (and perhaps also the recipient) may have an action in the tort of negligence - **Spring v Guardian Assurance [1994].**

4.8   Activity

If an employee is injured at work and decides to bring an action against his employer in the tort of negligence then what must he prove in order to succeed?

4.9   Activity solution

He must prove that (a) the employer owes him a duty of care and (b) the employer breached that duty of care by failing to provide reasonably safe plant, premises, system of work and competent fellow employees and (c) his injury was caused by the breach of duty and was not too remote.

5   IMPLIED TERMS - OTHER SOURCES

5.1   Custom and practice

Many employees are taken on at the factory gate. The employer selects those he wants from people waiting. There is little, if any, discussion of the terms of the contract. In addition, few contracts of employment will cover all eventualities expressly or by the use of the implied terms above. Many of the day to day matters will be governed by long standing custom and practice.

> **Definition**   To be legally recognisable a custom must be 'reasonable, certain and notorious'.
>
> Thus even if the individual employee is unaware of a custom it may be implied it if satisfies this test.

Sagar v Ridehalgh & Son Ltd [1931]

Facts: a deduction from weavers' wages was made in the same way for thirty years.

Held: this was an implied term of a weaver's contract even though she did not know of it. *(Note:* the decision in this case would now be affected by the Wages Act 1986).

5.2   Collective bargaining agreements

> **Definition**   A collective agreement is an agreement between a trade union and an employer.

It will contain a variety of provisions, some of them specifically covering matters of immediate interest to the employee, for example, pay, hours, disciplinary procedures etc, and others covering matters governing the relationship between the union and the employer, for example, negotiating rights, intervals at which meetings will be held etc.

The Trade Union and Labour Relations (Consolidation) Act 1992 provides that such agreements are presumed not to be binding between the parties unless expressly stated to be so. Thus, unless the parties expressly state that they intend to create legal relations the agreement is not a contract and neither the employer nor the union can sue for failure to carry out a promise contained in the agreement.

Many employees' terms and conditions are determined by such collective agreements. In order for this to happen the terms of the collective agreement must be incorporated in the individual employment contracts. This is not automatic. However there may be:

(a)   express incorporation - the employment contract expressly states that the terms of the collective agreement are incorporated;

(b)   implied incorporation - there is no express statement in the contract but it is well accepted by both parties that the terms are incorporated.

If the terms are incorporated into the employment contract the employee and employer can enforce them against each other even though the union and the employer cannot. Generally any alteration of the collective agreement will automatically alter the provisions in the employment contract.

5.3   Work rules and notices

In many businesses the employer issues a set of work rules made by the employer. They will be terms of the contract if they are incorporated into the contract by:

(a)   express incorporation - the contract expressly provides that the rules made by the employer are the terms of the contract;

(b)   implied incorporation - the contract has no express provision but it is well accepted that such rules form part of the contract.

5.4   Variation of the terms of the contract of employment

As with any attempted unilateral variation of a contract the effect will be in theory a breach of contract. However, it is becoming common for employers to wish to change the terms of a contract. The effect on the contract may vary according to the precise circumstances.

Four possible situations follow:

(a)   Employer gives employee lawful notice to terminate the existing contract followed by an offer to re-engage him on a different contract incorporating the new terms. (An attempt to do this by Timex UK in 1993 led to industrial action.)

(b)   Employer makes the change without giving the employee requisite notice. If the change is an important breach of contract the employee could treat it as a repudiation of their agreement, and claim damages.

(c)   Change is made by mutual agreement. This will only be binding if the variation is supported by consideration **or** one party is estopped from going back on his promise because the other party has acted in reliance on it. It is doubtful whether an employee's gratuitous promise to accept less than his agreed salary can ever be binding on him.

(d)   The variation may come within the terms of the original contract:

(i)   where the terms of an employment contract are incorporated from a collective agreement, the variation of the collective agreement may be an agreed variation of the employment contract;

(ii)   if the terms of the employment contract give the employer the discretion to change some of the terms eg, the place or type of work done by the employee, exercise by the employer of this discretion will come within the terms of the contract. It is important to remember that in certain circumstances the courts are prepared to imply such terms into contracts.

The problems of variation of a contract arise in cases of unfair dismissal (eg, is the employer in breach by requiring the employee to do different work or has he the discretion to require it and therefore the employee is in breach of his duty to obey?) and redundancy (eg, is the employee redundant when there is no longer work for him to do at X plant and he is required to move to Y plant some miles away or does the employer have the right to alter the place he works?).

5.5   Activity

Charlotte is employed as a clerk by a firm of accountants. She is asked by a friend, Beth, who runs her own dress design business, if she will do Beth's bookkeeping in her spare time. Under employment law will Charlotte be able to accept this offer?

5.6   Activity solution

The factors to consider are Charlotte's implied duty of loyalty to her employer and whether she has the capacity to harm the interests of her employer by working for Beth. Given Charlotte's junior status as a clerk and the fact that Beth's business is not in competition with the firm of accountants it would appear unlikely that this would be a problem.

6   CHAPTER SUMMARY

A contract of employment combines express terms agreed by both parties and terms implied by statute, common law, custom, collective agreements and work rules and notices. If these express or implied terms are breached by employer or employee then there may be a cause for legal action.

7   SELF TEST QUESTIONS

7.1   What is the difference between a contract of service and a contract for services? (1.1 and 1.2)

7.2   What is the alternative name for the economic reality test? (1.5)

7.3   Can a minor enter into a valid employment contract? (2.1)

7.4   Which Act of Parliament implies terms into employment contracts? (2.6)

7.5   On what time-scale must a written statement of particulars be issued to employees? (3.1)

7.6   List the required particulars of the written statement (3.1)

7.7   What type of order is it an employee's duty to obey? (4.2)

7.8   What was the decision in **Lister v Romford Ice**?(4.2)

7.9   At common law what length of notice must an employer give to terminate a contract of employment? (4.3)

7.10   Is an employer obliged to give a reference? (4.7)

8   EXAMINATION TYPE QUESTIONS

8.1   Contract of service and contract for services

What tests are used by the courts to distinguish between a contract of service and a contract for services? Why is this distinction important?

(15 marks)

8.2   Clutch

Clutch has recently obtained a job as a lorry driver and at the time he was engaged he was told that he would be employed 'on the usual terms'.

Advise Clutch where he may ascertain what these terms are and in what ways he is protected by statute with regard to them.

(20 marks)

9   ANSWERS TO EXAMINATION TYPE QUESTIONS

9.1   Contract of service and contract for services

The courts have, for various purposes, used the following tests over the years in deciding whether there is a **contract of service** (employment) or a **contract for services** (self-employment):

(a)   The **control** test ie, the greater the degree of control exercised, the more likely there is to be an employer/employee relationship.

(b)   The **integration** (or **organisation**) test ie, whether the work done is integrated into the business of the person for whom it is done so that it forms part of that business and is not a separate business carried on by an independent contractor.   This test was devised as appropriate for highly skilled professional men like surgeons, over whom the 'employer' could have little actual control in relation to matters he did not himself understand: **Cassidy v Ministry of Health.**

(c)   The **mixed** test (sometimes called the **multiple** test) is the modern approach and recognises that neither the control test nor the integration test will be adequate in all cases: it will be necessary to look at the entire arrangement, including the wording of the contract, the measure of control and who pays the social security contributions in addition to any other circumstances relevant in a particular case.

Thus, degree of control will not in itself be enough to establish conclusively that there is or is not a contract of employment.   There are many case law examples, but reference to one must suffice.   In **Ready-Mixed Concrete Ltd v Minister of Pensions and National Insurance** drivers who were assisted financially to purchase their own vehicles were held to be independent contractors, even though they had to paint them as instructed by the company and wear the uniform prescribed by the company.   Despite this degree of control, the drivers were carrying on businesses of their own, at their own financial risk.   Emphasis was placed on the fact that the drivers could always delegate their work.

Whether a person is employed or self-employed is important in many branches of the law.

The accountant encounters it mainly in relation to its effect on liability for income tax and social security contributions.   The lawyer thinks of it in the context of vicarious liability in the law of tort ie, the employer is liable for his employees' torts if they are committed in the course of the employment but not (with some important exceptions) for torts committed by self-employed sub-contractors (**independent contractors**).   A very important aspect is that one who is not an employee cannot secure the benefits and protection provided by the employment protection legislation eg, unfair dismissal and redundancy, nor can he benefit from all the provisions of the Health and Safety at Work Act 1974 or receive unemployment benefit.

9.2   Clutch

It may well be that the terms on which Clutch has been engaged do not amount to a contract at all. For a contract to exist, the main terms of the contract must be sufficiently certain.   An agreement to agree terms in the future is not a contract (**Scammel v Ouston**) but it may be possible in the circumstances to imply terms into a contract on the basis of a previous similar contract (**Hillas v Arcos**).   In any event a contract of employment need not be a single or even a written document and the terms are usually implied from a variety of sources.

Firstly, Clutch should be advised to see if express terms exist in the form of an employer's work handbook or a collective agreement with a trade union.   However, there is some uncertainty in the law as to the precise effect of collective agreements, as these are made between the employer and the union; and as such it is debatable whether they provide rights for individual employees such as Clutch as they are not parties to the contract.   Nevertheless, the reference to the 'usual terms' made by the employer could be argued as being an express incorporation of any collective terms into Clutch's individual contract.

Other terms on which Clutch is employed may be implied by the common law or by statute.   For example, at common law Clutch owes his employer a duty of skill and care, of fidelity and a duty to obey reasonable instructions. His employer in turn must, for example, treat him with respect and pay agreed wages. Moreover The Employment Protection (Consolidation) Act 1978 lays down certain minimum periods of notice which relate to the length of employment and allows time off work for various activities eg, jury service and trade union activities.

Clutch will additionally be assisted in ascertaining the terms on which he is employed by S1 Employment Protection (Consolidation) Act 1978 which requires his employer to provide him with particulars written within 2 months of commencing employment. The statement will cover such matters as his rate and date of pay, holidays, place of work and description of his job. Although the written statement is not his contract of employment it forms evidence of what the employer believes to be its terms and conditions.

14 EMPLOYMENT: STATUTORY REGULATION

INTRODUCTION & LEARNING OBJECTIVES

Syllabus area 8d. The contract of employment:
Engagement. (Ability required 3).
Terms (including wages). (Ability required 3).
Health and safety requirements. (Ability required 3).

In this chapter the legislation which has been designed to protect employees and restrict employers will be considered.

When you have studied this chapter you should be able to do the following:

- Calculate the period of continuous employment of an employee.

- Explain the statutory provisions which are intended to prevent discrimination.

- Discuss the legal provisions that relate to payment of wages and time off for various reasons.

- Outline the state benefits available to an employee

1 INTRODUCTION TO THE STATUTORY REGULATION OF EMPLOYMENT

1.1 Summary

There are a large number of statutory provisions giving protective rights to employees and these can be grouped into

(a) the anti-discrimination provisions relating to

- sex: the Equal Pay Act 1970 and the Sex Discrimination Acts 1975 and 1986
- race: the Race Relations Act 1976
- trade unionism: the Trade Union and Labour Relations (Consolidation) Act 1992
- health and safety complaints: the Employment Protection (Consolidation) Act 1978

(b) provisions regulating pay

- deductions: the Wages Act 1986
- pay statements: the EPCA 1978
- guarantee payments: the EPCA 1978
- suspension on medical grounds: the EPCA 1978

- time off: the EPCA 1978, TULRCA 1992 and the Health and Safety at Work Act 1974

- equal pay: the EPA 1970, RRA 1976, TULRCA 1992

(c)   provisions regulating dismissal

- minimum notice periods: the EPCA 1978

- written reasons for dismissal: the EPCA 1978

- unfair dismissal (covered in the chapter 'Employment: Termination of employment'): the EPCA 1978

- redundancy (covered in the chapter 'Employment: Termination of employment'): the EPCA 1978

(d)   state benefits including

- statutory sick pay
- statutory maternity pay
- industrial injury benefit

(e)   provisions relating to maintenance of health and safety (covered in the chapter 'Employment: Health and Safety')

- Health and Safety at Work Act 1974
- Factories Act 1961
- Office Shops and Railway Premises Act 1963

There are very few statutory provisions imposing duties on the employee. These are

(a)   minimum notice periods: the EPCA 1978

(b)   maintenance of health and safety (covered in the chapter 'Employment: Health and Safety'): the HSWA 1974, FA 1961 and OSRPA 1963.

1.2   EPCA 1978: Continuity of employment

Many of the rights given to employees under the EPCA 1978 are gained only once the employee has completed a minimum period of continuous employment with his employer and, once gained, become more valuable the longer the period of continuous employment. It is important, therefore, that you can calculate the length of an employee's continuous employment.

The period is counted in terms of weeks. The count begins at the first 'countable week' (usually when the employee begins to work for his employer) and ceases whenever there is a 'non-countable' week (usually when the employee ceases to work for that employer).

Thus there are two main aspects to consider

(a)   Breaks in employment

There is a presumption that employment is continuous. The onus is on the employer to show there has been a break in continuity. It is therefore important that the written statement of particulars sets out the commencement date of employment and periods of continuous employment. The effect of the statement is to enable the employee to calculate the period and prevent the employer from denying it.

If the employee does not work (or is not contracted to work) for one or more weeks there are two possible results:

(1)   the period will not count in computing continuous employment;

(2)   there will be a break of 'continuous employment' - when the employee resumes work he will have no continuous employment and will have to start from week one again.

However certain absences have neither possible result (ie, they count in calculating continuous employment and do not break continuity). These are absences because of:

(1)   sickness or injury (up to 26 weeks);

(2)   pregnancy (up to 26 weeks);

(3)   maternity leave under the right to return to work provisions;

(4)   temporary cessation of work (eg, teachers between academic sessions);

(5)   circumstances in which by arrangement or custom the employee is regarded as continuously employed (eg, a skipper of a trawler who signed off at the end of each trip and signed on again at the beginning of the next);

(6)   unfair dismissal followed by re-instatement by order of an Industrial Tribunal.

There are absences which do not count as weeks in calculating continuous employment but do not break continuity. These include absences:

(1)   during which the employee was on strike;
(2)   the employee was locked-out by his employer.

(b)   Transfer of the employer's business

At common law the transfer of a business from one employer to another automatically terminates the contract of employment. The employee has a new contract with the new employer. This breaks the continuity of employment. However, in certain circumstances the continuity is not broken.

The 1978 Act and the Transfer of Undertakings (Protection of Employment) Regulations 1981 provide for the continuity of employment where there is a:

(1)   transfer to an associated employer (ie, here one company controls another or both companies are under the control of the same person);

(2)   change of partners;

(3)   transfer of the trade, business or undertaking in which the employee was employed at the time of the transfer (ie, where a business is sold as a going concern including the goodwill, know-how and benefit of the employment contracts - **Melon v Hector Powe [1981]**). However, the employee must be employed by the transferor company at the exact time of the transfer. Thus the provisions will not apply if the transferor dismisses all the employees. If the transferor does dismiss them, their action is against him (for unfair dismissal or redundancy). If the transferor does not dismiss them then the transferee takes them with their accumulated continuous employment and all the rights which go with that.

1.3 Activity

X works full time for P Ltd in its shoe-making factory under a fixed term contract for 3 years. He then leaves and goes on an expedition to the South Pole. On his return a year later he is re-engaged by P Ltd on another 3 year contract doing the same job as before. After two years (during which time X was on strike for 6 months) P Ltd sells the shoe-making side of its business to Q Ltd and X continues working for Q Ltd for a further 6 months until he is dismissed.

Calculate X's period of continuous employment for the purpose of his statutory rights against Q Ltd.

1.4 Activity solution

X has actually worked for Q Ltd for 6 months. However, provided Q Ltd bought the shoe-making business including goodwill, the Transfer of Undertakings (Protection of Employment) Regulations 1981 will allow X to aggregate his continuous employment with P Ltd.

Continuity was broken after the initial 3 years by the South Pole absence so those 3 years are lost. Only 1½ years of his further 2 year period with P Ltd counts because although strike does not break continuity it does not count.

Thus X is treated as having been continuously employed by Q Ltd for 2 years.

1.5 Summary

Continuity is important for some rights given by the EPCA 1978. It is not relevant to rights given by other statutes.

2 EQUAL PAY ACT 1970

2.1 The equality clause

Despite its name, this Act deals not only with pay but with other **terms** of work such as overtime, bonuses, holiday and sick leave.

It applies equally to men and women: it implies an 'equality clause' into all contracts of employment whereby a woman's (or man's) terms must be as favourable as a man's (or woman's) in the same employment if she/he is employed on the following:

(a) **Like work** - this means work of the same or broadly similar nature as a man (or woman) in the same employment. This means comparison with another job which is so similar that the terms can be compared.

Maidment v Cooper [1978]

Facts: the work of women who cooked for large numbers of employees and a man who worked as a chef cooking for a smaller number of senior employees was compared.

Held: it was **like work**.

Eaton Ltd v Nuttall [1977]

Facts: a man production scheduler who dealt with 1,200 items worth £5 to £1,000 was compared with women production schedulers who handled 2,400 items worth below £2.50.

Held: it was not like work as a mistake by the man would produce more serious consequences.

(b)   **Work rated as equivalent** - this means jobs which although not the same have been given equal value under a job evaluation scheme. This is an evaluation of the demands of the jobs under various headings such as effort, skill, decision. Thus if the employer has carried out such a scheme the employee can compare her/his terms with the terms of other jobs which, although not the same, are rated as equivalent.

The weakness of this provision is that there is **no duty** on the employer to carry out such a job evaluation.

The UK was held to be in breach of **Article 119 of the Treaty of Rome** as it requires **'equal pay for equal work'** and a woman/man could not insist on a job evaluation. Thus the Act was amended to include the third type of comparison.

(c)   **Work of equal value** - this means jobs which are rated as being of equal value on the basis of a job evaluation done by an independent expert appointed through the Industrial Tribunal. A woman/man can only apply for such a study to be done if there is no existing job evaluation study.

Most claims are made by women and the rest of the points made here on the EPA 1970 are made from their point of view.

2.2   The comparator

A woman may choose her male **comparator** but he must be in the 'same employment' which means working for the same employer at the same establishment or at another of his establishments where similar terms and conditions apply. The male comparator may be a predecessor or successor in the job (although there then may be a defence to any difference in pay (see below)). She cannot compare herself with a 'hypothetical male'

Conclusion   She must compare herself with another real person even if he has since left the job or had the job she now has before her.

2.3   The comparison

Each distinct provision of the contract must be compared with similar provisions in the comparator's contract and there will be inequality if that provision is unequal even if overall the package of terms is not less favourable.

Hayward v Cammell Laird [1988]

Facts: a canteen cook claimed equal pay with painters, joiners and engineers employed in the same shipyard on the grounds that her work was of equal value, which was confirmed by an independent expert under five headings: physical demands, environmental demands, planning and decision-making demands, skill and knowledge demands, and responsibility demands. She had various benefits which the men did not have but received lower wages.

Held: the House of Lords ruled that her pay must be equal regardless of the fact that overall the terms might be equal.

The Act does **not prevent** differing terms to afford special treatment to women in connection with childbirth or pregnancy.

2.4   Defences

The employer may have a defence. Even if the woman can show that the work is like work and that a term is different the employer will have a defence if he can show that the difference in term (usually pay) is due to a 'genuine material difference'. This will include what is known as 'red circling' (transferring a man to a less senior post but protecting his pay to avoid a breach of contract) or the fact that a later occupier of the post legitimately has higher pay.

Shields v E Coomes [1979]

Facts: male counterhands at the defendant's betting shops were paid 14p per hour more than the female counterhands. The employer attempted to justify this pay differential on the ground that a man would more effectively be able to deal with violent customers.

Held: the Court of Appeal dismissed the employer's argument on the basis that a properly trained woman could equally well have dealt with any violence which might have arisen.

2.5   The claim

A woman who believes she is not receiving equal treatment in respect of any of the terms of her employment makes a claim to the industrial tribunal which, if it finds in her favour, may award up to two years of arrears of pay and damages for breach of the equality clause. There is no qualifying period of employment to make a claim – thus one could be made on the first day of employment. The Act applies to contracts of service and contracts for services.

Conclusion   The Equal Pay Act implies clauses into a contract of employment to ensure equality between the sexes

3   SEX DISCRIMINATION ACTS 1975 AND 1986

3.1   Introductory

The SDA operates differently from the Equal Pay Act 1970 in that it does not imply any terms into a contract. It prohibits certain types of discrimination.

The SDA prohibits discrimination in employment against women (and men) by reason of sex and married people by reason of their marital status. Again as most cases are situations where women are claiming sex discrimination the rest of the Act is considered here from the point of view of women.   However, you must remember men have equal rights to claim if they have been discriminated against - (except that special treatment of women in connection with child birth and pregnancy is permitted).

3.2   Discrimination defined

Discrimination can arise in two ways:

(a)   **Direct discrimination:** where on the ground of her sex an employer treats a woman less favourably than he treats or would treat a man. This requires the court to consider whether or not a man in comparable circumstances would have been treated differently and to her detriment.

Jeremiah v Ministry of Defence [1979]

Facts: male ordnance examiners were, on occasion, required to work in the colour-bursting shop, a very dirty part of the factory. Female examiners were not so required.

The CA **upheld** Mr Jeremiah's complaint of sex discrimination deciding that he was treated less favourably than a woman. It was also stated that it was no defence for the employer to allege:

- no protective clothing or separate showering facilities were available for women

- the women did not wish to work in the dirty colour-bursting shop

- the women might have gone on strike if they were so required

- there was no detriment to the men because they were paid extra for any shifts in the colour-bursting shop: ie, it is not possible to buy the right to discriminate.

Webb v Emo Air Cargo (UK) Ltd [1994]

Facts: the appellant was taken on to replace an employee who would be taking maternity leave in about 6 months time. Two weeks after starting work the appellant discovered she was pregnant and on informing her employer she was dismissed.

Held: in 1992 the House of Lords adjourned the hearing and made a reference to the European Court of Justice for a preliminary ruling - the SDA 1975 was enacted to implement the EC Equal Treatment Directive. In mid 1994 the ECJ ruled that dismissal of a woman because she is pregnant amounts to sex discrimination. It is expected that when the House of Lords resumes the hearing it will give judgement in favour of Mrs Webb.

Note: Mrs Webb was unable to claim 'unfair dismissal' under the EPCA 1978 because she had not been employed for 2 years (which, until 1993, was a pre-requisite for making an unfair dismissal claim on pregnancy grounds).

(b)   **Indirect discrimination:** when a requirement is applied to a woman which would equally be applied to a man but:

(i)   the proportion of women who can comply with it is smaller;
(ii)   it cannot be justified irrespective of sex; and
(iii) it is to the particular woman's detriment because she cannot comply with it.

Price v Civil Service Commission [1978]

Facts: the requirement was that applicants be under twenty-eight years of age.

Held: this was held to be sex discrimination as fewer women could qualify because at this age and under a large proportion of women would be occupied with child bearing and rearing.

When considering both direct and indirect discrimination minor differences in treatment are ignored.

Peake v Automotive Products [1977]

Facts: the employer allowed women employees to leave their shift 5 minutes earlier than men so as to avoid the crush at the factory gates. Mr Peake complained of sex discrimination.

Held: the court dismissed his claim on the ground that this difference was de minimis.

3.3   Extent of unlawful discrimination

It is unlawful to discriminate against a woman in relation to:

- advertising a post
- selection
- terms offered (not pay because this is covered by the EPA 1970)
- promotion, training, etc
- dismissal.

Summary: it is unlawful to discriminate directly or indirectly on grounds of sex or marital status at all stages of employment.

3.4   The genuine occupational qualification exception

It is **not unlawful** to discriminate where a person's sex is a genuine qualification for a job. A person's sex is regarded as a genuine occupational qualification:

- where the essential nature of the job calls for a man for reasons of physiology (excluding strength or stamina) eg, a fashion model;

- for reasons of authenticity in dramatic performances or other entertainment

- for reasons of decency or privacy where the job involves physical contact or where men might reasonably object to the presence of a woman because they are in a state of undress or using sanitary facilities eg, a changing room attendant

- in a private home for reasons of physical or social contact or intimacy

- where the job involves the provision of welfare or educational services which can be more effectively provided by a man

- where the job involves duties abroad in a country whose laws or customs are such that the duties could not, or could not effectively, be performed by a woman

- where the job is one of two to be held by a married couple.

A genuine occupational qualification exception cannot be relied on where the employer already has sufficient male employees who can conveniently do the special duties.

Wylie v Dee & Co (Menswear) Ltd [1978]

Facts: Mrs Wylie was refused employment as a sales assistant in a menswear shop.

This was **held** to be unlawful discrimination. The employer failed to justify the discrimination on decency grounds because customers changed in a private cubicle. The employer also failed on the ground of physical contact (taking inside leg measurement) because on the rare occasions this was required it could conveniently be carried out by one of the seven other assistants, all male.

3.5   The claim

Not only is an employer liable if he personally discriminates (or victimises a person who has complained of discrimination) but he is also liable, together with his employee or agent, if the employee or agent discriminates. It is also unlawful for a person to induce another to discriminate.

There is no qualifying period of employment to make a claim, although the applicant must claim within 3 months of the alleged discriminatory act. The tribunal may make an order declaring the rights of the parties, award compensation and recommend that the employer takes such action as the tribunal consider practicable for eliminating the discrimination.

3.6   The Equal Opportunities Commission

The Equal Opportunities Commission has the role of ensuring the eradication of discrimination. It can fund test cases, make recommendations for changes in the law, issue codes of practice and serve 'discrimination notices' on employers it considers to be contravening the provisions of the Act.

4   RACE RELATIONS ACT 1976

The Race Relations Act 1976 prohibits discrimination on **racial grounds.**

> **Definition**   Racial grounds is defined to include colour, race, nationality or ethnic or national origin.
>
> Discrimination on the grounds of religion is not covered although a number of religious groups will be ethnic groups eg, Jews and Sikhs.

The wording of the Act follows that of the Sex Discrimination Act 1975 as far as it is relevant. Thus:

(a)   discrimination can be direct or indirect (defined as in the SDA 1975);

(b)   discrimination is unlawful at all stages of employment (including pay)

(c)   there are only two 'genuine occupational qualification' exceptions, viz

- for reasons of authenticity in dramatic performances, photographers' or artists' models, or in the food and drink setting

- where the job involves the provision of welfare services for a racial group which can more effectively be performed by a person of that racial group

(d)   the claim and remedies are the same.

(e)   The Commission for Racial Equality (CRE) has the same role and powers in respect of racial discrimination as the Equal Opportunities Commission does in respect of sex discrimination.

5   EPCA 1978: RIGHT NOT TO SUFFER A DETRIMENT IN HEALTH AND SAFETY CASES

Under the Employment Protection (Consolidation) Act 1978 (as inserted in 1993) an employee has the right not to be subjected to any detriment on the ground that

(a)   having been designated by the employer to carry out activities in connection with preventing or reducing risks to health and safety at work, he carried out, or proposed to carry out, any such activities, or

(b)   having been appointed a safety representative or member of a safety committee (under the Health and Safety at Work Act 1974, covered later) he performed, or proposed to perform, any of his functions, or

(c)   he is an employee who

- brought to his employer's attention circumstances which he reasonably believed were harmful or potentially harmful to health or safety, or

- he refused, or proposed to refuse, to work in circumstances which he reasonably believed to be of serious and imminent danger, or

- in circumstances which he reasonably believed to be of serious and imminent danger he took, or proposed to take, appropriate steps to protect himself or other persons from the danger.

The EPCA 1978 does not specify what the 'detriment' might be but it is likely that it might include matters such as docking his pay and not promoting him.

Any complaint must be presented to the Industrial Tribunal within 3 months.

If the tribunal finds the complaint is well-founded it must make a declaration to that effect and may make an award of compensation to the complainant.

6   TRADE UNION AND LABOUR RELATIONS (CONSOLIDATION) ACT 1992

The TULRCA makes it unlawful to refuse a person employment either because he is, or is not, a member of a trade union. Further, an employer may not take action against an employee for the purpose of

- deterring him from being or seeking to become a union member; or
- deterring him from taking part in union activities; or
- compelling him to be or become a union member.

Any complaint must be made to the Industrial Tribunal within 3 months which may award compensation.

7   SUMMARY

Statute now prohibits discrimination on grounds of sex, race, trade unionism, and health and safety complaints. When we cover dismissal you will see that these four matters are also grounds for a complaint of unfair dismissal under the EPCA 1978.

You should be aware that there are no statutory provisions specifically outlawing discrimination on other grounds such as religion or age. There is, however, legislation on the statute book requiring employers to ensure that disabled persons make up a minimum of 3% of the workforce but currently this is not being enforced.

8   WAGES ACT 1986

8.1   Introductory

An employee's pay, being the most essential element for him, will almost invariably be an express term of the contract. Remember that the statutory statement of written particulars must include details of the rate of pay and the dates of pay: this will form evidence of the employer's view as to the contractual pay. There is no statutory intervention into levels of pay. There is no statutory minimum wage as there is in many countries. (Prior to 1994 there were Wages Councils which set minimum wages for certain classes of workers, such as agricultural workers, but the Wages Councils were abolished by the Trade Union Reform and Employment Rights Act 1993). Generally pay will be negotiated between the employer and employee or as part of the collective bargaining process where there is a trade union. In the absence of express agreement the employee is entitled to reasonable remuneration for the work he has done, (one of the common law duties of the employer).

The two most common pay systems are payment based on units of time (hourly, daily, weekly, monthly) and payment by result (piecework or commission). A person may have additional pay in the form of overtime or fringe benefits. Generally the pay for a manual worker is referred to as a wage and pay for a non-manual worker is referred to as salary, in law, however, the two words are used interchangeably.

Not only is the amount and frequency of pay a matter for agreement between the parties but so also is the form of the pay (ie, whether money, goods, or other benefits) and the manner of payment (eg, whether cash, cheque or direct transfer to the employee's bank account).

The provisions of the Wages Act 1986, given below, apply to all workers - not just employees.

8.2   Deductions: whether or not allowed

It is fairly common for employers to make deductions from an employee's wages for such things as shortages, breakages, negligence, disciplinary offences.

The Wages Act 1986 states that an employer may not make deductions or receive or demand payment from the worker unless it is authorised by a relevant provision in the contract or the worker has previously agreed in writing that the deduction can be made. The contractual provision or prior agreement in writing must set out not only the amount of deduction but also for what purpose it is made.

The inclusion of the provision on payment is to prevent the employer circumventing the terms of the Wages Act 1986 by not making a deduction but instead requiring the employee to pay. For simplicity we have referred only to deductions below but all the provisions cover both deductions and demands for payments.

8.3   Deductions: restriction on amount for retail workers

Special rules apply to deductions from retail workers in respect of cash shortages/stock deficiencies:

(a)   it must be made within 12 months of the date the employer discovered or ought reasonably to have discovered the shortage/deficiency;

(b)   the deduction must not on a particular pay day exceed 10% of the worker's gross wages on that pay day.

The 10% limit does not apply to the final payment. Thus the employer may discover the shortage, dismiss the worker and deduct the whole of his loss. Alternatively the employer may discover the shortage, not dismiss the worker but deduct 10% of his pay each pay day until he has recovered the full amount of his loss. If the employee leaves before the full amount has been recovered the employer can deduct the remaining amount from the final pay even if it more than 10%.

In no circumstance can an undeducted amount be carried forwards for more than 12 months.

8.4   Deductions: complaints procedure

The worker may complain to an industrial tribunal within three months of the deduction. The tribunal may make a declaration that the deduction is invalid and order it to be repaid. If the complaint is that more than 10% was deducted on any one occasion the tribunal may order repayment of the excess. Where such an order is made the amount repaid is still counted towards covering the employer's loss - ie, he cannot recover it again by going through the proper procedure.

8.5 Deductions: exceptions

The Wages Act 1986 does not apply to certain deductions which include:

(a)   where the deduction is authorised by statute (eg, PAYE);

(b)   where deductions are made because a worker has taken part in a strike or other industrial action;

(c)   where deductions are made to recover previous overpayments of wages or expenses.

Conclusion   pay is largely a matter for free bargaining between the employer and employee provided there is no infringement of the Equal Pay Act 1970 and other anti-discrimination legislation. Deductions from pay are regulated by the Wages Act 1986.

8.6 Activity

An employer wishes to reduce his factory workers' wages by £3 per week and give luncheon vouchers worth £3 instead. Can he legally do this?

8.7 Activity solution

This can only be done if each worker agrees; otherwise the employer commits a breach of contract which might amount to constructive dismissal.

9 EPCA 1978: ITEMISED PAY STATEMENT

The Employment Protection (Consolidation) Act 1978 gives every employee the right to a written pay statement at or before every payment of wages or salary which shows:

(a)   the gross amount of pay;
(b)   variable and fixed deductions;
(c)   the net amount of pay;
(d)   where different parts of the net amount are paid in different ways, the amount and method of each payment.

If the employer fails to provide the statement or there is a dispute over the details it contains, an application may be made to the industrial tribunal which may declare the particulars which must be included and, where there have been unnotified deductions, order the employer to pay any such deductions which were made within the 13 weeks preceding the application.

10 EPCA 1978: GUARANTEE PAYMENTS

An employer has no right to suspend an employee *without pay* unless there is agreement to that effect. Thus an employee is entitled to his contractual pay even though there is no work for him to do. Where there is insufficient work an employee may lose where he is paid by the piece or where his employment contract entitles the employer to suspend without pay.

Under the Employment Protection (Consolidation) Act 1978 an employee who has been continuously employed for four weeks is entitled to a guarantee payment for certain days when he is not provided with work and as a result receives no pay. He is entitled to a maximum (currently

£14.10) per day for each work day on which work was not provided up to a maximum of five days in any three month period.

An employee who has been continuously employed for 4 weeks and is not excluded by the Act is entitled to a guarantee payment for certain days when he is not provided with work. He can claim only for days on which he is normally required to work, and on which he had no work throughout the whole of the day because of diminution in the requirement of his employer's business for work of the kind he does or any other occurrence affecting normal working of the employer's business. Guarantee payments may not be claimed if the failure to provide work is the result of trade disputes, the employee unreasonably refusing an offer of suitable alternative employment or the employee failing to comply with reasonable requirements to ensure his safety.

Seasonal workers (ie, those with an expected employment of less than 3 months) are excluded from the guarantee payment scheme.

Any complaint must be made to the Industrial Tribunal within 3 months.

[Conclusion] these provisions are likely to apply only to *piece* workers who are laid off or put on short time because on any workless day where the employer is liable to pay contractual remuneration the guarantee payment is available only to the extent that it exceeds the contractual amount. The guarantee payment is very small and is only available for up to 5 days in any three months.

11 EPCA 1978: MEDICAL SUSPENSION

Under the Employment Protection (Consolidation) Act 1978 an employee who has been continuously employed for one month will be entitled to receive his normal week's pay during the period of medical suspension to a maximum of 26 weeks. An employee will be suspended from work on medical grounds where he is told not to report for work because there is a risk of coming into contact with something which will cause injury eg, radio-active material. He is not entitled to medical suspension pay if:

(a)   he is incapable because he is sick (he then claims statutory sick pay);

(b)   he unreasonably refuses a suitable offer of alternative work;

(c)   he does not comply with reasonable requirements imposed by his employer with a view to ensuring that his services are available.

An employee may complain to an Industrial Tribunal not later than 3 months after the first payment should have been made. The Tribunal can order the employer to pay the amount due.

12 TIME OFF WORK

12.1 Introductory

The employee's hours of work, leave entitlement etc, are determined by agreement between the employer and employee. The basic position then is that if an employee is absent from work otherwise than as permitted by his contract he is in breach of contract and has no right to pay for those absences. There are however a number of statutory inroads into this basic position. A number of miscellaneous provisions are covered in this paragraph. The next paragraph covers the very special position of pregnant women.

12.2 Trade union duties and activities

The Trade Union and Labour Relations (Consolidation) Act 1992 provides that if there is an independent trade union

- **Officials** may claim the right to time off **with pay** to carry out official duties concerned with industrial relations at the business or undergo industrial relations training approved by the union or the Trades Union Congress.

- **Members** of such trade unions are entitled to time off **without pay** to join in its activities or act as its representative. This right does not include activities which themselves constitute industrial action.

Complaint is to the Industrial Tribunal within 3 months of the refusal. The Tribunal can order in respect of union officials payment of wages wrongfully withheld and in respect of union members a declaration of their rights, and in respect of an official or a member compensation for any injury.

12.3   Public duties

The Employment Protection (Consolidation) Act 1978 entitles any employee to time off **without pay** for various public duties such as jury service.

The time off must be reasonable in the circumstances. Complaints are made to the Industrial Tribunal within 3 months of the refusal. The Tribunal can make a declaration of the employees rights and award compensation for any injury (eg, injured feelings).

12.4   Employees under notice of redundancy

Under the Employment Protection (Consolidation) Act 1978 where an employee is dismissed by reason of redundancy he is entitled to reasonable time off with pay during the notice period to look for other work or training. The employee is only entitled to such time off if he is entitled to redundancy payment. This normally means that he must have a minimum period of 2 years continuous service. Any complaint must be made to the Industrial Tribunal within 3 months of refusal. The Tribunal may award maximum compensation of two-fifths of a weeks pay.

12.5   Safety representatives

By virtue of regulations made under the Health and Safety at Work Act 1974 recognised safety representatives must be allowed to take such time off, with pay, as is necessary to enable them to carry out their duties and undergo training. The Health and Safety Commission have issued a Code of Guidance as to what is necessary. Complaint is to the Industrial Tribunal within 3 months of the refusal. The Tribunal can order payment of wages wrongfully withheld and compensation for any injury.

13   EPCA 1978: MATERNITY RIGHTS

13.1   Introductory

It is becoming increasingly common for a woman's contract of employment to give valuable rights in connection with pregnancy: often for example these might include maternity leave and pay whilst she is absent. Any such contractual right is labelled **contractual** to distinguish it from any right she might have under statute. The statutory provisions provide minimum rights: thus if an employee's contractual rights are more generous than the statutory rights she will choose to exercise her contractual rights rather than the statutory rights. It is for her to choose which to rely on.

You will see in the immediately succeeding paragraphs that the thrust of the statutory provisions is to ensure that employers allow women time off for childbirth.

You should realise that the statutory protection given to pregnant women does not require the employer to continue to pay her wages during her time off (though she might be entitled to state benefit called statutory maternity pay).

Later you will see that pregnant women also have statutory protection against unfair dismissal.

The statutory protection given to pregnant women is contained in the Employment Protection (Consolidation) Act 1978 (to which far reaching amendments were made by the Trade Union Reform and Employment Rights Act 1993). The statutory provisions are immensely complicated and are here covered only in outline (which is sufficient for your examination).

13.2   Ante-natal care

A pregnant woman is entitled to reasonable time off with pay to obtain ante-natal care (eg, to see a doctor). She must have an appointment and may be required to produce written confirmation of her pregnancy and the appointment. There is no qualifying period of employment. Complaint is to an Industrial Tribunal within 3 months of the refusal. The Tribunal may order the payment of a sum equivalent to her loss or the value of her time during the period she was refused time off.

13.3   General right to maternity leave: S33 EPCA 1978

An employee who is absent from work at any time during her maternity leave period shall be entitled to the benefit of the terms and conditions (except remuneration) of her employment provided

- she notifies the employer of the date she intends her leave to commence (called the notified leave date) at least 21 days beforehand.. No date may be notified which occurs before the beginning of the eleventh week before the expected week of childbirth.

- she notifies the employer in writing at least 21 days before her maternity leave period commences (a) that she is pregnant, and (b) the expected week of childbirth.

The maternity leave period commences with the notified leave date and continues for 14 weeks (or until the birth of the child, if later).

An employee who intends to return to work earlier than the end of her maternity leave period must give the employer at least 7 days notice of the date on which she intends to return.

13.4   Right to return to work: S39 EPCA 1978

An employee who has the general right to maternity leave conferred by S33 and who has a minimum period of continuous service of 2 years (as at the beginning of the eleventh week before the expected week of childbirth) has the right to return to work at any time during the period beginning at the end of her maternity leave period and ending twenty-nine weeks after the beginning of the week in which childbirth occurs. The employee must give written notice of her return date at least 21 days before she returns.

The right under S39 is to return to work for the same employer in the same job and on no less favourable terms. In particular her remuneration must be not less than that which she would have had had she not been on leave.

13.5   Summary

Every pregnant woman has the statutory right to time off for ante-natal care. Every pregnant woman has the statutory right to 14 weeks maternity leave (called the general right to maternity leave). Pregnant women with 2 years service have the statutory right to 40 weeks maternity leave (called the right to return to work). Any pregnant woman might have contractual rights to longer leave.

If an employer fails to allow a pregnant woman her leave rights this will be an automatically unfair dismissal (except that there are special provisions for redundancy during maternity leave).

14   EPCA 1978: MINIMUM NOTICE PERIODS

14.1   Notice to be given by the employer

Under the EPCA 1978 the length of notice of termination of employment, which the employer has expressly agreed in the contract of employment to give, cannot be less than certain minimum periods depending on the length of his continuous employment with the same employer.

The scale is (S49 EPCA 1978):

Continuous employment of employee	*Minimum notice to be given by employer*
Between four weeks and two years	One week
Between two and twelve years	One week for each complete year of employment
Twelve years or more	Twelve weeks

If an employee is dismissed with inadequate notice he may bring a claim for wrongful dismissal; his damages will be his lost wages for the period of notice which he should have been given, subject to his duty to mitigate by accepting reasonable employment.

14.2   Notice to be given by the employee

Under the EPCA 1978 an employee with at least 4 weeks continuous employment must give to his employer at least one week's notice of his intention to leave.

14.3   Activity

John's contract of employment entitles him to 1 month's notice.

What length of notice must his employer give him if John has been in his job for 6 years?

14.4   Activity solution

6 weeks. The contractual period is upgraded to the minimum required by the EPCA 1978.

15   EPCA 1978: WRITTEN REASONS FOR DISMISSAL

Under the Employment Protection (Consolidation) Act 1978 any employee who has completed at least two years' continuous employment is entitled to be provided by his employer on request with a written statement giving particulars of the reasons for dismissal within fourteen days of the employee's request. If an employee is dismissed whilst she is pregnant or on maternity leave the employer must give the written statement whether or not she makes a request and whether or not she has 2 years continuous employment. Any statement given will be admissible in evidence in any proceedings. If the employer fails to comply with these rules, then, upon a complaint being presented under the section, the tribunal may make a declaration as to what it finds were the employer's reasons for dismissing the employee and is bound to make an award that the employer pay to the employee a sum equal to two weeks' pay.

16   UNFAIR DISMISSAL/REDUNDANCY

Under the Employment Protection (Consolidation) Act 1978 certain employees have the right not to be unfairly dismissed and/or the right to a redundancy payment. This is covered as a separate topic in the next chapter.

17   HEALTH AND SAFETY

There are numerous statutory provisions intended to ensure the health and safety of the workplace. These provisions, which impose duties not only on employers but also on employees amongst others, are covered separately in the chapter 'Employment: Health and Safety'.

18   STATE BENEFITS

18.1   Introductory

Under the Social Security Contributions and Benefits Act 1992 a number of state benefits may be available to employees (often dependent on their record of national insurance contributions). The ones of relevance to your examination are considered below.

18.2   Sickness benefit

An employee who is absent from work through illness or injury may have an express contractual right to payment from his employer. This is called contractual sick pay. In the absence of an expressly agreed right the courts will not imply a duty on the employer to pay wages whilst an employee is absent and this is where state benefits become important.

Under the Social Security legislation persons unable to work through illness may claim state benefit. For the first 28 weeks of any period of illness this is paid by the employer and is called 'statutory sick pay'. It is not available for the first three days of any absence. The employer can offset any money he pays under a contractual right to sick pay and vice versa. A small employer can also recoup a certain amount of SSP payments from the government by way of deducting them from his national insurance contributions.

Where SSP is not available to a worker he may be eligible for invalidity benefit. Where an employee suffers lasting injury a claim may be made after six months for disablement benefit and even if by that time he has returned to work.

18.3   Industrial injuries disablement benefit

This state benefit is available if an employee is disabled as a result of an accident at work (or if he contracts certain prescribed industrial diseases). The amount depends on the severity of the disablement and nothing is payable unless he is at least 14% disabled.

Clawback The Social Security Act 1989 allows the Department of Social Security to clawback any benefit paid in respect of injuries. The clawback is made out of damages paid by an employer where the employee has successfully sued the employer in a civil claim. The amount subject to clawback is any damages over £2,500 but restricted to the amount of benefits received within the first 5 years of the injury. So as to ensure the DSS obtains these sums the employer is required to deduct them from the damages it would otherwise pay and transmit the sums to the DSS

18.4   Maternity benefit

A woman who is absent from work on account of maternity may have an express contractual right to payment from her employer. This is called contractual maternity pay. In the absence of an expressly agreed right the courts will not imply a duty on the employer to pay wages whilst an employee is absent and this is where state benefits become important.

Under the Social Security legislation women unable to work because of maternity may be able to claim state benefit. Much depends on her contribution record. For the first 18 weeks of her maternity leave this is paid by the employer and is called 'statutory maternity pay'. The employer may offset any money he pays under a contractual right to maternity pay and vice versa. A small employer can also recoup a certain amount of SMP payments from the government by way of deducting them from his national insurance contributions.

19   SELF TEST QUESTIONS

19.1   Name the three statutes which together prevent discrimination on grounds of sex. (1.1)

19.2   What is a 'countable week'? (1.2)

19.3   What is an 'equality clause'? (2.1)

19.4   List the 7 'genuine occupational qualifications' under which sex discrimination is lawful. (3.4)

19.5   Name the statute which outlaws race discrimination. (4)

19.6   What can an employee do whose employer brands him as a trouble-maker because he had complained of dangers at work? (5)

19.7   Is the 'closed-shop' lawful? (6)

19.8   X refuses to employ Z because he is a Roman Catholic. Is this lawful? (7)

19.9   In what circumstances may an employer make deductions from a worker's wages? (8.2, 8.5)

19.10   What must be itemised on a pay statement? (9)

19.11   For how many workless days is a guarantee payment available? (10)

19.12   List the circumstances in which statute allows an employee time off work. (12 and 13)

19.13   What is the minimum period of continuous employment which a woman must complete before she is allowed

    (a)   time off for ante-natal care? (13.2)
    (b)   maternity leave (14 weeks)? (13.3)
    (c)   the right to return to work? (13.4)

19.14   Set out the minimum statutory periods of notice which an employer must give his employee (14.1)

19.15   Distinguish contractual sick pay and statutory sick pay (18.2)

20   EXAMINATION TYPE QUESTION

20.1   **(a)**   Perhaps the most important obligation placed upon an employer is the payment of wages.

    What legal rules may be applied to determine the amount of the wage to be paid?

                  (10 marks)

    (b)   To what extent must an employer pay wages:

        (i)   during the absence of an employee through illness; and
        (ii)   when he is unable to provide work?

                  (10 marks)

              (Total: 20 marks)

21 ANSWER TO EXAMINATION TYPE QUESTION

21.1 (a) In determining the amount of wage to be paid the starting point is the express terms of the contract of employment. The contract (written or oral) may expressly state a figure based on units of time (hourly, weekly, monthly etc) or expressly state a figure by result (piecework or commission). The contract may (in addition, or alternatively, to specifying a figure) expressly incorporate whatever might be set from time to time in a collective bargaining agreement. If the employment contract was oral and there is a dispute as to what amount was actually agreed reference may be had to the written particulars of employment which the employee, by the EPCA 1978, should have received within 2 months of commencement of employment and within one month of any change in particulars. The written statement forms evidence (but no more) of the employer's view of what is the agreed position.

Where there is no expressly agreed term in the contract as to the amount of pay the courts will imply a term either based on what is the customary or usual amount in that industry or work place or, in the absence of custom or usage, based on the common law. At common law an employer has a duty to pay a reasonable wage.

Although there is no general statutory minimum (or maximum) amount of wage there is statutory intervention in particular circumstances. For example, the Equal Pay Act 1970 may imply an 'equality clause' into a worker's contract of employment. The general aim of this Act is that an employer must pay a woman employee doing like work or work of equal value to a man the same pay unless he can justify the pay differential by relying on a genuine material difference eg, that the man is more productive or better at the job than the woman. Other statutory examples include the Race Relations Act 1976 (which makes it unlawful for an employer to pay a worker more or less than another worker purely on account of his race, colour, nationality or ethnic or national origins); the Trade Union and Labour Relations (Consolidation) Act 1992 (which makes it unlawful to pay an employee more or less than another on the basis of his membership or non-membership of a trade union); and the Employment Protection (Consolidation) Act 1978 (which prevents victimisation (eg, as regards level of pay) on the basis that the employee complained of unsafe working conditions.)

Once the amount of wage is set (by whatever method, above) the employer is obliged to pay it and may only make deductions where they are permitted by the Wages Act 1986. The Wages Act forbids deductions unless the amount and purpose has previously been agreed to by the employee (either in his contract or in writing) or unless it is authorised by statute (as is the situation with the PAYE system for payment of tax). The Wages Act 1986 puts a further restriction on deductions on account of stock losses or shortages from wages of workers in retail employment (eg, petrol pump attendants). Even if the worker has agreed to the deduction that employer may not deduct more than 10% of his gross pay on any pay day except the last pay day.

(b) (i) An employee's contract will normally entitle him to wages only if he is ready and able to work. Thus if he is absent due to illness he would normally have no contractual right to pay. The courts will not imply a duty on the employer to pay an employee who is absent due to illness. If, on the other hand, the employee's contract expressly entitles him to payment while off work sick then the employer has a duty to pay the stated amount - called contractual sick pay.

Under the EPCA 1978 if an employee is suspended from work on medical grounds (this would normally be to prevent *anticipated* illness or injury) he must be paid his contractual pay for at least 26 weeks.

Under Social Security legislation an employee who is unable to work for more than 3 days because of illness receives state benefit. For the first 28 weeks this is automatically paid by the employer who may be able to recoup a certain amount from the state by deduction from his liability to pay national insurance. Any contractual sick pay is offset against this statutory sick pay and vice versa.

(ii)   The general rule is that the employer must pay the agreed amount even though there is no work for the employee to do. Thus where pay is calculated by intervals eg, weekly, monthly, the employee will be paid even though the employer cannot provide work.

However, some methods of pay depend on there being work available eg, piece work. In addition some employment contracts contain a term allowing the employer to suspend the employee on no pay when there is no work available. In these situations the Employment Protection (Consolidation) Act 1978 requires the employer to pay the employee a guarantee payment for certain days when he is not provided with work and as a result receives no pay. To be entitled to such guarantee payment the employee must have been employed for a minimum of four weeks. The entitlement is to a set amount for each work day on which work is not provided up to a maximum of five days in any three month period. The employee can only claim in respect of days on which he is normally required to work and on which no work is provided throughout the whole day because of a diminution in the requirement of his employer's business for work of the kind he does or any other occurrence affecting normal working of the employer's business. No guarantee payment is made if failure to provide work is due to trade disputes, the employee unreasonably refusing an offer of suitable employment or the employee failing to comply with reasonable safety requirements.

15 EMPLOYMENT: TERMINATION OF EMPLOYMENT

INTRODUCTION & LEARNING OBJECTIVES

Syllabus area 8d. Dismissal. (Ability required 3).

This chapter will consider the ways in which a contract of employment may be terminated. Examples of wrongful dismissal, unfair dismissal and redundancy will be considered together with the claims that are possible for employees in these situations.

When you have studied this chapter you should be able to do the following:

- Appreciate the ways in which a contract of employment may be terminated.
- Recognise a case of wrongful dismissal and advise an employee of his remedies.
- Discuss the remedies of an employer if an employee is in breach of contract.
- Understand the meaning of summary dismissal and of constructive dismissal.
- Distinguish between fair and unfair dismissal.
- Recognise special situations such as industrial action and maternity.
- Explain the remedies available to an employee unfairly dismissed.
- Define when redundancy takes place and the claim available to an employee made redundant.

---

1 METHODS OF TERMINATION OF THE EMPLOYMENT CONTRACT

1.1 Introduction

On ordinary contractual principles a contract of service may be terminated in a number of different ways:

1.2 Termination without notice by the employer

Definition Termination **without notice by the employer** is summary dismissal of the employee.

The general principle is that summary dismissal is justified if the conduct of the employee is such that it prevents further satisfactory continuance of the relationship ie, a serious breach of the contract of employment eg,:

(a) wilful disobedience of a lawful order;
(b) misconduct such as dishonesty, the use of violence or disclosure of trade secrets;
(c) habitual, serious and persistent neglect, carelessness, or laziness.

In contractual terms, the act of the employee must be such as to entitle the employer to repudiate the contract immediately ie, a very serious breach of contract.

If the employer unjustifiably terminates the contract, the employee may maintain an action for damages for wrongful dismissal.

1.3   Termination without notice by the employee

[Definition]   Termination **without notice by the employee** is where he repudiates the contract by leaving.

This would normally mean a breach of contract by the employee.

Note, however, that the employee may leave in circumstances which warrant his doing so because of the behaviour of the employer. This will amount to constructive dismissal by the employer and the employee will have an action for wrongful dismissal.

1.4   Termination by notice

Notice can be by either party giving notice for the specified period.

The period of notice may be:

(a)   Express: specified in the employment contract itself – but this must not be less than the statutory minimum.

(b)   Implied by the courts into the contract on the basis of the presumed intention of the parties ie, reasonable notice. An implied term as to notice cannot be less than the statutory minimum but it may provide for a longer period.

Hill v Parsons [1971]

Facts: what would be an appropriate notice period for a senior engineer? (One month's notice had been given.)

Held: (Court of Appeal): one month was inadequate and inappropriate in this case: reasonable notice in this case could be anything between 6 to 12 months.

1.5   Fixed term contract expires

A fixed term contract expires without notice at the end of the term: there is no breach by either party. If an employer wishes to reserve a right to determine such a contract before it expires he must do so in the contract in clear and unequivocal terms.

McClelland v Northern Ireland General Health Service Board [1957]

Facts: there was a clause providing for premature determination on grounds only of inefficiency or gross misconduct.

Held: this did not permit termination for redundancy.

If an employee is employed under a fixed term contract and is wrongfully dismissed before the expiry of that term, he may claim as damages his lost wages for the whole of the unexpired period of the contract, subject to his obligation to mitigate his loss.

1.6   Termination by agreement

Termination **by agreement** is when the parties to a contract of employment by agreement end their relationship at any time and upon any terms.

1.7   Termination by operation of law

(a)   Frustration.

Definition   'Frustration occurs whenever the law recognises that without default of either party the contract has become impossible to perform because the circumstances in which performance is called for would render it a thing different from that which was undertaken by the contract.'

Frustration could be caused by death, long illness, incapacity, or imprisonment:

(b)   Dissolution, winding up. The dissolution of a partnership where the partners are the employers will terminate the contracts; similarly the compulsory liquidation of a company, where the company is the employer will terminate employment contracts.

1.8   Activity

What are the statutory minimum periods of notice required to be given by

(a)   the employee
(b)   the employer?

1.9   Activity solutions

(a)   not less than one week

(b)   •   not less than one week where the employee has been continuously employed for one month or more but less than two years

•   not less than one week for each complete year of employment where the employee has been continuously employed for two years or more but less than 12 years.

•   not less than 12 weeks where the employee has been continuously employed for twelve years or more

1.10   Possible claims

An **employee** who is dismissed may have one or more of the following claims:

(a)   damages for **wrongful** dismissal at common law – this is for breach of the employment contract.

(b)   an order for reinstatement, re-engagement or a monetary award for **unfair** dismissal – even if there is no breach of the employment contract if the employee qualifies and he was unfairly dismissed under EPCA 1978;

(c)   a lump sum payment for **redundancy** payable under EPCA 1978 to qualifying employees.

A dismissal may be both wrongful at common law and unfair by statute; or lawful but unfair; or even fair yet wrongful. Independently of these categories a dismissal may give rise to a claim by reason of redundancy (although dismissal for redundancy will generally be fair – unless the employee was unfairly selected for redundancy).

Conclusion| It is important to distinguish between the three claims, the situations in which each of the claims arises, the legal basis of the claims, how they are made and what the employee is likely to get if he makes a claim.

An **employer** will have a claim for breach of contract if the employee is in breach eg, leaves employment without proper notice (unless there has been constructive dismissal).

2 BREACH OF CONTRACT - WRONGFUL DISMISSAL AT COMMON LAW

2.1 Introduction

Where an employment contract is terminated not in accordance with the terms of the contract there is a breach of contract and the innocent party will have a claim for damages. Remember, that the court will not usually grant specific performance of an employment contract.

2.2 Employer's breach

The **employer** will be in breach of his contract with his employee if he terminates the contract without giving proper notice. The length of notice required will be determined by the contract, subject to the statutory minimums imposed by the EPCA 1978. Also note that where a fixed term employment contract expires and is not renewed there is no breach of contract.

- Summary dismissal

  Definition| Summary dismissal is dismissal without notice

  This will be a wrongful dismissal unless:

  (a) the employee waives his rights, accepts payment in lieu or there is an agreement to discharge;

  (b) the employee has repudiated or is in fundamental breach of his own obligations eg,

      (i) Wilful refusal to obey lawful instructions eg, **Pepper v Webb [1968]** contrast **Laws v London Chronicle [1959]**

      (ii) Failure to show a professed skill eg, **Harmer v Cornelius [1858]**

      (iii) Serious or persistent negligence.

      (iv) Breach of duty of good faith eg, **Hivac v Park Royal Scientific [1946]**, **Sinclair v Neighbour [1967]** and **Boston Deep Sea Fishing v Ansell [1888]**

      (v) Immorality or drunkenness (even when outside working hours if it is important to the job).

- Constructive dismissal

  Definition| a serious breach of contract by the employer such as entitles the employee to treat the contract as discharged.

Western Excavation Ltd v Sharp [1978]

Facts: what conduct will amount to constructive dismissal?

Held: an employee is entitled to treat himself as constructively dismissed if the employer is guilty of conduct which is a significant breach going to the root of the contract of employment, or which shows that the employer no longer intends to be bound by one or more of the essential terms of the contract. Whether the employee leaves with or without notice, the conduct must be sufficiently serious to entitle him to leave at once. However, he must act quickly, for if he continues for any length of time without leaving, he will be regarded as having elected to affirm the contract and will lose his right to treat himself as discharged.

Where such a repudiatory breach occurs the employee resigns and will have an action against the employer for wrongful dismissal.

Donovan v Invicta Airways [1970]

Facts: the employer put pressure on the employee, an airline pilot, to take abnormal risks on a flight. The employer did this three times in rapid succession. Each time the employee refused. Relations with management deteriorated and he left.

Held: the employer had committed a serious breach of contract amounting to constructive dismissal. The employee succeeded in an action for wrongful dismissal.

2.3   Employee's remedies

The employee who has been dismissed has the following remedies at common law:

(a)   If he is dismissed rightfully with proper notice he has no claim if he is paid for the full period of notice. (There is no breach of contract.)

(b)   If he is dismissed rightfully without proper notice, he may claim for unpaid wages.

(c)   If he is dismissed wrongfully, without proper notice, he may:

   (i)   sue for wages accrued due, if any, and damages for wrongful dismissal;

   (ii)   sue on a *quantum meruit* basis for services rendered; or

   (iii)   sue for a declaration that the contract still subsists and for an injunction restraining breach. (However, an injunction would very rarely be granted.)

(Contrast this with an order for reinstatement or re-engagement for unfair dismissal. See below.)

Definition   A claim on a *quantum meruit* is one for fair payment for work done or services rendered.

Definition   An injunction is an equitable remedy, granted at the discretion of the court, ordering a person to do, or to desist from doing, some act as a remedy for a breach of duty (contractual or otherwise).

2.4   Damages

The damages which would be awarded will depend on the following principles:

(a)   The contractual remoteness rule applies: **Hadley v Baxendale**.

(b)   In practice, the measure is usually, the net wages which the employee would have received over the normal notice period. (Remember, damages are designed to restore the plaintiff's position. He would have received net pay (ie, after tax) had his employment continued.)

(c)   The following additional claims may be made:

(i)   loss of commission or tips and possibly pension rights;

(ii)   lost prospects if employee is an apprentice, but otherwise nothing for difficulty in getting a new job;

(iii)   loss of the right to claim unfair dismissal if the wrongful dismissal prevents him from having the qualifying continuous employment to claim.

(d)   deductions may be made as follows:

(i)   for mitigation or for failure to do so, (ie, did, or should, the employee have found new work?) - **Brace v Calder [1895]**

(ii)   unemployment pay received.

There is no set limit on the amount of damages. (Unlike unfair dismissal compensation, which is subject to a set maximum amount).

> Conclusion   An employee who has been wrongfully dismissed can recover damages.

The usual statutory periods of limitation relating to claims for breach of contract apply (six years - simple contract; twelve years - contract by deed) so that an employee wrongfully dismissed will not be restricted by the three month limitation period imposed in cases of unfair dismissal.

Claims are made to the County Court or High Court of Justice.

2.5   Employee's breach and employer's remedies

If the **employee** is in breach an employer has the following remedies:

(a)   Dismiss the employee without notice if the breach is serious enough to justify treating the contract as discharged.

(b)   If the employee wrongfully leaves without notice, sue him for breach. This is rarely pursued because the damages awarded would be so small (unless the employee is on a very high salary and a long period of notice).

(c)   Bring action to recover any secret profit **Boston Deep Sea Fishing v Ansell [1888],** or other loss caused by the breach of duty eg, **Lister v Romford Ice [1957]**.

(d)   Seek an injunction - generally, this will not be awarded to prevent an employee from leaving. However, it is often used to enforce the duty of confidentiality.

2.6   Activity

An employee is discovered to be accepting commissions unknown to her employer. Could the employee be summarily dismissed and on what grounds?

2.7   Activity solution

The employee could be summarily dismissed on the grounds of breach of duty of good faith.

3   UNFAIR DISMISSAL AND REDUNDANCY: FACTORS COMMON TO BOTH

3.1   General points

(a)   Both are statutory claims under the Employment Protection (Consolidation) Act 1978 (as amended).

(b)   Both are litigated at first instance in the Industrial Tribunal: appeal, on a point of law only, lies to the Employment Appeal Tribunal, then to the Court of Appeal, and finally to the House of Lords.

(c)   Neither claim depends on breach of contract, so the remedy is not damages. The remedy for redundancy is a redundancy payment. The possible remedies for unfair dismissal are re-instatement, re-engagement and a monetary award.

(d)   Only employees can claim, not independent contractors.

(e)   Employees in excluded classes of employment cannot claim. An example of relevance to your examination is employees who ordinarily work outside Great Britain.

3.2   Upper age limit

The claimant must be, at the effective date of termination, under the normal retiring age. This is whatever it might be for the job except that, for redundancy, it cannot exceed 65. It there is no normal retiring age, or if it is different for men and women, the normal retiring age is deemed to be 65.

3.3   Qualifying period of employment

Ending with the effective date of termination the employee must have been **continuously employed** for two years for those who work more than sixteen hours per week or five years for those who work between eight and sixteen hours a week.

The calculation of continuous employment has already been covered in the previous chapter.

3.4   Dismissal

The employee must prove he has been dismissed.

Under the EPCA 1978 an employee is dismissed if:

(a)   the contract is **terminated by the employer** with or without notice;
(b)   a **fixed term** contract expires and is **not renewed**;
(c)   the employee was **constructively dismissed.**

•   Resignation is not dismissal (unless in circumstances amounting to constructive dismissal)

Morton Sundour Fabrics v Shaw [1966]

Facts: an employee was warned that it was likely that he would be dismissed (for redundancy) at some unspecified date in the near future. He then left (because he had found another job).

Held: he had not been dismissed.

However, if an employee had actually been given notice of dismissal and leaves before the expiry of the notice this is still treated as a dismissal.

A difficult case showing the very narrow borderline between dismissal and resignation is

Saunders v Neale [1974]

Facts: the employees went on strike and were warned by the employer that if they did not return they would be dismissed. The employer did not actually dismiss them but when the strike was over the employer refused to take them back as there was no work for them because his business had disappeared during the strike.

Held: on the facts the employees had dismissed themselves ie, they had not been dismissed by the employer, they had resigned.

- Termination by mutual consent is not dismissal.

- Frustration is not dismissal.

3.5 Contracting out

Contracting out is possible as to either or both claims only if:

(a)   the contract is for a fixed term of one year or more (2 years for redundancy); **and**

(b)   the employee has agreed in writing before the expiry of the term that non-renewal will not give rise to a claim.

3.6 Effective date of termination

The **effective date of termination** varies according to the manner of termination:

(a)   In relation to an employee whose contract is terminated by notice, whether his employer's or his own, it means the date on which that notice expires.

(b)   In the case of an employee whose contract is terminated without notice, it means the date on which the termination takes effect.

(c)   In circumstances where a fixed term contract expires without being renewed, it will be the date on which that term expires.

If the circumstances are such that the statutory period of notice required under the EPCA 1978, if given, would have expired later than the effective date of termination as defined above, that later date is treated as the effective date of termination (amongst other things) for the purposes of computing the qualifying period of employment. This reduces the qualifying period.

For example, an employee who has been continuously employed for one week short of two years and who is then dismissed without notice will be deemed to have been given the statutory notice to which he would otherwise have been entitled, that is one week, and hence will have the protection of the unfair dismissal legislation.

A part of a week is deemed to be a full week, which, therefore, has the effect of reducing the qualifying period still further:

4   UNFAIR DISMISSAL

4.1   What must be proved

It is for the **employee to show** that he has been **dismissed**, but once this has been done, or if it is accepted by all parties that there was a dismissal, it is for the **employer** to show:

(a)   **what was the reason** or, if more than one, the principal reason for the dismissal; and

(b)   that this reason related to one or more of the **statutory fair reasons**.

4.2   What was the reason?

An employer can only rely on a given reason where he knew of it at the date of the dismissal.

Devis v Atkins [1977]

Facts: the employer dismissed the employee and afterwards discovered that the employee had been guilty of dishonesty.

Held: dishonesty was not the reason for the dismissal and therefore the employer could not rely on it in order to justify the dismissal as fair.

Note that the position is different in a wrongful dismissal action: the employer may rely on after discovered facts to defend an action for wrongful dismissal - **Cyril Leonard v Simo Securities Trust [1971]**

4.3   The statutory fair reasons for dismissal

S57(1) EPCA sets out five reasons on which the employer may rely in order to justify the dismissal as fair:

(a)   **The capabilities or qualifications** of the employee (ie, the lack of them) for performing work of the kind he was employed to do. Capability is to be assessed by reference to skill, aptitude, health or any other physical or mental quality; and qualification means any relevant degree, diploma or other academic, technical or professional qualification.

(b)   The **conduct** of the employee, for example:

Stevenson v Golden Wonder Ltd [1977]

Facts: a technical manager took part in a moderately serious and unprovoked assault on another employee at a company social function held outside working hours in the company canteen.

Held: this was a fair reason for the dismissal.

Any breach of the employee's contractual duties (express or implied) would also be misconduct.

(c)   The fact that the employee was **redundant.**

(d)   The fact that the employee could not continue to work in the position which he held without **contravention of a duty** or **restriction imposed by or under statute.**

(e)   **Some other substantial reason** of a kind such as to justify the dismissal of an employee from the position which that employee held.   The reason need only be one which **can possibly** justify dismissal, not one which in the court's opinion of the facts **does** justify it. There is an element of objective judgement, thus excluding mere personal motives. Examples of some other substantial reasons are as follows:

   •   conduct of the employee away from the employment where this impinges on the employment relationship eg,

       Foot v Eastern Counties Timber [1972]

       An employee married an employee of a direct competitor.

       Singh v London County Bus Services

       An employee in a position of trust was convicted of a criminal offence of dishonesty (which he committed off duty).

   •   the dismissed employee was recruited as a temporary replacement for an employee disabled through injury or illness or pregnancy provided this temporary status was set out in writing on engagement - EPCA 1978.

The EPCA 1978 specifically states that industrial action pressure or union pressure is not 'other substantial reason'.

4.4   Reasonableness of employer

Once the employee has shown he was dismissed and the employer has shown that it was for one or more of the five fair reasons it is then for the tribunal to decide whether the dismissal was fair or unfair.

S57(3) EPCA 1978 states that the determination of this question 'depends on whether in the circumstances (including the size an administrative resources of the employer's undertaking) the employer acted reasonably or unreasonably in treating the reason given as a sufficient reason for dismissing the employee; and that question shall be determined in accordance with equity and the substantial merits of the case'.

Case law shows that this 'reasonableness test' involves two questions:

   •   whether the reason given was sufficiently serious to justify dismissal. Thus it is unlikely that the tribunal would consider it reasonable to dismiss for a minor isolated act of misconduct.

   •   whether the employer adopted reasonable procedures both in coming to the decision to dismiss and in the manner of the dismissal.

       The Arbitration, Conciliation and Advisory Service (ACAS) has issued Codes of Practice for procedures to be followed in coming to the decision to dismiss an employee (eg, warnings, proper inquiry into alleged misconduct etc) which the Industrial Tribunal has regard to. These were illustrated by the House of Lords in **Polkey v AE Dayton Services**

[1987] where it was stated that in a case of incapability, the employer will normally not act reasonably unless he gives the employee fair warning and an opportunity to mend his ways and show he can do the job; that in a case of misconduct, the employer will normally not act reasonably unless he investigates the complaint fully and fairly and hears whatever the employee wishes to say in his defence or in explanation or mitigation; that in a case of redundancy (this was the situation in **Polkey**) the employer will normally not act reasonably unless he warns and consults any employees affected or their representative, adopts a fair basis upon which to select for redundancy and takes such steps as may be reasonable to avoid or minimise redundancy by redeployment within his own organisation.

4.5   Inadmissible reasons

The EPCA 1978 sets out a number of reasons on which the employer is not allowed to rely in order to justify the dismissal as fair. The 'inadmissible reasons' are important because:

- the dismissal is deemed 'automatically unfair' with the result that the 'reasonableness test' is not relevant.

- the qualifying conditions (age and period of continuous service) do not have to be satisfied.

- the monetary awards are substantially higher than for other reasons.

The inadmissible reasons are complicated and are given in outline.

(1)   Dismissal in health and safety cases: EPCA 1978

This includes:

- dismissal of a safety representative because he performed, or proposed to perform, any of his functions

- dismissal of any employee because he raises health and safety matters, refuses to work because of lack of health and safety or took steps to protect himself or other persons from danger.

(2)   Dismissal on ground of pregnancy or childbirth: EPCA 1978

This includes dismissal of a woman

- because she is pregnant

- for any reason connected with her pregnancy

- in connection with the exercise of her right to maternity leave or her right to return to work

(3)   Dismissal on grounds of trade unionism: TULRCA 1992. This includes dismissal of an employee because

- he is, or proposes to become, a member of a trade union

- he has taken part, or proposed to take part, in the activities of a trade union

- he has refused, or proposed to refuse to become or remain a trade union member.

(4)   Dismissal on grounds of assertion of a statutory right: EPCA 1978

Assertion of a statutory right includes not only where the employee has brought formal tribunal proceedings claiming a statutory right but also where he simply alleges that the employer has infringed a statutory right. It is immaterial whether or not it was eventually decided that the right was infringed provided the employee made his assertion in good faith.

The statutory rights which are relevant are:

- any right conferred by the Employment Protection (Consolidation) Act 1978

- any right conferred by the Wages Act 1986

- any right conferred by the Trade Union and Labour Relations (Consolidation) Act 1992.

(5)   Unfair selection for redundancy

An employer unfairly selects an employee for dismissal for redundancy if

- he does so in contravention of a customary arrangement or agreed procedure relating to selection

- the reason for selection was an inadmissible reason.

4.6   Complaint of unfair dismissal

(a)   General rule

A complaint of unfair dismissal must be presented to the Industrial Tribunal within **three months** from the effective date of termination or within such further period as the tribunal considers reasonable. However, the tribunal will not extend the period unless it is satisfied that it was not reasonably practicable for the complaint to be presented within the initial three months period: EPCA 1978.

(b)   Industrial action: loss of unfair dismissal protection

- Unofficial industrial action

  Under the Trade Union and Labour Relations (Consolidation) Act 1992 an employee cannot present a complaint to an Industrial Tribunal for unfair dismissal if at the date of his dismissal he was taking part in an unofficial strike or other unofficial industrial action.

  Broadly speaking, strike is unofficial if, where there is a recognised union, the members go on strike without the strike being authorised by the union after a proper ballot. Colloquially an unofficial strike is called a 'wild cat' strike.

- Non-unofficial industrial action (ie, where there is no recognised trade union or where the strike is official). If the employee is dismissed whilst he is on such a strike he may present a complaint to the Industrial Tribunal for unfair dismissal only if there has been victimisation ie,

(i)   one or more of the striking employees have not been dismissed, or

(ii)   within 3 months of the dismissal one or more striking employees have been offered re-engagement and the complainant has not been offered re-engagement.

In such situations the complainant has 6 months in which to present his case to the tribunal.

4.7   Reinstatement or re-engagement

If a complaint of unfair dismissal succeeds, the tribunal must explain to the complainant its powers to order reinstatement or re-engagement.

[Definition]   **Reinstatement** means resumption of work as though there had been no break and nullifies totally the effect of the dismissal.

[Definition]   **Re-engagement** does not have this effect on the dismissal and means re-employment under a new contract of employment.

In exercising its discretion, the tribunal must first consider reinstatement and if it decides not to make an order to this effect, it must then consider re-engagement. In both cases, however, it should take into account:

(a)   The wishes of the complainant.
(b)   Whether it is practicable for the employer to comply with such an order.
(c)   Whether it would be just having regard to the conduct of the complainant.

Very few reinstatement or re-engagement orders are made, principally because generally employees do not wish it.

4.8   Monetary award

Where the Tribunal does not make an order for re-instatement or re-engagement it must make a monetary award. Sometimes it will exercise its discretion to make a monetary award even though there is re-instatement or re-engagement.

The monetary award has three components: the basic award, the compensatory award, and the special, additional or higher award.

If an employee is guilty of misconduct, it may be that he will have no claim at all. However, if, despite his misconduct, his dismissal is nevertheless unfair, for example as a result of the employer's failure to give a warning or to comply with the practical guidance given in the Code of Practice, his compensation may be reduced by 100%. In these circumstances, a tribunal is not entitled to take account of misconduct subsequent to the dismissal in deciding the fairness or reasonableness of the dismissal, but it is nevertheless entitled in assessing compensation to have regard to subsequently-discovered misconduct and, if it thinks fit, to award nominal or nil compensation on this basis.

4.9   Basic award

The basic award depends on the age of the employee, his weekly pay and the length of his continuous employment.

For each year of employment,
where employee is wholly over the
age of 41 $1\frac{1}{2}$ weeks' pay

For each year of employment,
where employee is below the age
of 41 but over the age of 22   1 week's pay

For each year of employment,
where employee is below the age of 22 $\frac{1}{2}$ week's pay

There is a maximum of 20 years and a maximum of £205 weekly pay.

The tribunal may reduce this amount:

(1)   by any redundancy payment awarded by the tribunal; or
(2)   if the employee has caused or contributed to his dismissal.

However, it is payable regardless of actual loss.

4.10   Activity

If someone had worked for 23 years over the age of 41 (from 41-64) at a final week's pay of £300 per week what would be his basic award?

4.11   Activity solution

20 years x $1\frac{1}{2}$ weeks × £205 = £6,150

(A maximum of 20 years with the weekly pay rated at the statutory maximum of £205.)

4.12   Compensatory award

The second part of the award is within the tribunal's discretion and is known as a **compensatory award**, which will be of such amount as is just and reasonable having regard to the employee's losses and expenses through dismissal up to a maximum of £11,000. In assessing compensation, the tribunal will take into account immediate loss of wages based on net figures, the manner of dismissal, future loss of wages, loss of protection in respect of unfair dismissal and loss of pension rights, and will then deduct:

(a)   money received from the employer;
(b)   state benefits;
(c)   any failure to mitigate loss (in terms of weeks or months); and
(d)   damages received for wrongful dismissal.

4.13 Additional award

This special award of a high amount is made:

- where an employer ignores an order for re-instatement or re-engagement
- where the dismissal was unfair because of unlawful race or sex discrimination
- where the reason for the dismissal was an inadmissible one

5 STATUTORY REDUNDANCY

5.1 Introduction

Definition A person will be **redundant** ie, the dismissal will be taken to be by way of redundancy, if it was attributable wholly or mainly to the fact that:

(a) the employer has **ceased** or **intends to cease** to carry on the **business** for the purposes of which or in the place where the employee was employed, permanently or temporarily; or

(b) the **requirements** of that business for employees to carry out **work** of a **particular kind**, or **in a place** where they were so employed, have **ceased or diminished** or are **expected to cease** or **diminish**, permanently or temporarily: S81 EPCA 1978.

In proceedings before a tribunal, an employee who has been dismissed by his employer is presumed to have been so dismissed by reason of redundancy, unless the contrary is proved: the employer can only rebut the presumption of redundancy by proving some other main reason for dismissal, for example any of those arising under S57 EPCA 1978.

5.2 Type of work

European Chefs v Currell

Facts: a pastry cook was dismissed because the requirement for his speciality (eclairs and meringues) had ceased. He was replaced by a new pastry cook whose speciality was the new requirement (continental pastries).

Held: it was held that the dismissed pastry cook had been dismissed for redundancy as the need for the particular work he contracted to do had ceased.

If the employer wishes to alter the terms on which the work is done, that is not a case of redundancy unless there is a fundamental change in the type of work which becomes the reason for the dismissal of the employee.

Vaux & Associated Breweries v Ward [1969]

Facts: a quiet public house was modernised by, amongst other things, installing a discotheque. Mrs Ward, the 57 year old barmaid was dismissed in order to make way for a younger more glamorous 'Bunny girl' barmaid.

Held: Mrs Ward had not been dismissed for redundancy as there was no change in the nature of the particular work being done.

5.3 **Place of work**

The place where a person is employed means in this context the place where he is habitually employed and any place where under his contract he can be required to work. There will not, therefore, be a redundancy situation where the transfer of location is reasonable or where the contract gives the employer an express or implied right to move the employee in question from one place to another. This is not the case, though, if the employer has no such right: **O'Brien v Associated Fire Alarms [1969]**

5.4 **Offer of fresh employment**

A redundant employee will be disqualified from receiving a redundancy payment if he unreasonably refuses an offer made by his employer before the end of the previous contract to renew his contract or to re-engage him on the same terms as before. In addition, if the employer makes an offer to renew the contract or to re-engage the employee but on terms which differ from the previous contract, the employee will lose his right to a redundancy payment if he unreasonably refuses the offer, provided that it constitutes an offer of suitable employment in relation to that employee: S82 EPCA 1978.

Whether the alternative employment is suitable, or the offer was unreasonably refused, are both questions of fact to be determined by reference to such matters as the employee's skill and working conditions, the requirements of his family, change in earnings, age, health, sex, etc. Any dispute arising in this respect is for the tribunal to determine and the onus of proof is on the employer:

Taylor v Kent County Council [1969]

Facts: T was headmaster of a school. The school was amalgamated with another school and a new head appointed to the combined school. T was offered employment in a pool of teachers, standing in for short periods in understaffed schools. He would retain his current salary.

Held: T was entitled to reject this offer and claim a redundancy payment: the new offer was substantially different, particularly in regard to status.

If such an offer is made, the employee is entitled to have a four weeks trial period in the alternative employment, from the end of his employment under the previous contract. If the employer terminates the employment during this trial period for a reason connected with the change, the employee will be deemed to have been dismissed for redundancy on the date when the previous job ended.

The offer of further employment may be made by the employer himself or by an associated employer, that is a company of which the other employer has control or the other of two companies controlled by a third person. The offer may also be made by a new employer to whom the business has been sold as a going concern (as opposed to a sale of assets only); the situation will be the same as though an offer was made by the previous employer.

If the employee accepts the offer of further employment, whether made by the same or a new or associated employer, and retains it beyond the trial period, his employment will be regarded as continuous and unbroken by the change for the purposes of reckoning total employment.

5.5 **Lay-off and short time**

Definition An employee is taken to be **laid off** for any week in which his employer does not provide work for him to do and he is thereby deprived of his right to remuneration, such right being dependent upon the performance of work which he is employed to do.

Definition   An employee is taken to be kept on **short time** where, by reason of a diminution in the work provided for him, being work which he is employed to do, his remuneration for any week is less than half a week's pay.

To qualify for a redundancy payment in either of these cases, the employee must have been laid off or kept on short time for either:

(a)   four or more consecutive weeks; or

(b)   for a broken series of six or more weeks (of which not more than three were consecutive) within a period of thirteen weeks;

and must, within four weeks from the end of the relevant period, serve written notice on his employer of his intention to claim a redundancy payment. Within seven days after service of this notice, the employer may serve a counter notice and if this is not subsequently withdrawn in writing by the employer, the employee will not be entitled to a redundancy payment except in accordance with a decision of a tribunal.

If he wishes to pursue his claim the employee must also terminate his contract by a week's notice or alternatively by giving his contractual period of notice within the period allowed by EPCA 1978. An employee will also not be entitled to a redundancy payment pursuant to this notice of intention to claim if he is dismissed by his employer (but he may then have the more general right to redundancy pay for dismissal).

If laid off or put on short time, an employee having at least one month's service has an overriding right to claim **guarantee payments** for up to five days' pay, in any quarter, for days when no work is provided and no other suitable work is available.

5.6   Voluntary termination

An employee will be taken to have been dismissed by his employer if the employer first gives him notice of termination, and the employee later gives notice in writing to his employer to terminate his contract on a date earlier than that on which the employer's notice is due to expire. The employer may, however, exclude his liability for a redundancy payment if, before the expiry of the employee's notice he gives him written notice requiring him to withdraw his notice of termination and to continue in his employment until the date of expiry of the employer's original notice. Where the employee is given such a notice, he will not be entitled to receive a redundancy payment unless a tribunal decides that it is just and equitable for him to do so.

5.7   Death of employer

The general rule is that if the death of an employer operates under any enactment or rule of law to determine the contract of employment, it is regarded for the purposes of the EPCA 1978 as a termination by the employer. In these circumstances the employee will be regarded as dismissed for redundancy unless within a period of eight weeks after the death, a personal representative of the deceased employer offers to renew the contract or re-engage him under a new contract of employment. The offer must comply with the conditions regarding the terms and suitability in relation to the employee and must be in writing, to take effect within eight weeks from the employer's death.

5.8   Activity

An electrician had lived and worked in Newcastle all of his life and refused to move to a job in London when his company's Newcastle branch closed. Has he been made redundant?

5.9 Activity solution

From the facts it would appear that Newcastle was the place where he was habitually employed and the employer had no right to move him to another place. Therefore he has been made redundant.

5.10 Disqualification from payment - misconduct

An employee who is dismissed by reason of misconduct has no right to a redundancy payment.

5.11 Time limit for claim for redundancy pay

An employee shall not be entitled to a redundancy payment unless, before the end of the period of six months beginning with the date on which notice or a fixed term expired or, if no notice, the date on which termination takes effect:

(a)   payment has been agreed and paid; or
(b)   the employee has submitted a written claim for payment to his employer; or
(c)   a dispute as to the right to or amount of a payment has been transferred to a tribunal; or
(d)   a claim for unfair dismissal has been referred to a tribunal.

This six months period may be extended by a further six months if during that second period the employee makes any of the claims listed in (b) to (d) inclusive above and it appears just and equitable to a tribunal that he should receive a redundancy payment.

5.12 Calculation and payment of redundancy pay

The **amount** of redundancy pay is calculated by reference to **age, length of service** and **final remuneration**.

For every complete year of continuous employment (up to a maximum of 20 years) the entitlement is:

Employee's age at time of dismissal	*Amount to which entitled for each year*
41 – 64	$1\frac{1}{2}$ weeks' pay
22 – 40	1 week's pay
18 – 21	$\frac{1}{2}$ week's pay

A week's pay is a maximum of £205.

The amount due is paid by the employer and (except where the amount has been specified in a tribunal decision), he must give to the employee a written statement indicating how the amount of payment has been calculated.

The basic award on redundancy will be set against the basic award for unfair dismissal or an 'unfair redundancy claim'. However, damages awarded for wrongful dismissal do not affect or are not affected by a redundancy payment.

5.13 Activity

Robin has been made redundant on his 51st birthday after 30 years of continuous employment with Bear plc. His current salary is £1,000 per week.

Calculate his statutory redundancy payment.

5.14   Activity solution

Between 41 and 64: $10 \times 1\frac{1}{2} \times 205 =$	3,075
Between 22 and 40: $10 \times 1 \times 205 =$	2,050
	5,125

Note: limitation of pay to £205 and years service to 20.

5.15   Enforcement

Any question arising under the **EPCA 1978** as to the right or to the amount of a payment may be referred to a tribunal. There is also a right of appeal on a point of law to the EAT.

If the employer has defaulted in payment and is insolvent, the employee may apply to the Secretary of State for Employment for payment and if a payment is made by the Secretary of State in respect of an employer's payment, he will be subrogated to the employee's rights against the employer.

5.16   Activity

A married headmaster with a family is made redundant due to an amalgamation of schools and is offered alternative employment at the same salary, as part of a mobile pool of teachers. Due to this he would have to move home. Is his refusal to accept the job likely to be seen as reasonable?

5.17   Activity solution

The inconvenience of moving and the loss of status is likely to justify his refusal of the job.

6   REDUNDANCY: DUTY TO CONSULT

6.1   The duty

Where the employer is proposing to dismiss as redundant any employee and there is a recognised trade union he must consult representatives of the union about the dismissal - Trade Union and Labour Relations (Consolidation) Act 1992.

The consultation must include such matters as:

- reasons for the proposed redundancies
- number of employees involved
- proposed methods of selecting those to be made redundant
- timing of the dismissals
- ways of avoiding redundancy (eg, offers of alternative employment).

6.2   Timing

The employer must consult with the union at the earliest opportunity and, in any event:

- at least 90 days before the first of the dismissals take effect if there are to be 100 or more redundancies within a period of 90 days or less

- at least 30 days before the first of the dismissals take effect if there are to be 10-99 redundancies within a period of 30 days or less.

6.3   Breach of duty

If the employer fails to consult the trade union may complain to the Industrial Tribunal which may make a protective award to the redundant employees. A protective award is a sum of money calculated in accord with a statutory formula.

Apart from this statutory duty to consult with any recognised union an employer also ought to consult (or at least warn) a particular employee of impending redundancy. If he does not he may find himself successfully sued for unfair dismissal - see **Polkey v AE Dayton Services [1987]**.

7   REDUNDANCY: DUTY TO NOTIFY

7.1   The duty

Where the employer is proposing to dismiss as redundant ten or more employees he must notify the Secretary of State - Trade Union and Labour Relations (Consolidation) Act 1992. The notice must include such matters as

- numbers to be made redundant
- proposed date(s) of the dismissals
- identification of any trade union with which consultation is necessary

7.2   Timing

The employer must notify the Secretary of State:

- at least 90 days before the first of the dismissals take effect if there are to be 100 or more redundancies within a period of 90 days or less

- at least 30 days before the first of the dismissals take effect if there are to be 10-99 redundancies within a period of 30 days or less.

7.3   Breach of duty

Failure to consult is a criminal offence punishable by a fine in the Magistrates Court.

8   CHAPTER SUMMARY

A contract of employment can be terminated with or even without notice in certain circumstances. An employee can be dismissed with no notice but only if the employee has repudiated or is in fundamental breach of his obligations as an employee. An employee wrongfully dismissed can usually recover damages. If an employee is dismissed for some reason which is not set out in the Employment Protection (Consolidation) Act 1978 as a fair dismissal then the employee may have an action for unfair dismissal. The remedies for unfair dismissal are reinstatement or re-engagement or a financial award. Finally if a person can prove that he has been made redundant then he will have a claim for redundancy pay.

It is important to distinguish between the three claims (and particularly between wrongful dismissal and unfair dismissal). It is also important to realise that in an appropriate situation an employee might be able to bring all three claims against his employer. The last was the position of the employee in **Polkey v AE Dayton Services Ltd [1987]**.

9   SELF TEST QUESTIONS

9.1   What is summary dismissal? (1.2 and 2.2)

9.2   What is the remedy available to an employee wrongfully dismissed? (1.10 and 2.4)

9.3   What is constructive dismissal? (2.2)

9.4   How long must an employee have worked in order to qualify for unfair dismissal and redundancy? (3.3)

9.5   What are the five reasons set out in the Employment Protection (Consolidation) Act 1978 for fair dismissal? (4.3)

9.6   List the 5 'inadmissible reasons'. Why are they of importance? (4.5)

9.7   What is reinstatement? (4.7)

9.8   What is re-engagement? (4.7)

9.9   How is the basic award calculated? (4.9)

9.10   What is the definition of redundancy? (5.1)

9.11   What is the definition of lay-off? (5.5)

9.12   In the case of proposed redundancies with whom does the employer have a statutory duty to consult? (6.1)

9.13   In the case of proposed redundancies to whom does the employer have a statutory duty to give notice? (7.1)

10   EXAMINATION TYPE QUESTIONS

10.1   Industrial tribunal - unfair dismissal

If an industrial tribunal finds that an employee has been unfairly dismissed, what orders can it make, and under what circumstances will it make them?

(20 marks)

10.2   Statutory redundancy

(a)   How does an employee qualify for statutory redundancy pay?

(b)   What do you understand by the relevant date of dismissal in this connection?

(20 marks)

11   ANSWERS TO EXAMINATION TYPE QUESTIONS

11.1   Industrial tribunal - unfair dismissal

If an industrial tribunal finds an employee to have been unfairly dismissed it has power under Employment Protection (Consolidation) Act 1978 to make the following orders:

(a)   a reinstatement order;

(b)   a re-engagement order;

(c)   an order to an employer to pay a monetary award to his employee.

A reinstatement order is one which requires the employer to give the employee back his old job and treat him as if he had not been dismissed. A re-engagement order requires the employer or his successor or an associated employer to re-engage the employee either in a job which is comparable to the one from which he was dismissed or in other suitable employment.

Both an order for reinstatement and one for re-engagement require the consent of the employee. If the employee consents to an order being made, the tribunal will first consider the making of a reinstatement order. The tribunal must take two factors into account:

(a)   whether it is practicable for the employer to comply with the reinstatement order; and

(b)   whether it would be just to order the reinstatement of the employee in circumstances in which the employee has contributed to his dismissal.

The EPCA 1978 states that the engagement of a permanent replacement for the dismissed employee does not *per se* make it impracticable to take the employee back. Indeed, the tribunal may not take this fact into consideration unless the employer can prove either that it was not reasonably practicable for him to arrange for the dismissed employee's work to be done without engaging a permanent replacement, or that he engaged a replacement after the lapse of a reasonable period without having heard from the dismissed employee that he wished to be reinstated or re-engaged, and that when the employer engaged the replacement it was no longer reasonable for him to arrange for the dismissed employee's work to be done except by a permanent replacement.

When a tribunal makes a reinstatement order it must also specify the amount payable by the employer to the employee in respect of arrears of pay and the restoration of any rights and privileges, including seniority and pension rights, which must be restored to the employee.

A re-engagement order is more detailed than a reinstatement order and in addition to the matters referred to in the preceding paragraph it will contain details as to the nature of the employment, remuneration, etc.

If the tribunal does not order reinstatement or re-engagement it must order the employer to pay a monetary award to the employee. The monetary award normally consists of two parts. The basic award is calculated on the basis of the employee's age, length of service and final pay. The compensatory award is calculated to be a just and equitable amount, having regard to the loss suffered by the employee.

In special circumstances a higher award can be made. One circumstance occurs if the tribunal does order reinstatement or re-engagement and the employer fails to comply with the order. Others include dismissal for an inadmissible reason (such as pregnancy) and for reasons of race or sex. This additional award is calculated in accordance with a set statutory formula.

11.2   Statutory redundancy

(a)   In order to qualify for a redundancy payment, an employee must have been 'continuously employed' by his employer for a minimum of two years under a contract of employment (Employment Protection (Consolidation) Act 1978).

In addition to the requirement of continuous employment, in order to become entitled to a redundancy payment, an employee must have been dismissed, laid off or put on short time. According to the Employment Protection (Consolidation) Act 1978 (EPCA 1978), an employee is dismissed if his contract of employment is terminated, if his fixed-term contract is not renewed upon expiry or, where the employee has himself terminated the employment, if he has done so because of the employer's misconduct or breach of the terms of the contract. An employee may not claim a redundancy payment if he has voluntarily left the employment.   If the contract of employment has been frustrated there is no dismissal and, therefore, no redundancy entitlement.

An employee is laid off if his employer fails to provide work and this results in the employee not being entitled to remuneration.

Short-time working occurs where the amount of remuneration depends on the number of hours worked and because of a necessary reduction of hours, the remuneration is reduced to less than half of a week's pay.

It should be noted that in addition to the above rules regarding dismissal, lay off and short-time working, the Act provides that these situations must have occurred because of redundancy and not for some other extraneous reason. The Act provides that redundancy occurs where an employee is dismissed because the employer has ceased or intends to cease carrying on the business for the purposes of which the employee was employed by him; or business has ceased or is to cease in the place where the employee was so employed, or the work carried out by the employee has ceased to be necessary to the employer's business or has diminished or is expected to cease or diminish. The employee is presumed to have been dismissed for reasons of redundancy and the burden of proving otherwise falls upon the employer. It follows from this, that if any employee is in breach of his contract of employment so that an employer is entitled to dismiss the employee for misconduct, no entitlement to redundancy payment exists.

In addition to employees who are dismissed because of misconduct, certain other persons are excluded from any entitlement to redundancy payments. These are: firstly, those over the retiring age, secondly, certain employments which are excluded from any redundancy entitlement eg, those who ordinarily work abroad; thirdly, employees engaged on a fixed term contract of two years or more, who may contract out of the right to redundancy payment in respect of the non-renewal of the contract (this is an exception to the general rule which is that attempts to contract out of redundancy entitlements are void); and finally, if an employee has unreasonably refused an offer of new employment, he is deemed not to have been dismissed and is not, therefore, entitled to any redundancy payment.

(b)   The relevant date of dismissal is the expiry of the employee's notice period. This must not be less than the statutory minimum prescribed by the EPCA 1978. Such statutory length of notice is deemed to have been given in cases where no notice was given at all. Where a fixed-term contract expires in circumstances which constitute redundancy, the date of expiry is the relevant date.

16 EMPLOYMENT: HEALTH AND SAFETY

INTRODUCTION & LEARNING OBJECTIVES

Syllabus area 8d. Health and safety requirements and the consequences of breach. (Ability required 3).

This chapter concentrates on the legislative provisions which are intended to ensure that workplaces are safe and free from risks to health. It primarily deals with provisions of the criminal law but also reviews civil liability in tort and contract.

When you have studied this chapter you should be able to do the following:

- Outline the duties imposed by the Factories Act 1961.

- Outline the duties imposed by the Health and Safety at Work Act 1974.

- Recognise and distinguish between duties which are 'strict liability' and those which are 'so far as is reasonably practicable'.

- Understand the functions and powers of the Health and Safety Executive.

1   INTRODUCTION

1.1   Overview

The employer must ensure safe and healthy working conditions for his employees. There are several ways in which the employer may be made liable if he does not do so:

(a)   he may be in breach of his common law duty implied into the employment contract enabling the employee to make a civil claim for breach of contract;

(b)   he may be liable in tort for negligence or breach of statutory duty enabling the employee to make a civil claim in tort;

(c)   he may be guilty of criminal offence under a statutory provision or under the common law and be open to prosecution by the Health and Safety Executive.

These liabilities depend on both common law and statutory provisions.

It is important that you distinguish between civil liability and criminal liability and between the common law provisions and the statutory provisions.

1.2   Civil liability

If an employee has been injured at work he may have an action against his employer for damages

- in the law of contract for breach of the common law implied term to take reasonable care for the health and safety of his employees

- in the tort of negligence for breach of the common law duty of care or for breach of the Occupiers Liability Act 1957

- in tort for breach of statutory duty. The legislation relevant here are the two statutes (the Factories Act 1961 and the Office Shops and Railway Premises Act 1963) and delegated legislation (primarily regulations made under the provisions of the Health and Safety at Work Act 1974).

All these civil actions for damages will be brought in the County Court or High Court of Justice (Queens Bench Division) as appropriate.

Every employer is required to insure against liability to employees for personal injury arising in the course of employment - Employer's Liability (Compulsory Insurance) Act 1969.

Remember that under the EPCA 1978 an employee who has complained about safety at work and is consequently victimised or who is consequently dismissed may take action against his employer in the Industrial Tribunal.

1.3   Criminal liability

An employer (and sometimes others such as employees) may be prosecuted, and on conviction fined and/or imprisoned, for criminal offences created by

(a)   the common law eg, manslaughter

(b)   legislation. The legislative provisions creating criminal offences primarily comprise

- the Health and Safety at Work Act 1974
- the Factories Act 1961
- the Office, Shops and Railway Premises Act 1963
- regulations made under the Health and Safety at Work Act 1974

The statutory provisions creating criminal offences are now considered.

2   FACTORIES ACT 1961

The FA 1961 imposes a general duty on the occupier of a factory to ensure healthy and safe working conditions so far as is reasonably practicable. The general duty is supplemented by a number of specific provisions (eg, regarding cleanliness, temperature, ventilation, lighting, sanitary and washing facilities). The particular specific provision is the absolute duty to fence securely all dangerous machinery which was covered in detail in the chapter 'Tort: other torts'.

3   OFFICE SHOPS AND RAILWAY PREMISES ACT 1963

This Act makes provision for the safety, health and welfare of persons in all offices and shops and most railway buildings near the railway. Offices and shops which are only part of a building used for other purposes (eg, office in a school) are covered. The duties on the occupier are virtually the same as those under the FA 1961 (including the important strict liability provisions relating to the fencing of dangerous machinery.)

4   **HEALTH AND SAFETY AT WORK ACT 1974**

4.1   Introduction

When this Act was enacted it was envisaged that it would provide general statutory duties relating to all places of work and that regulations would be made under the Act imposing detailed and specific duties so far as would be relevant to different workplaces (for example quite different special rules on safety would be required on an oil rig as compared to an accountant's office) such that, once a comprehensive series of regulations was in place, other legislation such as the Factories Act 1961 could be repealed. Although numerous regulations have been made (and continue to be made) creating a vast and complex mass of law they are not yet comprehensive and thus the other statutes are still in force.

Although your examiner requires you to appreciate the existence of the regulations under the HSWA 1974 and the fact they create criminal offences and may be the basis of civil proceedings in tort for breach of statutory duty you are not required to know the detail of any of the regulations.

You are required, however, to have knowledge of the provisions of the Health and Safety at Work Act 1974 itself.

4.2   Health and safety provisions of the HSWA 1974

- **Employers' duties**

    (a)   The general duty to employees

    Every employer has a general duty to ensure the health, safety and welfare at work of all his employees so far as is reasonably practicable.

    This responsibility shall include, in particular:

    - The provision and maintenance of **plant and systems of work** that are, so far as is reasonably practicable, safe and without risk to health.

    - Arrangements for ensuring, so far as is reasonably practicable, safety and absence of risks to health in connection with the **use, handling, storage and transport of articles and substances.**

    - The provision of such **instruction, training and supervision** as is necessary to ensure, so far as is reasonably practicable, the health and safety at work of their employees.

    - So far as is reasonably practicable as regards any **place of work** under the employer's control, the maintenance of it in a condition that is safe and without risks to health and the provision and maintenance of means of **access to** and **exit** from it that are safe and without such risks.

    - The provision and maintenance of **working environment** for his employees that is, so far as is reasonably practicable, safe without risks to health, and adequate as regards facilities and arrangements for their welfare at work.

    Note that the duty is to make particular provision **'so far as is reasonably practicable'**. In **West Bromwich Building Society v Townsend** the court took into account the degree of risk against the sacrifice involved. If the sacrifice was disproportionately heavy then it was not reasonably practicable.

(b)   Written statement of policy

Unless otherwise prescribed, an **employer** must prepare a **written statement** of **his general policy on health and safety** at work for his employees and the **organisation and arrangements** that are in force for carrying out that policy and bring it to the **notice** of his employees. The statement may be revised from time to time as appropriate.

(c)   Consultation

It is the duty of the employer to consult representatives of the employees with a view to the making and maintenance of arrangements which will enable him and his employees to cooperate effectively in promoting and developing the health and safety at work of the employees and in making sure the measures are effective.

Under the Safety Representatives and Safety Committee Regulations 1977 a recognised trade union may appoint safety representatives to represent the employees in discussions with management, investigate potential hazards, accidents and complaints and the workplace generally. (Note these representatives are allowed time off with pay to carry out their duties). An employer must appoint a safety committee where safety representatives have been appointed and request such a committee. The committee, composed of employers representatives, safety representatives and trade union representatives, then monitors and safety etc of the workplace.

(d)   Duty to persons other than employees

The employer (and anyone who is self-employed) has a duty to conduct his undertaking in such a way as to ensure, so far as is reasonably practicable, that persons not in his employment are not exposed to risks to their health or safety.

- **Duties on persons controlling business premises**

(a)   Any such person (including employers) must take such measures, so far as is reasonably practicable, to ensure that all means of access thereto or egress therefrom and any plant or substance in the premises is safe and without risks to health.

(b)   Any such person must use the best practicable means for preventing pollution.

- **Duties on manufacturers etc**

Any person who designs, manufactures, imports or supplies any articles for use at work must ensure, so far as is reasonably practicable, that it will be safe and without risks to health.

- **Employees' duties**

Every employee must:

(a)   take reasonable care for the health and safety of himself and of other persons who may be affected by his acts or omissions at work; and

    (b)   as regards any duty or requirement imposed on his employer or any other person or under any of the relevant statutory provisions, cooperate with him so far as is necessary to enable that duty or requirement to be performed or complied with.

- **Duty on every person**

  No person shall intentionally or recklessly interfere with or misuse anything provided in the interests of health or safety.

    | Conclusion | the HSWA 1974 imposes health and safety duties of a general nature on everyone concerned with the workplace. The duty is, in most situations, 'so far as is reasonably practicable'. These general duties are supplemented by Regulations imposing specific and detailed steps.

4.3   Enforcement of health and safety legislation

The HSWA 1974 contains detailed provisions for enforcing, by use of criminal proceedings, *all* of the duties imposed by *all* health and safety legislation.

The Health and Safety Commission has the general duty of monitoring health and safety at work and of proposing new legislation on specific measures to the Secretary of State who will then make the appropriate regulations by Statutory Instrument.

The Health and Safety Commission also has an executive arm, called the Health and Safety Executive which monitors the health and safety of particular workplaces. HSE Inspectors have wide investigative powers. Thus, they have power to enter premises and make examinations and investigations, take pictures or samples, and require people to give information. Where appropriate they serve notices on the employer to ensure that they carry out their duties under the legislation. The two types of notice are:

- **Improvement notice.** An inspector may serve such a notice calling for the remedying of contraventions within a specified period. During the period specified in such a notice, work may be carried on, but if at the end of a specified period of time the remedial work has not been done, the inspector may prosecute or serve a prohibition notice.

- **Prohibition notice.** An inspector may serve notice which will prevent any activities at all being carried on, should an employer contravene the relevant statutory provisions and involve the risk of serious personal injury.

HSE Inspectors also have the duty of instituting criminal proceedings against any person who fails to discharge his legislative duties (including failure to comply with an improvement or prohibition notice.) Some offences are summary only whereas others are triable either way. The sanctions include fines and imprisonment and, in the case of directors and managers of companies, disqualification. HSE Inspectors may also prosecute common law offences such as manslaughter (which is triable on indictment only).

4.4   Activity

X, an employee, deliberately removes a guard from a dangerous machine which he is operating. Has he committed a criminal offence, and if so, who will bring the prosecution?

4.5   Activity solution

He commits a criminal offence under the HSWA 1974: 'No person shall intentionally or recklessly interfere with anything provided in the interests of safety.'

The prosecuting authority will be the HSE.

5   **SELF-TEST QUESTIONS**

5.1   List the three possible civil actions which an employee who is injured at work may have against his employer. (1.2)

5.2   What is the **extent** of the employer's duty to fence dangerous machinery under the Factories Act 1961 and Office, Shops and Railway Premises Act 1963? (2)

5.3   List the general duties of employers under the Health and Safety at Work Act 1974. (4.2)

5.4   What is an improvement notice? (4.3)

5.5   Who prosecutes for breach of health and safety legislation? (4.3)

6   **EXAMINATION TYPE QUESTION**

6.1   **Furniture factory**

Charles intends to open a small factory to make furniture. He has leased a small building in which he will install woodworking machinery.

You are required:

(a)   to explain the statutory requirements regarding safety with which he must comply;

(8 marks)

(b)   to explain the means by which these requirements are enforced;

(6 marks)

(c)   to explain Charles' liability if he fails to conform to them.

(6 marks)

(Total: 20 marks)

7   **ANSWER TO EXAMINATION TYPE QUESTION**

7.1   **Furniture factory**

(a)   In running a small factory in which woodworking machinery is to be used, Charles will have to comply with the provisions of the Factories Act 1961 and the Health and Safety at Work Act 1974.

The Factories Act 1961 only applies to a 'factory' which is defined as being any premises in which, or within the precincts of which, persons are employed in manual labour in any process for, or incidental to *(inter alia)* the making of any article or part of an article, being premises in which, or within the precincts of which, the work is carried on by way of trade or for purposes of gain and to or over which the employer of the persons employed therein has the right of access or control. Making furniture would clearly fall within the Act and the small building would undoubtedly be 'premises' covered by S175 of the Act. The Act contains general provisions dealing with health, safety and welfare in factories as well as specific provisions dealing with working conditions, accidents, diseases and the employment of young persons. Failure to comply with the Act is a breach of statutory duty and may lead to criminal prosecution. In practice the conditions in S14 relating to machinery are very important and obviously of relevance to Charles who is to use woodworking machinery. Every dangerous part of machinery must be securely fenced. A part is 'dangerous' if it is foreseeable that injury may occur to anybody acting in a way in which a human being may reasonably be expected to act in circumstances which may reasonably be expected to occur. The obligation to fence machinery is unqualified. Thus, it is not a defence that to fence dangerous parts of machinery would render it unusable. However, the Secretary of State is given power to modify or extend the duty to fence by regulations, and regulations are currently in force in respect of woodworking machines.

The Health and Safety at Work Act 1974 contains a number of general duties imposed on employers. It is the duty of every employer to ensure, so far as is reasonably practicable, the health, safety and welfare of all his employees. In particular, this involves providing and maintaining, so far as it is reasonably practicable, safe plant premises and systems of work; ensuring that 'articles and substances' are, so far as is reasonably practicable, safe and free from health risks; providing such information, training, instruction and supervisions as is necessary to ensure the safety and health of employees and ensuring that the environment is, as far as is reasonably practicable, free from risks to health, etc. Charles must provide his employees with a written statement of his health and safety policy and the organisation and arrangements for carrying it out.

(b)   The ultimate political responsibility for the enforcement of statutory requirements lies with the Minister, but the administration and enforcement of the provisions as they actually operate in the workplace is by the Health and Safety Executive and in some cases by the local authority. Inspectors of the Health and Safety Executive have wide powers under the Health and Safety at Work Act 1974. They may at any reasonable time enter premises to carry out an inspection and may prosecute for breach of any provision of the safety legislation and for failure to comply with any enforcement notice. If an inspector is of the opinion that a statutory provision is being contravened, he may serve on that person an 'improvement notice' providing details of the contravention and requiring that it be remedied within a specified period. If particular activities appear to involve serious risk of personal injury, the inspector may serve a 'prohibition notice' detailing the risk and directing that activities should not be carried on until the risks have been remedied.

(c)   Breach of statutory provision relating to safety at work may well entail liability to criminal prosecution. If such a breach causes injury to an employee who falls within the ambit of the statutory protection, the employee may have an action in tort for breach of statutory duty. It is specifically provided, however, that the general duties imposed by the Health and Safety at Work Act 1974 do not confer such a right of action although breaches of regulations made under the Act normally do. In contrast, it is well established that an action for breach of statutory duty will arise where an employee is injured as a result of certain provisions of the Factories Act 1961. In addition, it may be possible to bring a common law action against the employer in the tort of negligence. It should be noted, however, that some of the provisions of the Factories Act impose strict liability, in which case Charles would be liable without any proof of negligence.

If a prosecution is brought, it is normally in the Magistrates' Court where the penalty for conviction will be a fine; but in extreme cases imprisonment is possible. The fine may be of a fixed amount to take immediate effect or the decision may be postponed to allow the defaulter to remedy the situation within a stated time.

17 COMPANY FORMATION: INCORPORATION

INTRODUCTION & LEARNING OBJECTIVES

Syllabus area 8e. Company formation. (Ability required 2.)
Types of company formed under the Companies Act. (Ability required 2.)
Corporate personality 'lifting the veil of incorporation'. (Ability required 2.)
Company registration. (Ability required 2.)

This chapter introduces you to the different types of company which can be formed under the Companies Acts and to the concept of corporate personality. The latter is encapsulated in the phrase 'veil of incorporation' and much of the chapter concerns situations where by statute or by case the veil is lifted. The chapter then moves on to how a company is formed and how once having been formed a company can change from one type to another.

Finally, the chapter introduces you to the basics of insolvency and the concept of corporate governance - two matters which run throughout the whole of company law.

When you have studied this chapter you should be able to do the following:

- Identify the different types of company.

- Understand the doctrine of incorporation as established by **Salomon v Salomon**.

- Identify the main differences between a company and a partnership.

- Understand and give examples of lifting the veil of incorporation.

- Set out the steps for registering and re-registering a company together with the duties of promoters.

- Differentiate between receivership, liquidation and administration.

- Know in detail the statutory order of payment of an insolvent company's debts.

---

1 TYPES OF COMPANY FORMED UNDER THE COMPANIES ACTS

1.1 Methods of classification

S1 Companies Act 1985 (CA85) allows a company to be registered with or without limited liability.

S1 CA85 allows a limited company to be public or private. An unlimited company must be private.

1.2 Limited liability companies

Although the phrase 'limited liability company' is used it is the liability of the members which is limited. There are two forms of limiting liability - by shares and by guarantee.

(a) **Companies limited by shares**

In the case of a company limited by shares the liability of a member to contribute to the company's assets is limited to the amount, if any, unpaid on the nominal value of his shares.

Once the shares are fully paid there is, in general, no further liability; ie, if the company becomes insolvent the members are not required in this case to make any further contribution to discharge its debts. Companies of this type are the normal model used for business operations where there is a real risk of commercial loss. Limited liability is particularly useful where the shareholders leave the management of the company in the hands of its directors and have no immediate control over its financial situation and day to day transactions.

(b)   **Companies limited by guarantee**

In the case of a company limited by guarantee, the liability of members is limited to such amount as they undertake to contribute to the assets in the event of its being wound up. That amount is specified in the memorandum of association which is part of a company's constitution. If the company is wound up, each person who is a member at that time or has been a member within the preceding year may be required to contribute up to the amount of his guarantee towards payment of debts incurred while he was a member. Past members are liable only if present members default.

Many such companies are formed for non-profit making purposes and where the ability to raise capital is not important. Examples are most of the supervisory and regulatory bodies in the investment industry eg SIB. Such associations reckon to recover the cost of their services by charges or levies on those who use them. However, as companies limited by guarantee, they have the general advantages of corporate status and the members' guarantees are a form of reserve fund to be called on in case of crisis.

There are specific rules in the CA85 concerning the matters to be included in the memorandum and articles of association of a company limited by guarantee. In particular a guarantee company must register its own articles of association (unlike a company limited by shares which may adopt a model set of articles called Table A). A guarantee company must be private unless it also has a share capital; it may, but usually does not, have a share capital. No new company may now be formed or become a company limited by guarantee with a share capital: S1 CA85. If it does have a share capital, members are liable to the extent of the amounts (if any) unpaid on their shares as well as to the extent of their guarantees.

In addition in certain circumstances a company limited by guarantee may dispense with the word 'Limited' at the end of its name.

1.3   Unlimited companies

In the case of an unlimited company, there is no limit on the liability of members to contribute to the assets on a winding up. Past members who ceased to be members within the previous year may be liable in respect of debts incurred before they ceased to be members. However, there is no such liability of members until the company is wound up.

Special features of unlimited companies are:

(a)   they are not required to file their accounts at the Companies Registry for the information of the public;

(b)   they are free to purchase their own shares; and

(c)   they must have special articles of association.

However, rule (a) does not apply to an unlimited company which is controlled by one or more limited companies or which has a limited company as subsidiary.

1.4   Public companies and private companies

Until the passing of the Companies Act 1907, all companies were public companies and subject to rules appropriate to the issue of their shares to the public. This system was inconvenient to owners of small businesses who wished to secure the advantages of incorporation without having to comply with elaborate rules designed for a very different type of enterprise.

At the same time as the distinction between public and private companies was introduced the law of partnership was amended to allow some partners (but not all) to enjoy the protection of limited liability - the Limited Partnerships Act 1907. However, the introduction of the private company proved a more satisfactory expedient for the family business as all members could limit their liability. Private companies are now very much more numerous than public companies though the financial resources of the latter are larger.

The CA85 defines a public company as a company limited by shares or limited by guarantee and having a share capital, being a company:

(a)   the memorandum of which states that the company is to be a public company; and

(b)   in relation to which the provisions of the Companies Act as to the registration or re-registration of a company as a public company have been complied with – in particular the requirements relating to a minimum share capital.

A private company is any company which is not a public company.

The major differences between private (limited) companies and public companies are:

(a)   **Minimum number of members**

A public company is required to have two members - S24 CA85. A private company may have a single member - Companies (Single Member Private Limited Companies Regulations 1992.

(b)   **Minimum capital requirements**

A public company must have a minimum authorised capital of £50,000 and, in order to trade, must have allotted shares of at least that amount. There are no minimum (or maximum) requirements for a private company.

(c)   **Public subscription**

A public company may raise capital by advertising its securities (shares and debentures) as available for public subscription. It is illegal for a private company to advertise its securities to the public - Financial Services Act 1986. Because of this legal prohibition it follows that securities of a private company cannot be dealt with on the Stock Exchange (either by way of a full listing or on the Unlisted Securities Market): thus only securities of public companies are a medium for investment by the general public. Private companies are often therefore relatively small and controlled by family members. It is this difference between public and private companies (namely the ability of the public company to raise large capital sums from the public) which is the most important factor when choosing between the different types of company.

(d)   **Companies Act**

Some provisions of the Companies Act do not apply to private companies (particularly those concerning payment for shares) whilst many other provisions are relaxed, at least to some extent. The process of 'de-regulation' of private companies began in 1989 by allowing private companies to dispense, inter alia, with the holding of annual general meetings and it is likely that the future will see much of the 'red-tape' surrounding the administration of companies being lessened as regards private companies.

There are many other differences between public and private companies (dealt with throughout the text) but they are minor in the sense that they would not be a deciding factor when choosing which of the public or private company is appropriate to a given situation.

1.5   Other classifications

(a)   **Single Member Private Limited Companies**

As a general rule every company must have a minimum of two members - S24 CA85. In 1992, in response to a European Community directive, a statutory instrument called the Companies (Single Member Private Limited Companies) Regulations 1992 was made allowing a private limited company (whether newly incorporated as such or pre-existing) to have one member only. Thus if the membership of a private limited company falls to one, that member does not incur personal liability for the company's debts.

The CSMPLCR 1992 makes the following consequential amendments to existing law in relation to such single member companies:

(i)   Only one subscriber to the memorandum is needed.

(ii)   Where the membership of a company falls to one the fact, date and person's name and address must be entered on the Register of Members. A corresponding statement must be made where the membership of a single member company increases.

(iii)   The quorum at meetings is one member present personally or by proxy.

(iv)   Where the sole member takes a decision instead of holding a general meeting with himself he must (unless he uses the written resolution procedure) provide the company with a written record of that decision. Failure results in a fine but does not affect the validity of the decision.

(v)   S122(e) Insolvency Act 1986 (IA86) (which allows a company to be compulsorily wound up where the number of members is reduced below 2) does not apply.

(vi)   Where the sole member is also the sole director and he makes a contract with the company, the company must, unless the contract is in writing, ensure the terms are set out in a written memorandum or are recorded in the minutes of the first board meeting held after the making of the contract. Failure results in a fine but does not affect the validity of the contract.

(b)   **Small and medium-sized companies**

Ss246 - 249 CA85 provide, in line with the EC Fourth Directive, for exemptions from the full accounting disclosure for small and medium-sized companies. For the purposes of these accounting exemption provisions in respect of any financial year of the company and the financial year immediately preceding that year a company shall be classified as a small company if it satisfies any two or more of the qualifying conditions. These are:

•   The amount of its turnover must not exceed £2.8m.

- Its balance sheet total must not exceed £1.4m.

- The average number of persons employed by the company in the financial year in question (determined on a weekly basis) must not exceed fifty.

It is a medium-sized company if it satisfies any two or more of the qualifying conditions:

- The amount of its turnover must not exceed £11m.

- Its balance sheet total must not exceed £5.6m.

- The average number of persons employed by the company in the financial year in question (determined on a weekly basis) must not exceed 250.

However, companies so qualifying may not take advantage of the permitted exceptions if they are public companies, banking or insurance companies or an authorised person under FSA 1986 or members of a group including a company of one of these kinds.

(c)   **Welsh companies**

A company is Welsh if its registered office is stated in its memorandum to be in Wales. If it is a private company it may use the word **cyfyngedig (cyf)** instead of limited (Ltd) in its name, and if a public company, the words **cwmni cyfyngedig cyhoeddus (ccc)** instead of public limited company (plc).

(d)   **Overseas companies**

A company incorporated outside Great Britain which establishes a place of business in Great Britain is called an overseas company. S744 CA85 provides that place of business in this context includes a share transfer or share registration office; but it has been held that a company which only employs agents within Great Britain and has no office, has not established a place of business.

Such companies are, at least to some degree, regulated by UK company law. They must, for example, file accounts with the Registrar of Companies and must maintain an address within the jurisdiction where official communications (eg, writs) can be sent.

1.6   **Conclusion**   Companies registerable nowadays can be classified as follows:

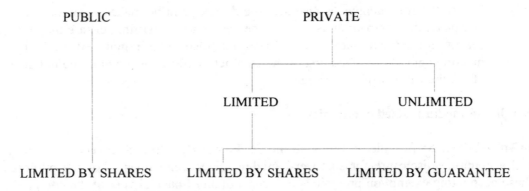

2   **CORPORATE PERSONALITY**

2.1   **Salomon v Salomon**

A company is a legal person ie, it is an entity in its own right - this is the doctrine of incorporation. Recognition that a company has legal personality independent of its members was established last century by the House of Lords in **Salomon v Salomon**.

Salomon v Salomon & Co Ltd [1897]

Facts: Mr Salomon had, for thirty years, carried on a successful business as a sole trader in the manufacture of boots and shoes. In 1892 he formed a company; in those days the minimum number of shareholders was seven and he had one share issued to himself, his wife and five of his children; his wife and children held their shares as his nominees. He then transferred his business to the company at a value of over £39,000. This price was very much in excess of the true value but as Salomon owned the company no one was thereby defrauded. He took the price partly in 20,000 £1 shares, partly in cash withdrawn from the business in the course of transfer, and partly in a £10,000 debenture issued by the company and secured by a floating charge on its assets. The nature of a floating charge will be explained later in this text; the effect was that whoever held the debenture had a claim to the assets (to the extent of £10,000) in priority to the claims of any other creditor of the company. So Salomon became a secured creditor of his own **one man company**.

The business of the company did not prosper. Salomon pledged his debenture to one Broderip who lent him £5,000 in cash, which Salomon in turn paid over to the company. Eventually the company became insolvent; if the debenture were repaid in full there would be nothing left for the other creditors.

In the confused lawsuit which followed, the main body of unsecured creditors advanced two main arguments:

(a)   the sale transaction was a sham and so Salomon was still the owner of the business and liable for its debts; and

(b)   the company was irregularly formed because six of the seven shareholders were mere nominees of Salomon.

Argument (a) prevailed in the High Court but was rejected by the Court of Appeal which upheld argument (b). The House of Lords turned down argument (b) also and held that Salomon and his company were two separate persons.

Held: it was held that:

(a)   the business was owned by and its debts were liabilities of the company, not of Salomon personally; and

(b)   although Salomon owned beneficially all the issued shares of the company he (and Broderip as his successor) could also be a secured creditor with enforceable rights against the company in that capacity.

A rather more extreme example of the effect of the doctrine of incorporation arose in **Lee v Lee's Air Farming**.

Lee v Lee's Air Farming Ltd [1960]

Facts: This case concerned an aerial crop-spraying business, in which Mr Lee, who owned the majority of the shares (all but one) and was the sole working director of the company, was killed while piloting the aircraft.

Held: that although he was the majority shareholder and sole working director of the company, he and the company were separate legal persons and therefore he could also be an employee of it with rights against it when killed in an accident in the course of his employment.

2.2   The veil of incorporation

The legal consequence of the doctrine of incorporation, namely that a company is a separate legal entity from its members, is expressed by saying that there is a veil of incorporation drawn down between the company and its members.

This legal separation and the concept of a company as an artificial entity means:

(a)   **Perpetual succession**

A company is not dependent for its legal existence on the existence of members or directors (although there are obvious practical problems with no humans to do the work): thus changes in membership (whether through death or otherwise) do not affect the legal existence of the company.

(b)   **Ownership of property**

The company itself owns its own property, not the members or directors.

Macaura v Northern Life Assurance [1925]

Facts: M owned a forest. He formed a company in which he beneficially owned all the shares and sold his forest to it. He, however, continued to maintain an insurance policy on the forest in his own name. The forest was destroyed by fire. Could M claim on the policy?

Held: he could not since the property, damaged belonged to the company, not him, and as shareholder he had no insurable interest in the forest.

This consequence of the doctrine of incorporation, that the property of the company belongs to the company and not the shareholders (nor directors) means that it is perfectly possible for members (and directors) to be convicted of theft from the company - and this can cause problems in the small 'one-man' type company where he may well be treating the company's assets as his own, which, in law, they are not.

(c)   **Limitation of liability**

Since a company is itself legally the party to contracts it makes, it and it alone can be sued for breach of contract. It follows that members are not liable to creditors for the company's debts. Further a member is able to contract with the company (the contract is contained in the Memorandum and Articles) to limit his liability to contribute to the company's debts.

(d)   **Separation of ownership and management**

Because the company, as a commercial enterprise, is distinct from its members as proprietors it must have its own **management** in the form of a board of directors.

(e)   **The company can sue and be sued in its own name**

The company as a legal person will sue if a wrong is done to it. Individual shareholders cannot generally sue in such circumstances and the decision as to whether the company will sue or not rests with the members collectively in general meeting or with the board of directors. The rule that only the company can sue is known as the rule in **Foss v Harbottle** but there are some exceptions to the rule. These exceptions are part of what is known as 'minority protection' and are discussed in detail in a later chapter.

3   **LIFTING THE VEIL OF INCORPORATION**

3.1   **Introduction**

The principle that a company is a person separate from its members and also from the directors and others who manage it can produce unsatisfactory results in particular circumstances. Company law, therefore, recognises a number of exceptions to the principle. In those exceptional contexts the company is treated as in some degree identified with its members or managers as if there were no distinction between them. Those exceptions are described as **lifting the veil of incorporation**.

Although there is no one consistent principle running through these various exceptions those provided by statute tend to penalise breaches of the legislation and those provided by case law tend to be a situation where 'special circumstances exist indicating that it (the corporate veil) is a mere facade concealing the true facts' per Lord Keith in **Woolfson v Strathclyde Regional Council [1978]**.

Where the veil is lifted, the usual result is either that some other person is made to share liability for the company's debts or the assets, liabilities, profits and losses of the company are attributed to its shareholders.

3.2   **Statutory examples**

(a)   **Minimum number of members: S24 CA85**

If the number of members of a company (other than a private limited company) falls below two and this situation continues for six months, the remaining member, if he is aware of the situation, is liable (jointly and severally with the company) for the company's debts contracted after the six months.

Note: private limited companies may have a single member - CSMPLCR 1992.

(b)   **Company name: S349 CA85**

If any officer (eg, a director or secretary) issues or signs, on behalf of the company, a bill of exchange or order for goods on which **the company's name is incorrectly stated** or is omitted he is liable if the company itself defaults. The principle can be seen in the case of

Penrose v Martyr [1858]

Facts: a company secretary 'accepted' a bill of exchange drawn on the company on which its name was incorrectly written by omitting the word 'limited' from the name. The company defaulted.

Held: the secretary was personally liable on the bill.

(c)   **Trading certificate: S117 CA85**

Where a public company trades or exercises borrowing powers before it has been issued with a 'trading certificate' the directors are jointly and severally liable to indemnify the other party in respect of any loss suffered by him as a result of the failure to comply with S117 CA85.

(d)   **Group accounts: S227-9 CA85**

If a group exists, a parent company must prepare group accounts consolidating the balance sheets and profit and loss accounts of it and its subsidiary undertakings.

Thus the veil is lifted between the individual entities within the group so that investors (and others) can judge the financial position of the group as a whole. Group accounts are considered further in the later chapter 'Company formation: publicity'.

(e)   **Fraudulent trading (S213 IA86) and wrongful trading (S214 IA86)**

Under S213 IA86 if the court finds that the business of a company has been carried on with intent to **defraud** it may declare any persons (eg, directors) who were **knowingly parties** to the fraud liable for all or any debts and other liabilities of the company. Under S214 IA86 if in the winding up of an insolvent company a past or present director (or shadow director) knew or ought to have known, before the commencement of the winding up, that there was no reasonable prospect that the company could avoid insolvent liquidation, and failed to take every step to minimise the loss to the company's creditors, then the court may declare on the application of the liquidator that the person is liable to make such contribution as the court thinks fit.

3.3   Case law examples

(a)   **Nationality**

In times of war it is illegal to trade with the enemy. It may be possible to lift the veil of incorporation so as to impute to a company the same nationality as its members.

Daimler v Continental Tyre & Rubber Co [1916]

Facts: the defendant, a UK incorporated company, was owned by five individuals and a company incorporated in Germany. Only one individual was British and he held one share

Held: the plaintiffs need not discharge the debt to the defendants since effective control of the latter was in enemy hands and hence to do so would be to trade with the enemy.

(b)   **Company liability – crime and tort**

Many crimes require that the accused party not only commits the act which constitutes the offence *(actus reus)* but also has the necessary mental element of guilty intention or knowledge *(mens rea)*. A company being an artificial legal person cannot have, as such, intention or knowledge and only acts through its servants or agents, particularly its directors. For the purpose of imposing criminal liability the state of mind and acts of the company's servants and agents may be imputed to the company. However, not all of the company's servants or agents will have their state of mind and acts so imputed. In **Tesco Supermarkets v Nattrass [1971]** Lord Reid said:

'It must be a question of law whether, after the facts have been ascertained, a person in doing particular things is to be regarded as the company or merely as the company's servant or agent.'

If it can be decided that the particular person or persons in question are 'an embodiment of the company' can it be said that their mind is the mind of the company thus making the company liable for a crime involving *mens rea*. The contrasting cases of **R v ICR Haulage Ltd [1944]** and **John Henshall (Quarries) Ltd v Harvey [1965]** illustrate this point.

R v ICR Haulage Ltd [1944]

Facts: a haulage contracting company was charged with ten others (one of whom was its managing director) with conspiracy to defraud, in that they agreed to charge another company with more goods than were actually delivered to it.

Held: the appellant company could be charged with the offence because the fraud of the managing director was the fraud of the company.

John Henshall (Quarries) Ltd v Harvey [1965]

Facts: H an independent contractor, was casually engaged for haulage by the company. His lorry was incorrectly weighed at the company's weigh-bridge by B the company's employee. H was charged with driving a lorry contrary to regulations and the company was charged with aiding and abetting this offence.

Held: the company should not be convicted. To support the conviction the company must have been shown to have known the facts out of which the offence arose and although B was a servant he was not a responsible officer and his mind was not the mind of the company.

A sole director cannot be convicted on a charge of conspiracy with his company as the court have held there are not two minds concerned: **R v McDonnell [1966].**

Certain crimes do not require a mental element at all. These crimes are known as crimes of strict liability and for most purposes the state of mind of the company's servants and agents is irrelevant. It may be relevant where the statute creating a crime involving strict liability provides for a defence of 'due diligence' by the accused ie, the person accused took all reasonable precautions and exercised all due diligence to avoid commission of such an offence by himself or any person under his control. A company may be able to argue that failure to exercise due diligence on its part would only occur where the failure was that of a director or senior manager who could be identified with the controlling mind or will of the company and not by a failure of a junior employee.

A company like any other employer is vicariously liable for the torts of its employees committed in the course of their employment. In general, liability in tort does not depend on any mental element being present.

(c)   **Mere facade (sham or puppet companies)**

The House of Lords in **Woolfson v Strathclyde [1978]** stated that it is appropriate for the courts to lift the veil of incorporation only where special circumstances exist indicating that it is a mere facade concealing the true facts. This judgement encapsulates the present reluctance of judges to lift the corporate veil: there had been a prior tendency to lift the veil very readily - a tendency culminating in the much criticised case, **DHN Food Distributors v London Borough of Tower Hamlets [1976]** .

Two cases, approved by **Woolfson**, are now given as examples of this 'mere facade' principle.

Gilford Motor Co v Horne [1933]

Facts: a restraint of trade clause was binding on a former employee. He set up a company in an attempt to circumvent its provisions. He claimed that the company could not be bound by the restraint clause because it was a separate legal person from himself and not a party to the contract between himself and his former employer.

Held: the company was a sham and an injunction was granted against the former employee and the company.

Jones v Lipman [1962]

Facts: L agreed to sell some land to J. L then changed his mind and, in order to evade specific performance of the contract, sold the land to a company of which he was the controlling member.

Held: the company was a sham and specific performance extended not only to L but also to the company.

3.4   Groups

A source of particular controversy over the years has been in relation to groups where each company, according to the doctrine of incorporation, is a separate entity ie, there is a veil of incorporation between a holding company and its subsidiary. Similarly there is a veil between co-subsidiaries.

There have, however, been a number of cases where the courts have been asked to lift the veil (or veils) of incorporation between a holding company and its various subsidiaries with two main aims:

(a)   to benefit the group by obtaining higher compensation payment on compulsory purchase of premises. Broadly, different rates are payable (in ascending order) to owners, occupiers and owner-occupiers. 'Occupiers' claim disturbance value to the business;

(b)   to benefit creditors of an insolvent company by making other companies within the group liable for its debts.

There are two main legal arguments on the basis of which the veil might be lifted: agency and the doctrine of economic reality. The latter has been much criticised by very recent cases.

Agency. The argument here is that the subsidiary is acting merely as an agent of its principal, the holding company.

Smith, Stone & Knight Ltd v Birmingham Corporation [1939]

Facts: SSK a paper manufacturer had a wholly controlled subsidiary, BW, which carried on a waste-paper dealing business operating from premises owned by SSK. On compulsory purchase of the premises the court was asked to lift the veil between SSK and BW to enable BW to claim compensation as owner-occupier.

Held: the veil would be lifted on the basis that BW was running the waste-paper business as agent for SSK. The main fact which led the court to this conclusion was that SSK controlled the business on a day-to-day basis through its nominees (who were also directors of SSK) on BW's board.

Doctrine of economic reality. The argument here is that the group, albeit each company is autonomous within its own sphere of business, nevertheless forms a single economic unit and the law ought to follow the economic reality.

DHN Food Distributors v London Borough of Tower Hamlets [1976]

Facts: DHN carried on business as grocers from premises owned by a subsidiary of DHN. The subsidiary itself had no business activities. Both companies had the same directors. The local authority acquired the premises compulsorily but refused to pay compensation for disturbance of the business since the subsidiary, which owned the premises, did not also carry on the business.

Held: each company was, in economic terms, mutually interdependent on each other and therefore they should be regarded as a single economic entity. Thus there was a valid claim for disturbance since ownership of the premises and business activity were in the hands of a single group.

In **Woolfson v Strathclyde [1978]** the House of Lords doubted the correctness of the **DHN** reasoning and refused to lift the veil on very similar facts stating that 'it is appropriate to pierce the corporate veil only where special circumstances exist indicating that it is a mere facade concealing the true facts'.

In 1990 the Court of Appeal in **Adams v Cape Industries** endorsed the **Woolfson** case's reluctance to lift the veil by stating 'the court is not free to disregard the principle of **Salomon v Salomon** merely because it considers that justice so requires . . .'.

Adams v Cape Industries [1990]

Facts: Cape was an English registered company involved in mining asbestos in South Africa and marketing it worldwide through various subsidiaries. One of its marketing subsidiaries CPC, a company incorporated and carrying on business in the United States, had a court judgement against it.

Held: it was unsuccessfully argued that the veil should be lifted between the companies so as to enable the judgement to be enforced against Cape. The Court of Appeal said there were no special circumstances indicating that CPC was a mere facade for Cape such as was the situation in **Jones v Lipman**. There was no agency as CPC was an independent corporation under the control of its chief executive, and the **DHN** doctrine of economic reality would not be extended beyond its own facts to facts such as these where the effect would be to make a holding company liable for its subsidiary's debts.

| Conclusion | Except where statute specifically provides, the courts' changed attitude to lifting the veil might best be summarised by comparing Lord Denning's statement in 1969 'The doctrine laid down in **Salomon v Salomon** has to be watched very carefully' with the riposte of Richmond P in 1978 'for myself, and with all respect, I would approach the question the other way round, that is to say that any suggested departure from the doctrine laid down in **Salomon v Salomon** should be watched very carefully'. |

3.5   Activity

For what reasons would the companies below have their veils of incorporation lifted?

(a)   Jim Brown, the company secretary of Lamplight Ltd orders some bulbs and signs the order form 'for and on behalf of Lighting plc'. The company later defaults on the order.

(b)   Sally is an accountant with Merger and Merger. Her contract of employment contains a restrictive covenant stating that when she leaves the firm she cannot induce her clients to move with her. Sally sets up Sal's Accounting Ltd and takes some of the clients, claiming that it is not she but her company that is dealing with the former clients.

(c)   Louise and Phil are the only two members of Harry plc. Phil sells all of his shares to Louise. Eight months later Harry plc enters into a contract with Exe Ltd.

3.6   **Activity Solution**

(a)   An officer has wrongly signed an order for goods S349 CA85 as illustrated by the case of **Penrose v Martyr**.

(b)   Sal's Accounting Ltd will be regarded as a 'bubble' or 'puppet' company as in **Gilford Motor Co v Horne**.

(c)   S24 CA85: the membership of the company has fallen to less than the statutory minimum of 2 for more than 6 months.

4   **COMPANIES AND PARTNERSHIPS COMPARED**

4.1   **Structure**

The essential distinction between a company and a partnership is that a company is a person separate from its members whereas a partnership is merely two or more persons in a particular form of relationship with each other; the partnership firm is a group of partners but not a separate legal entity.

4.2   **Detail**

Advantages and disadvantages of using a company or a partnership to carry on a business will often derive from special factors such as **taxation** and **limited liability**. Other points of comparison to be considered are:

	Company	**Partnership**
(a)	A company must have a **written constitution** ie, memorandum and articles of association.	There need not be a written partnership agreement though it is usual.
(b)	A company is a separate legal person so may (i) own property; (ii) contract in its own name; (iii) sue/be sued in its own name.	A partnership is not a separate person - the partners personally: (i) own property; (ii) are liable on contracts; (iii) are liable if sued.
(c)	**Shares** in a company are in principle **transferable** though the right of transfer may be restricted.	A partner cannot transfer his status as partner to someone else without the consent of all the other partners.
(d)	There is no **maximum number** of members; but for a public company there is a minimum of 2	The maximum number of partners is 20. However most professional partnerships are no longer subject to a maximum. The exemption is likely to be extended to multi-disciplinary partnerships with at least 75 per cent of the members drawn from one profession with up to 25 per cent drawn from other professions.
(e)	The owner (**members**) of a company as such are neither its managers (**directors**) nor its **agents**.	The owners (**partners**) are entitled to share in its management and are agents of the firm for carrying on it business in the usual way.

(f)	**Capital** subscribed by members for their shares cannot ordinarily be returned to them but (in a limited company) they are not liable for its debts once they hold fully paid shares.		Partners may withdraw capital but are still liable without limit for the firm's debts to its creditors.
(g)	Companies can **borrow** in the same way as individuals but only for purposes covered by their objects. They can use current assets as security by creating floating charges.		Partners have unrestricted powers of borrowing in terms of amount and purpose. They cannot create floating charges but can mortgage fixed assets.
(h)	Both in their formation and in their subsequent trading and other activities companies are subject to a number of **statutory rules** of **procedure** and supply of information available to the public.		Partnerships may be created informally and need not disclose any information about their affairs (except to the Inland Revenue over taxable profits).
(i)	The **dissolution** of a company usually entails a formal liquidation.		Partnerships can be dissolved by mere agreement of the partners but the creditors have first claim on the assets and some general legal principles apply.

In the above comparison no mention has been made of limited partnerships, the essential feature of which is that some inactive or sleeping partner may have limited liability. It is a hybrid form of organisation which is rarely used; a private company is generally a better solution.

Conclusion	There are many significant differences in the legal operation of companies and partnerships. All such factors are relevant in determining the type of business association best suited to a particular enterprise.

4.3 Limited liability

Although the most important reason for incorporating a company is likely to be the ability of members to isolate their personal assets from the company's creditors; in practice large creditors of small private companies such as the company's bankers, will inevitably require directors (who are often also the shareholders) to give personal guarantees of the company's borrowings.

4.4 Activity

List the principal disadvantages of setting up a business as a limited company rather than a partnership.

4.5 Activity solution

The principal disadvantages are usually identified as follows:

(a) Expense and formalities

It is more expensive to set up a company than a partnership. Furthermore during its lifetime, a company has to comply with all the registration and other formalities of the Companies Act.

(b)   **Publicity**

Because a company has to initially provide the registrar of companies with a certain amount of information, update that information, as well as provide financial information, there is much more data available to the public concerning the activities of that business.

(c)   **Taxation**

Whether or not there is a tax advantage or disincentive in setting up as a company will depend on the precise financial circumstances of that company

5   COMPANY REGISTRATION

5.1   Registration documents

In law a person who wishes to form a company is required merely to deliver to the Registrar of Companies certain documents and to pay a fee. In practice, however, prior to submission of the requisite documentation he would check the proposed name against the index of existing company names to ensure that it is not the same as an existing name and, if the name contains a restricted word, obtain consent to its use from the body designated by the Secretary of State.

To form a company it is necessary to deliver to the Companies Registry the following documents:

(a)   **Memorandum of association** signed by at least two persons (one for a private limited company) called the subscribers and dated. The signatures of the subscribers must be witnessed by a third person. Each of the subscribers undertakes to subscribe for one or more shares of the company. The memorandum contains several compulsory clauses, the detail of which is considered later.

(b)   **Articles of association** signed, dated and witnessed as for the memorandum (and by the same subscribers) or a statement that in lieu of special articles the company will adopt Table A.

(c)   **Directors, secretary and registered office** (Form 10). The name, address and other particulars of the first directors and secretary, with their consent to act in that capacity, must be given on a form signed by the subscribers to the memorandum. The same form also gives the first address of the registered office. All these particulars take effect from the date of incorporation: S10 CA85.

(d)   **Declaration of compliance** (Form 12). This is a sworn declaration made either by a person who is named in document (c) as a **director or secretary** of the company, or by a **solicitor** engaged in the formation of the company. The declaration is to the effect that the requirements of the Companies Act relating to formation have been complied with.

A registration fee is payable on presentation of the application.

5.2   Duties of the Registrar

On receiving the prescribed documents it is the duty of the Registrar of Companies (acting through his staff) to examine the documents and satisfy himself that:

(a)   the relevant requirements of the Companies Act have been complied with;

(b)   the memorandum and articles of association do not infringe the CA85;

(c)   the objects of the company set out in the memorandum are lawful;

(d)   the name of the company is not contrary to the provisions of the CA85; and

(e)   in the case of a public company that the company's share capital as stated in it memorandum is not less that the authorised minimum.

5.3 **Certificate of incorporation**

If the Registrar is satisfied that the registration requirements and the above points have been complied with, he must issue a certificate of incorporation which is conclusive evidence that:

(a)   the relevant requirements of the Companies Act have been complied with; and
(b)   the company is either a private or a public company as stated in the certificate.

The declaration of compliance with the Companies Act required by S12 CA85 can be accepted by the Registrar as sufficient evidence of compliance.

The procedure between delivery of documents and issue of certificate usually takes about two weeks. On due notice in advance the Registrar will issue his certificate on a pre-selected date, such as 1 January, so that a company can be formed on a timetable basis.

The Registrar's certificate is conclusive evidence that the company has been validly incorporated on the date stated in the certificate:

Jubilee Cotton Mills v Lewis [1924]

Facts: the certificate was dated 6 January although it was signed and issued on 8 January. On 6 January the directors allotted shares but the allottees refused to pay, arguing that the company did not exist on that date.

Held: the date on the certificate was conclusive as to the date of incorporation of the company. The allottees had to pay for the shares.

Despite S13 CA1985 the validity of a company's incorporation (and thus its very existence) can be challenged by way of judicial review proceedings on the basis that the Registrar had no legal power to register the company. Two instances of such are

•   where under other legislation the body is precluded from existing as a company. **Bowman v Secular Society [1917]**. This is the situation as regards a trade union.

•   where the company's objects are unlawful or contrary to public policy - **Attorney-General v Lindi St Clair (Personal Services) Ltd [1980]** - the company's trade was prostitution.

5.4 **The Companies Registry**

When a company is formed the Registrar opens a file for it and gives the company an identifying serial number which must be inserted on all documents subsequently presented for filing. The formation documents and a copy of the certificate of incorporation become the first enclosures on the file. As additional documents, such as each year's annual return or a notice of change of directors are presented to the Registry they are added to the file. The file thus increases by the addition in chronological order of documents received plus copies of any certificates (change of name, registration of a charge, etc) issued by the Registrar.

The contents of each file are copied on to microfilm and much of the public inspection is now by means of the microfiche copies.

There is at the Registry an alphabetical index of all companies on the register. Such an index may be purchased from the Registrar and is updated twice weekly. This is critical as Company Law is policed by the 'ethic of disclosure'. Vital issues must be made public.

The Registrar is required to give notice in the **London Gazette** of the receipt of documents of various classes relating to companies.

5.5   Activity

If a trader was considering acquiring an 'off the shelf' company, as opposed to incorporating a new company, what are the likely advantages of this approach?

5.6   Activity solution

The principal advantages are as follows:

(a)   speed. The company is already in existence. All that is required is to transfer existing shares to the new owners.

(b)   cheapness. A single fee is paid to the formation agent. The constitutional documents have already been drafted, and there is no additional fee payable to the Registrar. Any necessary changes to the constitution can easily be organised.

5.7   Certificate of entitlement to do business

Although every company is in existence as a legal person as from its date of incorporation (the date on the certificate of incorporation) a **public** company, incorporated as such, cannot do business or exercise any borrowing powers unless it has obtained from the Registrar a further certificate properly called the 'certificate of entitlement to do business' (more commonly called the trading certificate) - S117 CA85.

To obtain the trading certificate the public company must deliver to the Registrar a statutory declaration in the prescribed form signed by a director or secretary stating:

(a)   the nominal value of the company's allotted share capital is at least £50,000;

(b)   each allotted share is paid up to at least one-quarter on the nominal value and the whole of any premium;

(c)   the preliminary expenses of the company and who has paid, or is to pay, them;

(d)   any benefits given, or intended to be given, to promoters.

If a public company which does not have a trading certificate:

(a)   does business or exercises borrowing powers, the company and any officer in default commit a crime punishable by a fine;

(b)   enters into a transaction with a third party, the directors are jointly and severally liable with the company to the third party on the transaction;

(c)   has been in existence for more than one year (whether or not it has done business or borrowed money), this is a ground for its winding up under S122 IA86.

In practice most companies incorporate as private and then later 'go public' (called re-registration) thus avoiding the need for any trading certificate and the necessary hiatus period endured whilst obtaining it.

Conclusion   Every company (both private and public) is formally and legally incorporated on the date on its certificate of incorporation.

In addition a plc requires a trading certificate before it can legally trade (contracts made before this date will be valid but the directors and the company can be fined).

6 PROMOTERS

6.1 Who is a promoter?

Definition A promoter is a person who undertakes to form a company with reference to a given project and to set it going, and who takes the necessary steps to accomplish that purpose: **Twycross v Grant [1877].**

If, as in **Salomon's case** the promoter sells his own business or other property to the new company at an inflated value and retains the entire share capital no one else suffers. However, there were scandals in the nineteenth century when promoters sold shares of the company to the investing public thereby (through the previous sale to the company) defrauding the public. Such abuses are less likely to occur nowadays because modern law and practice stands in the way, but the legal rules applicable to promoters have to be understood as part of company law.

To combat these abuses the concept of the promoter's duties to the company was developed. The definition of 'promoter' has purposely been left vague. There is no statutory definition. However, it is clear that a promoter will include those who raise the capital, appoint solicitors, directors etc. The promoters are usually also the first directors. CA85 does specifically exclude from the definition a person who acts merely in a professional capacity eg, a solicitor or accountant who advises on the law or accounting rules.

6.2 Promoters' duties

The law does not prohibit a promoter from making and retaining a profit from his promotion, but it does require him to disclose his profit from the promotion (especially but not restricted to profit on resale of property) either:

(a)   to a board of directors of the company independent of himself; or
(b)   to existing and intended shareholders.

The principle here is that a promoter, although he is neither trustee for nor agent of the company does stand **in a fiduciary position** in his dealings with it. This is a professional position of trust and competence. Under that principle the company must be aware that it is buying his property or property in which he has an interest. If with that knowledge, imparted to shareholders or to an independent board of directors, the company completes the purchase it has by implication agreed that the promoter may obtain at its expense whatever benefit he may secure.

Erlanger v New Sombrero Phosphate Co [1878]

Facts: disclosure of the sale by the promoter to the company of a phosphates mining concession was made to a board of five consisting of two associates of the promoter, two who were abroad and the Lord Mayor of London (who was preoccupied with his other duties).

Held: proper disclosure to an independent board had not been made. The contract of sale was voidable at the option of the company.

The amount of detail which the promoter must disclose is now regulated by statute under FSA86.

Disclosure of indirect or additional interests must also be made.

Gluckstein v Barnes [1900].

Facts: a promoter disclosed in the prospectus that he (and his associates) were reselling to the company property (the Olympia Exhibition Hall) at a higher price than they had recently paid to acquire it, but he did not disclose that in addition his syndicate had bought up (for £20,000 less than its nominal amount) a mortgage on the property. The mortgage would be repaid by the company out of money received from the issue of shares to the public.

Held: by concealing this additional interest the promoter had failed to make proper disclosure of the extent of his interest in the property.

6.3   Remedies for non-disclosure

If the promoter fails to make proper disclosure the company may:

(a)   rescind the contract for the purchase of property; or

(b)   claim damages; or

(c)   recover any profit made by the promoter out of transactions effected during the period of promotion.

However, rescission may have become impossible if the company can no longer restore the property in the same condition as when it was purchased: or if third parties have meanwhile acquired an interest in it. In a claim for damages the company must prove that it has suffered a loss ie, the test is not whether the promoter made any profit on resale which was not disclosed but whether he resold the property to the company for more than it was worth: **Re Leeds & Hanley Theatres of Varieties [1902].**

Recovery of the promoter's profit is a useful alternative where the company wishes to retain the property which it has purchased (ie, does not wish to rescind) and cannot prove that it suffered loss by paying an excessive price for it. However, in order to be able to recover the promoter's profit the company must show, as in **Gluckstein's case**, both:

(a)   failure to disclose; and
(b)   that the profit arose from transactions within the promotion period.

There could be no such claim in **Salomon's case**, for example, because neither of the conditions (a) and (b) was satisfied; Salomon disclosed the facts to all the shareholders and he had owned his business for many years before he decided to form the company. The promoter's duty is merely to disclose, not to account for any profit made to the company.

Omnium Electric Palaces v Baines [1914]

Facts: the promoter agreed to sell to the company quite openly a lease which he was about to obtain. It was argued that because of his fiduciary position the promoter is accountable for any profit he makes out of transactions in the promotion, but that argument was rejected.

Held: his duty is to disclose; if he does so he may keep his profit. If the profit is made on property acquired before the promotion began the company cannot claim it even if the promoter does not make a proper disclosure.

In connection with prospectuses, it will be seen that there are now remedies under the Financial Services Act 1986 which could be more helpful to the investor if, as is likely in such a case, the promoter has become liable for a misleading prospectus.

6.4   S104 CA85 - Protection for public companies

To avoid founding members paying up the amount required on the shares of a public company, but later taking some of it back by way of an excessive payment from the company for property transferred to the company by them, S104 CA85 provides that if within two years of a public company being issued with its certificate of entitlement to commence business under S117 CA85, a subscriber to the memorandum transfers property to the company at a price which is equal in value at the time of the agreement to 10% or more of the company's issued nominal share capital, then:

(a)   The consideration must be valued, as under S103 CA85.

(b)   A report must have been given to the company within six months before the date of the agreement.

(c)   The terms of the agreement must have been approved by ordinary resolution.

(d)   Copies of the report must have been circulated to the members not later than the notice calling the meeting, and to the person with whom the agreement is made.

The same rule applies as regards existing members within 2 years of a private company re-registering as public.

The shares taken up by the signatories to the memorandum of a public company, in pursuance of the undertaking in the memorandum to do so, must be paid in cash (including any premium) (S106 CA85).

6.5   Formation expenses

Dispute may also arise between an honest promoter and the company he has formed over the recovery of his expenses. Some fees are payable to form a company; if there is a large operation involving transfer of property and flotation of the company on the Stock Exchange, expenses can be very large indeed. The promoter has no automatic right to recover his expenses from the company even if the company has benefited. The articles of association will usually authorise the directors, of whom the promoter may well be one, to repay the expenses. Even such a clause in the articles, however, is not a contract which the promoter can enforce because the articles only apply as a contract to dealings between the company and a shareholder as such.

There is no objection in law to the promoter becoming one of the first directors; he may also be a substantial shareholder. From that vantage point he should in practice be able to recover from the company his actual preliminary expenses.

6.6   Disqualification of promoters

The court has power to disqualify for up to fifteen years a person convicted on indictment of an offence in connection with the promotion, formation or management of a company. A person so disqualified may not be a liquidator or a director or a receiver or a manager of the property or otherwise concerned in the promotion, formation or management of any company. The articles of association of companies also usually disqualify any person so convicted from holding office as a director: Company Directors Disqualification Act 1986.

> **Conclusion** A promoter's principal duty is one of disclosure of any interest they have in or any profit they may make out of a transaction involving the company. In practice these days, the position is regulated by Stock Exchange requirements, the Financial Services Act 1986 and the more stringent attitude (these days!) of city institutions and merchant banks.

7   CHANGES IN A COMPANY'S STATUS - RE-REGISTRATION

7.1   Reasons

A company may initially register as one type of company, for example a private company, and then wish to change to a public company because eg, it has grown and wishes to offer its shares to the public. Alternatively, a public company may find that its business has reduced, and wishes to reduce its issued capital below the £50,000 required for a public company. Such changes are possible through a formal procedure of re-registering with the Registrar of Companies.

7.2   Re-registration of private companies as public companies: Ss43-47 CA85

A private company may re-register as a public company if:

(a)   a special resolution that it should be so re-registered is passed:

Such resolution must:

(i)   alter the company's memorandum so that it states that the company is to be a public company;

(ii)   make such other alterations in the memorandum as are necessary to bring it in substance and in form into conformity with the requirements Companies Act 1985 with respect to the memorandum of a public company; and

(iii)   make such alterations in the company's articles as are requisite in the circumstances; and

(b)   an application for the purpose in the prescribed form and signed by a director or secretary of the company is delivered to the Registrar accompanied by:

(i)   a printed copy of the memorandum and articles as altered;

(ii)   a copy of the company's balance sheet made up to a date not more than seven months prior to the application date accompanied by an auditor's report which is not materially 'qualified';

(iii)   a certificate by the company's auditors that the balance sheet shows the company's net assets to be not less than the aggregate of its called-up share capital and undistributable reserves; and

(iv)   a statutory declaration in the prescribed form made by a director or the secretary of the company stating that the re-registration requirements have been complied with and that between the balance sheet date and the application date the company's net assets have not become less than the aggregate of the company's called up share capital and undistributable reserves.

The Registrar will then issue a new 'public company' certificate of incorporation if he is satisfied that the company complies with the criteria for public status specified above, whereupon the special resolution passed by the company takes legal effect.

7.3   Re-registration of public companies as private companies: Ss53-55 CA85

A public company may re-register as private if:

(a)   a special resolution that it should be so registered is passed.

Such resolution must alter the company's memorandum so that it no longer states that the company is to be a public company and must make such other alterations in the company's memorandum and articles as are requisite in the circumstances; and

(b)   an application for the purposed in the prescribed form and signed by a director or secretary of the company is delivered to the Registrar; and

(c)   the period during which an application form the cancellation of the resolution may be made has expired without any such application having been made; or

(d)   where such an application has been made, the application has been withdrawn or a court order has been made confirming the resolution and a copy of that order has been delivered to the Registrar.

The right of objection referred to in (c) above is exercisable by 5% or more of the shareholders, or by shareholders holding 5% or more of the voting share capital or 50 or more members. It must be exercised within 28 days after the passing of the resolution.

Further, it should be noted that by S139 CA85 if the share capital of a public company is reduced below the authorised minimum, the company must at the same time be re-registered as private.

7.4   Re-registration of unlimited companies as private limited companies or vice versa

An unlimited company may re-register as a private limited company or vice versa, but re-registration may be done only once in the life of any company.

7.5   Limited to unlimited company

To make the change there must be filed at the Companies Registry:

(a)   An **application** signed by a director or by the secretary;

(b)   A **form of assent** signed by **all** the members;

(c)   A **statutory declaration** by the directors that all the members have signed the assent; and

(d)   A **copy of the memorandum and articles** incorporating the necessary changes: S49 CA85.

The Registrar then issues a new certificate of incorporation of the company as unlimited.

The existing members then have unlimited liability to contribute to the company's assets to pay its debts. The liability of a past member is still limited as before.

The special advantage of an unlimited company is that it is not required to file its accounts and can, therefore, maintain privacy on its affairs.

A company originally formed with limited liability can be converted to unlimited liability but cannot thereafter be converted back to limited ie, a change can be made only once.

No public company may apply under S49 CA85 to be re-registered as an unlimited company.

7.6   Unlimited to limited company

A company which was formed as unlimited (but not one already converted from limited to unlimited) can be re-registered as limited. In this case there must be filed at the Companies Registry:

(a)   an **application** signed by a director or by the secretary;

(b)   a **special resolution** (carried by a 75% majority of votes cast) making the necessary amendments of the memorandum and articles; and

(c)   a copy of the memorandum and articles as amended: S51 CA85.

In this case also the Registrar issues a new certificate of incorporation as a private limited company.

Members of an unlimited company which is insolvent might try to escape their liability to contribute for payment of its debts by converting it to a limited company. To counter such schemes it is provided that if the company goes into liquidation within three years of the conversion to limited liability any person who was a member at the time of the conversion has unlimited liability to contribute to the payment of outstanding debts incurred while the company was unlimited. A second complicated rule imposes a similar liability on any person who ceases to be a member of an unlimited company if (following conversion) it goes into liquidation within a year of his ceasing to be a member and at the time of liquidation no longer has any members who were members of the unlimited company at the time of the change.

No unlimited company can be a public company: S1(3) CA85.

If a company wishes to go from unlimited to a public limited company two steps are required:

(a)   by special resolution authorise alterations so that its liability is limited and the amount of the share capital is at least the authorised minimum (ie, to become limited); and

(b)   make such alterations in the company's memorandum to bring it into conformity with that required of a public limited company: S45 CA85 (ie, to become public).

Conclusion   A company can re-register and so change its classification. When re-registering as a public limited company remember that there are certain requirements for a plc which do not have to be complied with if the company is a private one. For example:

- a plc requires a minimum authorised and issued share capital of £50,000
- a plc must have a minimum of 2 directors and 2 members
- a plc must have a plc clause in its memorandum
- a director of a plc cannot be over 70 years old (unless excepted)
- the company secretary of a plc must be qualified.

Usually a special resolution of the members must be passed to successfully re-register. If re-registering from an unlimited company to a plc **two** steps should be taken; one from an unlimited company to a limited one and then another to a plc.

8   INTRODUCTION TO INSOLVENCY

8.1   Introduction

The law relating to insolvency of companies (and individuals, including partnerships) is contained in the Insolvency Act 1986 (IA86) which not only consolidated existing insolvency law but also made far-reaching changes.

Much of company law is directed towards protection of creditors and therefore can only be understood in the context of what happens when a company is unable to pay its debts. An example of this is **Salomon v Salomon** - the issues did not arise until the company had been put into liquidation.

There are three main formal ways of dealing with insolvency of a company, namely administrative receivership, administration, and liquidation. The latter is also called winding-up.

8.2   Administrative receivership

This is a remedy of secured creditors. If a company defaults on payment of its borrowings and the lender has security by way of a charge on the company's assets the secured creditor will wish to obtain payment out of the security. If the charge is a floating charge over the whole or substantially the whole of the company's assets he will appoint an administrative receiver whose basic function is to sell the charged assets in order to pay the secured creditor.

Definition An administrative receiver is a receiver of the whole or substantially the whole of a company's assets.

Every properly drawn loan contract (in company law called a debenture) which creates a charge will give the chargee the right to appoint a receiver. Although the receiver is appointed by contractual right the IA86 nevertheless imposes duties on him.

8.3   Dissolution and liquidation

As a company is an artificial legal entity it cannot die: there therefore has to be a legal procedure for terminating the legal existence of a company. The moment at which a company ceases to exist is called dissolution and the procedure which eventually leads to dissolution is called liquidation. Although the prime cause of liquidation is that the company is insolvent there are other reasons for liquidation of a company, for example it may be that the members wish the business to be ended and the company's property distributed to them; there are therefore a substantial number of solvent liquidations (to which the IA86, despite its title, applies).

There are two forms of liquidation:

(a)   The compulsory liquidation is so-called because the court has ordered that the company be wound up. S122 IA86 sets out the grounds on which a winding up order may be made. Of particular importance is ground (f) whereby a creditor can petition on the basis that the company is unable to pay its debts and ground (g) whereby a member can petition on the ground it would be just and equitable. S122(g) IA86 is covered in detail later.

(b)   The voluntary liquidation, so-called because the company (by resolution of its members in general meeting) has put itself into liquidation. If the company is insolvent it is called a creditors' voluntary (CVL) and if the company is solvent, it is called a members' voluntary (MVL). An extraordinary resolution is required for a CVL and normally a special resolution for a MVL.

Whatever the type of liquidation the liquidator is acting generally for the benefit of all concerned with the company. His aim is to obtain dissolution of the company and, inter alia, he will close down the business, realise all the assets, investigate the conduct of the company's officers (this is a statutory duty if the company is insolvent) and distribute the company's assets.

The statutory order of application of a company's assets is as follows:

(a)   Creditors secured by fixed charge obtain payment out of their charged asset.

(b)   Expenses of the liquidation.

(c)   Preferential debts. By Schedule 6 IA86 the preferential debts include:

- **VAT** falling due within the six months before the date of liquidation;

- **income tax** deducted under **PAYE** rules within the twelve months up to the date of liquidation from salaries and wages of employees;

- **national insurance contributions** due within the twelve months up to the date of liquidation;

- **wages and salaries** of employees due in respect of the four months ended on the date of liquidation up to a maximum of £800 in any one case. A director or company secretary as such does not fall into this category. But if he is also an employee he may be a preferential creditor for his salary (within the above limits);

- **accrued holiday remuneration** of an employee due on termination of his employment before or at the date of liquidation. There is no limit on this.

(d)   Creditors secured by floating charge.

(e)   Ordinary unsecured creditors. This category includes any debt not included elsewhere.

(f)   Post-liquidation interest. This is interest at a set rate on all the above categories of debt.

Should there still be assets at this stage, the company is solvent.

(g)   Adjustment of rights of contributories. This is the procedure for distributing the remaining assets amongst the members: in general, the order would be:

- deferred debts eg, debts due to members as members such as dividends declared, but not paid, before the date of liquidation.
- return of nominal value to preference shareholders.
- return of nominal value to ordinary shareholders.
- any remaining surplus then goes to ordinary shareholders.

Note: the Insolvency Act 1986 provides that a floating charge created by a company within a certain period before the commencement of its winding up or the making of an administration order shall be void as a security. The liquidator or administrator may then avoid the charge and the lender becomes an unsecured creditor. If the creditor is a connected person, that is a director or someone connected to a director by a family or business relationship, the period is two years. If the charge is in favour of any other person, it is one year.

The liquidator cannot avoid a floating charge created in return for new consideration, whether by way of cash or goods, to the extent of that consideration.

8.4   Activity

Runowt plc is in liquidation and the liquidator, after payment of expenses, has £125,000 available for distribution. The schedule of creditors shows the following debts:

(a)	Big Bank plc	£80,000 (all secured by floating charge)
(b)	British Gas plc	£10,000
(c)	KPMG (auditors)	£10,000
(d)	Local authority (business rates)	£5,000
(e)	Inland Revenue	£5,000 (corporation tax)
		£18,200 (PAYE, all within 12 months)
(f)	Galleon Ltd	£5,000
(g)	William Worker (employee)	£5,800 (wages, all within 4 months)
(h)	Lord Ingit (non-executive director)	£10,000 (fees voted by GM)

The share capital of the company comprises 50,000 fully paid £1 ordinary shares and 20,000 fully paid £1 preference shares. Prepare a distribution schedule for the liquidator.

8.5   Activity solution

Distribution schedule:

			Amount distributed	
			£	£
Realisation				125,000
1	Preferential creditors			
	Inland Revenue		18,200	
	William Worker		800	
			20,000	
				(20,000)
				105,000
2	Floating chargeholders			
	Big Bank plc		80,000	
				(80,000)
Amount available for ordinary unsecured creditors				25,000

		Due	
		£	
3	Ordinary unsecured creditors		
	British Gas plc	10,000	5,000
	KPMG	10,000	5,000
	Local authority	5,000	2,500
	Inland Revenue	5,000	2,500
	Galleon Ltd	5,000	2,500
	Lord Ingit	10,000	5,000
	W Worker	5,000	2,500
		50,000	25,000
			(25,000)
			-

There is nothing available for post-liquidation interest nor for shareholders.

Note: since there was insufficient to pay the ordinary unsecured creditors in full each received 50p for every £1 owed.

8.6   Administration orders

Neither liquidation nor receivership have the aim of rescuing a company which is in financial difficulties. The IA86 invented the concept of administration as a means of dealing with the affairs of a company in severe financial difficulty other than by way of liquidation of receivership.

The administrator is appointed by court order (on a petition, usually presented by the company and large creditors jointly). The administration order will set out the purpose or purposes which the administrator is expected to achieve - such a purpose might include the rescue of all or part of the company's business.

9   ISSUES IN CORPORATE GOVERNANCE

Your examiner expects you to be aware of topical issues in company law. One of these, generally referred to as 'Issues in Corporate Governance', is the question of who has control within a company or, to put it more bluntly - who is to stop directors feathering their own nests, whether by receiving large sums as remuneration or otherwise?

The answer given by the law is that it should be the shareholders and throughout this text you will see in detail what legal restrictions there are on the directors and the legal hurdles shareholders face in bringing the directors to book - the prime problem is that the law provides for action by the general body of shareholders, not, usually, for action by individual shareholders.

The articles of association of the company (ie, part of the constitution of a company) will usually provide that the directors are to have all the powers of the company and management of its affairs except insofar as the Companies Act or the articles themselves reserve powers to the shareholders in general meeting. In such a case the directors are entitled to exercise those powers so long as they have them, and the shareholders' remedy, if they are dissatisfied, is to restrict the directors' powers by altering the articles or to remove the directors from office - both of which is done at a General Meeting.

In a large company, particularly listed companies, not only is there the legal separation between ownership (shareholders) and management (directors) but there is also the separation in involvement; the shareholders merely receive the accounts and the directors' report on each year's results. They rarely attend general meetings (or even vote by proxy) though they have a right to do so.

In practical terms, rather than attempt to force directors to account, the solution opted for by shareholders of listed companies is to avoid the problem by selling their shares.

You are strongly advised during your course to read the financial pages of newspapers and to read professional journals, like Management Accounting, and to try to relate topical issues to what you are learning in company law.

10   SELF TEST QUESTIONS

10.1   What are the two forms of limitation of liability? (1.2)

10.2   Are the annual accounts of an *unlimited* company open for public inspection? (1.3 and 9.3)

10.3   What is the most important advantage a public company enjoys in comparison to a private company? (1.4)

10.4   What is the ratio of the case of **Salomon v Salomon and Co Ltd?** (2.1)

10.5   What is the 'veil of incorporation'? (2.2)

10.6   What is meant by 'lifting the veil'? (3.1)

10.7   What is the ratio of **Woolfson v Strathclyde Regional Council**? (3.1, 3.3, 3.4)

10.8   What is the main (ie, structural) difference between a company and a partnership? (4.1)

10.9   What form of security for loans can a company provide, but a partnership cannot? (4.2)

10.10   List the documents which must be forwarded to the Registrar in order to incorporate a company. (5.1)

10.11   On what date does a company legally come into existence? (5.3)

10.12   What type of newly incorporated company requires a trading certificate? (5.7)

10.13   Define a promoter. (6.1)

10.14   Is there any protection for minorities provided by statute when a company re-registers? (7.3)

10.15   What is the function of administrative receivership? (8.2)

10.16   What is the function of liquidation? (8.3)

10.17   List the preferential creditors. (8.3)

10.18   What is the function of administration (under the IA86)? (8.6)

11   EXAMINATION TYPE QUESTIONS

11.1   Susan, Mabel and Doris

Susan, Mabel and Doris wish to carry on business as caterers. They all intend to take part in the management of the business but would like to avoid personal liability for its debts. They are anxious that the affairs of the business and the arrangements between themselves should be kept secret as far as possible, and would like to be able to transfer their respective interests in the business without difficulty.

Disregarding tax considerations, advise them whether it would be better for them to form a company limited by shares or a partnership and state the advantages and disadvantages of each.

(10 marks)

11.2   Clipse Ltd

(a)   The general legal principle is that a company has a separate legal existence from that of its members. In what circumstances does the general principle not apply? Give examples of such situations.

(10 marks)

(b)   Walter is employed as managing director of Clipse Ltd whose main object is to retail office equipment. His contract of employment contains a clause which states that in the event of his leaving the employment of Clipse Ltd he will not solicit their customers for a period of two years. He resigns his employment and together with his wife Jean forms a new company, Desks Ltd, whose main object is also retailing office equipment. Bill is a salesman employed by Desks Ltd. He is given customer lists by Walter and immediately begins soliciting Clipse Ltd's customers.

In order to raise cash for his new business, Walter enters into a contract to sell his house to Wilf for £50,000. Bill who has always admired the house approaches Walter and makes him an offer of £60,000. Walter transfers ownership of the house to Desks Ltd, and on behalf of the company enters into negotiations to sell the house to Bill.

Advise Clipse Ltd and Wilf on any action they can take.

(10 marks)

(Total: 20 marks)

11.3 Registration of a new plc

Give an account of the legal procedure which must be followed in order to effect the registration of a new public limited company which is entitled to do business.

(20 marks)

12 ANSWERS TO EXAMINATION TYPE QUESTIONS

12.1 Susan, Mabel and Doris

As all three ladies intend to take part in the management of the business they must operate either as a partnership or as the directors of a limited company. A limited partnership would not be possible because limited partners' cannot take part in the management of a business.

Of the two alternatives, only a limited company would permit them to avoid personal liability. In this situation a private limited company would be appropriate unless is it intended to raise money from the public, which seem unlikely. However, all limited companies are required to prepare and to file at Companies Registry a memorandum and articles of association, annual return, accounts and other documents. If the ladies are determined that their affairs are kept secret they would be compelled to trade as an unlimited company or a partnership and thus lose limited liability. However, since 1981 'small companies' (as defined by the CA85) need only file a modified balance sheet (giving main headings, and little detail), and no profit and loss account or director's report need be filed. There is therefore less point in sacrificing limited liability by using an unlimited company or partnership to avoid filing accounts (although full accounts must still be prepared for members).

Additionally, one of the advantages of a limited company is that it is usually easier to transfer shares that to transfer an interest in partnership. Thus as the ladies wish to be able to transfer their interests, a limited company would probably be the most appropriate medium.

12.2 Clipse Ltd

(a)   The case of **Salomon v Salomon & Co** first raised the issue of the personality of a company incorporated by registration. In that case the promoter had sold his business to the company and received in part payment a fixed charge over the company's assets. When the company went into liquidation the promoter, as a separate person from the company, was able to claim its assets in priority to the unsecured creditors despite his connection with the company. The court held that Mr Salomon had not been fraudulent and thus raised the possibility of an exception to the separate legal entity doctrine.

Recent cases have stated that the veil will be lifted only where it is a mere facade concealing the true facts **Woolfson v Strathclyde.** Thus in **Adams v Cape Industries** the court refused to lift the veil between a holding company and its wholly owned subsidiary in order to make the holding company liable for the debts: there was no evidence to show the subsidiary was merely an agent carrying on the holding company's business (as in the **Smith, Stone, Knight case)** and the court refused to extend and apply the doctrine of economic reality raised in the **DHN** case where veils between companies in a group were lifted on the basis that the group was an economic entity and that the law should follow the economic reality. However, the courts have lifted the veil so as to impute the company with the German nationality of its members and directors so as to treat a UK registered company as an enemy alien in times of war - **Daimler v Continental Tyre & Rubber.** Further examples of the 'mere facade' exception are given in part (b).

In addition to these common law exceptions to lifting the veil there are a number of statutory examples eg,

(i) members' liability for the debts of the company if the number of members falls below the statutory minimum (now two unless it is a single member company): S24 Companies Act 1985 (CA85);

(ii) statutory provisions relating to holding and subsidiary companies and the preparation of group accounts;

(iii) offers of the company who carry on the business of the company with intent to defraud creditors may be called on to make such contributions to the company's assets as the court thinks proper; S213 Insolvency Act 1985 (IA 1985);

(iv) officers liable for wrongful trading may be required to contribute to the company's assets as above: S214 IA 1986;

(v) any person disqualified from acting as a director who acts in contravention of is disqualification will incur personal liability for the company's debts incurred whilst so acting: S15 Company Directors Disqualification Act 1986.

(b) The restraint of trade clause in Walters contract with Clipse Ltd restrains Walter from soliciting Clipse's customers within a two year period of his leaving Clipse's' employ. Such a clause does not bind a company with is a separate legal entity, unless that company is a party to the agreement. Desks Ltd is not a party to the agreement but is a company formed and partly owned by Walter who is bound by the clause. If it can be shown that the main purpose in forming the company was to avoid the application of the restrictive covenant, the court may lift the veil of incorporation and treat Walter and the company as one and extend the clause to the company. The case is similar to the **Gilford Motor Co v Horne.** It should perhaps be noted Clipse would also have to show that the restraint clause is valid for public policy reasons as there is a presumption against the validity of such clauses.

In land law there is a general principle that damages for a breach of contract of sale is an inadequate remedy and normally specific performance ie, an order to perform the terms of the contract is awarded. This is on the basis that every piece of land is unique and damages will not be adequate compensation.

Specific performance, unlike damages, is an equitable remedy and will only be awarded by the courts in certain circumstances, in particular no order for specific performance will be made if this would affect the rights of a *bona fide*, (good faith), purchaser.

Walter is in breach of contract with Wilf and specific performance would normally be available against Walter. Walter has already transferred ownership of the house to Desks Ltd with a view to selling it to Bill. Walter has done this hoping to prevent an order of specific performance in Wilf's favour. If the company is a separate legal entity and is a *bona fide* purchaser it is unlikely that the court will disturb the transaction despite Walter's ulterior motive. However, the court might equate the company and Walter and treat them as one to avoid a fraud being perpetrated on Wilfe, as in **Jones v Lipman.** Alternatively, the court might find that the company is not a *bona fide* purchaser, because there is no mention of the company having paid for the house. If this is the case an order for specific performance could be made anyway without lifting the veil of incorporation.

It seems that the house has not yet been transferred to Bill but if it had been unless Bill knows of the contract between Walter and Wilf, he would be a *bona fide* purchaser and no order for specific performance could be made against him.

12.3 Registration of a new plc

Note: the candidate should be careful to realise the significance of the phrase 'entitled to do business'.

Although the concept of a public limited company has been around for nearly a century, the procedure for registration of the significance of the designation 'plc' were substantially revised in 1980. There are two stages which must be complied with before a public limited company may do business. First, the company must obtain a certificate of compliance with certain share capital requirements before it may commence business and enter into contracts.

Registration requires the depositing of certain documents with the Registrar of Companies along with payment of the registration fee (currently £50). The documents to be registered are:

(a)   Memorandum of association. This must contain the name clause, a statement that the company is a public limited company, the situate clause, the objects of the company, a statement that the company's liability is limited and the capital clause. The memorandum can contain other clauses but, apart from class rights, any clauses contained in the memorandum which could have been contained in the articles are alterable as if contained in the articles, so there is no advantage in putting them in the memorandum. The memorandum must be signed by at least two people who have agreed to subscribe for shares in the company.

(b)   Articles of association. As it must be a company limited by shares it may rely on the standard form of articles found in Table A, or it may register its own. Together, the memorandum and articles form the company's constitution.

(c)   Details of directors and secretary and their signed consents to act. Details include their addresses and any other directorship and the company's address.

(d)   A statutory declaration that the Companies Act 1985 registration requirements have been complied with.

A public company must have at least two members who each agree to subscribe for a share in the company but the minimum issued share capital must be £50,000. Despite its name the public company does not have to offer its shares to the public, it may do so if it wishes, however ultimately the company may require a listing on the Stock Exchange in which case at least 25% of the shares must be available for purchase by the public.

Once the company has obtained its certificate of incorporation it has legal capacity as a separate person and can be bound by legal transactions. However, in order to protect the public from under-capitalised companies the Companies Act 1895 (CA85) now requires a public company to obtain a certificate of compliance with certain capital requirements before it may do business or exercise any borrowing powers: S117 CA85. The Registrar will grant a certificate of compliance if he receives:

(a)   an application in the prescribed form stating that the company's **issued** share capital together is at least £50,000 (the statutory minimum) and all issued share capital is paid up to at least 25% together with all of any premium: Ss117 and 101 CA85; and

(b)   a statutory declaration signed by a director or secretary of the company stating that the company's share capital is not less than the authorised minimum, the amount paid up on those shares, the company's preliminary expenses and who is entitled to them and the amount of any benefit given to any promoter of the company.

Once issued the certificate is conclusive evidence that the company is entitled to do business and borrow money. Failure to comply with S117 renders the company and any officer in default liable to a fine, but so that there is no detriment to creditors the transactions entered into a breach remain valid. If the company fails to honour such a transaction within twenty-one days of a request from the creditor to do so, the directors become jointly and severally liable to indemnify the other contracting party for any loss or damage suffered as a result of the company's failure to comply with S117.

18 COMPANY FORMATION: PUBLICITY

INTRODUCTION & LEARNING OBJECTIVES

Syllabus area 8e. Company formation: publicity, accounts and filing. (Ability required 2.)

An underlying philosophy of company law is that persons dealing with a company are protected by disclosure of information. Thus this chapter looks at where information can be found and what it consists of.

When you have studied this chapter you should be able to do the following:

- Know that publicly available documentation can be found at the Companies Registry and at each company's registered office.

- Know what information is available.

- List and know the contents of the statutory registers.

- Be able to advise a company as to its duties in relation to the Annual Return and the Annual Financial Statements.

---

1 SOURCES OF INFORMATION

1.1 Introduction

An underlying philosophy of company law is that persons dealing with a company are protected by disclosure of information. This is of importance not only to actual and potential investors but also to creditors particularly in relation to limited liability companies. The two locations where information is publicly available are at the company's own registered office and at the Companies Registry. In order to assist in ascertaining the address of the company's registered office and to enable a search to be made at the Companies Registry it is important that persons dealing with a company should be able to identify the company.

1.2 Name outside every place of business

Every company must paint or affix its name outside of every office or place in which its business is carried on - S348 Companies Act 1985 (CA85). This must be in a conspicuous position and in letters easily legible.

1.3 Letters and orders

All letters and order forms must give the following information:

(a)   the company name - S349 CA85;
(b)   place of registration - S351 CA85;
(c)   its registered number - S351 CA85;
(d)   address of its registered office - S351 CA85.

For this purpose an **order form** is one issued by the company (including, for example, a coupon in a newspaper advertisement) for use of customers.

A company must not state in any form the names of its directors (otherwise than in the text or as a signatory) on any business letter on which the company's name appears unless it states on the letter in legible characters the first name or the initials thereof, and surname of every director of the company who is an individual and the corporate name of every corporate director: S305 CA85.

1.4   Registered office

S287 CA85 provides that a company shall at all times have a registered office to which all communications and notices may be addressed. (Service of legal proceedings and documents on a company is good service if it is served on its registered office).

The intended situation of a company's registered office on incorporation must be notified to the Registrar on incorporation of the company. (This is part of the prescribed Form 10).

The address of the registered office may be freely changed (usually the Articles provide by board resolution) within the domicile, but notification of any such change must be given to the Registrar, who must record the change. The change is not effective until the notice is registered with the Registrar of Companies. On receipt of notice of such change the Registrar in accordance with S711 CA85 must advertise the same in the 'Gazette'.

S42 CA85 provides that if no Gazette notification has appeared the company cannot rely on the change of registered office against another person unless the other person was actually aware of it at the time. Even when the Gazette notification has appeared there is a period of fourteen days grace during which the company cannot rely on the change against a person who was unavoidably prevented from knowing of it (if the matter in dispute arose during or before the fourteen day period). Thus if a company fails to notify the Registrar of the change of registered office and documents are served at the old registered office, the company cannot plead that they were not properly served. The consequent alteration to its letterheads and relocation of documents required to be kept at the Registered Office must be effected within 14 days after it has notified the Registrar.

The law requires that certain registers and documents must be kept at the registered office, and in practice, various other registers, and documents will be kept there. The registers in question are:

(a)   Register of Members: S353 CA85;
(b)   Register of Directors and Secretaries: S288 CA85;
(c)   Register of Debenture Holders (if any): S190 CA85;
(d)   Register of Charges: S411 CA85;
(e)   Register of Directors' Interests: S325 CA85
(f)   Register of Interests in Shares (if applicable): S211 CA85.

In addition copies of instruments creating charges, minutes of general meetings and directors' service agreements must be held in the same way: (Ss411, 383 & 318 CA85 respectively).

Item (a) or (c) may be held at some place in England or Wales or (for Scottish company) in Scotland other than the registered office provided that notice of that other address is given to the Registry. Items (e) and (f) may be kept wherever the register of members is held and so may directors' service agreements (which may also be at the company's principal place of business in the country of domicile).

The maintenance of each statutory register is detailed below.

1.5   Activity

AT Foulks Lynch Ltd's registered office is properly situated in London at 100, Fetter Lane.

Could it change it to 100, MacSporran Lane in Glasgow?

1.6   Activity solution

No. Its registered office must be somewhere in England and Wales. (Glasgow is in Scotland.)

1.7   Companies Registry

The Companies Registry (commonly called Companies House) is an Executive Agency answerable to the Department of Trade and Industry. The Registry is now in Cardiff but with a branch in London. There is a separate Companies Registry in Edinburgh for companies incorporated in Scotland.

The important duties of the Registrar of Companies include:

(a)   the issue of a certificate of incorporation which is conclusive evidence that the company has been formed either as a public or private company and, where appropriate, that it is a limited company. It is for the Registrar to satisfy himself that the formalities have been properly observed; once he has issued his certificate the matter cannot be re-opened: S13 CA85;

(b)   keeping the index of companies names required by S714 CA85. Any change of name takes effect only on the issue of his certificate;

(c)   issue of a certificate of re-registration eg, limited company as unlimited and *vice versa*, public company as private and *vice versa*, the issue of a certificate of compliance with the capital requirements to a public company;

(d)   the receipt of the annual return and annual financial statements of each company and also notices of various changes eg, of directors or secretary, address of registered office, situation of registers (if not held at the registered office). All these, together with the formation documents and those referred to below, are put on file for public inspection;

(e)   the receipt of a return on allotments when shares are issued and of copies of orders and minutes of the court eg, for a reduction of share capital;

(f)   the receipt of signed copies of special and extraordinary resolutions and of resolutions affecting share capital or class rights, also amended copies of the memorandum and articles of association and details of special rights attached to shares;

(g)   the receipt of particulars of charges over the company's assets for registration, and the issue of a certificate of registration. He also receives the memorandum of satisfaction which clears a registered charge from the register;

(h)   the receipt of a signed copy of every prospectus and annexed documents before publication;

(i)   the receipt of various resolutions and notices relating to appointment of a receiver and the commencement of winding up and various reports, accounts and returns filed in the course of winding up;

(j)   the publication in the **London Gazette** of the fact of receiving or issuing various classes of documents;

(k)   striking a company off the register under S652 CA85 or at the end of winding up.

As it is, or should be, possible to see the file of any company within an hour of demand, the Companies Registry is an invaluable source of information to the public.

The main practical difficulty in operating the system is that companies are often very late or fail altogether in filing documents, notably annual returns. In the last resort the Registrar may commence criminal proceedings or strike a defaulting company off the register. He also may apply to the court for an order disqualifying a person in persistent default from being concerned in the management of a company - Company Directors Disqualification Act 1986. (CDDA86). Any three defaults in any period of five years is deemed persistent.

2   THE STATUTORY REGISTERS

2.1   Register of members

Every company is **required** by S352 CA85 to maintain a **register** in which must be entered:

(a)   The **name** and **address** of each member;

(b)   The **date** on which they were entered as a member and the eventual date on which they cease to be a member; and

(c)   Where the company has a share capital, the number and amount paid up on each share. Where the company has more than one class of issued shares, the **class of shares** which he holds.

In theory each share should also be distinguished by a serial number but this tiresome formality is now rarely followed as S182 CA85 permits de-numbering. If the shares have been converted into stock corresponding particulars of stock held are entered.

The register must be **kept** either at the **registered office** of the company or at some **other place** in the same country as the registered office (ie, either England, Wales or Scotland) of which **notice** has been given to the **Registrar of Companies**, who puts the notice on his file for public information. If the company has more than **fifty members** it must either keep the register in alphabetical order or provide an **index**: S354 CA85. If the company is a single member company (permitted in the case of private limited companies) a statement of the fact, the date it happened and the name and address of the member must be entered. A corresponding entry must be made if and when the membership increases.

Any person may obtain **information** from the register under S356 CA85:

(a)   by exercising their **right of inspection** (for which a small fee may be charged to non-members). The register must be open to inspection (subject to the company's right to close the register for not more than thirty days in the year eg, to prepare a list of dividend payments: S358 CA85); or

(b)   by requiring the company, for a small charge, to supply within ten days **a copy** of the register or any part of it (eg, a list of members holding at least 1,000 shares).

These rights are frequently used in preparation for takeover bids and by junk mail business.

The register is evidence of ownership of shares/membership of the company.

The **court** has power to **rectify** the register where a name is wrongly inserted or omitted: S359 CA85. A person whose name wrongly appears (because it should never have appeared or because they have rescinded their contract with the company) should have their names removed or they may be estopped from denying they are members, by letting their names remain. Conversely, a person who is a member but whose name does not appear on the register should apply to rectify the register.

Trusts

An English company is expressly forbidden to register or enter on its register of members any notice of a trust: S360 CA85. The company recognises **only the registered holder of shares.** This means that in the case of a trust only the name of the trustee appears and in the case of shares held by a nominee, the nominee's name: in both situations as if that named person were the outright owner - the company cannot take account of the fact that they hold them for someone else.

A beneficiary can protect their interest by a legal procedure known as a **stop notice**. If such a notice is served on the company it is required to inform the beneficiary of any impending transfer or dividend fourteen days in advance. It is then for the beneficiary to take appropriate legal steps against the trustee.

As the company only recognises the trustee shareholder they are liable to pay any calls made on their shares; they may exercise the voting rights and receive the dividends. The trustee in turn is accountable to and can claim against the beneficiary. But the company cannot deal direct with the beneficiary even if the trustee is a man of straw.

2.2   Register of interests in shares

The register of members only gives the identity of the registered proprietors of the shares and as has been seen Company Law expressly forbids the company to recognise a trust on its register. This can be highly inconvenient and is capable of abuse eg, it might enable insiders to trade in the company's securities without the company's knowledge, or enable someone to secretly acquire control of a sizeable holding through nominees ie, warehousing. To assist in preventing such abuses provisions exist to require a **public** company to maintain a register of the holdings and dealings by people with an interest in three percent or more of the company's issued share capital carrying unrestricted voting rights: S211 CA85. This register is sometimes called the Register of Notifiable Interests or the Register of Substantial Share Interests.

(a)   **Duty to disclose interests - substantial holdings**

Ss198-201 CA85 states that where a person **knows or becomes aware** that he:

- has **acquired** an interest in three percent or more of any class of a **public** company's issued share capital carrying unrestricted **voting rights;** or

- if already interested in three percent or more of such share capital of a public company they increase or reduce the extent of their interest by more than 1%; or

- ceases to have a three percent interest in such shares.

The 3% level is replaced by a 10% level for certain people such as the operators of an authorised unit trust.

They must notify the company in writing within **two** days. The notice must specify the share capital to which it relates and either the number of shares in which the person concerned has or still has an interest if they have or retain more than three percent of the company's relevant share capital or that he has ceased to hold more than three percent where such is the case.

Where a notification relates to other than a cessation of a substantial holding it will also have to state the identity of each registered holder of any shares to which the notification relates and the number of those shares held by such registered holder so far as known to the person making the notification at the date of the notification.

A person will have an interest in shares

- As a beneficiary under a trust;

- In which they have a right to acquire an interest in the shares (eg, an option to buy);

- In which they are entitled to exercise any rights which the registered holder would be entitled to exercise;

- In which their spouse, minor child or stepchild has an interest;

- In which a company has an interest if:

    (1)   the company acts in accordance with their instructions; or

    (2)   They have one-third or more of the voting power at general meetings.

He will cease to have an interest in shares held by someone else if:

- the relationship ceases; or

- that other person disposes of their interest.

Though an obligation to disclose under Ss198-201 CA85 through the interest of another person only arises when the person knows both the relevant facts relating to the other person's interest and those relating to his own.

Persons sometimes act together to acquire and build up large holdings in a (target) company. Individually, each of these holdings may be below 3%. Such arrangements are known as concert parties.

Each party to such an agreement is to be taken to be **interested** in **all shares** in the target company in which any other party to the agreement is interested (whether or not the interest of the other party in question was acquired or includes any interest which was acquired in pursuance of the agreement).

Where an obligation to notify arises under the concert party provisions, the notification to the company by a party must:

- State the person making the notification is a party to such agreement;

- Include the names and (so far as is known to him) the addresses of the other parties to such agreement;

- State the number of shares in which he is interested for the purpose of the concert party provisions: S205 CA85.

In order to effect the provisions, S206 CA85 imposes an additional obligation on any party to the agreement **to notify the other parties** thereto in writing of any interest in the capital of a target company. A person ceases to be interested in shares where they leave a concert party.

(b)   **Company's right to require members to disclose interest**

By S212 CA85 any **public company** may by notice in writing require any person whom the company knows or has reasonable cause to believe **to be** or, at any time during the three years immediately **preceding** the date on which the notice is issued to have been interested in shares forming part of the company's issued share capital carrying unrestricted **voting rights** to **confirm** that fact or (as the case may be) to **indicate** whether or not it is the case and whether he holds, or has during that time held any **interest** in shares so comprised.

An interest arising under the concert party provisions is deemed an interest within the terms of S212.

Information received under S212 is to be **entered** by the company against the name of the registered holder of those shares in a separate part of the company's register of interests in shares.

Under S214 the holders of not less than one-tenth of the company's share capital carrying the right to vote may, by requisition, require the company to exercise its powers under S212 CA85.

(c)   **Penalties for failure to disclose**

A person who fails to:

- disclose a substantial interest to the company either because he does not disclose at all; does so outside the stated time period; or provides false information;

- disclose information to other members of a concert party;

is guilty of an offence and liable to a fine or imprisonment, or both. If they are convicted the Secretary of State may order that the shares in question be subject to restrictions on transfer, voting and payments eg, of dividends or bonus shares.

In addition if a person fails to provide information as required by a company under (d) above the company may apply to the Court for an order restricting the use of the shares - in the same way as may be done by the Secretary of State above.

(d)   **The register of interests in shares**

As stated above every public company is required to keep a **register** and to enter into it against the name of the person concerned any information it receives from a person in consequence of the fulfilment of an obligation imposed on him by Ss198-208 CA85. The date of the entry must also be recorded in the register. Entries in the register have to be made within three days of receipt of the information. The register has to be kept at the **same place** as the **register of members** and is **open to public inspection**.

2.3   Register of debenture-holders

A company is not obliged by the Companies Act to keep and maintain a register of debenture-holders. However, if it chooses to do so then S190 CA85 obliges it to maintain and be open to inspection in the same way as the Register of Members.

2.4   Register of charges

S411 CA85 obliges every company to keep at its registered office a register recording all charges on its property. This Register is open for public inspection (members and creditors free).

The register must show an entry for each charge giving a short description of the property charged, the amount of the charge and the names of the persons entitled to it.

The company is also required to keep at its Registered Office for public inspection a copy of every instrument creating a charge over its property. The Register therefore constitutes a convenient summary: the detail can be ascertained by inspecting the debenture creating the charge.

Failure to comply with S411 CA85 is a criminal offence enforceable by way of a fine against the company and every officer in default.

2.5   Register of directors and secretary

By S288 CA85 every company is required to keep at its registered office a **register of directors and secretary** giving the following particulars in relation to every director:

(a)   name (where a director has changed his name, the former name must also be given);

(b)   usual residential address;

(c)   business occupation;

(d)   nationality;

(e)   directorships of other companies held by him or which have been held by him in the preceding five years (unless the same wholly-owned group of companies); and

(f)   his date of birth.

As regards the company secretary, the register will record his name and address only.

This register is also open for public inspection.

Failure to comply with S288 CA85 is a criminal offence enforceable by way of a fine against the company and every officer in default.

2.6   Register of directors' interests

Directors are required to inform the company of any interests he (or his wife, minor children or associated company) has in the company's shares or debentures within 5 days of becoming aware of his interest - S324 CA85.

This information (which not only must include details of the shares or debentures but also the price paid) must be entered by the company on a Register of Directors' Interests within 3 days - S325 CA1985.

The register also must record any share options which have been granted by the company to a director.

The register must be kept with the Register of Members and in the same way is open to public inspection.

Failure to comply with S324 or S325 or CA85 is a criminal offence enforceable by way of a fine against the company and every officer in default.

3 ACCOUNTING RECORDS

3.1 Content

S221 CA85 provides that every company shall keep accounting records in accordance with the provisions of that section.

> **Definition** Such records shall be sufficient to show and explain the company's transactions, disclosing with reasonable accuracy, at any time, the financial position of the company and enable the directors to ensure that any balance sheet or profit and loss account prepared by them gives a true and fair view of the company's state of affairs.

In particular the company's accounting records must contain:

(a) entries from day to day of all sums of money received and expended by the company and the matters in respect of which the receipt and expenditure takes place;

(b) a record of the assets and liabilities of the company; and

(c) where the company's business involves dealing in goods:

- statements of stock held by the company at the end of the each financial year of the company;

- all statements of stocktakings from which any such statement as is mentioned above has been or is to be prepared; and

- except in the case of goods sold by way of ordinary retail trade, statements of all goods sold and purchased showing the goods and the buyers and sellers to be identified.

3.2 Location and Inspection

Such records must be kept at the company's registered office or at such other place as the directors of the company shall think fit and shall at all times be open to inspection by the officers of the company. Such records must be preserved for six years in the case of a public company and for three years in the case of a private company.

4 ANNUAL FINANCIAL STATEMENTS

4.1 Introduction

A company's annual financial statements are comprised of its accounts (the balance sheet and the profit and loss account) and its reports (the directors' report and the auditor's report).

This paragraph introduces you not only to the content of each document but also to the company's obligations to send them to members (and others), to lay them before the members in general meeting and to deliver them to the Registrar of Companies. Group accounts are covered where relevant.

4.2   Accounting reference period

Every company must have an accounting reference date. A company must give notice in the prescribed form to the Registrar of Companies of its accounting reference date before the end of nine months of the date of the company's incorporation. As an accounting reference period cannot be less than 6 months nor more than 18 months and the first period starts with the date of incorporation, the company's chosen accounting reference date must be between 6 and 12 months after incorporation. Failure to give notice will mean that the company's accounting reference date will be the last day of the month in which the anniversary of its incorporation falls.

Accounts must be prepared up to the accounting reference date or such other date not more than seven days before or more than seven days after that date for each accounting reference period; ie, the period in which an accounting reference date falls. It is the duty of the directors to lay copies of the accounts before the company in general meeting and further to deliver to the Registrar a signed copy within:

(a)   for a **private company**, ten months after the end of the relevant accounting reference period, and

(b)   for a **public company**, seven months after the end of that period.

These intervals may be extended by three months if the company gives notice to the Registrar that it carries on business or has interests abroad. An unlimited company which is neither a parent nor a subsidiary of a limited company does not have to deliver a copy of its accounts to the Registrar. Small and medium-size private limited companies may file modified accounts (see below).

A company may alter its accounting reference date by notice to the Registrar but subject to certain conditions and limitations.

A company's first accounting reference period for which accounts must be prepared is such period ending with its accounting reference date as begins on the date of its incorporation and is a period of more than six months and not more than eighteen months. Thereafter the company must prepare accounts for each calendar year ending on its accounting reference date (plus or minus seven days).

Members, debentureholders and other entitled persons (eg, the auditors) are entitled to receive a copy of the accounts before the meeting at which they are to be laid.

The parent company of a group is in principle required:

(a)   to ensure that its subsidiaries have the same financial year; and
(b)   to produce group accounts in respect of itself and its subsidiaries.

4.3   The balance sheet

The directors of every company must prepare a balance sheet. The balance sheet must give a true and fair view of the state of affairs of the company as at the end of the financial year: S226 CA85.

The general provisions relating to the form, content and format of the balance sheet are set out in Sch 4 CA85. However, if a balance sheet drawn up in accordance with those requirements would not provide sufficient information to comply with the need to give a true and fair view any necessary additional information must be provided in that balance sheet or in a note to the accounts.

4.4   The profit and loss account

The directors of every company must prepare a profit and loss account. The profit and loss account must give a true and fair view of the profit or loss of the company for the financial year: S226 CA85.

The general provisions relating to the form, content and format of the profit and loss account are set out in Sch 4 CA85. However, as with the balance sheet if a profit and loss account drawn up in accordance with those requirements would not provide sufficient information to comply with the need to give a true and fair view, any necessary additional information must be provided in that profit and loss account or in a note to the accounts.

4.5   Form and content of group accounts

S227-9 CA85 (as amended) require group accounts to be in the form of consolidated accounts. The format and content is set out in Sch 4A CA 1985.

If a subsidiary has a different year-end to the holding company then the subsidiaries' last financial year-end should be used providing that this is not more than three months before the holding company year-end. If it is more than three months then coterminous (same in range and time) interim accounts must be used.

4.6   Definitions of a subsidiary company, subsidiary undertaking, holding company, parent company

As a result of extensive changes made in 1989 there are now two sets of definitions in use in relation to groups. A narrow set of definitions using the terminology 'holding company' and 'subsidiary company' is used for all non-accounting purposes. An extended set of definitions using the terminology 'parent company' and 'subsidiary undertaking' is used for all accounting purposes. The wide term 'undertaking' in the accounting definition includes not only a company but may also include a partnership or other unincorporated business.

The wide and extended accounting definitions were introduced to counter what had come to be called 'off-balance sheet' activities. Broadly, some business activity was carried on by an entity which was controlled by a company (or as a joint venture with another entity) but the entity was not, under pre-1989 law, a subsidiary and so its accounts were not required to be consolidated.

[Definition]   The wide and extended accounting definition of a subsidiary defines it as where any of the following are satisfied:

(a)   The parent holds a majority of the rights to vote at general meetings of the undertaking on all or substantially all matters.

(b)   The parent is a member and has a right to appoint or remove directors having a majority of the rights to vote at board meetings of the undertaking on all or substantially all matters.

(c)   The parent is a member and has the right to control alone a majority of the rights to vote at general meetings of the undertaking pursuant to an agreement with other shareholders.

(d)   The parent has a right to exercise a dominant influence over the undertaking by virtue of provisions in the memorandum or articles or by a lawful control contract.

(e)   The parent has a participating interest and actually exercises a dominant influence or the parent and subsidiary undertaking are managed on a unified basis.

For definition (d) above the existence of a dominant influence is only deemed to apply if the parent has a right to give directions on operating or financial policies and the subsidiary directors are obliged to comply with those directions whether or not they are for the benefit of the subsidiary.

For definition (e) above a participating interest means an interest in shares, held for the long-term, to secure a contribution to its activities by the exercise of control or influence. A holding of 20% or more is presumed to be a participating interest unless the contrary can be shown.

For accounting purposes all five definitions apply. For non-accounting purposes only the first three definitions apply using 'holding company' rather than 'parent' and 'company' rather than 'undertaking'.

4.7   Exemption from the requirement for group accounts

(a)   **Intermediate parent company**

An intermediate parent company (ie one which is itself a subsidiary undertaking) is exempt from the requirement to prepare group accounts, if:

- none of its securities are listed anywhere in the EU; and

- its immediate parent undertaking is incorporated in the EU.

Providing that:

- it is wholly owned by that immediate parent; or

- its immediate parent holds more than 50% and notice for the preparation of group accounts has not been served from shareholders owning either more than one-half of the remaining shares or 5% of the total shares.

Various detailed conditions apply for this exemption including the need for the intermediate parent to be included in the group accounts of an EU parent. A copy of these accounts must be filed with the Registrar of Companies together with an English translation.

(b)   **Small and medium-sized groups**

A parent company need not prepare group accounts if the group headed by that parent satisfies at least two of the following conditions:

	Small	*Medium-sized*
Annual turnover	£3.36m gross or £2.8m net	£13.44m gross or £11.2m net
Balance sheet assets	£1.68m gross or £1.4m net	£6.72m gross or £5.6m net
Average employees	50	250

The right to exemption does not apply if any company in the group is either:

- a public company;
- a banking or insurance company; or
- a company authorised under the Financial Services Act 1986 (FSA86)

(c)   **Subsidiaries excluded from consolidation: S229 CA1985**

A subsidiary may be excluded from consolidation in the following situations:

(i)   if its inclusion is not material for giving a true and fair view, or

(ii)   if severe long-term restrictions substantially hinder the rights of the parent over the assets or management of the subsidiary, or

(iii)   if the information necessary for the preparation of group accounts cannot be obtained without disproportionate expense or undue delay, or

(iv)   the interest of the parent is held exclusively with a view to subsequent resale and the undertaking has not previously been included in the consolidated group accounts.

A subsidiary must be excluded from consolidation if its activities are so different that its inclusion would be incompatible with the obligation to give a true and fair view.

If, as a result of the above, there are no subsidiaries to be consolidated then the parent is exempt from the need to prepare group accounts.

Conclusion   Any company that has subsidiary undertakings and is not a small or medium-sized group or an intermediate parent company must prepare consolidated group accounts.

4.8   Additional information

In addition to the contents specified in Sch 4 CA85, the accounting documents to be laid before the company in general meeting and delivered to the Register must also show those matters specified in Sch 5 CA85 relating to the identities and places of incorporation of companies which are not subsidiaries whose shares the company holds, and particulars of those shares etc.

4.9   Activity

Stables Ltd has an accounting reference date of 31 December. When must it have delivered its accounts to the Registrar of Companies each year?

4.10   Activity solution

By 31 October of the following year ie, 10 months after the end of the accounting reference period.

4.11   Summary accounts: S251 CA 1985

Listed companies are allowed to issue summary financial statements to their shareholders instead of the full annual report and accounts. The full annual accounts and reports still have to be prepared, audited and filed. The summary financial statements must be derived from the full accounts and directors' report. Copies of the full accounts and reports must still be sent to any entitled person who wishes to receive them.

The Secretary of State has issued regulations which prescribe the contents of the summary financial statements and which prescribe how the company ascertains where a particular member wishes for full or summary accounts.

The auditors have to report on whether or not the statement is consistent with the full accounts and whether it complies with the relevant statutory requirements. If the audit report on the full accounts is qualified then details of the qualification must be included in the notes in the summary statements.

4.12 Directors' report

S234 CA85 requires the directors to prepare a report with respect to the company's affairs.

In addition to stating the amount of any recommended dividend and proposed transfer to reserves the directors' report must include names of the directors, particulars of any important events affecting the company or any of its subsidiaries which have occurred since the end of that year, an indication of likely future developments in the business of the company and of its subsidiaries, an indication of the activities (if any) of the company and its subsidiaries in the field of research and development, information regarding the health, safety and welfare at work of employees of the company and its subsidiaries, and in respect of political donations in excess of £200 the name of the political party, the amount and purpose for which the money was given. If particulars of directors' interests in shares or debentures are not given in a note to the accounts they must be given in the directors report.

If the company is a listed company the Stock Exchange requires the directors' report to state many other matters in addition to those required by the CA 1985. In particular the company is required to state whether or not it complies with the Code of Best Practice (published as part of the Cadbury Committee's report on financial aspects of corporate governance) and if it does not comply then in what respect and why.

The Directors' report must be approved by the board and signed on behalf of the board by a director or secretary of the company.

As with the accounts, the directors's report must be sent, laid and delivered.

4.13 Auditors' report

The auditors must report to the company on the accounts examined by them, and on every balance sheet, every profit and loss account and all group accounts laid before the company in general meeting during their tenure of office. The report must state whether or not the accounts are properly prepared in accordance with the Companies Act and whether or not the accounts give a true and fair view: S235 CA85. The auditors must carry out investigations such as will enable them to form an opinion whether:

(a)   proper accounting records have been kept, and proper returns adequate for their audit have been received from branches not visited by them;

(b)   the accounts are in agreement with the accounting records and returns.

If the auditors are of the opinion that either requirement (a) or (b) has not been satisfied or if they fail to obtain the information and explanations which they consider necessary for the purpose of their audit, they must state any such conclusion in their report on the accounts: S237 CA85.

The auditor must give particulars of directors' emoluments or loans to directors, or transactions with directors, if these are not adequately or correctly disclosed in the accounts, so far as they are reasonably able to do so.

Further, it shall be the duty of the auditors of the company, in preparing their report under the Act on the company's accounts to consider whether the information given in the directors' report relating to the financial year in question is consistent with those accounts. If the auditors are of opinion that the information given in the directors' report is not consistent with the company's accounts for the financial year they shall state that fact in their report.

In the preparation of their report in respect of a parent company the auditors may require information from any subsidiary undertaking; it is a criminal offence for any officer of a company knowingly or recklessly to supply false or misleading information to auditors: S389A CA85.

The auditors report, which must contain the auditors' names and signatures, must be sent with the accounts to members, be laid before the general meeting and filed with the Registrar.

> **Conclusion**   A company's annual financial statements will consist of a balance sheet, a profit and loss account, a directors' report and the auditor's report.

4.14   The filing exemptions

As a general rule all **limited** companies must deliver their annual financial statements to the Registrar of Companies but there are exemptions for certain small or medium sized private limited companies (see definitions in the earlier chapter 'Company formation: incorporation).

S246 CA85 provides, in line with the EC Fourth Directive, for exemptions from the full accounting disclosure for such small and medium-sized companies. Such companies are permitted to deliver to the Registrar modified accounts containing less information than the full accounts required to be prepared for shareholders. For medium-sized companies the information that may be omitted relates mainly to details of turnover but for small companies much more extensive abridgement is permitted and, in particular, no profit and loss account need be delivered to the Registrar, the notes to the delivered accounts are severely abbreviated and no directors' report need be delivered to the Registrar.

As regards the operation of these exemptions in relation to group accounts, the Act requires a parent company to deliver full individual accounts to the Registrar unless the group as a whole is exempt (see above, group accounts).

4.15   Dormant and small companies

> **Definition**   S250 CA85 provides that where a company is one that is small as defined for exemption purposes and has had no significant accounting transactions in the period concerned, it is a dormant company

A dormant company can relieve itself of the obligation to appoint auditors and deliver an auditors' report by passing a special resolution.

Certain small companies which meet certain qualifying conditions eg, as to turnover in respect of a financial year are exempt from the obligation to have their annual accounts audited. However, members holding 10% of the company's issued share capital may require the company to obtain an audit.

4.16   Private companies

A private company may by elective resolution dispense with the laying of the annual accounts and reports before a general meeting. Any member or the auditor may, however, require the calling of a general meeting for this purpose. Where such an elective resolution is in force, copies of the accounts must be sent to the members not less than 28 days before the end of the period allowed for laying and delivering.

4.17   Revision of accounts and directors' report

The CA 1989 introduced a new procedure for the revision of defective accounts and reports. The procedure is contained in S245-245C CA 1985 as supplemented by regulations made by statutory instrument.

Accounts and reports are defective if they do not comply with the CA 1985 (ie, they are not properly prepared or they do not show a true and fair view).

S245 CA 1985 empowers the directors to revise defective accounts and reports. S245B allows the Secretary of State or the Financial Reporting Review Panel to apply to the court for an order to compel the directors to prepare revised accounts. No-one else (eg a member) can apply to the court.

5   ANNUAL RETURN

5.1   Timing: S363 CA 1985

A company is required to deliver to the Registrar of Companies once a year the annual return within 28 days after the return date (which is the anniversary of the company's incorporation or, if the company's last return was made in accordance with CA85 to a different date, the anniversary of that date).

5.2   Content: S364 CA 1985

The return must contain the following information:

(a)   the address of the registered office and, if the register of members or the register of debentureholders is not kept at that office, the address (eg, of a professional registrar) at which it is kept;

(b)   the type of company it is and its principal business activities;

(c)   particulars of directors and secretary taken from the register;

(d)   a company having share capital must also state the total number of shares issued, the aggregate nominal value of the shares, the classes of shares, a list of names and addresses of members at the date of the return (a full list every three years, alterations in the other two years).

(e)   if relevant, statement that the company has passed an elective resolution to dispense with the laying of accounts and/or holding of AGMs.

The annual return must be signed by one director or the secretary: S365 CA85.

5.3   Penalties

Failure to deliver it in the required format and on time is an offence by the company and every director or secretary unless he shows that he took all reasonable steps to avoid the omission or continuance of the offence: S363 CA85. The penalty is a fine and, for continued contravention, a daily default fine.

6   SELF TEST QUESTIONS

6.1   List the information which must be on all company letters. (1.3)

6.2   How is the address of the registered office changed? (1.4)

6.3   List the 6 statutory registers which must be kept at the company's registered office. (1.4 and 2)

6.4   Within what time periods must accounts be filed? (4.2)

6.5   Which type of company may send summary accounts to members instead of full accounts? (4.11)

6.6   Which type of company may dispense with laying accounts before members in general meeting? How is this dispensation made legal? (4.16)

6.7   What are the consequences, and for whom, of failure to file an Annual Return? (5.3)

19 COMPANY FORMATION: MEMORANDUM OF ASSOCIATION

INTRODUCTION & LEARNING OBJECTIVES

Syllabus area 8e. Company formation:
Memorandum of association (Ability required 2)
Corporate capacity to contract (Ability required 2).

The memorandum of association is one of the two constitutional documents which a company must have (the other is the articles of association).

The most important clause is the objects clause which sets out the type of business the company may engage in and therefore its capacity to make contracts. Corporate capacity and the *ultra vires* rule overlaps with directors duties in later chapters.

When you have studied this chapter you should be able to do the following:

- List the clauses set out in the memorandum.

- Explain the contents of each clause.

- Know if and to what extent each may be altered.

- Understand who is liable on pre-incorporation contracts and why the company is not.

- Understand the *ultra vires* doctrine and S35 CA89.

1 THE MEMORANDUM - GENERAL

1.1 Memorandum and articles of association

Every company is required to have a written constitution in the form of two documents. The memorandum of association defines the essential components of the structure of the company, partly for the information of those who do business with it. The second document is the articles of association (or Table A adopted in place of articles) which is the code of internal regulations applicable to the company and its members in their dealings with each other.

In the earliest period of company law the memorandum, as the essential definition of company structure, could only be altered to a very limited extent. Over the years many of the restrictions have been removed; but the principle still remains - the various clauses of the memorandum cannot be altered except as specified by the Companies Act 1985 (CA85). The articles, as working bye-laws, are in principle generally alterable by the members by special resolution but this general power is subject to some restrictions.

1.2   Contents of the memorandum

The mandatory clauses of the memorandum of a public company limited by shares state the following matters:

(a)   the name of the company which must end with the words 'public limited company' (plc) or Welsh equivalent:

(b)   that the company is a public company;

(c)   the situate of the company's registered office;

(d)   the objects of the company;

(e)   that the liability of the members is limited;

(f)   the nominal amount of the authorised share capital (at least £50,000) divided into a specific number of shares of specific value; and

(g)   after the main clauses of the memorandum comes a declaration of association which must be signed by a minimum number of subscribers (ie, two); they must each agree to take one or more shares – in practice usually one only; their signatures must be witnessed by a witness who signs as such; the date of signature must also be inserted.

The Secretary of State, by statutory instrument, has prescribed model forms for a company's memorandum. In practice the objects clause will deviate considerably from the model. The model for a public company is Table F.

TABLE F

A PUBLIC COMPANY LIMITED BY SHARES

MEMORANDUM OF ASSOCIATION

1.   The company's name is 'Western Electronics Public Limited Company'.

2.   The company is to be a public company.

3.   The company's registered office to be situated in England and Wales.

4.   The company's objects are the manufacture and development of such descriptions of electronic equipment, instruments and appliances as the company may from time to time determine, and the doing of all such other things as are incidental or conducive to the attainment of that object.

5.   The liability of the members is limited.

6.   The company's share capital is £5,000,000 divided into 5,000,000 shares of £1 each.

We, the subscribers of this memorandum of association, wish to be formed into a company pursuant to this memorandum; and we agree to take the number of shares shown opposite our respective names.

Names and Addresses of Subscribers	Number of shares taken by each Subscriber
1. James White, 12 Broadmead, Birmingham.	1
2. Patrick Smith, 145A Huntley House, London Wall, London EC2.	1
Total shares taken	2

Dated   XX-X-19XX

Witness to the above signatures,
Anne Brown, 13 Hute Street, London WC2.

Where the company is a private company limited by shares, the memorandum must be in a similar form, but there are four differences:

(a)   the name of the company must end with the word 'limited' (Ltd) or Welsh equivalent;

(b)   the second clause ie, that the company is public, is omitted;

(c)   there is no minimum share capital requirement; and

(d)   the association (or subscription) clause needs only one subscriber - Companies (Single Member Private Limited Companies) Regulations 1992.

The model for a private company limited by shares is contained in Table B.

In the memorandum of a guarantee company, the amount which members may be required to contribute on a winding up to pay its debts must be stated.

1.3   Name clause

The name in the name clause of the memorandum is the legal corporate name of the company. Thus, the choice of the name is important. There are also restrictions on the use of any name other than the proper corporate name and change of name. The detail of this important clause is covered in detail below.

1.4   Public company clause

Only companies registered as public companies must include this clause in their memorandum. A public company may re-register as a private company if, *inter alia*, the company passes a special resolution altering the company's memorandum so that it no longer states that the company is to be a public company: S53 CA85. Conversely, when a private company wishes to become a public company it must pass a special resolution altering the memorandum so as to include a statement that it is a public company.

1.5   Registered Office clause

The next clause of the memorandum states that the registered office of the company is situate in England and Wales, or Wales, or in Scotland as the case may be. This fixes the domicile and nationality of the company (but not its residence eg, for tax purposes, which can be in another country). The exact address is not given in this clause. This clause cannot be altered otherwise than by Act of Parliament.

1.6   Objects clause

The CA85 requires the objects clause to set out expressly the business (or businesses) of the company. The CA85 assumed that powers (ie, things a company can do in order to achieve its objects such as borrowing money) would be implied and therefore are not statutorily required to be expressly stated. In practice many companies choose to expressly detail powers in the objects clause.

The objects clause is intended to provide a measure of protection for investors in that they are aware of what type of business they are investing in.

This very important clause is covered in detail later.

1.7   Liability clause

In the case of a company limited by shares or by guarantee, the memorandum states that the liability of members is limited. As we have seen this means limited to the unpaid part of their shares.

There is no liability clause in the memorandum of an unlimited company.

1.8   Capital clause

This clause of the memorandum of a company limited by shares must state:

(a)   the total amount of the share capital which the company is authorised to issue; and

(b)   how that amount is divided into shares of specified value; eg, the share capital of the company is £100 divided into 100 shares of £1 each.

There may be more than one class of shares. It is possible, but not necessary or usual, to specify here the rights attached to, for example, preference shares. These are called 'class rights'. Class rights are usually given in detail in the articles.

No minimum share capital is required for a private company but a public company must have a minimum authorised share capital of at least £50,000.

The equivalent clause for a company limited by guarantee is a clause which states that every member undertakes to contribute such amount as may be required (not exceeding £x) to the company's assets if it is wound up while he is a member or within one year after he ceases to be a member. This clause cannot be altered. A company limited by guarantee and having a share capital (must have been formed before 1980) will also have a statement as set out above for companies limited by shares showing its share capital.

S121 CA85 allows the capital clause to be altered, if so authorised by the company's articles, for the following purposes:

(a)   to increase the authorised capital;

(b)   to decrease authorised capital (ie, to cancel shares which have not been issued)

(c)   to consolidate or sub-divide shares into different nominal values (the overall nominal amounts may not be altered); and

(d)   to convert fully paid shares into stock or vice versa.

S121 CA85 requires this power of alteration to be done by the company in general meeting. In the absence of an alternative majority specified in the company's articles this will be by ordinary resolution (simple majority).

1.9   Association clause

This clause is explained above.

1.10   Additional clauses

There may be additional clauses covering other matters apart from the compulsory ones referred to above.

1.11   Alteration of the memorandum

It will be seen from the preceding that only the registered office clause and the association and subscription clause cannot be altered in some way subject to special rules of procedure.

If in addition to the compulsory clauses the memorandum contains any other clause:

(a)   If that clause is **entrenched** ie, expressed as unalterable, it cannot be altered by any act of the members of the company. For example, prohibition on payment of dividends may be entrenched in this way. If it is alterable only by a specified procedure, that procedure is obligatory and has precedence over the statutory rule.

(b)   If the clause defines the rights of a class of shares and specifies a procedure for alteration (or refers to a procedure in the articles) the procedure must be followed. If no procedure is stated it can only be altered by agreement of all members.

(c)   If there is no restriction on alterations the clause (unless it relates to share rights) can be altered in the same way and to the same extent as if it had been part of the articles ie, by special resolution) instead of the memorandum but subject to the same procedure for objection by a 15% minority and appeal to the court as are given on an alteration of the objects clause with the exception that debenture holders cannot apply for cancellation: S17 CA85.

Conclusion   The main clauses can be summarised as follows:

- Name Clause   -   the corporate identity of the company

- Objects Clause   -   what the company's business is and its powers

- Capital Clause   -   the authorised share capital of the company and the number and nominal value of shares

- Public Clause   -   stating that the company is a plc (plc's only)

- Liability Clause   -   stating that the liability of the members of the company is limited

- Registered Office Clause   -   the legal jurisdiction of domicile of the company

1.12   Activity

Draft the memorandum of association for a private limited company whose registered office is to be located at 32, Coal Way, Cardiff.

It is to operate as a passenger and freight carrier under the name of 'The South Wales Motor Transport Company'.

It has sufficient share capital to register as a public company if it chooses. Initially the original shareholders are to be Thomas Jones of 138 Mountfield Street, Tredegar and Mary Evans of 19 Merthyr Road, Aberystwyth, and they will take one share each.

(Your answer need not be in Welsh.)

1.13   Activity solution (taken from the statutory model)

TABLE B

A PRIVATE COMPANY LIMITED BY SHARES
MEMORANDUM OF ASSOCIATION

1.   The company's name is 'The South Wales Motor Transport Company Ltd'.

2.   The company's registered office is to be situated in Wales.

3.   The company's objects are the carriage of passengers and goods in motor vehicles between such places as the company may from time to time determine and the doing of all such other things as are incidental or conducive to the attainment of that object.

4.   The liability of the members is limited.

5.   The company's share capital is £50,000 divided into 50,000 shares of £1 each.

We, the subscribers to this memorandum of association, wish to be formed into a company pursuant to this memorandum; and we agree to take the number of shares shown opposite our respective names.

Names and Addresses of Subscribers	Number of shares taken by each Subscriber
1. Thomas Jones, 138 Mountfield Street, Tredegar.	1
2. Mary Evans, 19 Merthyr Road, Aberystwyth.	1
Total shares taken	2

Dated   19

Witness to the above signatures,
Anne Brown, 'Woodlands', Fieldside Road, Bryn Mawr.

2   THE COMPANY NAME

2.1   Choice of name

The name in the memorandum of association is the company's legal name in which it will contract and sue and be sued.

S26 CA85 provides that a company shall not be registered under the CA85 by a name:

(a)   which includes otherwise than at the end of the name any of the following words and expressions that is to say **limited, unlimited**, or **public limited company** or their Welsh equivalents **or** which includes, otherwise than at the end of the name, abbreviations of any of those words or expressions;

(b)   which is the **same** as a name appearing in the index of names which the Registrar is required to keep under S714 CA85;

(c)   the use of which by the company would in the opinion of the Secretary of State constitute a **criminal offence**; or

(d)   which in the opinion of the Secretary of State is **offensive**.

Further, except with the **approval of the Secretary of State**, a company may not be registered under the CA85 by a name which:

(a)   in the opinion of the Secretary of State would be likely to give the impression that the company is connected in any way with Her Majesty's Government or with any local authority; or

(b)   includes any word or expression for the time being specified under regulations made under S29 CA85. Examples of these are the words National, Registered, International, Trust, Scottish, Royal, etc.

2.2   Detail on this area

(a)   A **private** company must have as the final word in its name **Limited** or **Ltd**; a **public company** must have as the final words in its name **public limited company** or **plc**.

(A **private** company which by it memorandum stipulates that it is registered office must be in Wales may use **cyfyngedig** instead of **limited** in its name or, if it is **public**, the words **cwmni cyfyngedig cyhoeddus** instead of **public limited company**: S25 CA85.)

Moreover, new offences have been created to protect the new classification of companies. It is an offence for a person who is not a public company to trade under a name which includes the words **public limited company**. Similarly, a public company must not imply that it is a private company in circumstances in which the fact that it is a public company is likely to be material: S33 CA85.

However a company is permitted under S30 CA85 to omit the word **'limited'** from its name if it fulfils the following conditions (and submits a statutory declaration to that effect):

(i)   it is or is about to be registered as a **private company limited by guarantee**; or

(ii)   it was immediately before the day on which the provision came into force a private company limited by shares the name of which did not by virtue of a licence granted under the repealed S19 CA48, include the word limited and which satisfies the following requirements:

- its **objects** are or, in the case of a company to be registered, are to be the **promotion of commerce, art, science, education, religion, charity or any profession** and any thing incidental or conductive to any of those objects; and

- the **memorandum** or **articles** of association:

  (1)   requires its **profits**, if any, or other income to be **applied in promoting its objects**;

  (2)   **prohibit** the payment of **dividends** to its members; and

  (3)   **require** all the **assets** which would otherwise be available to its members generally to be **transferred** on its **winding up** either to **another body** with objects similar to its own or to another body, the objects of which are the promotion of charity and anything incidental or conductive thereto (whether or not the body is a member of the company).

A company so exempted from the requirements of the CA85 relating to the use of the word 'limited' as any part of its name is also exempted from the requirements of the Companies Act 1985 relating to the publishing of its name and the sending of lists of members to the Registrar of Companies.

(b)   **Name same as another**

Under S714 CA85 the Registrar is required to keep an index of the names of existing companies, incorporated and unincorporated bodies and limited partnerships for the purpose of Ss26 & 28 CA85. It is this index that promoters of a company check against to ensure that the proposed name of the company they intend to form is not 'the same' as that of an existing company. Assuming that such is not the case, that the proposed name ends with the relevant designation and is not in the opinion of the Secretary of State offensive or the use of which would be a criminal offence, the proposed name will be accepted by the Registrar.

(c)   **Illegal words**

A company shall not be registered by a name if, in the opinion of the Secretary of State, the use by the company would be a criminal offence. Certain statutes have prohibited the use of certain words which are recognised as being associated with charitable or other organisations. Thus it is unlawful to use the words 'Boy Scouts' 'Girl Guides', 'Red Cross' or to represent oneself as a building society when not registered as such.

(d)   **Consent of Secretary of State required**

Consent of the Secretary of State is necessary to register with a name likely to give the impression that the company is connected in any way with the government or any local authority. In addition there is a long list of words that may only be used in company names with the consent of the Secretary of State or, in some cases, of a specified Department of State or public authority. Thus consent of the Secretary of State is required to use the words 'England', 'Ireland', 'Scotland', 'Wales', or 'Great Britain', 'British', 'Queen' 'International', 'European', 'association', 'chartered', 'council', 'society', 'group' and 'trust'.

2.3   The tort of passing off

Acceptance of a name by the Registrar of Companies does not relieve those concerned of liability under other branches of the law.

There is also the risk of a **passing off** action by some other person (not necessarily another company) on the ground that the company is by the use of its name leading the public to believe that the company's products are those of the person who makes the complaint ie, that his business goodwill is being damaged. In a suitable case the court may restrain the company from trading under its registered name and order that damages be paid to the person whose business has suffered loss. This is not an action under company law but seeking redress for a civil wrong under the law of tort.

2.4   Change of name

(a)   By Secretary of State

(i)   In spite of these precautions a company may be formed with or may by change of name adopt a name which is too much like that of some existing company. Accordingly S28 CA85 provides that where a company has been registered by a name which is **the same** as or, in the opinion of the Secretary of State, **too like** a name appearing or which should have appeared at the time of the registration in the index of names kept by the Registrar under S714 CA85, the Secretary of State may within 12 months of that time, in writing, direct the company to change it name within such period as he may specify.

(ii)   The Secretary of State has an additional power within five years of registration to order an existing company to change its name on the ground that the company presented misleading information for the purpose of being registered with a particular name.

(iii)   The Secretary of State may also direct a change of name if it is so misleading as to the nature of its activities as to cause harm to the public. There is no time limit within which the Secretary of State must act but the company has a right to appeal to court. The name must then be changed within six weeks of the order of the Secretary of State.

(b)   By the company

It happens more frequently that a company, of its own initiative, decides to change its existing name to some other. The company changes its name by passing a special resolution to that effect and presenting a signed copy of the resolution to the Companies Registry (with a fee): the change of name takes effect a few days later when the Registrar issues his certificate of change of name; he may refuse to do so and in that case the resolution has no legal effect: S28 CA85.

A change of name by a company under S28 CA85 does not affect any rights or obligations of the company or render defective any legal proceedings by or against the company, and any legal proceedings that might have been continued or commenced against it under its former name may be continued or commenced against it under its new name.

Conclusion   A company may have to change its name. This could be by order of the Secretary of State or the Court (as a remedy following a successful action under the tort of passing off). It may also change the name voluntarily.

Either way the procedure is contained in S28 CA85:

- call an Extraordinary General Meeting (EGM)

- give those members who are entitled to attend and vote at the meeting a minimum of 21 days notice that a special resolution to change the name is to be moved at the meeting

- pass the special resolution (with a minimum of 75% of the votes which are cast being cast in favour)

- send the special resolution and the new Memorandum of Association (containing the new name clause) to the Registrar of Companies within 15 days of the passing of the resolution

- Registrar will issue a new certificate of incorporation containing the new name.

2.5   Business Names Act 1985

Providing that the company complies with the above rules (even in small print) it is free within the provisions of Business Names Act 1985 to adopt some other name (trade name) under which to carry on business.

The Act requires the prior approval of such name by the Secretary of State if that name would be likely to give the impression that the business is connected with Her Majesty's Government or with any local authority; or includes any word or expression specified under regulations made under the Act (as for the company's legal name - see above).

Further, where the company is using a trade name it must:

(a)   stage in legible characters on all business letters, invoices and receipts issued in the course of the business and written demands for payments of debts arising in the course of the business its corporate name and an address for service of documents;

(b)   in any premises where the business is carried on and to which the customers of the business or suppliers of any goods or services to the business have access, display in a prominent position so that it may easily be read by such customers or suppliers a notice containing such name and address; and

(c)   provide its name and address for service immediately, in writing, to any person with whom anything is done or discussed in the course of the business and who asks for such.

Failure to comply with the provisions of BNA 1985 is an offence.

In additional any legal proceedings brought by a person to enforce a right arising out of a contract made in the course of a business in respect of which he was, at the time the contract was made, in breach of the provision shall be dismissed if the defendant shows:

(a)   that he has a claim against the plaintiff arising out of that contract which he has been unable to pursue by reason of the latter's breach; or

(b)   that he has suffered some financial loss in connection with the contract by reason of the plaintiff's breach;

unless the court before which the proceedings are brought is satisfied that it is just and equitable to permit the proceedings to continue.

Conclusion   The principal restrictions on the choice of a name are:

- it must not be the same as one currently on the index

- it must not be too like one currently on the index

- it must not be offensive or be a criminal act

- it must not use the words ltd, plc or unltd otherwise than at the end of the name

- It must not, without the prior permission of the DTI, use restricted words (such as 'National', etc), or refer to local or central Government.

2.6   Activity

What, if any, objections are likely to be made to the following proposed company names?

(a)   Ministry of Defence Suppliers plc
(b)   The Ace Trading Company
(c)   Whiplash Personal Services Ltd
(d)   The International Trading Company Ltd
(e)   The Small Trades Bank plc
(f)   Smith Brothers Ltd

2.7   Activity solution

(a)   Permission would be required for this name as it suggests a connection with government
(b)   There is no apparent reason why the word 'limited' is not in the name.
(c)   This is likely to be perceived as an offensive name.
(d)   The word 'International' is included in the list of words for which permission is required.
(e)   Calling a company a Bank, unless it is one as defined by the Banking Acts is an offence.
(f)   There may be a problem if an existing company has a name similar or the same as this.

3   CORPORATE CAPACITY: PRE-INCORPORATION CONTRACTS

Definition   A pre-incorporation contract is one made by a person on behalf of or purporting to be the company at a date prior to that on the company's certificate of incorporation.

3.1   Position at common law

A company cannot be bound by a contract which was made on its behalf by any person (including a promoter) before the company itself had been formed. At the time when the contract is made, the company is non-existent; it cannot after its formation ratify (or formally adopt) a contract to which it could not have been a party when the contract was made.

Kelner v Baxter [1866]

Facts: A, B and C entered into a contract with the plaintiff to purchase goods on behalf of the proposed Gravesend Royal Alexandra Hotel Co. The goods were supplied and used in the business. Shortly after incorporation the company collapsed.

Held: as the Hotel Co was not in existence when the contract was made it was not bound by the contract and could not be sued for the price of the goods.

In **Kelner v Baxter** goods had been ordered for the company's business before the company was formed, and the company was not bound by a contract merely because it later performed it eg, by accepting the goods or services. The company will, of course, be liable if it makes a fresh contract after the company is formed; but there must be clear evidence that it intended to do so.

3.2   S36C CA85

S36C CA85 provides that where a contract purports to be made by a company, or by a person as agent for a company, at a time when the company has not been formed, then subject to any agreement to the contrary the contract shall have effect as a contract entered into by the person purporting to act for the company or as agent for it and he shall be personally liable on the contract accordingly.

Phonogram Ltd v Lane [1981]

Facts: prior to the formation of F Ltd, which was to manage a pop group, the defendant, their manager, reached an agreement with the plaintiffs regarding finance. The defendant signed an undertaking, 'for and on behalf of F Ltd' to repay the monies advanced, if the contract was not completed within a certain period. The plaintiffs sued for the money advanced, the defendant denied that he was personally liable to repay the sum as the words 'for and on behalf of F Ltd' was 'agreement to the contrary' under S36C.

Held: that the words did not amount to such agreement and the defendant was personally liable. To exclude personal liability, clear words must be used.

3.3   Possible solutions

(a)   The simplest and safest course for a promoter is to bring the negotiations to the point of agreement but to postpone any binding contract until the company is formed and can enter into the contract for itself.

(b)   However, if it is essential to commit the other party before the company exists, the promoter can try to persuade the other party to some formula of **assignment** or novation (by which the company is to take over his obligations **as a new contract**) to be made after incorporation and when it does so, or if it does not within a specified time, he is then to be released.

(c)   Buy an 'off the shelf' company. Fully formed and legally constituted companies can be purchased on a 'ready made' basis.

(d)   Agree that there will be no personal liability on his part once the company has been formed and taken over the obligations. S36C CA85 appears to allow this as it does state that the promoter will be liable 'unless otherwise agreed'. This probably means that it could be agreed that the benefits and burdens of the contract could be assigned to the company once it is formed and once assigned the promoter will no longer be liable.

(e)   Purchase an 'option'. An option is contract to keep an offer open to a specified person. Thus if, for example, the promoter wished to buy a factory/land for the company which cost £1 million he would not wish to take on potential liability for that amount. However, the seller may be prepared to grant him an option ie, a promise that he will offer the factory to the company at the stated price as soon as it is formed. To bind the seller the promoter will have to pay something for the option but the price he pays will be considerably less than the full purchase price of the factory.

(f) Agree a term of the contract that either party may rescind if the company is not formed within a specified period of time. On rescission the parties will be restored to their pre-contractual positions.

| Conclusion | Prior to the certificate of incorporation:

- the company does not legally exist

- the promoters are personally liable on all contracts entered into (even if in the name of the company): S36C CA85

- the company cannot ratify (formally adopt by way of an ordinary resolution of the members) a contract made before it is incorporated

- contracts are known as pre-incorporation contracts

After the certificate of incorporation:

- company is now a separate legal entity. It can form contracts in its own name (but cannot ratify pre-incorporation contracts)

- the promoters (usually) become the first directors and can now bind the company in contract

- the company may enter into a novation/assignment to contractually replace the pre-incorporation contract

3.4   Activity

On 1 June a promoter acquires a mining lease. On 3 June he sends off the incorporation documents to the Registrar. On 4 June he enters into a contract to acquire mining equipment for the company. The same day the registrar signs the certificate of incorporation for the 'Acme Mining Company plc'. The certificate is dated 5 June. On 8 June he sells the mining lease to the newly formed company at 100% profit.

Describe the status of the contracts entered into on 4 June and 8 June?

3.5   Activity Solution

(a)   Contract 4 June.

This is a pre-incorporation contract. It is dated prior to the date on the certificate of incorporation of the company.

However it is a valid contract. It is just that it is not enforceable by or against the company. If the supplier failed to provide the equipment, the company, as a third party, would not be successful in any action against the supplier.

It would make no difference that the company had ratified the contract.

(b)   Contract 8 June

On the facts given it would appear that the promoter has made a profit out of the promotion of the company without disclosing the fact to the shareholders or the board of directors. This is a breach of fiduciary duty.

The contract is therefore a voidable contract, which can be rescinded by the company, as long as the company does not delay and can restore the mining equipment to the supplier in the same condition, it will recover any monies paid out.

4   CORPORATE CAPACITY: OBJECTS CLAUSE

4.1   The *ultra vires* concept

The **memorandum** of association of every company must state the **objects** of the company. This requirement was intended to be satisfied by a short statement of the type of business which the company was formed to undertake. Thus, see Table F in which the objects are set out very briefly. However, modern practice is very different and the objects clause of most companies is two or three pages long with many sub-clauses.

The purpose of the objects clause is to define and limit the activities which the company is permitted to undertake. It defines the contractual parameters within which the company can contract.

Anything not authorised expressly or impliedly by the objects clause is *ultra vires* the company (the converse of *ultra vires* is *intra vires*). Literally, the words *ultra vires* mean 'beyond the powers'

> **Definition**   In company law the phrase '*ultra vires*' is used to describe transactions entered into by a company which are not within the capacity of the company as delimited expressly or impliedly by the company's objects clause.

Ashbury Railway Carriage v Riche [1875]

Facts: The **objects clause** of the company set out **purpose** of the company as the making and selling of railway carriages. The company entered into a contract to purchase a concession for constructing a railway.

Held: The contract was *ultra vires* and beyond the capacity of the company.

In addition to the **matters set out expressly** in the objects clause, a company has **implied powers** to do things incidental or consequential to carrying out the stated matters: For example the implied powers of a trading company will include the power to borrow for the purpose of business, and to pledge its assets as security for loans. Other implied powers include powers to employ staff, pay wages, gratuities and pensions, to sell assets and to institute or defend legal proceedings. However, it is common for an objects clause to expressly list powers as well as objects.

Rolled Steel v British Steel Corporation [1985]

Facts: the objects clause contained a number of sub-clauses:

(A)   To carry on business or businesses as exporters and importers of, and manufacturers of, and dealers in, and buying and selling agents for, iron, steel, copper, bronze, aluminium, lead, tin, zinc and other metal goods of all descriptions . . ..

(K)   To lend and advance money or give credit to such persons, firms or companies and on such terms as may seem expedient . . . and to give guarantees . . ..

Held: clause A contained an object. Clause K contained two powers (to loan money, to give guarantees). Since the objects clause allowed guarantees any guarantee was *intra vires* the company, albeit only a power and despite the fact that the particular guarantee resulted in no benefit to the company's actual business of steel retailing.

4.2   Alteration of the objects clause

In practice, a company which makes extensive changes in the nature of its business will be advised to bring its objects clause into line with the new situation by exercising the statutory power of alteration. A lender may stipulate that the borrower's objects clause shall be altered to the satisfaction of their advisers as a precondition of their loan.

The powers of alteration are of much practical importance and application where the inadequacy of the existing objects clause is realised before the transaction takes place, but alteration will **not operate retrospectively to make** an *ultra vires* transaction *intra vires*.

S4 CA85 as amended by CA89 permits a company, by special resolution, to alter its objects clause. However S5 CA85 gives a right of objection on the following terms:

(a)   Objection may be made by members, holding at least **15% of the issued shares or of some class of shares** or certain debentures, who did not vote in favour of the resolution.

(b)   Objection to be made by application to the court **within twenty-one days** of the passing of the resolution.

(c)   The court has power to confirm or cancel the proposed alteration or to impose a compromise. It might, for example, require the company to adopt some name suitable to its altered objects or to give security to debenture holders. In particular, the court is empowered to provide for the purchase by the company of members' shares and the consequent reduction of capital and can make the necessary alterations to the memorandum and articles.

The company must wait twenty-one days to see whether objection will be raised. It then has fifteen days in which to file at the Companies Registry a copy of the memorandum as amended. If application is made by the objectors to the court there is a similar period of fifteen days for filing after the court has given its decision (unless, of course, the alteration is completely rejected by the court).

4.3   Effect of an *ultra vires* transaction

(a)   **Introduction**

At common law an *ultra vires* transaction is void. However, beginning in 1972 this rule has been changed in stages by statute, culminating in 1989 when the CA89 rewrote S35 CA85 to provide that an *ultra vires* transaction is not void for being *ultra vires*. Many of the existing cases, therefore, now remain relevant only to the extent of deciding whether a transaction is *intra* or *ultra vires* and not as to the legal effect of an *ultra vires* transaction.

(b)   **S35   CA85 (as amended by CA89): A company's capacity is not limited by its memorandum.**

ss1   The validity of an act done by a company shall not be called into question on the ground of lack of capacity by reason of anything in the company's memorandum.

ss2   A member of a company may bring proceedings to restrain the doing of an act which but for subsection (1) would be beyond the company's capacity; but no such proceedings shall lie in respect of an act to be done in fulfilment of a legal obligation arising from a previous act of the company.

ss3   It remains the duty of the directors to observe any limitations on their powers flowing from the company's memorandum; and action by the directors which but for subsection (1) would be beyond the company's capacity may only be ratified by the company by special resolution.

A resolution ratifying such action shall not affect any liability incurred by the directors or any other person ; relief from any such liability must be agreed to separately by special resolution.

Thus it would appear, that:

- once the contract has been made neither the outsider nor the company may challenge it on the ground that it is *ultra vires;*

- the directors commit a breach of duty for which the company may sue them. The members could choose to relieve the directors from liability by special resolution;

- the company may, by special resolution, ratify an *ultra vires* transaction and thereby enforce it against third party even though the directors are committing a breach of duty;

- even in the absence of a ratifying special resolution, the third party may enforce the contract against the company if he is in good faith (this is S35A CA85, covered in the later chapter 'Corporate management: the board');

- a member may obtain an injunction to prevent the directors from entering into an *ultra vires* transaction.

(c)   **Failure of the substratum**

Where a company is not carrying on a business as covered by the objects clause, a member can petition the court for a winding up order on the grounds that as the substratum of the company has failed it is just and equitable to bring the company to an end: S122(g) Insolvency Act 1986 (IA86). This might provide a member with an alternative remedy to an injunction if a company is committing an *ultra vires* act which is evidence of failure of the substratum.

Re German Date Coffee Co [1882]

Facts: There was failure to carry out the object of making coffee from dates by means of a German patent (although the company did manufacture it with a Swedish patent).

Held: The company would be wound up.

For a member to succeed under S122(g) IA86 all the main objects of the company must have failed.

Re Kitson & Co. [1946]

Facts: The objects were to carry on the business of general engineering and to acquire a specific, existing business – the business was acquired but then sold. An application was made to wind up the company.

Held: This failed as the company was still intending to carry on a general engineering business.

4.4   Format of an objects clause

A company may choose to state (often in very great detail) its objects and its powers or it may take advantage of S3A CA85 (inserted in 1989) to state its objects in very general terms.

S3A CA85 allows a company's objects clause to state that its object is **to carry on business as a general commercial company.** S3A explains this as meaning:

(a)   the object of the company is to carry on any trade or business whatsoever; and

(b)   the company has power to do all such things as are incidental or conducive to the carrying on of any trade or business by it.

Many companies (both newly incorporated and pre-existing) have chosen not to have the new S3A format. It is therefore necessary to examine the court's interpretation of detailed objects clauses.

4.5   Company practice - courts' interpretation

(a)   **Strict interpretation**

The approach of the courts is to interpret the wording of an objects clause very restrictively. For example in **Ashbury Railway Carriage v Riche** it was held that building railway carriages did not encompass building a railway line. For example in **Re German Date Coffee** it was held that making coffee from dates using a German patent meant that making coffee from dates using a Swedish patent was *ultra vires*.

(b)   **Many sub-clauses**

This attitude of the courts led to companies drafting very long clauses attempting to cover just about every conceivable activity (both powers being included as well as objects) the company might wish to engage in.

(c)   **Rules of construction**

However, the courts subverted this practice by the use of two rules of construction.

*   the **main objects rule of construction.** By this rule the courts identified, as the main objects of the company, the activities described in the opening paragraphs of the objets clause with the result that businesses in later sub-clauses would be *ultra vires* unless carried on as an adjunct of the main business.

*   the **eiusdem generis rule of construction.** By this rule the courts restrict the meaning of general words following on after specific words to the same kind of thing as the specific words.

(d)   **The independent clause**

This clause is usually inserted as the last sub-clause and is intended to prevent use of the main objects rule of construction and of the eiusdem generis rule of construction.

A typical such independent clause is the following taken from the Memorandum of British Telecommunications plc.

. . . AND IT IS HEREBY DECLARED . . .

References to 'other' and 'otherwise' shall not be construed eiusdem generis where a wider construction is possible . . .   The objects of the company as specified in each of the foregoing paragraphs of this Clause 4 of this Memorandum of Association (except only if and so far as otherwise expressly provided in any paragraph) shall be separate and distinct objects of the company and shall not be in any way limited or restricted by reference to or inference from the terms of any other paragraph or the order in which the same occur or the name of the company and none of the paragraphs shall be deemed merely subsidiary or incidental to any other paragraph. . . .

The validity of this type of clause, known variously as an independent clause, a separate clause, or a **Cotman v Brougham** clause, was tested in the leading case of:

Cotman v Brougham [1918]

Facts: The objects clause contained thirty subclauses which enabled the company to carry on a number of types of business.   The first sub-clause authorised it to develop rubber plantations.   The twelfth sub-clause authorised it to deal in shares in other companies.   The final sub-clause stated that each sub-clause was to be construed as a substantive clause, and not limited or restricted by reference to the other sub-clauses, and none of the sub-clauses were to be deemed to be subsidiary to the objects in the first sub-clause.   The company underwrote shares in an asphalt company and had shares allotted to it.   It was argued that the contract for the allotment was *ultra vires*.

Held: The 'independent objects sub-clause' was valid and, therefore, the contract was not *ultra vires*.

(e)   **Objects and powers**

The courts also reduced the effect of the wide drafting of objects clauses by construing some sub-clauses as objects and some sub-clauses as powers.   This approach is based on the concept that some activities, because of their very nature, cannot stand as independent objects but must confer 'mere powers'.   Generally, an object is an activity which is an end in itself eg, manufacturing and selling cars, and a power is an activity which can only be carried out to achieve some purpose eg, borrowing money must be done for some purpose.

A clause allowing a company to borrow money can only ever be a power, not an object, and it therefore follows that an independent clause cannot convert such a power into an object - **Introductions Ltd v NPB [1970]**.

Some activities are, however, theoretically capable of being either objects or powers.   In this situation whether a sub-clause is an 'object' or 'power' will depend on the construction of the memorandum in each case.

This distinction is important, not for the purpose of the capacity of the company but for the purpose of directors' duties - directors commit a breach of duty if they abuse the company's powers.

Rolled Steel v BSC [1985]

Facts: the objects clause contained a number of sub-clauses:

(A)   To carry on business or businesses as exporters and importers of, and manufacturers of, and dealers in, and buying and selling agents for, iron, steel, copper, bronze, aluminium, lead, tin, zinc and other metal goods of all descriptions . . ..

(K)   To lend and advance money or give credit to such persons, firms or companies and on such terms as may seem expedient . . . and to give guarantees . . ..

The objects clause also contained the usual form 'independent' clause.

The director of RS caused it to give a guarantee to BSC for money which another company, SSS, owed to BSC. This guarantee conferred no benefit on RS: it did however benefit BSC, SSS and the director of RS (because he was also director and shareholder of SSS).

During the subsequent liquidation of RS, the liquidator challenged the validity of the guarantee.

Held:

(1)   On a proper construction and despite the independent clause the giving of guarantees was a power not an object.

(2)   Nevertheless, by virtue of this express power, the guarantee was *intra vires* the company.

(3)   However, the director was abusing RS's powers since the guarantee conferred no benefit on RS as it was not exercised in furtherance of RS's business.

(4)   Since BSC knew of this abuse the guarantee was voidable by RS, and therefore could not be enforced against the liquidator.

> *Note:* since the decision in the Rolled Steel case S35A CA85 (inserted by CA89) became law and may have an impact on this part of the judgement. S35A is considered in the later chapter 'Corporate management: the board'.

(f)   **The subjective clause**

Another development by companies in an attempt to widen the scope of a company's authorised activities is to include a sub-clause 'to carry on any other trade or business whatsoever, which can, in the honest opinion of the board of directors, be advantageously carried on by the company in connection with, or ancillary to ... the general business of the company'. This type of clause is known as a **subjective objects clause**. This quote is taken from the objects clause of a company Bell Houses Ltd which was challenged in the leading case of:

Bell Houses Ltd v City Wall Properties Ltd [1966]

Facts: Bell Houses Ltd's main business was property development. Its objects clause contained as a subclause the words quoted above. A contract was entered into with City Wall Properties Ltd., under which Bell Houses Ltd would introduce City Wall Properties Ltd to financiers to enable it to obtain finance. Bell Houses Ltd charged a fee for this service. City Wall Properties Ltd having agreed to pay the fee then refused on the grounds that it was *ultra vires* as the arranging of finance was not one of the objects of Bell Houses Ltd. Bell Houses Ltd argued that the contract was covered by the 'subjective objects clause' as the decision to enter the contract was one which the person having the management powers of the board had considered could be advantageously carried on with the general business of the company.

Held: The Court of Appeal upheld the validity of such a sub-clause.

The effect of the subjective objects clause is restricted by the need to have an existing business (covered by express objects) with which to combine the new activity.

Summary and conclusion

Some companies will have a short objects clause in the format permitted by S3A CA 1985: the effect of which is to entitle it to carry on any business whatsoever. Other companies' objects clauses will achieve the same result by virtue of length, and careful drafting.

4.6   Activity

Stephen is setting up a private limited company for the purpose of the repair, and retailing of tyres and all other associated activities. He has heard of the *ultra vires doctrine* and is concerned to draft the memorandum to ensure that any legal difficulties are kept to a minimum.

How would you advise him?

4.7   Activity solution

The doctrine of *ultra vires* means that any transactions entered into which are not permitted by the company's objects clause are in principle void. These days the effect on a third party, or even the company, has been largely nullified by the Companies Acts.

However acting *ultra vires* is a breach of the director's duty to manage the company in accordance with the constitution.

Stephen should therefore be advised as follows:

(1)   Register with the object of carrying on business as a 'general commercial company', which allows it to carry on any trade or business whatsoever.

(2)   Include specific clauses to cover all intended and foreseeable activities of the company.

(3)   When limiting activities in a single clause and concluding with a general statement, bear in mind the effect of the eiusdem generis rule.

(4)   Use a **Cotman v Brougham** clause to ensure that all businesses described in separate clauses are treaded as substantive clauses.

(5)   Consider the use of a 'subjective objects clause' as in the **Bell Houses** case.

4.8   Provision for employees

At common law it was established that a company could have implied powers to pay employees gratuities and pensions while the company was a going concern provided it was for the benefit of the company to do so. This was distinguished in:

Parke v Daily News [1962]

Facts: A bonus payment to employees who were redundant on the closing down of the entire business.

Held: It was *ultra vires* as it could not be said to be in the interests of the company.

Note: even if the company's objects clause had contained an express power to make bonus payments to employees the exercise of the power would have been a breach of directors duties to act in the interests of the company because it could not be said that such payments benefited a company whose entire business was closed. Contrast the situation if, for example, some only of the employees are being made redundant: it is strongly arguable that a perceivably generous employer would have the effect of promoting good industrial labour relations with those remaining.

Two statutory provisions now affect employees:

(a)   S309 CA85 requires the directors to have regard to the interest of the employees generally although it reiterates that the directors' duty is to the company. The precise meaning of this provision is not clear.

(b)   S719 CA85 which reverses the effect of **Parke v Daily News** and provides that a company's powers include power to make provision for the benefit of employees of the company or subsidiary on the cessation or transfer of the whole or part of the company's (or subsidiary's) undertaking. This statutory power is exercisable even though its exercise is not in the best interests of the company but may only be exercised by:

(i)   ordinary resolution of the members; or

(ii)   if the memorandum or articles require sanction by the members otherwise than by ordinary resolution, by the sanction so required; or

(iii)   if the memorandum or articles delegate the power to directors, by resolution of the directors.

Such payment under S719 CA85 may be made only out of assets available for members ie, distributable profit. This is to protect creditors.

5   SELF TEST QUESTIONS

5.1   List the 6 clauses which must be contained in the Memorandum of a private limited company. (1.2)

5.2   List the 7 clauses which must be contained in the Memorandum of a public limited company. (1.2)

5.3   What type of resolution is normally necessary to increase authorised capital? (1.8)

5.4   What two categories of name require approval of the Secretary of State? (2.1)

5.5   How does a company change its name? (2.4)

5.6   Who is liable and on what authority for a pre-incorporation contract? (3.2)

5.7   The phrase *ultra vires* literally means 'beyond the powers', but what does it mean in relation to company law? (4.1)

5.8   How can a company alter its objects clause? (4.2)

5.9   What is the purpose of the objects clause and what is the effect of breaching it? (4.3)

5.10   What is the effect of a 'general commercial company clause'? (4.4)

5.11   What is the effect of a **Bell Houses** clause? (4.5)

6   EXAMINATION TYPE QUESTIONS

6.1   Plum Pie Ltd

(a)   The directors of Plum Pie Ltd wish to change the name of the company to Apple Pie Ltd.

What procedure should they adopt, and what requirements must be satisfied?

(5 marks)

(b)   Bubble Ltd wishes to trade as South Birmingham Pigeon Breeders.

What requirements must be satisfied?

(5 marks)

(Total: 10 marks)

6.2   Don plc

Don plc, has as its main object the business of travel agents, but there are subsidiary objects including one which authorises the company 'to borrow money' and another which permits the company 'to carry on any business which the directors consider to be profitable'. The travel agency has closed and the directors have now approached Money Bank for a loan to build a factory for the manufacture of shoes.

Discuss the position of the bank.

(6 marks)

6.3   Alteration of objects clause

How, and to what extent, may a company alter its objects clause, and what are the rights of a shareholder who disagrees with an alteration?

(6 marks)

7   ANSWERS TO EXAMINATION TYPE QUESTIONS

7.1   Plum Pie Ltd

(a)   A company may change its name of its own initiative by passing a special resolution (75%) and without obtaining Department of Trade approval. However, the change does not take effect until the registrar issues a certificate of incorporation under the new name, which will only be issued if the restrictions imposed when the company is incorporated have been complied with.

A company may not have a name which likely to mislead the public as to its real status or activities or have offensive or criminal connotations. Certain words would also require Department of Trade approval.

The directors should first check that no company is **registered** with a similar name and then call an extraordinary general meeting of members, or put a resolution to the next AGM resolving that the name be changed. Plum Pie Ltd could then change its name to Apple Pie Ltd by passing a special resolution and applying for a new certificate of incorporation which would be granted provided the alteration was not misleading as to the company's activities.

(b)   A company is not obliged to trade under its own name. If it elects to carry on business under a different name, then like any other person in that situation, it must comply with the rules on 'business names'.

The Business Names Act 1985 regulates the use of business names. A company is subject to these rules if it carries on business under a name which does not consist of it corporate name without any addition. It must state its company name on all business letters, written orders for goods or services, invoices, receipts or written demands for payment of debts and display its company name in a prominent position so that it may easily be read at all premises where the name is carried and to which customers or suppliers have access: S4 BNA 1985.

In addition, certain sensitive words may not be included in a company name without official approval. This prevents a company which has been refused a company name from getting around the bar by trading under a similar business name.

Bubble may therefore trade under a business name provided it displays all the required information. It may however require approval for its proposed name as the word 'breeder' is a regulated word which requires clearance from the Ministry of Agriculture. If approval is given, the company may then trade under its business name.

Note:

(1)   Note that parts (a) and (b) are separately answered and properly labelled.

(2)   In a problem question it is standard practice to set out the law first and then apply it to the facts of the question. Note that in both (a) and (b) the last paragraph of each applied the law as stated in the earlier paragraph adding any relevant detail.

(3)   A plan for this answer could be:

(a)   Change by special resolution when effective prohibitions on names selected

application   - check name acceptable
               - call meeting
               - apply for new certificate of incorporation

(b)   Can trade under another name - 'business name'

BNA 1985   - when apply
               - requirements
               - prohibitions on choosing - like (a)

Application   - can - if display
               - obtain consent

When answering questions try to state the law first and then apply it. If you find this too difficult then you must nevertheless ensure that you state the legal principles clearly and do not just given an answer without stating the principles on which you reach your conclusion. You will see that model answers vary in the method of approach - some stating legal principles first and then applying them and others applying the legal principles as they are stated.

(4)   In this question you could not be expected to know that the word 'breeder' is a regulated word. However, you would be expected to know that there are regulated words and this it is essential to obtain approval for such words. Thus a satisfactory alternative would be - 'The use of the words 'pigeon' or 'breeder' may require approval. If so this must be obtained.' Obviously if you did know it was a regulated name you should say so.

7.2   Don plc

A company can only do those things stated in its objects clause or ancillary to those objects – otherwise it is acting *ultra vires:* **Ashbury Railway Carriage v Riche.**

The question describes the other two objects as **subsidiary.** This probably is to be taken to mean that there is no independent object clause declaring all the clauses to be independent and not subsidiary or ancillary: **Cotman v Brougham.** Even if there were such an independent objects clause it seems that an inherently subsidiary power to borrow cannot be converted into an independent object. In **Rolled Steel** it was held that exercise of an express power for a purpose not ancillary to the objects would not be *ultra vires* but could be an abuse of power. A clause similar to the one which permits the company to carry on any profitable business was upheld in **Bell Houses v City Wall Properties;** thus the new activity might come within this clause and be *intra vires* in which case the bank could sue to recover any loan made.

Even if the contract is *ultra vires,* S35 Companies Act 1985 (CA85) (as amended by CA89) provides that an act done or promise given cannot later be challenged on the grounds that it is not within the objects clause. However a member may restrain an action not yet taken and the company could sue the directors for breach of duty if the company is bound.

7.3   Alteration of objects clause

An alteration of objects may be made under (S4 Companies Act 1985 (CA85)) by special resolution. A company may not alter its objects to validate retrospectively an *ultra vires* transaction **(Ashbury Railway Carriage Co v Riche).** Although it used to be necessary to specify certain grounds on which the alteration was made under CA89 the grounds have been removed. The company can alter its objects clause for any reason and to any extent.

Holders of   15% in nominal value of the company's issued share capital or any class thereof; or

15% in number of the company's members, if the company is not limited by shares;

may object to the court within twenty-one days of the date of the authorising resolution. The court will do as it thinks fit.

20 COMPANY FORMATION: ARTICLES OF ASSOCIATION

INTRODUCTION & LEARNING OBJECTIVES

Syllabus area 8e. Articles of association. (Ability required 2)

The articles are one of the two critical documents of incorporation and are examined on a fairly regular basis. It is important to know how S14 CA85 impacts upon the members and how the articles can be altered.

It is important to know the principal contents of Table A, as this gives an indication of the matters usually dealt with in a company's articles of association.

When you have studied this chapter you should be able to do the following:

- Identify the principal provisions of Table A or other properly drafted articles.

- Understand the legal effect of the articles.

- Describe how a company may alter its articles and outline the main restrictions on such alterations.

1 TABLE A

Definition   Table A is a model or standard set of articles laid down in the Companies Acts. The latest is contained in a statutory instrument made in 1985. It will apply to all companies limited by shares unless it is expressly excluded.

1.1 Introduction

Every company must have a memorandum and every unlimited company or company limited by guarantee must also have articles. Companies with a share capital must have articles or be subject to Table A.

A company limited by shares may either have its own special articles or, alternatively, it can adopt or allow Table A to apply wholly or in part: S8 Companies Act 1985 (CA85). There are the following alternatives:

(a)   a company may have its own articles and expressly exclude Table A from applying;

(b)   a company may expressly adopt Table A with or without alterations and exclusions; and

(c)   in any other case ie, if the company neither excludes nor adopts Table A, then Table A applies to the extent that any articles of the company fail to provide for matters covered by Table A.

It is not necessary to learn Table A but this examination text contains numerous references to it. You should be familiar with the main topics covered by Table A or any other properly drafted articles; these topics are the issue and transfer of **shares** and the rights attached to them, company **meetings** and the appointment, powers and proceedings of **directors**.

1.2   Table A (SI 1985/805)

The following regulations are those set out in Table A (1985 version). **There is no need to learn them** but it is useful, for reference purposes, to have the provisions of Table A available, as they govern the internal operations of many companies and in the absence of specific provisions in questions you are to assume that the articles are those in Table A. It would be useful to read once through them quickly now to gain an understanding of what is included.

Article 1 - contains definitions (not reproduced).

Articles 2 - 118 are the regulations and are reproduced below.

Share capital

2.   Subject to the provisions of the Act and without prejudice to any rights attached to any existing shares, any share may be issued with such rights or restrictions as the company may by ordinary resolution determine.

3.   Subject to the provisions of the Act, shares may be issued which are to be redeemed or are to be liable to be redeemed at the option of the company or the holder on such terms and in such manner as may be provided by the articles.

4.   The company may exercise the powers of paying commissions conferred by the Act. Subject to the provisions of the Act, any such commission may be satisfied by the payment of cash or by the allotment of fully or partly paid shares or partly in one way and partly in the other.

5.   Except as required by law, no person shall be recognised by the company as holding any share upon any trust and (except as otherwise provided by the articles or by law) the company shall not be bound by or recognise any interest in any share except an absolute right to the entirety thereof in the holder.

Share certificates

6.   Every member, upon becoming the holder of any shares, shall be entitled without payment to one certificate for all the shares of each class held by him (and, upon transferring a part of his holding of shares of any class, to a certificate for the balance of such holding) or several certificates each for one or more of his shares upon payment for every certificate after the first of such reasonable sum as the directors may determine. Every certificate shall be sealed with the seal and shall specify the number, class and distinguishing numbers (if any) of the shares to which it relates and the amount or respective amounts paid up thereon. The company shall not be bound to issue more than one certificate for shares held jointly by several persons and delivery of a certificate to one joint holder shall be sufficient delivery to all of them.

7.   If a share certificate is defaced, worn-out, lost or destroyed, it may be renewed on such terms (if any) as to evidence and indemnity and payment of the expenses reasonably incurred by the company in investigating evidence as the directors may determine but otherwise free of charge, and (in the case of defacement or wearing-out) on delivery up of the old certificate.

Lien

8.   The company shall have a first and paramount lien on every share (not being a fully paid share) for all moneys (whether presently payable or not) payable at a fixed time or called in respect of that share. The directors may at any time declare any share to be wholly or in part exempt from the provisions of this regulation. The company's lien on a share shall extend to any amount payable in respect of it.

9.   The company may sell in such manner as the directors determine any shares on which the company has a lien if a sum in respect of which the lien exists is presently payable and is not paid within fourteen clear days after notice has been given to the holder of the share or to the person entitled to it in consequence of the death or bankruptcy of the holder, demanding payment and stating that if the notice is not complied with the shares may be sold.

10.   To give effect to a sale the directors may authorise some person to execute an instrument of transfer of the shares sold to, or in accordance with the directions of, the purchaser. The title of the transferee to the shares shall not be affected by any irregularity in or invalidity of the proceedings in reference to the sale.

11.   The net proceeds of the sale, after payment of the costs, shall be applied in payment of so much of the sum for which the lien exists as is presently payable, and any residue shall (upon surrender to the company for cancellation of the certificate for the shares sold and subject to a like lien for any moneys not presently payable as existed upon the shares before the sale) be paid to the person entitled to the shares at the date of the sale.

Calls on shares and forfeiture

12.   Subject to the terms of allotment, the directors may make calls upon the members in respect of any moneys unpaid on their shares (whether in respect of nominal value or premium) and each member shall (subject to receiving at least fourteen clear days' notice specifying when and where payment is to be made) pay to the company as required by the notice the amount called on his shares. A call may be required to be paid by instalments. A call may, before receipt by the company of any sum due thereunder, be revoked in whole or part and payment of a call may be postponed in whole or part. A person upon whom a call is made shall remain liable for calls made upon him notwithstanding the subsequent transfer of the shares in respect whereof the call was made.

13.   A call shall be deemed to have been made at the time when the resolution of the directors authorising the call was passed.

14.   The joint holders of a share shall be jointly and severally liable to pay all calls in respect thereof.

15.   If a call remains unpaid after it has become due and payable the person from whom it is due and payable shall pay interest on the amount unpaid from the day it became due and payable until it is paid at the rate fixed by the terms of allotment of the share or in the notice of the call or, if no rate is fixed, at the appropriate rate (as defined by the Act) but the directors may waive payment of the interest wholly or in part.

16.   An amount payable in respect of a share on allotment or at any fixed date, whether in respect of nominal value or premium or as an instalment of a call, shall be deemed to be a call and if it is not paid the provisions of the articles shall apply as if that amount had become due and payable by virtue of a call.

17.   Subject to the terms of allotment, the directors may make arrangements on the issue of shares for a difference between the holders in the amounts and times of payment on calls of their shares.

18.   If a call remains unpaid after it has become due and payable the directors may give to the person from whom it is due not less than fourteen clear days' notice requiring payment of the amount unpaid together with any interest which may have accrued. The notice shall name the place where payment is to be made and shall state that if the notice is not complied with the shares in respect of which the call was made will be liable to be forfeited.

19.   If the notice is not complied with any share in respect of which it was given may, before the payment required by the notice has been made, be forfeited by a resolution of the directors and the forfeiture shall include all dividends or other moneys payable in respect of the forfeited shares and not paid before the forfeiture.

20.   Subject to the provisions of the Act, a forfeited share may be sold, re-allotted or otherwise disposed of on such terms and in such manner as the directors determine either to the person who was before the forfeiture the holder or to any other person and at any time before sale, re-allotment or other disposition, the forfeiture may be cancelled on such terms as the directors think fit. Where for the purposes of its disposal a forfeited share is to be transferred to any person the directors may authorise some person to execute an instrument of transfer of the share to that person.

21.   A person any of whose shares have been forfeited shall cease to be a member in respect of them and shall surrender to the company for cancellation the certificate for the shares forfeited but shall remain liable to the company for all moneys which at the date of forfeiture were presently payable by him to the company in respect of those shares with interest at the rate at which interest was payable on those moneys before the forfeiture or, if no interest was so payable, at the appropriate rate (as defined in the Act) from the date of forfeiture until payment but the directors may waive payment wholly or in part or enforce payment without any allowance for the value of the shares at the time of forfeiture or for any consideration received on their disposal.

22.   A statutory declaration by a director or the secretary that a share has been forfeited on a specified date shall be conclusive evidence of the facts stated in it as against all persons claiming to be entitled to the share and the declaration shall (subject to the execution of an instrument of transfer if necessary) constitute a good title to the share and the person to whom the share is disposed of shall not be bound to see to the application of the consideration, if any, nor shall his title to the share be affected by any irregularity in or invalidity of the proceedings in reference to the forfeiture or disposal of the share.

Transfer of shares

23.   The instrument of transfer of a share may be in any usual form or in any other form which the directors may approve and shall be executed by or on behalf of the transferor and, unless the share is fully paid, by or on behalf of the transferee.

24.   The directors may refuse to register the transfer of a share which is not fully paid to a person of whom they do not approve and they may refuse to register the transfer of a share on which the company has a lien. They may also refuse to register a transfer unless:

(a)   it is lodged at the office or at such other place as the directors may appoint and is accompanied by the certificate for the shares to which it relates and such other evidence as the directors may reasonably require to show the right of the transferor to make the transfer;

 (b) it is in respect of only one class of shares; and

 (c) it is in favour of not more than four transferees.

25. If the directors refuse to register a transfer of a share, they shall within two months after the date on which the transfer was lodged with the company send to the transferee notice of the refusal.

26. The registration of transfers of shares or of transfers of any class of shares may be suspended at such times and for such periods (not exceeding thirty days in any year) as the directors may determine.

27. No fee shall be charged for the registration of any instrument of transfer or other document relating to or affecting the title to any share.

28. The company shall be entitled to retain any instrument of transfer which is registered, but any instrument of transfer which the directors refuse to register shall be returned to the person lodging it when notice of the refusal is given.

Transmission of shares

29. If a member dies the survivor or survivors where he was a joint holder, and his personal representatives where he was a sole holder or the only survivor of joint holders, shall be the only persons recognised by the company as having any title to his interest; but nothing herein contained shall release the estate of a deceased member from any liability in respect of any share which had been jointly held by him.

30. A person becoming entitled to a share in consequence of the death or bankruptcy of a member may, upon such evidence being produced as the directors may properly require, elect either to become the holder of the share or to have some person nominated by him registered as the transferee. If he elects to become the holder he shall give notice to the company to that effect. If he elects to have another person registered he shall execute an instrument of transfer of the share to that person. All the articles relating to the transfer of shares shall apply to the notice or instrument of transfer as if it were an instrument of transfer executed by the member and the death or bankruptcy of the member had not occurred.

31. A person becoming entitled to a share in consequence of the death or bankruptcy of a member shall have the rights to which he would be entitled if he were the holder of the share, except that he shall not, before being registered as the holder of the share, be entitled in respect of it to attend or vote at any meeting of the company or at any separate meeting of the holders of any class of shares in the company.

Alteration of share capital

32. The company may by ordinary resolution:

 (a) increase its share capital by new shares of such amount as the resolution prescribes;

 (b) consolidate and divide all or any of its share capital into shares of larger amount than its existing shares;

(c)   subject to the provisions of the Act, sub-divide its shares, or any of them, into shares of smaller amount and the resolution may determine that, as between the shares resulting from the sub-division, any of them may have any preference or advantage as compared with the others; and

(d)   cancel shares which, at the date of the passing of the resolution, have not been taken or agreed to be taken by any person and diminish the amount of its share capital by the amount of the shares so cancelled.

33.   Whenever as a result of a consolidation of shares any members would become entitled to fractions of a share, the directors may, on behalf of those members, sell the shares representing the fractions for the best price reasonably obtainable to any person (including, subject to the provisions of the Act, the company) and distribute the net proceeds of sale in due proportion among those members, and the directors may authorise some person to execute an instrument of transfer of the shares to, or in accordance with the directions of, the purchaser. The transferee shall not be bound to see to the application of the purchase money nor shall his title to the shares be affected by any irregularity in or invalidity of the proceedings in reference to the sale.

34.   Subject to the provisions of the Act, the company may by special resolution reduce its share capital, any capital redemption reserve and any share premium account in any way.

Purchase of own shares

35.   Subject to the provisions of the Act, the company may purchase its own shares (including any redeemable shares) and, if it is a private company, make a payment in respect of the redemption or purchase of its own shares otherwise than out of distributable profits of the company or the proceeds of a fresh issue of shares.

General meetings

36.   All general meetings other than annual general meetings shall be called extraordinary general meetings.

37.   The directors may call general meetings and, on the requisition of members pursuant to the provisions of the Act, shall forthwith proceed to convene an extraordinary general meeting for a date not later than eight weeks after receipt of the requisition. If there are not within the United Kingdom sufficient directors to call a general meeting, any director or any member of the company may call a general meeting.

Notice of general meetings

38.   An annual general meeting and an extraordinary general meeting called for the passing of a special resolution or a resolution appointing a person as a director shall be called by at least twenty-one clear days' notice. All other extraordinary general meetings shall be called by at least fourteen days' notice but a general meeting may be called by shorter notice if it is so agreed:

(a)   in the case of an annual general meeting, by all the members entitled to attend and vote thereat; and

(b)   in the case of any other meeting by a majority in number of the members having a right to attend and vote being a majority together holding not less than ninety-five per cent in nominal value of the shares giving that right.

The notice shall specify the time and place of the meeting and the general nature of the business to be transacted and, in the case of an annual general meeting, shall specify the meeting as such.

Subject to the provisions of the articles and to any restrictions imposed on any shares, the notice shall be given to all the members, to all persons entitled to a share in consequence of the death or bankruptcy of a member and to the directors and auditors.

39   The accidental omission to give notice of a meeting to, or the non-receipt of notice of a meeting by, any person entitled to receive notice shall not invalidate the proceedings at that meeting.

Proceedings at general meetings

40   No business shall be transacted at any meeting unless a quorum is present. Two persons entitled to vote upon the business to be transacted, each being a member or a proxy for a member or a duly authorised representative of a corporation, shall be a quorum.

41   If such a quorum is not present within half an hour from the time appointed for the meeting, or if during a meeting such a quorum ceases to be present, the meeting shall stand adjourned to the same day in the next week at the same time and place or to such time and place as the directors may determine.

42.   The chairman, if any, of the board of directors or in his absence some other director nominated by the directors shall preside as chairman of the meeting, but if neither the chairman nor such other director (if any) be present within fifteen minutes after the time appointed for holding the meeting and willing to act, the directors present shall elect one of their number to be chairman and, if there is only one director present and willing to act, he shall be chairman.

43.   If no director is willing to act as chairman, or if no director is present within fifteen minutes after the time appointed for holding the meeting, the members present and entitled to vote shall choose one of their number to be chairman.

44.   A director shall, notwithstanding that he is not a member, be entitled to attend and speak at any general meeting and at any separate meeting of the holders of any class of shares in the company.

45.   The chairman may, with the consent of a meeting at which a quorum is present (and shall if so directed by the meeting), adjourn the meeting from time to time and from place to place, but no business shall be transacted at an adjourned meeting other than business which might properly have been transacted at the meeting had the adjournment not taken place. When a meeting is adjourned for fourteen days or more, at least seven clear days' notice shall be given specifying the time and place of the adjourned meeting and the general nature of the business to be transacted. Otherwise it shall not be necessary to give any such notice.

46.   A resolution put to the vote of a meeting shall be decided on a show of hands unless before, or on the declaration of the result of, the show of hands a poll is duly demanded. Subject to the provisions of the Act, a poll may be demanded:

    (a)   by the chairman; or

    (b)   by at least two members having the right to vote at the meeting; or

(c)   by a member or members representing not less than one-tenth of the total voting rights of all the members having the right to vote at the meeting; or

(d)   by a member or members holding shares conferring a right to vote at the meeting being shares on which an aggregate sum has been paid up equal to not less than one-tenth of the total sum paid up on all the shares conferring that right;

and a demand by a person as proxy for a member shall be the same as a demand by the member.

47.   Unless a poll is duly demanded a declaration by the chairman that a resolution has been carried or carried unanimously, or by a particular majority, or lost, or not carried by a particular majority and an entry to that effect in the minutes of the meeting shall be conclusive evidence of the fact without proof of the number or proportion of the votes recorded in favour of or against the resolution.

48.   The demand for a poll may, before the poll is taken, be withdrawn but only with the consent of the chairman and a demand so withdrawn shall not be taken to have invalidated the result of a show of hands declared before the demand was made.

49.   A poll shall be taken as the chairman directs and he may appoint scrutineers (who need not be members) and fix a time and place for declaring the result of the poll. The result of the poll shall be deemed to be the resolution of the meeting at which the poll was demanded.

50.   In the case of an equality of votes, whether on a show of hands or on a poll, the chairman shall be entitled to a casting vote in addition to any other vote he may have.

51.   A poll demanded on the election of a chairman or on a question of adjournment shall be taken forthwith. A poll demanded on any other question shall be taken either forthwith or at such time and place as the chairman directs not being more than thirty days after the poll is demanded. The demand for a poll shall not prevent the continuance of a meeting for the transaction of any business other than the question on which the poll was demanded. If a poll is demanded before the declaration of the result of a show of hands and the demand is duly withdrawn, the meeting shall continue as if the demand had not been made.

52.   No notice need be given of a poll not taken forthwith if the time and place at which it is to be taken are announced at the meeting at which it is demanded. In any other case at least seven clear days' notice shall be given specifying the time and place at which the poll is to be taken.

53.   A resolution in writing executed by or on behalf of each member who would have been entitled to vote upon it if it had been proposed at a general meeting at which he was present shall be as effectual as if it had been passed at a general meeting duly convened and held and may consist of several instruments in the like form each executed by or on behalf of one or more members.

Votes of members

54.   Subject to any rights or restrictions attached to any shares, on a show of hands every member who (being an individual) is present in person or (being a corporation) is present by a duly authorised representative, not being himself a member entitled to vote, shall have one vote and on a poll every member shall have one vote for every share of which he is the holder.

55.　In the case of joint holders the vote of the senior who tenders a vote, whether in person or by proxy, shall be accepted to the exclusion of the votes of the other joint holders; and seniority shall be determined by the order in which the names of the holders stand in the register of members.

56.　A member in respect of whom an order had been made by any court having jurisdiction (whether in the United Kingdom or elsewhere) in matters concerning mental disorder may vote, whether on a show of hands or on a poll, by his receiver, curator bonis or other person authorised in that behalf appointed by that court, and any such receiver, curator bonis or other person may, on a poll, vote by proxy. Evidence to the satisfaction of the directors of the authority of the person claiming to exercise the right to vote shall be deposited at the office, or at such other place as is specified in accordance with the articles for the deposit of instruments of proxy, not less than 48 hours before the time appointed for holding the meeting or adjourned meeting at which the right to vote is to be exercised and in default the right to vote shall not be exercisable.

57.　No member shall vote at any general meeting or at any separate meeting of the holders of any class of shares in the company, either in person or by proxy, in respect of any share held by him unless all moneys presently payable by him in respect of that share have been paid.

58.　No objection shall be raised to the qualification of any voter except at the meeting or adjourned meeting at which the vote objected to is tendered, and every vote not disallowed at the meeting shall be valid. Any objection made in due time shall be referred to the chairman whose decision shall be final and conclusive.

59.　On a poll votes may be given either personally or by proxy. A member may appoint more than one proxy to attend on the same occasion.

60.　An instrument appointing a proxy shall be in writing, executed by or on behalf of the appointor and shall be in the following form (or in a form as near thereto as circumstances allow or in any other form which is usual or which the directors may approve):

PLC and Limited

I/We, ..., of ...., being a member/members of the above-named company, hereby appoint .... of ...., or failing him, ... of ...., as my/our proxy to vote in my/our name(s) and on my/our behalf at the annual/extraordinary general meeting of the company to be held on .... 19 ..., and at any adjournment thereof.

Signed on .... 19 ...'

61.　Where it is desired to afford members an opportunity of instructing the proxy how he shall act the instrument appointing a proxy shall be in the following form (or in a form as near thereto as circumstances allow or in any other form which is usual or which the directors may approve):

PLC and Limited

I/We, ..., of ...., being a member/members of the above-named company, hereby appoint .... of .... or failing him, ... of ...., as my/our proxy to vote in my/our name(s) and on my/our behalf at the annual/extraordinary general meeting of the company to be held on .... 19 ..., and at any adjournment thereof.

This form is to be used in respect of the resolutions mentioned below as follows:

Resolution No.1 *for *against
Resolution No.2 *for *against

*Strike out whichever is not desired.

Unless otherwise instructed, the proxy may vote as he thinks fit or abstain from voting.

Signed this .... day of .... 19 ...'

62.   The instrument appointing a proxy and any authority under which it is executed or a copy of such authority certified notarially or in some other way approved by the directors may:

    (a)   be deposited at the office or at such other place within the United Kingdom as is specified in the notice convening the meeting or in any instrument of proxy sent out by the company in relation to the meeting not less than forty-eight hours before the time for holding the meeting or adjourned meeting at which the person named in the instrument proposes to vote; or

    (b)   in the case of a poll taken more than forty-eight hours after it is demanded, be deposited as aforesaid after the poll has been demanded and not less than twenty-four hours before the time appointed for the taking of the poll; or

    (c)   where the poll is not taken forthwith but is taken not more than forty-eight hours after it was demanded, be delivered at the meeting at which the poll was demanded to the chairman or to the secretary or to any director;

and an instrument of proxy which is not deposited or delivered in a manner so permitted shall be invalid.

63.   A vote given or poll demanded by proxy or by the duly authorised representative of a corporation shall be valid notwithstanding the previous determination of the authority of the person voting or demanding a poll unless notice of the determination was received by the company at the office or at such other place at which the instrument of proxy was duly deposited before the commencement of the meeting or adjourned meeting at which the vote is given or the poll demanded or (in the case of the poll taken otherwise than on the same day as the meeting or adjourned meeting) the time appointed for taking the poll.

Number of directors

64.   Unless otherwise determined by ordinary resolution, the number of directors (other than alternate directors) shall not be subject to any maximum but shall be not less than two.

Alternate directors

65.   Any director (other than an alternate director) may appoint any other director, or any other person approved by resolution of the directors and willing to act, to be an alternate director and may remove from office an alternate director so appointed by him.

66.   An alternate director shall be entitled to receive notice of all meetings of directors and of all meetings of committees of directors of which his appointor is a member, to attend and vote at any such meeting at which the director appointing him is not personally present, and generally to perform all the functions of his appointor as a director in his absence but shall not be entitled to receive any remuneration from the company for his services as an alternate director. But it shall not be necessary to give notice of such a meeting to an alternate director who is absent from the United Kingdom.

67.   An alternate director shall cease to be an alternate director if his appointor ceases to be a director; but, if a director retires by rotation or otherwise but is reappointed or deemed to have been reappointed at the meeting at which he retires, any appointment of an alternate director made by him which was in force immediately prior to his retirement shall continue after his reappointment.

68.   Any appointment or removal of an alternate director shall be by notice to the company signed by the director making or revoking the appointment or in any other manner approved by the directors.

69.   Save as otherwise provided in the articles, an alternate director shall be deemed for all purposes to be a director and shall alone be responsible for his own acts and defaults and he shall not be deemed to be the agent of the director appointing him.

Powers of directors

70.   Subject to the provisions of the Act, the memorandum and the articles and to any directions given by special resolution, the business of the company shall be managed by the directors who may exercise all the powers of the company. No alteration of the memorandum or articles and no such direction shall invalidate any prior act of the directors which would have been valid if that alteration had not been made or that direction had not been given. The powers given by this regulation shall not be limited by any special power given to the directors by the articles and a meeting of directors at which a quorum is present may exercise all powers exercisable by the directors.

71.   The directors may, by power of attorney or otherwise, appoint any person to be the agent of the company for such purposes and on such conditions as they determine, including authority for the agent to delegate all or any of his powers.

Delegation of directors' powers

72.   The directors may delegate any of their powers to any committee consisting of one or more directors. They may also delegate to any managing director or any director holding any other executive office such of their powers as they consider desirable to be exercised by him. Any such delegation may be made subject to any conditions the directors may impose, and either collaterally with or to the exclusion of their own powers and may be revoked or altered. Subject to any such conditions, the proceedings of a committee with two or more members shall be governed by the articles regulating the proceedings of directors so far as they are capable of applying.

Appointment and retirement of directors

73.   At the first annual general meeting all the directors shall retire from office, and at every subsequent annual general meeting one-third of the directors who are subject to retirement by rotation or, if their number is not three or a multiple of three, the number nearest to one-third shall retire from office; but, if there is only one director who is subject to retirement by rotation, he shall retire.

74.   Subject to the provisions of the Act, the directors to retire by rotation shall be those who have been longest in office since their last appointment or reappointment, but as between persons who became or were last reappointed directors on the same day those to retire shall (unless they otherwise agree among themselves) be determined by lot.

75.   If the company, at the meeting at which a director retires by rotation, does not fill the vacancy the retiring director shall, if willing to act, be deemed to have been reappointed unless at the meeting it is resolved not to fill the vacancy or unless a resolution for the reappointment of the director is put to the meeting and lost.

76.   No person other than a director retiring by rotation shall be appointed or reappointed a director at any general meeting unless:

   (a)   he is recommended by the directors; or

   (b)   not less than fourteen nor more than thirty-five clear days before the date appointed for the meeting, notice executed by a member qualified to vote at the meeting has been given to the company of the intention to propose that person for appointment or reappointment stating the particulars which would, if he were so appointed or reappointed, be required to be included in the company's register of directors together with notice executed by the person of his willingness to be appointed or reappointed.

77.   Not less than seven nor more than twenty-eight clear days before the date appointed for holding a general meeting notice shall be given to all who are entitled to receive notice of the meeting of any person (other than a director retiring by rotation at the meeting) who is recommended by the directors for appointment or reappointment as a director at the meeting or in respect of whom notice has been duly given to the company of the intention to propose him at the meeting for appointment or reappointment as a director. The notice shall give the particulars of that person which would, if he were so appointed or reappointed, be required to be included in the company's register of directors.

78.   Subject as aforesaid, the company may by ordinary resolution appoint a person who is willing to act to be a director either to fill a vacancy or as an additional director and may also determine the rotation in which any additional directors are to retire.

79.   The directors may appoint a person who is willing to act to be a director, either to fill a vacancy or as an additional director, provided that the appointment does not cause the number of directors to exceed any number fixed by or in accordance with the articles as the maximum number of directors. A director so appointed shall hold office only until the next following annual general meeting and shall not be taken into account in determining the directors who are to retire by rotation at the meeting. If not reappointed at such annual general meeting, he shall vacate office at the conclusion thereof.

80.   Subject as aforesaid, a director who retires at an annual general meeting may, if willing to act, be reappointed. If he is not reappointed, he shall retain office until the meeting appoints someone in his place, or if it does not do so, until the end of the meeting.

Disqualification and removal of directors

81. The office of a director shall be vacated if:

    (a) he ceases to be a director by virtue of any provision of the Act or he becomes prohibited by law from being a director; or

    (b) he becomes bankrupt or makes any arrangement or composition with his creditors generally; or

    (c) he is, or may be, suffering from mental disorder and either:

        (i) he is admitted to hospital in pursuance of an application for admission for treatment under the *Mental Health Act 1983* or, in Scotland, an application for admission under the *Mental Health (Scotland) Act 1960*, or

        (ii) an order is made by a court having jurisdiction (whether in the United Kingdom or elsewhere) in matters concerning mental disorder for his detention or for the appointment of a receiver, curator bonis or other person to exercise powers with respect to his property or affairs; or

    (d) he resigns his office by notice to the company; or

    (e) he shall for more than six consecutive months have been absent without permission of the directors from meetings of directors held during that period and the directors resolve that his office be vacated.

Remuneration of directors

82. The directors shall be entitled to such remuneration as the company may by ordinary resolution determine and, unless the resolution provides otherwise, the remuneration shall be deemed to accrue from day to day.

Directors' expenses

83. The directors may be paid all travelling, hotel, and other expenses properly incurred by them in connection with their attendance at meetings of directors or committees of directors or general meetings or separate meetings of the holders of any class of shares or of debentures of the company or otherwise in connection with the discharge of their duties.

Directors' appointments and interest

84. Subject to the provisions of the Act, the directors may appoint one or more of their number to the office of managing director or to any other executive office under the company and may enter into an agreement or arrangement with any director for his employment by the company or for the provision by him of any services outside the scope of the ordinary duties of a director. Any such appointment, agreement or arrangement may be made upon such terms as the directors determine and they may remunerate any such director for his services as they think fit. Any appointment of a director to an executive office shall terminate if he ceases to be a director but without prejudice to any claim to damages for breach of the contract of service between the director and the company. A managing director and a director holding any other executive office shall not be subject to retirement by rotation.

85.   Subject to the provisions of the Act, and provided that he has disclosed to the directors the nature and extent of any material interest of his, a director notwithstanding his office:

    (a)   may be a party to, or otherwise interested in, any transaction or arrangement with the company or in which the company is otherwise interested;

    (b)   may be a director or other officer of, or employed by, or a party to any transaction or arrangement with, or otherwise interested in, any body corporate promoted by the company or in which the company is otherwise interested; and

    (c)   shall not, by reason of his office, be accountable to the company for any benefit which he derives from any such office or employment or from any such transaction or arrangement or from any interest in any such body corporate and no such transaction or arrangement shall be liable to be avoided on the ground of any such interest or benefit.

86.   For the purposes of regulation 85:

    (a)   a general notice given to the directors that a director is to be regarded as having an interest of the nature and extent specified in the notice in any transaction or arrangement in which a specified person or class of persons is interested shall be deemed to be a disclosure that the director has an interest in any such transaction of the nature and extent so specified; and

    (b)   an interest of which a director has no knowledge and of which it is unreasonable to expect him to have knowledge shall not be treated as an interest of his.

Directors' gratuities and pensions

87.   The directors may provide benefits, whether by the payment of gratuities or pensions or by insurance or otherwise, for any director who has held but no longer holds any executive office or employment with the company or with any body corporate which is or has been a subsidiary of the company or a predecessor in business of the company or of any such subsidiary, and for any member of his family (including a spouse and a former spouse) or any person who is or was dependent on him, and may (as well before as after he ceases to hold such office or employment) contribute to any fund and pay premiums for the purchase or provision of any such benefit.

Proceedings of directors

88.   Subject to the provisions of the articles, the directors may regulate their proceedings as they think fit. A director may, and the secretary at the request of a director shall, call a meeting of the directors. It shall not be necessary to give notice of a meeting to a director who is absent from the United Kingdom. Questions arising at a meeting shall be decided by a majority of votes. In the case of an equality of votes, the chairman shall have a second or casting vote. A director who is also an alternate director shall be entitled in the absence of his appointor to a separate vote on behalf of his appointor in addition to his own vote.

89.   The quorum for the transaction of the business of the directors may be fixed by the directors and unless so fixed at any other number shall be two. A person who holds office only as an alternate director shall, if his appointor is not present, be counted in the quorum.

90.   The continuing directors or a sole continuing director may act notwithstanding any vacancies in their number, but, if the number of directors is less than the number fixed as the quorum, the continuing directors or director may act only for the purpose of filling vacancies or of calling a general meeting.

91.   The directors may appoint one of their number to be the chairman of the board of directors and may at any time remove him from that office. Unless he is unwilling to do so, the director so appointed shall preside at every meeting of directors at which he is present. But if there is no director holding that office, or if the director holding it is unwilling to preside or is not present within five minutes after the time appointed for the meeting, the directors present may appoint one of their number to be chairman of the meeting.

92.   All acts done by a meeting of directors, or of a committee of directors, or by a person acting as a director shall, notwithstanding that it be afterwards discovered that there was a defect in the appointment of any director or that any of them were disqualified from holding office, or had vacated office, or were not entitled to vote, be as valid as if every such person had been duly appointed and was qualified and had continued to be a director and had been entitled to vote.

93.   A resolution in writing signed by all the directors entitled to receive notice of a meeting of directors or of a committee of directors shall be as valid and effectual as if it had been passed at a meeting of directors or (as the case may be) a committee of directors duly convened and held and may consist of several documents in the like form each signed by one or more directors; but a resolution signed by an alternate director need not also be signed by his appointor and, if it is signed by a director who has appointed an alternate director, it need not be signed by the alternate director in that capacity.

94.   Save as otherwise provided by the articles, a director shall not vote at a meeting of directors or of a committee of directors on any resolution concerning a matter in which he has, directly or indirectly an interest or duty which is material and which conflicts or may conflict with the interests of the company unless his interest or duty arises only because the case falls within one or more of the following paragraphs:

(a)   the resolution relates to the giving to him of a guarantee, security, or indemnity in respect of money lent to, or an obligation incurred by him for the benefit of, the company or any of its subsidiaries;

(b)   the resolution relates to the giving to a third party of a guarantee, security, or indemnity in respect of an obligation of the company or any of its subsidiaries for which the director has assumed responsibility in whole or part and whether alone or jointly with others under a guarantee or indemnity or by the giving of security;

(c)   his interest arises by virtue of his subscribing or agreeing to subscribe for any shares, debentures or other securities of the company or any of its subsidiaries, or by virtue of his being, or intending to become, a participant in the underwriting or sub-underwriting of an offer of any such shares, debentures, or other securities by the company or any of its subsidiaries for subscription, purchase or exchange;

(d)   the resolution relates in any way to a retirement benefits scheme which has been approved, or is conditional upon approval, by the Board of Inland Revenue for taxation purposes.

For the purposes of this regulation, an interest of a person who is, for any purpose of the Act (excluding any statutory modification thereof not in force when this regulation becomes binding on the company), connected with a director shall be treated as an interest of the director and, in relation to an alternate director, an interest of his appointor shall be treated as an interest of the alternate director without prejudice to any interest which the alternate director has otherwise.

95.   A director shall not be counted in the quorum present at a meeting in relation to a resolution on which he is not entitled to vote.

96.   The company may by ordinary resolution suspend or relax to any extent, either generally or in respect of any particular matter, any provision of the articles prohibiting a director from voting at a meeting of directors or of a committee of directors.

97.   Where proposals are under consideration concerning the appointment of two or more directors to offices or employments with the company or any body corporate in which the company is interested the proposals may be divided and considered in relation to each director separately and (provided he is not for another reason precluded from voting) each of the directors concerned shall be entitled to vote and be counted in the quorum in respect of each resolution except that concerning his own appointment.

98.   If a question arises at a meeting of directors or of a committee of directors as to the right of a director to vote, the question may, before the conclusion of the meeting, be referred to the chairman of the meeting and his ruling in relation to any director other than himself shall be final and conclusive.

Secretary

99.   Subject to the provisions of the Act, the secretary shall be appointed by the directors for such term, at such remuneration and upon such conditions as they may think fit; and any secretary so appointed may be removed by them.

Minutes

100.   The directors shall cause minutes to be made in books kept for the purpose:

   (a)   of all appointments of officers made by the directors; and

   (b)   of all proceedings at meetings of the company, of the holders of any class of shares in the company, and of the directors, and of committees of directors, including the names of the directors present at each such meeting.

The seal

101.   The seal shall only be used by the authority of the directors or of a committee of directors authorised by the directors. The directors may determine who shall sign any instrument to which the seal is affixed and unless otherwise so determined it shall be signed by a director and by the secretary or by a second director.

Dividends

102.   Subject to the provisions of the Act, the company may by ordinary resolution declare dividends in accordance with the respective rights of the members, but no dividend shall exceed the amount recommended by the directors.

103. Subject to the provisions of the Act, the directors may pay interim dividends if it appears to them that they are justified by the profits of the company available for distribution. If the share capital is divided into different classes, the directors may pay interim dividends on shares which confer deferred or non-preferred rights with regard to dividend as well as on shares which confer preferential rights with regard to dividend, but no interim dividend shall be paid on shares carrying deferred or nonpreferred rights if, at the time of payment, any preferential dividend is in arrears. The directors may also pay at intervals settled by them any dividend payable at a fixed rate if it appears to them that the profits available for distribution justify the payment. Provided the directors act in good faith they shall not incur any liability to the holders of shares conferring preferred rights for any loss they may suffer by the lawful payment of an interim dividend on any shares having deferred or non-preferred rights.

104. Except as otherwise provided by the rights attached to shares, all dividends shall be declared and paid according to the amounts paid up on the shares on which the dividend is paid. All dividends shall be apportioned and paid proportionately to the amounts paid up on the shares during any portion or portions of the period in respect of which the dividend is paid; but, if any share is issued on terms providing that it shall rank for dividend as from a particular date, that share shall rank for dividend accordingly.

105. A general meeting declaring a dividend may, upon the recommendation of the directors, direct that it shall be satisfied wholly or partly by the distribution of assets and, where any difficulty arises in regard to the distribution, the directors may settle the same and in particular may issue fractional certificates and fix the value for distribution of any assets and may determine that cash shall be paid to any member upon the footing of the value so fixed in order to adjust the rights of members and may vest any assets in trustees.

106. Any dividend or other moneys payable in respect of a share may be paid by cheque sent by post to the registered address of the person entitled or, if two or more persons are the holders of the share or are jointly entitled to it by reason of the death or bankruptcy of the holder, to the registered address of that one of those persons who is first named in the register of members or to such person and to such address as the person or persons entitled may in writing direct. Every cheque shall be made payable to the order of the person or persons entitled or to such other person as the person or persons entitled may in writing direct and payment of the cheque shall be a good discharge to the company. Any joint holder or other person jointly entitled to a share as aforesaid may give receipts for any dividend or other moneys payable in respect of the share.

107. No dividend or other moneys payable in respect of a share shall bear interest against the company unless otherwise provided by the rights attached to the share.

108. Any dividend which has remained unclaimed for twelve years from the date when it became due for payment shall, if the directors so resolve, be forfeited and cease to remain owing by the company.

Accounts

109. No member shall (as such) have any right of inspecting any accounting records or other book or document of the company except as conferred by statute or authorised by the directors or by ordinary resolution of the company.

Capitalisation of profits

110.   The directors may with the authority of an ordinary resolution of the company:

(a)   subject as hereinafter provided, resolve to capitalise any undivided profits of the company not required for paying any preferential dividend (whether or not they are available for distribution) or any sum standing to the credit of the company's share premium account or capital redemption reserve;

(b)   appropriate the sum resolved to be capitalised to the members who would have been entitled to it if it were distributed by way of dividend and in the same proportions and apply such sum on their behalf either in or towards paying up the amounts, if any, for the time being unpaid on any shares held by them respectively, or in paying up in full unissued shares or debentures of the company of a nominal amount equal to that sum, and allot the shares or debentures credited as fully paid to those members, or as they may direct, in those proportions, or partly in one way and partly in the other: but the share premium account, the capital redemption reserve, and any profits which are not available for distribution may, for the purposes of this regulation, only be applied in paying up unissued shares to be allotted to members credited as fully paid;

(c)   make such provision by the issue of fractional certificates or by payment in cash or otherwise as they determine in the case of shares or debentures becoming distributable under this regulation in fractions; and

(d)   authorise any person to enter on behalf of all the members concerned into an agreement with the company providing for the allotment to them respectively, credited as fully paid, of any shares or debentures to which they are entitled upon such capitalisation, any agreement made under such authority being binding on all such members.

Notices

111.   Any notice to be given to or by any person pursuant to the articles shall be in writing except that a notice calling a meeting of the directors need not be in writing.

112.   The company may give any notice to a member either personally or by sending it by post in a prepaid envelope addressed to the member at his registered address or by leaving it at that address. In the case of joint holders of a share, all notices shall be given to the joint holder whose name stands first in the register of members in respect of the joint holding and notice so given shall be sufficient notice to all the joint holders. A member whose registered address is not within the United Kingdom and who gives to the company an address within the United Kingdom at which notices may be given to him shall be entitled to have notices given to him at that address, but otherwise no such member shall be entitled to receive any notice from the company.

113.   A member present, either in person or by proxy, at any meeting of the company or of the holders of any class of shares in the company shall be deemed to have received notice of the meeting and, where requisite, of the purposes for which it was called.

114.   Every person who becomes entitled to a share shall be bound by any notice in respect of that share which, before his name is entered in the register of members, has been duly given to a person from whom he derives his title.

115.   Proof that an envelope containing a notice was properly addressed, prepaid and posted shall be conclusive evidence that the notice was given. A notice shall be deemed to be given at the expiration of forty-eight hours after the envelope containing it was posted.

116.   A notice may be given by the company to the persons entitled to a share in consequence of the death or bankruptcy of a member by sending or delivering it, in any manner authorised by the articles for the giving of notice to a member, addressed to them by name, or by the title of representatives of the deceased, or trustee of the bankrupt or by any like description at the address, if any, within the United Kingdom supplied for that purpose by the persons claiming to be so entitled. Until such an address has been supplied, a notice may be given in any manner in which it might have been given if the death or bankruptcy had not occurred.

Winding up

117.   If the company is wound up, the liquidator may, with the sanction of an extraordinary resolution of the company and any other sanction required by the Act, divide among the members in specie the whole or any part of the assets of the company and may, for that purpose, value any assets and determine how the division shall be carried out as between the members or different classes of members. The liquidator may, with the like sanction, vest the whole or any part of the assets in trustees upon such trusts for the benefit of the members as he with the like sanction determines, but no member shall be compelled to accept any assets upon which there is a liability.

Indemnity

118.   Subject to the provisions of the Act but without prejudice to any indemnity to which a director may otherwise by entitled, every director or other officer or auditor of the company shall be indemnified out of the assets of the company against any liability incurred by him in defending any proceedings, whether civil or criminal, in which judgement is given in his favour or in which he is acquitted or in connection with any application in which relief is granted to him by the court from liability for negligence, default, breach of duty or breach of trust in relation to the affairs of the company.

Conclusion   The key provisions are article 24 relating to a transfer; article 32 concerning increase in share capital; articles 38-63 about proceedings at general meeting; article 70 on powers of directors and articles 84-87 on the directors' conflict of interest.

1.3   Activity

Answer the following questions by reference to Table A:

(a)   Which article sets out the directors discretion to refuse to register transfers of shares?

(b)   Which article permits an increase in the company's authorised share capital?

(c)   Is the company authorised to purchase its own shares?

(d)   What period of notice must be given for general meetings as a general rule?

(e)   What happens if there is an equality of votes (on a poll or by show of hands) at a general meeting?

(f)   How many directors must there be?

(g)   Where are the power of the directors set out?

(h)   Which article deals with a directors vacation of office?

(i)   Which article requires directors to disclose to the board any material interest they have in transactions to which the company is also a party?

(j)   Which article restricts the ability of directors to vote on matters such as that referred to in (i)?

1.4   Activity solution

(a)   Article 24.

(b)   Article 32.

(c)   Yes, under article 35.

(d)   21 or 14 days, (article 38).

(e)   The chairman has a casting vote (article 50).

(f)   At least two (article 64).

(g)   Article 70.

(h)   Article 81.

(i)   Article 85.

(j)   Article 94.

2   FORM OF ARTICLES

If a company has its own articles they must be:

(a)   printed;

(b)   divided into paragraphs numbered consecutively; and

(c)   signed (if they are the original articles delivered to form the company) by each subscriber to the memorandum whose signature of the articles must also be dated and witnessed.

3   LEGAL EFFECT OF ARTICLES

3.1   The Articles as a contract: S14 CA85

The memorandum and articles, when registered, bind the company and its members as if they have been executed under seal by the members and the members had agreed to observe them: S14 CA85.

The articles are enforceable by the company against its members.

Hickman v Kent or Romney Marsh Sheepbreeders Association [1920]

Facts: the company's articles included a clause to the effect that all disputes between the company and its members were to be referred to arbitration. A member brought court proceedings against the company.

Held: the proceedings were stayed. The company could enforce the arbitration clause against a member.

The articles are binding on both sides.

Pender v Lushington [1877]

Facts: the articles provided for one vote per ten shares. With no member to have more than one hundred votes. A member with more than one thousand shares, transferred the surplus to a nominee and directed him how to vote. The chairman refused to accept the nominee's votes.

Held: the right to vote was enforceable against the company.

The articles also operate as a contract between individual members in their capacity as members.

Rayfield v Hands [1960]

Facts: the articles required the directors to be members ie, to hold qualification shares and to purchase shares from any member who wished to sell.

Held: this was enforceable against the directors in their capacity as members.

The contract only relates to matters arising between the company and its members as **members**.

Eley v Positive Government Security Life Assurance [1876]

Facts: the articles provided that Eley should be solicitor to the company.

Held: this was not a right given to him as a **member** and he could not rely on the articles as a contract for professional services. The right to be a director of a company has also been held to be an outsider right.

Beattie v EF Beattie [1938]

Facts: the company's articles contained an arbitration clause (in the same wording as in **Hickman's** case). B, a member and director of the company, was in dispute with the company. It was a wide ranging dispute concerning his rights as director. He brought court proceedings against the company.

Held: he was not bound by the arbitration clause since he was acting in his capacity as director, not a member.

However, even where the articles are not a relevant contract for this purpose they may be evidence of another contract made independently.

Re New British Iron Co, ex parte Beckwith [1898]

Facts: the articles stated that directors were entitled to be paid £1,000 on taking office.

Held: the contract was implied from the directors' action in taking office. The provision in the articles was merely evidence of that separate contract.

Conclusion   S14 CA85 states that the articles of association form a contract between company and members, and members between themselves, even if they do not in fact sign the articles.

They are contractually binding and the individual articles are the terms of the contract.

It is important to check in the exam question the **capacity** in which the person is claiming? Is it as a member, or in some other capacity, such as a director or an accountant?

Obviously the articles have no effect as a contract between the company and a person who is not a member even if they are named in them and given apparent rights against the company. In **Eley's** case above, Eley's membership was irrelevant to his claim; as solicitor he had no claim - he was attempting to enforce a non-member's right. But see the case of:

Salmon v Quin & Axtens [1909]

Facts: a joint managing director was allowed to exercise his power of veto over board decisions, a power which was included in the articles and given to him in his capacity as managing director. However, Salmon sued in his capacity as a member claiming that he as a member had a right to ensure that the articles were complied with including the article giving veto powers to managing directors.

Held: he was merely enforcing a member's right, whereas Eley brought a personal action requesting reinstatement (or damages) for the loss of work as a solicitor.

The same principles apply to the memorandum but its contents do not generally give rise to such claims.

3.2   Activity

State whether the following provisions in the Articles would be enforceable under S14 in each situation.

(a)   Member's right to vote?

(b)   Member's right to attend general meetings?

(c)   Pre-emption rights in favour of existing shareholders on a proposed transfer of shares?

(d)   Member's right to receive a dividend?

(e)   An arbitration clause (similar to the one in the **Hickman** case) against the company by a director/shareholder being sued by the company for breach of directors duty?

(f)   An article requiring directors to purchase the shares of a member who wishes to sell?

3.3 Activity solution

(a) Yes - **Pender v Lushington.**

(b) Yes - This is a right given to a member in that capacity.

(c) S14 has been interpreted to allow the enforcement of pre-emption rights on transfer by member against members.

(d) Yes - this is the same as (a) and (b).

(e) No - the director would be seeking to enforce the clause in his capacity as director not member. See **Beattie v EF Beattie**

(f) It depends on whether the articles require the directors to be shareholders as well. See **Rayfield v Hands.**

4 ALTERATION OF ARTICLES

4.1 Procedure and Restrictions

In contrast to the specially defined powers to alter the memorandum, a company has a general power to alter its articles by passing a special resolution: S9 CA85. This general power, however, is subject to overriding restrictions as follows:

(a) the alteration must not conflict with the memorandum nor with the Companies Act or other relevant laws: S9 CA85;

(b) the number of shares which a member is bound to subscribe for (and the amount payable on his shares) may not be increased without his consent: S16 CA85. Any rights of a class of shares may only be altered in accordance with the relevant rules and procedure contained in the memorandum or articles: S125 CA85.

(c) the alteration may not override an order of the court under for example S459 CA85;

(d) the alteration must be for the benefit of the company;

(e) no contract extraneous to the articles can prevent a company from altering its articles but the company is liable for damages if, in altering the articles, it commits a breach of any such contract.

4.2 Alteration for benefit of the company

When there is a conflict between members over a proposed alteration the question which may arise is whether the majority are seeking an unfair advantage for themselves or merely exercising their right as a majority to make changes for the benefit of the company, even if a minority thereby lose some advantage.

The general test of validity is whether the alteration is proposed **in good faith for the benefit of the company as a whole - Allen v Gold Reefs of Africa [1900]**. This test includes two elements (good faith and benefit) but it is a single principle:

Greenhalgh v Arderne Cinemas (1950)

Facts: the issue was the removal from the articles of the members' right of first refusal of any shares which a member might wish to transfer; the majority wished to make the change in order to admit an outsider to membership in the interests of the company.

Held: the benefit to the company as a whole was held to be a benefit which any individual hypothetical member of the company could enjoy directly or through the company and not merely a benefit to the majority of members only. The test of good faith did not require proof of actual benefit but merely the honest belief on **reasonable grounds** that benefit could follow from the alteration. In several cases the court has held that actual and foreseen detriment to a minority affected by the alteration was not in itself a sufficient ground of objection if the benefit to the company test was satisfied.

An alteration to remove a fraudulent director has been upheld.

Shuttleworth v Cox [1927]

Facts: the purpose of the alteration was to remove from office a director who had repeatedly failed to account to the company for money in his hands.

Held: the alteration was valid.

Alteration to remove members by enforcing a transfer of their shares will not be upheld unless restricted.

Sidebottom v Kershaw Leese & Co [1920]

Facts: the alteration was to expel a member who carried on a business in competition with the company.

Held: it was a valid alteration. (Compare **Dafen Tinplate Co v Llanelly Steel Co [1907]** where there was no such restriction and the alteration was invalid).

An alteration, which is otherwise valid, may be made with retrospective effect:

Allen v Gold Reefs of West Africa [1900]

Facts: Z held fully paid up and partly paid up shares in the company. The company's articles provided for a lien for all debts and liabilities of any member upon all partly paid shares held by the member. The company by special resolution altered its articles so that the lien was available on fully paid up shares as well.

Held: that the company had power to alter its articles by extending the lien to fully paid shares.

However, it cannot deprive members or directors of accrued rights, eg, to dividend or to remuneration.

4.3   Breach of contract

If the proposed alteration of the articles (or of the memorandum) will put the company in breach of contract, the company cannot by injunction be restrained by the other party to the contract from exercising its statutory power to alter its articles, but the other party may sue for damages for breach of contract.

Southern Foundries v Shirlaw [1940]

Facts: alteration of the articles to empower the holding company to remove the managing director of the subsidiary from his office of director. He thereby ceased to be managing director in breach of the company's contract to employ him in that capacity.

Held: the alteration was valid but the company was in breach of the service contract and liable for damages.

Conclusion   Articles can always be altered by special resolution of the members of the company in General Meeting.

This subject to the following limitations that an alteration of the articles:

- cannot conflict with the memorandum;
- cannot conflict with company law;
- cannot be illegal;
- cannot alter class rights;
- cannot override an order of the Court; and
- cannot be otherwise than for the best interests of the company.

4.4   Activity

In what way and subject to what limitations may the shareholders of a company alter its articles of association?

4.5   Activity solution

A company may alter its articles of association by passing a special resolution: S9. As the articles are a document of public record a copy of the altered articles and the resolution must be delivered to the Registrar within 15 days.

An alteration is ineffective if it contravenes the Companies Acts or the memorandum of association. If there is a conflict between the latter document and the articles, the memorandum prevails.

It is not possible to increase a members liability by altering the articles, without the members express consent, S16.

Alteration must be bona fide in the interests of the company as a whole; **Greenhalgh v Arderne Cinemas.** Alterations to expel a member will not be permitted unless that individual has been defrauding the company **(Shuttleworth v Cox)** or competing with the company **(Sidebottom v Kershaw, Leese & Co).**

There are two other statutory restrictions. If the alteration amounts to a variation of class rights, the appropriate statutory or constitutional procedure must be followed as well: S125.

Furthermore alteration cannot override an order of the court: S459.

5   SELF TEST QUESTIONS

5.1   What are the three alternative ways for a company to devise the articles? (1.1)

5.2   In respect of what type of share may directors refuse to register a transfer according to Table A? (1.2)

5.3   How can a company increase its share capital under Table A? (1.2)

5.4   Who can demand a poll of general meetings? (1.2)

5.5   What is the principal authority for the binding nature of the articles? (3.1)

5.6   Why could the members enforce the articles in **Pender v Lushington** but not in **Eley's** case? (3.1)

5.7   How do you alter the articles? (4.1)

5.8   What is the principal case law test of whether the alteration is valid? (4.2)

5.9   Can an alteration of articles have retrospective effect? (4.2)

5.10   Can the existence of a separate contractual obligation prevent an alteration of the article? (4.3)

6   EXAMINATION TYPE QUESTIONS

6.1   Aire Ltd

The articles of association of Aire Ltd provide that Donald and Charles are to be employed as sales manager and accountant respectively at salaries of not less than £10,000 pa until they attain the age of sixty five years. They have both been so employed for many years and are now in their late fifties.

(a)   Advise Donald who has received notice from the company purporting to discharge him. He does not wish to leave.

(b)   Advise Charles who has offered his resignation which has been rejected by the company.
(15 marks)

6.2   Beta Ltd

John has for several years asked numerous awkward questions at the annual general meetings of Beta Ltd and has become very unpopular with the board. One of the directors has suggested that the articles of association be altered to enable a majority of the members of the company to buy out John's shareholding at a fair value as certified by the company's auditor.

What principles would be applied by the court in deciding whether such an alteration was valid?
(10 marks)

6.3   Articles and Members

S14 CA85 states that the memorandum and articles of association of a company shall, when registered, bind the company and the members to the same extent as if they respectively had been signed and sealed by each member, and contained covenants on the part of each member to observe all the provisions of the memorandum and of the articles.

Explain the effect of this section on the relationships between shareholders and their company and between the shareholders themselves. Illustrate your answer with decided cases.
(20 marks)

7   ANSWERS TO EXAMINATION TYPE QUESTIONS

7.1   Aire Ltd

The memorandum and articles of association are by S14 Companies Act 1985 (CA85) a contract binding as if executed under seal between the company and its members and between the members themselves. But it is a contract binding only in respect of rights and obligations of members; only members are bound and then only in respect of membership matters.

In **Eley v Positive Government Security Life Assurance Co** the articles provided that Eley, who was a member, should be employed as the company's solicitor (without any time limit being specified). It was held that Eley could not enforce the articles as a contract of employment because this was not a right of membership. But in **Salmon v Quin & Axtens** a managing director was able to enforce a power of veto over board decisions relying purely on the contract in the articles provided for in S14 CA85, even though this was a non-members (ie, an outsider) right. In both these cases the plaintiff was a member but in the problem there is no indication that either Donald or Charles are members. If they could rely on **Salmon's** case they must at least be members themselves.

However, where companies have in fact employed directors in the absence of an express agreement it has been held **(Re New British Iron Co. ex parte Beckwith)** that a separate contract of service may be established by the parties' course of dealing with each other ie, implied from their conduct, which may include terms found in the articles. In effect the articles are not in such a case a contract but they offer evidence of what has been agreed in a separate contract between the parties. In **Beckwith's** case the articles were referred to as evidence of the salary which the company had agreed to pay. In **Eley's case** however, the court refused (partly for technical reasons abolished by the subsequent repeal of S4 Statute of Frauds) to treat the articles as evidence of an agreement to employ Eley indefinitely merely because his services had been used by the company for a time (ie, there was no evidence of a contract separate from the Articles).

The company will rely on **Eley's case** and Donald will argue that the article in question and his long service are evidence of a contract to employ him to the age of sixty five. The court would have to decide which of the two conflicting precedents it preferred. If, as is probable, the court follows **Beckwith's case** and holds that the contract binds the company until Donald is sixty five, damages will be payable for premature termination by his dismissal.

The same principle applies to employer and employee. If Donald is subject to dismissal Charles is entitled to resign (on reasonable notice). If Donald cannot be dismissed Charles cannot resign.

7.2   Beta Ltd

A company may alter or add to its articles of association by special resolution, S9 Companies Act 1985 (CA85).

However, an alteration must be exercised *bona fide* for the benefit of the company as a whole. This does not prevent a company altering its articles retrospectively. Thus in **Allen v Gold Reefs of West Africa** an alteration to give a company a lien on fully paid shares for debts due was held to be effective, even in respect of shares that were already issued and fully paid.

It is for the company itself ie, the shareholders and not for the court to determine if the alteration could benefit the company, unless it is quite impossible for it to benefit the company.

Where there is a compulsory acquisition of a minority's shareholding the courts will be very careful to scrutinise whether the alteration proposed is *bona fide*.

Thus in **Sidebottom v Kershaw Leese & Co. Ltd,** an alteration was made to the articles to provide for the acquisition of any shareholder's holding where he competed with the company's business. This was held to be a valid alteration.

However, in **Brown v British Abrasive Wheel** the court considered the alteration to provide for compulsory acquisition was not *bona fide*. A large majority of the shareholders wished to buy up the minority with a view to extending the capital. The minority refused to sell, and the majority then passed special resolutions altering the articles so as to enable the minority to be bought out. It was held that the alteration of the articles would be restrained as it was not for the benefit of the company. The decision in **Dafen Tinplate v Llanelly Steel** is to a similar effect.

It seems that on the facts of this case the alteration will fail as it is not proposed in the interests of the company, but to assist a shareholder who is 'a thorn in the side' of management.

7.3   Articles and Members

S14 Companies Act 1985 (CA85) is a very important section for every shareholder. This section deems there to be a contract between the company and a member on the terms of the memorandum and articles. In addition, it seems that S14 constitutes a contract between the members *inter se*. This section is essential as without it a member obtaining his shares by way of transfer, as opposed to an issue, would have no contract at all with the company because of the contractual doctrine of privity. Even where a member has a contract with the company because he purchased the shares directly from the company, S14 is important because it provides what the terms of that contract are - ie, the articles.

The contract is binding on both parties thus the company can sue to enforce its provision, **(Hickman v Kent or Romney Marsh Sheepbreeders Ass.)** and the member can sue: **Pender v Lushington**. However, it is unusual in that the normal remedy for breach of contract is damages, yet damages have never been awarded for breach of this contract. The usual remedy obtained by the company is for a liquidated sum and by the shareholder an injunction or declaration. It is an unusual contract in another respect also. Most contracts once entered into are not capable of alteration unilaterally but the S14 contract is made specifically alterable by the company. S9 CA85 provides for alteration of the articles by special resolution passed in a general meeting by the shareholders, this right to alter the articles cannot be contracted out of. There are limits on the way in which the articles can be altered but the courts do not countenance many such limitations.

There has been considerable discussion regarding the extent to which a shareholder can rely on the S14 contract to enforce his rights. In **Eley v Positive Life Assurance**, the court refused to allow a solicitor (who was also a member) to enforce the S14 contract which provided that the company would use his services as a solicitor. The rule developed that the S14 contract was only available to shareholders for the enforcement of shareholders personal rights - ie, rights given to them as members such as attending and voting at general meetings and receiving dividends and not for non-members rights eg, right to act as a solicitor. Such rights are commonly referred to as outsider rights. The discussion continues, clearly the S14 contract cannot be used by a non-member to enforce a non-member's right but it has been argued that any member has a general right to see that the articles are complied with and if by forcing a company to comply with the articles, the court is incidentally enforcing an outsider right, so be it. In **Salmon v Quin and Axtens** the court allowed a joint managing director to enforce an article giving him a power of veto over board decisions. The director was also a member but the case is quite inconsistent with **Eley's** case as the right of a managing director to veto board decisions cannot really come within the description of members' personal rights. Occasionally however, this issue is avoided by the courts implying a contract outside of the articles in favour of an outsider and using the terms contained in the articles as evidence of the terms of the contract outside the articles: **Re New British Iron ex parte Beckwith**.

It is generally thought that the decision in **Eley** is to be preferred as this case is also consistent with the rule in **Foss v Harbottle** that shareholders cannot interfere with management. If a shareholder could sue for every breach of the articles there would be considerable interference with the directors' powers of management. A compromise might be that a shareholder has a personal right to see that the proper organ of management is carrying out the duties described to it, so for eg, if the managing director has a certain right the board may not carry out that right, nor can the shareholders, as in **Salomon**.

The literal interpretation of S14 also gives rise to the idea of a contract between members inter se and this has been approved of in the rather doubtful decision in **Rayfield v Hands**. In this case the directors were given a right in the articles to purchase the shares of any member wishing to transfer them. The court held that this right could be enforce because the reference to directors was construed as a reference to them as members and as against other members they had a contractual right to rely on this article. It is an unusual case as the right to purchase the shares was only given to the directors and not all other members of the company and the right was given to the directors in their capacity as such, not as members though incidentally they were members.

21 CORPORATE FINANCE: RAISING OF SHARE CAPITAL

INTRODUCTION & LEARNING OBJECTIVES

Syllabus area 8f. Types of shares, raising share capital, increase of share capital. (Ability required 3)

The two main sources of finance for a company are share capital and loan capital. In this chapter the legal rules on types of shares and their issue are covered. This includes rules on the amount of share capital which can be issued, who has authority to do so, to whom it can be issued and what forms payment may take.

When you have studied this chapter you should be able to do the following:

● Understand the characteristics of the two most common types of share, the preference share and the ordinary share.

● Distinguish between authorised capital and allotted capital.

● State that private companies cannot raise capital from the public.

● Explain how S80 and 89-96 restrict directors' powers to allot shares.

● State and explain why there are restrictions on the type and amount of consideration a company receives in payment for its shares.

---

1 TYPES OF SHARES

1.1 The nature of a share

The share capital of a company is divided into shares which are units defining the shareholder's proportionate interest in the company.

> **Definition** A share is the interest of the shareholder in the company measured by a sum of money, for the purpose of liability in the first place and of interest in the second, but also consisting of a series of mutual covenants as provided by S14 Companies Act 1985 (CA85).

The main elements and characteristics of a share are:

(a) it gives a right to receive **dividends** declared on that class of shares;

(b) unless it is a non-voting share, it carries a right to **vote** at general meetings; such rights are usually defined in relation to shares eg, one vote for each share or ten shares;

(c) on a liquidation or reduction of capital a share defines the **right to receive assets** distributed to members of that class;

(d) where there is **liability** eg, to subscribe capital, it is measured by reference to shares: if £1 shares are issued at par, the liability is to pay £1 for each share;

(e)   various **rights of membership** are given by the CA85 and by the memorandum and articles of association in terms of shares eg, the right to requisition the holding of a general meeting or to receive notices. All these rights depend on holding shares sometimes to the extent of a special percentage of all issued shares (or voting shares);

(f)   subject to any restrictions of the articles of association, a share is **transferable** by its nature.

1.2   Calls

Shareholders in a public company are legally bound to pay 25% of the nominal value of each share on application for allotment (S101 CA85) and the remaining instalments as specified in the contract for the shares. If the contract contains no stipulation, the company may make calls for the benefit of the company in order to raise unpaid capital from shareholders. Calls must be made in the manner provided by the articles. Of course shareholders are liable up to the full amount of the unpaid nominal value of their shares on a winding up. The articles of association often empower the company, if acting in good faith, to **forfeit** the shares of a member who fails to fulfil his obligations to pay calls. But the subject is of little practical importance as most shares nowadays are fully paid up.

1.3   The company's lien

The rights of a shareholder will be subject to any lien (or right) which the company has over the shares. The articles must expressly confer a lien, if it is to exist. The lien may be for calls on unpaid shares in which case it is effective once the shares are issued (although in that case it is of minimal practical importance as most shares are fully paid up and, if not, the remedy of forfeiture would be more effective). But it may be for any debt due to the company from the member, in which case it will be effective from the time the debt becomes due. A lien is an equitable charge on the share in favour of the company.

The lien enables the company to set off against dividends payable on the shares any money owing to it, present or future. It will be able to enforce the lien by selling the shares if it applies to the court or if the articles confer such right (or possibly under S101 Law of Property Act 1925 if the lien qualifies as a **mortgage** under that Act). In the event of sale, the company must give effect to any restrictions on transfer of shares.

1.4   Classes of shares

In the absence of contrary provision in the memorandum or articles, it is presumed that the rights of all shareholders are equal. These include rights to equal liability to calls (where shares are not fully paid up) dividends (however much is paid up on each share), attendance and voting at meetings and return of capital on an authorised reduction of a winding up.

In many cases a company has only one class of share. But if it has more than one class, the shares will be differentiated by reference to special rights of the shares of each class.

Class rights will generally consist in one or more rights distinguished from rights of other classes as follows:

(a)   in respect of **dividends** paid out of profits;
(b)   in respect of **assets** distributed on a winding-up or a reduction of capital;
(c)   in respect of **voting rights**.

The exact mix is a matter for determination by the company and its members when the class of shares is created. In appropriate cases shares can be given other rights eg, the right to appoint one or more directors.

Some of the common different types of shares are:

Ordinary shares (the equity) typically carry normal rights without special definition. If there is only one class it need not be explicitly described as **ordinary**.

Preference shares carry rights in preference to other shares.

Redeemable shares carry a right by the company to redeem (ie buy back) the shares. As this would reduce the capital of the company, there are strict rules about the issue and redemption of such shares. These rules are covered in the chapter on the maintenance of capital.

Deferred or founders' shares rank after ordinary shares for dividend and sometimes return of capital. They may have additional voting rights. In a typical case such shares were taken by promoters in recognition of their special position. They are now not often found.

Non-voting shares: the term explains itself: they can be of any class. The first employee shares tended to be of this type.

1.5   Preference shares

Preference shares are shares which carry rights in preference to other shares.

The usual preferences given are:

(a)   payment of dividend; and
(b)   return of capital on winding up of the company.

The shares may also be subject to restrictions eg, voting rights.

(a)   Dividend

A preference share generally confers the right to receive a **dividend** up to a specified amount eg, 6% of its paid up value, before any dividend is paid on the ordinary shares.

The rights of preference shares depend essentially on what is **expressly** stated of them in their terms of issue; to this principle there is one exception ie, that the preferential dividend is **deemed to be cumulative** unless expressly described as **non-cumulative.** Cumulative means that the preference shareholder will be entitled to arrears in dividend if not paid out in one year.

The preference shareholder is only entitled to receive a dividend out of **available profits** out of which the **dividend** is **declared** payable. The power to declare preference dividends is usually given to the directors. Available profit of the latest year may be transferred to reserves even though it thereby becomes insufficient to pay the preference dividend. However, if the dividend is **passed** ie, not declared, the priority right is carried forward unless the right to dividend is expressly non-cumulative eg, a 6% dividend unpaid in Year 1 creates a 12% priority right (6 + 6) in Year 2, and so on. If these arrears are later paid off the dividend is entirely payable to the holders of the shares at the time of payment even if others held them when the arrears first arose.

The right to a preference dividend is **exhaustive**. Thus, if the preference dividend is paid in full there is no further right to dividend unless there is an **express right** ie, to participate equally with ordinary shares as soon as the latter have received a dividend of a specified amount. Such shares are called **participating preference shares** and rank as equity share capital.

If a **company goes into liquidation** with arrears outstanding of preference dividends, the right to receive arrears (other than any dividend already declared which a member can claim as an unsecured but deferred debt) lapses unless the articles provide that the arrears shall be paid out of the assets available in winding up. They have no claim on any reserves which could have been applied in paying their dividends. If dividend arrears are payable on liquidation, payment may come from the assets of the company even if before liquidation they represented capital but not available profits.

(b)   **Capital**

Unless expressly so provided in winding up (or return of capital on reduction) preference shares do not have any priority over ordinary shares in return of capital. They then rank *pari passu* with ordinary shares in bearing their proportion of any deficiency of paid up capital.

If, as is usual, however, the preference shares are given priority in any return of capital that priority right is **exhaustive** ie, they are entitled to be repaid capital as so provided but not to participate in any surplus assets. In addition, participating preference shares have no claim on repayment to assets which represent reserves out of which dividends could have been paid to their benefit:

Re Saltdean Estates [1968].

Facts: the company had ordinary and preference shares, the preference shareholders having priority on the return of capital. The company proposed to reduce capital (with the court's permission under S135 CA85) by way of returning capital (ie, nominal value) to them to eliminate the class.

Held: the preference shareholders had received what their class right entitled them to - repayment of nominal value before the ordinary shareholders. They were not entitled to more.

1.6   Activity

A company has an issued ordinary share capital of £50,000 and a preference share capital of £25,000 with priority on a winding up.

On a winding up, how much does each class receive assuming the company has net assets available for contributories amounting to:

(a)   £20,000;
(b)   £135,000.

1.7   Activity solution

(a)   Preference shareholders   -£20,000.
       Ordinary shareholders   - nil.

(b)   Preference shareholders   - £25,000.
       Ordinary shareholders   - £110,000.

2   TYPES OF CAPITAL

2.1   Introduction

In most cases companies are set up to make money. The company will need to fund its activities to make profits - it needs money to make money. Like any sole trader or partnership a company may buy on credit, hire-purchase or obtain an overdraft from the bank.

2.2   Sources of finance

The two major sources of finance however, will be:

(a)   **share capital** - members purchase shares in the company; and

(b)   **loan capital** - persons lend money to the company under a debenture.

In the case of a company with liability limited by shares, the members of the company provide the necessary capital be means of their shareholdings ie, the sum which is actually paid for the shares; or, if some is unpaid, the sum liable to be called in by the company.

The holder of a debenture is also an investor but his investment can be recovered by repayment of his investment, the safety of which is protected by the debenture.

The shareholder is, as a rule, able to recover his investment by selling his shares to a third party who takes his place. Nevertheless, both shareholder and debenture-holder can be seen as investors who put money (their capital) into the company until they want it to be returned and who meanwhile receive some return on their capital, either (if shares) by way of dividends or (if debentures) by way of interest.

2.3   Limited liability company

The limited liability company is one of the leading forms of business association by which persons are encouraged to combine in order to trade. Limiting liability by shareholdings is intended to be a protection to third parties at least as much as to shareholders. Thus, third parties can, in principle at least, rely on the share capital of the company as representing a sum which can be used to satisfy claims against the company, whether the company is actually in possession of the money or able to call it in from the shareholders.

2.4   Share capital - terminology

Definition   The term share capital is used to describe the capital of a company represented by shares.

It is important to be able to differentiate between:

(a)   **authorised share capital** - the amount of share capital which a company **is authorised by its memorandum to issue** eg, £100 divided into 100 shares of £1 each: S2(5) CA85. This will be contained in the capital clause; and

(b)   **issued or allotted share capital** - the nominal amount of the share capital **actually issued** at any time eg, £100 authorised capital of which 50 £1 shares have been issued.

This represents the liability of the members of the company. They are liable to the extent of the nominal (par) value of their shares, which means that the company is entitled to use the full amount of the sum received for the shares in order to satisfy claims against it.

Issued share capital may be:

(a)   **Paid up capital** - the amount so far paid on partly-paid shares eg, 50 £1 shares 50p paid is a paid up capital of £25.

(b)   **Uncalled capital** - the amount which the company is entitled to call on the shareholders to contribute. The other 50p in the £1 share in the above example, once the company has called on the shareholders to pay it.

Uncalled capital is unusual. Shares are generally fully paid, particularly as shares are often worth more than their nominal amount. S101 CA85 requires shares in a public company to be paid up at least as to 25%. Where it exists the company may resolve that uncalled capital be treated as **reserve capital** ie, capital which is only to be called up on a winding up.

Conclusion   Thus, a company may have the following structure of its share capital:

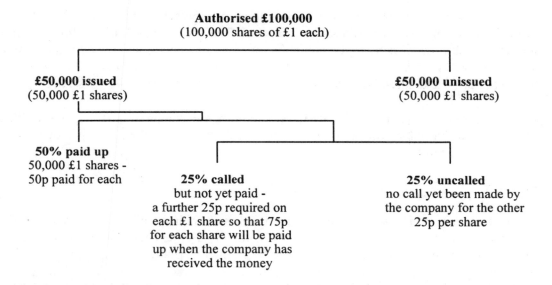

Authorised £100,000
(100,000 shares of £1 each)

£50,000 issued
(50,000 £1 shares)

£50,000 unissued
(50,000 £1 shares)

50% paid up
50,000 £1 shares -
50p paid for each

25% called
but not yet paid -
a further 25p required on
each £1 share so that 75p
for each share will be paid
up when the company has
received the money

25% uncalled
no call yet been made by
the company for the other
25p per share

2.5   Activity

A company has 250,000 50p shares in issue with 30p paid up. The remainder has been called. What is the paid up capital?

2.6   Activity solution

250,000 shares at 30p each, £75,000.

3   PUBLIC SUBSCRIPTION

3.1   Public companies only

It is illegal for a private company's securities (shares or debentures) to be advertised as being available for public subscription - Financial Services Act 1986.

Thus it is public companies only which can raise capital by public subscription.

3.2   Methods of public subscription

There are a variety of ways in which capital can be obtained from the public by the issue of shares.

(a)   **Direct invitations to the public (also called offers for subscription)**

A large company of well-known financial standing may be able to attract sufficient subscriptions from the public by issuing a prospectus and inviting subscriptions for shares directly.

To ensure that the issue of shares is a success, and that all the shares issued are sold, the company will usually arrange **underwriting**. This is an agreement with the issuing house that it undertakes to subscribe for all the shares that are not otherwise sold. Underwriters usually spread the risk by sub-underwriting agreements. The underwriters and sub-underwriters are paid a commission for their services.

(b)   **Offers for sale**

An offer to the public may be made in an indirect way be selling the shares directly to an issuing house (an institution whose function is to float off company shares) for the issuing house to resell them directly to the public by issuing a prospectus and inviting applications. The public will have confidence in the reliability of the investment since the issuing house would not undertake direct responsibility for the issue if the shares were not sound.

Issuing houses are generally also used as agents of the company where it makes direct invitations to the public ((a) above), in which case they make their money not from the profit on resale but by commission.

(c)   **Placings**

A company may **place** shares with an issuing house, either for it to buy and resell to selected clients or to act as the company's agent in finding clients to subscribe for the shares. Such issues do not usually therefore take effect as issues to the public at large but, since one of the advantages of shares is their free transferability, it will usually be necessary to obtain a Stock Exchange listing and, as a result of the Stock Exchange requirements, to make a significant amount available to the public.

The issue may be at a fixed price or it may be on a tender basis ie, persons are in effect being asked to put in written bids for shares. Usually there is a minimum price and the issue price reflects the average price of tenders (or of the higher tenders if the issue is over-subscribed).

3.3   Regulation of public subscription

Acting under powers vested in him by the Financial Services Act 1986 the Secretary of State has delegated the regulation of issues of securities which are to be the subject of dealing on the stock market to the Stock Exchange.

As regards public issues where no application is to be made for the securities to be dealt on the stock market, regulation remains with the Secretary of State.

The level of regulation and disclosure of information, particularly under Stock Exchange requirements, is high and is not within your company law syllabus.

4 ISSUE OF SHARES

4.1 Authorised capital

A company can only issue available unissued shares. If there are none or not enough it will be necessary to create additional shares by an increase of share capital. This entails an alteration of the capital clause. Under S121 CA85 there must be authority in the articles for the purpose of increase. Thus it may be necessary to alter the articles (special resolution) to give the company power to increase which it would then exercise by ordinary resolution.

4.2 Authority of directors to allot shares

S80 CA 1985 states that directors may not allot **relevant** securities (ie, all shares except subscriber shares and employee shares, but including convertible securities) without first obtaining authority from the shareholders. Such authority may be general or specific, conditional or unconditional but in no circumstances may it exceed five years: S80 CA85, unless in the case of a private company an elective resolution has been passed extending the period beyond five years or for an indefinite period.

The authority must state the maximum amount of relevant securities that may be allotted under it and the date on which it will expire, which must usually be not more than five years from:

(a)   in the case of an authority contained in the **company's articles** at the time of its original incorporation, the date of that incorporation; and

(b)   in **any other case**, the date on which the resolution is passed;

but such an authority (including an authority contained in the articles) may be revoked or varied by the company in general meeting.

The authority may be renewed or further renewed by the company in general meeting for a further period not exceeding five years.

A resolution of a company to give, vary, revoke or renew such an authority may, notwithstanding that it alters the company's articles, be an ordinary resolution, but in any case a copy is to be forwarded to the registrar within fifteen days.

A director who knowingly and wilfully contravenes, or permits or authorises a contravention of, this section is liable to a fine but the validity of any allotment is not affected.

> **Conclusion**   In general the directors of a company must have the authority of the shareholders to allot shares. An unauthorised allotment is a criminal offence.

4.3 Pre-emption rights (statutory)

Shareholders have often complained that the lack of pre-emption rights can lead to a watering down of the value of their shareholding eg, by the issue of new shares of the same class ranking *pari passu* (or equally) for dividend and voting. Until 1980 the usual response was to include some sort of pre-emption rights in the company's articles but this was not obligatory. The problem is made more acute as the allotting of additional shares of the same class may lead to a reduction in the value of the existing shares and it is not regarded as a variation of class rights such that the special rules relating to variation and objection would apply: **White v Bristol Aeroplane [1953]**.

The Companies Act, S89-96 , attempts to deal with this problem by providing that no company can allot **equity securities** without first offering them *pro rata* to existing equity shareholders on the same or more favourable terms than it is proposing to offer them to other people. The shareholders must be given twenty-one days in which to decide whether to accept or reject the offer.

Definition Equity securities are, basically, shares other than shares which as respects dividends and capital carry a right to participate only up to a specified amount in a distribution. In short, equity shares are generally the ordinary shares.

There are a number of exceptions to this requirement, *inter alia*:

(a) where the securities are part of an employees' share scheme; or

(b) where the securities are to be paid for otherwise that in cash;

(c) in the case of a private company, this requirement may be excluded by a provision in the memorandum or articles: S91 CA85;

(d) where general authority has been given to the directors to allot shares under S80, the directors may be given, by special resolution or by the Articles, discretion to exclude or modify the statutory pre-emption rights. However, the exclusion or modification will cease to have effect on the lapse of the directors' S80 authority.

(e) by special resolution the statutory pre-emption rights may be excluded or modified in relation to a particular allotment. The directors are required to circularise the members before the meeting justifying the proposal.

An allotment in contravention of S89 is not invalid but, the company, and every officer if it who knowingly authorised or permitted the contravention, are jointly and severally liable to compensate any person to whom an offer should have been made under the subsection for any loss, damage, costs or expenses which the person has sustained or incurred by reason of the contravention.

4.4 Issue for an improper purpose

As with all powers exercised by directors they must be exercised for the purpose for which they were conferred - the proper purposes rule. The prime purpose of an issue of shares is that the company is in need of further finance. Any other purpose is at least questionable.

It would be an improper purpose to issue shares to defeat a take-over bid - **Hogg v Cramphorn**: to facilitate a take-over bid - **Howard Smith v Ampol Petroleum**; to prevent the removal of directors - **Piercy v Mills**; to secure the passing of a special resolution - **Punt v Symons**; or to deprive a shareholder of his special voting weight - **Clemens v Clemens Bros Ltd**.

The courts have not, however, concluded that the only proper purpose of an issue of shares is the need to raise finance. It was recognised in **Clemens v Clemens** that it could be a proper purpose to issue shares to employees and directors in order to given them an equity interest in the company's fortunes.

If the directors do make an issue for improper purposes the issue is voidable and may be ratified by the company - **Bamford v Bamford** and **Hogg v Cramphorn** - provided no votes are exercised by the members to whom the shares were improperly issued. Exceptionally, ratification was not allowed in **Clemens v Clemens Bros** since this amounted to the director ratifying her own breach of duty.

Hogg v Cramphorn [1967]

Facts: the directors of a company learned of a proposed take-over bid which they genuinely believed would not be to the benefit of the company. In order to defeat the bid, they issued 5,000 shares to be held on trust for the company's employees.

Held: the issue was an improper exercise of directors' powers and thus invalid. However, the court ordered a general meeting of the company to be held so that consideration could be given to ratifying the issue. The 'new' shares would not be allowed to vote.

Howard Smith Ltd v Ampol Petroleum Ltd [1974]

A and B owned 55% of the issued share capital of M Ltd between them. They made an offer for all the share capital of M Ltd. At the same time another company, X Ltd, made a similar offer. Although the directors of M Ltd favoured X Ltd's offer, there was no chance that it would succeed because A and B as majority shareholders of M Ltd would vote to reject offers from any other source. In order that X Ltd's offer would stand the greatest chance of success, the directors of M Ltd issued 10 million dollars worth of shares to X Ltd, thereby converting A and B's holding into a minority one.

Held: The issue was an improper exercise of directors' powers and therefore invalid since the sole motive was to enable a take-over to succeed which the majority shareholders were otherwise in a position to block.

Piercy v S Mills & Co [1920]

Facts: the directors made a fresh issue of shares to themselves and their supporters with the object of maintaining control and resisting the election of three additional directors which would have made them a minority on the board.

Held: the issue of shares was improper.

Punt v Simons & Co Ltd [1903]

Facts: the directors issued shares to five additional members in order to secure the passing of a special resolution.

Held: the issue was improper.

Bamford v Bamford [1970]

Facts: in order to fight off a take-over bid the directors of X Ltd issued 5 million shares to B Ltd for cash. The shareholders who supported the take-over complained and the directors called an extraordinary general meeting of the company which approved and ratified the directors' action. B Ltd did not vote.

Held: Although the issue of shares by directors to defeat a take-over bid was an improper exercise of their powers, the issue would remain valid because it had been ratified by the company in general meeting.

Clemens v Clemens Bros Ltd [1976]

Facts: P held 45% of the shares in the company and D held 55%. D was a director; there were also six other directors. The board (ie, D) wished to increase the nominal share capital declaring that the purpose was to issue further shares to long-term employees. A general meeting was called in order to pass an ordinary resolution to ratify this issue. D used her voting weight in favour of the resolution. P alleged that the real purpose of the share issue was to dilute her voting control to below 25% and thereby deprive her of her power to veto special resolutions.

Held: on the evidence the court accepted that the true purpose of the share issue was to dilute P's negative voting weight. The share issue was therefore an improper exercise of directors' powers.

The court declared the resolution ratifying this improper exercise to be invalid; the judge stated that the votes of a majority shareholder are subject to 'equitable considerations which may make it unjust to exercise those votes in a particular way'.

4.5   Partly paid shares

This issue of shares creates a debt owing by the allottee to the company but it is not essential that it should be paid (in cash or kind) at once. But a public company must not allot a share unless at least one quarter of the nominal value and the whole of any premium is paid up - S101 CA85. Shares may be issued on the basis of payment either by instalments at fixed dates (so that a company raises money for an expanding business or long-term project by stages as required) or by instalments (**calls**) when demanded by the company. The directors are usually given the power under the articles of association to make such calls. They must use this power for the benefit of the company as a whole eg, they cannot make calls exclusively on shareholders other than themselves.

A company may by special resolution decide that part of the amount payable on its shares shall only be called up for payment when the company is wound up. This creates **reserve capital** and it is rather similar in the result to a company limited by guarantee. **Reserve capital** in this sense should be clearly distinguished from **capital reserves** which are quite a different thing: S120 CA85.

Forfeiture and **surrender** of shares on failure to pay subscription moneys on shares or for sums owing to the company are possible if the articles contain appropriate provisions.

4.6   Issue of shares at a discount on their market value

In general it is for the directors to fix the price at which shares are to be issued and, particularly in the case of rights issues to existing members, it is common practice to issue shares at a discount to the market value in order to encourage take-up.

As with all powers of directors, they have a fiduciary duty to exercise it in the interest of the company as a whole: shares issued to friends and relatives of directors at below market value may be questioned as a breach of fiduciary duty.

4.7   Issue of shares at a discount on the nominal value

A company may not issue its shares for a consideration which is less then the nominal value of the shares. If a company did enter into a contract to issue shares at a discount it could not enforce it against the allottee but if he took the shares he would be liable to pay the amount of the discount as unpaid share capital and interest on that amount at 5%: S100 CA85.

This rule does not apply to debentures which may be issued at a discount unless they carry an **immediate** right of conversion into shares on such terms that in effect a right to take shares at a discount is given through the debentures.

The ban on issue of shares at a discount can be inconvenient if the market price of a company's shares has fallen below par and the company wishes to raise cash by the issue of additional shares.

There are two ways shares may be issued at a discount:

(a)   in exchange for property which is in fact overvalued. As far a public companies are concerned, this loophole has been filled (see below);

(b)   at up to 10% discount as underwriting commission.

4.8   Issue of shares at a premium

A company is always free to issue shares at a premium eg, to obtain £2 each for £1 shares. No special power in the articles is required nor is any other sanction required. If it is possible to issue shares at a premium the directors should do so (to secure a benefit to the company). As stated above unless the shares are offered entirely to existing shareholders as a rights issue, failure to obtain the best price may be evidence of a breach of duty by the directors.

Share premium account

Any premium obtained must be treated as equivalent to capital and safeguarded accordingly; S130 CA85. This is effected by requiring the premium to be credited to a **share premium account** which can only be distributed to members under the same procedure as in a reduction of share capital. The share premium account can also be applied for certain capital purposes, however ie,:

(a)   to pay up bonus shares to be issued as fully paid to members;

(b)   in writing off:

•   preliminary expenses; or
•   expenses, commission or discount incurred in the issue of shares or debentures;

(c)   in paying the premium (if any) on redemption of debentures.

With reference to (a), note that share premium account cannot be used for a bonus issue of **debentures**.

With reference to public companies there is a further restriction on the use of the share premium account. A public company must not make a distribution of profit by way of dividend if to do so would reduce its net assets below the aggregate of its called up share capital and undistributable reserves. The share premium account is an undistributable reserve for the purposes of this section: S264 CA85.

Apart from S130 there are other provisions in the CA 1985 where a debit can be made to share premium - notably on redemption or purchase by a company of its own shares.

A shareholder who pays a premium for his shares obtains no rights to the premium in the hands of the company. His dividends are calculated by reference to the par value of his shares. On a liquidation or return of capital, no extra sums payable to those shareholders who subscribed for their shares at a price above par value.

The rule that a premium must be credited to share premium account applies to an issue for cash and to an issue for a consideration other that cash eg, to acquire shares of another company: **Henry Head v Ropner Holdings [1952]**.

Merger relief

Ss131 & 132 CA85, which are concerned with merger and acquisition accounting, seek to provide relief from S130 CA85 in certain defined situations.

S131 CA85 will not apply to any premium on the shares issued for the purpose of a merger, if the issuing company has secured an equity holding in another company of not less than ninety percent, in pursuance of an arrangement providing for the allotment of equity shares in the issuing company, where the consideration is the issue or transfer to the issuing company of equity shares in the other company, or the cancellation of any such shares not held by the issuing company. Schemes of arrangement are included. Where the equity capital of the other company is divided into separate classes the ninety percent requirement must be satisfied, even though not all the shares were acquired as a result of the arrangement.

S132 CA85 gives relief where a wholly owned subsidiary allots shares to its holding company or to another wholly owned subsidiary of the group, in consideration for the transfer to it of shares in another subsidiary (which need not be wholly owned).

Further, S134 CA85 enables the Secretary of State by statutory instrument to make further provision of relief from S130 CA85.

4.9 Payment for shares - cash or kind

Shares are normally paid for in cash although the full issue price need not necessarily be received on allotment. A debt owing by the company may be capitalised by the issue of shares in exchange; this is an issue for cash.

The company may agree with subscribers that they shall pay for their shares in kind eg, by transferring property or even rendering services to the company instead of paying cash. In any case a company should obtain property or services of a value at least equal to the nominal value of the shares.

In the case of a **private company** it enjoys a surprising freedom to determine whether the value of what is received is in fact adequate. If a company chooses to acquire property at a rather high price and in payment allot shares of a nominal value equal to that price, the decision of the directors cannot generally be challenged: **Re Wragg [1897]**. But if the consideration is patently inadequate or it is clear on the face of the documents that it is illusory or fraudulent, the courts might query the adequacy of the consideration: **Hong Kong & China Gas Co v Glen [1914]**. This is an application of the contractual rule - consideration must be valuable and sufficient but need not be adequate.

However, a **public company** may not:

(a)   issue subscribers' shares other than for cash;

(b)   allot shares for consideration which includes an **undertaking** which may be performed more than five years after the allotment: S102 CA85;

(c)   accept in payment for its shares performance of **services** for the company: S99 CA85;

(d)   (to avoid problems with inadequate consideration) allot shares for non-cash consideration unless:

- the consideration for the allotment has been independently valued; and

- a report with respect to its value has been made to the company by a person appointed by the company during the six months preceding the allotment of shares; and

- a copy of the report has been sent to the proposed allottee: S103 CA85.

A report and calculation is not required where the allotment by the company is in connection with a takeover or merger.

The valuation and report must be made by an independent person, that is, a person qualified at the time of the report to be appointed, or continue to be, an auditor of the company.

However, where it appears to the independent person to be reasonable for the valuation of the consideration , or part of it, to be made (or for him to accept such a valuation) by another person who:

- appears to have the requisite knowledge or experience to value the consideration or that part of it; and

- is not an officer or servant of the company or being a body corporate a member of the same group;

the independent person may arrange for or accept a valuation, together with a report which will enable the independent person to make his report: S108 CA85.

A copy of the report must be filed with the Registrar at the same time as the return of the allotments is made: S111 CA85.

If a public company does issue shares in contravention of these rules, the allotment is valid but the allottee will be liable to pay the nominal value or so much as is treated as paid up to a minimum of ¼ of the nominal value plus any premium plus interest. In **Re Bradford Investments Plc (No 2) [1991]** full value was not obtained for the shares which were exchanged for non-cash consideration and the shareholders were accordingly liable for the shortfall.

4.10   Bonus issues

Definition   A **bonus** or **capitalisation issue** of shares is effected by appropriating some part of the company's reserves (including share premium account or capital redemption reserve fund) to paying-up unissued shares in full and then distributing those shares as a bonus to shareholders eg, if a company has an authorised share capital of 200,000, it can capitalise £100,000 from its reserves to issue the remaining 100,000 shares as fully paid on the basis of one new share for each share already held.

This is not the same as the company issuing shares without receiving consideration for them. The reserves are shareholders' funds and the effect of the transaction is to reduce the reserves in providing consideration for the shares. The individual shareholder is, of course, no better off since he owns the same proportion of the increased issued share capital as before. Power under the articles is required to make an issue of this kind.

4.11   Rights issue

Definition   In a rights issue the shares are offered to existing shareholders (in proportion to their shareholding) usually at somewhat less than the current market value of the shares.

Eg, a company whose £1 shares stand at, say, 190p each, may offer new shares at, say, 170p on the basis of one new share for every four shares already held. On the allotment of new shares a company should first offer them to existing shareholders; S89 CA85.

Conclusion   Both bonus issue and rights issue shares are offered to existing shareholders in proportion to their shareholdings. However a rights issue is an issue to raise money from the shareholders whereas in a bonus issue reserves are capitalised rather than cash being raised.

4.12   Application for shares and allotment of shares

The subscribers to the memorandum of association agree to take at least one share each. The company when formed is entitled to enter their names in its register of members as holders of those shares and to require the subscribers to pay the money due on those shares.

In other cases a company will generally obtain from potential shareholders a written application for shares to be issued to them. The directors of the company then pass a resolution to allot and issue the shares to the applicants. A letter of allotment is written to inform the applicants that in response to their application shares have been allotted to them. If payment (in cash or kind) has not already been made for the shares it will then become due.

The allottee has a contractual right to have his name entered on the register of members.

Frequently the contract expressly provides that the contract may be assigned to a third party, who is then entitled to be entered on the register. This is common where a company wishes to raise capital without incurring the expense of a public issue. It invites applications for shares from its existing members at a consideration below market value (so the shareholder is induced to apply for shares which he can immediately sell for a profit). On accepting the offer, the company sends out renounceable letters of allotment to the offeree, who can then either be registered himself as the holder of the new shares or renounce in the favour of a third party, who will be registered instead. The renouncement will, of course, take place where the third party pays for the contractual right to be registered as the shareholder.

There are variations of this standard procedure when a company makes a **rights issue** or a **bonus issue** or if the shares are issued as part of a transaction by which the company acquires property in exchange for its shares. A private company may issue shares in a rather more informal way without the use of written letters of application and allotment.

Once the company and the prospective shareholders have agreed to the terms of issue of available new shares, the transaction should appear in the books of the company in the form of a board resolution to allot the shares, an entry in the register of members and receipt or appropriation by the company of cash or other assets as consideration for the shares.

4.13   Return of allotment

A company which has issued shares in any way whatever is required within **one month** to deliver to the Companies Registry a signed return of allotments containing:

(a)   particulars of the shares issued (ie, details of class rights);

(b)   details of the consideration received; and the

(c)   names of the allottees: S88 CA85.

Where shares have been issued for a consideration other than cash the return must be accompanied by a contract relating to the issue or by a summary, setting out the consideration received, and a copy of the report as required by S103 CA85.

4.14   Activity

Why might bonus shares be issued by a company?

4.15   Activity solution

Bonus shares might be issued in order to reduce the market value of the shares. Eg, a company has 200,000 shares in issue with a market value of £5 each, total market value, £1 million. If a bonus issue of 300,000 shares is made then there are 500,000 shares in issue, total market value still £1 million. This has theoretically reduced the value of one share to £2.

4.16   Activity

The three directors of Court Ltd, F,G and H, each hold one third of the company's issued share capital. It has been decided to issue 50,000 further ordinary shares to X in order to purchase his business. The company has sufficient authorised capital, but neither the Articles nor any existing resolutions make provision for issue of shares. What is necessary for this allotment to be legal?

4.17   Activity Solution

The shares can only be allotted if the members (ie, F, G and H) pass a resolution in general meeting giving themselves as directors the authority to issue the shares (S80 CA85). This must specify the maximum amount of shares that may be allotted and must be for a period of not more than five years.

The consideration for the shares is a business, therefore not cash. As Court Ltd is a private company there is no necessity for an independent valuation to be made of this non-cash consideration.

There is no need to pass a special resolution disapplying the S89 CA85 pre-emption rights since, although the shares are equity securities, they are not being issued for cash.

5   CHAPTER SUMMARY

This chapter considered the law surrounding the issue of share capital by a company and therefore the chapter commenced with an explanation of the nature of shares, the distinction between share and loan capital and the terminology surrounding share capital.

Issues of shares by companies in general were then considered. This included the rules on allotment of shares and the authority required by the directors of a company in order to be able to issue shares. Shares may be issued at a premium, thereby setting up a share premium account, but not a discount. Shares may also be issued for non-cash consideration but in the case of public companies there are a number of rules for such a situation. The distinction between a rights issue and a bonus issue was also considered.

There are various methods of offering shares to the public and the rules regarding applications for listing on The Stock Exchange and offer of unlisted securities are mainly covered by FSA86.

6   SELF TEST QUESTIONS

6.1   What two priority rights are commonly given to preference shares? (1.5).

6.2   What is the difference between authorised and issued share capital? (2.4).

6.3   What are the various methods of issuing shares to the public? (3.2).

6.4   Where must authority be in order to pass an ordinary resolution to increase authorised capital under S121 CA85? (4.1).

6.5   Explain the requirements of S80 CA85. (4.2).

6.6   What can be the effect of shareholders not having pre-emption rights? (4.3).

6.7   What is the one-quarter rule? To what type of company does it apply? (4.5).

6.8   What are the allowed uses of share premium account? (4.8).

6.9   What are the provisions of S131 CA85? (4.8).

6.10   List the special statutory rules regulating payment for shares issued by a public company. (4.9).

7   EXAMINATION TYPE QUESTIONS

7.1   Rakolite plc

(a)   What are the differences between shares issued at a discount and shares issued at a premium? What are the legal consequences of each type of issue?

(10 marks)

(b)   Rakolite plc wishes to raise capital in order to finance expansion of its activities and is considering the following alternative methods of attracting capital in a highly competitive market by public issue:

(i)   A series of debentures with a nominal value of £1. The debentures will be issued at 80p. The debentures are redeemable at nominal value on 1 January 1992;

(ii)   A series of debentures with a nominal value of £1 also to be issued at 80p and redeemable at nominal value of 1 January 1992. One of the terms of issue is that debenture holders will be entitled at any time after 1 July 1991 to convert their debentures into fully paid £1 ordinary shares:

(iii)   A series of debentures with a nominal value of £1 also to be issued at 80p and redeemable at nominal value on 1 January 1992. One of the terms of issue is that debenture holders will be entitled at any time after 1 July 1991 to convert their debentures into fully paid ordinary shares with a nominal value of 75p;

Advise Rakolite plc on the legal validity of the above proposals.

(10 marks)

(Total: 20 marks)

7.2   A Ltd

The directors of A Ltd which was incorporated last month propose to issue £1 shares of the company in exchange for 50p shares of B Ltd on the basis of a straight 1 for 1 exchange of shares.

State the relevant legal rules if the net asset value of the shares of B Ltd at the time of the exchange is:

(a)   £1.25 per share; and
(b)   75p per share.

None of the existing members of A Ltd wish to purchase additional shares. Would your answer differ if A were a public limited company?

(10 marks)

8   ANSWERS TO EXAMINATION TYPE QUESTIONS

8.1   Rakolite plc

(a)   A company may not issue its shares at a discount: S100 Companies Act 1985 (CA85). This rule was first applied in **Ooregum Gold Mines v Roper** as part of the capital maintenance provisions. If shares are issued at a discount this would mislead the creditors who are entitled to assume that at least the full par value of the shares issued has been received by the company. An issue at a discount means an issue at a price less than the par value of the share, there is no rule to prevent the company issuing shares at a price less than their current market price as long as the company receives the par value. An issue by the company at par when the shares have a higher market value might constitute a breach of directors' duty because they are obliged to obtain the best possible price for the company's shares: **Head v Ropner Holdings.** An issue at par when the shares have a higher market value results in a 'watering down' of the value of the existing shares as the profits available for distribution will have to be spread more thinly. This is one of the reasons for the introduction of pre-emption rights in 1980. Existing shareholders, therefore, get first chance to take up any new shares and the value of their shareholding overall should not be affected if they take a proportionate interest.

A public company which issues shares in exchange for non-cash assets must have the assets independently valued (S103 & S108 CA85) and shares may be allotted only to the value of the asset. Failure to do so will condemn the allotter liable to pay the company the full value of the shares (nominal values plus premium). This provision was introduced to avoid the possibility of shares being issued at a discount through exchanging them for a non-cash asset.

This is no such restriction for a private company and the court will only interfere if there is evidence of fraud or the value of the asset in illusory: **Re Wragg.**

An issue at a premium is where the company issues shares at a price higher than the par value. This price might still be less than the current market price and is likely to be so in order to attract investors - this would not constitute a discount. Any sum received by the company as premium must be paid into a separate share premium account which for most purposes is treated as share capital - in particular it is not available for distribution by way of dividend and it cannot be reduced except by a reduction of capital duly authorised: S130 CA85.

The share premium account can be used for certain purposes:

(i)   paying fully paid bonus shares,

(ii)   paying the company's preliminary expenses,

(iii)   paying discounts, expenses or commission where allowed on any issue of shares or debentures;

(iv)   paying for the premium on redemption of debentures.

A company may not issue shares at a discount but if it does the share issue remains valid and the discount is treated as unpaid up share capital which the shareholder is liable to pay with interest at the appropriate rate.

If the company distributes funds to the shareholders which should have been retained in the premium account, the company and the officers may be liable to a fine and the officers of the company may be called upon to make up the deficit.

(b)   (i)   Shares may not be issued at a discount but debentures maybe. Debentures are not covered by the capital maintenance provisions.

        (ii)   The one exception to (i) is where debentures have an immediate right to be converted into shares. An issue of debentures at a discount would then be tantamount to an issue of shares at a discount and a breach of S100 CA85: **Mosely v Koffeyfontein Mines.** In this case the option to convert is not immediate and thus does not fall within the exception. The issue will be valid.

(iii)   In this case the par value of any shares converted is 75p, therefore there is no suggestion at the time of issue of a discount, in fact the reverse is true. At the time of conversion it could be argued that the shares are issued at a premium, ie, 80p is paid for a 75p share. If this is so, the difference of 5p per share must be transferred to the share premium account and may not be used except in accordance with S130 CA85.

8.2   A Ltd

(a)   It is assumed that the directors have the requisite authority from the shareholders to make this issue, (S80 Companies Act 1985 (CA85)) and the issue is within the authorised share capital.

The issue of shares for a consideration other than cash ie, in this case in exchange for shares of B Ltd, is permissible but the return of allotment must have attached to it a copy or particulars of the contract of acquisition: S88 CA85. Consideration to support a contract must be sufficient ie, of some monetary value, but need not be adequate and the parties to the contract are free to make their own bargain.

Where, as in **Henry Head v Ropner Holdings** the net asset value of the company whose shares are acquired exceeds the nominal value of the shares issued (in this case by A Ltd) the excess should be treated as share premium subject to the restrictions of S130 CA85. Thus, a notional 25p per share should be placed in the share premium account. This case and **Shearer v Bercain** effectively outlawed 'merger accounting' whereby (under the then ED3) the creation of a share premium account could (it was thought) be ignored in certain types of merger. CA85 therefore modifies the position and relaxes the rules on share premium accounts to make it unnecessary to 'lock' the excess of the true value of the assets of the acquired company into a share premium account where (*inter alia*) a 90% minimum holding is acquired. It is not possible to tell from the question whether there has been such a merger here.

(b)   In this case the yardstick of net asset value suggests that A Ltd is not obtaining full consideration for its shares; if that is so it would on these facts be issuing its shares at a discount on their nominal value which is not permitted **Ooregum Mining Co. v Roper** and now Ss100 and 112 CA85. It is, however, permissible for a shareholder to undertake to contribute more for his shares than their nominal value, the excess is called share premium.

However, asset value is merely one indication of the value to be put on shares of B Ltd. The merger of A and B may offer prospects of greater profitability for both companies. If the directors consider that the shares of B Ltd are worth an amount at least equal to the nominal value of the shares of A Ltd to be issued in exchange and enter the shares of B Ltd in their books at that value, their judgement, unless it is obviously not made in good faith and for sufficient reason, is unlikely to be set aside: **Re Wragg.** In that case there is no issue of shares of A Ltd at a discount; there is an acquisition of assets (shares of B Ltd) at a possible over-value, which may be evidence of a breach of directors' duty ie, the duty to act in the best interest of the company.

If the company were a public company on issuing the shares for a consideration other than cash, it must obtain an independent valuation of the proposed consideration: Ss103, 108 and 112 CA85, but this provision is dispensed with if the shares are issued in connection with a merger which might be the case in the problem.

22 CORPORATE FINANCE: MAINTENANCE OF SHARE CAPITAL

INTRODUCTION & LEARNING OBJECTIVES

Syllabus area 8f. Maintenance of capital, increase and reduction of share capital, purchase by a company of its own shares, financial assistance in the purchase of shares. (Ability required 3).

Distribution of profit. (Ability required 3).

The law provides rules on maintenance of capital in order to prevent a company reducing its capital by returning it to members, whether directly or indirectly: capital of limited companies is regarded as a guarantee, or buffer, fund for creditors.

When you have studied this chapter you should be able to do the following:

- Understand why a company must maintain capital.

- Understand in detail S135 CA85.

- Set out the procedures for redemption and purchase of own shares and the various methods of funding.

- Know that financial assistance for acquisition of own shares is generally prohibited but also know the exceptional situations where it is lawful.

- Understand the dividend rules.

---

1 INTRODUCTION TO CAPITAL MAINTENANCE

1.1 Introduction

The liability of the members of a company limited by shares is restricted to the nominal value of the shares issued to them. If the company is prosperous it will have assets worth more than the nominal value of its issued share capital out of which to satisfy claims against it. If it falls on hard times it may have lost capital so that the sum total of its assets is less than its issued share capital; and if its shares are paid up, no money may be obtained by making calls on the members. The law does not seek to avoid all the consequences necessarily attendant on the speculative ventures it encourages by permitting limited liability companies. But it does take steps to safeguard the capital to which outsiders are entitled to look. The rules on maintenance of capital prevent the company from reducing its share capital by obtaining less than the value of the shares on issue (it cannot issue shares at a discount: S100 Companies Act 1985 (CA85)) or by returning capital to members. The rules do **not** prevent the company from using the capital to trade (that is what it is there for).

The capital which a limited company must maintain as a guarantee or buffer fund for creditors includes not only share capital, but also share premium account (S130 CA85) and capital redemption reserve (S170 CA85). Loan capital (ie, borrowings) is not subject to maintenance.

1.2   Rules on capital maintenance

Once capital has been raised it must be maintained. The law attempts to achieve this by:

(a)   forbidding a company from acquiring its own shares - S143 CA85 which is a statutory enactment of the common law rule in **Trevor v Whitworth**.

There are a number of exceptions to this maintenance rule, in particular:

- S135 CA85 - reductions of capital;
- S159 CA85 - redemption of redeemable shares;
- S162 CA85 - purchase of own shares.

(b)   forbidding a company from giving financial assistance for the acquisition of its own shares - S151 CA85. There are a number of exceptions to this rule of maintenance;

(c)   forbidding a company from making distributions except out of profit - the dividend rules of S263 and S264 CA85.

2   INCREASE AND REDUCTION OF CAPITAL

2.1   Increase of capital

Definition   The expression increase of share capital usually denotes an increase of authorised share capital, but it can also be used to denote the actual issue of shares.

A company may alter its capital clause to increase its authorised share capital if so authorised by its articles (eg Art 32 Table A) by passing an ordinary resolution: S121 CA85. Clearly there are no difficulties for the maintenance principle produced by increasing authorised capital.

The procedure for issue of shares was covered in the previous chapter. The rules on maintenance are underpinned by S100 CA85 (which prohibits the issue of shares at a discount on their nominal value), by S130 CA85 (which requires the creation of a share premium account if shares are issued at more than their nominal value), and by the special rules for public companies in relation to non-cash consideration as payment for shares (in particular the requirement for the independent valuation and report which is intended to prevent manipulation of the discount and premium rules).

2.2   Other capital changes

Subject always to appropriate powers existing in the articles a company may by S121 CA85:

(a)   **consolidate or divide** its shares eg, £1 shares can be consolidated into half the number in £2 shares or divided into twice the number in 50p shares. However the proportions of amounts paid and unpaid must remain the same where shares are partly paid eg, before sub division every £1 share was 50p paid then the new shares of 50p must be treated as 25p paid. Since the overall nominal values remain the same, this alteration does not contravene the maintenance principle;

(b)   convert its shares into **stock** and **vice versa**.

The difference between stock and shares is that shares are regarded as units whereas stock is conceived to be a single fund of a given total value but for convenience it is transferable in multiples of a similar amount. There is very little difference in practice between, say, 100 shares of £1 and £100 stock transferable in stock units of £1. Again this alteration does not contravene the maintenance principle.

At one time companies were disposed to convert shares into stock because stock, unlike shares, did not have distinguishing serial numbers for its units. Share numbers caused much difficulty. But it is now unnecessary to have distinguishing numbers for shares which rank *pari passu*, and are fully paid: S182 CA85.

A company cannot, however, issue stock nor can stock be partly paid. A company issues shares which when fully paid may be converted into stock. This can be done in one sequence of resolutions eg, when making a bonus issue, at the same meeting.

A company may **convert its shares** or some of them into different classes of shares with special rights eg, preference shares can be converted to ordinary and *vice versa*. But if any of these shares are already issued the consent of the class must be obtained by following a special procedure called variation of class rights - S125 CA85. This though, would not contravene the maintenance principle as again capital is not reduced.

2.3   Diminution of capital

A company may cancel **unissued** shares in the same way (see above) as it can increase its unissued shares: S121 CA85. This is not a reduction in capital as, although the company had the power to issue shares, it had not actually done so, and merely lowering the amount of shares which the company (usually through the directors) has the power to issue without approval of members in no way reduces the capital available to the company.

2.4   Reduction of capital

If a company wishes to reduce its **issued** share capital it must obtain the approval of the court: S135 CA85.

But a public company cannot reduce its capital below the statutory minimum using S135 procedure unless it is first re-registered as a private company, or the court otherwise directs: S139 CA85.

The price of limited liability is a restriction on the return to members of money subscribed as share capital. A reduction of share capital can effect such a repayment. The restrictions, however, extend to all methods of reducing share capital with or without repayment of money etc.

S135 CA85 specifies three possible modes of reduction:

(a)   Cancellation wholly or in part of liability on issued shares not fully paid up.

In a simple example of an issued capital 50 £1 shares 50p paid, the unpaid sum of 50p on each share could be cancelled; this would reduce the authorised and issued capital by £25 leaving 50 shares of 50p fully paid as the reduced issued capital; the resources of capital available to pay the company's debts are thereby reduced.

(b)   Cancellation of some part of the paid up value of the issued shares which is lost or unrepresented by available assets; eg, if a company had an authorised, issued and fully paid capital of £100 in £1 shares, it could cancel, say, 50p per share and reduce its authorised issued and fully paid capital to £50 in 100 issued shares of 50p. The £50 cancelled in this way would permit a corresponding reduction in, for example, a debit balance on profit and loss account in the balance sheet.

(c)   Repayment to members of some part of the paid up value of their shares which is in excess of the needs of the company eg, taking the same initial situation as in (b) above the company might repay to members 50p per share in cash and so reduce its capital to £50 in 100 shares of 50p. In this case the asset side of the balance sheet would be reduced by £50 in cash paid out to members.

In cases (a) and (c), where the effect is to reduce the actual or potential fund available to meet the company's debts, the creditors would have grounds for objection and accordingly they are given a right to object. It is possible (though unusual) to reduce share capital by means other than the standard ones described in (a), (b) and (c) above. It is common to reduce the share premium account and capital redemption reserve under S135 as although S135 specifies three examples (all relating to share capital) it allows reduction of any capital for any reason.

2.5   Procedure for reduction of capital

The procedure is laid down by Ss135-138 CA85 as follows:

(a)   the company must have power in its **articles** (eg, Art. 34 of Table A) to reduce its capital. If necessary the articles must be altered to this effect before proceeding to stage (b) below but the alteration may be made at a prior stage of the same meeting;

(b)   the company must pass a **special** resolution setting out the terms of the reduction;

(c)   it then **applies to the court** by petition for an order confirming the reduction (the resolution is not effective until confirmed);

(d)   the court is then required to consider the **position of creditors** of the company in cases (a) and (c) of the preceding paragraph and may do so in any other case. But the court has a general discretion as to what should be done.

   If the company has more than one class of shares, the court will also consider whether the reduction is **fair between classes**. In this it will have regard to the rights of the different classes in a liquidation of the company since a reduction of capital is by its nature similar to a partial liquidation.

   •   An affidavit will be made by one of the directors setting out all the circumstances and reasons and submitting a statement of assets and liabilities. If possible the position of creditors will be safeguarded in advance by producing, for example, a bank guarantee that all creditors will be paid in full. It is only creditors to whom debts are owing at the time who must be considered (and also landlords to whom the company has future obligation to pay rent under existing leases). If the creditors are not afforded safeguards in this way the court may order that an advertisement be published inviting creditors to appear; the court may later refuse to approve the reduction until creditors have consented or been paid off.

   •   If the **preference** shares carry **no priority** in repayment of capital they are likely to suffer a reduction of capital rateably with ordinary shares. This result follows even if the dividend on the preference shares, expressed as x% on the amount paid up on the shares, must thereby be reduced: **Re Mackenzie & Co [1916]**. This is not regarded as a variation of rights, thus no separate class consent would be required.

   •   If preference shares carry a right to **repayment of capital in priority** to ordinary shares if surplus cash is returned, no class consent of the preference shareholders is required to a reduction of share capital which eliminates that class as this merely reflects their rights to priority in liquidation.

Scottish Insurance Corp Ltd v Wilsons & Clyde Coal Co [1949]

Facts: a company proposed to reduce its capital by paying off all the holders of preference shares. The preference shareholders had priority on a liquidation to a return of capital. The preference shareholders objected to the scheme on the ground that it deprived them of the opportunity of sharing in a distribution of surplus assets on the liquidation of the company.

Held: the court held that the articles made it clear that, subject to the payment to the preference shareholders of their capital and any outstanding preferential dividend, the whole of any reserve fund and other assets, including the sale of the capital assets, belonged to the ordinary shareholders to the exclusion of the preference shareholders. The reduction was confirmed.

The **Scottish Insurance** decision has been followed in later cases eg, **Re Saltdean Estate [1968]** and **House of Fraser plc v ACGE Investments [1987]**.

- If capital is lost and written off then, if preference shares have priority to return of capital on liquidation, the ordinary shares should bear the loss first.

- But the court may decline to confirm a reduction which is demonstrably unfair.

Re Holders Investment Trust Ltd [1971]

Facts: it was proposed to reduce capital by cancelling cumulative redeemable preference shares in exchange for unsecured loan stock. The majority (90%) preference shareholders held 52% of the ordinary stock and shares. The reduction was approved by a special resolution of the company and an extraordinary resolution of a separate class meeting of the preference shareholders.

Held: this was not confirmed by the court on the grounds:

    (1)   that there was no effectual sanction for modifying the class rights because the majority of the preference shareholders acted in their own interests as ordinary shareholders (in which capacity they stood to gain); and

    (2)   the company had not discharged the onus of showing that the proposed reduction was fair - moreover, the minority had shown it was unfair because the advantages of conversion were not greater than the compensation for the disadvantages.

- If the company has reserves, whether statutory (eg, share premium account) or general, it is normal practice to utilise those reserves to absorb losses before resorting to a reduction of share capital for that purpose.

(e)   if the **court** is satisfied it may make any **order** confirming the reduction on such conditions and terms as it thinks fit. It may order the words **'and reduced'** to be added to the company's name and may order publication of details of, including reasons for, the reduction;

(f)   a copy of the order which will show in respect of the share capital as altered by the order the amount of share capital, the number of shares, the amount of each share and the amount paid up on each share and of a minute approved by the court setting out the reduced share capital is **delivered to the Registrar of Companies** who registers it. The reduction then takes effect and the Registrar issues a certificate.

Conclusion   Reduction of capital flies in the face of the whole tenet of the concept of maintenance of capital.

A company can reduce its capital by:

- cancellation of some or part of the debt on partly paid shares
- cancellation of some part of the value of paid up shares
- repayment of some part of the value of paid up shares

To do this directly affects two groups of people:

(i)   the shareholders: protection is afforded to them by the procedure laid down under S135 CA85. The company must have power in its articles of association to reduce capital and the members must agree to the reduction by passing a special resolution;

(ii)   the creditors: where reduction reduces the fund available to pay unsecured creditors, protection is afforded to them by the court. The court has to agree to the reduction and can vary, cancel or allow it with conditions.

2.6   Serious loss of capital

There is, of course, no means of ensuring that a company does not reduce its capital merely by trading at a loss; S135 CA85 recognises this situation by **permitting** a reduction of capital where capital is lost or unrepresented by available assets. This type of reduction is a book transaction and no money is usually handed back to the shareholders. There is, however, **no obligation** to reduce in this situation so a company's capital may be whittled away by trading losses.

Under S142 CA85 the directors of a **public** company are obliged to call an extraordinary meeting of the company within twenty-eight days from the earliest date on which any director knew the company had suffered a serious loss of capital.

Definition   A serious loss of capital is where the net assets of the company are half or less of the amount of the company's called up share capital.

The meeting must be fixed for a date not later than fifty-six days from when **a** director was aware of the loss. It is to consider whether any, and if so what, measures should be taken to deal with the situation.

S142 provides that the meeting may not be used to discuss anything 'which could not have been considered at that meeting apart from this section'. There is some uncertainty as to what this includes but it may include a resolution to dismiss or censure the directors.

Directors who knowingly and wilfully authorise or permit a failure to convene such a meeting are liable on conviction to a fine.

2.7   Capital redemption reserve

As will be seen later a capital redemption reserve is created where shares are purchased or redeemed out of distributable profit. In the same way as share capital, this reserve must be maintained, except that it may be used to pay for bonus shares - S170 CA85.

2.8   Share premium account

Alterations permitted by S130 CA85 to the share premium account were covered in the previous chapter.

3 REDEMPTION OF REDEEMABLE SHARES

3.1 The rules

> **Definition** Redeemable shares are those which, under their contractual terms of issue, must be bought back by the company at a certain time.

Under S159 CA85 a company limited by shares or limited by guarantee and having a share capital may, if **authorised by its articles**, issue shares which are, or at the option of the company or the shareholder, are to be liable, to be redeemed. However:

(a)   no such shares may be issued at any time when there are no issued shares of the company which are not redeemable;

(b)   redeemable shares may not be redeemed unless they are fully paid; and

(c)   the terms of redemption must provide for payment on redemption.

(d)   the articles must, at the time of issue, set out the terms of redemption.

In general redemption may only take place by using the proceeds of a fresh issue, distributable profits and any premium payable on redemption must also be paid out of the company's distributable profits.

On redemption out of the profits of the company, the company is required to establish a capital redemption reserve equivalent to the amount by which the company's issued share capital is thereby reduced. Such fund is a capital fund, though it may be used to pay up unissued shares for the purpose of a bonus issue: S170 CA85.

Shares redeemed under S159 are treated as cancelled on redemption, reducing the company's issued share capital.

A company which has issued shares up to its maximum authorised capital is allowed to issue fresh shares for the purpose of redeeming an existing issue of redeemable shares.

S171 CA85 extends the power given by S159 even further in relation to private companies, in that such companies may redeem shares out of capital where so authorised by their articles. The procedure to be followed, called a 'permissible capital payment', is covered later in this chapter.

3.2 Activity

A limited company has in issue 100,000 £1 redeemable preference shares, partly paid up to 75p. The terms of redemption allow redemption at any time and the company also has in issue 400,000 50p ordinary shares. Can the redeemable preference shares be redeemed immediately?

3.3 Activity solution

No, as only fully paid shares can be redeemed.

4 PURCHASE OF OWN SHARES

4.1 The rules

S162 CA85 permits a company limited by shares or limited by guarantee and having a share capital which is **authorised** to do so by its **articles** to purchase its own shares. The shares may be redeemable shares or they may not be.

However a company may not purchase any of its shares if, as a result of such purchase, there would no longer be any member of the company holding shares other than redeemable shares; and any such purchase must be in accordance with the provisions set out in the Act.

The rules on the financing of the purchase are the same as the rules on financing of redeemable shares (see above).

The shares purchased are treated as cancelled.

The procedure followed depends on whether it is a market purchase or an off-market purchase.

(a)   **Market purchases** ie, on the stock exchange. Prior approval by an **ordinary resolution** is required for the purchase of a number of shares within a specified price band (ie, the resolution must state the maximum and minimum price which may be paid) and within a specified time, not greater than eighteen months. Thus the approval is general rather than specific.

(b)   **Off-market purchases** ie, not on stock exchange. This requires a **special resolution** of the company authorising it to make the contract to purchase (not the purchase itself). For a public company such approval must be limited to a contract made within a period of no more than eighteen months from the date of approval.

The contract must be available for inspection for at least fifteen days before the meeting (at the company's registered office) and at the meeting itself. The name of the vendor must be made clear as vendors may not vote with the shares concerned on the resolution and failure to abstain may invalidate the resolution. He can, however, vote with any other shares owned.

In either case, within twenty-eight days of the transfer to the company of the shares concerned the company must deliver to the Registrar a return stating with respect to shares of each class purchased the number and nominal value of the shares and the date on which they were transferred to the company. Further, in the case of a public company this return must also state the aggregate amount paid by the company for the shares and the maximum and minimum prices paid in respect of shares of each class purchased.

4.2   Activity

X plc wishes to purchase 600 of its shares. The current market value of such a block is £8,000. X plc has distributable profits amounting to £6,000.

Can it achieve its aims?

4.3   Activity solution

Yes, but only if it first makes a fresh issue of shares raising at least £2,000 in order to fund the purchase. A **public** company may only use distributable profit and/or proceeds of a fresh issue for purchase (or redemption) of own shares.

4.4   Activity

A public company purchases, out of distributable profit, 20,000 of its own £2 ordinary shares at a price of £3 each. What amount must be transferred to capital redemption reserve?

4.5   Activity solution

£40,000. (20,000 shares at £2 nominal value.)

5   PERMISSIBLE CAPITAL PAYMENT

5.1   Redemption and purchase of own shares - additional provisions for private companies

S171 CA85 extends the powers provided by S159 CA85 and S162 CA85 in that it enables a **private** company limited by shares or limited by guarantee and having a share capital, if authorised to do so by its articles, to redeem or purchase its own shares **out of capital** through a permissible capital payment, **but only** to the extent that its distributable profits (and proceeds of a new issue, if any) are insufficient.

A payment out of capital will not be lawful, however, unless:

(a)   The directors of the company make a **statutory declaration** specifying the amount of capital required and stating that having made full inquiry into the affairs and prospects of the company they have formed the opinion that the company will not thereby become insolvent and will still be able to continue to carry on business as a going concern. Such declaration must be supported by and have annexed to it an **auditors' report**.

(b)   A **special resolution** approving the payment out of capital is passed within the week immediately following the date on which the directors make the statutory declaration.

(c)   Within the week immediately following the date of the resolution for payment out of capital, and having delivered a copy of the statutory declaration and the auditors' report to the Registrar, the company must cause to be **published in the London Gazette** and in an appropriate newspaper (or give notice in writing to that effect to each of its creditors) a notice detailing its intention and actions and bringing to the attention of creditors the statutory rights of objection.

(d)   The **payment** out of capital must be made not earlier than five nor more than seven weeks after the date of the resolution.

During the five weeks before payment any member, other than one who voted in favour of the resolution, or any creditor may apply to the court for cancellation of the resolution. On the hearing of such an application the court may make such order as it thinks fit.

(S173 CA85 provides that a director who makes a declaration without reasonable grounds for the opinion expressed is liable to imprisonment or fine or both.

S76 Insolvency Act 1986 (IA86) provides that directors who signed the statutory declaration and shareholders from whom the shares were purchased out of capital are liable to meet any insufficiency of assets up to the amount of the payment made for the shares on a winding up commencing within one year of the date of purchase. The section enables a director who acted on reasonable grounds to be exempted from liability.)

5.2   Activity

A Ltd wishes to purchase 200 of its £1 ordinary shares at 25p above par. It has distributable profit amounting to £190 and is not proposing to fund the purchase by a new issue.

What is the amount of capital payment which is permissible under S171 CA85?

5.3   Activity solution

	£
Purchase price (200 × 1.25)	250
Less: All distributable profit	(190)
Permissible capital payment	60

6   FINANCIAL ASSISTANCE FOR THE ACQUISITION OF OWN SHARES

6.1   The rule

S151 CA85 provides that it is unlawful for a company to give financial assistance, directly or indirectly, for the acquisition of its own shares. The assistance is unlawful whether it is given before, at the same time or after the acquisition. It is similarly unlawful for a subsidiary to give financial assistance for the acquisition of shares in its holding company.

The Act defines financial assistance very broadly to include:

(a)   a gift;

(b)   an indemnity;

(c)   a guarantee or security for a third party loan.

Heald v O'Connor [1971]

Facts: P sold his shares in X Ltd to D for £35,000. D borrowed £20,000 of this from P and X Ltd guaranteed that loan.

Held: the guarantee amounted to illegal financial assistance;

(d)   a loan;

(e)   assuming by assignment a third party loan or security;

(f)   the release or waiver of an obligation; or

(g)   any other financial assistance whereby the net assets of a company are materially reduced.

Belmont Finance Corporation v Williams Furniture Ltd (No. 2) [1979]

Facts: G wished to purchase the shares of X Ltd for £489,000, but did not have the money to do so. X Ltd thus arranged to buy an asset from G for £500,000 in order to assist G. The asset was in fact worth about £60,000.

Held: the transaction amounted to illegal financial assistance.

6.2   Effect of breach of prohibition

The CA85 states that:

(a)   the company is liable to a fine;

(b)   every officer in default is liable to a fine and/or imprisonment;

(c)   the transaction is unlawful.

Case law has established:

(a)   any guarantee or other security issued in connection with the transaction is void: **Heald v O'Connor [1971]**;

(b)   if the company provides financial assistance in the form of an unlawful loan it cannot sue on the **contract** to recover the loan because the contract is illegal: **Selangor United Rubber Co v Craddock [1967]**;

(c)   the company may sue its directors for breach of duty **(Steen v Law [1964])**, because they have wrongfully dissipated the company's assets in breach of their fiduciary duty;

(d)   the company may sue other persons involved in the transaction (particularly the person who received the assistance) for breach of trust. In **Belmont Finance v Williams Furniture [1979]**, it was stated that a person will be liable as constructive trustee to return the money or compensate the company for its loss if:

   •   he knowingly receives company property, in breach of S151 CA85; or

   •   he knowingly participates in a dishonest design on the part of the directors to mis-apply company property;

(e)   the company may sue for damages in the tort of conspiracy if two or more persons combine to effect the unlawful transaction: **Belmont Finance v Williams Furniture [1979]**.

6.3   Exceptions

The following exceptions are designed to exclude from the scope of S151 CA85 certain transactions which the law regards as legitimate.

(a)   If the company's principal purpose in giving the assistance is not that of financing an acquisition, or the giving of the assistance for that purpose is but an incidental part of some larger purpose of the company, then, always provided that the assistance is given in good faith in the interests of the company, the transaction is a lawful one,- S153 CA85.

This exception contains two alternative situations within it

   (i)   The principal purpose of giving the assistance is not to finance an acquisition.

      An example perhaps could be if the company purchases an asset at full market value for the purposes of its business and not with the aim of putting the vendor in possession of liquid funds to enable him to purchase the company's shares. If the vendor of the asset did then happen to use the purchase money to buy shares in the company, this exception would prevent a breach of S151 CA85.

   (ii)   The principal purpose is to finance an acquisition but this is incidental to some larger purpose of the company.

      The meanings of 'principal purpose' and 'some larger purpose' are obscure. In **Brady v Brady [1988]** the House of Lords gave this exception a narrow meaning. In that case, in a complicated arrangement of family companies, to enable the assets to be split between the factions (where the family had fallen out) the court differentiated between reasons and purpose. Thus the reasons for giving assistance might be to enable the assets to be split but the purpose was to acquire shares and was therefore illegal.

Brady v Brady [1988]

Facts: two brothers, Jack and Bob Brady owned and ran a group of companies. The businesses were prosperous but Jack and Bob fell out and in consequence there was complete deadlock in management. The only solutions were either for the companies to be wound-up (which no-one wanted) or for the group to be re-organised such that Jack had the haulage business and Bob the drinks business. The scheme eventually devised involved merging all the businesses into one company B Ltd which was then divided and transferred to two new companies, M Ltd controlled by Jack and A Ltd controlled by Bob. Part of the scheme involved B Ltd giving financial assistance to M Ltd to enable M Ltd to discharge its liability incurred to A Ltd in purchasing shares in B Ltd. After the first stages of the scheme were put into effect Bob refused to complete the deal in actuality because he had now decided that he had got a bad deal but on the legal ground that the financial assistance given by B Ltd was unlawful. Jack sued for specific performance contending that although the principal purpose of the assistance was to finance an acquisition this purpose was incidental to some larger purpose of the company.

Held by the House of Lords: the exception did not apply. Although the assistance would be given in good faith and in the interests of the company and although the overall **reason** or **motive** for the scheme was to save the group from extinction the **only purpose** of the assistance would be acquisition of shares: there therefore was no larger **purpose,** as distinct from 'reason' to which it could be incidental.

Note: the House of Lords then pointed out that since B Ltd was a private company and had distributable profits it could lawfully give the assistance under S155 (covered in the next paragraph), thus the Lords ordered specific performance on an undertaking being given that the procedural requirements of S155 be complied with.

(b)   Where the lending of money is part of the ordinary business of the company, the loan will be lawful. In order for the loan to be in the ordinary course it must be at the free disposition of the borrower.

Fowlie v Slater Ltd

Facts: Slater Walker Ltd loaned money to B Ltd for the purpose of assisting B Ltd to purchase shares in Slater Walker Securities Ltd, of which Slater Walker Ltd was a subsidiary. Slater Walker Ltd was a banking company.

Held: the loan by Slater Walker Ltd amounted to financial assistance for the purchase of shares in its holding company. The **ordinary course of business** exception did not apply because, although the lending of money was part of Slater Walker Ltd's ordinary business, that particular loan was not in the ordinary course of that business because Slater Walker Ltd had stipulated that the loan was only for the purpose of purchasing shares in its holding company.

(c)   It is lawful to provide, in good faith in the interests of the company, money for the purchase of shares under an employee share scheme. The scheme may include salaried directors.

(d)   Where loans are made to employees (other than directors) to enable them to purchase fully paid shares.

In the exceptions (b), (c) and (d) assistance given by a public company must either not reduce net assets, taken at book value, or in the alternative, be provided out of distributable profits.

6.4   Relaxation of the restrictions for private companies

A private company (only) may give any assistance for the acquisition of shares in itself or in its (private) holding company, providing that either the net assets are not reduced thereby, or, if they are, the assistance is provided out of distributable profits: S155 CA85.

The statutory procedure, which must be followed, requires:

(a)   The directors must make a statutory declaration. It must describe the assistance to be given, identify the recipient and declare that the company is solvent. Solvency here means that the company will be able to pay its debts as they fall due within the following year or, if it is intended to wind up within the next 12 months, that the company will be able to pay its debts within 12 months of commencement of winding up.

(b)   A report by the auditors must be annexed to the declaration. The report must state that the auditors have enquired into the state of affairs of the company and are not aware of anything to indicate that the opinion of the directors as to solvency is unreasonable.

(c)   A special resolution must be passed by the company (except where it is a wholly owned subsidiary) within the week following the statutory declaration.

(d)   The statutory declaration and report must be filed together with the special resolution within 15 days after the passing of the resolution (or within 15 days of the declaration if no special resolution is necessary).

(e)   The assistance must be given not earlier than four weeks after the resolution (unless all members voted for the resolution) and not later than eight weeks after the statutory declaration (unless the court orders otherwise after objection has been made).

The purpose of the four weeks' hiatus period after the special resolution is to enable objection to be made to the court by members who did not vote for the resolution provided they are holders of at least 10% by nominal value of any class of issued share capital.

Conclusion   The general rule under S151 CA85 is that a company cannot give financial assistance to a person to buy its own shares (this would be by way of an indirect purchase of its own shares).

The exceptions are:

• for **all** companies (ltd and plc):

-      the principal purpose of the assistance is not the purchase of shares

-      the principal purpose of the assistance is the purchase of shares but it is incidental to some larger purpose of the company.

-      if it is in the ordinary course of the company's business (eg, a bank, etc) and no pressure as to how the money given should be used

-      an employee share scheme

-      loans to employees (not directors)

- for **ltds** only:

  - as long as net assets are not reduced and the assistance is approved by a special resolution backed by directors' and auditors' reports.

6.5   Activity

A company X Ltd controls all the shares in Y Ltd X Ltd wishes to sell its shares in Y Ltd and the employees of Y Ltd wish to set up a new company Z Ltd in order to purchase the shares. The employees wish Y Ltd to agree to allow its assets to be used as security for a bank loan to Z Ltd in order to buy the shares in Y Ltd. Does the law permit this?

6.6   Activity solution

The security for a bank loan on Y Ltd's assets would be classed as financial assistance to purchase its own shares, S151 CA85. However as Y Ltd is a private company it may give this assistance for the acquisition of shares in itself providing that the net assets are not reduced or if they are then the reduction is out of distributable profits, and provided the set procedure under S155 CA85 is followed.

7   DISTRIBUTIONS OF PROFIT

7.1   Introduction to the dividend rules

It is a basic principle of company law that a company with limited liability may not return capital to members. This principle is designed to safeguard the rights of creditors to be paid what is owing to them before capital is returned to members.

As already seen this maintenance principle underlies such specific rules as the treatment of share premiums, capital applied in redemption of shares, reduction of share capital and the basic ban on purchase of its own shares by a company or lending money to finance the purchase of its shares. Further, a company may only make a distribution (pay dividends) out of profits available for the purpose, S263 CA85, not capital.

7.2   Practical pointers

Apart from legal rules there are a number of practical constraints on dividend policy:

(a)   if the company becomes insolvent and goes into liquidation the directors and others may be liable for defrauding creditors;

(b)   dividends, unless paid *in specie* require cash (and entail cash to be paid in ACT to the Revenue). There are practical limits on what can be borrowed to finance dividend payments. The accounts will, after the event at least, reveal the depletion of liquid assets;

(c)   the articles of association may restrict payment of dividends eg, by limiting distributions to trading profit (thereby excluding profits arising from sale of fixed assets);

(d)   the commercial standing and credit rating of a company depends to some extent on financial prudence and some retention of profits for expansion.

The principle that a company may only pay dividends out of available profits cannot, of course, safeguard the company from a loss of capital by unprofitable trading or unwise investment.

7.3   Profits available for dividend: rules for all companies

All companies, including private companies, are prohibited from paying dividends **(making a distribution)** except out of profits available for that purpose: S263(1) CA85.

Definition   Profits available for dividend are accumulated, realised profits so far as not previously utilised (whether by distribution or capitalisation) less the accumulated, realised losses, so far as not previously written off: S263(3) CA85.

This definition permits the distribution as dividend of a **capital profit** ie, a surplus over book value realised on sale of a fixed asset. But the key words are:

(a)   **accumulated** - which means that the balance of profit or loss from previous years must be brought into account in the current period; and

(b)   **realised** - which prohibits the inclusion of unrealised profits arising from the revaluation of fixed assets retained by the company.

There are the following supplementary rules:

(a)   if fixed assets are revalued and as a result more has to be provided for depreciation than would have been necessary if the original value had been retained, the additional depreciation may be treated as part of the realised profit for dividend purposes;

(b)   if a provision (eg, for bad debts) is made in the accounts it is to be treated as a realised loss unless it is merely a diminution in value of fixed assets or of all fixed assets other than goodwill appearing on revaluation;

(c)   if there is no available record of the original cost of an asset its cost may be taken as the value put on it in the earliest available record;

(d)   if it is impossible to establish whether a profit or a loss brought forward was realised or unrealised, any such profit may be treated as realised and any such loss as unrealised.

7.4   Profits available for dividend: additional rules for public companies

In addition to the rules set out above a public company may not pay a dividend unless its net assets are at least equal to the aggregate amount of its called-up share capital and undistributable reserves. It may not pay a dividend so as to reduce its net assets below that aggregate amount: S264 CA85. If, for example, the share capital plus undistributable reserves is £1 million and the net assets are £999,999, no dividend may be paid; if the net assets are £1,000,001, the dividend is limited to that amount which would leave the net assets at £1 million ie, £1.

Definition   Undistributable reserves are:

(a)   share premium account;

(b)   capital redemption reserve;

(c)   unrealised profits (less unrealised losses unless previously written off);

(d)   any other reserve which the company is prohibited from distributing by any statute or by its memorandum or articles of association.

7.5   Profits available for dividend: additional rules for investment companies

There are complicated rules for investment companies that are public limited companies. In essence they may make distributions out of any undistributed excess of realised **revenue** profit and realised **revenue** losses provided this does not reduce the assets to below one and a half times the aggregate liabilities: Ss265-268 CA85.

7.6 Relevant accounts: Ss270-273 CA85

The basis of calculation of what is available for dividend is the **relevant accounts**:

(a) in the ordinary course the relevant accounts are the latest audited annual accounts laid before the company in general meeting;

(b) if figures derived from the latest annual accounts would preclude the payment of a dividend, interim accounts may be used but they must be **such as are necessary to enable a reasonable judgement to be made**;

(c) if the company has not yet produced its first annual accounts, interim accounts (as described in (b) above) may be used.

When the annual accounts are the basis of calculation the rules are:

(a) the accounts must have been properly prepared and also audited;

(b) the report of the auditors must either be unqualified or if qualified must be accompanied by a statement by the auditors as to whether in their opinion the subject of their qualification is material to determine whether a dividend may be paid. In this context an unqualified report is one which states without qualification that the accounts have been **properly prepared**.

Re Precision Dippings [1986]

Facts: the audit report qualified the accounts. The company paid a dividend. The auditors had not made a materiality statement (no-one had realised that one was necessary).

Held: the dividend payment was unlawful (even though in actuality it had been paid out of distributable profit).

When annual accounts are used under (a) or interim accounts are used under (b) or (c) above, they must be **properly prepared** ie, they must comply with various rules on statutory accounts and they must give a true and fair view. It is not necessary, however, that they should deal with matters which are not material to the dividend rules. In case (c) the auditors must report whether in their opinion the accounts have been properly prepared.

7.7 Consequences of making an unlawful distribution

If a member of a company receives a dividend which is wholly or in part paid in breach of the rules and he either knows (when he receives it) or has reason to believe that it is paid in breach of the rules, he is liable to repay to the company all or so much of it as is paid in breach of the rules. There is no time limit for this liability: S277 CA85.

There is nothing in these statutory rules to alter the existing common law liability of directors or other officers of a company who recommend payment of a dividend out of capital: **Flitcroft's case [1882]**. They must make good to the company the unlawful distribution of capital. But they are not liable if at the time they relied on accounts which had been properly prepared and which showed profits sufficient to cover the dividend: **Stringer's** case.

7.8 Scope of the dividend rules

The dividend rules apply to every description of distribution of a company's assets to its members, whether in cash or otherwise - S263(2) CA85 with the following exceptions:

whether in cash or otherwise - S263(2) CA85 with the following exceptions:

(a)   bonus issues of shares;

(b)   the redemption or purchase of any of the company's own shares;

(c)   reductions of share capital under S135 CA85;

(d)   distribution of capital on a winding-up.

In **Aveling Barford Ltd v Perion Ltd [1989]** a sale at an undervalue of an asset belonging to AB Ltd to another company controlled by the sole beneficial shareholder of AB Ltd was held to be a distribution to him.

7.9   Payment of dividends

A dividend is due when it has been declared and has become payable in accordance with the relevant provisions of the articles which usually permit the directors to declare interim dividends but reserve to the company in general meeting power to declare a final dividend not exceeding the amount recommended by the directors (Art. 102 Table A).

Scott v Scott [1943]

Facts: the company in general meeting resolved to pay dividends to ordinary shareholders.

Held: in the absence of a recommendation by the directors the general meeting has no power to declare a dividend. The resolution was of no effect.

Once a dividend has become payable it is a debt for which the limitation period is twelve years.

Dividends are payable in proportion to the nominal value of shares unless the articles relate them to the amount paid up on shares: S119 CA85 (eg, Art. 104 Table A).

A preference shareholder is not entitled to his dividend until it is declared and the directors may, if the articles permit, transfer the entire profit to reserve with the result that none is available for preference dividend.

Payment of dividends implies a cash payment unless the articles (eg, Art. 105 Table A) permit distribution of assets such as shares in other companies *in specie:* **Wood v Odessa Waterworks Co [1889]**.

7.10   Activity

A company had a balance on its profit and loss account reserve at the beginning of its accounting year of losses of £3,000. During the year the company made trading profits of £7,000 and revalued its fixed assets by £5,000. What are the profits available for distribution?

7.11   Activity solution

£4,000. Profit for the year £7,000 less accumulated losses of £3,000. The unrealised profit on the revaluation of fixed assets is excluded.

8   CHAPTER SUMMARY

A limited company may not generally buy its own shares as this will reduce its creditors buffer. However there are certain situations in which the acquisition of shares by a company is lawful.

If a company provides financial assistance for purchase of its own shares this will only be lawful if it is a private company and follows a certain statutory procedure or, if a public company, the provision of finance follows within a number of exceptional circumstances.

The final area of consideration is that of dividend payments. The rules regarding the profits available for distribution are basically that only accumulated realised profits less accumulated realised losses are available for distribution. There are also additional rules for public and investment companies.

9   SELF TEST QUESTIONS

9.1   What capital constitutes a buffer fund for creditors? (1.1).

9.2   List the three circumstances envisaged by S135 CA85 for a reduction of capital. (2.4).

9.3   Define serious loss of capital. (2.6).

9.4   Must redeemed shares be cancelled? (3.1).

9.5   What type of resolution is needed for a:

    (a)   market purchase;
    (b)   off-market purchase of a company's own shares? (4.1).

9.6   How is the amount of a permissible capital payment calculated? (5.1).

9.7   What does S151 CA85 provide? (6.1).

9.8   List the five exceptional circumstances where financial assistance, exceptionally, is lawful. (6.3 and 6.4).

9.9   Define profit available for distribution as per S263 CA85. (7.3).

9.10   Define the net assets test as per S264 CA85. (7.4)

9.11   What is a materiality statement with regard to dividends? (7.6)

10   EXAMINATION TYPE QUESTIONS

10.1   Zed Ltd - cancellation of shares

Zed, a limited company has an authorised share capital of £100,000 in £1 ordinary shares of which 60,000 have been issued and are fully paid. The company intends:

    (a)   to cancel the 40,000 unissued shares;
    (b)   to repay in cash 50p per share to the holders of the 60,000 issued shares.

What is the procedure for effecting each of these changes? The company's articles of association are in the form of Table A.

(10 marks)

10.2   Seasky Ltd

Seasky Ltd has an issued share capital of £150,000 divided into 100,000 ordinary shares and 50,000 10% preference shares all of £1 each. The terms of issue of the preference shares are that they may be redeemed at par at the option of the company at any time after 31 December 1994.

The board wishes to exercise the option to redeem because the company has surplus cash.

Explain to the board the legal requirements with which the company must comply.

(10 marks)

10.3   Rundown plc

The directors of Rundown plc, which has called-up share capital of £2,000,000, are presented with the latest balance sheet of the company which shows net assets of £800,000, a very substantial deterioration over the last twelve months.

(a)   Advise the directors as to what action they should take and of the results of their failure to heed your advice.

(b)   What is the purpose of the action which has to be taken by the directors?

(10 marks)

10.4   Esk Ltd

Esk Ltd incurred trading losses during each of the four years of its existence and its net assets only represent one half of the nominal value of its issued share capital. In the fifth year it made a profit which the directors now wish to distribute as dividend.

Discuss.

(10 marks)

11   ANSWERS TO EXAMINATION TYPE QUESTIONS

11.1   Zed Ltd - cancellation of shares

(a)   If its articles so provide a company may (S121(2)(e) Companies Act 1985 (CA85)) cancel any unissued shares. The procedure prescribed by the articles must be followed and a copy of any resolution (and also a copy of the memorandum showing the change in the share capital clause) must be filed at the Companies Registry Ss121-122 CA85. Under Table A Article 32 unissued shares may be cancelled by ordinary resolution.

(b)   The repayment of part of money paid as subscription for issued shares is a reduction of share capital to which Ss135-138 CA85 apply.

There must be authority in the articles (in this case Table A Article 33) and a special resolution must be passed in general meeting: S135. Application is then made to the court for approval and the relevant financial information to show that the company can afford to repay £30,000 is provided. Creditors have a right to object if the reduction consists of a diminution of liability or a return of paid-up share capital, as in this case. The court is required (S136) to consider the effect of the repayment on the company's creditors. Unless some bankers guarantee or other adequate security is obtained to ensure that all existing creditors will be paid in full the court will order an advertisement to be published and will later consider any objections raised by creditors.

If the court is satisfied that the interests of creditors are safeguarded it will make an order approving the reduction. The order is produced to the Registrar of Companies with a 'minute' setting out the details of the change of capital. The reduction takes effect and the cash may be paid out as soon as the court order is registered.

The court may require the words 'and reduced' to be added to the company's name but in practice this is not usually done.

As there is only one class of shares in this case the court is not concerned, as it would be if there were more than one class, with class rights in respect of capital and its repayment.

11.2   Seasky Ltd

As a general rule, a company may not reduce its share capital by returning the capital to the shareholders. There are a number of exceptions to this, in particular a company may use the statutory reduction of capital procedure or the shares may be redeemed.

In this particular case, the company need not use the statutory procedure for reduction as the shares are expressly created as redeemable preference shares.

The provisions relating to redeemable preference shares are set out in S159 Companies Act 1985 (CA85). A company may if authorised by its articles issue shares which are to be redeemed or are liable to be redeemed at the option of the company or its shareholders. Redemption may only be out of distributable profits of the company or out of the proceeds of a fresh issue of shares made for the purpose of redemption.

If a premium is payable on redemption it must be out of distributable profits of the company.

Shares which are redeemed are treated as cancelled, thus reducing the company's issued share capital.

S170 CA85 requires the creation of a capital redemption reserve where the redemption has been financed otherwise than out of the proceeds of a fresh issue of shares. Where the redemption is solely out of the profits of the company the amount transferred to the capital redemption reserve (from distributable profits) will be equivalent to the amount of share capital cancelled due to redemption. Where the redemption is partly out of profits the amount transferred to the capital redemption reserve will be computed as:

	£
Nominal value of shares redeemed	X
Less: Aggregate amount of proceeds	
of fresh issue of shares	X
Amount to CRR	X

The capital redemption reserve is a quasi-share capital and may only be used for the issue of fully paid bonus shares.

Seasky would therefore require £50,000 of distributable profits to redeem all the redeemable preference shares and a transfer of this amount from distributable profits to capital redemption reserve would be required.

Note the company's capital remains at £150,000, which is now represented by 100,000 £1 ordinary shares and £50,000 in the capital redemption reserve.

As long as the company complies with the above requirements it may redeem the shares. The preference shareholders cannot claim that this is a variation of rights as the company is merely doing what it is permitted to do both by company law and its articles.

In addition, as a private company it may under S171 CA85 purchase shares with payment out of capital, but only to the extent its distributable profit is insufficient, provided the proper procedure is followed ie,

(a)   The directors of the company make a statutory declaration that the company will not thereby become insolvent and will still be able to continue to carry on business as a going concern. Such declaration must be supported by an auditors' report.

(b)   A special resolution approving the payment out of capital is passed within the week following the statutory declaration.

(c)   Within the week immediately following the date of the resolution the company publishes in the Gazette and in an appropriate newspaper a notice detailing its intention.

(d)   The payment out of capital is made not earlier than five nor more than seven weeks after the date of the resolution. Any creditor or any member who did not vote for the resolution may apply to court to have it cancelled. On the hearing of such an application the court may make such order as it thinks fit.

Under S76 Insolvency Act 1986 directors are jointly and severally liable as contributors together with any person whose shares were purchased or redeemed, in the event of a winding up commencing within one year of the date of purchase. The section enables a director who acted on reasonable grounds to be exempted from liability, but otherwise the liability extends to the *permissible capital payment* ie, the capital element in the redemption or purchase and not the whole of the purchase price.

11.3   Rundown plc

(a)   Action to be taken, results of failure to do so

The Companies Act 1985 (CA85) contains provisions for the directors of a public company to advise their members of serious losses of capital. S142 CA85 requires the directors to convene an extraordinary general meeting where the net assets are half or less of the company's called-up share capital. This is the situation of Rundown Plc The directors are therefore required to call a meeting within twenty eight days of discovering Rundown's position. The meeting must be held not later than fifty six days from the day of that discovery. It is called for the purpose of considering what measures, if any, should be taken to deal with the situation. The meeting will be an extraordinary general meeting, all business transacted at it will be deemed 'special business'. Clear notice must therefore be given of any resolution which it is proposed to put to the meeting.

S142 provides sanctions for failure to comply. Each director who knowingly and wilfully fails to convene an extraordinary general meeting commits a criminal offence punishable by a fine. The Act does not prescribe any civil liability. An action for breach of statutory duty by the company against the defaulting directors might be possible. Rundown Plc would need to show that such a duty was owed by the directors of the company, and that failure to call the meeting had itself caused further losses. Since S142 does not require any action to be taken by the extraordinary meeting even if it is properly summoned, it may be difficult to show that any loss arose from the directors' failure to call a meeting.

(b)   **Purpose**

The purpose is to ensure timely disclosure of the company's position so that the general meeting may, if it wishes, resolve to take remedial action before conditions deteriorate to the point of insolvency. Article 70, Table A places the power of management in the hands of the directors; the general meeting may only instruct the directors how to exercise that power by a special resolution. It thus seems uncertain how far the general meeting could go without the directors' collaboration. Timely disclosure of the company's position would give the opportunity for an ordinary resolution (after special notice) dismissing the directors and replacing them by others more competent. Boyle and Birds' Company Law describes the provisions as a 'new and rather curious concept' introduced to comply with the Second EC Directive on Company Law.

11.4   Esk Ltd

A company cannot reduce its share capital, this general principle is reflected in a number of rules relating to the raising and maintenance of capital one of which is the rule that dividends can only be paid out of profits ie, profits available for distribution: S263 Companies Act 1985 (CA85). These are defined as 'accumulated realised profits less accumulated realised losses'. Thus the directors of Esk must bring forward the previous trading losses and only if the profit of the fifth year is sufficient to wipe out the losses of the previous years, can they declare a dividend and then only of the excess.

Moreover the directors of a company are obliged to consider the interests of the company ie, the shareholders and the employees. They should act in good faith in respect of both categories.

If Esk were a public limited company, there are two further provisions the directors must consider:

(a)   They can only pay a dividend out of profits available for distribution and only if net assets would not be reduced below the aggregate of the company's called-up share capital and its undistributable reserves: S264 CA85. The undistributable reserves are made up of the share premium account, the capital redemption reserve fund, unrealised profits and any other reserves retained by the company. It is unlikely in this case that the profit made by the company could make up the capital and provide sufficient available profits for a legal distribution.

(b)   As the company's net assets only represent half of the nominal value of the company's capital the directors should summon an extraordinary general meeting of the company of the company to consider whether and if so what measures could be taken to deal with the situation. This obligation imposed on directors of public limited companies by the S142 CA85 as an additional capital maintenance provision. It seems unlikely that the directors could make a dividend distribution whether Esk is a public or private company. If they did, they are in breach of their duties to the company, and any member who knows or who has reasonable grounds for believing that the distribution is in breach shall be liable to repay the whole of part of the dividend paid in excess of these provisions: S277 CA85.

23 CORPORATE FINANCE: LOAN CAPITAL

INTRODUCTION & LEARNING OBJECTIVES

Syllabus area 8f. Loan capital: raising loan capital, secured and unsecured loans, fixed and floating charges, registration of charges, priority of charges. (Ability required 3).

This chapter looks at borrowing by the issue of debentures: concentrating in particular on secured borrowings. Thus the distinction between the fixed and the floating charge, their relative priorities and the different remedies on default available to the chargee are covered. The publicity requirements for charges and their validity are also considered. The whole of this chapter must be viewed in relation to the order of application of an insolvent company's assets.

When you have studied this chapter you should be able to do the following:

- Understand how debentures differ from shares.

- Describe in detail and differentiate between the fixed charge and the floating charge.

- Understand how the system of registration of charges not only affects the validity of a charge but also enables later creditors to discover the extent to which company's assets are already charged.

- State the order of priority of charges where more than one is secured on the same asset.

- Recognise the situations in which a charge is invalid thereby depriving a creditor of his status as secured.

- Describe the actions a debentureholder can take where a company defaults, concentrating in particular on his contractual right to appoint a receiver.

1   RAISING LOAN CAPITAL

1.1   Borrowing powers of a company

In addition to capital raised by the issue of shares companies may need to borrow. This may be done in several ways such as the issue of debentures or unsecured loans, bills of exchange and other commercial short-term loans, or obtaining an overdraft or loan from the bank. Obtaining goods on normal trade credit is not usually treated as borrowing.

A trading company has an implied power to borrow for purposes incidental to its business. In practice the memorandum is likely to include in the objects clause an express power to borrow. A non-trading company can only borrow if it has an express power. If the power to borrow is implied it is limited to borrowing for purposes incidental to the company's business. If the power to borrow is express then borrowing for a purpose other than to fulfil an object will be *intra vires* the company but an abuse of the directors powers: **Rolled Steel v BSC [1985]**.

Borrowing is a contract to repay the loan. Even if it is within the company's powers it can still be unenforceable against the company if the directors or other representatives of the company borrowed on its behalf without being authorised to do so. The directors' powers to borrow may be limited in amount by the articles. But if they exceed their powers the company can ratify the borrowing by ordinary resolution in general meeting and it may be prevented from denying that the directors had authority.   Borrowing powers are usually exercised by the board; however, an individual director may be expressly authorised to exercise the company's borrowing powers.   In the absence of express authority a single director has little implied authority to borrow.

Whether a loan to a company is *ultra vires* or merely beyond the directors' powers it may be enforceable by reason of S35 Companies Act 1985 (CA85) or S35A CA85.

1.2   Nature of a debenture

The term **debenture** is used to denote the document issued by a company setting out the terms of a loan; such loans are usually medium or long term borrowings.

> [Definition]   A debenture is defined in company law as including **debenture stock, bonds or other securities of a company whether constituting a charge on the assets of the company or not** ie, it may be secured or unsecured: S744 CA85.

An ordinary mortgage of freehold land by a company is a debenture.

1.3   Debentures and shares compared

Both debentures and shares are commonly grouped together as **securities**.

Holdings in company debentures or loan stocks are dealt with on the Stock Exchange under similar procedure to share dealings. The same prospectus rules apply to both. But there are essential distinctions between the two:

(a)   a debenture-holder is a **creditor**; a shareholder is a **member** of the company;

(b)   a company may freely **purchase** its own debentures;

(c)   **interest** on a debenture is a debt which may be paid out of capital if there are no profits. It is a charge on income for tax purposes (unlike a dividend payable out of taxed profits when available);

(d)   debentures **may be issued at a discount** eg, £100 nominal for £95 cash, but not if they carry an **immediate** right to convert into shares so as to confer a right to acquire shares at a discount in contravention of S100 CA85;

(e)   a debenture is a document evidencing a chose in action (the indebtedness) whereas a share **is** a chose in action evidenced by a document called a share certificate.

> [Conclusion]   Debenture-holders and shareholders are both providers of finance to a company. Shareholders are members whose dividends are appropriations of profit whereas debenture-holders are creditors and their interest is an expense of the company.

1.4   Law relating to debentures

The Companies Act 1985 provides various specific rules applicable to debentures but not a comprehensive code. On a number of points the lender and the company are left to make their bargain as they see fit subject to general rules of contract and, where security is given, of mortgages.

Equitable principles protect a mortgagor against **clogging the equity of redemption** either by:

(a)   the lender making the mortgage perpetual or redeemable only after a long period; or

(b)   securing to the lender commercial advantages on terms which are unfair especially if they are to continue for a further period after the repayment of the mortgage debt.

However, rule (a) does not apply to debentures issued by a company: S193 CA85.

Knightsbridge Estates Trust v Byrne [1940].

Facts: an estate company borrowed a sum of £310,000 from an insurance company and as security mortgaged to the lenders property consisting of seventy-five houses, eight shops and a block of flats. The loan was to be paid by eighty half yearly instalments, and the mortgagee's remedies became immediately exercisable if the mortgagors sold the mortgaged property without the consent of the mortgagee. The mortgagors claimed to redeem the mortgaged property giving six months notice, they contended that a provision that a mortgage would last forty years was void as a clog on the equity of redemption.

Held: that the mortgage was a debenture within the Companies Act and accordingly the provisions which postponed the right of redemption were valid.

However, rule (b) does apply.

If a debenture is **perpetual** or repayable at some future time which has not yet arrived it nonetheless becomes immediately due for repayment if the company defaults on the terms of the loan eg, by failing to pay interest when due, or if the company goes into liquidation.

1.5   Debentures - terminology

Although technically the term debenture means a document evidencing any loan to a company the terminology used is somewhat different in contexts other than legal contexts.

In stock exchange terminology a debenture is a secured borrowing; if unsecured it is an **unsecured loan**. A debenture secured by a charge on fixed assets is in that context a **mortgage debenture**. A **convertible debenture** is one which carries a right at the option of the holder to convert into shares of the company on terms fixed in advance.

1.6   Debentures - types

There may be a **single debenture** (eg, to a bank to secure an overdraft).

There may be a **series of debentures** in identical form (eg, a number of individual loans to the company) all ranking for repayment equally or *pari passu*.

There may be a the loan raised from a large number of lenders, typically through an offer to the public, in the form of a **debenture stock** ie, a single debt in which each lender has a holding of specified value.

If there is debenture stock there must be (and if there is a series of debentures there may be) a **trust deed** (see below) setting out the terms of the loan and the safeguards to the lenders.

1.7   Bearer debentures

Debentures may be issued in **bearer form** (ie, made payable to bearer). These are transferable by delivery. Interest is paid on production of coupons attached to the debenture.

1.8   Registered debentures

The more common form of debenture is **registered debentures**. These will state that the monies and interest are payable to the person named in the debenture (the registered holder). Title to the debenture depends on the holder's name being entered in a register maintained by the company. Transfer is effected in the same way as shares are transferred (ie, a proper instrument must be delivered to the company - see later). The company would, at common law, have the right to set off against the money it owes to the original debenture-holder any money owed by the debenture-holder to the company (the right of set off). A transferee of the debenture will take subject to such rights of the company (ie, the company could set off against them too). However, the debenture will usually exclude the company's right to set off against a transferee any existing claims against the transferor.

1.9   Issue of debentures

Debentures are subject to many of the rules which apply to shares. In particular an offer of debentures to the public is subject to the same general prospectus requirements as for an issue of shares and an offer of debentures to the public by a private company is an offence: S170 Financial Services Act 1986 (FSA86). Debentures are normally issued under the common seal affixed by authority of the board of directors. A contract to subscribe for debentures may be enforced by an order for specific performance: S195 CA85.

Debentures may be issued at a discount unlike shares. But the rule against the issue of shares at a discount may not be evaded by issuing debentures with an **immediate** right of conversion into shares on such terms that the shares will have been issued for less consideration than their par value:

Moseley v Koffyfontein Mines [1904].

Facts: a company proposed to issue to its shareholders debentures at a discount of 20%, payable on 1 November 1909, upon the terms that the registered holder could before 1 May 1909 exchange his debentures for fully paid up shares in the company at a rate of one £1 share for every £1 of the nominal amount of the debenture. In the event of the debenture-holder giving to the company a written demand for shares in exercise of this right, the principal moneys were to become immediately repayable.

Held: that the proposed issue of debentures was void, in as much as it was capable of being used as a means of issuing shares at a discount.

If debentures are issued at a premium ie, for more than their nominal value, there is no restriction on the use of the premium when received but it would normally be transferred to capital reserve. If the debentures are issued at a discount or on terms requiring a premium to be paid on redemption the discount or premium may be charged to the share premium account: S130 CA85.

Where identical debentures are issued as a series but to different lenders, possibly on different dates, it is usual to exclude the normal principle of priority of the earlier over the later claim by providing that they shall all rank *pari passu*. This may be so even if the amounts subscribed by the lenders are unequal.

Where a convertible debenture is issued additional restrictions are imposed:

(a)   the directors must be authorised by the company in general meeting or by its articles to make the issue: S80 CA85; and

(b)   the company must not allot any such securities unless it has offered them first to existing members or debentureholders on equal or more favourable terms: S89 CA85.

The restrictions are necessary anti-avoidance provisions in view of the additional restrictions on the allotment of shares.

1.10   Redemption of debentures

Unless the debentures are **perpetual** the company is bound to repay the debentures by the specified final date for redemption and may by the terms of the debenture have the option to repay within some specified period before the final date.

The terms of the debenture may require the company to make an annual payment into a sinking fund for eventual redemption or alternatively to redeem a proportion of the outstanding debentures each year. Unless the debentures prohibit it the company is free to purchase its own debentures in the market.

When debentures have been redeemed the company is free to re-issue them unless the articles or any contract (ie, the terms of the debentures) prohibit re-issue or the company has by some formal act eg, a resolution passed in general meeting, shown an intention to cancel the redeemed debentures: S194(1) CA85. Where debentures have been issued eg, to a bank, to secure advances made from time to time on current account, the debentures are not treated as redeemed by reason only of the company's account going into credit: S194(3) CA85.

| Conclusion | Debentures can be issued at a premium or at a discount. They may also be redeemed at a premium in which case the premium may be charged to the share premium account. |

1.11   Debenture trust deeds

Where large sums are raised from the public (usually by way of loan stock) a trust deed will nearly always be drawn up appointing trustees for debentureholders. The trustee is in effect the creditor of the company. He is the representative of the debenture stockholders with the duty of enforcing their rights and protecting their interests as set out in the debentures or (in the case of debenture stock) in a trust deed.

The debenture (loan contract) will contain a number of terms. Some of the terms are common to all debentures (whether trust deeds or not). The terms common to all debentures (which will also be contained in any trust deed) are:

(a)   the covenant of the company to repay the amount of the debenture at the due time and meanwhile to pay interest on the due dates; in default the whole loan becomes immediately repayable;

(b)   the creation of a fixed charge over the company's fixed assets as security;

(c)   the creation of a floating charge over some or all of the companies assets;

(d)   a covenant by the company to keep the property subject to the charge(s) in good repair and insured (to safeguard the security given for the loan);

(e)   on the happening of various events, such as the company ceasing to trade the whole amount is to become immediately due for repayment and the debenture-holder (charge holder) then has various rights to step in to ensure payment, for example, sell the property subject to the charge or appoint a receiver.

Trust deeds will usually deal with the following additional matters:

(a)   the appointment of the trustee;

(b)   holding meetings of debentureholders to give necessary authority to the trustee on occasion.

(c)   the powers and duties of the trustee including the events on which the trustee may (and should) act to enforce the security on behalf of the debentureholders. The trustee will usually have power to appoint a receiver or to sell assets and to agree to modifications with approval of a meeting of debentureholders;

(d)   a provision that trustees will be paid for the work they do and will be indemnified for any liabilities incurred.

The trustee is liable if he fails to perform his duties properly and may not be relieved in **advance** of that liability by the terms of the trust deed. But if liability has already arisen the trustee may then be released with the consent of a majority of the debentureholders having at least three quarters in value of the debentures: S192 CA85.

1.12   Advantages of a trust deed

The advantages of a trust deed should be evident from the above summary of its contents. The main points are:

(a)   it would not be practicable to create a specific charge in favour of a number of debentureholders separately but a single trustee can hold the security for any number;

(b)   the trustee receives periodic information from the company and can act promptly on behalf of the debentureholders if default or insolvency of the company is revealed;

(c)   the trustee enforces the obligations of the company eg, to insure and keep its property in repair (if so required by the trust deed);

(d)   the power to appoint a receiver under the terms of a trust deed is a useful and prompt safeguard;

(e)   various acts or omissions are specified as defaults by the company. The whole amount becomes due for payment immediately as soon as any event occurs.

1.13   Activity

Can X Ltd make an offer of debentures to the public?

1.14   Activity solution

No, because X Ltd is a private company, S170 FSA86.

2   FIXED CHARGES AND FLOATING CHARGES

2.1   Introduction

A lender to a company may obtain security in the form of a personal guarantee of a director or shareholders. Otherwise he is likely to demand security in the form of a charge over its assets if his bargaining position enables him to insist upon it.

A company which has either an express or implied power to borrow also has an implied power to charge its assets as security for the loan.

In addition to creating mortgages (in this context called **fixed or specific charges**) of land or other fixed assets a company has a unique ability to create **floating charges** of an equitable nature over any assets, fixed or current, present or future, including the equity of redemption of property already subject to fixed charges having priority. These terms will be explained later.

2.2   Fixed charge

> **Definition**   A **fixed charge** has the essential features of a normal mortgage and is created by the procedure appropriate for mortgaging property of any particular type; eg, a mortgage of land by deed, a mortgage of shares of another company by transfer to the mortgagee.

The essential feature of a fixed charge is that if properly created it **attaches from the moment of creation** (the company cannot deal with the property without the lender's consent) to the property in question and (subject to registration) gives the holder of the charge an immediate security over the property in priority to subsequent claimants.

2.3   Floating charge

A fixed charge over fluctuating assets is obviously inappropriate as the company's freedom to dispose of its stock-in-trade, for example, is essential if it is to carry on its business efficiently. On the other hand, if it cannot create a suitable security interest over such assets, it is deprived of the means of raising a loan secured by the use of what is likely to be a substantial part of its assets. This difficulty has been overcome by the invention of the **floating charge**.

A **floating charge** does not attach to the property until the charge **crystallises** (this means that it fixes onto certain property). Until crystallisation of the charge the company is free to dispose of assets subject to it: the person to whom the assets are transferred takes them free of the charge. It is also possible for the company, while still owning the assets subject to the floating charge, to create fixed charges over them in priority to the floating charge. The holder of a floating charge may also be postponed to certain creditors of an insolvent company.

> **Definition**   A floating charge has been defined in **Re Yorkshire Woolcombers Association** as having three characteristics:
>
> (a)   it is a charge on a **class of assets** present and future; eg, if it applies to stock in trade or book debts it comprises whatever assets of that class the company may own at the moment of crystallisation;
>
> (b)   the class of assets will **change from time to time** in the ordinary course of the company's business; and
>
> (c)   the company may carry on its business and **dispose of the assets in the course of business** until the charge crystallises.

It is point (c) which makes the crucial distinction between fixed and floating charges. Which type of charge has been created is not determined by the nature of the property over which it is created but rather by the degree of freedom accorded to the company to deal with the charged property in the course of its business.

Siebe Gorman v Barclays Bank [1979]

Facts: the company created a charge over book debts. The charge provided that the company could not charge or assign these debts and had to pay the proceeds into an account with the chargee bank which the company could not operate without the consent of the bank.

Held: this was a fixed charge: the absence of the ability to use the book debts in the normal course of business deprived the charge of the character of being floating.

Re Brightlife Ltd [1987]

Facts: the company created a charge over book debts. The company retained the freedom to pay the proceeds into its bank account and use them in the normal course of its business.

Held: the charge was a floating charge.

A charge of this nature is the only means by which a company can pledge its current assets (often a major asset financed with the borrowed money) as security for loans to it. But a floating charge may also be expressed to apply to the company's **undertaking and property**: it then comprises the fixed as well as the current assets.

It may be noted, however, that there are limitations on the value of the floating charge, in that if the company's fortunes fall so drastically that it has little property in its possession then there is little on which the floating charge can fix.

2.4   Crystallisation of floating charges

A floating charge crystallises in any of the following circumstances:

(a)   the liquidation of the company;

(b)   the cessation of the company's business: **Re Woodroffe's (Musical Instruments) Limited [1986]**;

(c)   if a receiver is appointed of the company's assets either by the court or under the terms of the debenture or other powers;

(d)   if an event occurs which by the terms of the debenture causes the floating charge to crystallise. Thus the debenture may contain provisions eg, that the charge will crystallise if the company fails to keep the property subject to the charge repaired/insured or (very important for floating charge holders) if the company fails to keep stock levels sufficiently high (ie, of a value equal to or more than the amount of the loan).

There is some doubt as to whether crystallisation will occur automatically on the occurrence of the event specified or whether that happening merely permits the debentureholders to take action to bring about crystallisation eg, by giving notice of their decision, and that crystallisation will only occur when the debenture-holders take action.

CA89 empowers the Secretary of State to make regulations to clarify this. In particular they may require that notice be given to the Registrar of the occurrence of events which cause crystallisation and that crystallisation shall be treated as ineffective until notice is given. (No such regulations have yet been made).

2.5   Activity

Is a charge on a company's undertaking and property a fixed or floating charge?

2.6   Activity solution

A floating charge.

3   REGISTRATION OF CHARGES

3.1   Registration at Companies House

A fixed or floating charge may become invalid on failure to **register it at the Companies Registry**. This rule is mainly to enable other creditors to discover the existence of the charge by searching the file at the Companies Registry before making a loan or otherwise giving credit to the company.

If the prescribed particulars are not delivered to the Registrar within 21 days of creation of the charge then the charge is void against the administrator or liquidator of the company and any person who for value acquires an interest in or right over the property subject to the charge where commencement of insolvency proceedings or acquisition of the interest occurs after the charge's creation whether before or after the end of the 21 days - S399 CA85.

The duty to register is on the company and failure is an offence by the company or any officer at fault. However, because the creditor may be prejudiced by failure to register the charge may be registered by him - S398 CA85.

S396 CA85 lists a number of charges to which the section applies. These include charges on land and various forms of personalty, tangible and intangible. The only significant omission is a charge on shares or other securities (unless these are caught as part of the **undertaking or property** of the company). The list also includes charges created to secure an issue of debentures and floating charges on the undertaking or property of the company.

The twenty-one days for registration runs from the time when the document creating the charge is executed and not from the date of the loan thereby secured.

3.2   Procedure for registration

The **procedure for registration** is that the original instrument of charge (CA89 does not require the instrument to be sent but regulations may require this as it has been required to date) and the **prescribed particulars** (a form showing date of creation, property charged, amount secured and name of chargee) are delivered to the Registrar of Companies who returns the original instrument and sends to the company and the chargee (the lender) a copy of the particulars and the note made by him of the date particulars were delivered. Any person may require the Registrar to provide a certificate of the date on which the particulars were delivered. Such a certificate is conclusive evidence that the particulars were delivered no later than the date stated in the certificate. However the certificate may not be conclusive evidence that the provisions of CA85 are fulfilled (as the actual charge instrument may not need to be delivered) - exactly what the position will be will depend on regulations made.

3.3   Failure to register

The effect of failure to register is that the charge but not the debt secured, becomes void against the liquidator or administrator of the company or any person who for value acquires an interest in or right over the property subject to the charge where commencement of insolvency proceedings or acquisition of the interest occurs after the creation of the charge (whether before or after the end of the 21 days). The loan becomes repayable immediately notwithstanding any fixed period in the loan agreement. Thus the creditor becomes an unsecured creditor in a liquidation or an administration.

Late registration used to be possible only if the court sanctioned it. Court sanction is no longer required under S400 CA85 (inserted by CA 1989) which provides that where particulars are delivered late the charge is not void against an administrator or liquidator or a person acquiring an interest where the event occurs after the actual date of delivery, unless at the date of delivery the company was unable to pay its debts or became so because of the transaction, and insolvency proceedings began within 2 years (floating charge to connected person), 1 year (floating charge to non-connected person) 6 months (fixed charges) then it is void against the administrator or liquidator. Insolvency proceedings include making an administration order or commencement of liquidation.

CA85 (inserted in 1989) also provides that where particulars are inaccurate or incomplete the charge is void to the extent of the error or omission. However the chargee may apply to the court for an order that the charge is effective against the administrator or liquidator on the grounds that the error in the particulars did not mislead or prejudice an unsecured creditor. He may also apply for an order that the charge is effective against a person who acquired an interest in the property on the grounds that he did not rely on the particulars.

CA85 (inserted in 1989) specifically provides that a person taking a charge over a company's property shall be taken to have notice of any matter requiring registration and disclosed on the register at the time the charge is created. The specific provision for charges is included in CA89 as it otherwise abolishes the concept of constructive notice (see earlier *ultra vires*).

It is only **charges created by the company** which require registration under the above. A charge created by a previous owner and in force when the company acquires the asset must be registered within twenty-one days of acquisition (but does not lose its validity if not registered in time).

3.4   Register of charges

There is a completely separate statutory requirement that a **company** shall maintain a **register of charges** at its registered office S411 CA85. Here must be registered **all charges** on the property of the company. A company must also keep a copy of all charges requiring registration. The register and the copies are open to inspection by members and creditors.

3.5   Activity

A bank is considering making a loan to H plc. H plc has offered a floating charge over the assets and undertaking of the company. What steps should the bank take to ensure that the assets and undertaking of H plc are not already the subject of a charge?

3.6   Activity solution

The bank should initiate a search at Companies House to determine whether there are any charges already registered over H plc's assets. Any charges not registered will be void against the bank.

3.7   Discharge of charges

A charge on property of the company may be released by the creditor eg, when the property is sold and substitute security is given in its place, or the company may become entitled to discharge of the charge on repayment of the debt which it secures. In any such case the proper formalities of mortgage law must be observed. The company is then entitled to present to the Companies Registry a **memorandum of satisfaction** (or in an appropriate case of partial satisfaction eg, where several properties have been jointly charged). This memorandum must be in the prescribed form and be signed by both the company and the chargee.

The Registrar places the memorandum on file but leaves the particulars of the charge on the file as before. The satisfaction is noted on the index of charges kept at the back of the file.

Where a duly signed memorandum is delivered when in fact the charge continues, the charge is void against an administrator or liquidator or any person who for value acquires an interest in the property where insolvency occurred or the interest was acquired after the delivery of the memorandum.

4 PRIORITY OF CHARGES

4.1 Priority of charges generally

The following rules apply provided that any registration requirements have been duly satisfied:

(a) a **fixed charge** attaches to the property at the moment of creation. It will generally take priority over any subsequent fixed charge of the same property and over a floating charge created at any time.

This is so even if the fixed charge was created after the floating charge unless:

- the floating charge **prohibits** the creation of subsequent charges with priority over itself; and

- the holder of the fixed charge had actual **notice** of the restriction (ie, registration *per se* does not constitute notice of the prohibition).

(b) a **floating charge** attaches to the property only when it crystallises. It will generally take priority (by order of creation) over a subsequent floating charge but be postponed to any fixed charge.

4.2 Priority of floating charges

When a floating charge crystallises the debentureholders entitled to the benefit of the charge have priority over the relevant assets except to the following extent:

(a) the holders of any **fixed charge** on the company's assets have priority over a floating charge on the same assets.

(b) - the owner of goods let to the company under a **hire-purchase** agreement retains title to them and has priority over the floating charge.

- the seller of goods may reserve title to goods until he has received payment from the buyer, if the **reservation of title clause** is effective the property in the goods will not pass until the buyer pays, until such time the seller may claim his own goods back.

(c) the company's **preferential debts** (see later chapter), even if unsecured, are to be paid out of assets subject to a floating charge, insofar as any other assets not subject to the charge are insufficient. This rule applies even if the company is not in liquidation: S40 Insolvency Act 1986 (IA86);

(d) special situations:

- a **judgement creditor** probably has priority if at the time the charge crystallises he has been paid or the company's goods have been seized and sold;

- a **landlord** may retain goods of the company (and the subsequent proceeds of sale) seized in course of distraining for rent before the floating charge crystallises.

In addition the receiver must bear in mind that a **floating charge** may be invalid if the company becomes insolvent (the date of a petition on which an administration order is made or the commencement of winding up) within twelve months (or two years if the charge is made in favour of a **connected** person): S245 IA86. A receiver who is appointed within two years of the creation of the charge should, therefore, act with caution (though his proper acts as receiver are not invalidated by the subsequent invalidity of the charge itself).

4.3   Activity

Z Ltd creates a floating charge on its undertaking and property on 1 June 19X2. On 30 November 19X2 a fixed charge is attached to Z Ltd's factory building which it owns. Which charge takes priority?

4.4   Activity solution

The fixed charge providing that the floating charge does not prohibit the creation of the fixed charge and the holder of the fixed charge was not given actual notice of that prohibition.

> **Conclusion** In general a fixed charge has priority over a floating charge on the same assets no matter when the two charges were made. The only exceptions to this are if the fixed charge is not properly registered or if the floating charge is specifically stated to rank above all later created floating charges.

5   VALIDITY OF CHARGES: IA86

5.1   Introduction

If a loan is invalid any charge securing it will be invalid. In this paragraph, however, it is accepted that the loan is valid: it is the validity of the **charge** which is in question. In general, if the charge is invalid the erstwhile secured creditor is an unsecured creditor. It is therefore of vital importance that his charge is valid.

The Companies Act requirement of registration at Companies House has already been covered. This paragraph deals with provisions in the IA86 which may invalidate charges.

5.2   Avoidance of certain floating charges: S245 IA86

S245 IA86 provides that a floating charge created in favour of an unconnected person within 12 months prior to the commencement of winding up or the making of an administration order is invalid unless it is proved that the company was solvent immediately after the creation of the charge. If this condition is not met such a floating charge will be invalid except to the extent of money, goods or services advanced to the company at the same time as, or after, the creation of the charge.

Where the floating charge is in favour of a connected person of the company (eg, director, his relatives and other companies within the group) the period within which the charge is vulnerable is two years and there is no need to show that at the time the charge was created that the company was insolvent.

5.3   Transactions at an undervalue and preferences

The liquidator or administrator may apply to the court to set aside company **transactions at an**

undervalue (S238 IA86) or where the company gives a **preference**: S239 IA86.

(a)   A company enters into a transaction at an **undervalue** if:

- the company makes a gift or otherwise enters into a transaction on terms that the company receives no consideration; or

- the company enters into a transaction for a consideration significantly less than that provided by the company.

The transaction would not be set aside if it was entered into in good faith on the reasonable belief that it would benefit the company.

(b)   A company gives a **preference** if it does anything to put a creditor, surety or guarantor in a better position in the event of the company's insolvent liquidation than he would otherwise be. The court will not make an order under S239 IA86 unless the company was influenced by a desire to prefer the creditor. Thus, a payment made or charge created in favour of a creditor who is threatening legal proceedings might be a defence to an action under this section. If the preference is given to a connected person it is presumed that the company was influenced by its desire to give a preference (ie, it is for the 'connected person' to show there was no such influence).

The transaction or preference will only be set aside by the court if the company is insolvent and the transaction or preference was made within the relevant period which is:

(a)   any transaction at an **undervalue** or a **preference** to a **connected person** (as for invalidity of floating charge, except that employees are not connected persons under Ss238 & 239) within **two years** of the onset of insolvency; or

(b)   **preferences** to **other persons** within **six months** of the onset of insolvency.

The onset of insolvency is the commencement of the liquidation or presentation of the petition for an administration order.

The transaction or preference will not be set aside unless at the time it was made the company was not able to pay its debts or the company became unable to pay its debts as a result. The burden of proving this is on the person seeking to have it set aside except where a transaction at an undervalue is alleged to a connected person in which case it is presumed (ie, the connected person will have to show that the company is not insolvent).

S241 IA86 gives the court wide powers in the orders it may make eg, release any security, invest property in the company. However, a *bona fide* purchaser for value without notice of the relevant circumstances who was not party to the transaction or preference is protected.

6   DEBENTUREHOLDERS' REMEDIES

6.1   Introduction

A debentureholder is in a contractual relationship with the company. The terms of the contract, and obligations thereunder, are fixed when the debenture is issued and are not variable subsequently, except on normal contractual principles (unlike the articles of association between the members). Therefore the debentureholder is entitled to seek a remedy for action taken by the company in breach of contract.

A debentureholder such as the company's bank may be the only creditor who holds a debenture. Alternatively, he may hold one of a series of debentures ranking equally with others or he may hold debenture stock and in either case be represented by a trustee in the enforcement of his rights against the company. According to these different situations there are differences of procedure in enforcing a remedy against the company. In principle an action against the company is likely to be brought either by a sole debentureholder or by one of several debentureholders as representative of them all or by the trustee on behalf of all. For brevity reference below to action by debentureholders includes all the possibilities just mentioned.

6.2   Unsecured debentures

The second and important question is whether the debenture is unsecured or secured. If it is unsecured any action to enforce payment of principal or interest is limited to an action for debt or steps are taken to have the company wound up or to apply for an administration order ie, the normal remedies of an unsecured creditor.

6.3   Secured debentures

If, however, the debenture is secured the debentureholder has the normal rights of an unsecured creditor and in addition he may enforce his security in the following ways:

(a)   if his debenture is (as is normal) issued under the common seal of the company he has a statutory power to sell the property or to appoint a receiver of its income in specified circumstances of default: S101(1) Law of Property Act 1925;

(b)   he can resort to any **express power given by the debenture** to be exercised on the occurrence of any one of specified happenings or defaults of the company. Typical instances of events on which the power is exercisable are default in payment of principal or interest; commencement of winding up; appointment of a receiver (by another secured creditor); ceasing to carry on business; breach of various restrictions imposed by the debenture such as a substantial disposal of assets without the debentureholder's consent. If the company is a holding company many of the restrictions will be expressed to apply to its subsidiaries also;

(c)   he can in the last resort **apply to the court** for an order for:

- sale;
- delivery of possession;
- foreclosure; or
- appointment of a receiver of the property subject to the charge.

The court will order sale or appoint a receiver only in three cases ie, when principal or interest is in arrears, when the company has gone into liquidation and when the security is **in jeopardy**. The last of these situations is generally established by showing that other creditors are about to seize assets in execution of a judgement for debt or are about to petition for a compulsory winding up or by showing that the company has or is about to cease to carry on its business or to transfer its assets to its shareholders or some other person.

The fact that the assets on realisation would not repay the debenture in full has been held insufficient.

Since a forced sale of assets is often an uncompromising means of realising the security, the secured creditor is most likely to appoint (or apply to the court to appoint) a **receiver** (who is usually an accountant specialising in insolvency). The receiver may be able to restore the financial position of the company and discharge the secured debt, by sale or otherwise. If he is unable to do so his receivership may be a preliminary to the company going into liquidation.

7 RECEIVERSHIP

7.1 Appointment

A **receiver** is appointed to get in the assets charged (if any - there usually will be), to collect income due on them, to realise the assets and to pay the proceeds to the debentureholders in reduction of what is owed to them. If something has happened to destroy or reduce the value of the security (eg, a factory has burned down) or if there is no security, the debenture-holders, or trustees for debenture stockholders, may petition for a winding up (so may a receiver). But this is a drastic remedy and it will generally be preferable for the company to carry on business but for the receiver to be appointed as a **receiver and manager** so that he has the additional power of carrying on the company's business.

A receiver must be an individual: S30 IA86. A body corporate may not be appointed nor may an individual so long as he is an undischarged bankrupt or is subject to a disqualification order under the Company Directors Disqualification Act 1986.

The Insolvency Act 1985 introduced new statutory provisions regulating the appointment and vacation of office of a receiver, his status while acting and his powers. It also introduced the need for a specific qualification, that of Insolvency Practitioner to act in certain circumstances. All these provisions are now contained in the Insolvency Act 1986.

The receiver may be appointed as receiver of **part only** of the company's property or only of the **income** or part of the income arising from the property. He is then called a **receiver**. An example of this would be a receiver appointed under a fixed charge on a factory owned by the company. If the receiver is appointed under a floating charge over **the whole**, or **substantially the whole**, of the company's property he is called an **'administrative receiver'**: S29 IA86. Nearly all receivers nowadays are administrative receivers.

An **administrative receiver** must be a qualified Insolvency Practitioner but a receiver need not be: S388 IA86.

The **appointment** made under the debenture (as usually happens) is of no effect unless it is accepted by the person before the end of the business day following the day he receives notice of the appointment. If he does accept his appointment it takes effect from the date he received notice of appointment: S33 IA86. If the appointment is for some reason invalid the court **may** order the person appointing or the debentureholder to indemnify the receiver/administrative receiver for any liability incurred because of the invalidity: S34 IA86.

The court may also appoint a receiver/administrative receiver. If the company is being wound up by the court, the court may appoint the official receiver (an official of the Department of Trade and Industry) to act.

The receiver/administrative receiver will ensure that the terms of his appointment include provisions as to his pay. This can be challenged by a liquidator (if the company is being wound up) by applying to the court to fix the receiver's pay if he considers it excessive.

The appointment is a sign that the company is or may be in financial difficulty. Accordingly every invoice, order or business letter of the company must state that a receiver has been appointed: S39 IA86. Notice of the appointment must also be given to the Companies Registry within seven days by the person who made or applied for it: S405 CA85. The appointment causes any floating charge to crystallise unless this has already occurred.

7.2 Control of assets/position of directors

On taking up his appointment the receiver assumes control of the assets subject to the charge. The powers of the directors with regard to those assets are in suspense so long as the receiver is in control although it appears they can pursue a right of action provided the interests of the debentureholders are not threatened: **Newhart Developments v Co-op Commercial Bank**. In particular the receiver may have to get the tangible and intangible assets into the possession of himself or his representatives and bring or threaten legal proceedings to enforce the company's rights against other persons. The restoration of the company's financial position may require a variety of drastic measures.

7.3   Application to court for directions

A receiver appointed by the court will be an officer of the court and will act according to the court's directions. A receiver appointed by the debentureholders will act according to their instructions. However, if he has doubts as to any particular matter he may apply to the court for directions: S35 IA86.

7.4   Liability on contracts

If the company is carrying on its business at the time of his appointment the receiver is likely to find that a number of substantial contracts are in course of performance eg, the employment of staff, the purchase of materials, the sale of finished goods. The appointment in no way terminates the **existing contracts**. He has no personal liability on these contracts since he did not make them.

If appointed by the court, employees are dismissed. However, if he is appointed by debentureholders as agent for the company it will not automatically terminate the employment contracts. S37 IA86 provides that the receiver will be personally liable on any contract of employment adopted by him. However, S37 IA86 provides that he will not be taken to have adopted a contract of employment within the first fourteen days after his appointment. Thus, it would appear that he is given fourteen days to decide whether to adopt them or not.

The receiver may also have to make **new contracts** in order to carry on the business. On such contracts he is personally liable but has a right of indemnity out of the company's assets: S37 IA86. He may contract out of personal liability on the contracts.

In principle, the receiver has power to break the outstanding contracts. But if such actions would injure the company's goodwill (as well as expose it, as it must, to liability for breach of contract) the receiver, whether appointed in or out of court, should apply to the court for approval of his proposed action. The court would not sanction permanent damage to the company's long-term future merely to secure some immediate advantage to its creditors. But, on the other hand, it would not compel a receiver to go on with existing contracts if he had to assume personal liability for new loans raised to finance them.

7.5   Statement of affairs

The administrative receiver must require any or all officers, employees (current or within the previous year) or persons who took part in forming the company within the previous year to submit a statement of affairs showing details including:

(a)   the company's assets, debts and liabilities; and

(b)   the creditors' names and addresses and securities held by them.

The statement must be verified by an affidavit sworn by the person giving the statement: S47 IA86.

7.6   Report by administrative receiver

Within three months of his appointment the administrative receiver must send a report to the Registrar of Companies and to all secured and unsecured creditors setting out details of:

(a)   events leading to his appointment;

(b)   disposals or proposed disposals of company property by him;

(c)   carrying on or proposed carrying on of the company's business by him;

(d)   principal and interest payable to the debenture-holders who appointed him; and

(e)   the amount, if any, likely to be available to pay other creditors.

In addition he must call a meeting of all unsecured creditors unless the court allows him to dispense with the meeting. If the meeting is called it may establish a creditors' committee to maintain contact with the administrative receiver and obtain information from him on a regular basis.

If the company is in or goes into liquidation the administrative receiver must also send a copy of his report to the liquidator.

7.7   General powers of administrative receiver

By S42 & Sch 1 IA86 the powers conferred on the administrative receiver by the debenture are deemed to include the following, so far as they are not inconsistent with the provisions of the debenture:

(a)   take possession of and realise company property;

(b)   sell or dispose of company property;

(c)   borrow money and give securities over company property;

(d)   bring/defend legal proceedings or refer matters to arbitration;

(e)   insure the business and property;

(f)   appoint agents;

(g)   carry on the business;

(h)   use the company seal, execute deeds, bills of exchange, etc, in the company's name;

(i)   make payments;

(j)   grant or accept surrender of leases or take a lease;

(k)   establish subsidiaries, transfer business or property to a subsidiary, make any arrangements or compromise on behalf of the company;

(l)   call up any uncalled capital;

(m)   claim in any bankruptcy, insolvency, etc;

(n)   present or defend a petition to wind up the company;

(o)   change the registered office; and

(p)   anything incidental to the above.

7.8   Power to dispose of charged property

In addition to the above powers, S43 IA86 gives the administrative receiver specific power to dispose of any company asset which is subject to a charge other than the one under which he is appointed as if it were not subject to a charge. To do so he must apply to the court for leave which will be granted if the court is satisfied that the sale is likely to promote a more advantageous sale of the asset and the proceeds will be used to pay the sums secured by the charge.

7.9   Vacation of office

The administrative receiver may resign or be removed by court order. He cannot be removed by the debentureholders. He must vacate his office if he ceases to be a qualified Insolvency Practitioner. On vacation of office he must notify the Registrar of Companies.

7.10   Payments by the receiver/administrative receiver

There is a set order of priority in which the receiver should apply the moneys which he can raise. In brief:

(a)   he must first pay the **expenses** of his operations (including his own remuneration) and the fees, etc, due to the debenture-holders' trustee and the expenses (if any) of the court proceedings leading to his appointment;

(b)   if the security for the debentures is a floating charge only, the receiver must next discharge the debts owing by the company to its **preferential creditors**;

(c)   he may then repay the **debenture debt and interest** thereon.

7.11   Activity

A bank has made a long term loan to F Ltd. The loan is secured by a combination of a fixed charge over the company's property and floating charges over the other assets. F Ltd is defaulting on the interest payments. What are the remedies available to the bank?

7.12   Activity solution

(a)   Sue for breach of contract.
(b)   Threaten to present a winding-up petition.
(c)   Apply to the court for an administration order.
(d)   Appoint a receiver.

8   ADMINISTRATION ORDERS

8.1   Introduction

This procedure (new in 1986) enables an attempt to be made to rescue a company in financial difficulty by placing its affairs in the hands of an administrator. While the order is in force the leave of the court is needed before any winding-up proceedings can be taken or any process, charge, hire-purchase or other agreement can be enforced. Thus, the idea is that the granting of an administration order will 'buy time' for the company and give a procedure similar to that of receivership used by secured creditors to secure the company in financial difficulties.

8.2   Application for orders

An application may be made to court for an order by petition presented by the company, the directors, or a creditor (or creditors), or any combination of them. Notice of the petition must be given to any persons entitled to appoint an administrative receiver: S9 IA86.

Once the petition has been presented:

(a)   **No** resolution may be passed to wind up the company. However, a petition may be presented for a compulsory winding up or an administrative receiver may be appointed.

(b)   A **moratorium** is imposed on the company's debts until such time as the court decides to make the order or dismiss the petition. This means that creditors may not:

   •   Take any steps to enforce any security over the company's property.

- Repossess goods under a hire-purchase agreement, leasing agreement, retention of title or conditional sale agreement.

- Commence legal proceedings or levy executions or distress.

However, these actions may be taken with the court's permission.

8.3   Making the order

The court must dismiss the petition and may not make an order if an administrative receiver has been appointed unless it is satisfied that the persons on whose behalf the receiver was appointed have consented to the making of the order or the charge under which he was appointed would be set aside under S245 IA86 or as a transaction at an undervalue or a preference.

This is an important provision as it means that holders of floating charges, who have appointed an administrative receiver, may block the making of an order **and** may appoint the administrative receiver **after** the petition has been presented.

In addition, before making such an order, under S8 IA86, the court must be convinced that the order would be likely to achieve one or more of:

(a)   the survival of the whole or part of the company as a going concern;
(b)   the approval by creditors of a composition or scheme of arrangement;
(c)   a more advantageous realisation of assets than a winding-up would bring.

8.4   Consequences of administration order: S11 IA86

If the court makes an order:

(a)   The prohibitions against enforcing securities, repossessing goods etc, contained in S10 IA86 (effect of presentation of petition) continue.

(b)   Every invoice, order or letter issued must contain the administrator's name and a statement that the company is being managed by him.

(c)   Any petition for winding up the company is dismissed.

(d)   Any administrative receiver must vacate office. In addition, any receiver must also vacate office if the administrator requires him to do so.

Thus, the holders of a floating charge may feel less protected by an administration order than by appointing their own administrative receiver. However, there are other reasons why they may prefer an administration order, in particular the wide powers of an administrator.

(e)   A qualified insolvency practitioner is appointed to administer the affairs of the company. The administrator is given the same wide powers as an administrative receiver (see above) to manage the business and property of the company, including the power to bring and defend legal proceedings, sell assets, borrow money, insure and appoint agents. In case of difficulty the administrator may apply to the court for directions.

However, S14 IA86 gives the administrator additional powers to remove any directors and appoint directors and call meetings of members and creditors.

In addition, S15 IA86 gives the administrator the following powers:

(a)   S15(1) IA86 allows property subject to a floating charge to be disposed of as if unencumbered;

(b)   S15(2) IA86 provides that property subject to a fixed charge and property held under a hire-purchase agreement, conditional sale agreement or lease may be disposed of providing the court is satisfied that the disposal is likely to promote the administration. The court must order that the proceeds of sale be used to discharge the liability of the secured creditors or the owners of the goods.

8.5   Carrying out the order

(a)   Once the order has been made the administrator must send notice to the company forthwith, to all creditors within twenty-eight days, and to the Registrar of Companies within fourteen days. (He may be fined for default.)

(b)   He must also require a statement of affairs from officers (current and past) employees or independent contractors (current or in the past year) or persons who have taken part in the company's formation within the year before the order. This statement must show the company's assets, debts and liabilities, creditors' names and addresses and details of securities held by them, and be provided within twenty-one days of the date on which it was required, unless the administrator extends the time period.

(c)   The administrator must, within three months of the order, send a statement of his proposals to the Registrar and to all creditors. In addition he must send a copy of his proposals to all members, or he may publish a notice giving members an address from which they can obtain copies instead of sending copies to members.

(d)   A copy of the proposal must be presented to a meeting of creditors at which they shall decide whether to approve them. They may only make modifications to the proposals with the administrators consent.

(e)   The administrator must report the results of the meeting to the Registrar and to the court. If the meeting did not approve the proposals the court may dismiss the order or make such provisions as it thinks fit.

If the proposals are approved the administrator must carry out the proposals as stated. If he wishes to make any 'substantial' revisions he must call a further meeting of creditors and obtain their approval.

(f)   S27 IA86 allows any creditor or member to apply to the court on the ground that the company's affairs, business and property are being managed in a manner which is unfairly prejudicial to the interests of its creditors or members generally, or of some part of its creditors or members (including at least himself) and that any actual or proposed act or omission of the administrator is or would be so prejudicial. The court may make such order as it thinks fit. In particular:

- regulate the future management by the administrator of the company;

- require the administrator to do or not to do specified acts of which the applicant has complained;

- require meetings of creditors or members to be called; and

- discharge the order. However, if the application is made more than twenty eight days after the proposal is approved the court cannot prejudice or prevent the implementation of the proposals.

8.6   Discharge and the administrator: S18 IA86

The administrator may apply to the court for discharge at any time. He must make such an application when it appears that the purpose of the order has been achieved or is incapable of being achieved.

> **Conclusion** The purpose of an administration order is to place the company in the hands of an administrator for a period in order to attempt to allow the company to recover rather that winding it up.

9   CHAPTER SUMMARY

Debentureholders and shareholders are both providers of capital to a company. However whereas shareholders are members of the company debentureholders are simply creditors.

There are various different types of debentures and only a public company may offer debentures to the public. Debentures may be issued at a discount or at a premium and the terms of the debenture will specify the date and amount of redemption of the debentures.

Debentures will generally be secured by either a fixed or a floating charge on the assets of the company. Such charges must be registered at the Companies Registry and the company itself must keep a register of charges at its registered office.

If the company does not pay the interest or capital repayments on the loan then the secured debentureholder has a number of options which may result in the appointment of a receiver to the company.

10   SELF TEST QUESTIONS

10.1   How is a debenture defined? (1.2).

10.2   What is debenture stock? (1.6).

10.3   What are registered debentures? (1.8).

10.4   What are the additional restrictions imposed on an issue of convertible debentures? (1.9).

10.5   What is a fixed charge? (2.2).

10.6   What are the three characteristics of a floating charge? (2.3).

10.7   What is a register of charges? (3.4).

10.8   What rights of action does a holder of unsecured debt have? (6.2).

10.9   What is an administrative receiver? (7.1).

10.10   Why might a secured creditor prefer administration rather than administrative receivership? (8.4).

11   EXAMINATION TYPE QUESTIONS

11.1   Forms of security

Describe the different forms of security available to debentureholders and state the rules governing their priority.

(20 marks)

11.2   Rights of a preference shareholder

(a)   Preference shareholders share the disadvantage of debentureholders but lack their advantages. They can only receive a return on their money if profits are earned and dividends declared, they rank after creditors on a winding-up, and they have less effective remedies for enforcing their rights. 'Suspended midway between true creditors and true members they get the worst of both worlds': Gower - *The Principles of Modern Company Law.*

Examine, by reference to the distinction between preference shares and debentures, the proposition that preference shareholders 'get the worst of both worlds'.

(10 marks)

(b)   To what extent (if at all) are the rights of preference shareholders implied if not stated in the articles of association?

(5 marks)

(Total: 15 marks)

12   ANSWERS TO EXAMINATION TYPE QUESTIONS

12.1   Forms of security

A debentureholder is a person who has a written document evidencing a loan repayable to him. In company law it is usual for a debenture to be for a long period and to be secured.

There are two main types of security which a company may offer a debentureholder ie, a **fixed** or a **floating** charge. A fixed charge is where the debt is secured over specific property which can be readily identified; such a charge attaches to the property at the time of creation of the charge and the company is unable to deal with the property charged until the debt has been paid and the charge satisfied. A fixed charge may be created over any type of property. A floating charge is a charge over a class of assets present and future. The idea of the floating charge is that the class of assets will be constantly changing and being constantly replaced by the company in its ordinary course of business. The company has the right to deal with the assets which belong to the class of assets subject to the charge. **Re Yorkshire Woolcombers Association.** The floating charge is an immediate charge (and thus like other charges requires registration within twenty one days of creation) but the charge does not attach to specific property until the charge crystallises. Crystallisation usually takes effect on the appointment of a receiver by other debentureholders, on liquidation or on the happening of certain events specified in the debenture itself.

If the company issuing the debentures goes into liquidation the secured creditors may take their security and do not have to prove in the liquidation along with the unsecured creditors. The secured creditors may, if their security does not adequately cover their debt, prove as unsecured creditors for the balance.

If there is any conflict between the holders of a fixed and the holders of a floating charge to a specific asset, the holders of the fixed charge will usually take priority. A floating charge is always equitable whereas a fixed charge may be legal or equitable, legal charges prevail over equitable ones. Moreover, a fixed charge created after a floating charge will usually take priority over the latter unless the floating charge prohibited the creation of subsequent fixed charges over the same property and the holder of the fixed charge knew of the existence of the floating charge and the restriction.

Finally, in relation to priorities between holders of fixed and floating charges is the rule that a specific charge usually takes priority over a general charge, as it is more likely for a floating charge to be general and a fixed to be specific, the holder of the fixed charge will have the prior claim.

Most charges must be registered by the company at Companies House under the Companies Act 1985 (CA85). Failure to register invalidates the security against the liquidator, administrator or person acquiring for value an interest in or right over property subject to the charge. If there is any conflict between secured debentureholders over a particular security, the charge which is registered will prevail though the other debentureholder may still claim the debt from the company.

Where particulars are delivered late the charge is not void against an administrator/liquidator or person acquiring an interest where these events occur after the actual date of delivery unless insolvency proceedings commence within the relevant period and when the particulars were delivered the company was unable to pay its debts or become so as a consequence of the transaction.

Generally, if the assets subject to the charge are available on liquidation, the debentureholders take the property charged and take no further part in the liquidation. Sometimes, however, the holder of a floating charge may find himself subject to other claims.

On liquidation if there is insufficient money raised from the company's assets to pay the preferential creditors in full, the property secured by a floating charge may be realised and used to pay the preferential creditors: S175 Insolvency Act 1986 (IA86). Any money left after the preferential creditors have been paid belongs to the debentureholders secured by the floating charge.

A floating charge may be avoided under S245 IA 1986 if no consideration was given for it and it was created within two years of commencement of liquidation or petition for an administration order if made in favour of a connected person which includes a director or associate. If the charge is created in favour of anyone else the period is one year and the charge may only be avoided if the company could not pay its debts when the charge was created or became unable to pay as a result of the transaction.

In addition a transaction at an undervalue or a preference given by the company may also be set aside under Ss238 and 239 IA 1986. A transaction at an undervalue is one whereby the company receives no or inadequate consideration. A company gives a preference if it does anything to put a creditor in a better position than he would otherwise have been in an insolvent liquidation. The court will not make an order unless the company was influenced by a desire to prefer the creditor.

12.2   Rights of preference shareholder

(a)   The holder of a preference share is a member of the company; the holder of a debenture is a creditor. Many distinctions between them are derived from this basic contrast. The similarity of their position is that both are usually providers of capital to be employed in the company's business on a long-term basis at a fixed rate of return.

Gower's first point of contrast is that a preference shareholder is only entitled to receive a dividend if:

(i)   there are profits from which a company may properly pay a dividend; and
(ii)   a dividend is declared.

Preference dividends, like all other dividends, may not be paid out of capital but only out of profits: S263 Companies Act 1985 (CA85). If the company makes losses and has no distributable reserves, no dividend can be paid. However, the interest on a debenture is a debt, and the company may pay this out of capital if it has no other resources. A second point on preference dividend is that the holder of a preference share has no right to insist that any available profit shall be distributed as dividend. If the company prefers to transfer its profits to reserve and to leave the dividend in arrears, he can do nothing (unless the articles - as is not uncommon - give him some special rights in such circumstances).

Finally, if there are arrears of preference dividend (on cumulative shares) when the company goes into liquidation, the arrears cease to be payable unless the right to receive them is specially conferred by the articles. The holder of a debenture has a contractual right to interest, whether or not there are profits and whether the company is trading or has gone into liquidation. His claim is limited merely by the company's financial ability to meet it.

Gower's second point is that in a winding-up the holders of preference shares rank after the creditors ie, nothing can be repaid on the preference shares until all debts have been paid in full. The preference shareholder also has no priority right to be paid before capital is returned to ordinary shareholders, unless that right is expressly given to him.

Lastly, holders of preference shares have fewer effective remedies than holders of debentures. A debentureholder, as a creditor, may sue the company for debt if it defaults in payment of interest or repayment of capital when due. He may also petition for the compulsory winding-up of the company, on the grounds that it is unable to pay its debts: S122 Insolvency Act 1986 (IA86). A preference shareholder has only such rights (if any) when his dividend is not paid as he may be given by the articles.

(b)   The only special right of preference shares which is implied if not stated expressly is that the entitlement to a preference dividend is cumulative (unless otherwise stated). Hence, if a company which has issued '6% preference shares' fails to pay a dividend on them in Year 1, the priority entitlement to dividend of the shareholders is increased to 12% in Year 2, and so on. Other special rights (if any) of preference shares must be expressly given; otherwise the shares carry the same rights, no more and no less, as ordinary shares. If additional rights are expressly given, it is presumed that no further rights are to be implied. If, for example, the shares carry a priority right to repayment of capital in a winding-up, there is no implied right to participate in any surplus assets remaining after the subscribed share capital has been repaid: **Scottish Insurance Corporation v Wilson's & Clyde Coal Co.**

24 CORPORATE MANAGEMENT: THE BOARD

INTRODUCTION & LEARNING OBJECTIVES

Syllabus area 8g. Directors: appointment, retirement, removal and disqualification, powers. (Ability required 3.)

Issues in corporate governance. (Ability required 2.)

When you have studied this chapter you should be able to do the following:

- understand the legal terms 'director' and 'shadow director'

- know how directors are appointed and who can be appointed

- understand how the law attempts to regulate remuneration, loans and compensation for loss of office paid to directors

- explain in detail the overriding power of members to dismiss directors under S303 CA85

- understand how power in a company is divided between the board and the general meeting

- explain the legal provisions intended to ensure that third parties are protected even though directors are exceeding their powers.

1 APPOINTMENT OF DIRECTORS

1.1 Introduction

The members are free to decide, in the articles, on the way in which the company is to be managed eg, by a board of directors, managers, a managing committee, etc. Normally, it will be by a board of directors elected by the general meeting (and most likely according to the provisions of Table A).

> **Definition** The term director includes **any person occupying the position of director by whatever name called**: S741(1) Companies Act 1985 CA85.

The test is one of **function** not of title: the terms **governors, managers or trustees** are occasionally used in articles instead of **directors**. Similarly the mere description of someone as a director (eg, where an employee is referred to as an **associate director**) will not necessarily make them one for present purposes. Thus, the articles may provide for the appointment of senior employees as **special directors,** etc, but without the right to attend board meetings. These are not directors, however, for purposes of company law.

Certain provisions of the Companies Act apply to persons who are not appointed directors but who are **shadow directors.**

> **Definition** A shadow director means a person in accordance with whose directions or instructions the directors of the company are accustomed to act: S741(2) CA85. However, a person is not a shadow director by reason only that the directors act on advice given by him in a professional capacity.

The meaning of the terms 'director' and 'shadow director' was extensively canvassed in a recent case - **Re Hydrodan [1994]** - in the context of an application under S214 Insolvency Act 1986 (IA86) by the liquidator of an insolvent company for a court order compelling contribution to the company's assets. The S214 IA86 wrongful trading provision applies to 'directors' and 'shadow directors'. In the case Millett J divided up into first, *de jure* directors (validity appointed directors); second, *de facto* directors (those who assume to act as directors without having been validly appointed or at all); and third, shadow directors (who are not directors, whether de jure or de facto). He considered that the three terms did not overlap, and that to establish that a person is a shadow director it is necessary to prove the following:

- First, who the company's directors (whether de jure or de facto) are;
- Second, that the person alleged to be a shadow director directed those directors how to act
- Third, that those directors acted in accordance with such instructions; and
- Fourth, that the directors were accustomed so to act

A director need not necessarily be a human person - thus a company can be a director of another company. The same is the case with shadow directors but with the limitation that for most CA85 purposes a holding company is specifically stated not to be a shadow director of its subsidiary. This limitation does not apply to the definition of shadow director for IA86 purposes, with the result that it is possible for a holding company to be liable for wrongful trading by its subsidiary if the holding company can be proved to be a shadow director of its subsidiary.

A distinction is drawn in practice - though not by the law - between executive directors and non-executive directors. A non-executive director's function is to attend board meetings whilst the executive director's function includes not only attendance at board meetings but also day-to-day responsibility for the management of the business. In his capacity as an executive, such a director will often be a full-time employee of the company. The Cadbury Report on corporate governance recommends that the boards of all listed companies consist of both executive and non-executive directors and further recommends that non-executive directors' functions should be clearly set out and should include a supervisory role over the executive directors.

1.2   Numbers

A public company must have a minimum of at least two directors; a private company one, as long as this one is separate from the company secretary: S282 CA85. The maximum number of directors is usually fixed by the articles but there is no requirement that there shall be a specified maximum nor is there any statutory limit on the number.

Table A specifies a minimum of two directors; it does not specify a maximum number.

The secretary of the company may also be a director but a sole director may not also be secretary.

1.3   Method of appointment

The **first directors** are either named as such in the articles or alternatively the articles give authority, usually to the subscribers to the memorandum, to appoint the directors. The documents delivered to the Registrar to secure incorporation of a new company must include particulars of the first directors and their signed consent to act as such: S10 CA85. They are not the first directors unless this is done.

The appointment of **subsequent directors** is regulated by the articles. The articles of most public and many private companies follow Table A. The main points are:

(a)   at each **annual general meeting one-third of** the non-executive directors (to the nearest whole number) **retire** but are **eligible for re-election**. A managing director or other executive director (Article 84) or any director for whom the articles make specific provision (eg, X is to be director for life) and any director retiring under rule (b) below is disregarded in arriving at the numbers to retire. Those longest in office since their last election should retire first (Article 74). The chairman, unless also a managing director, is subject to normal retirement by rotation. A non-executive director is one who does not take part in the day to day management of the company.

(b)   the **board of directors** has power to **appoint** a new director either to fill a **vacancy** or as an **addition** to their number (subject to any maximum permitted number). A director so appointed holds office only until the next annual general meeting at which he retires and is eligible for re-election (Article 79).

However, this system is optional. Private companies with a small number of members may have articles providing that the directors shall be appointed by the members (or be the members themselves) in due proportion. A wholly-owned subsidiary may, by its articles, authorise its holding company to appoint and remove its directors. The articles may merely provide for the directors to continue in office indefinitely and without retiring at intervals. Sometimes the holders of debenture stock are given the right to appoint a director; or the appointment of directors is granted to an outsider in a separate agreement.

When directors of a public company are elected in general meeting the appointment of each director must be voted on separately unless the meeting previously agrees without any dissentient to waive the rule: S292 CA85. A procedural defect in the appointment of a director does not usually invalidate the acts of that director (or of the board of which they are an apparent member): S285 CA85; but there must have been a purported appointment.

Over age directors. A public company and a private company which is a subsidiary of a public company are subject to S293 CA85, which provides that:

(a)   no person is capable of being appointed a director if at the time of their appointment they have attained seventy years of age; and

(b)   a director must retire at the AGM next following their seventieth birthday.

These provisions do not apply:

(a)   if excluded by the articles; or

(b)   if the director's appointment was made at a general meeting by passing an ordinary resolution of which special notice which stated their age was given. (S379 CA85)

S294 CA85 imposes a duty on the directors to disclose their ages to the company.

1.4   Activity

List the principal ways by which directors may be appointed to office.

1.5   Activity solution

(a)   Co-opted by board (eg, Table A Art 79).

(b)   By members in general meeting by ordinary resolution (eg, Table A Art 78).

2   QUALIFICATION AND DISQUALIFICATION OF DIRECTORS

2.1   Who may be a director

Generally, any person may be a director. In addition, a company may be a director of another company in which case it is usual to appoint an individual to represent it at board meetings.

A director need not be a member of the company.

There are certain **situations** in which a person will not be entitled to be a director of a company. These situations are ones where the same person holds more than one office thereby infringing the rule that a company must have a minimum number of directors, as explained above.

Certain **persons** because of their own conduct or characteristics may not act as directors. These break down into several categories.

(a)   **Disqualification by age** - subject to contrary resolution, a person aged over seventy cannot be a director of a public company. An overage director can be appointed by passing an ordinary resolution with 'special notice', (see later).

(b)   **Disqualification because not a member** - the law does not require a director to be a member, but the articles may.

(c)   **Other grounds for disqualification** - the articles may so provide.

(d)   **Statutory disqualification** - where the court has made a **disqualification order** against a person ie, an order that that person cannot act in, among other roles, a director of a company for a specified number of years. These provisions are all set out in the Company Directors Disqualification Act 1986 (CDDA 86).

2.2   Share qualification

There is no rule of law that a director must also be a member of the company. But the articles may impose such a requirement ie, a **share qualification** clause to ensure that as they have a stake in the company they will work harder for it.

Where the requirement exists it is only satisfied by the director being the **registered holder** of the required number of shares (called 'qualification shares'). Beneficial ownership eg, from purchase of shares not yet registered in their name, is not enough. To hold shares as nominee of the owner or jointly with another person will, however, suffice.

The requirement to acquire shares in the company, if imposed, must be satisfied within two months (or such shorter period as the articles may provide) from their appointment taking effect (S291 CA85). They vacate office immediately if they cease to hold the required qualification shares.

However, even if disqualified under S291 their act will be valid (S285 CA85 and Article 92 of Table A). So if a director remains in office without buying at least one share in a company, a contract made by him will not be invalid on that ground.

2.3   Articles

The articles often provide that a director shall cease to hold office if they become insolvent or insane or are absent from board meetings for a specified minimum period (usually 6 months) without leave: see Table A and in particular note Article 81 which provides that a director will cease to hold office on a resolution of the board if he is absent from board meetings for more than six consecutive months without permission of the directors.

2.4   Company Directors Disqualification Act 1986

S1 Company Directors Disqualification Act 1986 contains the general provisions whereby the court has the power in certain circumstances and in other circumstances has a **duty** to make an order disqualifying a person for a specified period from being:

(a)   a director;

(b)   a liquidator or administrator;

(c)   a receiver or manager; or

(d)   in any way, whether directly or indirectly, concerned in the promotion, formation or management of a company.

The period of disqualification runs from the date of the order and depends on the grounds on which the order was made and the court making the order.

The Act groups the grounds for disqualification into three groups:

(a)   Ss2-5 relating to misconduct (from CA85);
(b)   Ss6-9 relating to unfitness (from IA86); and
(c)   Ss10-12 relating to various grounds (from CA85 and IA86).

2.5   Grounds for disqualification - general misconduct

(a)   S2 CDDA 1986 **empowers** a court to make a disqualification order against a person who is **convicted of an indictable offence in connection with the promotion, formation, management or liquidation** of a company or with **the receivership or management** of company property. The maximum period of such an order is fifteen years. The court making the order may be the court convicting them or the court winding up the company.

Recent cases indicate that the courts are taking a very broad view of 'in connection with ...... management'. Thus, in an unreported case, a director of a building company, who was convicted of offences under the Health and Safety at Work Act 1974 in relation to an unsafe building site operated by the company, was also disqualified under the CDDA86. Another example arose recently where a director (who was the chairman and a qualified accountant), having been convicted of insider dealing and sent to prison for 18 months under what is now the Criminal Justice Act 1993, was then disqualified under the CDDA86 for 10 years - **R v Goodman [1994].**

(b)   (i)   S3 CDDA 1986 **empowers** a court which is **winding up a company** to make a disqualification order against directors if it appears that they have **persistently defaulted in their duty to file documents or notify the registrar of companies** as required by the Companies Act 1985. Persistent default will be conclusively proved by showing that the person has been adjudged guilty of three or more defaults in the previous five years in respect of the duty to file accounts and make returns, etc.

The maximum period for an order under this section is five years.

(ii)   S5 **empowers** a court which **convicts** a person of a summary offence in relation to **persistent default of their duty** to file documents or notify the Registrar of Companies as required by the Companies Act 1985 to make an order disqualifying that person for a maximum period of five years. This is basically the same as the power under S3 given to a court winding up a company.

(c)   S4 **empowers** the court **winding up a company** to make a disqualification order if it appears that the person has been **guilty of an offence of fraudulent trading whilst the company is a going concern, or any fraud** in relation to the company.

The maximum period is fifteen years.

2.6   Grounds for disqualification - unfitness

(a)   Under S6 CDDA 1986 the court **must** make a disqualification order against a person if it is satisfied that:

   (i)   he or she is or has been a director of a company which has at any time become **insolvent** (whether while they were directors or subsequently); and

   (ii)   their conduct as a director of that company (taken alone or with their conduct as a director of any other company or companies) makes them **unfit** to be concerned in the management of a company.

A shadow director is regarded as a director for this purpose.

The application to the court is made by the Secretary of State (or the Official Receiver as directed by the Secretary of State) where it appears to the Secretary of State to be expedient in the public interest that such an order should be made. It must be made within two years of the company winding up or going into administration unless the court gives leave for a later application.

There is a duty on the Official Receiver, a liquidator, an administrator or an administrative receiver to report to the Secretary of State if he considers that a director's conduct in relation to the company, considered individually or taken together with their conduct as director of another company, makes them unfit to be concerned with the management of a company. In addition the Secretary of State or Official Receiver may require any of these people to furnish them with information and documents relating to the director's conduct as he may be reasonably required to decide whether or not to apply for a disqualification order.

Sch1 CDDA 1986 sets out various criteria to be considered by the court in determining the unfitness of a director. These include any breach of fiduciary duty and general misfeasance.

A disqualification order under S6 will last for a minimum of two years and a maximum of fifteen years.

(b)   S8 CDDA 1986 provides for disqualification following **investigation of a company** by the DTI. The court **may** make the order if it is satisfied that the person's conduct in relation to the company makes them unfit to be concerned in the management of a company.

Director includes shadow director.

An application under this section may be made whether the company is insolvent or not and the court has a discretion as to whether it makes an order or not.

There is no minimum period of disqualification but there is a maximum of fifteen years.

2.7   Other cases of disqualification

(a)   S10 CDDA 1986 provides that the court may make a disqualification order against any person against whom it makes an order to contribute to the company's assets under S213 IA86 (fraudulent trading) or S214 IA86 (wrongful trading).

There is no minimum period for an order under S10. The maximum period is fifteen years.

(b)   S11 CDDA 1986 provides that it is an offence for an **undischarged bankrupt** to be a director of or otherwise concerned in the management of any company without leave of the court.

(c)   S12 CDDA 1986 provides that, where a person fails to make any payments as required by an administration order, the court may make a disqualification order against that person not exceeding two years. An administration order is an order providing for the administration by the county court of a debtor's estate.

2.8   Consequences of contravening a disqualification order

(a)   S13 CDDA 1986 - any person who acts in contravention of a disqualification order or while an undischarged bankrupt is guilty of an **offence** - maximum penalty two years imprisonment and or a fine.

(b)   S14 CDDA 1986 - where a company is guilty of an offence under S13 any person who consented to or contributed to the company so acting is also guilty of an **offence** and may be prosecuted.

(c)   S15 CDDA 1986 - provides that anyone who is involved in the management of a company while disqualified (under a disqualification order or while an undischarged bankrupt) or who acts or is willing to act on the instructions of a person who is disqualified shall be **personally liable** for the company's debts incurred during the time he acts.

The Secretary of State maintains a register of disqualification orders which is open to public inspection: S18 CDDA 1986.

Conclusion   A director can be disqualified under the CDDA 1986 in the following circumstances:

- S2:   if he is convicted of an indictable offence (ie, a serious crime) relating to the promotion, formation or management of a company

- S4:   if he is found guilty of a fraudulent offence relating to the management of a company

- S6:   if he is considered unfit to be involved in the management of a company considering breaches of fiduciary duty, and misapplication or wrong dealing with the funds of the company

- S8:   If he is considered unfit following investigation of the company

- S10:   if an order is made against him in respect of fraudulent or wrongful trading

- S11:   if he is an undischarged bankrupt

2.9   Activity

What are the principal restrictions on appointment to or a continuation in office as a director?

2.10   Activity solution

(a)   Where the director is a sole director and is also the company secretary;

(b)   Where the director of a public company is over 70 years;

(c)   Non compliance with a share qualification clause in the articles;

(d)   Disqualification by the articles;

(e)   Disqualification under the CDDA 1986.

3   SERVICE CONTRACTS OF DIRECTORS

3.1   Introduction

A person who acts as a director may be:

(a)   An **officer** of the company only. A director is an **officer** of the company S744 CA85. A director may serve in an office other than that of director although he cannot be an auditor (S389) and if he is the sole director he cannot be the company secretary (S282(2)).

(b)   An **officer and an employee** of the company under a contract **of** service. Thus, they might be a director of and also a lecturer employed by the company. This is fairly clear. What is less clear is where they are an officer and an employee of the company in their capacity as director. Thus, a person who is a director (an officer) may also be the managing director (an employee).

(c)   An **officer and** an **independent contractor** of the company under a contract **for** services. Thus, a person who is a director (an officer) may also be the finance director who merely provides occasional services and therefore in law be an independent contractor as they merely **provide** services as opposed to actually being in the service of the company as an employee under a contract **of** service.

Whether or not a director has a contract for services or a contract of service (the latter meaning he is an employee) is important for employment law but in company law the importance is limited to liquidation where money due under a contract of service is a preferential debt but money due under a contract for services is an ordinary debt.

What is important for company law is whether or not the director has a contract (the general term service contract is now used to cover both types) as there are statutory rules on the length of service contracts; in addition whether or not a director has a service contract is relevant to remuneration and any claim for damages on dismissal (remember that the Articles are not a contract between the company and a director in that capacity).

3.2   Who negotiates directors' service contracts?

This is dealt with by the company's Articles.

Table A Reg 84 allows the board to enter into an agreement with any director for his employment by the company on such terms as they think fit. The director concerned may not vote on his contract at the board meeting nor may he be counted towards the quorum (Arts 94, 95 and 97).

3.3   Long-term service contracts

A company cannot include a term in a director's service contract that it should continue for more than five years during which time it cannot be terminated by the company by notice or can only be terminated in specified circumstances, without first obtaining the approval of the shareholders in general meeting by an ordinary resolution: S319 CA85. If a clause is included in the contract in contravention of the section it is void and the contract is deemed to contain a clause entitling the company to terminate it at any time by giving reasonable notice. The Cadbury Report recommends that for listed companies the period should be reduced to three.

3.4   Contracts of service to be open for inspection

The company is required to keep at its registered office (or other **appropriate place**) a copy of the service agreements of all its directors and directors of its subsidiaries who are **employees** (or a written summary if there is no contract in writing). There is an exception for directors who work wholly or mainly abroad and where the unexpired period of the contract is less than 12 months. Members of the company have a statutory right of inspection: S318 CA85.

4   REMUNERATION OF DIRECTORS

Except to the extent of requiring disclosure in the annual accounts of the aggregate of directors' emoluments, the amount paid to the highest paid director and chairman, and a breakdown in bands, and forbidding payment without deduction of income tax, the CA85 does not regulate who is to set what amount, if anything, a director receives as remuneration (whether money or other benefits). This matter is dealt with by common law rules and the company's articles.

At common law a director has no entitlement for his services as director except as provided by the articles - **Guinness plc v Saunders [1990]**.

Table A provides:

(a)   directors shall be entitled to such remuneration as the company by ordinary resolution may determine - Art 82;

(b)   the board may remunerate as they think fit directors appointed to executive office and directors who provide services outside the scope of their normal duties - Art 84. Normal duties would appear to mean attendance at board meetings. The director concerned may not vote on his remuneration at the board meeting nor may he be counted towards the quorum - Arts 94, 95 and 97). The Cadbury Report on corporate governance recommends that a committee consisting only of non-executive directors should set the remuneration of executive directors.

Such articles are interpreted strictly by the courts.

Guinness plc v Saunders [1990]

Facts: Ward, a director of Guinness, received £5.2m from the company as special remuneration for services in connection with a take-over bid which the company had made. The remuneration was authorised by a sub-committee of the board.

Held: as the articles required such remuneration to be authorised by the board (ie, the whole board) Ward had no entitlement to the £5.2m and it was recoverable by the company. His subsidiary argument that he should be entitled to a quantum meruit (since he had provided valuable services) was rejected because such would be contrary to the nature of the directors' fiduciary relationship with the company which requires him not to profit from his position.

| Conclusion | The shareholders have little direct control over remuneration paid to the directors - directors, if they comply with the company's articles, have the ability to set their own remuneration. This is a topical issue of corporate governance and, as recommended by the Cadbury Report, many listed companies, in an attempt to deal with the problem require the GM to set fees of non-executive directors who then set the fees of the executive directors. |

5   LOANS TO DIRECTORS

5.1   Scope

S330-344 CA85 contain complex rules which in general seek to prevent a company loaning money to its directors and shadow directors. The rules also extend to guarantees and securities of third-party loans and for relevant companies to quasi-loans and credit transactions and to connected persons of a director.

Definition A **quasi loan** is a transaction in which one party, for example the client company, agrees to pay or actually pays a sum for or on behalf of a director or, alternatively, reimburses expenditure incurred by a third party on behalf of the director in each case in circumstances where the director is obliged or is liable to reimburse the company. An example of a quasi loan is where the director buys some personal items with a credit card, the company pays the credit card company and the director later repays his company.

Definition A **credit transaction** is one under which one party (eg, the company) sells goods or land to another party (eg, the director) under hire purchase or conditional sale arrangements, leases or hires goods or land, or otherwise supplies anything on deferred payment terms.

Definition Relevant companies are public companies, and any private company which is part of a group containing a public company.

5.2   The prohibitions

(a)   **The general rule for all companies**

All companies are prohibited from making a **loan** or entering into any guarantee or providing any security in connection with a loan made by any person to a **director** of the company or its holding company: S330 CA85.

(b)   **Additional restrictions for 'relevant companies'**

They are prohibited from:

(i)   making a **loan** or guaranteeing or providing security for a loan to a **person connected** with a director of the company;

(ii)   making a **quasi loan** or guaranteeing or providing security for a quasi loan to a **director or persons connected** to him or her; and

(iii)   entering into a **credit transaction** or guaranteeing or providing security for a credit transaction to a **director** or **persons connected** with him or her.

Definition The definition of connected person of a director (in S346 CA85) is complex, but can be summarised as follows:

(a)   spouse, children (under eighteen) or step children;

(b)   a company in which the director or his connections control at least 20% of the equity or votes;

(c)   a trustee of a trust from which the director or his connections may benefit;

(d)   a partner or director of any of his connections.

5.3   Anti avoidance provisions

The company is prohibited from entering into 'arrangements' with another person which if entered into by the company with its directors or his connections would be illegal (eg, arrangements would include a non-contractual understanding that directors of one company (A) would authorise loans from that company (A) to the directors of another company (B) in return for loans to the directors of A by B).

5.4   Lawful transactions

There are **exceptions** from the prohibitions of S330. The exceptions are:

(a)   **Loans**

    (i)   any company may make a loan to a **director** not exceeding **£5,000;**

    (ii)   loans and guarantees, etc, between **group companies**;

    (iii)   loans made to **directors** to enable them to **perform their duties**. There is no limit for non-relevant companies but for **relevant companies** the **maximum is £20,000**. All such loans must have prior approval in general meeting or the funds are provided on condition they are repaid six months after the next annual general meeting of the company unless at that meeting approval is given;

    (iv)   loans made to an **employee** before appointment to the board;

    (v)   loans and quasi loans made by **money lending companies** (ie, a company whose business is that of making loans):

        (1)   a recognised **bank** may make such loans **without limit** provided the loan was made within the **ordinary course of business** and not on especially favourable terms;

        (2)   where the company is a money-lending relevant company **not** being a recognised **bank** the limit is **£100,000;**

        (3)   all money-lending companies may make loans up to **£100,000** on favourable terms for **house purchase**, provided the terms are no more favourable than those available to employees of the company. In the case of money-lending relevant companies which are **not** recognised **banks** the house **loans** have to be **aggregated** with other loans and the overall limit of £100,000 is applied.

(b)   **Quasi loan**

    Small quasi loans are permissible for relevant companies provided that they are for no more than **£5,000** for no more than **two months**. *Note:* no prohibition against quasi loans at all for non-relevant companies.

(c)   **Credit transactions**

    Small credit transactions are permissible for relevant companies provided that they are not on specially favourable terms and that they are not more than **£10,000** if not lent in the normal course of business. *Note:* no prohibition against credit transactions at all for non-relevant companies.

5.5   Effect of an unlawful transaction

If a company enters into a transaction arrangement in contravention of S330 the transaction or **arrangement is voidable** by the company unless:

(a)   restitution is no longer possible or the company has been indemnified for the loss or damage suffered by it; or

(b)   any rights have been acquired by *bona fide* purchaser for value without actual notice.

The section further provides that the director and any person connected with him or her in contravention of S330 and any director who authorised the transaction or arrangement is liable;

- to account to the company for any gain which they have made; and
- (jointly and severally with any other person liable under the section) to indemnify the company for any loss or damage.

Criminal liability is imposed on directors of **relevant companies** who authorise or permit the company to enter into a transaction or arrangement knowing or having reasonable cause to believe that the company was contravening S330.

5.6   Disclosure

All **loans, quasi loans or credit transactions with directors**, whether made in contravention of S330 or not must be **disclosed** in the company's annual accounts: S232 CA85. If the directors fail to make such disclosures the auditor of the company is required to do so in his report: S237 CA85 .

6   COMPENSATION FOR LOSS OF OFFICE

6.1   Introduction

Although directors may lose **office** in various ways, it does not necessarily follow that they will not be able to obtain compensation for the loss. Thus (apart from the restrictions on payments for loss of office contained in Ss312-316 discussed below) they may obtain:

(a)   damages for wrongful dismissal (ie, breach of employment contract); and

(b)   compensation for unfair dismissal (ie, as an employee): **Parsons v Albert J. Parsons Limited.**

6.2   Ss312-316 CA85

Ss312-316 CA85 regulate the payment to directors of compensation for loss of **office** (and other terminal payments or inducements). The underlying principle is that a director should only be allowed to receive and retain sums, whether provided by the company or a third party, in connection with the termination of their appointment if the company in general meeting after full disclosure approves the payments .

There are three possibilities:

(a)   a director may receive **compensation for loss of office** paid by the company on their retirement, whether voluntary or enforced: S312 CA85;

(b)   a payment may be made to a director (usually by the purchaser) on their retirement from office following the **sale of the company's undertaking**: S313 CA85;

(c)   a payment may be made to a director as compensation for loss of office in connection with **an offer for all or even part of the share capital** of the company. Where the offer is for part only of the capital the rules apply if the offer is for at least one-third of the voting capital or if the offer is conditional on acceptance to a given extent: S314 CA85.

In any of these cases there must be disclosure to shareholders and approval of the payment in general meeting.

Re Duomatic [1969]

Facts: compensation for loss of office payments were made to a director after having been approved by the voting shareholders. No disclosure had been made to the non-voting shareholders except by way of disclosure in the accounts after the payment had been made.

Held: the payment was unlawful. Disclosure must be made to **all** shareholders (even though they would not be entitled to vote) and **prior** to the payment being made.

Failure to disclose in cases (a) and (b) leads to a return of the compensation to the company. In case (c) the payments are held on trust by the director for the accepting shareholders.

In cases (b) and (c) above ie, where the payment may be made to the director by someone other than their company, any payment within one year before and two years after the relevant transaction is subject to the code. The purchase of a director's shares at a higher price than is offered (in case (c) above) for the shares of other members is subject to the code to the extent of the excess.

It is important to remember that these provisions do not apply to payments to which a director is contractually entitled (eg, *bona fide* payment by way of damages for breach of contract) nor compensation for unfair dismissal; or to a pension benefit: S316 CA85.

> **Conclusion**   S312 requires directors' 'golden handshakes' to be approved by the members.

7   REMOVAL OF DIRECTORS

7.1   Introduction

A director may cease to hold office in various ways:

(a)   Directors may be removed from office by disqualification arising under statutory provisions or under the terms of the articles set out above.

(b)   If the articles provide for the removal of a director for other reasons, removal according to those provisions will be effective.

(c)   A director may relinquish office by resignation (Article 81 Table A provides that a director ceases to hold office if he resigns by notice to the company) or by not standing for re-election.

Note also that:

(a)   If appointed under a fixed term contract, expiry of the term means termination of the directorship.

(b)   Winding up and administration does not necessarily operate to terminate directors' contracts of employment, although they lose their powers to act. An administrator has power under the IA86 to appoint and remove directors.

(c)   The appointment of a receiver out of court by debentureholders does not necessarily terminate directors' contracts of employment, at least so long as the role and function of the receiver is not inconsistent with the continuation of those contracts.

7.2   Removal of directors under S303

S303 CA85 lays down a **statutory rule** which can be exercised by the company by ordinary resolution in any case, provided the procedure laid down by the section is followed. This confers on the director certain safeguards of natural justice. The person proposing their removal must give twenty-eight days' advance warning to the company, which must inform the director and circulate any representations they wish to make to the members and allow them to address the meeting before a vote is taken.

The statutory power **cannot be excluded** but it may be possible to **circumvent** it by weighted voting rights.

Bushell v Faith [1970]

Facts: a provision in the Articles which tripled the votes of shares held by directors on a resolution to remove a director. Parliament only required an ordinary resolution and made no provision as to how the resolution could be obtained or defeated, although it was pointed out that such an Article, as the one in question, was sometimes necessary in a family company in order to reduce repercussions from family quarrels in the boardroom and general meetings.

Held: the provision was upheld. The ratio of the case probably limits the application of this principle to private companies.

S303 does **not** carry with it the power to **deprive a director of compensation** for dismissal to which they are otherwise entitled. This will depend upon whether they have a right to compensation arising from a contract of employment with the company, distinct from any right solely as a member under the Articles (assuming the director is a shareholder).

Managing directors often have contracts of service and rights over and above those of directors in general.

Articles may enable the directors to appoint a **managing director** on such terms as they think fit.

Removal of a director may found a claim by that director for breach of a service contract.

Southern Foundries (1926) Ltd v Shirlaw [1940]

Facts: a managing director was appointed under a contract with the company for ten years but, after the articles had been changed empowering his removal as director, he was dismissed.

Held: the House of Lords awarded them damages for wrongful dismissal since the alteration of the articles, although effective, constituted a breach of their contract of service; it was contrary to the agreement that he should serve for ten years, which became impossible when he lost their directorship.

Dismissal of a director of a small partnership type company may give rise to the compulsory winding up of the company.

Ebrahimi v Westbourne Galleries [1973]

Facts: Mr Ebrahimi had been in business with a colleague for 25 years, the last ten as a company. He agreed to transfer some of his shares to his colleague's son, who then combined with his father to dismiss Mr Ebrahimi from the board.

Held: the company would be compulsory wound up on the ground that it was just and equitable under IA86 S122(g).

Alternatively to winding up such a director may petition for relief from unfair prejudice under S459 CA85 - **Re Bird Precision in Bellows [1986].**

7.3   Procedure for removal of a director

S303 CA85 states that a director can be removed by the passing of an ordinary resolution with special notice. Notice is given by the person(s) wishing to remove.

This person(s) should give a minimum of 28 days' notice to the company. The company must then inform the director 'forthwith'.

The company should then give notice to all members who are entitled to attend and vote at the general meeting. This notice is:

(a)   a minimum of 14 days if the motion to remove is to be voted on at an Extraordinary General Meeting (EGM)

(b)   a minimum of 21 days if the motion to remove is to be voted on at an Annual General Meeting (AGM).

The director has various rights to protest his removal (this is the purpose of the special notice provision). He may require the company to circulate his written representations (they must be read out at the meeting if there was no time for prior circulation). He must be allowed to attend and vote at the meeting.

If a director is deprived of the rights to protest his removal, his removal is not valid under S303. Exceptionally in **Bentley-Stevens v Jones [1974]** a director who was not allowed to protest his removal was held validly removed because those denying him his rights had ordinary resolution control of the company.

| Conclusion | Removal of directors is an important area of the syllabus. The most examinable part of this subject is the procedure under S303 CA85. |

The key points to remember are:

- removal under this section requires an ordinary resolution

- special notice is given to the director(s) who is/are to be removed. This is to give time to write to all members who will be involved in the vote at the general meeting

- a director can block the passing of the ordinary resolution to remove him by having more than 50% of the voting power.

- the company may not be able to afford to remove the director if he has a long term service contract which, if breached, will entitle him to a balance of the salary owing to him under the fixed term.

7.4   Activity

The directors of Northgate Forest Football Club want one of their number to step down from the board. They believe that the director concerned, named Read, has been supplying the media with confidential information about the state of health of their ailing manager, Brian Clogg.

Set out the advice you would give to Read, who is reluctant to resign.

7.5   Activity solution

Assuming the articles are in the form of Table A there is no provision whereby the board of a company can require a director to vacate his position provided he attends board meetings.

By Table A, a director may resign by notice, or by 'not standing for re-election when he is required to do so' (for example under the retirement by rotation provisions of Table A).

The usual method of removing a director from office is to utilise the procedure of S303. This required the general meeting to pass an ordinary resolution of which special notice has been given. The notice must be given at least 28 days before the meeting, and the director concerned has a right to circularise the company with a statement, as well as to speak at the meeting, in his support.

If Read were to be removed under this procedure (or under any other procedure set out in the articles, if they are not in the form of Table A), he may well have a claim against the company for wrongful and/or unfair dismissal, if he is an executive director: **Shirlaw v Southern Foundries Ltd.**

8   POWERS OF DIRECTORS

8.1   Introduction

Companies invariably **delegate extensive powers of** management to their **directors**.

Article 70 Table A states that 'subject to the provisions of the Companies Act, the memorandum and the articles and to any directions given by special resolution, the business of the company shall be managed by the directors who may **exercise all the powers** of the company'.

Two points to remember:

(a)   **Acts *ultra vires* the company**

The company must obviously be deemed only to delegate such powers as the company itself may have ie, the directors are not competent to engage in *ultra vires* transactions. They may, however, (when Article 70 applies) do anything which the company in general meeting could do (unless reserved as above - ie, 'subject to ...').

(b)   **Directors acting for an improper purpose**

In connection with the duties of directors there is a rather different limiting factor ie, that directors can only validly exercise their powers in the interests of the company and for the purposes for which the powers are conferred unless the company in general meeting authorises what they have done or intend to do. Anything done by directors which, although *intra vires* the company, is not done for an authorised purpose is an unauthorised act and may not be binding on the company.

The delegation of powers is to the **directors collectively** ie, acting as a **board of directors** the board may, of course, be authorised by the articles to sub-delegate powers to an individual director eg, by appointing them to be managing director or by express delegation of powers to a director or to a committee of directors. In either case such delegation is possible **only if authorised** by the articles since the directors are themselves delegatees of the company.

Article 72 provides that the directors may delegate any of their powers.

An individual director has no direct authority from the company to act on its behalf except, perhaps, to sign documents as a director (for which a single director's signature suffices unless the articles require more than one).

Two types of legal problem may arise in connection with directors' powers.

First, the **company** in general meeting may wish to **exercise or control** the directors in the exercise of their powers. **Secondly**, the company may deny that the directors or a single director **were authorised** to commit the company in some transaction with an outsider.

8.2   Table A, Art 70

At the very root, authority to act so as to bind the company stems from the agreement of the members of the company, the shareholders. Authority issues from them in two basic ways:

(a)   from the terms to which they are taken to have agreed for the regulation of company affairs in the **articles of association**; and

(b)   from **decisions in general meeting** (in which there may be participation by others afforded the right to vote eg, debentureholders).

Remember that by virtue of S14 CA85 the Articles are a contract between the company and shareholders and can only be altered by special resolution - S9 CA85.

Salmon v Quin & Axtens Ltd [1909]

Facts: under the articles of a company, the general management of the company was vested in the directors. The articles also provided that either of the two managing directors could veto certain matters if they dissented from a board resolution. The plaintiff, one of the managing directors, dissented from a resolution. The company in general meeting by a simple majority purported to ratify the director's resolution. The plaintiff sued on behalf of himself and all the other shareholders in the company against the directors for an injunction restraining them from acting on the resolutions of the board and the general meeting.

Held: that the resolutions were inconsistent with the articles: an attempt to alter the terms of the contract between the parties by ordinary resolution instead of by special resolution.

To a large extent, in practice, the decisions of the general meeting in large public companies will coincide with the wishes of the directors since the directors will control the proxy voting machinery. In other cases, it may be important to decide the effect of the division of power between the general meeting and the board of directors.

The general view appears to be that powers delegated to the board by the articles cannot be exercised by the members in general meeting: **Breckland Group Holdings v London & Suffolk Properties Ltd [1989]** and **Scott v Scott [1943]**; and nor can the general meeting instruct the board in the exercise of their delegated powers - **Shaw v John Shaw [1935]** and **Automatic Self-Cleansing Filter Syndicate Company Limited v Cuninghame [1906].**

Breckland Group Holdings v London & Suffolk Properties Ltd [1989]

Facts: C held 51% of the company's voting shares and instructed solicitors to commence an action in the company's name against six defendants (one of whom included the company's managing director).

Held: where a company's articles vest the right to commence legal proceedings in the company's name in the board (it was assumed this was the effect of an Article similar to Art 70 of Table A): the board, alone, and not the general meeting, is able to exercise that right. Thus C could not cause the company to commence litigation and accordingly the solicitors had no claim against the company for their fees.

Shaw v John Shaw [1935]

Facts: the company's board (acting by a majority of its directors) resolved that the company commence litigation against two errant directors. A shareholders' meeting resolved, by ordinary resolution, that the action be discontinued.

Held: the ordinary resolution could not overrule the board's decision.

Automatic Self-Cleansing Filter Syndicate v Cuninghame [1906]

Facts: the board, which was authorised to sell company property on terms they saw fit, was instructed by an ordinary resolution of shareholders to sell the company's undertaking.

Held: the board was not bound to comply with the resolution.

The ability of the general meeting to control the board (or rather, the lack of ability) is a topical issue of corporate governance. The principle arises not only when the company should litigate but also when the general meeting wishes the board to adopt or discontinue certain policies (this is a particularly contentious issue where shareholders disapprove of the company doing business with companies or governments with oppressive regimes).

Art 70, does not, however vest every power of the company in the board.

The opening words of Art 70 subject the powers of the directors to manage the company to:

(a)   provisions of the Act;

(b)   provisions of the memorandum and articles; and

(c)   directions given by special resolution (except that no such direction shall invalidate any prior act of the directors).

The first two provisos are clear cut:

(a)   Certain powers are expressly reserved to members in general meeting by the Act itself. These powers include alteration of the memorandum, articles and share capital, removal of directors and a decision to voluntarily wind up the company.

(b)   The memorandum or articles may expressly reserve powers to the members in general meeting. Thus, under Table A appointment of directors, declaring of dividends and decisions to capitalise profits are specifically reserved to members (subject to some conditions).

(c)   The third provision is much less clear. Cases under the old (1948) Table A which had similar wording stating that the third proviso was subject to 'regulations' indicated that such 'regulations' by members were generally ineffective. It may be that 'directions given by special resolution' will be more effective. However, as the voting required for this and to alter the articles to remove the directors powers is the same it would seem more prudent to alter the articles which has a certain effect (or remove the directors which takes less voting power).

Thus, the members are not solely without power to control directors whose actions are not in accord with members wishes.

8.3   Ultimate control lies with the General Meeting

(a)   It may remove the directors (S303 CA85 - by ordinary resolution) and appoint a board more in sympathy with its wishes.

(b)   It may withdraw the powers by altering the articles (S9 CA85 by special resolution).

Neither of these will invalidate authorised acts already done by the directors but will ensure (hopefully) more unity in the future.

At common law there are other situations in which members may (or have at least in the past been held to be entitled to) step in. These are:

(a)   Where the directors decline to exercise their discretion to act or are otherwise unable to act (eg, because the board is deadlocked) then the general meeting can exercise the board's powers:

Barron v Potter [1914].

Facts: the two directors refused to meet to appoint the third director.

Held: the members could break the deadlock.

(b)   The general meeting may act where there is no board.

Alexander Ward & Co v Samyang Navigation Co [1975]

Facts: two persons took legal steps to protect the interests of the company at a time when it had **no directors** and subsequently the company went into liquidation and the liquidator, as successor to the members in general meeting, ratified what had been done.

Held: this validated what had been done and that in principle if the directors could not exercise their powers, the company might protect its rights through other means.

(c)   The company in general meeting may **ratify or authorise** in advance an act which is beyond the directors' powers. The most usual case is where the directors' personal interests conflict with those of the company or they wish to exercise a power for some purpose other than that for which it was given. But a majority in general meeting cannot sanction an act of the directors to defraud the company: **Cook v Deeks [1914]**. Under S35 CA85 the members can even ratify an *ultra vires* act by passing a special resolution.

8.4   How directors' powers are exercised

It should be clear that the directors' only have such powers as are delegated to them, and that the articles will usually delegate wide powers to the board of directors. Unless there is then a power to sub-delegate, all decisions and actions must be by the board collectively. Thus:

(a)   We consider the very limited rules for the calling and conduct of board meetings.

(b)   We consider the position of a managing director to whom the board, if empowered to do so, may delegate its powers.

(c)   Then in the next section we deal with the wider and more difficult area of liability of the company for acts of individual directors, including other officers in this discussion as many of the basic principles are the same for directors and other officers.

8.5   Board meetings

Unless the articles otherwise provide **any director may call** a board meeting. Article 88 expressly empowers them to do so. But a meeting must be called at a reasonable time and place.

No minimum **notice** is prescribed and it is unusual for the board to fix a standard period of notice. Where notice is given it need not specify the business to be transacted.

The board may expressly or by custom establish a **quorum** ie, minimum number of members to be present. This may be fixed at one; if no quorum is fixed Article 89 Table A provides a quorum of two. A director who cannot vote because of their interest in a contract cannot be counted for quorum purposes (Article 95). But the articles may expressly permit a director to be counted in such a case. If the total number of directors falls below the quorum figure the articles (Article 90) may permit the surviving directors to hold a valid meeting for the purpose only of increasing their number or calling a general meeting.

The board is usually (Article 91) empowered to appoint a **chairman** either for a limited period or until the board terminates their appointment. In their absence from a meeting the directors present may appoint a substitute for the meeting.

Unless the articles otherwise provide each director present has **one vote** and a resolution is not carried unless a majority of votes is cast in its favour. The chairman only has a **casting vote** if the articles give it to him or her (eg, Article 88). A director may be expressly disqualified from voting on a matter in which they are interested (Article 94).

The articles may provide that a **resolution** signed by all directors entitled to notice of a meeting shall be as valid a decision as if it had been passed at a meeting (Article 93). This is particularly useful where the directors cannot conveniently meet.

Minutes of meetings of the directors must be kept. If signed by the chairman the minutes are *prima facie* evidence, which may, however, be rebutted, of the proceedings. Directors have a right to inspect the minutes of their meetings for the purposes of discharging their duties but not to further their own ends; the same principle applies to their statutory right to inspect the books of account: S222(1) CA85. The auditors also have a right of access to the directors' minutes.

It is the normal practice to draft the minutes as a brief formal record of information received and decisions taken and not to attempt to summarise discussion and argument. But a director who votes against or abstains from voting on a resolution is entitled to have that fact recorded.

The articles may require the directors to sign an **attendance book** as a record of their presence. If a director is absent from part of a meeting it is usual to record this fact in the minutes.

8.6   Managing director

The articles (eg, Article 84 Table A) may permit the appointment of a managing director (or more than one) and delegation to them of any of the powers of the board to be exercised by them either **collaterally with or to the exclusion of** the board. Note that it is the function of the board, and not the general meeting, to appoint a managing director.

The board may be authorised to delegate any or all of its powers to the managing director, who will thus have complete control over their exercise until their authority is revoked. In such a case, the general meeting, the board and the managing director will each have exclusive jurisdiction over their respective spheres of power.

A managing director is something more than a director with management functions. They are deemed to have general powers **as an individual** to commit the company to contracts. However, as between a managing director and the board they are the board's delegate only; thus they have no power to exercise those residual powers of the shareholders.

A managing director's appointment ceases if they cease to be a director. If he or she has a separate service agreement providing for their employment as managing director their removal from office as director may be a breach of contract: **Southern Foundries v Shirlaw**; but they cannot prevent, by injunction, an alteration of articles affecting their removal, or the passing of an ordinary resolution by the company removing them from office.

8.7   Activity

Identify the possible recourses of the general meeting if the board of a company refuses to undertake a commercial project which has been approved by a resolution of the meeting.

8.8   Activity solution

(a)   Remove the board under S303;

(b)   Alter the articles by special resolution (S9) to make the board subject to the direction of the general meeting;

(c)   If the articles are in the form of Table A, pass a special resolution in accordance with Article 70 to direct the board;

(d)   It may be possible to bring an action under S459 of CA85 on the basis of 'unfair prejudice' or S122 of IA86 (to wind the company up on the just and equitable ground), although the court will probably need evidence of more than just a disagreement with the company's commercial policy.

9   LIABILITY OF THE COMPANY FOR ACTS OF DIRECTORS (AND OTHERS)

9.1   Introduction: agency in company law

We have seen that there are certain circumstances in which a company may incur liability (ie, for contracts, torts and crimes). This may be because the company itself has committed an act, through one of its organs, the constitutional position of which means that its acts are the acts of the company. More likely, an act will be done on behalf of the company not by an organ but by a servant or agent. Whether or not such an act will make the company liable depends on the power of the company to act in such a situation (the *ultra vires* rule and its exceptions) and on whether or not the person acting is capable of binding the company, which is the point we must consider now.

The issue is basically one of the law of agency so far as it is applicable in the context of company law. A principal (here, the company) will be liable for the acts of its agent if the agent has acted within either:

(a)   the **actual** scope of the authority conferred on him by his principal prior to the transaction or by subsequent ratification, or

(b)   the **apparent** scope of his authority. This last is based on representations by the principal. It is based on estoppel.

- Thus if a person has been appointed to the office of Managing Director he will appear to a third party to have authority to bind the company in all contracts connected with the management of the company. Similarly other agents will have apparent authority from what is usual to their position or office. Remember that a non-executive director has no usual authority by virtue of that office.

- Thus if the company holds a person out as occupying a particular office or position it will then be estopped from denying to a third party who relies on the representation that the person has authority usual to that position. This doctrine of holding out is illustrated by the leading case of:

Freeman & Lockyer v Buckhurst Park Properties (1964).

Facts: Kapoor, a property developer, and Hoon, formed a private company which purchased Buckhurst Park Estate. The board of directors consisted of Kapoor and Hoon and a nominee of each. The company's articles gave the company power to appoint a managing director but none was appointed. Kapoor, however, acted as such. He instructed the plaintiffs, a firm of architects, to do work for the company which was completed. The company refused to pay claiming that Kapoor had no authority to bind the company to this type of transaction.

Held: Kapoor had been held out as having apparent authority to enter into this transaction by those having actual authority to commit the company in this way ie, the board. The company is, therefore, estopped from denying to anyone who has entered into a contract with an agent in reliance upon such apparent authority that the agent had authority to contract on behalf of the company.

A third party cannot rely on apparent authority when he knows, or perhaps ought to know, of the lack of actual authority. Prior to amendments made in 1989 a third party was also unable to rely on apparent authority where he could have found out about the lack of actual authority by reading the company's publicly available documents (eg, the Memorandum and Articles). This, the doctrine of constructive notice, was abolished in this area of law by S711A CA85 (as inserted in 1989) except in circumstances where the third party should reasonably have made enquiries. It is not clear how the courts would interpret this.

9.2   Royal British Bank v Turquand (or the 'Indoor Management' Rule)

This rule is often expressed as a particular aspect of the general agency rule. However, it should be learned as a separate rule as some people treat them as two different rules.

Facts: the facts of the case were that the articles authorised the directors to borrow such sums as might be authorised by (ordinary) resolution passed in general meeting. A resolution was passed but it did not specify any amount which the directors were authorised to borrow. The directors issued debentures; the company became insolvent; Turquand was sued as its liquidator.

Held: the plaintiff bank was deemed to be aware that the directors could only borrow up to the amount authorised by ordinary resolution since the articles, which imposed that limit, were a document available for public inspection at the Companies Registry. But as an outsider the bank had no means of knowing whether an adequate ordinary resolution (or any resolution at all) had been passed: ordinary resolutions do not have to be filed at the Companies Registry. In the circumstances the bank **had a right to infer the fact of a resolution authorising that which on the face of the document (the debentures) appeared to be legitimately done.**

In general terms the rule (sometimes called **the indoor management rule**) is that an outsider dealing with a company is entitled, in the absence of knowledge or suspicion to the contrary, to assume that the company has properly complied with internal procedures required by its articles.

The rule does not apply to all transactions of a company. It does apply to internal matters such as the appointment of directors and to the proper conduct of board meetings and signature of documents ie, the outsider may assume that requirements of internal procedure and authorisation have been satisfied in such cases. Also the rule does not apply where a document purportedly issued on behalf of a company is a forgery.

9.3   Irregularities in the appointment of directors

When powers are delegated to **directors** this means to directors properly appointed. A **director** who is invalidly appointed or who has ceased to be a director but who continues to act as such is not a director at all. But there are **two** rules of law which tend to validate the acts of a **director** (and of a board of which they are a member) in spite of any irregularities in their appointment.

(a)   A person who deals with a company through persons who purport to be its **directors** and who could have been properly appointed directors (but who in fact have not been) may be entitled to assume that they are directors and to hold the company bound by their acts: **Mahony v East Holyford Mining Co.** (This is a particular application of the rule in **Turquand's Case**).

Facts: W, along with some friends, started a mining company. Subscriptions were obtained from shareholders and paid into the bank. The bankers received a formal notice signed by the 'company secretary' asking the bank to pay out on the signatures of any two of the following three directors, and countersigned by himself. Three specimen signatures were attached. The bankers honoured cheques signed in this fashion. When the fund had been almost entirely drawn out, the company was ordered to be wound up.

It then appeared that there had been no meeting authorising the signatures, no appointment of any director or secretary, but that the promoters of the company had treated themselves as directors and secretary and appropriated the subscription money.

Held: the liquidator could not recover from the bank the amount of the cheques which had been paid *bona fide*. Where those who draw and those who honour cheques intend them to operate on a certain account, no objection can afterwards be taken that the account is not specifically mentioned on the face of the cheques.

(b)   There is also a statutory rule that the acts of a director or manager shall be valid notwithstanding any defect that may afterwards be discovered in their appointment or qualification: S285 CA85. The two rules overlap, but only partially, in their application.

S285 CA85 is expressly limited in its scope to **initial defects** of appointment or qualification but it could apply to **internal** transactions of irregularly appointed directors as well as to their dealings with outsiders. S285 CA85 will only **validate** transactions where the sole defect is in relation to the directors' qualification or appointment. It **cannot** be used to **validate** transactions entered into by an **unauthorised** person or in excess of the directors' authority.

9.4   Personal liability

Although the third party cannot sue the company on a transaction which is outside the scope of the agent's actual or apparent authority, he may sue the agent personally for breach of warranty of authority and thereby recover damages for any loss.

It should also be remembered that if an agent acts outside his actual authority he commits a breach of duty and the principal could sue him and, in a serious case, dismiss him.

9.5 Transactions beyond the board's powers

This section is concerned with company transactions with a third party made by the board (or by a person who has authority from the board).

A transaction might be beyond the powers of the board for several reasons.

(a)   the transaction is *ultra vires* the company as delimited by its memorandum;

(b)   the transaction, although *intra vires* the company, is an abuse by the directors of the company's powers: the situation in **Rolled Steel v BSC [1985]** is an example of this;

(c)   the transaction was beyond the directors' powers as set out by the company's articles or by the general meeting. Nowadays articles of companies will commonly delegate all the company's powers to the board (Table A does this in Art 70) but in the past it was extremely common for Articles to subject the exercise of borrowing powers by the board to the sanction of the members in general meeting.

In the absence of ratification by the members in general meeting - usually ordinary resolution but remember S35 CA85 requires a special resolution in relation to *ultra vires* - the transaction would not be binding on the company at common law unless **Turquand's** rule applies.

S35A CA95 (inserted by CA89) now provides considerable protection to third parties.

It provides that in favour of a person dealing with the company in good faith the power of the board to bind the company or authorise others shall be deemed to be free of any limitations in the company's constitution including by resolution or agreement by members. It further states:

(a)   a person 'deals with' a company if they are party to any transaction or other act to which the company is a party;

(b)   a person shall not be regarded as acting in bad faith by reason only of their knowledge that an act is beyond the powers of the directors under the company's constitution;

(c)   a person shall be presumed to have acted in good faith unless the contrary is proved;

and S35B states:

(d)   a party to a transaction with a company is not bound to enquire as to whether it is permitted by the company's memorandum or as to any limitation on the powers of the board of directors to bind the company or authorise the others to do so.

However, the provision does not affect any right of a member of the company to bring proceedings to restrain the doing of an act which is beyond the powers of the directors. Thus, prior to the directors acting a member could seek an injunction to prevent the directors from acting beyond their powers, but could not do so once they have acted. The provision does not affect the liability of directors to the company for acts done beyond their powers. This section probably supersedes the rule in **Turquand's** case and should be considered first when answering an examination question in this area.

9.6   Invalidity of transactions involving directors

S322A CA85 (inserted by CA89) provides that where a company enters into a transaction to which the parties include a director or person connected with a director of the company or its holding company and the board have exceeded the limitation in their powers under the company's constitution the transaction is voidable by the company. This provision therefore modifies the rules in S35A CA85 when a director or connected person contracts with the company and renders the contract voidable. Connected person is defined as for substantial property transactions basically close relatives, companies under the directors control etc.

S322A CA85 provides that the transaction will cease to be voidable if:

(a)   the restriction is no longer possible; or

(b)   the company is indemnified for any loss suffered; or

(c)   a *bona fide* purchase for value without notice of directors exceeding their authority acquire rights on the subject matter of the transaction; or

(d)   the company in general meeting ratifies the transaction by ordinary or special resolution.

However, S322A CA85 also provides that whether the transaction is avoided or not any director or connected person who was a party to it and any director of the company who authorised it is liable to account to the company for any gain or indemnify the company for any loss.

10   SELF TEST QUESTIONS

10.1   Who is a shadow director? (1.1)

10.2   How many directors must a company have? (1.2)

10.3   What is the age qualification for directors and when does it apply? (1.3)

10.4   What are the grounds for disqualification under the CDDA 1986? (2.5 - 2.7)

10.5   How long is a long-term service contract as per S319 CA85? (3.3)

10.6   Where must directors' service contracts be kept? (3.4)

10.7   Who is empowered by Table A to set directors' remuneration? (4)

10.8   Which type of company may make a director a loan for house purchase? (5.4)

10.9   Is an unlawful loan a criminal offence? (5.5)

10.10   Who must approve a compensation for loss of office payment to a director in order to render it lawful? (6.2)

10.11   How is a director removed from office under S303 CA85? (7.2 & 7.3)

10.12   Where are the directors' powers stated? (8.1)

10.13   What is the indoor management rule? (9.2)

10.14   In what circumstances is a third party protected by S35A CA85? (9.5)

11   EXAMINATION TYPE QUESTION

11.1   Division of authority

How is authority divided between the members of a company in general meeting and the board of directors of the company?

(10 marks)

12   ANSWER TO EXAMINATION TYPE QUESTION

12.1   Division of authority

A company must have at least one director if it is a private company and at least two if it is a public company: S282 Companies Act 1985 (CA85). The written constitution of the company ie, its memorandum and articles of association, define the extent of the directors' powers of management. Most articles follow the model of Article 70 of Table A in conferring on the directors all the powers of the company which are not either by the Companies Act or by the articles themselves reserved to the company in general meeting. Some major decisions such as an alteration of the articles or a reduction of share capital are by the Companies Act reserved to the members in general meeting. The directors cannot have greater powers than the company itself ie, they are subject to the doctrine of *ultra vires*.

As the directors' powers are conferred by the articles of association, the directors must exercise them as they see fit, acting *bona fide* and in the interests of the company. The members in general meeting cannot instruct the directors on the exercise of their powers: **Salmon v Quin and Axtens**. If the members are dissatisfied, their proper course is either to remove the directors from office (by their statutory power under S303 CA85 or under the articles) or to alter the articles (though not with retrospective effect) to curtail the directors' powers. When the directors wish to exercise their powers for a purpose other than that for which they were conferred by the articles, the members in general meeting may sanction this course: **Bamford v Bamford.**

Any powers of the company which are not delegated to the directors remain with the members in general meeting. There is also a limited and rather uncertain doctrine of **concurrent powers**. The effect of this doctrine is that in some matters the general meeting has a residual or concurrent power to act if the directors cannot or will not exercise their powers. The scope of this doctrine is narrow. It does not extend to the exercise of the directors' general powers of management: **Quin and Axtens Case** above. However, if two directors are in a state of deadlock and cannot agree to appoint a third director, the general meeting may do so: **Barron v Potter.**

25 CORPORATE MANAGEMENT: DIRECTORS' DUTIES

INTRODUCTION & LEARNING OBJECTIVES

Syllabus area 8g. Directors' duties, the liability of directors to shareholders, creditors and employees, fraudulent and wrongful trading.

Issues in corporate governance. (Ability required 3)

This chapter considers the duties which every director owes to his company deriving from both the common law and statute. It considers the conceptual question of whether or not duties owed to the legal entity, the company, also encompasses members, creditors and employees. The accountability of directors and to whom they are accountable is one of the contentious issues of corporate governance.

When you have studied this chapter you should be able to do the following:

- Understand to whom directors owe their duties.

- Explain and describe the common law duty and the extent to which statute imposes additional requirements.

- Describe the common law duty of care and skill.

- Understand the Insolvency Act 1986 (IA86) provisions relating to fraudulent trading and wrongful trading.

- Appreciate in outline how a director may be relieved from liability.

1 NATURE OF THE DUTIES OF DIRECTORS

1.1 The Director's roles

There may be several different types of director in a company, depending upon the functions of each director and his function in the company. Two points, however, are reasonably clear.

Firstly, the directors of a company are persons of some importance and with a definite place in the constitutional structure of the company. It is they who, in practice, control the company and upon whom the fortunes of the company largely depend. But this does not mean that they can treat the company as their own.

Secondly, the directors have certain duties which they are obliged to fulfil. These derive from the various roles which a director has and the roles which he fills within the company.

(a) Director as employee

Although a director may be an employee, he need not necessarily be one, so his duties are not necessarily related to a contract of service. Generally speaking, an employee's duty of fidelity may impose lesser obligations than the director's duties of good faith.

(b)   **Director as agent**

They will be in the position of an **agent** (although the precise nature of the agency will depend upon the particular circumstances) and so will owe the duties of an agent. But their relationship with the company cannot be determined solely by reference to the law of agency, especially as they do not necessarily have all the rights of an agent.

(c)   **Director as trustee**

It has been said that directors are in the position of **trustees** and this is accurate insofar as it suggests, quite rightly, that the director is in a fiduciary position and owes duties of good faith. The quasi-trusteeship position of director has great significance with reference to breach of duty in that if a director in breach of fiduciary duty misapplies company assets he commits a breach of trust and under trust law principles becomes liable to restore the misapplied property. The same liability attaches to any person who knowingly assists in a breach of trust or who knowingly receives company assets misapplied in breach of trust. We earlier saw this principle in operation when considering the effect of a company giving unlawful financial assistance for the acquisition of its own shares.

The position of director is not, however, wholly analogous to that of a trustee. A trustee must be cautious and safeguard the trust property; the director, however, is engaged in a speculative undertaking and the likelihood of their having to take risks is such that their obligation to refrain from negligence is far less onerous than that of a trustee.

1.2   To whom are the duties owed?

There are potentially a number of individuals or bodies to whom the director owes duties, the company, the members, the employees, the creditors, the board. We shall deal with all of these in turn.

(a)   **The company**

The general rule is that directors owe their duties to the **company as a whole** and this has traditionally been taken to mean to the shareholders as a collective body; which includes present and future shareholders.

They may **take account** of their own interests as shareholders and of the interests of particular sections of shareholders; they are not required to think of the company as an entity which is completely distinct from its members. S309 Companies Act 1985 (CA85) requires them **to take into account** the interests of employees and members but their **duty** is to the company.

(b)   **The members**

The directors owe no general duty to individual members:

Percival v Wright [1902]

Facts: some shareholders wrote to the secretary of a company asking if he knew of anyone wishing to purchase shares in the company. After negotiations, the shareholders sold their shares to the chairman of the company and two directors at £12.10s 0d per share. Subsequently, the plaintiffs discovered that during the negotiations the board had been engaged in talks with another party concerning a takeover of the company, at a price which was considerably more than £12.10s 0d a share. The attempted takeover did not take place. The shareholders wished to have the sale of their shares set aside on the basis that the directors should have disclosed the negotiations with the bidder.

Held: the directors must act *bona fide* for the interests of the company but they are not in a fiduciary position in relation to individual shareholders. Therefore the individual shareholders had no action against the directors. (Presumably the company itself could have sued).

The same principle was applied in **Scottish Co-operative Wholesale Society v Meyer [1958]** where the majority shareholder in a holding company had appointed its nominees as directors of the subsidiary and it was stated by the Court of Appeal that their first duty was to the subsidiary, the company of which they were directors, and not to the holding company, the majority member and their nominator.

However, despite the general rule, particular circumstances may give rise to a duty owed by directors to particular shareholders, for example where they are authorised to act as agents for particular shareholders in relation to sale of their shares.

(c)   **The employees**

S309 CA85 insists that the directors take into account the interests of the company's employees as well as the members. However, the duty is to the company; there is no duty to the employees and any breaches of the directors' duties are enforceable by the company as the proper plaintiff.

(d)   **The creditors**

The law does not recognise a duty to others eg, creditors, customers or (for example, in environmental matters) to the community, but there are numerous provisions designed to protect such persons and in practice this point is much affected by the factor that it will generally be in the interests of the company that its relations with creditors, etc, should be harmonious and that the company should be of good repute.

A director appointed by holders of debentures under a power in the debentures owes his duties primarily to the company and not to the debentureholders. This might appear to detract from the protection given to debentureholders, in that their appointee will not be obliged merely to promote their interests, unless it is remembered that the appointee should be able to see, by their membership of the board, that the affairs of the company are properly conducted and in the manner presumably expected by the debentureholders.

(e)   **The board**

It might be argued that the directors are responsible to the board of directors, of which they are a member and which may have initially secured their appointment as directors. But, although directors may derive power from their activities as a board (their authority to bind the company generally depends on whether or not they act as a board) their duties are not owed to the board (ie, to themselves). Thus, they cannot control the extent and exercise of their duties, or excuse breaches of them, by board decisions.

A further aspect of this is that although directors exercise their powers collectively as a Board, their duties are owed individually.

Conclusion   Each director owes a duty to the company. The significance of this is that since the company is a legal entity it is the company who sues. This is an aspect of the rule in **Foss v Harbottle** which, in general, prevents a member suing where wrongs have been done to the company.

1.3   Acting in the interests of the company as a whole

Directors are bound to carry out their duties (to exercise the powers and discretion given to them) but the means by which they do so will not generally be specified. They are, however, obliged to adhere to their overriding duty of good faith and to act in what they consider to be in the **interests of the company as a whole**. There are two aspects of this well-worn phrase:

(a)   Who decides what is in the best interests of the company?

The test here is subjective ie, did the directors themselves honestly believe that they were acting in the best interests of the company? If so, their judgement will not be impugned even if the outcome shows or the opinion of the court is that they showed bad judgement.

As an example, a director and controlling shareholder must not procure a service agreement for himself entirely to provide a pension for his widow: **Re Roith [1967].** He was held to be in breach of duty because he had given no thought to the benefit of the company.

Rather similarly in **Bishopsgate Investment Management Ltd v Maxwell (No 2) [1994]** - one of the many cases spawned out of the huge exercise of unravelling the tangled affairs of the late Robert Maxwell and the companies he controlled - summary judgement was given against Ian Maxwell (one of Robert Maxwell's two sons, the other being Kevin) who, as director of Bishopsgate, signed stock transfer forms transferring shares, forming part of the company's pension fund for employees, to another company controlled by Robert Maxwell. Judgement was given against Ian mainly because he had given no thought to the benefit of Bishopgate, merely by signing because Kevin told him to do so. *Note:* there are many other allegations in this case (eg negligence, ie breach of duty of care and skill) which have not yet come to a full trial. As Ian Maxwell has been made bankrupt this may never happen.

(b)   What are the interests of the company as a whole?

This is really another aspect of the problem posed above ie, to whom is the duty owed and what happens if there are conflicting duties?

As we have seen the interests of the company are at one remove from the interests of its shareholders collectively and now the employees. The directors are entitled to take account of these interests in a collective sense: eg, the declaration of a dividend is to the advantage of shareholders and in its direct effect disadvantageous to the company as a separate person eg, making *ex gratia* redundancy payments is advantageous to the employees concerned but not the company. The directors are entitled to act accordingly although they themselves, if they are shareholders or employees, will secure a benefit.

Company law gives no clue as to how directors are to reconcile any competing interests between employees and shareholders, now that they are obliged to consider both. It can be assumed, however, that as long as the directors take their decisions in good faith, the court will remain reluctant to impugn them.

Where a director has been appointed to represent some particular interest eg, a debentureholder, it is doubtful whether he is entitled to subordinate the interests of the company to the non-members' interests whom he specifically represents.

It may be that it is becoming accepted that directors must take account of the interests of the company **and** that this requires taking account of all relevant interests (whether of shareholders, creditors, employees, etc) in deciding what is in the overall interests of the company. In other words, it may be antiquated and misconceived to assume that the interests of the company must be the interests of the shareholders alone. Of course, it would be naive to assume that directors could in any case act in the best interests of the shareholders if they ignored related interests.

A number of statutory provisions of the IA86 are designed to protect creditors (notably the fraudulent and wrongful trading provisions of S213 and S214 IA86 under which the liquidator can take action against errant directors. Although such action by the liquidator is theoretically taken by him on behalf of the company it is the creditors who stand to benefit where the company is insolvent.

Conclusion   Although directors owe their duties to the company and it is the company which sues them for breach, whether or not they are in breach of their duty will entail consideration of their treatment of members, employees and perhaps creditors.

1.4   In what capacity do directors owe duties?

Directors owe duties whilst acting in the capacity of director - thus, for example, at a board meeting each director must exercise his vote in the interests of the company and not, for example, in his own personal interest.

The position is different at general meetings where, if a director is a member, he will be voting, not in his capacity as director but in his capacity as member - **North-West Transportation v Beatty [1887]**.

1.5   Summary of directors duties

It is not easy to summarise or categorise directors' duties as they are wide ranging, depend on the articles and are changing both through legislation and case law which are increasing the standard and the scope of the duties.

At common law there are two main duties of directors:

(a)   the fiduciary duty;

(b)   the duty of care and skill.

Both are supplemented by statute: the fiduciary duty by for example Part X CA85 Enforcement of Fair Dealing by Directors; the duty of care and skill by for example certain provisions of the IA86 intended to deal with malpractice which has become apparent once the company has gone into liquidation.

2   THE FIDUCIARY DUTY OF DIRECTORS

2.1   Introduction

Every director has a fiduciary duty to act in good faith for the benefit of the company as a whole.

Although there is one overriding fiduciary duty it has a number of different, but overlapping applications.

2.2   Duty to exercise powers for the proper purpose (the proper purposes rule)

Although the directors themselves must decide how to exercise their powers, and although actions taken by them outside their powers may be ratified by the company in general meeting, this does not permit the directors to exercise their powers other than for the purposes for which they are given.

Obviously the exercise of a discretion may require the taking account of many factors and the influence of mixed motives. But the directors will be justified if their main purpose is a proper one.

Mills v Mills [1938].

Facts: directors, who were majority ordinary shareholders, capitalised dividends and issued bonus shares to the ordinary shareholders and thereby the position of preference shareholders was weakened.

Held: this was permitted as the main purpose was in the interests of the company.

The most common instance of challenge of directors' exercise of powers for a proper purpose is the issue of shares by directors for the purpose of creating additional votes at a general meeting in order to resist a takeover bid or otherwise to affect voting control. The power to issue shares is given to directors by the articles for the purpose only of raising additional capital or acquiring assets which the company needs for its business. The issue of shares for any other purpose, even if the directors honestly believe that to do so is in the interests of the company, is a breach of their duty. A number of illustrative cases were given in the earlier chapter 'Corporate finance: raising of share capital.'

In the two leading cases on this point the courts have ruled that the company in general meeting may, by ordinary resolution, authorise in advance or ratify after the event an issue of shares made for a wrong purpose but in the honest belief that it was in the interests of the company.

Hogg v Cramphorn [1967].

Facts: the company had a capital of 96,000 £1 preference shares, 40,000 £1 ordinary shares, of which 90,293 preference and 35,888 ordinary shares were issued. The company's articles gave the directors the power to issue new shares. The articles also provided that every share was to carry one vote.

The directors learnt of a takeover bid and, believing such a takeover would not be in the company's best interest, decided to forestall the bid. They issued 5,707 preference shares, each carrying ten votes per share, to a trust, which was controlled by the chairman of the board, a partner in the company's auditors and an employee. The company advanced an interest free loan of £28,293 to the trustees for the purchase of further preference shares. The allotment was challenged.

Held: the directors were in breach of their duty to the company by manipulating the voting position and their belief that it was for the benefit of the company was irrelevant. The matter was adjourned so that the company should be given an opportunity to decide whether it approves or disapproves of the issue of these shares. At such a meeting the trustees were not to vote. The shareholders subsequently approved the issued.

In **Bamford v Bamford [1970]** an equally well-known and quoted case, the facts were similar except that the members had ratified the directors actions before the court action which, therefore, held the allotment to be valid.

Further points to note are:

(a)   If the shares have already been issued the votes attached to the new shares must not be used when the matter is put to the vote: an independent vote must be obtained.

(b)   If the purpose which the directors had in view was proper their judgement as to the means used to achieve it will not usually be questioned.

(c)   A purpose cannot be a proper one if it is *ultra vires* the company.

(d)   The courts now distinguish between transactions which are *ultra vires* the company and those which are *intra vires* the company but beyond the powers of the directors or an abuse of the directors powers.

Rolled Steel Products Ltd v British Steel Corporation [1985]

Facts: the giving of a guarantee and the giving of security was undertaken by the board and not properly ratified by the members.

Held: RSP was not bound by the directors' acts as there was an abuse of power and BSC were aware of this. The company had not ratified the transaction and was, therefore, not bound.

(e)   Although the company may ratify the transaction the ratification will not be valid if there is a fraud on the minority.

Clemens v Clemens [1976]

Facts: 45% of the shares were owned by the plaintiff and 55% were owned by her aunt who was also a director of the company and as such issued shares to reduce her niece's shareholding and, therefore, control in the company. The aunt then used her voting power in an ordinary general meeting to 'ratify' the issue of shares.

Held: that the purported ratification was ineffective as a fraud on the minority.

2.3   Duty to avoid a conflict of interest

A director may be in a position where there is a conflict between their duty to the company and their own personal interests. For example, they become a director of a company which provides training to accountants while working as an independent tutor teaching at rival colleges. There is a general rule that this should not be allowed. Thus, a director must not do or omit to do something if that gives rise to a conflict, or might reasonably be expected to give rise to a conflict, between the duties of his office and either their private interest or any duties they owes to any other person. The possibility of such a conflict arises in a number of circumstances:

(a)   where a director is in a position to compete with the company;
(b)   where a director makes a profit from their position as director;
(c)   where a director contracts with the company. Here there are:

  (i)   general rules which relate to **any** contract;
  (ii)   specific rules about transactions of **substantial** value;
  (iii)   specific rules on **loans** and other forms of credit being given to a director; and

(d)   where a director owns shares or debentures in the company and as a result of their position has information which gives him an advantage in dealing in them.

We shall deal with each of these in turn.

2.4   Not to compete with company

(a)   **Competing businesses**

   A director should not compete with the company of which they are directors and, despite the possible advantages of having non-executive directors who are involved with other businesses, he should not serve as a director of another company, at least where he has a contract of employment with the first company.

Other problems of conflict of interest can arise where:

(i)   a director is appointed to the board as a nominee of some outside interest eg, a major loan creditor;

(ii)   a director of company A is also a director of company B which is a competitor of company A.

There is apparently no objection in principle to making either arrangement but there is a very real conflict of interest if at any time the director has to (or chooses to) advance the interest of the other party whom he represents rather than that of the company. It has been said that if such a situation develops the director must either put the interest of the company first or resign the directorship. It is an uncertain area of law and much depends on the facts of the case.

(b)   **Confidential information**

They should not abuse the confidence placed in them by disclosing to others, or using for their own purposes, confidential information obtained by virtue of their being in office as a director.

2.5   Profits obtained from the position of director

One potential breach of duty that the company is not likely to allow concerns the making of profits which the director would not have made if he were not a director.

Directors may **actively divert** property or, in some cases, opportunities to themselves which would otherwise have gone to the company. The law will not allow them to keep the benefits and provides that it is a breach of his fiduciary duty to obtain any benefit from their office without the company's consent given by the articles or a resolution in general meeting. They are accountable to the company as constructive trustee for any such profit.

Cook v Deeks [1916]

Facts: the shares of a railway company, T, were held in equal shares by four people who also constituted the board. The company carried out several large construction contracts for the Canadian Pacific Railway Co. Three of the directors, hearing that there was a new contract coming up, obtained it in their own names to the exclusion of the company and formed another company, D, to carry out the work. They then passed resolutions by virtue of their shareholding approving the sale of plant by T to D and declaring that T had no interest in the new contract with the Canadian Pacific. The fourth director, Cook, brought an action against the others claiming that the benefit of the contract properly belonged to T and the directors could not use their voting power as shareholders to vest it in themselves.

Held: the opportunity to obtain the new contract came to the directors whilst acting as directors of T, the contracts belonged in equity to the company and the directors could not retain the benefit of it for themselves. Moreover, the directors could not use their voting control to appropriate the interest and property of the company.

Thus, the directors could not keep the benefit of the contracts even though it had been ratified by the general meeting as it had been their own voting power which had resulted in the ratification.

Another situation occurs where the directors have acted openly and honestly but still obtained a benefit from their position. The rule appears to be strict and to depend on the mere making of a profit from his position as director, regardless of his motives or the consequences for the company.

Regal (Hastings) Ltd v Gulliver [1942]

Facts: Regal owned a cinema. The directors wished to acquire the leases of two other cinemas with a view to selling the whole as a going concern. Regal had insufficient funds to purchase the leases and the directors were unwilling to purchase in their own names, thereby making themselves personally liable without limit. So they formed a company, Amalgamated, with a capital of 5,000 £1 shares. Regal subscribed for 2,000 shares and the directors and their friends subscribed for the rest. Eventually the three cinemas were sold as a going concern by a sale of the shares in both companies. The directors received £2.16sh.1d profit per share on the sale of their shares in Amalgamated. The company sued for the recovery of this profit.

Held: the directors used their opportunities and special knowledge as directors to make a secret profit for themselves. They were accountable to the company for the profits made. In their decision the House of Lords recognised that the directors, as controlling shareholders, could have passed a resolution in general meeting to approve the retention of their profit. But they had not done so. Thus, the (potential or actual) breach of duty may be authorised or ratified by the general meeting provided the effect of this is not to permit fraud on the minority shareholders as in **Cook v Deeks [1916]**.

The fiduciary duty can survive even after the director has left the company.

IDC v Cooley [1972]

Facts: Cooley, the managing director of IDC, had been negotiating a contract on behalf of the company but the third party wished to award the contract to him personally and not to the company. Without disclosing his reason to the company (or its board) he resigned in order to take the contract personally.

Held: he was in breach of fiduciary duty as he had profited personally by use of an opportunity which came to him through his directorship: it made no difference that the company itself would not have obtained the contract. He was therefore accountable to the company for the benefits gained from the contract.

Cooley's case has recently been distinguished in

Island Export Finance v Umunna [1986]

Facts: U was managing director of IEF and in 1976 he secured a contract for it from the Cameroon postal authorities. In 1977 he resigned from IEG due to general dissatisfaction with it and subsequently obtained orders from the Cameroon postal authorities for his own company. IEF sued him for breach of fiduciary duty.

Held: he was not in breach of fiduciary duty. There were 2 main reasons behind the decision. First that while U may have in a general way contemplated that Cameroon authorities might be a good source of business for his own company on resignation, the exploitation of the opportunity was not his primary or indeed an important motive for his resignation. Second, neither when U resigned nor when he obtained the orders was IEF actively pursuing further business with the Cameroon authorities: at most it had a hope of obtaining further orders but that could not in any realistic sense be said to be a maturing business opportunity of IEF.

There is a dicta to support the view (and applied in cases from Canada such as **Peso Silver Mines v Cropper [1965]**) that if a company bona fide for good business reasons rejects a corporate opportunity then a director who takes the opportunity personally is not in breach of fiduciary duty.

You should also remember that under the general law of restraint of trade (see the earlier chapter 'Contract: terms) that a director who is an employee cannot be injuncted from using, after his employment has ceased, personal skills and knowledge gained during his employment, as distinct from using confidential information.

2.6   Contracts with the company

(a)   The general rule

A director should not generally **contract** with his company, otherwise he might be dismissed as a director; he must account for profits; and the company may avoid the contract (it need not do so). It is immaterial that the contract is made on fair terms and after full disclosure.

Aberdeen Railway v Blaikie [1854]

Facts: the defendant company entered into a contract to purchase a quantity of chairs from the plaintiff partnership. One of the directors of the company was also a member of the partnership at the time of contract.

Held: the director was interested in both sides of the bargain. Therefore, he could not make the best bargain for the company. No question should be raised as to the fairness or unfairness of a contract so entered into. The company was entitled to avoid the contract.

This situation necessarily exists where the director contracts directly or has an interest (eg, as director or shareholder of another company) in a contract with his company.

(b)   Exceptions to the rule

(i)   Articles allow

The practical inconvenience of the strict principle (eg, it would apply to contracts of service with working directors) is such that the articles usually permit directors to be interested in certain specified types of contract and to retain any profit realised from such contracts provided he discloses the nature and extent of his interest to the board. There are also standard provisions prohibiting directors from voting on and being counted for quorum purposes at board meetings considering contracts in which they may be interested (see **Articles 85, 86 & 94).**

Guinness plc v Saunders & Another [1990]

Facts: a payment of £5.2 m was made to a director for work on a takeover bid. The director argued that disclosure had been made to a sub-committee of the board.

Held: the disclosure must be made to a full board meeting and not to a committee of the board.

S317 CA85 (directors to disclose interest in contracts), later, contains a similar disclosure rule.

(ii)   Approval by general meeting of members

Where the articles do not provide an adequate remission in a particular case the company in general meeting can, after full disclosure of the terms of the contract, **approve** it and exempt the director from the rule.

S320 CA85 (substantial property transactions), later, **requires** approval of the general meeting for certain contracts whatever the company's articles might say.

3   STATUTORY INTERVENTION

3.1   Introduction

In general any statutory provision must be complied with in addition to the common law fiduciary duty. It is important that you realise, in relation to breach of each statutory provision, whether it provides for civil remedies or criminal penalties (or both) as examination questions will often require you to make the distinction.

3.2   Part X CA85 Enforcement of Fair Dealing by Directors

Some aspects of Part X (sub-headed Restrictions on directors taking financial advantage) have been covered in detail, and they are merely listed here.

(a)   **Prohibition on tax-free payments to directors:** S311 CA85.

(b)   **Compensation for loss of office:** S312-316 CA85.

(c)   **Directors to disclose interests in company contracts:** S317 CA85.

A director who is interested directly or indirectly in a contract (arrangement or transaction) or proposed contract with their company must **declare the nature of his interest** at a meeting of **the directors**: S317 CA85. The disclosure should be made at the first meeting at which the proposed contract is considered by the board or when the director's interest first arises (if later). In **Guinness plc v Saunders [1990]** it was stated that board means a full board, not merely a committee of the board even where the company only has 1 Director, he must declare his interests to himself, and ensure this is recorded in the minutes of the board meeting. A director may, however, give a general notice that they are a shareholder of another company or a partner of a firm and so is interested in any future contract made with it. It is only the **nature of the interest** and not all the material facts which have to be disclosed. A director who fails to comply with the section is liable to a fine.

The purpose of this provision is to enable the board to comply with their statutory duty of disclosing in the annual accounts detailed particulars of transactions or arrangements with the company in which a director had directly or indirectly a material interest: S232 CA85.

(d)   **Directors' service contracts to be open to inspection:** S318 CA85.

(e)   **Directors' long term service contracts:** S319 CA85.

(f)   **Substantial property transactions:** S320 CA85

S320 CA85 provides that a company shall not enter into an agreement:

(a)   whereby a director of the company or its holding company or a person connected with such a director is to acquire one or more **non-cash assets** of the requisite value from the company; or

(b)   whereby the company acquires one or more **non-cash assets** of the requisite value from such a director or a person so connected;

unless the arrangement is first **approved by an ordinary resolution** of the company in **general meeting** and, if the director or connected person is a director of its holding company or a person connected with such a director, by a resolution in general meeting of the holding company.

A non-cash asset is of the requisite value if at the time the arrangement in question is entered into its value is not less than £2,000 but, subject to that, exceeds £100,000 or ten percent of the amount of the company's assets, whichever is less.

S322 CA85 provides that should the resolution not be obtained, the transaction is voidable unless:

(a)   restitution is no longer possible or the company has been indemnified for loss or damage suffered by it; or

(b)   any rights have been acquired *bona fide* for value without actual profit; or

The section further provides that the director and any person connected with them in contravention of S320 and any director who authorised the arrangement is liable:

(a)   to account to the company for any gain which they have made; and

(b)   (jointly and severally with any other person liable under the section) to indemnify the company for any loss or damage.

Note that S320 extends to persons connected with the director.

Definition   The definition of connected persons of a director (in S346 CA85) is complex, but can be summarised as follows:

    (a)   spouse, children (under eighteen) or step children;

    (b)   a company in which the director or his connections control at least 20% of the equity or votes;

    (c)   a trustee of a trust from which the director or his connections may benefit;

    (d)   a partner or director of any of his connections.

Conclusion   Where a director sells an asset worth more than £100,000 to the company not only must the transaction be disclosed to the board (in order to comply with his common law fiduciary duty as modified by Table A, Art 84 and in order to comply with S317 CA85) but it must also be approved by the general meeting by ordinary resolution (in order to comply with S320 CA85). The same is the position where a director buys such an asset from the company.

(g)   **Invalidity of certain transactions involving directors:** S322A CA85.

(h)   **Share dealings by directors**

There are a number of aspects to this topic (many of the statutory rules applying beyond directors) and it is covered in the next section.

(i)   **Loans to directors:** S330-344 CA85.

4   SHARE DEALING BY DIRECTORS

4.1   Introduction

A general problem of company law, which is particularly relevant to directors, concerns the acquisition of information by virtue of being in a particularly advantageous position, which may be used unfairly in dealing in securities. A director might, by virtue of his position, get advance warning of a movement in share prices enabling him to sell or buy early so as to avoid a loss or make a profit.

Discounting the view that this is a legitimate prerequisite of the job, how can the problems posed be solved? How can the director deal in their own shares and act fairly to the other party to the deal, to whom they should not disclose confidential information?

(a)   The position at **common law** is that:

   (i)   it is a breach of a director's fiduciary duty to the company if he obtains and uses for his own purpose information acquired while a director or officer of the company. The director is accountable for the profit made even though the company suffers no loss: **Regal (Hastings) v Gulliver [1942]**;

   (ii)   this accountability is to the company not to individual shareholders directly - **Percival v Wright [1902]**.

Both of these developments have proved inadequate, in particular because legal action is rarely taken by companies against their directors unless there is a complete change of administration, as occurred in the **Regal case,** and so statute supplements the common law with a range of criminal penalties.

4.2   Prohibition on dealing in share options: S323 CA85

A director (or a shadow director) or spouse or child under 18 of such commits an offence if they buy options on the shares or debentures of his company, its holding company or any subsidiaries, if these are listed on any stock exchange anywhere; the penalty is up to two years imprisonment and/or a fine: S323 CA85..

4.3   Disclosure of interests in shares

A director is required to give notice to the company of their or their spouse or children's' interest in its shares or debentures and of any changes in his interest: S324 CA85. Failure to do so is an offence.

For the purpose of this rule a director's interest is elaborately defined to include a beneficial interest in shares or debentures **(securities)** held in a trust (other than a discretionary trust), securities which they have contracted to buy or which they have an option to acquire or over which they have control, or securities held by a company over which they have *de facto* control or in which they have at least one-third of the voting rights: Sch 13 Part 1.

Where a director is required to give notice of an interest or of a change of interest they must do so within five days: S328 CA85. The company must enter the information in the Register of Directors' Interests within 3 days - S325 and Sch 13 CA85.

If the company is a listed company the company must forward the information to the Stock Exchange before the end of the next day after it receives the information - S329 CA85.

4.4   Insider dealing: CJA93

(a)   **Introduction**

   In 1985 Parliament made insider dealing a criminal offence. Between 1985 and 1993 there were very few successful prosecutions and it was thought this was largely due to the wording of the legislation which was not only convoluted but also required the prosecution to prove to the court facts and states of mind of the accused neither of which were possible except in the most blatant of cases. Consequently 'clever' criminals were escaping liability. In 1993 the existing legislation was repealed and replaced by Part V of the Criminal Justice Act 1993 (CJA93) not only to make it easier to secure convictions but also to comply with European Union obligations.

Although the CJA93 talks of the offence of insider dealing, it actually creates three offences. The sub-categories of the offence of insider dealing are: **dealing, encouraging** another to deal, and **disclosing** information.

(b)   **The offence**

An individual who has information as an insider is guilty of insider dealing if he:

(i)   deals in securities that are price-affected securities in relation to the information; or

(ii)   encourages another person to deal in securities that are price-affected securities in relation to the information (knowing or having reasonable cause to believe that dealing would take place); or

(iii)   discloses the information (otherwise than in the proper performance of the functions of his employment, office or profession) to another person.

The word securities has a wide definition and includes such things as shares, debentures and options.

The word deal encompasses both buying and selling and a person deals whether he himself deals or whether he procures another to deal.

It is very important to realise that the word deal is restricted to dealing on a regulated market. Thus if an insider buys or sells shares without doing so on the stock exchange he does not commit the offence of insider dealing.

(c)   **Who is liable?**

The CJA 1993 states: . . . an individual who has information as an insider is guilty of insider dealing . . .

- **individual**. The use of the word individual means that it is only human persons who can commit the offence of insider dealing: not companies.

- **insider**. The CJA93 states that a person has information as an insider if and only if:

    (i)   it is, and he knows that it is, inside information; and
    (ii)   he has it, and knows that he has it, from an inside source.

- **inside information**. The CJA93 states that inside information means information which:

    (i)   relates to particular securities or to a particular issuer of securities or to particular issuers of securities and not to securities generally or to issuers of securities generally;

    (ii)   is specific or precise;

    (iii)   has not been made public; and

(iv)   if it were made public would be likely to have a significant effect on the price of any securities. (This last condition is often summarised by the phrase 'price-sensitive information' and also leads to the use of the phrase 'price-affected securities')

- **inside source**. The CJA93 states that a person has information from an inside source if and only if:

    (i)   he has it through being a director, employee, or shareholder of an issuer of securities; or

    (ii)   he has it through having access to the information by virtue of his employment, office or profession; or

    (iii)   the direct or indirect source of his information is a person within (i) or (ii) above.

Colloquially, individuals within (i) or (ii) are called primary insiders and individuals within (iii) are called secondary insiders or tippees.

(d)   **Defences**

The CJA93 provides three general defences which are available to an individual accused of insider dealing. They are:

- He shows that he did not at the time expect the dealing to result in a profit (or the avoidance of a loss) attributable to the fact that the information in question was price-sensitive.

- He shows that at the time he believed on reasonable grounds that the information had been widely disclosed.

- He shows that he would have done what he did even if he had not had the information.

In relation to the disclosure offence there is the additional defence of showing that he did not at the time expect any person to deal because of the disclosure.

There are also special defences for market makers and others.

(e)   **Penalties and prosecution**

The possible penalties are imprisonment (up to a maximum of seven years) and an unlimited fine. But the transactions entered into are not void or unenforceable merely by reason of contravention of the CJA93 and neither does the CJA provide for any other civil compensation such as damages, restitution, or recovery of profit - this is the province of the common law.

A prosecution under Part V of the CJA can only be instituted by or with consent of the Secretary of State or the DPP.

Under S177 of the Financial Services Act 1986 the DTI may mount an investigation where it appears that an offence under the CJA insider dealing provisions may have been committed.

4.5   Summary

The law which affects directors' dealing in shares and debentures of their company encompasses:

(a)   the common law fiduciary duty, breach of which enables the company to recover any profit from him;

(b)   the CA85, which requires disclosure to the company of his interests. Non-disclosure may result in a fine;

(c)   the CJA93, which relates to misuse of confidential information in relation to securities dealing on a stock market. Breach of the CJA is a criminal offence.

5   DUTY OF CARE AND SKILL OF DIRECTORS

5.1   Introduction

Unlike the above elaborate rules, the standard of competence required of company directors is fairly simple. Directors as such are supervisors rather than working executives (they may, of course, double both roles as director employees) and it would hardly be practicable to prescribe professional standards of qualification.

5.2   The duty

The standard of care and skill required of a director has been described in:

Re City Equitable Fire Insurance Co [1925].

Facts: The company was in liquidation and it was discovered that there was a shortage of funds of over £1,200,000 due, in part, to depreciation of investments, but mainly to the instrumentality of the managing director and largely to his deliberate fraud for which he had been convicted and sentenced. Article 150 of the company's articles excluded the officers of the company from liability in respect of the acts, defaults or neglects of others. The liquidator on a misfeasance summons brought action against the other directors of the company, who had acted honestly throughout, for negligence.

Held: the points established were:

(a)   A director need not exhibit in the performance of their duties a greater degree of **skill** than may reasonably be expected from a person of their knowledge and experience. Directors are not liable for mere errors of judgement. (In one case a company director who was a country gentlemen and not an accountant was held not liable for recommending a payment of a dividend out of capital: **Re Denham (Charles) & Co [1883]**).

(b)   A director is **not** bound to give **continuous attention** to the affairs of their company. Their duties are of an intermittent nature to be performed at periodical board meetings and at meetings of any committee of the board upon which they happen to be placed. They are not, however, bound to attend all such meetings, though he ought to attend whenever, in the circumstances, he is reasonably able to do so. (In **Re Cardiff Savings Bank [1892]**, a director who attended only one board meeting in 38 years was held not liable in negligence for mismanagement that had occurred during that time).

(c)   In respect of all duties that, having regard to the exigencies of business, and the articles of association, may properly be left to some other official, a director is, in the absence of grounds for suspicion, **justified in trusting** that official to perform such duties honestly. In **Dovey v Cory [1901]**, it was held that a director of a joint stock banking company was entitled to rely on the judgement and advice of the general manager of the bank.

Such duties are, in practice, even less onerous than the wording might suggest. It has been said that a director must do their best without having to be competent. Certainly one cannot say whether a person has been guilty of negligence unless one can determine what is the extent of the duty which they have alleged to have neglected. This requires consideration of the nature of the company's business and of the manner in which the company's work is distributed among officials.

Different expectations will be made of different directors eg, of executive and non-executive directors, the latter being potentially useful in being able to bring to the board a breadth of knowledge and experience which the company's own management may not possess and in increasing the element of independence and objectivity in board decision-making.

A recent reported case on directors' negligence is:

Dorchester Finance Co Ltd v Stebbing [1989]

Facts: the company was a money-lending company and had three directors, Parsons, Hamilton and Stebbing. All three had considerable accountancy and business experience (Parsons and Hamilton were chartered accountants). No board meetings were ever held and Parsons and Hamilton left all the affairs of the company to Stebbing. Parsons and Hamilton did however turn up from time to time and sign blank cheques on the company's account which they left Stebbing to deal with. Stebbing loaned the company's money without complying with statutory regulation applying to moneylending such that the loans were unenforceable.

Held: all three were liable in negligence.

6   STATUTORY INTERVENTION

6.1   Introduction

Although the common law duty of care and skill is not an exacting duty it is supplemented by statute both generally and in relation to specific matters.

Remember that directors adjudged 'unfit to be concerned in the management of a company' are liable to be disqualified by court order - Company Directors' Disqualification Act 1986.

Here, specific provisions of the IA86 are covered. These, although not generally relevant whilst the company is a going concern, may nevertheless serve to concentrate directors' minds.

6.2   Fraudulent trading

If in a **winding up** it appears that the company's business has been carried on with intent to defraud creditors or for any fraudulent purpose, the court may declare that any persons who were knowingly parties to the fraudulent trading shall make such contribution to the company's assets as the court thinks proper: S213 IA86.

It is necessary to establish **dishonest intent**. In **Re William C Leith Bros [1932]** it was said that if the directors carry on the business and cause the company to incur further debts at a time when they know that there is no reasonable prospect of those debts being paid this is a proper inference of dishonesty. The court also added that if the directors honestly believed the debts would eventually be paid there would be no intent to defraud.

R v Grantham [1984]

Facts: the directors ordered a consignment of potatoes on a month's credit at a time when they knew that payment would not be forthcoming at the end of the month when it was due (the company was hopelessly undercapitalised so there was no suggestion that the goods would eventually be paid for.)

Held: the directors were convicted of fraudulent trading.

A person is not liable for fraudulent trading where he has no dishonest intention.

Re EB Tractors Ltd [1986]

Facts: the directors caused the company to incur debts at a time when they would not be paid on the due date. They however showed that they thought the company would survive and the debts eventually paid.

Held: the directors' honest belief (although unrealistic) negatived the intention to defraud: they were not liable.

The second point required to establish liability is that the person concerned shall be a **party** to the fraudulent trading.

In **Re Maidstone Buildings [1971]** it was established that a person is not 'party' merely by reason of knowledge, he must take some active step, such as the ordering of goods.

The following are the possible consequences of fraudulent trading:

(a)   The court may order the person liable to make such contribution to the company's assets as it thinks fit - S213IA 1986. The application is made by the liquidator.

(b)   Criminal liability. The punishment includes not only an unlimited fine but also up to seven years imprisonment. Criminal liability can lie whether or not the company is in liquidation, - S458 CA 1985.

(c)   Fraudulent trading is a specific ground for disqualification under the CDDA86

6.3   Wrongful trading

A new provision of 'wrongful trading' contained in the Insolvency Act 1985 came into force on 28 April 1986. It was designed to remove one of the difficult obstacles to the establishment of being party to fraudulent trading - namely proving dishonesty.

It is now contained in S214 IA86 and applies only to directors, former directors and shadow directors.

Under S214 IA86 a liquidator may apply to the court for an order that a **director** of a company which has gone into **insolvent liquidation** should make such contribution to the company's assets as the court thinks proper. The court will need to satisfy itself that at some time before the commencement of the winding up the **director knew or ought to have known that there was no reasonable prospect** that the company would avoid going into insolvent liquidation and that he was a director at that time.

The court will not make an order if it is satisfied that as soon as the director knew or ought to have concluded there was no reasonable prospect of avoiding insolvent liquidation he took every step he ought to have taken to minimise the potential loss to the company's creditors.

The director is expected to reach those conclusions and take such steps as a reasonably diligent person would take. The legislation also expects such a director to have the general knowledge, skill and experience which may reasonably be expected of a person carrying out the same functions as were carried out by that director (objective test). In addition, it expects the director to use the general knowledge, skill and experience he himself has (subjective test) ie, the director is expected to use his specialist knowledge and experience. This is far more onerous than the previous statement of a director's duty of skill and care.

When considering the director's functions the court will have regard not only to those functions he carried out but also to those entrusted to him. This means that the director could be made liable for those actions he should have carried out but failed to.

The effect of this provision is that a director may be made personally liable for the debts and liabilities of the insolvent company if he knew that it could not avoid insolvent liquidation and did not take all reasonable steps open to him to prevent its creditors from suffering greater loss than they would have suffered by an immediate cessation of the company's activities or if a reasonable director with the knowledge available to him would have concluded that the company could not have avoided insolvency and would have taken more effective steps to minimise the loss to creditors.

Anything obtained as a result of these provisions would go to the liquidator for the payment of the company's debts.

In **Re Produce Marketing Consortium [1989]**, the first case heard under the new provision of wrongful trading, the court held that:

(a)   directors cannot rely on the fact that they were unaware of facts which they could and should have ascertained from documents (eg, the accounts);

(b)   the standard required is that of a reasonable director of that type of company (ie, higher standard for directors of larger companies). However, certain minimum standards must be maintained;

(c)   here the directors had received the accounts two years late but had known that the company was in financial difficulty - they were ordered to pay £75,000 contribution.

Wrongful trading is not a criminal offence but it is a specific ground for the making of a disqualification order - CDDA86.

6.4   Transactions at an undervalue and preference

The liquidator (or administrator) may apply to the court to set aside company transactions at an undervalue (S238 IA86) or where the company gives a preference (S239 IA86).

(a)   A company enters into a transaction at an **undervalue** if:

- the company makes a gift or otherwise enters into a transaction on terms that the company receives no consideration; or

- the company enters into a transaction for a consideration significantly less than that provided by the company.

The transaction would not be set aside if it was entered into in good faith on the reasonable belief that it would benefit the company.

(b)   A company gives a **preference** if it does anything to put a creditor, surety or guarantor in a better position in the event of the company's insolvent liquidation than he would otherwise be. The court will not make an order under S239 IA86 unless the company was influenced by a desire to prefer the creditor. Thus, a payment made or charge created in favour of a creditor who is threatening legal proceedings might be a defence to an action under this section. If the preference is given to a connected person it is presumed that the company was influenced by its desire to give a preference (ie, it is for the 'connected person' to show there was no such influence).

The transaction or preference will only be set aside by the court if the company is insolvent and the transaction or preference was made within the relevant period which is:

(a)   any transaction at an **undervalue** or a **preference** to a **connected person** (as for invalidity of floating charge, except that employees are not connected persons under Ss238 & 239) within **two years** of the onset of insolvency; or

(b)   **preferences** to **other persons** within **six months** of the onset of insolvency.

The onset of insolvency is the commencement of the liquidation or presentation of the petition for an administration order.

The transaction or preference will not be set aside unless at the time it was made the company was not able to pay its debts or the company became unable to pay its debts as a result. The burden of proving this is on the person seeking to have it set aside except where a transaction at an undervalue is alleged to a connected person in which case it is presumed (ie, the connected person will have to show that the company is not insolvent).

S241 IA86 gives the court wide powers in the orders it may make eg, release any security, invest property in the company. However, a *bona fide* purchaser for value without notice of the relevant circumstances who was not party to the transaction or preference is protected.

6.5   Invalidation of floating charges

The liquidator (or administrator) may invalidate any floating charge created by an insolvent company within 12 months before liquidation except to the extent of advances to the company before or at the time of the creation of the charge: S245 IA86.

Where the chargee is a connected person of the company the time period is two years and there is no need for proof of insolvency at the time the charge was created.

7   RELIEF FROM LIABILITY (SUMMARY)

The director may be able to avoid the usual consequences of breach of duty in several ways:

(a)   The company may, of course, approve what the directors have done or intend to do by a resolution to that effect passed in general meeting. If the directors are also shareholders they may, in principle, cast their shareholders' votes in favour of a resolution to approve their action (and the retention of benefit obtained from it):

North West Transportation Co v Beatty [1887].

Facts: the company purchased a boat from one of its directors for a reasonable price. The purchase was ratified by a general meeting, including the votes of the director.

Held: every shareholder has a right to vote upon any question; the fact that this shareholder had a controlling shareholding and had an interest in the contract made no difference.

However, in this difficult area of law there are at least two limiting conditions:

(i)   if the irregular act to be approved is the issue of shares made for the improper purpose of altering the balance of voting power, the votes attached to the new shares may not be used in voting on the resolution: **Hogg v Cramphorn [1967]**;

(ii)   if the directors are also controlling shareholders they may not exercise their control to carry a resolution approving the transfer to themselves of property or profits which otherwise belong to the company: **Cook v Deeks [1916]**. But, they may apparently use their control to approve the retention of a personal profit which could not have accrued to the company: **Regal (Hastings) v Gulliver [1967]**. See also **Clemens v Clemens [1976]**

(b)   In the **City Equitable Case [1925]** the innocent directors were relieved of any possible liability by an exemption given to them by the articles. Such exemption may no longer be given in advance: S310 CA85. Thus an article which provides that the directors will not be sued if they are in breach of duty will be void.

(c)   The court may exercise its discretion to relieve them under S727 CA85 if they have acted honestly and reasonably and ought fairly to be excused. This section cannot be used to excuse wrongful trading - **Re Produce Marketing [1989]**.

(d)   He might be insured. S310 CA85 does not prevent the company from insuring officers against liability.

8   SELF TEST QUESTIONS

8.1   To whom does a director owe his duties? (1.2)

8.2   State the two common law duties of directors. (1.5)

8.3   What did the leading case of **Regal (Hastings) v Gulliver** establish? (2.5)

8.4   Define a substantial property transaction. (3.2)

8.5   Name the Act of Parliament which contains the criminal offence of insider dealing. (4.4)

8.6   State the propositions established in **Re City Equitable Fire Insurance**. (5.2)

8.7   What is fraudulent trading? (6.2)

8.8   Who can be liable for wrongful trading? (6.3)

8.9   What is a preference? (6.4)

9   EXAMINATION TYPE QUESTIONS

9.1   Griff plc

John is a non-executive director of Griff plc, a listed company. Shortly after attending a board meeting where arrangements were finalised for an agreed take-over bid for the company by Whale plc, John bought two blocks of shares in Griff plc. One block he bought on the London Stock Exchange. The other block he bought from Adam as a result of a direct approach from Adam. Once the bid was made public John re-sold both blocks of shares at a profit.

You are required

(a)   to advise Griff plc, Adam and Whale plc whether any or all of them have an action against John for recovery of the profit.   **(10 marks)**

(b)   to explain whether John has committed the criminal offence of insider dealing.

                                                                    (10 marks)
                                                            (Total: 20 marks)

9.2   Williams Ltd

Ellen and Freda are the only directors of Williams Ltd, each holding 20% of the company's issued share capital. The remaining 60% of the shares are held by their father, Bill, the founder of the company. Although Bill is no longer a director, he continues to exert considerable influence over the policy and management of the company.

For some time Ellen and Freda have been aware of a serious drop in turnover and profits. An extraordinary general meeting was called on 1 November 19X2 to discuss the situation, and Bill warned his daughters that insolvency appeared inevitable. They, however, remained convinced that the profitability of the company would be restored in line with the expected upturn in the economy generally. Bill was persuaded to support his daughters' desire to continue trading, in return for their promise to arrange for Williams Ltd to make an early repayment of Bill's unsecured loan of £10,000 over the following three months. Bill was repaid on 1 January 19X3.

On 1 June 19X3 Williams Ltd's bankers cancelled the company's overdraft facilities, and at an extraordinary general meeting on 20 June 19X3 the shareholders reluctantly passed a resolution placing Williams Ltd in creditors voluntary liquidation.

You are required to discuss whether Ellen, Freda or Bill have acted in breach of company law, and if so, the possible consequences of the breach.

                                                                        (20 marks)

10   ANSWERS TO EXAMINATION TYPE QUESTIONS

10.1   Griff plc

(a)   It is possible that Griff plc has an action against John for breach of fiduciary duty.

A director owes a fiduciary duty to his company to act in good faith for the benefit of the company. In particular he may not make a personal profit out of his position or knowledge as director - **Regal (Hastings) v Gulliver**. He is accountable to the company for any such profit and he is accountable whether or not the company itself was able to make the profit: it is not a question of loss to the company. Accordingly it would seem that Griff plc may recover the profit John made on the share deals.

A director owes his fiduciary duty to the company, not to individual shareholders. In **Percival v Wright** (a case with the same material facts as the instant problem) it was therefore held that an individual shareholder could not sue to recover the profit the director had made on the share deal. Accordingly Adam has no action against John.

On the same principle no fiduciary duty is owed by John to Whale plc and therefore it has no action against John for breach of fiduciary duty.

(b)   Under the Criminal Justice Act 1993 an individual who has information as an insider is guilty of insider dealing if he deals in price-affected securities in relation to the information.

In order for John to be liable the prosecution must prove that he has information as an insider ie, that it is, and John knows that it is, inside information and that he has it, and knows that he has it, from an inside source. Inside information means information which relates to particular securities (or to a particular company or companies), which is specific or precise, and which has not been made public, and which if it were made public would be likely to have a significant effect on the price of any securities. It would seem that advance knowledge of Whale plc's bid for Griff plc is inside information. A person has information from an inside source if, inter alia, he has it through being a director of a company. John is therefore an insider.

The offence of dealing (here buying shares) is committed only where the insider deals on the stock exchange. Thus, although John commits the criminal offence of insider dealing when he bought on the stock market, he commits no criminal offence when he bought from Adam.

There are three main defences to the charge of insider dealing. First, where the defendant shows that he did not at the time expect the dealing to result in a profit, or the avoidance of a loss, attributable to the fact that the information in question was price-sensitive. Second, where he shows that at the time he believed on reasonable grounds that the information had been widely disclosed. Third, he shows that he would have done what he did even if he had not had the information.

10.2   Williams Ltd

The facts evidence a possible breach of S213 of the Insolvency Act 1986 (IA86) 'fraudulent trading', S214 of the IA86 'wrongful trading', and S239 of the IA86 'preferences'.

Fraudulent trading

Fraudulent trading occurs where the business of the company is carried on with intent to defraud creditors or for any fraudulent purpose. It is therefore necessary to establish dishonest intent. This will be inferred where a company carries on business and continues to incur liabilities where there is no reasonable prospect of those liabilities being met - **Re William C Leitch Bros**. Thus in **R v Grantham** two directors who ordered a consignment of potatoes on one month's credit at a time when they knew payment would not be forthcoming at the end of the month were found guilty of fraudulent trading. However, **Re William C Leitch Bros** established that because its directors were honestly of the opinion that the debts they caused the company to incur would eventually be paid they were not liable for fraudulent trading. The later case of **Re EB Tractors** confirms this contention. S213 identifies the persons liable for fraudulent trading as those knowingly party to the carrying on of business in the fraudulent way.

The facts of the question, which state that Ellen and Freda were 'convinced' that the company would be restored to profitability, would seem to suggest that they genuinely believed its debts would be paid. Thus, although they were mistaken and possibly foolish, they did not have the necessary dishonest intent to constitute fraudulent trading.

As to Bill: the facts given state that he believed that insolvency was inevitable; he therefore has the necessary dishonest intent. However, the case of **Re Maidstone Buildings** established that a person is not a 'party' to fraudulent trading solely by reason of knowledge, he must also take active steps to defraud, such as the ordering of goods. Thus if Bill, as stated, merely exerted influence over policy and management but did not actively manage the business he is not party to fraudulent trading.

Should it be the case the court decides that any one or all of Ellen, Freda and Bill are liable for fraudulent trading, the possible consequences are first, criminal (fine and/or imprisonment) and second civil liability. Under the latter each will be liable to contribute to the company's assets such sum as the court thinks fit. As a rule of thumb the court would probably order the payment of a sum equal to the unpaid debts incurred during the fraudulent trading period. Additionally, fraudulent trading is a specific ground for the making of a disqualification order under the Company Directors Disqualification Act 1986.

Wrongful trading

Under S214 IA86 persons potentially liable for wrongful trading are directors and shadow directors. Clearly Ellen and Freda, as directors, are within the ambit of S214. Bill will be if he can be classed as a shadow director, that is, a person in accordance with whose instructions or directions the board are accustomed to act. More facts will be needed to ascertain whether Bill was in the habit of giving instructions which his daughters were in the habit of abiding by.

In order for a person to be liable for wrongful trading the liquidator has the burden of proving the following two matters:

(a)   that the company is in insolvent liquidation - Williams Ltd is in creditors voluntary liquidation and it is therefore very likely insolvent;

(b)   that the person was a director (or shadow director) of the company at a time when he knew or ought to have known that there was no reasonable prospect of avoiding insolvent liquidation. The facts given clearly show Bill had this knowledge. As to Ellen and Freda the question is whether they ought to have known. Unlike fraudulent trading, what they personally honestly believed is not material since S214 states that what a director ought to know and deduce is judged according to the standard of reasonably skilled, experienced and diligent directors. As shown in **Re Produce Marketing Consortium** the court will examine the history of the company to establish objectively whether there was a 'moment of truth' when the directors should have known insolvency was inevitable. The given facts tend to suggest Ellen and Freda were over-optimistic and either knew or ought to have known at an early stage that insolvent liquidation was a likely prospect.

S214 states that the person is not liable for wrongful trading if he can prove that he took every step with a view to minimising the potential loss to the company's creditors he ought to have taken. Such steps would include such matters as cessation of business where continued trading is incurring losses, and taking expert advice on, for example, applying for administration order sooner rather than later. Merely continuing to trade in the hope of better times is not such a step.

An action for wrongful trading may only be brought by a liquidator (it is not a criminal offence) and in the same way as fraudulent trading civil liability will result in the court ordering personal contribution to the company's assets and may result in disqualification.

Preference

A preference occurs where a company does anything or suffers anything to be done which puts a creditor in a better position in the event of insolvent liquidation than he would otherwise have been in. The repayment to Bill of his £10,000 loan is a preference.

The liquidator may set aside a preference in favour of a connected person of a company if he can prove that the preference took place within the two years immediately preceding the commencement of liquidation and at a time when the company was unable to pay its debts. Bill, being the father of the directors, is a connected person, he was paid on 1 January, commencement of liquidation was 20 June and the facts point to the company being insolvent on 1 January. The action to set aside the payment will be successfully resisted by Bill if he can prove that the company, in deciding to make the payment, was not influenced by a desire to better his position. His evidence appears very weak.

If, as seems likely, the liquidator can set aside the preference the most likely result would be an order that Bill return the £10,000 to the liquidator. He would then rank for payment as the court so directs.

26 CORPORATE MANAGEMENT: COMPANY SECRETARY AND AUDITORS

INTRODUCTION & LEARNING OBJECTIVES

Syllabus area 8g. The company secretary: powers and duties. (Ability required 3).
Auditors: powers and duties. (Ability required 2).
Issues in corporate governance. (Ability required 2).

The chapter begins by considering the position of the company's chief administrative officer: the Company Secretary. It then moves to the auditors and their function of providing an independent check on the accuracy of the company's accounts. It concludes with an outline of the Cadbury Committee's recommendations on the financial aspects of corporate governance.

When you have studied this chapter you should be able to do the following:

- Know that every company must have a company secretary.

- Know the qualifications of the company secretary of a public company.

- Explain the extent to which a company secretary can bind the company to contracts.

- Know how auditors are appointed and removed.

- Know the duties of auditors and explain to whom their duties are owed.

- Be aware of current issues in company law.

---

1 THE COMPANY SECRETARY

1.1 Role and qualifications

Every company must have a secretary and the role cannot be doubled with that of sole director: Ss283-284 Companies Act 1985 (CA85). The post may be held by another company or by joint secretaries; any formal act of a secretary may in their absence be performed by a deputy or assistant.

In a public company the secretary is required to be a person with the requisite knowledge and experience to discharge the function of a secretary and who holds a relevant qualification ie:

(a)   have had three of the previous five years acting as company secretary of a public company; or

(b)   is a member of a recognised body; or

(c)   is a barrister, advocate or solicitor admitted in the UK; or

(d)   any other person who appears to the directors as being capable of discharging those functions: S286 CA85.

Recognised bodies are the Institute of Chartered Accountants in England and Wales, the Institute of Chartered Accountants of Scotland, the Institute of Chartered Accountants in Ireland, the Chartered

Association of Certified Accountants, the Institute of Chartered Secretaries and Administrators, the Chartered Institute of Management Accountants and the Chartered Institute of Public Finance and Accountancy.

These rules imposing duty on directors to see the secretary is qualified were new in 1980 and there is a transitional provision allowing the person who was secretary of the company on 22 December 1980 to continue in office in relation to that company.

1.2   Appointment and removal

The articles usually provide for the appointment of a company secretary by the directors.

Table A provides the secretary shall be appointed by the directors for such term, at such remuneration and upon such conditions as they may think fit; and any secretary so appointed may be removed by them.

1.3   Duties

There are no specific duties imposed on the Company Secretary by the CA85 (although various documents, such as the Annual Return, require the signature of a director or secretary). His duties, therefore, are whatever the board chooses to entrust to him. These duties might include:

(a)   preparing for, attending and taking action after meetings of the board of directors and also general meetings. These tasks will include preparation of notices and agenda, or working papers and information summaries and of minutes of the proceedings;

(b)   maintaining the statutory registers (though the register of members of a large company is now often entrusted to professional registrars using computers); this includes dealing with share transfers and the issue of share certificates;

(c)   witnessing ie, signing as witness (together with a director) the company seal when applied to documents;

(d)   the generation and delivery of returns of all kinds to the Companies Registry;

(e)   preparation of the numerous returns required by government departments and official bodies.

Depending on the size of the headquarters staff the secretary may also be the chief accounting officer, have charge of staff employment and pension matters, obtain legal advice from solicitors, confer with the auditors and deal with the Stock Exchange.

1.4   Status

A company secretary may be a director but is not automatically a director and if not a director they will not be a member of the board. However, the secretary is an **officer** and often is also an employee of the company.

The statutory register of directors must also include the secretary's particulars: S288 CA85. The first appointment of the secretary and any subsequent change must be notified to the Companies Registry. They must give their written consent in the notification: S10 CA85.

1.5   Liability

Many sections of the CA85 impose criminal liability on 'officers in default'. A company secretary is an officer and if the board have entrusted him with discharging such statutory duties and he fails he is liable as an officer in default. In addition some sections of the CA85 (notably S363 in relation to delivery of the Annual Return) specifically impose criminal penalties on him by name.

At common law he, as officer and/or employee, will owe a fiduciary duty and a duty of care and skill to the company.

If he acts as agent for the company and makes a contract for which he has no authority, he, like any agent, will be personally liable to the third party in damages for breach of warranty of authority.

1.6   Authority

Like all of the company's agents he will bind the company to third parties in contract where he acts within his authority, actual or apparent.

Prior to 1971 the Company Secretary had no authority by virtue of his office or position independent of that expressly given to him by the board.

This was changed in 1971 where Lord Denning in **Panorama Developments v Fidelis Furnishing Fabrics** stated:

'He is an officer of the company with extensive duties and responsibilities. This appears not only in the modern Companies Acts, but also by the role which he plays in the day-to-day business of companies. He is no longer a mere clerk. He regularly makes representations on behalf of the company and enters into contracts on its behalf which come within the day-to-day running of the company's business. So much so that he may be regarded as held out as having authority to do such things on behalf of the company. He is certainly entitled to sign contracts connected with the administrative side of a company's affairs, such as employing staff, and ordering cars, and so forth. All such matters now come within the ostensible authority of a company's secretary.'

Panorama Developments v Fidelis Furnishing Fabrics [1971]

Facts: Bayne was company secretary of the defendant. Without authority from directors he ordered from the plaintiffs, a car hire firm, self-drive limousines stating that they were for the business purposes of the company. In fact he used the cars for his personal purposes. The company refused to pay for the cars.

Held: the contract was binding on the company since hiring of cars was usual to the office of company secretary.

Although Lord Denning in his speech seemed to imbue the office with authority to make contracts within 'the day-to-day running of the business' it is questionable whether this extends beyond the administrative side of the business to commercial activities. In the same year the Court of Appeal (but differently constituted) stated '. . . it is established beyond all question that a secretary, while performing the duties appropriate to the office of secretary, is not concerned in the management of the company. Equally, I think he is not concerned in carrying on the business of the company' - **Re Maidstone Buildings [1971].**

Other cases, some prior to **Panorama** but which still appear to be good law, are:

- **Re Cleadon Trust [1968]:** borrowing of money held not within usual authority of office of company secretary.

- **Re State of Wyoming Syndicate [1901]:** summoning of a general meeting held not within the usual authority of the office of company secretary.

- **Re Zinotty Properties [1984]:** registering a transfer of shares (ie making an entry in the Register of Members) held not within the usual authority of the office of company secretary.

- **Daimler v Continental Tyre & Rubber Ltd [1916]** commencement of litigation in the company's name held not within the usual authority of the office of company secretary.

2   THE AUDITOR

2.1   Appointment of auditors

By S384 CA85 registered companies have to pass a resolution appointing auditors each year, such auditors holding office from the conclusion of the particular meeting at which appointed until the conclusion of the next general meeting at which the company's annual accounts are to be considered. If no such auditor is so appointed or re-appointed the Secretary of State may appoint a person to fill the vacancy and the company shall, within, one week of the Secretary of State's power becoming operative, give the Secretary of State notice of that fact.

The first auditors of a company may be appointed by the directors at any time before the first general meeting of the company at which the annual accounts are presented and auditors so appointed shall hold office, until the conclusion of that meeting. If the directors fail to make such an appointment their powers may be exercised by the company in general meeting.

Any casual vacancy in the office of auditor may be filled by either the directors or the company in general meeting but while any such vacancy continues, the surviving or continuing auditor or auditors, if any, may act.

By S388A CA85 dormant companies may, by special resolution, be exempted from appointing auditors. Such a company must be entitled to the benefit of the exemptions for individual accounts as a small company, or be excluded from so benefiting only because it is a member of an ineligible group. A company is regarded as dormant during any period in which no significant accounting transaction has occurred. A significant accounting transaction being one required by S221 CA85 to be entered in a company's accounting records, though there is an exception for shares taken under an undertaking in the company's memorandum by a subscriber thereto, thus enabling a newly-founded company to be considered dormant from its formation.

S386 CA85 (new in 1989) enables a private company by elective resolution to dispense with appointing auditors annually. The auditors are then reappointed automatically until there is a resolution that the appointment should end.

S385A CA85 (new in 1989) also sets out a special procedure for private companies which have elected not to lay accounts annually but have not elected not to annually appoint auditors. In this case auditors must be appointed within 28 days of the date on which copies of the accounts are sent to members.

2.2   Remuneration of auditors

In the case of an auditor appointed by the directors or by the Secretary of State the auditor's remuneration may be fixed by the directors or by the Secretary of State, as the case may be. Subject to this, however, their remuneration shall 'be fixed' by the company in general meeting or in such manner as the company in general meeting may determine. Remuneration of the auditors in that capacity must be stated in a note to the accounts - S390A. The CA 1985 empowers the Secretary of State by regulation to require disclosure of pay to auditors for other services in the accounts, and in 1991 he did so.

2.3   Qualifications for appointment as auditor

CA89 contains provisions to establish a new regulatory system for the auditing profession to ensure compliance with the EC 8th Directive. The government has decided to apply the 8th Directive through the existing professional accountancy bodies, but the Secretary of State has power to set up a corporate body to oversee the profession.

2.4   Eligibility for appointment

A person will not be eligible for appointment as auditor unless:

(a)   he is a member of a recognised supervisory body (RSB); and

(b)   he is eligible under the rules of the RSB.

An auditor may be an individual or a firm, including a corporate body.

2.5   Ensuring the independence of auditors

An auditor may not be:

(a)   An officer or employee of the company.

(b)   A partner or employee of (a).

(c)   A partnership in which a partner is one of (a).

(d)   A person who is ineligible as auditor of the parent or subsidiary or fellow subsidiary of the company.

The Secretary of State may add to this list of prohibitions by statutory instrument.

If an ineligible auditor acts for a company he may be liable to a fine. The Secretary of State may order a second audit to be carried out and this may be at the expense of the original auditor.

2.6   Recognised supervisory bodies

Under CA89 audits must only be performed by persons or firms who are authorised by a RSB.

The RSB is only allowed to authorise those who:

(a)   hold a recognised professional qualification; or

(b)   hold an approved overseas qualification; or

(c)   are members of the bodies currently recognised (ICAEW, ICAS, ICAI and ACCA) who are treated as qualified for twelve months after the appointed day and who must apply to the Secretary of State to retain that right of qualification within that twelve months;

(d)   are on a course of study or practical training before 1 January 1990 and obtain their qualification before 1 January 1996.

CA89 allows the Secretary of State to recognise appropriate overseas qualifications having regard to the eligibility of UK qualified auditors to practice in the country in question.

CA89 provides for the cost of implementing the new regime to be borne by the RSB and passed on to those registering.

The duties of a RSB include the keeping of a register showing:

(a)   individuals and firms eligible for appointment as auditors;

(b)   individuals who are responsible for company audit work for firms;

(c)   names, addresses and the name of the RSB.

The RSB must also provide a register of firms giving the names and addresses of each director and member (if a body corporate) or each partner (if a partnership).

The Secretary of State is left to settle the detailed arrangements. He may require a RSB to provide him with information, change its rules, revoke recognition or apply to the courts for a compliance order.

2.7   Recognition as a RSB

The requirements for recognition as a RSB are laid down in Sch 11 & 12 CA89.

Briefly, the body must have rules which ensure the following:

(a)   that an individual most hold an appropriate qualification;

(b)   that a firm has individuals who hold an appropriate qualification;

(c)   that the firm is controlled by qualified persons (ie, a majority of its members and its management board are qualified as auditors);

(d)   that audit work is conducted properly and with integrity; and

(e)   that conflicts of interest are not likely to arise.

The RSB must have procedures governing:

(a)   the content and application of technical standards;

(b)   maintenance of an appropriate level of technical competence.

(c)   effective monitoring and enforcement;

(d)   investigation of complaints; and

(e)   the ability of its members to meet claims.

2.8   Recognised professional qualification

A RSB may apply to the Secretary of State for an order recognising its professional qualification.

The basic requirements are:

(a)   entry requirements are restricted to those with university entrance level qualifications or a sufficient period of professional experience;

(b)   qualification is given only to those who have passed an examination to test theoretical knowledge and the ability to apply that knowledge;

(c)   a minimum of three years of professional training must be given. The practical training element must include a substantial part in company audit work or similar work;

(d)   the training must be provided by persons approved by the RSB and at least two-thirds by a fully qualified auditor; and

(e)   the RSB must have adequate arrangements to monitor compliance.

2.9   The rights of auditors

The rights of auditors are:

(a)   to receive notices of all general meetings and any other communication sent to the members in connection with them;

(b)   to attend general meetings, and to speak on any business that concerns them;

(c)   to have access to the books, accounts and vouchers of the company;

(d)   to require from the officers of the company all information and explanations thought (by the auditors) necessary for the performance of their duties; it is an offence to give false information;

(e)   to obtain information about a company's subsidiaries where this is necessary for the fulfilment of their duties as auditors of the company; and

(f)   to require the directors to call an extraordinary general meeting (or in default to call such a meeting themselves) when the auditors cease to hold office by way of resignation.

2.10   The duties of auditors

The auditors must report to the members on the accounts examined by them, and on every balance sheet, every profit and loss account and all group accounts laid before the company in general meeting during their tenure of office. The report must state whether or not in the auditor's opinion the annual accounts have been properly prepared in accordance with the Companies Act and whether or not they give a true and fair view: S235 CA85. The auditors must carry out investigations such as will enable them to form an opinion whether:

(a)   proper books of accounting records have been kept, and proper returns adequate for their audit have been received from branches not visited by them;

(b)   the accounts are in agreement with the books of account and returns.

If the auditors are of the opinion that either requirement (a) or (b) has not been satisfied or if they fail to obtain the information and explanations which they consider necessary for the purpose of their audit, they must state any such conclusion in their report on the accounts: S237 CA85.

The auditor must give particulars of directors' emoluments or loans to directors, or transactions with directors, if these are not adequately or correctly disclosed in the accounts, so far as they are reasonably able to do so.

Further, it shall be the duty of the auditors of the company, in preparing their report under the Act on the company's accounts to consider whether the information given in the directors' report relating to the financial year in question is consistent with those accounts. If the auditors are of opinion that the information given in the directors' report is not consistent with the company's accounts for the financial year they shall state that fact in their report.

In the preparation of their report in respect of a parent company the auditors may require information from any subsidiary undertaking; it is a criminal offence for any officer of a company knowingly or recklessly to supply false or misleading information to auditors: S389A CA85.

2.11   Liability of auditors

This topic was covered fully in the earlier chapter 'Tort: negligence'.

Summary - if auditors have failed to exercise **reasonable** care and skill they may be liable:

(a)   to the company for breach of contract and in the tort of negligence;

(b)   in the tort of negligence to the members as a body in general meeting - dicta in **Caparo Industries v Dickman [1990]**;

(c)   in the tort of negligence to persons they know will rely on their statements for a known purpose - dicta in **Caparo Industries v Dickman [1990]**;

but not to investors generally (including individual members) - **Caparo Industries v Dickman [1990]**.

2.12   Removal of auditors

A company may by ordinary resolution (with special notice) remove an auditor before the expiration of his term of office, notwithstanding anything in any agreement between it and him, and where a resolution removing an auditor is passed at a general meeting of a company, the company shall within fourteen days give notice of that fact in the prescribed form to the Registrar of Companies: S391 CA85. A special notice of twenty-eight days to the company is required for an ordinary resolution at a general meeting:

(a)   appointing as auditor a person other than a retiring auditor; or
(b)   removing an auditor before the expiration of his term of office.

In both cases the auditor must be sent a copy of the notice and may make representations in writing to the company and require the notification of these representations to the members of the company. Failing such notification he may require that the representations be read out at the meeting and in any case he has the right to be heard orally at the meeting.

The auditor of a company who has been removed from office has a right to attend the general meeting at which his term of office would otherwise have expired and any general meeting at which it is proposed to fill the vacancy caused by his removal. He may speak on any matter concerning him as former auditor.

2.13   Resignation of auditors

An auditor of a company may resign his office at any time by depositing at the company's registered office a notice in writing to that effect S392 CA85. The date of his resignation is the date of the notice or such later date as therein specified, but it shall not be effective unless it includes either a statement of any circumstances connected with his resignation which he considers should be brought to the notice of the members or creditors or a statement that there are no such circumstances.

Where an auditor's notice of resignation contains a statement of circumstances he may deposit with the notice a requisition signed by himself calling on the directors of the company to convene an extraordinary general meeting of the company for the purposes of receiving and considering such explanation of the circumstances connected with his resignation as he may wish to place before the meeting.

Within twenty-one days of the receipt of such a requisition the directors must convene a meeting to be held within twenty-eight days of the date of the notice convening the meeting. If the auditor requests this statement must be accompanied by a statement in writing not exceeding a reasonable length setting out the circumstances connected with his resignation.

The resigning auditor has a right to attend any such meeting and to be heard on any part of the business of the meeting which concerns him as a former auditor.

The auditor must within twenty-eight days of receipt of such a notice send a copy to the Registrar of Companies and, if it contains a statement of circumstances, to members and debentureholders. The court may direct that the statement not be sent to the Registrar or circulated if it is satisfied that the auditor is using the statement to secure needless publicity for defamatory matter.

2.14   Statement by person ceasing to hold office as auditor

S394 CA85 requires a statement by an auditor when he ceases to hold office for any reason. Previously this was only required when an auditor resigned. The statement must state whether or not there are any circumstances which ought to be brought to the attention of members or creditors of the company. If there are such circumstances, they must then be set out.

2.15   Activity

If a company's auditor is to be removed before the expiration of his term of office what type of resolution is required and what period of notice?

2.16   Activity solution

An ordinary resolution at a general meeting and special notice of 28 days to the company.

3   ISSUES IN CORPORATE GOVERNANCE

3.1   Introduction

There is, and have been, many matters debated under the general rubric 'corporate governance' which is the system by which companies are directed and controlled. At its narrowest, issues in corporate governance cover the concept of how companies should be governed (ie, how power is divided between the board and the general meeting and the accountability of the board to the members) and, at its widest, includes further questions such as

(a)   are companies accountable to employees, creditors and even to society or the community generally? (the latter in the sense of - should listed companies, in view of their economic power, have social consciences?) and

(b)   in the absence of effective shareholder control, how are the public agencies set up by the state performing? The role and effectiveness of the various supervisory bodies such as the Department of Trade and Industry, the Bank of England, the Securities and Investment Board (and its associated Self Regulatory Organisations) and the Stock Exchange have come in for considerable comment not only by academics and the professions but also, in the wake of the collapse of the Maxwell group and the Bank of Credit and Commerce International (BCCI), by the media.

It is the narrower issues in corporate governance which are of greatest relevance to your examination ie, that of the financial accountability of the board.

3.2   The Cadbury Committee

This committee was set up by the Financial Reporting Council, the London Stock Exchange, and the accountancy profession, in 1991 under the chairmanship of Sir Adrian Cadbury to report on the 'Financial Aspects of Corporate Governance' with the objective of helping to raise the standards of corporate governance and the level of confidence in financial reporting and auditing by setting out clearly what it sees as the respective responsibilities of those involved and what it believes is expected of them. The committee's remit was the narrower issues in corporate governance.

The resultant 'Cadbury Report' in 1992

- recognised that whilst the country's economy depends on the drive and efficiency of its companies and thus their boards must be free to drive their companies forward, that freedom must be exercised within a framework of effective accountability.

- stated that effective accountability is the essence of good corporate governance

- focused its recommendation on the control and reporting functions of boards, and on the role of auditors

- published a 'Code of Best Practice' designed to achieve the necessary high standard of corporate behaviour

- recommended that the Stock Exchange require all listed companies, as a continuing obligation of listing, to state whether or not they are complying with the Code and to give reasons for any areas of non-compliance.

3.3   The Code of Best Practice

The Cadbury Committee's Code of Best Practice is set out verbatim.

1   **The Board of Directors**

1.1   The board should meet regularly, retain full and effective control over the company and monitor the executive management.

1.2   There should be a clearly accepted division of responsibilities at the head of a company, which will ensure a balance of power and authority, such that no one individual has unfettered powers of decision. Where the chairman is also the chief executive, it is essential that there should be a strong and independent element on the board, with a recognised senior member.

1.3   The board should include non-executive directors of sufficient calibre and number for their views to carry significant weight in board's decisions.

1.4   The board should have a formal schedule of matters specifically reserved to it for decision to ensure that the direction and control of the company is firmly in its hands.

1.5   The should be an agreed procedure for directors in the furtherance of their duties to take independent professional advice if necessary, at the company's expense.

1.6   All directors should have access to the advice and services of the company secretary, who is responsible to the board for ensuring that board procedures are followed and that applicable rules and regulations are complied with. Any question of the removal of the company secretary should be a matter for the board as a whole.

2   **Non-Executive Directors**

2.1   Non-executive directors should bring an independent judgement to bear on issues of strategy, performance, resources, including key appointments, and standards of conduct.

2.2   The majority should be independent of management and free from any business or other relationship which could materially interfere with the exercise of their independent judgement, apart from their fees and shareholding. Their fees should reflect the time which they commit to the company.

2.3   Non-executive directors should be appointed for specified terms and reappointment should not be automatic.

2.4   Non-executive directors should be selected through a formal process and both this process and their appointment should be a matter for the board as a whole.

3   **Executive Directors**

3.1   Directors' service contracts should not exceed three years without shareholders' approval.

3.2   There should be full and clear disclosure of directors' total emoluments and those of the chairman and highest-paid UK director, including pension contributions and stock options. Separate figures should be given for salary and performance-related elements and the basis on which performance is measured should be explained.

3.3   Executive directors' pay should be subject to the recommendations of a remuneration committee made up wholly or mainly of non-executive directors.

4   **Reporting and Controls**

4.1   It is the board's duty to present a balanced and understandable assessment of the company's position.

4.2   The board should ensure that an objective and professional relationship is maintained with the auditors.

4.3   The board should establish an audit committee of a least 3 non-executive directors with written terms of reference which deal clearly with its authority and duties.

4.4   The directors should explain their responsibility for preparing the accounts next to a statement by the auditors about their reporting responsibilities.

4.5   The directors should report on the effectiveness of the company's system of internal control.

4.6   The directors should report that the business is a going concern, with supporting assumption or qualifications as necessary.

3.4   Summary of the Code's main points

- appointment of non-executive directors (at least 3)
- appointment of an audit committee
- non-executive directors to set remuneration of executive directors
- imposition of a three year maximum term on executive directors' service contracts

3.5   Further developments

The Stock Exchange has adopted the final recommendation and as a result requires every listed company incorporated in the UK to state in the directors' report whether or not it has complied with the Code of Best Practice over the accounting period and if not, to what extent and why not. This 'statement of compliance' requirement applies for all accounting periods ending on after 30 June 1993. The Stock Exchange requires the company's statement of compliance to be reviewed by the auditors before publication.

According to a survey published in early 1994 43% of listed companies do not intend to comply with the Code.

4   SELF TEST QUESTIONS

4.1   Are there any statutorily required qualifications for the Company Secretary of a **private** company? (1.1)

4.2   To whom and why might a company secretary be liable in damages for breach of warranty of authority? (1.5)

4.3   How is an auditor appointed? (2.1)

4.4   How is an auditor removed from office? (2.12)

5   EXAMINATION TYPE QUESTION

5.1   Duties and powers of an auditor

(a)   What relationships disqualify an auditor from appointment as auditor to a company?

(5 marks)

(b)   You are required to explain:

(i)   the principal duties of an auditor; and

(ii)   the powers he has been granted by statute to discharge such duties.

(10 marks)

(Total: 15 marks)

6   EXAMINATION TYPE ANSWER

6.1   Duties and powers of an auditor

(a)   An auditor, although properly qualified and a member of a recognised professional accountancy body, is nevertheless disqualified from acting as auditor by the Companies Act 1985 (CA85) as a result of certain relationships. A person cannot be appointed auditor of a company if he is an officer or servant of the company or of any other company which is a subsidiary company or a holding company of that company or any of the subsidiary companies of such a holding company; or if he is a partner of or in the employment of an officer or servant of the company or any such companies.

(b)   (i)   The principal duties of auditors consist of the common law duties of skill and care and those statutory duties contained in CA85. This provides that the auditors shall make a report to the members on the accounts examined by them, and on every balance sheet, every profit and loss account and all group accounts laid before the company in general meeting during their tenure of office. The general requirement is that the auditor's report must state whether or not the accounts of the company have been properly prepared in accordance with the Companies Act and whether or not they give a true and fair view of the financial affairs of the company. CA85 provides that the auditor is under a duty in preparing his report to carry out such investigations as will enable him to form an opinion in these respects; whether proper accounting records have been kept by the company and proper returns adequate for their audit received from branches not visited; and whether the balance sheet and profit and loss account are in agreement with the accounting records and returns. If the auditor is not satisfied in any such respect he must state this fact in his report. Likewise, if he fails to obtain all the necessary information and explanations which are required for the audit, he must qualify his report accordingly. A specific duty is laid on an auditor who resigns his appointment before the expiry of his term of office. CA85 requires him to file a statement with his notice of resignation at the company's registered office (and the company must send a copy to the Registrar and every person entitled to notice of general meetings) to the effect that there are no circumstances connected with his resignation which ought to be made known to the company's members or creditors or, if there are such circumstances, an account of them. Additional detailed duties also devolve upon auditors, including making reports in connection with the filing exemptions in respect of small and medium-sized companies, companies financing the purchase of or otherwise purchasing their own shares, and also a statutory duty to ensure that the directors' report is consistent with the financial statements and if not to state the fact in the audit report.

(ii) CA85 gives the auditor rights to demand information and explanations from the company's officers to assist him in the discharge of the aforementioned statutory duties. CA85 gives the auditor right of access at all times to the books and accounts and vouchers of the company; additionally, he is empowered to require from the officers of the company and its subsidiaries such information and explanations as he thinks necessary for the purpose of his duties. Further, as regards the collection of information from the officers of the company generally, CA85 creates a criminal offence of making a misleading, false or deceptive statement to an auditor when pursuing his statutory duties.

27 SHAREHOLDERS: COMPANY MEETINGS

INTRODUCTION & LEARNING OBJECTIVES

Syllabus area 8h. Company meetings: conduct, resolutions, the relationship between the board and the general meeting. (Ability required 3).

It is important to understand the main procedures at general meetings in order to be able to advise shareholders how to exercise their rights as shareholders. Knowledge of the different types of resolutions affects all areas of company law.

When you have studied this chapter you should be able to do the following:

- Identify who can call general meetings (EGMs and AGMs) and set out the period of notice required in each case.

- Distinguish the different types of resolutions which can be passed at meetings.

- Explain the voting procedures and general conduct of meetings.

- Explain the elective regime for private companies.

---

1 GENERAL MEETINGS

1.1 The importance of rules about meetings

The ultimate control of the company rests with its members in general meeting. There are, therefore, rules to ensure that there is at least one meeting in every year and that additional meetings be called when required and must be called on the requisition of a sufficient number of members. Adequate notice must be given to members of any meeting which is to be held and minimum attendance (the *quorum*) is required to transact business. The conduct of meetings is regulated both by general law and by special rules on company meetings.

Decisions at meetings are taken by majority vote on resolutions. For some decisions a 75% majority is required of the votes cast. The right of the majority to impose its views on the dissenting minority is limited in various ways.

1.2 Types of meeting

The two important types of general meeting are the **annual general meeting (AGM)** and **extraordinary general meeting (EGM)**.

Definition As a rule, a **general meeting** is one in which all shareholders may take part and which decides on matters binding the whole membership.

Class meetings may be held by particular classes of shareholder and decide matters relating to that particular class (eg, for a variation of class rights): the rules of procedure are much the same as those of general meetings.

There may also be class meetings of debentureholders or other creditors.

1.3   Annual general meetings

(a)   Every company must hold a first AGM within eighteen months of incorporation and thereafter no more than fifteen months apart and once in every calendar year - S366 Companies Act 1985 (CA85).

(b)   If the company fails to hold an AGM within the prescribed time the Department of Trade, on the application of any member, may order it to be held. The Department of Trade can give directions for holding the meeting and may fix the quorum at one member only: S367 CA85.

(c)   The following business is usually transacted at an AGM:

(i)   consideration of accounts and reports of directors and auditors;
(ii)   declaration of a dividend;
(iii)   election of directors in place of those retiring;
(iv)   appointment of auditors and fixing their remuneration.

Table A does not prescribe the business to be conducted at an AGM. Accordingly, full details of the business have to be set out in the notice convening the meeting. Some companies' articles, however, set out the above as 'ordinary' business with the intention that full details are not necessary in the notice convening the meeting.

Appointment of auditors must be made at the meeting which considers the accounts: S384 CA85; this is usually the AGM. The articles will typically require some non-executive directors to retire at each AGM, with the right to offer themselves for re-election **(Article 73 Table A)**. Accordingly, items (i)-(iv) are the standard minimum agenda for an AGM. Other business can be taken as well.

CA89 inserts a provision into CA85 (as S366A), allowing a private company to elect (by elective resolution (a resolution of which not less than 21 days' notice has been given and to which **all** members who are entitled to attend and vote agree)) to dispense with the holding of an AGM. However, any member of the company may, by notice to the company not later than three months before the end of the year, require the holding of an AGM in that year.

1.4   Extraordinary general meetings

[Definition]   Any general meeting which is not an AGM is an EGM.

There is no limit on the number of such meetings in a year or the intervals between them. But as convening a meeting entails formalities and sometimes expense, the directors convene such meetings infrequently. Non-urgent matters ie, technical amendment of the articles, can often conveniently be taken as an addition to the business of the next AGM.

1.5   Persons able to convene meetings

(a)   **Directors**

The articles (eg, **Article 37 Table A**) usually authorise the **directors** to call an EGM whenever they think fit.

Where it becomes known to any of the directors of a public company that there has been a serious loss of capital ie, if the company's net assets are half or less than its called up share capital, the directors **must** convene an EGM to consider whether any, and if so what, measures should be taken to deal with the situation: S142 CA85.

(b)   **Members**

(i)   **Members** also have a statutory **right to require the directors to convene** an EGM. To be valid the requisition must be signed by:

(1)   members holding at least one-tenth of the issued and paid up shares carrying voting rights; or

(2)   if the company has no share capital, members having at least one-tenth of the rights to vote at general meetings.

The requisition must state the objects of the meeting and be signed by the requisitionists and deposited at the registered office. If, within twenty-one days of the deposit of the requisition, the directors have not convened the meeting, the requisitionists, or a majority of them (in voting rights) may themselves convene a meeting to be held within three months of that date. In that case the company refunds their costs to the requisitionists and may recover them from the defaulting directors: S368 CA85.

The directors can, in theory, defeat the requisition by convening the meeting for a date which lies a long way ahead (there is no maximum period of notice - however **Table A** provides that it must be held within eight weeks of receipt of the requisition) but the court's powers, referred to below, could then be invoked. CA89 plugs this loophole by providing that directors are deemed not to have duly convened a meeting if they convene a meeting for more than twenty-eight days after the date of the notice convening the meeting.

(ii)   Members may also have the power to **call** an EGM themselves.

Unless the articles otherwise provide two or more members holding at least one-tenth of the share capital (even if it has no voting rights), or it there is no share capital, 5% of the members (even without voting rights) may call a meeting: S370 CA85. In practice articles (eg, **Article 37 Table A**) do usually have the effect of excluding these extended rights which are, therefore, of little importance.

(c)   **Auditors**

The **auditors** have special rights to require a meeting to be held following their resignation in certain circumstances.

Thus, where an auditor's notice of resignation contains a statement as to the circumstances of their resignation which they consider should be brought to the notice of the members or creditors, they may requisition the directors to call an extraordinary general meeting for considering their explanation: S392A CA85.

(d)   **Department of Trade and Industry**

If default is made in holding the annual general meeting, the Department of Trade and Industry may, on the application of any member, call such a meeting and give such ancillary or consequential directions as it thinks expedient: S367 CA85.

(e)   **The court**

The **court** has a general power to order a meeting to be held, either on its own initiative or at the request of a director or a single member having the right to vote. The court may give directions and fix the quorum as low as one member: S371 CA85. This is a cumbersome procedure and little used; but it can resolve a deadlock eg, where a company has two members only and one, by refusing to attend, denies to the other their right to have a general meeting.

[Conclusion] The following groups have the power to convene or require the convening of a general meeting:

- **Directors:**

   usually it is the directors who call general meetings (rights will be outlined in the articles of association);

- **Members:**

   (i)   S368 CA85 - if they hold 10% or more of paid up voting capital;

   (ii)   S370 CA85 - two or more members holding 10% or more of voting capital and there is no power to call a meeting set out in the articles;

- Auditors;

- Department of Trade and Industry;

- Court.

1.6   Class meetings

Such meetings are not meetings of the company but of a class of its shareholders usually for the purpose of considering a proposed variation of class rights. The articles may require that decisions in order to be binding on the class shall be taken by extraordinary resolution requiring a three-quarters majority.

S125(6) CA85 provides that the provisions of S369 (length of notice for calling company meetings), S370 (general provisions as to meeting and votes) and Ss376-377 (circulation of members' resolutions) and the provisions of the articles relating to general meetings shall as far as applicable, apply in relation to any meeting of shareholders required by S125 or otherwise to take place in connection with the variation of the rights attached to a class of shares and shall so apply with the necessary modifications and subject to:

(a)   the necessary quorum at any such meeting other than an adjourned meeting shall be two persons holding or representing by proxy at least one-third in nominal value of the issued shares of the class in question and at an adjourned meeting one person holding shares of the class in question or his proxy;

(b)   any holder of shares of the class in question present, in person or by proxy, may demand a poll. A poll is one vote per share, as opposed to the usual show of hands.

2   CALLING A MEETING

2.1   Introduction

A meeting will not be properly held unless proper notice has been given to persons entitled to receive it. The question of notice is usually determined by the articles but is subject to statutory provisions, in particular that notice must be served on every member in the manner required by

Table A, except insofar as the company's articles have made alternative provision: S370(1) CA85.

It is necessary to consider the various requirements of a valid notice which are:

(a)   length of notice;
(b)   persons entitled to receive notice; and
(c)   contents of a notice.

2.2   Length of notice of meetings and resolutions

The statutory minimum:

(a)   twenty-one days written notice for an AGM;

(b)   fourteen days written notice for an EGM (seven days if unlimited company) except that if a special resolution is to be moved twenty-one days notice is required for an EGM.

The articles can impose a requirement of longer but not shorter notice. Many articles (eg, **Article 115 Table A**) provide that in reckoning the period notice is deemed to be given forty-eight hours after posting; that day and the meeting itself are excluded from the period. Where **clear notice** rules of this kind apply a notice must be posted eg, on Monday for a meeting to be held on a Thursday (two or three weeks later).

The notice requirements can, however, be waived:

(a)   in the case of an AGM if so agreed by **all** the members entitled to attend and vote;

(b)   in the case of an EGM by a majority of members holding not less than 95% of the voting shares (or if there is no share capital) by 95% of the members having the right to attend and vote: S369 CA85.

CA89 inserts into S369 CA85 a provision that a private company may by elective resolution (see below) elect to substitute another percentage in (b) for 95%, but this may not be below 90%.

2.3   Persons entitled to receive notices

The articles will usually state who is entitled to receive a copy of the notice. If they do not, Article 38 Table A applies and the persons entitled to notice are every member; the personal representative of a deceased member provided he himself would have been entitled to notice; the trustee of a bankrupt provided the member would have been entitled to notice and the auditor: S370 CA85.

The general law is that failure to give notice even to one member entitled to it invalidates the meeting. It is usual (eg, Article 39 Table A) to provide that accidental failure to give or non receipt of notice shall not invalidate the proceedings.

It is also usual to provide (eg, Article 115 Table A) that notices may be sent by ordinary (ie, unregistered) post and are deemed to arrive (be served) forty-eight hours after posting.

2.4   Contents of a notice

The business of an AGM need only be specified in the notice in general terms eg, **"to elect a director"** is sufficient notice even if the meeting unexpectedly elects a different candidate from the director offering himself for re-election.

In the case of other business sufficient detail must be given in the notice to enable a member to be aware of what is proposed. Thus a proposal on directors' fees must disclose the exact amount involved. This duty is nowadays discharged by setting out in the notice the full and exact text of the resolution to be moved. But for an ordinary resolution this is a matter of practice and not a rule of law.

If the notice includes a special or extraordinary resolution the text of the resolution must be set out in full because the statutory definition of such a resolution makes this necessary.

In every case the notice must state that a member entitled to attend and vote may appoint a proxy or proxies to attend and vote on his behalf: S372 CA85. An AGM and a special or extraordinary resolution must be specified as such.

The date, time and place of the meeting must be given.

Whether any notice given is satisfactory, depends on the requirements of the statute and of the articles and, generally speaking, on whether in the particular circumstances it is reasonably adequate to enable an ordinary member to decide whether or not he ought to attend the meeting to safeguard his interests.

2.5   Circulation of members' resolutions and statements

Members have a statutory right (S376 CA85) to require the company:

(a)   to give to members entitled to receive notice of the AGM, notice of any **resolution** which is to be moved by them at the next AGM; and

(b)   to circulate to members entitled to receive notice of **any general meeting** any **statement** of not more than 1,000 words on any resolution or business to be discussed at that meeting.

To have such a right the members must be either:

(a)   members having at least 5% of the total voting rights of all members entitled to attend and vote; or

(b)   at least 100 members holding paid up shares to an aggregate of at least £10,000 (ie, £100 average),

and must deposit a copy of the requisition signed by the requisitionists not less than 6 weeks before the meeting (if a resolution is to be put an agenda of AGM) a week (in the case of a statement to be circulated). However the directors cannot defeat the requisition by calling an AGM after the deposit of the requisition: S377 CA85.

The members must bear the expense involved.

The intention is to give members an opportunity to put forward views or proposals which the directors may not favour. It is rarely used in practice. Firstly, directors have the advantage with circulars as they have better opportunity to prepare them and, if prepared for the benefit of members, to finance their circulation from company funds (but they must be truthful).

Secondly, when there are rival appeals for the votes of members at a forthcoming meeting, the opposition prefer to issue their circulars direct to members rather than give the directors the advantage of seeing them in advance.

If a company fails to comply with S376 the member may seek an order of the court permitting the resolution to be moved at the appropriate meeting.

2.6   Special notice

Special notice should be clearly distinguished from a special resolution.

Definition   Special notice, when required, is given **to the company by a member** at least twenty-eight days before the meeting. It is notice that the member intends to move a resolution at the meeting: S379 CA85.

If the company ie, the directors, agree or are by law required, to include the resolution (of which special notice has been given) in their notice of the meeting, the company includes the resolution in a twenty-one days notice issued to members to convene the meeting if the motion is put before an AGM or fourteen days if the motion is to be put before an EGM. But unless the member who gave the special notice has the minimum support described above the directors are entitled to refuse to include his resolution in their notice of the meeting and it cannot then be moved.

Pedley v Inland Waterways Association [1977]

Facts: the plaintiff was a shareholder in the defendant company. On 29 October 1975 he sent notice to the company that he wished to propose at the next AGM the removal of the directors of the company. The notice was headed 'Special Notice' and was in accordance with S379 CA85. The company secretary wrote to the plaintiff saying that S376 CA85 had not been complied with and thus the company did not have to include the proposal in the agenda. The plaintiff claimed that S376 was irrelevant to S379 and issued a summons against the company.

Held: the company was under no obligation to give notice to its members of the plaintiff's resolution. S379 did not confer on shareholders the right to compel the inclusion of a resolution in the company's agenda. Therefore, unless a member could rely on S376 or a provision of the articles, the member had no right to insist on his item being included in the agenda.

If, after receiving a special notice, the directors call a meeting for a date which is less than twenty-eight days later, the special notice is still treated as valid.

The purpose of these complex rules is to give to directors, members and to any individual (director or auditor) concerned ample warning of the proposer's intentions.

Special notice is only required for resolutions of three types:

(a)   To remove a director from office or to appoint a substitute in his place under S303 CA85;

(b)   To elect a director aged seventy or more where that age limit applies under S293 CA85;

(c)   To remove an auditor from office or to appoint any auditor other than the retiring auditor: S388 CA85.

In cases (a) and (c) where the special notice of an intended removal is received by the company, a copy of it must be sent forthwith to the director or auditor concerned.

2.7   Activity

Produce a table showing the type of meeting that can be called, the period of notice required and the percentage of shareholders required to approve a waiver of the notice period (using information from part of this chapter).

2.8   Activity solution

Meeting	Days notice	% required to waive notice
AGM	21	100
EGM	14 (or 21)	95*
EGM of unlimited company	7 (or 21)	95*

* Private company can reduce this figure but not below 90% by passing elective resolution.

3   CONDUCT OF MEETINGS

3.1   Introduction

The following are the main requisites of a valid meeting:

(a)   It must be properly **convened** by notice.

(b)   A **quorum** must be present.

(c)   There should be a **chairman** who should discharge his duties in a proper manner.

(d)   If the meeting is to reach decisions, **resolutions** and any amendments, should be proposed for discussion and then put to the **vote** in a proper manner.

(e)   There are subsidiary rules on such matters as **adjournment, proxies** to resolutions, etc.

3.2   Quorum at meetings

Definition   A quorum is the minimum number of persons whose presence is requisite in order that a meeting may validly conduct business.

If the articles do not make special rules for a quorum (eg, Article 40 Table A) then two members personally present is the quorum for a meeting of a company. Articles often provide that proxies may be counted in the quorum: S370 CA85.

In general one member cannot constitute a quorum. But there are a number of exceptions:

(a)   One member can be a quorum for a class meeting if he holds all the shares of the class and the regulations allow it.

(b)   If a meeting is ordered by the Department of Trade and Industry or by the court the quorum may be fixed at one member.

(c)   At an adjourned class meeting the quorum shall be one person holding shares of the class: S125(6)(a) CA85.

(d)   Where the company is a single member private limited company.

One member who attends in his own right and as proxy for another does not constitute a quorum of two members present in person or by proxy; he is still one member and that is insufficient.

In practice the directors themselves will often be shareholders and the numbers of them present will assure a quorum. Problems can arise when a company has, for example, only two members and one refuses to attend to prevent a valid meeting being held. Case (b) above affords a solution.

Where the articles provide that a quorum shall be present **when the meeting proceeds to business** it has been held that the meeting can validly continue even after part of the quorum originally present has withdrawn. Most companies' articles, though, require a quorum throughout (eg, Table A, Art 41)

3.3 Resolutions - introduction

The business of the meeting is conducted by the putting of, voting on and passing or not of resolutions.

For the business to be properly conducted each resolution must be properly put, any amendment properly put, discussed and voted on and the resolution (as amended if this is the case) properly discussed and voted on. It is therefore necessary to know:

(a)   The types of resolution and requirements for each to be properly put to the meeting;

(b)   Moving and discussion of resolutions;

(c)   Amendments; and

(d)   Voting.

3.4 Types of resolution

The three important types of resolution are:

(a)   An **ordinary** resolution passed by a **simple majority** of votes cast (this is **more** votes in favour of the resolution than against). The **period** of notice required **depends on the type of meeting** at which the resolution is moved (twenty-one days for an AGM and fourteen days for an EGM). In two cases only ie, the removal of a director from office under S303 CA85 and the removal of an auditor under S391 CA85, an ordinary resolution is expressly specified by law. It is also required wherever the law does not call for a special or extraordinary resolution. References to **'a resolution'** mean an ordinary resolution.

(b)   A **special** resolution requires at least a **three-quarters majority** and **notice** of at least **twenty-one days:** S378 CA85.

Special resolutions are prescribed for a number of important company decisions eg, an alteration of the articles and reduction of share capital.

(c)   An **extraordinary** resolution is one passed by at least a three-quarters majority of votes cast at a meeting convened by a notice specifying the intention to propose the resolution as an extraordinary resolution. The period of notice can, therefore, be fourteen days. It is used, among other things, to begin a voluntary winding up on grounds of insolvency, and, at class meetings, to vary class rights.

3.5 Written resolution

It is possible that a **written** resolution signed by all members entitled to vote will be as valid as resolutions passed in the normal way at meetings. In addition, the articles of association (eg, Article 53 Table A) may provide that instead of a meeting a decision of the members may be taken by a written resolution duly signed by all members entitled to attend and vote. This is a common practice in private companies if the number of members is small and it is not convenient to hold a meeting. It appears that such an article will apply to all types of resolutions, ordinary, extraordinary and special. CA89 extends these concepts in the case of private companies.

Written resolutions will, under the new provisions (S318A CA85), have effect notwithstanding anything in the company's memorandum or articles. The Act enables any resolution, whether normally requiring a general meeting or a class meeting, to be passed as a written resolution.

Such a resolution, which must be contained in a document or series of documents, must be signed by all shareholders who would have been entitled to attend and vote at the meeting. The date of the resolution will be the date upon which the last signature is appended. The resolution must be entered in the minutes.

An auditor or a director may not be removed from office by written resolution.

The auditors must be sent copies of written resolutions. If any such resolution 'concerns them as auditors' they have seven days to require that it be put to a general meeting or class meeting (as the case may be).   The resolution is therefore ineffective for the seven day period unless in the meantime the auditors notify the company that either the matter does not concern them as auditors, or if it does, that it need not be considered at a meeting.

3.6   Moving and discussion of resolutions

A member may move any resolution of which the general nature of the subject-matter has been indicated in the notice calling the meeting (even if the resolution differs from a specific resolution actually set out *verbatim* in the notice) unless the resolution had to be set out *verbatim*, in which case, that particular resolution is the one to be moved. However, an amendment may be moved if it is in the scope of the notice, but this depends on the leeway allowed by the wording of the notice. A reasonable opportunity must be extended to members to speak on the motion or any permissible amendment. Thereafter, it may be put to the vote.

3.7   Amendments of resolutions

Among the chairman's duties and powers is the acceptance or rejection (for discussion and later voting) of **amendments** to resolutions. It is not legally necessary that an amendment should be supported by a seconder. But the chairman should reject an amendment which is outside the scope of the notice given of the business to be done at the meeting. For example, if the notice contained a resolution authorising the directors to borrow, say £50,000 it is doubtful whether it can be amended to increase the amount. An amendment to reduce it might be permissible unless it is really a rejection of the resolution eg, to reduce the amount to a nominal £50 (in that case those who oppose the resolution should simply vote against it as it stands).

It is doubtful whether an amendment (except on a small point of drafting) can be accepted to alter a special or extraordinary resolution since such resolutions are required to be set out in the notice of the meeting: S378 CA85.

The effect of the notice requirement is generally taken to mean that the exact text of an extraordinary or special resolution must be set out *verbatim* in the notice convening the meeting and in **Re Moorgate Mercantile Holdings** it was **held** that a special resolution could not be amended. The period of notice can be waived with the consent of a majority of members entitled to vote and holding 95% of the voting shares: S378(3) CA85.

When an amendment has been accepted for discussion it should be voted on before the resolution which it amends. If the amendment is carried the resolution, as thus amended, is then put to the vote.   If, however, the amendment is rejected the original resolution (unless there are other amendments to discuss and put to the vote) is then voted on.

3.8   Voting - show of hands/poll

In votes on resolutions the three-quarters majority is of votes cast; members who do not vote are disregarded. The majority is required both on a show of hands and, if a poll is held, on a poll.

In the first instance, voting will be on a show of hands. This will be a rough guide as it will generally be on the basis of one vote per person, whatever the size of his actual shareholding and voting rights.

The standard practice is:

(a)   first to take a vote on a **show of hands** in which each member present in person has one vote regardless of the number of his shares; proxies are not usually entitled to vote on a show of hands;

(b)   then if a poll is properly demanded (this is a rare occurrence - see below) to take a vote on a **poll** in which voting rights depend on shareholdings and proxies are entitled to vote. A vote on a poll overrides a previous vote on the same point by a show of hands.

Voting rights are specified in the articles; one vote for each ordinary share is normal. But there may be non-voting ordinary shares and or preference shares carrying the right to vote only in special circumstances.

The chairman's declaration of the result of a vote on a show of hands is conclusive unless either a poll is properly demanded or his declaration is manifestly wrong (eg, **carried by eleven to ten** in a case where 75% majority is obligatory).

The articles may prescribe the rules for demanding and holding a poll. The **right to demand a poll** cannot be totally excluded by the articles except on the election of a chairman and the adjournment of the meeting: S373(1)(a) CA85. Furthermore, the articles may not set the minimum support required to obtain a poll at a higher level than five members entitled to vote, or any number holding at least 10% of the total voting rights or of the paid up shares carrying votes: S373(1)(b) CA85. Article 46 Table A provides that a poll may be demanded by the chairman, at least two voting members or members representing not less than 10% of total voting rights. A proxy has the same right to demand a poll as the member whom he represents. These rules are to safeguard a minority against restrictive provisions in the articles designed to make it difficult to obtain a poll.

Subject to any provisions of the articles the chairman may decide, when a poll is properly demanded, whether it should be held at once or later when the necessary arrangements have been made.

When a poll is held at a later date and not at the meeting itself, members may only send in proxies during the interval if the articles permit this to be done.

Where there is to be a vote on a poll the first step (apart from deciding when it should be held ie, forthwith or later) is to appoint **scrutineers** (a task often given to the auditors). Members either sign voting lists **for** or **against** the resolution or hand in signed voting cards. The scrutineers check the signatures against the register of members and report the result to the chairman who declares it.

3.9   Proxies

Definition   The expression **proxy** is used both to denote a person authorised to vote on behalf of a member and the paper or **proxy card** which gives him that authority.

Members of any company have important rights - S372 CA85 (which override any contrary provisions of the articles). These are:

(a)   Every member entitled to attend and vote at a meeting of a company having a share capital may appoint a proxy to attend and vote on their behalf:

    (i)   a proxy need not be a member of the company eg, a member can appoint his solicitor to be their proxy;

    (ii)   in the case of a private company, the proxy has the right to speak at the meeting;

(iii)   in the case of a public company only, the member may appoint more than one proxy eg, a bank nominee company holding shares for several different customers might wish to appoint one proxy to vote for and against a resolution in accordance with the instructions given by each beneficial owner.

(b)   Every notice issued to convene a meeting must specify the right to appoint one or more proxies and that a proxy need not be a member.

(c)   Proxies may be deposited at any time up to forty-eight hours before the meeting begins ie, the articles may fix a shorter but not longer time.

(d)   If the company issues proxy cards (ie, invites proxies) it must issue them to all members and not only to some (ie, to drum up support from its selected supporters): S372 CA85.

The same rules apply to class meetings.

The Stock Exchange requires listed companies to issue **two-way proxies** ie, forms on which the member can instruct his proxy to vote **against** (as well as **for**) the resolution.

A member who has sent in a proxy card may nonetheless attend the meeting in person. If he does so the authority of the proxy is automatically revoked. Death or insanity of the member would also revoke it unless the articles (eg, Article 63 Table A) provide that **until notice is received by the company** such a proxy continues in force.

Note that as a corporation is an artificial person it cannot attend the meeting itself. Thus, a member which is a **corporation** may by resolution of its own directors authorise another person to act as its **representative** (not a proxy) and exercise the same powers at a meeting of the company as the corporation would if it were a member.

3.10   The chair and procedure

As can be seen the chairman's role is a crucial one - **Byng v London Life Assurance [1988]**. Therefore, it is essential that there should be a chairman to preside over the meeting. The articles usually (eg, Articles 42 & 43 Table A) provide that the chairman of the board of directors, failing him another director or failing that, one of the members present chosen by them, shall act as chairman.

The chairman has a general duty to act in good faith in the interests of the company as a whole and in fairness to all sections of opinion present. If the chairman fails to conduct the meeting properly - the meeting and any purported resolution passed thereat is void.

Byng v London Life Assurance [1988]

Facts: a general meeting was called, to pass a special resolution to approve a merger, for 12 noon at Cinema I at the Barbican centre in London. The merger had aroused some opposition and critical press comment and as a result far more members attended than could be accommodated in the cinema. Adjacent rooms for the overflow were taken with audio-visual links but these did not work and at about 12.30 the chairman opened the meeting even though members were still pressing to get in. After one member proposed a vote of no confidence in the board the chairman decided to move the meeting to the Café Royal (a mile down the road) at 2.30pm. Far fewer members were able to attend at this later time and at this different venue, but the chairman went ahead and the special resolution was carried.

Held: in the chaotic circumstances the meeting, (whether at the Barbican or at the Café Royal) was not effective to pass the resolution.

In conducting the meeting the chairman should take it through its business in an orderly fashion, ensuring that one particular resolution at a time is proposed for discussion and that members relate what they say to the item then before the meeting. He must maintain order and for that purpose may require members to desist from making irrelevant or provocative remarks. When he judges that all points of view have been adequately expressed he may put the resolution then under discussion to the vote and declare the result. He has a casting vote only if the articles give him one (eg, Article 50 Table A).

Subject to any provisions of the articles the chairman may **adjourn** the meeting if the meeting agrees or if he considers it necessary to adjourn to avoid disorder. If he adjourns the meeting improperly before its business is concluded the meeting may elect another chairman and continue.

3.11   Adjournment and dissolution

Meetings may be adjourned and the business completed at a later date. Motions for closure of discussion, adjournment or dissolution of the meeting may generally be passed by ordinary resolution.

Where a resolution is passed at an adjourned meeting it is deemed to have been passed on the date it was in fact passed and not deemed to be passed at an earlier date.

3.12   Minutes of meetings

(a)   **Must be kept**

A company is required to maintain minutes of its general meetings to be entered in a minute book: S382 CA85. Such minutes are usually a brief formal record of resolutions passed. A company must also keep minutes of board meetings.

(b)   **Signing**

The minutes are usually signed by the chairman of the meeting or of the next succeeding meeting. Signed minutes are evidence of the proceedings but it is permissible to call other evidence, if any exists, to rebut the minutes. However, the articles may provide that a signed minute recording that a resolution was carried by a specified majority shall be conclusive (if the chairman declared that result at the meeting). This is to prevent argument later on points which should have been challenged at the time.

Failure to keep minutes is an offence and the company and any officer in default is liable to a fine.

(c)   **Inspection**

The minute book of general meetings must be kept at the registered office and must be open to inspection by members: S383 CA85. A member may also on payment of a small fee obtain a copy from the company which must be provided within seven days of the request. Failure to allow inspection and supply copies is also an offence. There is no similar right to inspect and have copies of minutes of board meetings.

3.13   When a meeting need not be held

This overlaps with the topic of resolutions above. Thus meetings may be dispensed with where a written resolution has been passed. But note also the new right of a private company to dispense with having an AGM by elective resolution.

These CA89 provisions are important as they are an attempt to distinguish between a small private company and a large public company and reduce the burden of regulation on private companies.

3.14   Registration and publicity

Details of, and resolutions in, meetings are generally the private concern of the company and its members. However, certain resolutions which may affect third parties must be registered. Thus, a signed copy of certain resolutions must be filed at the Companies Registry: Ss123, 380 & 572 CA85. Resolutions to be filed include:

(a)   All special resolutions;

(b)   All extraordinary resolutions;

(c)   All resolutions to increase or decrease authorised share capital;

(d)   All resolutions of class meetings (agreeing to vary class rights); and

(e)   Resolutions for voluntary winding up.

Note that an ordinary resolution, unless it falls within these categories (as some do), does not, however, have to be filed.

Such resolutions are thereafter annexed to the articles and become part of the company's public documents: S380.

3.15   The elective regime: S379A CA85

CA89 introduces for private companies the **elective regime,** this permits companies unanimously to dispense with certain formalities. Elective resolutions allow the company:

(a)   to fix the duration of the authority of the directors to allot shares (which may be longer than five years);

(b)   to dispense with the requirements to lay accounts and reports before the company in general meeting;

(c)   to dispense with the requirement to hold an annual general meeting;

(d)   to dispense with the requirement to appoint auditors annually;

(e)   to reduce the majority required to consent to the holding of a general meeting of the company at short notice from members holding 95 per cent to not less than 90 per cent in nominal value of shares having the right to attend and vote at a general meeting.

An elective resolution can be revoked by ordinary resolution.

Conclusion   This is a detailed area but for the purpose of the examination you should be aware of:

- the different types of resolution;

  (a)   ordinary
  (b)   extraordinary
  (c)   special
  (d)   written
  (e)   elective

- the contents of a notice (and what 'special notice' means);

- what the words 'quorum' and 'proxy' mean and when they apply; and

- how and when voting occurs at general meetings.

3.16   Activity

Produce a table showing the different types of resolution, the notice period (if any), the percentage of 'votes required to pass them' and if a copy of the resolution has to be forwarded to the Registrar.

3.17   Activity solution

Type of Resolution	Notice period	% of those voting to pass	To Registrar?
Special	21	75	Yes
Ordinary	14	Majority	Sometimes (eg, increase of ASC)
Extraordinary	14 or 7	75	Yes
Elective	21	100	Yes
Written	-	100	Sometimes

4   SELF TEST QUESTIONS

4.1   When must a company hold AGMs? (1.3 (a))

4.2   What is the usual business conducted at an AGM? (1.3(c))

4.3   Who can convene meetings? (1.5)

4.4   How can shareholders compel the inclusion of a resolution on the agenda of an AGM? (2.5)

4.5   For what three purposes is special notice of a resolution required? (2.6)

4.6   What is the quorum for a company meeting? (3.2)

4.7   What is the difference between voting on a show of hands and voting on a poll? (3.8)

5   EXAMINATION TYPE QUESTIONS

5.1   Dozy plc

The directors of Dozy plc have not called an annual general meeting of the company for nearly two years and a shareholders' committee has been formed. It wishes to call a meeting in order to remove the directors.

Advise the committee how they may proceed to call a general meeting or to have one called.

(10 marks)

5.2   Fork Ltd

Fork Ltd has a fully paid up share capital of £10,000 divided into 10,000 £1 shares. The two directors, Bill and Ben, each hold 150 shares. The remaining 9,700 shares are held by six other shareholders. These six shareholders requisition an extraordinary general meeting of the company to pass a vote of no confidence in the board of directors.

Say why these shareholders are in a position to make a valid requisition. What are the requirements of a valid requisition? If Bill and Ben ignore the requisition, what further action can the shareholders take?

(10 marks)

6   ANSWERS TO EXAMINATION TYPE QUESTIONS

6.1   Dozy plc

The holders of at least 10% of the voting shares of a company may (S368 Companies Act 1985 (CA85)) require the directors to call a general meeting. This is done by depositing at the registered office a requisition signed by the shareholders and stating the purpose for which the meeting is to be called. The directors must within three weeks of the deposit of the requisition call a meeting and the meeting must then be held within 28 days. If the directors do not convene the meeting the requisitionists, or a majority of them, may convene the meeting themselves for a date within three months of the deposit of the requisition. Their expenses are paid by the company and deducted from sums payable by the company to the directors.

As the purpose of the meeting is to remove the directors from office the requisitionists would also, in depositing their requisition, give special notice (S379 CA85) of their intention. This is notice to the company given twenty eight days before the meeting. The notice of the meeting would set out the resolution for removal of the directors. The directors themselves are entitled to receive a copy of the special notice from the company; to circulate 'representations' in their defence to members; and to be heard at the meeting itself.

Any members may under this procedure (Ss303-304 CA85) propose the removal of directors, but, unless there is some special provision in the Memorandum and Articles to the contrary, the directors can refuse to include the resolution in the notice covering the meeting unless the requisitionist(s) can muster at least 1/20-th of the voting rights or a hundred or more members holding at least £100 on average of the nominal share capital: **Pedley v Inland Waterways.** The resolution itself will be passed only if a majority of votes is cast in its favour at the meeting. The shareholders' committee must therefore have or obtain a majority of votes cast for their resolution.

Since no annual general meeting has been held for almost two years, the shareholders' committee could as an alternative procedure apply to the Department of Trade under Ss366-367 CA85 for an order that an annual general meeting be held. This might suit them if they lack the 10% support required for S368 procedure but reckon to attract sufficient support when the meeting is convened to carry a resolution under Ss303-304 CA85.

*(**Tutorial note:** if the company's name in the question had been Dozy **Ltd,** rather than Dozy **plc,** your answer should have included the possibility of the company having passed an elective resolution to dispense with the holding of AGMs.)*

6.2   Fork Ltd

Shareholders holding at least one-tenth of the company's paid up share capital (with voting rights) have a right to requisition an extraordinary general meeting of the company: S368 Companies Act 1985 (CA85). The requisition must state the objects of the meeting and be signed by those requisitioning it. It must be deposited at the company's registered office. As the business of the meeting might lead to the dismissal of a director by ordinary resolution, the shareholders should give notice to the company that this is their intention ie, special notice requiring twenty-eight days. If the directors fail to call a meeting within twenty-one days of the requisition, the shareholders requisitioning the meeting may convene it themselves but must do so within three months: S368(4).

The company will be liable to pay the reasonable expenses of the requisitionists in holding the meeting and the company is given the right to retain this sum from the remuneration normally given to the directors for these services.

28 SHAREHOLDERS: RIGHTS

INTRODUCTION & LEARNING OBJECTIVES

Syllabus area 8g. Shareholders rights: class rights and their variation; transfer, transmission and mortgage of shares; the protection of minority shareholders. (Ability required 3).

In contrast to the previous chapter which looked at shareholders' rights as a body, this chapter looks at shareholder's rights as individuals. Lastly the chapter goes outside company law to see how shareholders may use contract law to give themselves rights.

When you have studied this chapter you should be able to do the following:

- Identify class rights and set out how they may be varied.

- Understand the distinction between transmission of shares and transfer of shares.

- Set out the necessary steps in order to transfer shares.

- Explain how a shareholder might use his shares as security for a loan.

- Understand the rule in **Foss v Harbottle** and be able to explain how both common law and particularly statute provide exceptions to it which protect minority shareholders.

---

1   CLASS RIGHTS AND VARIATION OF CLASS RIGHTS

1.1   Introduction

Shareholders are given rights by the common law, the Companies Acts, the Memorandum, the Articles and also perhaps by the terms of a resolution authorising the issue of shares. Class rights are those enjoyed by a class of shares to distinguish them from rights enjoyed by all shareholders (the latter are commonly called shareholder rights). The significance of identifying what are class rights as opposed to shareholder rights is that the former can be varied only by compliance with S125-127 Companies Act 1985 (CA85). S125 begins by explaining that: 'This section is concerned with the variation of rights attaching to any shares in a company whose share capital is divided into shares of different classes' and carries on by requiring that a variation of class rights must be consented to by the shareholders of that class. Whereas if a company has only one class of share the rights (which would normally be in the articles) can be changed by special resolution under S9 CA85: if the rights are in the memorandum they may be changed under S17 CA85 (special resolution with right of objection by 15%).

1.2   What are class rights?

 Where a company has more than one class of share class rights are the special rights attached to each class such as dividend rights, distribution of capital on a winding up and voting.

The usual classes of shares are ordinary shares and preference shares. A full explanation of these rights were given in an earlier chapter 'Corporate finance: raising of share capital'.

Recent case law has extended the concept of class rights beyond those special rights attaching to particular **shares** but also to special rights conferred on a **person** (or persons) in his capacity as member.

Cumbria Newspapers Group v Cumberland & Westmorland Herald [1987]

Facts: the plaintiff held 10% of the shares in the defendant company. When the plaintiff bought the shares the articles were altered to grant the plaintiff, by name, rights of pre-emption on a transfer of any shares and the right to appoint a director (this latter so long as it held at least 10% of the company's shares). Subsequently the company proposed to cancel those articles in GM by special resolution under S9 CA85. The plaintiff objected on the basis that the articles conferred class rights on it and therefore S125 CA85 (requiring its consent) must be complied with in order to vary them.

Held: these were class rights since they were particular rights conferred on him as a member even though not attached to particular shares. Therefore S125 must be complied with.

The judge was also of the opinion that the weighted voting rights in **Bushell v Faith [1970]** given to members who were also directors and the right of members in **Rayfield v Hands [1960]** to compel members who were directors to buy their shares were class rights.

1.3   Variation of class rights

(a)   Procedure

The special rights of any class of shares are defined either by the articles or less commonly by the memorandum. In either case it is usual but not obligatory to provide in the same context for variation of class rights with consent of a three-quarters majority of the class.

If the rights are defined in the memorandum they can only be varied by the procedure contained in the memorandum or contained in the articles **and referred to** in the memorandum. If the memorandum is silent altogether on variation those rights may be varied by consent of all the members of all classes of shares: S125(5) CA85, or resort can be made to S425 CA85 ie, a scheme of arrangement.

Where rights are attached to a class of shares otherwise than by the memorandum, and the articles do not contain any provision for the variation of those rights (Table A does not), those rights can only be varied with the consent of the holders of three-quarters in nominal value of the issued shares of that class or with the sanction of an extraordinary resolution passed at a separate class meeting of the holders of that class of shares: S125(2) CA85.

On a variation of rights (whether as in accordance with the company's own articles or memorandum or S125 CA85) minority shareholders holding at least 15% of the class of shares whose rights are being varied, who did not consent to the variation may, within twenty-one days of consent being given, apply to the court: S127 CA85. The variation does not then take effect unless the court confirms it. The court is required to hear the interested parties and may disallow the variation (but not impose a compromise) if it would unfairly prejudice the members of the class represented by the objectors.

The most usual ground of objection under S127 CA85 is that the majority who consented did so not in the interest of the class whose consent was required but to secure some other advantage eg, where the majority also held shares of another class which would benefit from the change **Re Holders Investment Trust [1971]**; but any sufficient evidence of bad faith or discrimination against the minority would suffice.

(b)   **What is a variation of class rights?**

The safeguards of variation procedure are available only where there is a variation (or abrogation) of rights. It also includes varying a clause setting out the procedure for varying class rights. But a change in capital structure which adversely affects a class of shareholders is not necessarily a variation. This is so even where the article dealing with variation of rights is expressed to apply to anything which **affects** the rights. Most of the case law on this point is concerned with the grant or increase of rights to other members which reduces the **value** of existing rights without directly diminishing the **rights themselves**.

Examples of actions which do **not** amount to variation of class rights are:

- **White v Bristol Aeroplane Co [1953]**

  Facts: a bonus issue of new shares was made to holders of existing ordinary shares.

  Held: this does not **affect** the rights of existing preference shareholders even though their class rights become less valuable (in votes and in dividend priority) than before. A distinction is here made between rights and the enjoyment or effectiveness of rights.

- **Greenhalgh v Arderne Cinemas [1946]**

  Facts: ordinary shares of 50p each and preference shares of 10p each all had one vote per share. Sub-division of each ordinary share into five 10p shares, quintupled the votes of the ordinary shareholders.

  Held: this did not vary the voting rights of the preference shareholders although it reduced their effectiveness.

- A company which has preference shares may create and issue a new class of preference shares with priority over the existing class without thereby varying the rights of the latter.

[Conclusion]   When answering an examination question which appears to involve variation of class rights, consider:

- Are they class rights?

- Are they being varied?

- Where are the class rights contained?

- What is the S125 CA85 procedure to alter those rights?

- What is the S127 CA85 protection afforded to minorities who dissent and does it apply?

If the class rights are contained in the articles of association either follow the procedure to vary laid down or, if no procedure is contained therein, use S125 to vary.

If the class rights are contained in the memorandum of association either follow the procedure to vary laid down, or if no procedure is contained therein all shareholders of all classes must agree to vary.

It is only a 'variation' if it alters the structure of the shareholders rights (such as change the amount of dividend) but not if it merely makes those rights 'less enjoyable' as in the case of **White v Bristol Aeroplane**.

Only then will the specific protection afforded by S127 CA85 apply - petition to the court. If not, ordinary minority protection will have to be used: this is covered later in this chapter.

1.4 Activity

Draw up a table to show how class rights can be varied.

1.5 Activity solution

Class Rights stated where?	Variation procedure stated?	How to vary?
Memorandum	No	Consent of all members
Articles	No	Extraordinary resolution of class or consent in writing of ¾ of class (S125 CA85)
Memorandum or articles	Yes	Follow that procedure

Note: Minority protection procedures under S127 apply in each case.

2 TRANSFER AND TRANSMISSION OF SHARES

2.1 Share certificates

Following registration of any person as holder of its shares a company must within two months of the presentation of the transfer issue a share certificate stating that he is the registered holder of the shares: S185 CA85.

Definition A share certificate is not a document of title nor is it a negotiable instrument capable of transferring ownership of the shares by mere delivery (or delivery and endorsement). But it is a representation by the company of *prima facie* **evidence of title to the shares** of the person named in it: S186 CA85.

For this reason a company always insists that the transferor's share certificate shall be surrendered for cancellation before his transfer to someone else is registered and a new certificate issued.

But the company is not liable if the share certificate is itself a forgery issued without its authority.

The share certificate operates as a statement by the company that at the time it was issued the person named in it held the specified number of shares and that those shares were paid up to the extent specified. It is not evidence of that person's continuing membership.

The company is estopped (or prevented) as against a person relying on a statement contained in it from denying the statement. Hence, if the person relying on the certificate sues the company, the company is estopped from pleading in its defence that the statements were untrue.

Re: Bahia & San Francisco Railway Co [1898]

Facts: the owner of the shares passed to the certificates to a broker who forged a transfer of the shares into his own name, registered the transfer and sold to an innocent third party.

Held: the true owner's name should be restored to the register and the company was liable to the third party in damages (the broker having disappeared).

Thus if A is the name on the register, his share certificate is stolen by B, who forges A's name on a transfer and sells it to C, who presents the transfer to the company who register C as the new owner and issue a share certificate in his name, and C then sells to D (who relies on the share certificate) and A by this time, having found out about the theft, has his name restored to the register, D can sue the company for damages.

In this case the company must restore A's name to the register, this is called 'rectification', but D may sue the company because he relied on the certificate issued by the company. The company could in turn claim an indemnity from C for loss suffered by the company even if he was innocent as to the theft. This is because it is C who has passed the forged documentation to the company for transfer, even though unaware of the forgery.

The company will also be estopped from denying the truth of the false statement where it is acting against the person relying. For example the latter has a defence to calls where the share certificate states that the shares are fully paid up.

But it will be difficult for such a person to rely on the estoppel for the following reasons:

(a)   A person cannot rely on the estoppel if he has not relied and acted on the representation in the share certificate. In particular, this will not be so when he is aware of the truth.

(b)   A person who has put forward a forged transfer cannot rely on a statement made by the company as a consequence of it.

(c)   The company is not estopped by a statement contained in a forged share certificate unless it is represented as true by a person or persons with authority to bind the company.

2.2   Transfer and transmission generally

There are various ways in which a shareholder may cease to be a shareholder.

Transfer of shares means the actual transfer of shares to another, who becomes the shareholder. **Transmission** of shares means the control of the shares moves from the shareholder to someone else eg, personal representatives of a deceased shareholder. Transmission occurs by operation of law.

Note that because one person ceases to be a shareholder, it does not necessarily follow that the person who is then otherwise entitled to the shares can be registered as a member in his place, for the articles may give the directors discretion to refuse to register transfers and may require a sale to a specified person or persons.

The effect of a transfer of shares when duly registered is to make the transferee the holder of the shares subject to the memorandum and articles. There is a new contract between him and the company rather than an assignment of the transferor's existing rights against the company: S14 CA85.

2.3   Transfer procedure - general

A share is a legal **chose in action** and is transferable subject to any restrictions and procedural requirements of the articles: S182 CA85. In modern practice, however, a transfer in the common form authorised by the Stock Transfer Act 1963 (STA 1963) setting out the amount of consideration, the name of the company, the name, address and description of the transferor and transferee and the description and amount/number of the securities being transferred is sufficient notwithstanding additional formal requirements of the articles. In addition it must be dated and signed by the transferor. The special procedure for transfer of securities sold through a stock exchange is considered later. Under STA 1963 there is a simple standard procedure which takes two alternative forms depending on whether the transferor is or is not transferring his entire shareholding to one transferee. A transfer must be by written instrument: S183 CA85. However, CA89 empowers the Secretary of State to make regulations to enable securities to be transferred without a written instrument. These regulations will become effective as and when the Stock Exchange can install a computer system able to cope with computerised transfers.

Where the transfer is of the **entire shareholding** to a single transferee the transferor (on receiving payment of the price if it is a sale) delivers to the transferee a signed transfer and the share certificate. The transferee has the transfer stamped and delivers the stamped transfer with the transferor's share certificate to the company for registration. The company enters the name of the transferee in the register of members, cancels the old share certificate and issues a new one to the transferee. If the articles so provide the company may require payment of a small transfer fee. The company must either issue a new share certificate within two months of receiving the transfer or give notice within that period that the directors (if they are so empowered) have refused to approve the transfer: Ss183 & 185 CA85.

Where the transfer is of **part of the shareholding** to one transferee with the balance either being retained by the transferor or transferred to a second transferee, the procedure begins with the transferor sending the signed transfer to the company together with the share certificate. The company endorses the transfer **'certificate lodged'** and returns the transfer to the transferor who then passes it over to the transferee. But the certificate is retained by the company for cancellation. The procedure gets round the difficulty that if the holding is to be split, no transferee is entitled to receive with his transfer a certificate covering the entire holding.

If the transfer is returned certified by a duly authorised officer of the company, the company is estopped from denying to any person who acts on the faith of the certification that documents have been provided to the company showing *prima facie* title to the shares in the transferor named in the transfer: S184 CA85. In effect the company has confirmed that the transferor is at the time of certification the registered holder of the shares and has surrendered the share certificate. But certification does not warrant that the transferor has good title to the shares.

Having certified the transfer the company should retain the share certificate. But the duty to do so is owed only to the person named as transferee in the certified transfer and not to any third party.

2.4   Valuation of shares

Articles (especially of private companies) may provide that a member who wishes to sell their shares must offer them to another person or other persons at, for example, a fair value to be fixed by an auditor. The court will not enquire into the valuation unless there is evidence it was improperly made (a controversial exercise of discretion is insufficient) or unless reasons for the valuation are given which are patently wrong. However, a valuation which on its face demonstrates an erroneous calculation may be challenged.

The seller or purchaser of shares at a wrong valuation can sue a valuer for damages if they have acted negligently. Shares should normally be valued at their market price although it is conceivable that a block of shares will be worth more per share if the buyer of them is thereby enabled to obtain **control** of the company through the strength of their voting power.

2.5   Restrictions on transfer

Prima facie, shares are **freely transferable**. The knowledge that they can sell their shares and recover their market value is one of the inducements to a person who wishes to buy shares.

Shares are transferable except to the extent that the articles may restrict the right of transfer. The same principle applies to transmission to personal representatives and trustees in bankruptcy. Where a restriction on transfer exists the restriction is usually in one of two forms or a combination of them ie,:

(a)   a power to the directors to **decline to register** a transfer of shares either in their absolute discretion or on one or more specific grounds; and

(b)   a right of other members of **pre-emption** or first refusal of shares which a member wishes to transfer.

2.6   Directors' power to veto transfers

This is called directors' discretion. Such a power is subject to three requirements:

(a)   if the directors wish to veto a transfer they must exercise their power by a decision properly reached at a board meeting. Mere failure to consider the transfer at all or to approve it is not an exercise of a veto.

(b)   the power of veto lapses unless it is exercised within a reasonable time. The directors are required by statute to give notice of any refusal within two months of the presentation of the transfer: S183 CA85;

(c)   the power must be exercised **in good faith for the benefit of the company**. If power of veto is limited to specific grounds eg, that it is **undesirable to admit the transferee to membership of the company,** one of those grounds must exist and be the reason for the decision.

Where the directors have absolute discretion they cannot be required to disclose their reasons. But if they elect to give reasons these may be challenged under rule (c) above. Where specific grounds of refusal are stated in the articles the directors may be required to identify the grounds which they rely on, but need not enter into their reasons in detail.

2.7   Pre-emption rights of members on transfer of shares

The articles, which usually contain elaborate rules of procedure if a right of pre-emption is given, must be followed exactly. The other members must exercise their right within the time allowed and take all and not merely a part of the shares offered (unless the articles otherwise provide). Both parties are bound by any **fair value** fixed as the price to be paid in accordance with the articles.

If a member ignores any such pre-emption rights, any other member can obtain an injunction preventing the transfer (remember the articles, by S14, are a contract binding the members to the members) and, moreover, the directors must, on behalf of the company, refuse to register a transfer in breach of pre-emption provisions - **Tett v Phoenix Property [1972].**

A right of pre-emption only becomes exercisable if the member wishes to transfer their shares. The articles may, however, give the directors or the company in general meeting a power to compel a member to transfer their shares. The power is valid if exercised (in accordance with the articles) in good faith for the benefit of the company.

2.8   Contracts for the sale of shares

There will often be an interval of time between the making of a contract for the sale of shares and the transfer of legal title by registration of the transferee in the register of members in place of the transferor.

Under normal principles of contract law the beneficial ownership of **identified** shares passes to the transferee as soon as the contract is made. Unless otherwise agreed (eg, a sale on an **ex div**. basis) the transferee is entitled to any dividend declared and to any rights issues, voting rights or other benefits incidental to the shares arising after the transfer of ownership. They are correspondingly liable eg, for any calls made on partly paid shares after the date of the contract. (Although the company will seek the payment from the transferor as long as their name remains on the register, the transferor will have the right to an indemnity from the transferee.)

The transferor holds the shares (after the contract) on trust for the transferee pending registration. He should not impede registration of the transfer but if the directors refuse to approve it he is still entitled to receive the price and he will continue to hold the shares in trust for the transferee. In a transfer on sale the transferor is entitled (unless otherwise agreed) to receive the price in exchange for the signed transfer and may withhold it until he is paid. He will vote the shares as he see fit until the price is paid and after payment as the transferee directs.

2.9   Transmission of shares

The personal representatives of a deceased member establish their legal position with the company by production of the **grant of probate** of the will or **letters of administration: S187 CA85.** They can then claim legal ownership of the shares with effect from the death. Subject to any restrictions of the articles they may:

(a)   apply by **letter of request** for their names to be entered in the register of members as holders of the shares with full rights of membership;

(b)   without becoming members **transfer the shares** by presenting an ordinary transfer signed by them as transferors: S183 CA85; and

(c)   without becoming members **receive dividends** and other payments relating to the shares.

Articles (eg, Article 30 Table A) may make the rights in (b) and (c) subject to the same restrictions (if any) as normal transfers of shares. As an inducement to personal representatives to register as members the directors may be given power to withhold dividends, etc, if the personal representatives decline the directors' request to become members. They are entitled to receive notices but have no right to attend and vote at meetings unless they become members or the articles expressly confer such a right without membership. The estate is liable for calls on the shares whether made before or after death; the personal representatives also become personally liable if they become members.

A beneficiary of the estate has only an equitable interest in the shares until they are transferred. They can protect their position by a **stop notice** like any other person entitled to an equitable interest.

2.10   Transfer of share warrants

Share warrants are freely transferable. They are negotiable instruments and may be transferred, free from equities, by delivery. They are not particularly common, however, although they may become more so since the UK's entry into the European Community, as they are popular with continental investors. Subject to the articles, the bearer is entitled, on surrendering the share warrant for cancellation, to have their name entered on the register of members.

2.11   Activity

Mary deposited her share certificate for 500 ordinary £1 shares in Ereweo plc with Alan her broker. Alan forged his own name on a form of transfer and registered himself as the owner of the shares. He then sold them to Paula and disappeared with the proceeds.

State the legal position of Mary and Alan.

2.12   Activity solution

Mary is not estopped from asserting her ownership of the shares. She does not contribute to the fraud by the act of depositing a share certificate with a broker. She can therefore insist upon the rectification of the register to show her as the true owner.

Paula will still be entitled to recover compensation from the company which has wrongly issued the share certificate to Alan on the strength of the forgery. Had Alan forged the transfer into Paula's name, she would have been unable to claim against the company although she would have had an action against Alan.

3   MORTGAGE OF SHARES

Shares may be mortgaged in one or other of two ways as security for a loan.

On a **legal mortgage** the borrower transfers their shares to the lender who is registered as the new shareholder. Under the loan agreement the borrower is entitled to have his shares transferred back to him when the loan is repaid.

A legal mortgage gives the lender maximum security against evasion since they have the legal title. He would not generally accept partly paid shares in this way as he would be liable on them for calls made by the company. The risk remains that the shares may fall in value and cease to be adequate security. The directors of the company may be able to prevent such a form of security being given by refusing to approve the transfer to the lender.

As an alternative the lender may take an **equitable mortgage** of the shares. The share certificate is deposited with the lender and sometimes also a blank transfer. In contrast with the legal mortgage the lender does not become owner of the shares. The lender may also take a power of attorney in their favour authorising him to complete the transfer. The additional risk in an equitable mortgage is that a dishonest borrower may persuade the company to give them a duplicate certificate or persuade a purchaser to accept a transfer without their certificate. The lender can, be protected by the service of a stop notice.

A judgement creditor may apply to the court for a **charging order** in respect of shares owned by the debtor whether registered in the name of the debtor or his trustee (unless there are other beneficiaries). After six months from the making of the charging order the creditor may apply to the court for an order to sell the shares.

Except in certain circumstances a charge created by a public company over its own shares is void: S150 CA85.

4   MINORITY PROTECTION

4.1   Introduction

The control of the company rests with the members acting through votes at general meetings or the directors to the extent that the powers to manage have been delegated to them. However, the members will have such control over the directors as are set out in the articles and provided by statute, in particular the right to remove directors or alter the articles to remove the directors' powers.

The members decisions are, usually, by simple majority. Thus, an individual member, or a group of members with a small percentage shareholding may be bound by decisions with which they disagree. In particular in smaller companies the directors may also be the majority shareholders and thus the minority shareholders have virtually no control over the company's activities.

However, there are certain situations where minority shareholders may be able to influence the companies activities.

These circumstances can be divided into:

(a)   Statutory protection given to the minority on various aspects of the general conduct of the company meetings.

(b)   Statutory provisions allowing institution of court proceedings - specific statutory minority protection.

(c)   Common law rules governing the institution of court proceedings in matters relating to the conduct of companies affairs: exceptions to the rule in **Foss v Harbottle**.

(d)   The right of a member to petition the court if he proves the company's affairs are being conducted in a manner unfairly prejudicial to him - S459 CA85.

(e)   The right to petition (which means to formally apply to) the court to have the company wound up on the ground that it is just and equitable in the circumstances - just and equitable winding up - S122(g) IA 1986.

(f)   Administrative protection through DTI investigations.

4.2   Conduct of company meetings

There are certain statutory provisions to protect the minority.

(a)   Some changes of the company's constitution or affairs are considered sufficiently major that they require a 75% majority of votes cast. Thus, the holders of just over 25% of the voting shares have a veto in these cases. The important examples are to:

      (i)   alter the objects S4 CA85;
      (ii)   alter the articles S9 CA85;
      (iii)   alter the name S28 CA85; and
      (iv)   reduce the capital S135 CA85.

(b)   There are some things which the company cannot do unless each member's consent is obtained:

      (i)   It cannot increase a member's liability unless he agrees in writing: S16 CA85.

      (ii)   It cannot re-register as an unlimited company unless all members agree: S49 CA85.

(c)   Certain provisions give members the power to call meetings or require information to be circulated to members. These are important because the directors who have power to manage, have a degree of control, partly just through the fact that they will be the ones who usually call the general meetings, set out the agenda and circulate the information to members. The powers are:

      (i)   Require directors to call EGM (if 10% of paid-up voting capital): S368 CA85;

      (ii)   Require a resolution to be put to AGM (if 5% voting rights or 100 members): S376 CA85; and

      (iii)   Require a statement to be circulated (if 5% voting rights or 100 members): S376 CA85

The practical difficulty which confronts a shareholder of a large company is how to contact and cooperate with other dissatisfied members and also the expense of such action. By contrast the directors representing the majority have the records, resources and organisation of the company under their control.

4.3   Institution of court proceedings - specific statutory minority protection

Certain provisions give members a right to object to the court even though a resolution has been passed with the requisite majority. Thus:

(a)   Members having 15% of voting shares and who did not vote in favour of the resolution can apply to the court to set aside an alteration of objects: S4 CA85, or class rights: S127 CA85. Where additional clauses are entrenched in the memorandum there is a right of appeal to the court if they are at all alterable: S17 CA85;

(b)   Members holding 10% of the issued share capital can apply to the court where a private company gives financial assistance for the purchase of its own shares: S157 CA85.

(c)   Members holding 5% of voting shares can apply to the court to set aside a resolution for re-registering a public company as a private company, but no person can apply who consented or voted in favour of the resolution: S54 CA85.

(d) Any member may apply to the court to object to a private company making a permissible capital payment: S176 CA85, or to injunct an ultra vires transaction: S35 CA85.

4.4 Institution of court proceedings - the rule in Foss v Harbottle

A breach of duty owed to the company may arise from statute, contract, tort or the fiduciary position of the party in breach. The duty may be owed by a third party, a director or other servant, or even perhaps by a member (eg, in the unlikely case of his having to pay calls on shares not fully paid up). Since the duty breached is one owed to the company, which is a separate person in law, the company is the proper person to seek a remedy for the breach. Further, where the majority of members may ratify or excuse a breach, given that the will resides in the decisions of the majority, it would be futile (in the absence of fraud or other inequitable conduct) for the minority to litigate against the wishes of the majority. There is much to be said for the view that any action taken by the company must be taken via the methods provided by its constitutional structure and in that way only.

Foss v Harbottle [1843]

Facts: individual shareholders brought action against directors alleged to have misapplied company property.

Held: the company, as the victim of the alleged misdeeds, was the proper plaintiff to complain.

The company will act through whichever of its organs has the authority to act in such situations. Usually the articles will have devolved this power on the board of directors. If so, the majority in general meeting cannot generally restrain or compel directors in the exercise of their powers of litigation - **Shaw v John Shaw [1935]**.

The rule, therefore, prevents each and every shareholder from taking whatever form of action they wish, whenever they wish to complain of an alleged wrong by directors, servants or third parties, in situations where the company itself, either by decision of the board or a resolution of the general meeting, can decide whether or not to take action.

The rule in **Foss v Harbottle** has two principles:

(a) To redress a wrong done to a company or to recover money or damages alleged to be due to the company, the action should prima facie be brought by the company itself. The company is, in law, a separate person from its members; where a wrong is done to the company the company alone should vindicate its own rights. The company is the only proper plaintiff.

(b) If the thing complained of is a thing which in substance the majority of the company are entitled to do . . . there can be no use in having litigation about it, the ultimate end of which is only that a meeting has to be called and then ultimately the majority gets its wishes. Where the majority does not wish the company to sue, the court will not generally permit the minority to sue on its behalf nor interfere in the internal management of the company.

It is thought that these principles represent different aspects of the majority rule in company law ie, if the majority can do something the minority cannot interfere.

These principles can, however, produce an unfair or unsatisfactory result. There is some uncertainty under proposition (b) as to how far a majority should be permitted to authorise an irregularity which infringes the company's constitution.

Is the individual shareholder to be deprived by the company of insisting on his right to have its affairs conducted in accordance with the regulations? Can the company act capriciously in disregard of the interests of all but the majority shareholders? Can the directors, by decisions in board meetings and by their ability to control decisions of the general meetings (see above), treat the company as their own and act as they wish, taking account only of their own interests?

Before exploring the exceptions to the rule it is necessary to look at how court actions are instituted.

4.5   Types of court action - procedure

(a)   The personal action

This is an action by a member to enforce their own personal rights against the company and the wrongdoers, for example, where there has been a breach of the articles.

(b)   The representative action

Where a number of members have the right to bring personal action one may (but need not) sue in a representative action on behalf of himself and the members or class of members. The courts are reluctant to allow a representative action. However, it can be brought by a plaintiff shareholder on behalf of shareholders if:

(i)   All the members on whose behalf the action is brought have a separate cause of action.

(ii)   The relief claimed would not confer a right of action where none previously existed.

(iii)   An 'interest' was shared by all members of the class complaining.

(iv)   It was for the benefit of the class to permit the plaintiff to sue in a representative capacity.

(c)   The derivative action

This is an action brought by a member (or members) on behalf of the company. This is unusual as the members' right to sue derives from a wrong done to another legal person (the company). It has been described as a procedural device to enable the courts to give relief where a company is controlled by 'miscreant directors or shareholders'.

As the action is based on the company's rights any property or damages recovered will belong to the company and not the members who instituted the action. Similarly, any costs awarded against the loser will not include the member's costs, only the company's costs. However, the company may be ordered to indemnify the member if he can show that he acted in good faith and it was an action that a reasonable board would have brought.

A member could combine a personal and a derivative action or a representative and a derivative action.

4.6   The powers of the majority

The ordinary member's right to participate in the running of the company finds expression in their ability to take part in the discussion and voting in the general meeting. Resolutions passed in general meeting are, therefore, the practical result of the collective will of the various members - the majority decision displays the fact that more of the individual members, whatever their many and varied motives may be, have wanted one decision rather than another.

If all this is true, it is quite justifiable for the individual shareholders to exercise their votes in whichever way they wish, and to take their chance on whether the majority of the other voters agree with them or not. Their vote has been regarded, like their share, as their personal property which they can use as they wish, even if their action as a shareholder runs contrary to the path they must pursue in some other capacity eg, as a director (it being a separate issue whether or not he is in breach of any duties as a director and, if so, what are the effects of the breach).

Northern Counties Securities Ltd v Jackson and Steeple Ltd [1974]

Facts: a director had complied with an obligation to call a general meeting and to advise the members to vote for a resolution which had to be passed if the company were not to be in contempt of court. In his capacity as shareholder voted against it.

Held: the director was entitled to vote in this way. A similar decision was reached in **North-West Transportation v Beatty [1887]**.

However, if a shareholder owes no duties to the company (which is, of course, partly their property), does it follow that they owe no duties to their fellow members? Or, and this is a different point, does it follow that there are no restrictions on the manner in which they may exercise his vote? Certainly, there are a number of specific instances in which majority decisions have been regarded as intolerable because of their effect on certain shareholders.

Definition   Accordingly, the exceptions to the rule in **Foss v Harbottle** may be summarised as a right of individual shareholders to raise objection:

(a)   Where the individual rights of a member are infringed.

(b)   Where action is taken in disregard of the company's articles or by some other irregularity such as convening a general meeting by an inadequate notice. The extent of this exception is doubtful.

(c)   Where the approval of the majority is given to an *ultra vires* or illegal transaction. This has been modified by S35 CA85 (as amended by CA89). An *ultra vires* act can now be ratified by a special resolution.

(d)   Where the transaction is a fraud on the company by those who control it; which includes, possibly, where the power of the majority is exercised in an unjust manner and not *bona fide* in the interests of the company as a whole. This exception is commonly called 'fraud on the minority'.

4.7   Infringement of a member's personal rights

The articles may give to each member personal rights which they can use almost as a form of property eg, their right to cast the votes attached to their shares. A member is generally entitled to enforce these rights *against* the company as personal rights (rather than on the company's behalf to protect its constitution). In **Pender v Lushington [1887]** the court enjoined the directors from acting on the basis of a resolution not having been carried because votes attached to the plaintiff's nominee shareholding were improperly rejected. The plaintiff sued in a representative capacity but it was held that he could sue personally in respect of his individual right to have his vote recorded.

4.8   Irregularity in conduct of a company's business

It has been argued that every member has, by virtue of the rights and obligations binding the company and the members recognised by S14, a right to have the affairs of the company conducted in accordance with the regulations by which he has agreed to be bound. However, the individual member's right to participate is subject to the rules in the company's regulations as to how the company is to be run and to the general rules of company law. So, even where there is a potential irregularity of which they can feel justifiably aggrieved, they may be unable to take any action if it is something which could have or would be condoned or ratified by the general meeting. Taken a step further this means that the court may restrain action on the part of shareholders to give the general meeting the opportunity of condoning the irregularity. In **Hogg v Cramphorn Ltd [1987]**, the minority shareholder maintained a representative action in respect of a defensive issue of shares; but the case was adjourned to give the company the opportunity to ratify the issue.

However, situations where successful action have been brought include:

Edwards v Halliwell [1950]

Facts: a trade union had increased its rate of subscription without altering its rules.

Held: the challenge was upheld. The proper procedure for altering the rules should be followed. (The decision was based on company law).

4.9   Fraud on the minority by controlling majority

This is the most difficult area to produce comprehensive principles established in different cases. It can be pleaded even if there is no infringement of a personal right, no irregularity in the conduct of the business and the transaction in question is *intra vires* the company.

If the majority have defrauded, or plan to defraud, the company of its property, any resolution passed to approve their action (by use of their votes) is invalid: **Cook v Deeks [1916]**. This exception to the general principle of majority control is necessary to protect the company - and indirectly its minority shareholders - against a fraudulent majority.

To bring this exception into operation there must be:

(a)   misappropriation of the company's property; and

(b)   control of the company by those who misappropriate it.

Condition (a) was satisfied in the case cited above. **Mere negligence** of a controlling shareholder in disposing of the company's property to a third party is not enough. However, if the facts have not yet been fully established and the directors' negligence has yielded a profit at the company's expense to one of themselves, the court will allow the action to proceed so that the full facts may be elicited.

Daniels v Daniels [1977]

Facts: the plaintiffs, minority shareholders in a company, brought an action against two directors and the company. They alleged that the company, on the instructions of the directors, who were also majority shareholders, sold the company's land to one of the directors (who was the wife of the other) for £4,250 and that the directors knew, or ought to have known, that was an undervalue. Four years later the land was sold for £120,000. The directors claimed that there was no reasonable cause of action.

Held: the exception to the rule in **Foss v Harbottle**, enabling a minority shareholder to bring an action against a company for fraud where no other remedy was available, should include cases where, although there was no fraud alleged, there was a breach of duty by the directors and majority shareholders to the detriment of the company and the benefit of the directors. Accordingly, the minority had a cause of action.

Condition (a) is not satisfied, however, unless the property or benefit in question was or at least could have been acquired by the company: **Regal (Hastings) v Gulliver [1967]**.

In **Prudential Assurance v Newman Industries [1982]** the court held day to day management control was sufficient control to satisfy (b).

Prudential Assurance v Newman Industries [1982]

Facts: Newman agreed to take over the assets of TPG Co. and the liabilities of £1,117,000 for £325,000. Two of the directors of Newman held, through a wholly-owned company, 35% of the issued share capital of TPG Co. Newman issued a circular to the shareholders explaining the proposed transaction and the majority of shareholders in Newman approved the transaction by passing a resolution. The Prudential, the plaintiff, a minority shareholder, voted against the resolution. Prudential then brought an action claiming, *inter alia*, damages for conspiracy against the directors, alleging that the circular was tricky, misleading and contained statements which the defendants could not honestly have believed and alleged further misconduct on the part of the directors. The action brought was framed as a derivative action by the plaintiff against the directors for damages on behalf of Newman; the plaintiff combined a personal action claiming damages. Later this personal action was amended to a representative action on behalf of all the shareholders in Newman.

Held: jurisdiction to entertain a representative cause of action by a plaintiff suing on behalf of all the members.

Where there is no actual fraud ie, misappropriation to themselves of the company's property, the majority may use their votes to approve a transaction beneficial to themselves: **Regal (Hastings) Case [1967]**. They may also approve mere negligence on the part of the directors or the exercise by the directors of their powers for an irregular but not dishonest purpose: **Bamford v Bamford [1970]**.

It has recently been held that if the majority exercise their rights merely to discriminate against the minority, this can be challenged in the courts and set aside.

Clemens v Clemens [1976]

Facts: the plaintiff owned 45% of the issued share capital of the defendant company and her aunt held the remaining 55%. The aunt, who was a director of the company, and her fellow directors proposed to increase the share capital by the creation and issue of further shares; 200 to the aunt and 850 to be held on trust for the benefit of employees. Resolutions were passed adopting these proposals notwithstanding the plaintiff's objection. The new share issue meant that the plaintiff's 45% holding would be reduced to marginally less than 25%. She sought a declaration that the resolutions were oppressive and asked the court to set them aside.

Held: the resolutions were specifically and carefully designed to ensure not only that the plaintiff could never get control of the company but to deprive her of what has been called her 'negative control' - the power to prevent the passing of a special resolution. The resolutions were accordingly set aside.

4.10   S459 CA85 - Relief from unfair prejudice

Any member of the company who complains that the affairs of the company are being conducted in a manner **unfairly prejudicial** to the interests of some or all of the members (including at least themselves) may petition for an order under S459.

(a)   **Who may petition?**

Any single member may sue, notwithstanding the rule in **Foss v Harbottle**. It appears that it must be the petitioner who is being unfairly prejudiced; it would no doubt be insufficient to plead that some other of the members are being unfairly prejudiced.

S459(2) CA85 provides that the provisions apply to a person who is not on the register as a member of a company but to whom shares in the company have been transferred or transferred by operation of law (eg, to the personal representatives of a deceased member).

However, by its express terms, S459 is limited to members, and so would not justify a petition by a debentureholder, or other creditor or third party.

If, after an inspector's report or the production of documents, it appears to the **Department of Trade** that the company's affairs are being conducted in a manner unfairly prejudicial to any part of its members, the Department may (either as well as, or instead of, petitioning for a winding up) petition for an order under S459: S460(1).

It has been held that there is no requirement that the petitioner comes to court with 'clean hands' ie, they acted fairly themselves. Such a requirement probably does exist where a petition is presented to wind up the company under the just and equitable ground in S122(g) Insolvency Act 1986. It does, however, appear that the petitioner's conduct for the purposes of S459 may be material in one of two ways:

(i)   it might render the other side's conduct, even if prejudicial, not unfair; and
(ii)   it might affect the relief which the court might think fit to grant.

(b)   **What is 'unfairly prejudicial'?**

Although *prima facie*, any member may petition, they will probably not obtain relief if they are not being unfairly prejudiced as a **member.**

Re A Company [1983]

Facts: an application was made under S459 by executors who wished to sell shares to provide maintenance for a deceased's children.

Held: the application was refused. A shareholder's right to bring an action under *S459* was held to be confined to acts or omissions which unfairly prejudiced him as member of the company, not as executor.

However, in **Re Bird Precision Bellows [1984]** the exclusion from the management of a company that was a quasi partnership was the successful basis of a petition under S459 on the argument that in such a company it is an expectation of a member to participate in management.

The unfair prejudice does not have to be caused by a majority; it is quite possible for a minority to cause the unfair prejudice (eg, through a voting agreement, or control of the proxy voting machinery).

CA89 amends the wording to read 'unfairly prejudicial to the interests of its members generally or some part of its members'. The words added by this amendment are 'of its members generally'. This presumably makes it clear that an application can now be made even though the conduct affects all members and not just part of the membership.

Re a Company (No 00370 of 1987) [1988]

Facts: a family company was successful and clearly solvent at all material times (at the date of court hearing £12m on P & L). Between 1975 and 1988 no dividends had been paid and a 31½% shareholder presented an unfair prejudice petition under S459 CA85.

Held the petition failed. Prior to the amendment in 1989, S459 required unfair prejudice to some **part** of the members: non-payment of dividends had an equal effect on all members and was not discriminatory between members. It is likely nowadays that a petition could be presented on this ground. Whether the petition would succeed would depend on the court's view of 'unfairness'.

The courts give a very broad interpretation to the meaning of 'unfair' and 'interests' of members. Unfair extends beyond legal wrongs and 'interests' extends beyond shareholder rights to such things as expectations.

The cases are varied and the court looks at all the circumstances.

Scottish CWS v Meyer [1959] HL

Facts: CWS was majority shareholder in a subsidiary company and through its nominees controlled the board. It was in the business interests of CWS to run down the business of the subsidiary and this they did by withholding supplies from it. Mr Meyer's shares in the subsidiary, which at one time were worth £6, were now virtually worthless.

Held: his petition succeeded.

Remedy: CWS to purchase his shares at a fair value (which the court set at £3.15s).

Re London School of Electronics [1986]

Facts: X and CTC were shareholders and directors in LSE, a company running a tutorial college. CTC diverted LSE's students to another company which it controlled and when X complained it removed X from the board. X then retaliated by setting up a company to which he diverted students.

Held: X's petition succeeded. Unlike S122(g) IA86 a petitioner is not barred from relief by the maxim 'He who comes to equity must come with clean hands'.

Remedy: Order that respondents purchase petitioner's shares.

Re Elgindata (No 1) [1991]

Facts: (i) numerous complaints of bad management, and (ii) MD used the company's assets for his personal benefit and for the benefit of his family and friends.

Held: petition granted on basis of (ii), but not (i): the court stating . . . 'although, in an appropriate case, serious mismanagement of a company's affairs would constitute unfairly prejudicial conduct, the court would normally be very reluctant to accept that managerial decisions can amount to unfairly prejudicial conduct. It is not for the court to resolve differences of commercial judgement. It is not unfair for a member of a company to suffer the consequences of poor management of the company: it is one of the risks of investing in a company that its management may turn out to be not of the highest quality. The petitioners had no right to expect a reasonable standard of general management from the managing director.'

Remedy: Order that respondents purchase petitioner's shares.

Re Cumana [1986]

Facts: oral agreement between the two shareholders that they would share the profits of their business ventures $\frac{2}{3} : \frac{1}{3}$. The one who was to get $\frac{2}{3}$ devised various schemes to cut the other out of his $\frac{1}{3}$ viz (i) he diverted the company's business to another controlled by himself, (ii) he caused the company to make a large rights issue which he knew the other could not afford to take up, (iii) he caused the company to pay him an excessive bonus and to make excessive contributions to his pension funds.

Held: all three complaints amounted to unfair prejudice.

Remedy: Order that respondents purchase petitioner's shares.

(*Note:* there was also an interim injunction to prevent the rights issue.)

Re Bird Precision Bellows [1984]

Facts: X owned 26% of the shares in a quasi-partnership company and he was removed from his directorship by the majority.

Held: his petition succeeded.

Remedy: Order for purchase of his shares by the majority at a fair value (here the court fixed this on a pro-rata basis without any discount to reflect the fact that the shares constituted a majority holding).

Re Blue Arrow plc [1967]

Facts: petition presented on the basis that the company had failed to alter its Articles so as to enable the petitioner to remain in office.

Held: petition dismissed. Unlike the position in small private companies (where to deprive a person of his participation in management contrary to a mutual understanding can sustain a petition - **Re a company (No 00477 of 1986)**): investors in public listed companies are entitled to expect that the whole of the way in which the company is to be run is contained in the publicly available documents such as the Articles and that the company is not subject to undisclosed expectations, agreements or understandings.

Re R A Noble [1983]

Facts: B and N set up a business on the basis that B put up the capital and N ran it on the understanding that N would consult B on major matters. B petitioned on the basis that he was not informed of or adequately consulted on important matters.

Held: the petition was dismissed. The evidence showed that the situation arose largely because of B's lack of interest (he had confined himself to vague questions at social occasions).

Re a company, ex parte Kremer [1989]

Facts: breakdown in the relationship between the members of a small private company because the petitioner (one of the member-directors) had, due to old age, lost his business acumen. The articles gave power to force the transfer of shares in such circumstances.

Held: the petition of the expelled member was dismissed.

Re H R Harmer [1959]

Facts: H (aged 77) and his wife controlled 78.6% of the voting capital (but only about 10% of the share capital). H took the view he was entitled to disregard board decisions because he controlled so many voting shares. He disregarded board decisions (amongst other things causing the company to embark on a disastrous Australian venture) and acted foolishly (amongst other things engaging a private detective to watch the staff).

Held: the petition of his two sons (the directors and other shareholders) succeeded.

Remedy: court altered articles to appoint H president for life (an office carrying no rights or duties) and further ordered him not to interfere in management decisions.

(c)   **Powers of the court**

The court has a free hand in making such order as it thinks fit for giving relief in respect of the matters complained of once it is satisfied that a petition under the section is well founded S461 CA85. Specific examples of possible orders are given in S461 without prejudice to the generality of the provision. The specific examples are that the court may:

(i)   Regulate the conduct of the company's affairs in the future.

(ii)   Require the company to refrain from doing or continuing an act complained of by the petitioner, or to do an act which the petitioner has complained it has omitted to do.

(iii)   Authorise civil proceedings to be brought in the name and on behalf of the company by such person or persons and on such terms as the court may direct.

(iv)   Provide for the purchase of the shares of any members of the company by the other members or by the company itself and in the case of a purchase by the company itself, the reduction of the company's capital accordingly. The problem here is that where a minority is disposing of its shares the price is usually discounted to take account of the fact that the vendor does not have control. On occasion it may be that the court orders that the respondents purchase the shares from the petitioner. This is rare but it occurred for example in:

Re Nuneaton Borough Association Football Club [1991]

Facts: the petitioner was 'allotted' 24,000 shares in the company at a time when its authorised capital was only 2,000 (and 1,700 had earlier been allotted to the respondent). The petition was on the basis that he had bought something which did not exist.

Held: his petition succeeded.

Remedy: the court ordered that he buy out the respondent's shares (who was, of course, the majority shareholder). The fair value was the open market of a controlling holding. The court also ordered the repayment of substantial loans to the respondent.

In **Re Bird Precision Bellows Ltd** Nourse J considered that it was erroneous to assume that a minority shareholder in a quasi partnership company was selling freely. If the sale was not from a willing vendor the shares should be valued on a pro rata basis with no element of discount.

On the other hand if the holding has simply been acquired as a minority holding with no participation in management rights or if the minority has been blameworthy to some extent then the holding will be discounted as a minority shareholding.

Re a company, ex parte Harries [1989]

Remedy: on making an order for the purchase of the petitioner's shares the value was discounted to reflect the fact that the shares were a minority holding. Unlike **Re Bird Precision Bellows** where the petitioner had come into the business from the beginning with 26% capital, here the petitioner had come into the business by buying a minority holding (on that basis) from an existing member.

The other controversial feature of valuation is the date when the valuation is to be made. There is no fixed rule on this matter. The date of valuation may be the date of the purchase order but it could also be the date when the unfairly prejudicial conduct began. Another possibility is a valuation of the shares at the date the petition is presented as in **Re London School of Electronics** and **Re Cumana Ltd.**

The court has accepted that compensation should take account not merely of matters such as prospective dividends and the financial value of the shares but also, in some circumstances, of other matters such as prestige. This was discussed in **Re Nuneaton Borough AFC Ltd** where it was stated that prestige is a relevant factor in valuing football club shares.

Where the court makes an order requiring alterations to a company's memorandum and articles of association, the company then does not have the power without leave of the court to make any alteration in breach of the order.

4.11   'Just and equitable' winding up

It may be that the person complaining of the behaviour of the majority wishes to get their capital out of the company to invest elsewhere or start in business on their own or with other persons. An application under S459 CA85 may result in an order that their shares be purchased. Alternatively, they may apply for the company to be wound up completely and their capital returned to them. In this case they would apply to the court under S122(g) Insolvency Act 1986 that the company be wound up. The justice and equity depend on all the circumstances of the case; considerations that may incline the court to wind up include: changes in personal relationship which have rendered the operation of a small company unfair to the petitioner.

Ebrahimi v Westbourne Galleries [1973]

Facts: the company carried on business as dealers in Persian carpets. It was formed in 1958 to take over a business founded by Nazar. From 1945, however, the business had been carried on in partnership with Ebrahimi, sharing the management and profits equally. When the company was formed Nazar and Ebrahimi were the only shareholders and directors, holding 500 £1 shares each. Soon Nazar's son, George, was made a director and Nazar and Ebrahimi each transferred 100 shares to him. Soon there were disputes and Nazar and George passed an ordinary resolution in general meeting removing Ebrahimi from office. Ebrahimi petitioned for a winding-up order on the **just and equitable** ground: S122(g) IA 1986.

Held: the company would be wound up on the just and equitable ground. The company was founded on the basis that the character of the association would remain ie, a matter of personal relation and good faith. This had failed and thus by analogy to partnership law the court would order a winding-up.

Other examples are:

(a)   that the **substratum** of the company has gone ie, that the principal object or objects of the company cannot ever or can no longer be achieved.

Re German Date Coffee Co [1882]

Facts: the memorandum of the company stated that its object was the working of a German patent to manufacture coffee from dates. It was also empowered to acquire or produce any other inventions for similar purposes and to import and export all descriptions of produce for the purpose of food. The company failed to acquire the German patent but acquired a Swedish one and established works in Hamburg where it manufactured coffee from dates without a patent. Some shareholders withdrew from the company when they discovered that a German patent would not be obtained. The large majority wished the company to continue but two shareholders petitioned the court for a winding up order on the basis that as the main object for which the company had been formed was impossible to carry out, it was just and equitable to wind the company up.

Held: the whole substratum of the company was gone, the business was to make coffee from dates using a German patent in Germany and not to enter into business generally; the shareholders were entitled to say that they did not enter into the company on these terms, and so the company ought to be wound up.

It is necessary that all the main objects and not merely some of them should now be unattainable.

Re Kitson [1946]

Facts: a company was formed with the objects to purchase a particular engineering business and carry on the business of general engineering. The company did not acquire the business. Certain shareholders petitioned to have the company wound up.

Held: the substratum had not failed as the company also had as an object the carrying on of a general engineering business.

(b)   that a state of **deadlock** exists in the management of the company: **Re Yenidje Tobacco Co [1916]**. This situation is most likely to occur when the company has a small number of directors who are also the majority shareholders;

(c)   where the company is like a small partnership based on mutual trust and confidence and that trust and confidence is broken, the court might consider it just and equitable to wind the company up: **Ebrahimi's Case**;

(d)   if the company was formed for some fraudulent purpose;

(e)   the situation in **Loch v John Blackwood Ltd [1924]** where the directors failed to hold general meetings, recommend a dividend or lay and deliver accounts. The objective was to keep the shareholders in the dark in order to acquire their shares cheaply. There was a justifiable lack of confidence in the management and the court ordered the company to be wound up.

Re Lundie Brothers Ltd [1965]

Facts: the directors used their power for their own interests and not for the interests of the company. The petitioner was ousted as chairman of the printing company and his employment as a working director was terminated. Instructions were given to the bank for cheques signed by any two directors to be honoured thus rendering the petitioner's signature unnecessary. Lundie Brothers Ltd acquired another business, Stanwell & Co Ltd but the petitioner was excluded from management of this company.

Held: his petition was successful. It was based on the sharp practice of the other directors and the breakdown of trust and confidence.

(f)   If the company is a trading company and is incapable of making a profit a winding up order may be made, but it is not sufficient to show that it has merely not made a profit. In **Re Suburban Hotel Co [1867]**, the court refused a winding up order as most members wished to continue the business of running the Hampstead Heath Hotel although the company was trading at a loss.

There are legal problems with S122(g) IA86 which are not the case with S459 CA85.

(a)   under S122(g) IA86 'He who comes to equity must come with clean hands;

(b)   case law shows that a petitioner must have an interest in the winding up of the company eg, it is most likely that there will be surplus assets.

(c)   By S124 IA86 a contributory shall not be entitled to present a petition unless the shares in respect of which he is a contributory or some of them were

   •   originally allotted to him; or

   •   have been held by him and registered in his name for at least six months during the eighteen months before the commencement of the winding up; or

   •   have devolved upon him through the death of a former holder.

(d)   S125 IA 86 gives the court a discretion to refuse winding-up on the ground that the petitioner acted unreasonably in not pursuing an alternative remedy.

Re A Company [1983]

Facts: the petitioner had refused an improved offer to buy his shares, even though the facts of the case came within the above.

Held: winding up was refused and the court ordered that his shares be valued for purchase.

There are also non-legal considerations such as the fact that it might be financially disadvantagous to the petitioner to have the company wound up. For all these reasons the petitioner may prefer S459 CA89 as an alternative to S122(g) IA86.

Conclusion   Minority shareholders are protected by court action as follows:

   •   Statute provides some specific protection eg:

      -      S5 CA85:   objecting to an alteration in articles; and
      -      S127 CA85: objecting to a variation of class rights.

- Equity can intervene to prevent a majority of members ratifying a fraudulent act as it did in the case of **Clemens v Clemens** (this is rare, and intervention happens only very infrequently).

- An exception to the Rule in **Foss v Harbottle**. This will often be a derivative action (ie, one taken on behalf of the company). The usual route for this action will be where there has been a fraud on the minority. This is where the directors have acted fraudulently and they, also being majority members, benefit as a result.

- S459 CA85 where a member has been unfairly prejudiced by the actions of the company he can petition the court for an order to be made relieving this unfair prejudice. The court has a complete discretion to make any order that it sees fit.

- S122(g) IA86: a member can petition the court for the company to be wound up on the basis that it is just and equitable to do so. This is a final and extreme remedy and the court will not grant it unless nothing else is available.

5 DEPARTMENT OF TRADE AND INDUSTRY INSPECTIONS AND INVESTIGATIONS

5.1 The need for inspections and investigations

There are situations in which it might be said that the remedies available to a minority shareholder are insufficient to enable him to obtain adequate redress in a given situation. In such cases it is arguable that his position should be strengthened by intervention by some public body. In response, it could be said that the securities industry provides to some extent its own forms of redress under powers vested in the Stock Exchange and the Council for the Securities Industry, the supervisory body in which the major organisations active in the securities industry (eg, the Bank of England, the Confederation of British Industry, the Issuing Houses Association and the Council of the Stock Exchange) participate together with lay members to represent the individual investor and the wider public interest. The self-regulatory rules of the securities industry may be stricter, and possibly more effective, than legal rules. Of course, the industry is obliged to make them so, to avoid the need for intervention by the legislature. But self-regulatory rules are not legally binding and there is easily room for argument that they should be at least under-pinned by minimal legal powers for intervention by a publicly accountable body, whether in order to control the controllers of a company or to protect the public interest (not that the two purposes are necessarily independent of each other). This is achieved to some extent by the powers given to the Department of Trade and Industry where serious irregularities are suspected.

The exercise of these powers can have various effects. The mere fact of their existence, the threat of using them or the actual use of them may deter the company from undesirable conduct. More positively, their use may result in desirable conduct, namely the provision to the members of information about the company's affairs, which may be a useful end in itself or an essential basis for proceedings either by the member or the Department itself.

5.2 Production of documents

The Department of Trade and Industry has a number of powers one of which is the production of documents. If it thinks there is good reason so to do, the Department of Trade and Industry may give directions to a company requiring it to produce, at such time and place as may be specified, or may authorise an officer or the Department to require the company to produce to him any documents which he may specify: S447. The power extends over a person in possession of such documents (S447(4)) and is underlined by powers under a search warrant issued by a justice of the peace to enter and search premises: S448. Non-compliance and destruction, mutilation and falsification of documents are punishable by fine and or imprisonment: S450.

Documents must also be produced in an investigation under Ss431-433 (below).

5.3   Inspection and investigation

In certain situations, the Department of Trade and Industry can appoint an inspector to investigate and report on the affairs of a company, its ownership and its directors' share dealings.

The Department may begin its enquiries by calling for the production by the company of relevant documents under S447 CA85 (above). If it concludes that a full-scale investigation is necessary the Department appoints an **inspector**. By custom two joint inspectors are appointed in each case - one is usually a barrister and the other a chartered accountant. For convenience reference will be made to the **inspector**. The decision of the Department of Trade and Industry to appoint an inspector is final and unchallengeable so long as exercised *bona fide*.

Such investigations may be made into any of three aspects of a company's affairs:

(a)   the **affairs** of the company ie, the manner in which they have been conducted;

(b)   the **ownership** of its shares; and

(c)   **dealings** in its shares.

5.4   Investigation of the affairs of a company

In certain cases the Department of Trade and Industry **must** and in other cases it **may**, if it sees fit, investigate the affairs of a company. The rules are:

(a)   an investigation **must** be held if the court orders: S432 CA85;

(b)   an investigation **may** be held if the Department sees fit:

•   on the application of the company, 200 shareholders or holders of one tenth of the share capital or on the application of one fifth of the members if there is no share capital (eg, a guarantee company). In any such case the applicants must produce evidence in support of their application: S431 CA85;

•   if the Department considers that:

(1)   the affairs of the company have been conducted with intent to defraud its creditors or in a manner unfairly prejudicial to some part of its members or for an unlawful or fraudulent purpose;

(2)   that the promoters or managers have been guilty of fraud or misconduct; or

(3)   that proper information has not been given to its members: S432 CA85.

In practice the Department will only order an investigation if a very strong case is made out and in cases falling within (b)(i) above may require the applicant(s) to give security to an amount not exceeding £5,000 for payment of the costs of the investigation.

The inspector has extensive powers to:

(a)   require production of company documents;

(b)   question on oath officers and agents of the company or of any other company and to bring other persons before the court for questioning;

(c)   to investigate the affairs of related companies.

Ss434-436 CA85 extends these powers and provides that an inspector who considers that a person other than a director or officer is or may be in possession of information about its affairs, may require him to produce documents, attend before him and give all reasonable assistance with the investigation.   Answers given under these powers may be used in evidence against the person giving them. Affairs of subsidiaries and holding companies may also be investigated if necessary.

The inspector presents his findings in one or more reports to the Department. Where the inspector is appointed by the court a copy of the inspector's report must be forwarded to the court but in all other cases the Department has a discretion as to supplying a copy of the report: S437 CA85. The Secretary of State may also serve copies on the company or, on request and payment, on any member or person whose conduct is referred to in the report (auditors, applicants for investigation or other persons whose financial interests appear to be affected by the matters dealt with by the report). He **may** also have the report published.

On receiving the Report the Department of Trade and Industry may take any of the following actions which it considers appropriate:

(a)   refer the matter to the appropriate authority to bring criminal proceedings against any person believed to be guilty of offences;

(b)   institute civil proceedings on behalf of the company if it appears to be in the public interest to do so;

(c)   petition for winding up of the company on the **just and equitable** ground;

(d)   as an alternative to (c) the Secretary of State may petition for an order under S459 CA85 on the grounds of unfairly prejudicial conduct.

The expenses of an investigation are borne by the Department of Trade and Industry but it may, in appropriate cases, recover them from certain persons, including persons convicted on prosecutions instituted as a result of the investigation.

5.5   Investigation of ownership of a company

(a)   The Department of Trade and Industry **must** make an investigation of the ownership of shares of a company on the application of 200 shareholders or holders of 10% of the share capital or on the application of one fifth of the members if there is no share capital unless it considers that the application is vexatious (he may require security of up to £5,000); and

(b)   the Department **may** do so if it sees good reason: S442 CA85.

'The inspector has the same general powers as in an investigation of the affairs of the company, but he does not possess all the extended powers in Ss434-436 CA85. In this respect his powers do not go beyond persons financially interested in the company, or persons able to influence the policy of the company materially, or nominees of such persons, to any other person whom the inspector believes to have information relevant to the investigation. Further, any person (save in a case covered by professional privilege) having or being able to obtain information concerning the ownership of shares and debentures, must if required to do so give any such information to the Secretary of State. The court has power to impose restrictions on shares or debentures so as to enable the Department to ascertain the information required'.

5.6   Investigation of share dealings

Under S446 CA85 the Department of Trade and Industry may appoint inspectors to investigate if it appears that there has been an infringement of:

(a)   S323 CA85 - which prohibits directors, spouses and children dealing in options to buy or sell shares (if quoted) in their company; or

(b)   S324 CA85 - which requires directors, spouses and children to disclose to their companies their interest in the company's shares or debentures.

S177 Financial Services Act 1986 extends the powers of the Department of Trade and Industry to include investigation of circumstances which suggest contravention of the Criminal Justice Act 1993. The inspectors appointed to investigate have wide powers to require people to produce documents and give assistance. If any person refuses to comply with any request of the inspectors under S177 or to answer any of the inspector's questions the inspector may refer the matter to court. The court may then give direction to that person and punish him as though he had been guilty of contempt of court if it is satisfied the person refused to comply without reasonable excuse. In such a case the Department of Trade may disqualify the person from carrying on an in vestment business.

6   SHAREHOLDERS AGREEMENTS

It has become increasingly common for shareholders to enter into an agreement with other shareholders (or perhaps management, or others) as to how the company should be run. These agreements, which are outside the Memorandum and Articles, are enforceable by injunction and damages under the normal rules of contract law.

They are often used to agree how members should exercise their votes at general meetings in order to subvert the statutory right of a company to alter, for example, its articles. S9 CA85 specifies special resolution and this can be disadvantageous to a member with less than 25% of the voting rights. To get around the problem shareholders will often agree between themselves that they will not alter the articles unless everyone agrees. This device of the voting agreement is also used in relation to altering the memorandum (particularly the power to increase authorised capital by ordinary resolution - **Russell v Northern Bank [1992]**), and also to subvert the S303 power to remove a director from office by ordinary resolution.

Although such an agreement is valid and binding between the parties to it there are some limitations:

(a)   it is **personal** to those who are parties to the agreement and therefore if a member transfers his shares the new member is not subject to the agreement - **Greenhalgh v Mallard [1943]**. On similar principles the House of Lords in **Russell v Northern Bank [1992]** stated, obiter dicta, that a voting agreement contained in the company's articles drafted so as to be binding on all persons who were or might become shareholders would be invalid.

(b)   it is not valid so as to be binding on the **company** as this would be contrary to the company's unfettered statutory right to alter its Memorandum and Articles.

Russell v Northern Bank [1992] HL

Facts: a company was incorporated with five members, four of whom held 20 shares, the fifth holding 120 shares. A shareholders' agreement was made by the five members and the company (the fact that the company itself is party to the agreement is the novel feature of this case). Amongst other things the agreement provided that it had precedence between the shareholders over the articles of association and that 'no further share capital shall be created or issued in the company without the written consent of the parties to the agreement'. Some years later the board of the company gave notice to its shareholders of an ordinary resolution under S121 CA85 to increase the issued share capital to £4m and of an ordinary resolution to authorise the board to allot the new shares. Before the general meeting the plaintiff (one of the 5 members and who held 20 shares) sought an injunction against the defendants (the other 4 members) to restrain them from voting on the resolutions on the basis that if they did so this would breach the shareholders' agreement. The company was added as a defendant during the trial of the action. The defendants argued that the shareholders' agreement constituted an attempt to fetter the company's statutory power to increase its capital and was accordingly invalid and ineffective in law.

The House of Lords **held**:

- As far as the 5 shareholders were concerned the shareholders' agreement did not constitute an unlawful and invalid fetter on the company's statutory power to increase its capital but was merely a personal agreement outside the articles between the shareholders who executed it as to how they would exercise their voting rights in relation to the creation or issue of shares in the company and did not purport to bind future shareholders.

- As far as the company was concerned the agreement was unenforceable as being an unlawful and invalid fetter on its statutory power to increase its capital.

(c) an agreement whereby a **director** fetters his discretion at a **board** meeting would be contrary to his fiduciary duty to act in good faith for the benefit of the company.

[Conclusion] Voting agreements can be an effective way of providing protection for a minority under contract law rather than having to rely on the difficulties of company law protection.

7   SELF TEST QUESTIONS

7.1   Describe what is meant by 'class rights'. (1.2)

7.2   How are class rights varied where they are contained in the Articles of a company to which Table A otherwise applies? (1.3)

7.3   What is the difference between transfer and transmission of shares? (2.2)

7.4   When is the 'certificate lodged' procedure used for the transfer of shares? (2.3)

7.5   Who is the member of the company where there is an equitable mortgage of shares? (3)

7.6   What is the effect of the rule in **Foss v Harbottle**? (4.4)

7.7   What 2 matters must normally be shown in order for a shareholder to bring himself within the 'fraud on the minority' exception to the rule in **Foss v Harbottle**? (4.9)

7.8   Which section allows a member to petition for relief from unfair prejudice? (4.10)

7.9   What powers does the court have in relation to giving relief from unfair prejudice? (4.10)

7.10   List the restrictions on a petition by a member for just and equitable winding up. (4.11)

7.11   What percentage of members may apply to the DTI for an investigation of the company's affairs? (5.4)

7.12   Can the company be party to a voting agreement? (6)

8   EXAMINATION TYPE QUESTION

8.1   Z Ltd

The authorised issued and fully paid share capital of Z Ltd is £10,000 divided into 4,500 6% preference shares of £1 each all held by Smith and 5,500 ordinary shares of £1 each all held by Jones. Under the articles of association which follow the model of Table A:

(a)   each share of every class carries one vote;
(b)   a subdivision of shares may be effected by passing an ordinary resolution; and
(c)   dividend entitlement is in proportion to the amount paid up on each share.

Jones proposes at the next general meeting to pass a resolution to subdivide his £1 ordinary shares into 22,000 ordinary shares of 25p each. Smith considers that such a change would be prejudicial to him and that it amounts to a variation of his rights as holder of the preference shares.

How would it be prejudicial to Smith and can he prevent it?

(20 marks)

9   ANSWER TO EXAMINATION TYPE QUESTION

9.1   Z Ltd

As both classes of shares carry equal voting rights the present position is that Smith has 45% and Jones 55% of the votes. Jones cannot carry a special resolution against the opposition of Smith. If, however, Jones can multiply his votes fourfold by dividing his £1 shares into 25p shares, each carrying one vote, he will command a majority in excess of 75%. This would mean that Jones has the voting power to alter the articles as and when he wishes (S9 Companies Act 1985 (CA85)), a power which cannot be restricted. In this sense Jones' action would be prejudicial to Smith.

If the change proposed were a variation of the rights attached to the preference shares it would require Smith's consent under the express variation procedure since he holds all those shares.

However, Jones' scheme does not entail any **direct** change in the rights attached to the preference shares. Smith will have 4,500 votes as before even though there will be a smaller proportion of the total votes available. Such a change does not amount to a variation of the rights of the preference shares: **Greenhalgh v Arderne Cinemas** - where the facts were similar.

Jones' scheme might however be restrained by the court on a different ground ie, that it was an improper use of Jones' powers as controlling shareholder. In **Clemens v Clemens Bros. Ltd** the holder of the majority of ordinary shares proposed to issue additional ordinary shares to fellow directors who were likely to support her. The shareholding of the only other holder of ordinary shares would thereby be reduced to less than 25% of the increased issued capital. As this scheme was designed entirely to weaken the position of the minority shareholder and not for the benefit of the company the court forbade the majority shareholder to use her controlling voting power in this way.

Alternatively, Smith could claim that the affairs of the company are being conducted with an unfairly prejudicial manner: Ss459-461 CA85. It would appear that it is no bar to Smith's success that the proposed act by Jones is perfectly constitutional. If Smith were successful the court may make an order it thinks fit eg, it could order Jones to purchase Smith's shares at a fair market value.

A1 Saudi Banque v Clarke Pixley [1989]   197
Aberdeen Railway v Blaikie [1854]   502
Adams v Cape Industries [1990]   311
Adams v Lindsell [1818]   14
Alcock v Chief Constable of South
   Yorkshire [1991]   199
Alexander Ward & Co v Samyang
   Navigation Co [1975]   485
Allcard v Skinner [1887]   76
Allen v Gold Reefs of West Africa [1900]   395
Andrew Bros (Bournemouth) Ltd v Singer
   & Co Ltd [1934]   104
Andrews v Hopkinson [1957]   209
Arcos Ltd v EA Ronaasen [1933]   96
Armstrong v Jackson [1917]   162, 163
Ashbury Railway Carriage v Riche [1875]   362
Atlas Express v Kafco [1989]   74
Attwood v Small [1838]   58
Automatic Self-Cleansing Filter Syndicate
   Company Limited v Cunninghame [1906]   483
Aveling Barford Ltd v Perion Ltd [1989]   438
Avery v Bowden [1855]   125

Baker v Hopkins [1959]   185
Baker v James [1921]   184
Balfour v Balfour [1919]   37
Bamford v Bamford [1970]   410, 498, 561
Bannerman v White [1861]   84
Barclays v O'Brien [1993]   77
Barron v Potter (1914)   485
Beale v Taylor [1967]   95
Beard v London General Omnibus Co [1900]   180
Beattie v Beattie [1938]   393
Bell Houses Ltd v City Wall Properties Ltd [1966]368
Bell v Lever Bros [1932]   67
Belmont Finance Corporation v Williams
   Furniture Ltd (No. 2) [1979]   431
Belmont Finance v Williams Furniture [1967]   432
Beloff v Pressdam [1973]   233
Bentley-Stevens v Jones [1974]   481
Bernstein v Pamsons Motors [1987]   93
Beswick v Beswick [1968]   147
Bettini v Gye [1876]   90, 124
Bisset v Wilkinson [1927]   56
Bolt v WM Moss   185
Bolton v Mahadeva [1972]   121
Bolton v Stone [1951]   203
Boston Deep Sea Fishing & Ice Co v
   Ansell [1888]   163, 241, 273
Bourhill v Young [1942]   200
Bowater v Rowley Regis Corporation [1944]   184
Brace v Calder [1895]   139, 275
Brady v Brady [1988]   432
BRB v Herrington [1972]   214
BRC v Schelff   111
Breckland Group Holdings v London &
   Suffolk Properties Ltd [1989   483
British Railway Board v Herrington   214
British Reinforced Concrete v Schelff [1921]   110
British Syphon v Homewood [1956]   242

Brogden v Metropolitan Railway [1877]   13
BTC v Gourlay   139
Bull v Pitney Bowes [1966]   111
Burnard v Haggis [1863]   45
Burnard v Harris   46
Bushell v Faith [1970]   480, 547
Butler v Ex-Cell-O Corp [1979]   17
Bux v Slough Metals Ltd [1973]   218
Byrne v Leon Van Tienhoven [1880]   7
Re Blue Arrow plc [1967]   564
Re Bradford Investments Plc (No 2) [1991]   415
Re Brightlife Ltd [1987]   450
Re Bahia & San Francisco Railway Co [1898]   550
Re Bird Precision Bellows [1984]   481, 562, 564

Caparo Industries plc v Dickman and others
   [1990]   196,524
Car & Universal Finance v Caldwell [1964]   62
Carlill v Carbolic Smoke Ball [1893]   4, 11, 23, 39
Cassidy v Minister of Health [1951]   233
Cassidy v Osuustukkukauppa [1957]   129
Cellulose Acetate Silk Co v Widnes Foundry
   [1933]   135
Central London Property Trust Ltd v High
   Trees House Ltd [1947]   30
Century Insurance Co Ltd v Northern
   Ireland Transport Board [1942   180
Chadwick v BRB [1967]   199
Chapelton v Barry UDC [1940]   103
Chaplin v Hicks [1911]   139
Chappell & Co v Nestle Co Ltd [1960]   24
Charles Rickards Ltd v Oppenheim [1950]   121
Christmas v General Cleaning Contractors
   Ltd [1952]   214
CIBC Mortgages plc v Pitt [1993]   75, 77
Clemens v Clemens   569
Clemens v Clemens [1976]   4, 10, 499, 561
Clements v London and North Western Rail
   Co [1894]   42
Close v Steel Company of Wales [1961]   224, 225
Collier v Sunday Referee [1940]   244
Collins v Godefroy [1831]   25
Combe v Combe [1951]   31
Condor v The Barron Knights [1966]   128
Cook v Deeks   513
Cook v Deeks [1914]   485
Cook v Deeks [1916]   500, 501, 560
Cooper v Phibbs [1867]   66
Cornwal v Wilson [1750]   155
Corpe v Overton [1833]   43
Cotman v Brougham [1918]   366
Couturier v Hastie [1852]   66
Cowern v Nield   42
Craven-Ellis v Cannons Ltd [1936]   143
Cresswell v Inland Revenue [1984]   239
Cumbria Newspapers Group v Cumberland
   and Westmorland Herald [19   547
Cumming v Ince [1847]   73
Cundy v Lindsay [1878]   70
Currie v Misa [1875]   23

Curtis v Chemical Cleaning Co [1951]   103
Cutter v Powell [1795]   119
Cyril Leonard v Simo Securities Trust [1971]   278
Re Cardiff Savings Bank [1892]   508
Re Casey's Patents [1892]   27
Re City Equitable Fire Insurance Co [1925]   508
Re Cumana [1986]   564

D&C Builders v Rees [1966]   29
Dafen Tinplate Co v Llanelly Steel Co [1907]   396
Daimler Co Ltd v Continental Tyre & Rubber
   Co (GB) Ltd [[1916]   50, 308
Daniels v Daniels [1977]   560
Davis Contractors v Fareham UDC [1956]   129
De Francesco v Barnum [1889]   43
Derry v Peek [1889]   60
Devis v Atkins [1977]   278
Dewey v White [1827]   186
DHN Food Distributors v London Borough of
   Tower Hamlets [1976]   310
Dick Bentley Productions Ltd v Harold
   Smith (Motors) Ltd [1965]   85
Dickinson v Dodds [1876]   7
Dimmock v Hallet [1866]   57
Donoghue v Stevenson   194, 195, 208
Donovan v Invicta Airways [1970]   274
Dooley v Cammell Laird [1951]   199
Dorchester Finance Co Ltd v Stebbing [1989]   509
Dovey v Cory [1901]   508
Doyle v White City Stadium [1935]   42
Dulieu v White [1901]   199
Dunlop Pneumatic Tyre Co v New Garage [1915]   135
Dunlop Pneumatic Tyre Co v Selfridge [1915]   23, 143
Re Denham (Charles) & Co [1883]   508
Re Duomatic [1969]   479

Easson v LNER [1944]   204
Eaton Ltd v Nuttall [1977]   253
Ebrahimi v Westbourne Galleries [1973]   481, 566
Edgington v Fitzmaurice [1885]   57, 58
Edwards v Halliwell [1950]   560
Edwards v Skyways [1964]   38
Eley v Positive Government Security Life
   Assurance [1876]   393
Ellis v Sheffield Gas Consumers Co [1853]   182
Entores v Miles Far East Corporation [1955]   15
Erlanger v New Sombrero Phosphate Co [1878]   317
Errington v Errington [1953]   7
Esso Petroleum v Mardon [1976]   61, 197
Esso v Harper's Garage [1968]   111
European Chefs v Currell   284
Re EB Tractors Ltd [1986]   510
Re Elgindata (No 1) [1991]   563

Faccenda Chicken v Fowler [1986]   242
Felthouse v Bindley [1863]   13
Fisher v Bell [1960]   10
Fitch v Dewes [1921]   109
Foakes v Beer [1884]   28

Foley v Classique Coaches [1934]   87
Foot v Eastern Counties Timber [1972]   279
Forster & Son Ltd v Suggett [1918]   109
Foss v Harbottle [1843]   546, 555, 306, 495, 569
Foster v Driscoll   50
Fowlie v Slater Ltd   433
Freeman & Lockyer v Buckhurst Park
   Properties (1964)   157, 488
Frost v John Summers   224

G N Railway v Swaffield [1874]   157
Gallie v Lee   71
Galloway v Galloway [1914]   66
Gibson v Manchester City Council [1979]   6, 10
Gilford Motor Co v Horne [1933]   309
Glasbrook Brothers Ltd v Glamorgan
   County Council [1925]   25
Gluckstein v Barnes [1900]   317
GNR v Swaffield [1974]   158
Godley v Perry [1960]   99
Gorris v Scott [1874]   224
Great Northern Railways v Witham [1873]   16
Greenhalgh v Arderne Cinemas [1950]   396
Greenhalgh v Arderne Cinemas [1946]   548
Greenhalgh v Mallard [1943]   572
Gregory v Ford [1951]   239
Griffiths v Peter Conway Ltd [1939]   98
Guinness plc v Saunders [1990]   475, 502
Re German Date Coffee Co [1882]   364, 567

H Parsons Livestock v Uttley Ingham &
   Co [1978]   138
Hadley v Baxendale [1854]   137, 138, 275
Hardaker v Huby [1962]   218
Hare v Murphy Bros [1974]   128
Harlingdon Ltd v Hull Fine Art [1990]   95
Harmer v Cornelius [1858]   241, 273
Harris v Nickerson [1873]   11
Hartley v Ponsonby [1857]   25
Harvey v Facey [1893]   11
Haynes v Harwood [1935]   205
Hayward v Cammell Laird [1988]   254
Heald v O'Connor [1971]   431, 432
Hedley Byrne & Co Ltd v Heller & Partners
   Ltd [1963]   196
Henry Head v Ropner Holdings [1952]   413
Herbert Clayton and Jack Waller Ltd v
   Oliver [1930]   244
Herne Bay Steamboat Co v Hutton [1903]   127
Hickman v Kent or Romney Marsh
   Sheepbreeders Association [1920]   393
Hilder v Associated Portland Cement
   Manufacturers Ltd [1961]   203
Hill v Parsons [1971]   271
Hirachand Punamchand v Temple [1911]   29
Hivac Ltd v Park Royal Scientific Instruments
   Ltd [1946]   242, 273
Hochester v De La Tour [1853]   125
Hoenig v Isaacs [1952]   120
Hogg v Cramphorn [1967]   410, 498, 512

Hogg v Cramphorn Ltd [1987]   560
Hillsborough disaster   199
Hollier v Rambler Motors [1972]   104
Holwell Securities v Hughes [1974]   15
Honeywill and Stein v Larkin Bros [1934]   183
Hong Kong & China Gas Co v Glen [1914]   414
Horsfall v Thomas [1862]   58
Household Fire Insurance v Grant [1879]   14
Howard Smith v Ampol Petroleum   410
Hudson v Ridge Manufacturing Co Ltd [1957]   217
Hughes v Lord Advocate [1963]   206
Humble v Hunter [1948]   161
Hyde v Wrench [1840]   8
Re a company, ex parte Harries [1989]   566
Re H R Harmer [1959]   565
Re Holders Investment Trust Ltd [1971]   425, 547

IDC v Cooley [1972]   501
Introductions Ltd v NPB [1970]   366

J Spurling Ltd v Bradshaw [1966]   104
James McNaughten Paper v Hicks
  Anderson [1991]   198
James v Hepworth & Grandage Ltd [1967]   218
Jarvis v Swan's Tours Ltd [1973]   138
Jayes v IMI (Kynoch) Ltd   187
JEB Fasteners v Marks Bloom [1982]   202
Jennings v Rundall [1799]   45
Jeremiah v Ministry of Defence [1979]   255
John Henshall (Quarries) Ltd v Harvey [1965] 308, 309
John v Mendoza   50
Jones v Associated Tunnelling [1981]   239
Jones v Boyce [1816]   187
Jones v Lipman [1962]   310
Jones v Livox Quarries Ltd [1952]   187
Jones v Vernon's Pools Ltd [1938]   38
Joscelyne v Nissen [1970]   72
Jubilee Cotton Mills v Lewis [1924]   315

Keighley, Maxsted v Durant [1901]   155
Kelner v Baxter [1866]   46, 155, 359
King's Motors (Oxford) Ltd v Lax [1969]   87
King's Norton Metal Co v Edridge, Merrett
  & Co [1897]   70
Kleinwort Benson Ltd v Malaysia Mining
  Corp [1989]   38
Knightsbridge Estates Trust v Byrne   445
Kores Manufacturing Co v Kolok
  Manufacturing Co [1959]   111
Krell v Henry [1903]   127
Re a company, ex parte Kremer [1989]   564

L'Estrange v Graucob [1934]   103
Latimer v AEC Ltd [1952]   204, 217
Law v London Chronicle [1959]   240,273
Leaf v International Galleries [1950]   63, 67, 72
Lee v Lee's Air Farming Ltd [1960]   305
Lewis v Averay [1972]   63, 71
Lewis v Clay [1897]   72

Limpus v London General Omnibus Co [1862]   180
Lister v Romford Ice & Cold Storage Co
  Ltd [1957]   181, 241, 275
Liverpool City Council v Irwin [1977]   88
Lloyd v Grace, Smith & Co [1912]   181
Lloyds Bank v Bundy [1974]   76
Loch v John Blackwood Ltd [1924]   567
Long v Lloyd [1958]   62
Lucifero v Castel   164
Re Leeds & Hanley Theatres of Varieties [1902]   320
Re London and Northern Bank ex parte
  Jones [1900]   15
Re London School of Electronics [1986]   563
Re Lundie Brothers Ltd [1965]   568

Macaura v Northern Life Assurance [1925]   306
Mahony v East Holyford Mining Co   489
Maidment v Cooper [1978]   253
Maritime National Fish v Ocean Trawlers [1935]   130
Market Investigations Ltd v Minister
  of Social Security [1969]   233, 234
McClelland v Northern Ireland General
  Health Service Board [1957   271
McFarlane v EE Caledonia Ltd [1993] -
  the 'Piper Alpha' disaster   201
McLoughlin v O'Brian [1982]   200
McWilliams v Sir William Arrol Ltd [1962] 205, 220
Melon v Hector Powe [1981]   252
Merritt v Merritt [1970]   38
Mersey Docks & Harbour Board v Coggins
  & Griffiths [1947]   182, 232
Metropolitan Electric Supply v Ginder [1901]   141
Metropolitan Water Board v Dick Kerr &
  Co Ltd [1918]   129
Microbeads AG v Vinhurst Road Markings Ltd
  [1975]   94
Mills v Mills [1938]   498
Morgan Crucible v Hill Samuel [1991]   198
Morris v Murray [1990]   184
Morton Sundour Fabrics v Shaw [1966]   277
Moseley v Koffyfontein Mines   446
Re Mackenzie & Co [1916]   424
Re Maidstone Buildings [1971]   510
Re McArdle [1951]   26
Re Moore & Landauer [1927]   119
Re Moore and Co & Landauer and Co [1921]   96
Re Moorgate Mercantile Holdings   539

Napier v National Business Agency   50
Nash v Inman [1908]   41
Nethermere v Taverna & Gardiner [1984]   235
Nettleship v Weston [1971]   202
Newhart Developments v Co-op Commercial Bank 458
Niblett v Confectioners' Materials Co. [1921]   94
Nichol v Godts [1854]   99
Nicolene v Simmonds [1953]   87
Nordenfelt v Maxim-Nordenfelt Guns
  & Ammunition Co Ltd [1894]   110
North-West Transportation v Beatty [1887] 497, 512, 559

Northern Counties Securities Ltd v Jackson
and Steeple Ltd [1974   559
Nottingham Patent Brick v Butler [1886]   55, 57
Nova Plastics Ltd v Froggatt [1982]   242
Re Nuneaton Borough Association Football
Club [1991]   565
Re R A Noble [1983]   564

O'Brien v Associated Fire Alarms [1968]   239, 285
O'Kelly v Trusthouse Forte [1983]   234
Olley v Marlborough Court [1949]   103
Omnium Electric Palaces v Baines 1914   318
Oscar Chess Ltd v Williams [1957]   85
Re O C (Transport) Services Ltd   566

Page One Records Ltd v Britton [1967]   142
Panorama Developments v Fidelis
Furnishing Fabrics [1971]   166, 519
Paradine v Jane [1647]   126
Paris v Stepney Borough Council [1951]   203
Parke v Daily News [1962]   369
Parker v Clark [1960]   37
Parkinson v College of Ambulance   50
Parsons v Albert J. Parsons Limited   478
Partridge v Crittenden [1968]   11
Payne v Cave [1789]   17
Peake v Automotive Products [1977]   256
Pearce v Brooks [1866]   50
Pedley v Inland Waterways Association [1977]   536
Peek v Gurney [1873]   59
Pender v Lushington [1877]   393, 559
Penrose v Martyr [1858]   213, 307
Pepper v Webb [1968]   239, 240, 273
Percival v Wright [1902]   494, 505
Petrofina v Martin [1966]   111
Pharmaceutical Society of Great Britain v
Boots Cash Chemists [1953]   10
Phillips v Brooks [1919]   70
Philmore v Hood [1838]   57
Phonogram Ltd v Lane [1981]   360
Photo Productions Ltd v Securicor [1980]   104
Piercy v S Mills & Co [1920]   410
Planché v Colburn [1831]   120, 142
Polkey v AE Dayton Services [1987]   280, 289
Poussard v Spiers [1876]   90, 124
Powell v Lee [1908]   14
Prager v Blatspiel [1924]   157
Price v Civil Service Commission [1978]   256
Prudential Assurance v Newman Industrial [1982]561
Punt v Simons & Co Ltd [1903]   410
Re Precision Dippings [1986]   437
Re Produce Marketing Consortium [1989]   511

R v Clarke [1927]   6
R v Grantham [1984]   509
R v ICR Haulage Ltd [1944]   308
R v McDonnell [1966]   309
Raffles v Wichelaus [1864]   68
Rayfield v Hands [1960]   393, 547

Re a Company (No 00370 of 1987) [1988]   563
Re a company (No 00477 of 1986)   564
Re A Company [1983]   562, 568
Re Roith [1967]   496
Ready Mixed Concrete v Ministry of
Pensions [1968]   233
Redgrave v Hurd [1881]   58
Regal (Hastings) Ltd v Gulliver [1942]   501, 505
Regal (Hastings) v Gulliver [1967]   561
Roberts v Gray [1913]   42
Robinson v Davison [1871]   128
Roe v Minister of Health [1954]   202
Rolled Steel v British Steel Corporation
[1985]   362, 409, 443
Rondel v Worsley [1969]   199
Rose v Plenty [1976]   181
Routledge v Grant [1828]   8
Rowland v Divall [1923]   94
Royal British Bank v Turquand   488
Russell v Northern Bank [1992]   572

Sagar v Ridehalgh & Son Ltd [1931]   245
Salmon v Quin & Axtens Ltd [1909]   394, 483
Salomon v Salomon   300, 305, 312, 324
Saunders v Anglia Building Society [1970]   71
Saunders v Neale [1974]   277
Scammell v Ouston [1941]   87
Schawel v Reade [1913]   85
Scott v London and St Katherine Docks Co [1865]204
Scott v Scott [1943]   438,483
Scott v Shepherd [1773]   205
Scottish Co-operative Wholesale Society v
Meyer [1958]   495, 563
Scottish Insurance Corp Ltd v Wilsons & Clyde
Coal Co [1949]   425
Scriven v Hindley [1913]   69
Secretary of State for Employment v ASLEF [1972]240
Selangor United Rubber Co v Craddock [1967]   432
Shadwell v Shadwell [1860]   26
Shanklin Pier Ltd v Detel Products Ltd [1951]   146
Shaw v John Shaw [1935]   483, 484, 557
Shields v E Coomes [1979]   255
Shirlaw v Southern Foundries Ltd   482
Shuttleworth v Cox [1927]   396
Sidebottom v Kershaw Leese & Co [1920]   396
Siebe Gorman v Barclays Bank [1979]   450
Simaan General Contracting Co v Pilkington
Glass Ltd [1988]   207
Simpkins v Pays [1955]   37
Sinclair v Neighbour [1967]   241, 273
Singh v London County Bus Services   279
Smith, Stone & Knight Ltd v Birmingham
Corporation [1939]   310
Smith v Bradford Metropolitan Council   216
Smith v Charles Baker [1891]   184
Smith v Eric S Bush [1989]   188, 197
Smith v Hughes [1871]   69
Smith v Land and House Property
Corporation [1884]   56
Smith v Leech Braine [1962]   206

Solle v Butcher [1950] 67
Southern Foundries (1926) Ltd v Shirlaw
 [1940] 397, 480
Spartan Steel and Alloys Ltd v Martin
 & Co Ltd [1973] 207
Spring v Guardian Assurance [1993] 199, 244
Springer v GWR [1921] 158
Steen v Law [1964] 432
Steinberg v Scala (Leeds) Ltd [1923] 44
Stennett v Hancock & Peters [1939] 208
Stevenson v Golden Wonder Ltd [1977] 278
Stevenson v McLean [1880] 8
Stilk v Myrick [1809] 25
Sumpter v Hedges [1898] 120
Surrey County Council v Bredero Homes
 Ltd [1993] 139
Sword v Cameron [1839] 219
Re Saltdean Estate [1968] and House of Fraser
 plc v ACGE Investments [1987] 405, 425
Re Shipton, Anderson & Co [1915] 128
Re Suburban Hotel Co [1867] 568

Tamplin v James 64
Taylor v Caldwell [1863] 127
Taylor v Kent County Council [1969] 285
Tesco Supermarkets v Nattrass [1971] 308
Thomas v Thomas [1842] 24
Thornton v Shoe Lane Parking [1971] 103
Tinn v Hoffman [1873] 6
Trevor v Whitworth 422
Tsakiroglou v Noblee Thorl [1960] 129
Turner v Goldsmith [1891] 244
Turner v Mason [1845] 240
Turpin v Bilton [1843] 161, 162
Tweddle v Atkinson [1861] 28, 144
Twine v Bean's Express [1944] 181
Twomax v Dickson [1983] 202
Twycross v Grant [1877] 317

Uddin v Associated Portland Cement [1965] 188, 225
Universe Tankships of Monrovia v ITWF [1982] 73

Varley v Whipp [1900] 95
Vaughan v Taff Vale Railway [1890] 186
Vaux & Associated Breweries v Ward [1969] 284
Victoria Laundry v Newman Industries [1949] 137

Ward v London County Council [1938] 186
Ward v Tesco Stores [1976] 204
Wares v Caithness Leather Products [1974] 243
Warner Brothers Pictures Inc v Nelson [1936] 142
Warren v Henly's Ltd [1948] 180
Watt v Hertfordshire County Council [1954] 204
Watteau v Fenwick [1891] 159, 168
Webb v Emo Air Cargo (UK) Ltd [1992] 256
Webster v Cecil [1861] 69
West Bromwich Building Society v Townsend 295
Western Excavation Ltd v Sharp [1978] 274
Wheat v E Lacon and Co Ltd [1966] 213

White & Carter Council v McGregor (1961) 126, 140
White v Bluett [1853] 24
White v Bristol Aeroplane [1953] 409, 548
Williams v Roffey Brothers [1990] 26
Wilson and Clyde Coal Company Ltd v
 English [1938] 182, 217
Wilson v Rickett Cockerell and Co Ltd [1954] 97
With v O'Flanagan [1936] 55
Wood v Odessa Waterworks Co [1889] 438
Woolfson v Strathclyde Regional
 Council [1978] 307, 311
Wylie v Dee & Co (Menswear) Ltd [1978] 257
Re William C Leith Bros [1932] 509
Re Woodroffe's (Musical Instruments)
 Limited [1986] 450
Re Wragg [1897] 414

Yates Building v R J Pulleyn & Sons [1975] 13
Yewens v Noakes [1880] 232
Re Yenidje Tobacco Co [1916] 567
Re Yorkshire Woolcombers Association 449

Abnormal loss   137
Abuse of confidence   56, 77
Accord and satisfaction   29
Accounting reference period   341
Act of God   185
Action for the price   140
Additional award   284
Adequacy   24
Adjustment of rights of contributories   326
Administration   324
Administration orders   325, 460
Administrative receiver   323, 407
Administrator   327
Agency   152
Agency in company law   487
Allotment of shares   415
Alteration of articles   395
Alteration of the memorandum   353
Alteration of the objects   363
Annual general meetings   531
Annual return   340
Anticipatory breach   125, 140
Apparent authority   159
Appointment of directors   467
Assignment   146, 147
Association clause   353
Auctions   16
Auditor   520
Auditors' report   345
Authorised share capital   406
Authority of directors to allot shares   409
Avoidance of certain floating charges: S245 IA86 454

Balance sheet   341
Basic award   283
Board meetings   486
Bonus issues   415
Borrowed employees   182
Borrowing powers of a company   443
Breach of duty of care   201
Breach of statutory duty   179, 223
Breach of warranty of authority   489
Business efficacy   88, 238
Business Names Act 1985   358

Companies Act 1985   303, 424, 562
Cadbury Report   475, 526
Calls   403
Capacity to contract   40
Capital clause   352
Capitalisation issue   415
Care and skill of directors   508
Certainty of terms   87
Certificate of incorporation   315
Change of name   357
CJA93   506
Class meetings   533
Class rights   546

Classes of shares   403
Code of Best Practice   526
Collective bargaining agreements   39, 245
Communication of acceptance   13
Communication of the offer   6
Companies (Single Member Private
   Limited Companies Regulations 1992   302, 307
Companies limited by guarantee   301
Companies limited by shares   300
Companies Registry   334
Company Directors Disqualification
   Act 1986   321, 470, 510, 511, 515
Company name   307
Company secretary   517
Compensation for loss of office   503
Compensatory award   283
Concert parties   337
Conditions   89
Conflict of interest   499
Connected persons of a director   476, 504
Consideration   24
Constructive dismissal   273
Consumer Protection Act 1987   179
Continuity of employment   251
Contract for services   232
Contract of employment   231
Contract of guarantee   48
Contract of service   232
Contract   5
Contributory negligence   186
Control   232
Conversion   227
Corporate capacity   359, 362
Corporate governance   326, 475, 484, 493, 517, 525
Corporate personality   304
Counter-offer   8
Cross-offers   6
Crystallisation of floating charges   450
Custom and usage   89

Damages   190
Damages in contract   135
Dangerous machinery   224
Debenture   444
Debentureholders' remedies   455
Deed   3, 47, 143
Defamation   227
Department of trade and industry inspections
   and investigations   569
Derivative action   558
Director   467
Directors interests in company contracts   503
Directors' duties   493
Directors' long term service contracts   503
Directors' report   345
Discharge by acceptance of breach   124
Discharge by agreement   122
Discharge of charges   452
Discharged   119
Disclosure of interests in shares   505

Discount on a nominal value	412
Discount on market value	412
Disqualification of directors	470
Dissolution	323
Distributions of profit	435
Dividend rules	435
Doctrine of incorporation	305
Dormant companies	346
Duress	73
Duties of directors	493
Duty of care	194
Economic duress	73
Economic reality	311
Economic reality test	233
Effect of articles	393
Eiusdem generis rule of construction	365
Elective resolution	346, 543
Equal pay	253
Exclusion clauses	102
Executed consideration	23
Executory consideration	23
exemption clause	102
Exemption notices	188
Express terms	86
Extraordinary general meetings	531
Extraordinary resolution	538
Failure of the substratum	364
Fair reasons for dismissal	278
Fiduciary duty of directors	497
Financial assistance for the acquisition of own shares	422, 431
Fitness for purpose	96
Fixed charges	448
Floating charges	448
Form of a contract	47
Fraudulent misrepresentation	60, 227
Fraudulent trading	308, 509, 473
Frolic of his own	180
Frustration	126
General commercial company	365
General meetings	530
Group accounts	307, 342
Guarantee payments	261, 286
Guarantees	314
Health and Safety Commission	297
Insolvency Act 1986	303
Illegality	50
Implied terms	87, 238
Improvement notice	297
Inadmissible reasons	280
Increase and reduction of capital	422
Increase of capital	422
Indoor management rule	488
Independent clause	366
Industrial accidents	216
Industrial injuries disablement benefit	266
Inevitable accident	185
Injunction	141, 191, 309
Innocent misrepresentation	62
Innominate terms	91
Insider dealing	505
Integration test	233
Intention to create legal relations	36
Intermediate terms	89
Intra vires	362
Invalidity benefit	266
Invitation to treat	10
Issued or allotted share capital	406
Itemised pay statement	261
Just and equitable winding up	566
Lay-off	285
Letters of comfort	38
Liability clause	352
Lien	403
Lifting the veil of incorporation	307
Limitation	189
Limitation of actions	143
Limitation of liability	306
Limited liability	312
Liquidated damages	135
Liquidation	324, 325
Loan capital	443
Loans to directors	476, 504
Main objects rule of construction	365
Managing director	480
Materiality statement	437
Maternity benefit	266
Maternity rights	263
Measure of damages	138
Medical suspension	262
Medium-sized companies	303, 346
Meetings	530
Memorandum of association	349
Mental distress	138
Mere representations	84
Minimum notice periods	265
Minimum number of members	307
Minority protection	555
Minors	41
Minutes of meetings	542
Misrepresentation	54
Mistake	64
Mitigation	139
Monetary award	282
Mortgage of shares	554
Multiple test	233
Name	332, 355
Name clause	351
Necessity	185

Negligence 194
Negligent misrepresentation 60
Negligent misstatement causing economic loss 195
Neighbour principle 194
Nervous shock 199
Nominal damages 139, 190
Non est factum 71
Normal loss 137
Notice of meetings and resolutions 534
Novation 123, 360
Novus actus interveniens 205

Objects clause 352, 362
Occupiers liability 213
Ordinary resolution 538
Overage directors 469
Overseas companies 304

Paid up capital 407
Part-payment problem 28
Particulars of employment 237
Partly paid shares 412
Partnerships 313
Passing off 357
Past consideration 26
Payment for shares 414
Penalty clauses 135
Performance 119
Permissible capital payment 427
Perpetual succession 306
Postal rule 14
Powers 366
Powers of directors 482
Pre-emption rights (statutory) 409
Pre-emption rights of members on transfer of shares 553
Pre-incorporation contracts 359
Preference 454, 511
Preference shares 404
Preferential debts 323
Premium 413
Priority of charges 453
Private companies 302
Privity of contract 143
Product liability 207, 210
Professional negligence 195
Profit and loss account 342
Profits obtained from the position of director 500
Prohibition notice 297
Promissory estoppel 30
Promoters 317
Proper purposes rule 410, 497
Provision for employees 369
Proxies 540
Public companies 302
Public company clause 351
Public subscription 407
Publicity 332
Purchase of own shares 422
Pure economic loss 206, 207

Qualification 470
Quantum meruit 142
Quorum at meetings 537

Race discrimination 258
Reasonable care and skill 240
Reasonable foreseeability 206
Reasonableness test 279
Receivership 324, 457
Rectification of written agreement 72
Redeemable shares 422, 427
Reductions of capital 422
Redundancy 281
Re-engagement 282
Reference 228
References 244
Regal Case 505
Register of charges 339, 452
Register of debenture-holders 339
Register of directors and secretary 339
Register of interests in shares 336
Register of Notifiable Interests 336
Registered office 333
Registered Office clause 352
Registrar of Companies 334
Registration 315
Registration of charges 451
Reinstatement 282
Rejection of an offer 8
Remoteness of damage 136, 206
Remuneration of directors 475
Re-registration 319
Res ipsa loquitur 204
Rescission 62
Resolutions 538
Restraint of trade 108, 309
Resultant loss 205
Return of allotment 416
Revocation of offer 7
Rights issue 415
Rule in Pinnel's case 28

Sale by description 95
Sale of Goods Act 1979 91
Satisfactory quality 96, 207
Separate clause 366
Serious loss of capital 426
Service contracts of directors 474
Sex discrimination 255
Shadow director 467
Share certificates 549
Share dealing by directors 504
Share dealings by directors 504
Share options 505
Share premium account 413
Share qualification 470
Share warrants 554
Shareholders agreements 572

Shareholders: rights 546
Shares 402
Short time 285
Sick pay 244
Sickness benefit 266
Simple contracts 3, 143
Single Member Private Limited Companies 303
Small 346
Small companies 303
Special award 284
Special notice 536
Special resolution 538
Specialty contract 3, 22
Specific performance 141, 311
Standard of care 201
Standing offer 16
State benefits 266
Statutory authority 186
Stock 422
Strict liability 188, 207, 210, 223, 294
Subject to contract 12, 48
Subjective clause 367
Substantial property transactions 503
Sufficiency of consideration 24, 74
Summary accounts 344
Summary dismissal 273
Supply of Goods and Services Act 1982 Implied
    Terms 100

Table A 373
Tenders 16
Termination of an offer 7
Terms of a contract 83
The available market rule 140
Time off work 262
Tort of deceit 227
Tort of negligence 179
Tortfeasor 179, 182
Trade union 259, 262
Trading certificate 307, 316
Transactions at an undervalue 454, 511
Transfer of shares 549
Transmission of shares 549
Trespass 225
Trespassers 214
Trust deeds 447
Trustees for debentureholders 447
Types of capital 406
Types of company 300

Ultra vires 46, 362
Uncalled capital 407
Undisclosed principal 146
Unfair Contract Terms Act 1977 188
Unfair dismissal 278
Unfair prejudice 561
Unfit to be concerned in the management 472
Unlimited companies 301
Utmost good faith 55

Validity of charges 454
Valuable consideration 24
Variation of class rights 547
Veil of incorporation 306
Vicarious liability 179
Volenti non fit injuria 183
Voluntary liquidation 323
Voting agreement 572

Wages 259
Warranties 89, 92, 124
Welsh companies 304
Written reasons for dismissal 265
Written resolution 538
Wrongful dismissal 273
Wrongful trading 308, 473, 510